The Embassy of Sir Thomas Roe to India

SIR THOMAS ROE
From the portrait in the National Portrait Gallery
By permission of Emery Walker Ltd.

The Embassy of Sir Thomas Roe to India 1615-19

As Narrated in his Journal and Correspondence

Edited by
Sir William Foster

New and revised edition

Munshiram Manoharlal
Publishers Pvt Ltd

ISBN 81-215-0509-5
First Indian Edition 1990
Reprinted from the 1926 edition
All rights reserved with the publisher

Published by Munshiram Manoharlal Publishers Pvt. Ltd.,
Post Box 5715, 54 Rani Jhansi Road, New Delhi 110 055,
and printed at New Gian Offset Printers, Indralok Extension, Delhi 110 035

PREFACE

This work was originally published in 1899 by the Hakluyt Society. The edition was a small one, and the copies remaining after the usual distribution to the members were quickly absorbed, with the result that for many years the book has been out of print. Its consequent scarcity, and the interest taken of late in seventeenth-century India, suggested the advisability of preparing a new edition. To that course the assent of the Council of the Hakluyt Society was readily given; and an appropriate publisher was found in the Press of Roe's own university of Oxford. The result is the volume now placed before the reader.

The first step in the preparation of the new edition was to collate the text of the old with the manuscript and printed sources. The next was to review the selection that had been made from Roe's letters and other illustrative documents. As the result, nearly thirty fresh letters were drawn upon. To balance this increase, several formal documents given previously were omitted, as well as one short letter; while a few excisions were also made in the portion of the journal describing the outward voyage. These passages relate to matters of navigation, and therefore, while quite in place in the Hakluyt Society's edition, were felt to be superfluous in one intended mainly for historical students. The notes and introduction have of course been revised; while new illustrations have been substituted for most of those given in the earlier version. In this connexion warm thanks are due to Sir John Marshall, C.I.E., the Director-General of the Indian Archaeological Survey, for the photographs of the Fort at Ajmer and of the mosque at Māndu in which Roe is supposed to have stayed; also to Mr. B. K. Parry, I.C.S., for the two interesting views of Burhānpur.

LIST OF CONTENTS

	PAGE
PREFACE	v
FULLER TITLES OF CHIEF AUTHORITIES QUOTED	xi
INTRODUCTION	xiii
ROE'S JOURNAL	1

The voyage to the Cape, 1 ; events at Table Bay, 4 ; the Comoro Islands, 8 ; Sokotra, 18 ; arrival at Swally, 26 ; Roe lands and proceeds to Surat, 31 ; he leaves for Ajmer, 65 ; visits Prince Parwīz at Burhānpur, 70 ; arrives at Ajmer and is presented to the Emperor, 84 ; visits Prince Khurram, 92 ; the *Nauroz* festival, 125 ; Roe submits his proposed treaty, 132 ; he demands the repayment of the exactions of Zūlfakār Khān, 139 ; dispute over an English runaway, 158 ; arrival of some Portuguese merchants, 161 ; Roe is forbidden the court, 164 ; Khurram appointed to the command of the operations in the Deccan, 171 ; Roe goes again to court, 179 ; presents a miniature, 189 ; Zūlfakār Khān agrees to satisfy his demands, 196 ; Roe is puzzled to distinguish his miniature from the copies, 199 ; news of a Dutch ship at Swally, 202 ; Roe is entertained by Jamāl-uddīn, 209 ; Jahāngīr gives him his portrait, 214 ; death of Roe's chaplain, 216 ; the birthday festivities, 221 ; Roe presents another miniature, 222 ; and is given a gold cup, 225 ; his negotiations with Khurram, 226 ; his draft treaty is rejected, 228 ; his new proposals, 229 ; these are likewise rejected, 231; Jahāngīr refuses to see Parwīz, 235 ; Pepwell's fleet arrives, 240 ; Abdullah Khān comes to court, 242 ; an embassy from Bījāpur, 242 ; Khurram attempts to secure Khusrau, 245 ; the latter is handed over to Āsaf Khān, 256 ; arrival of a Persian ambassador, 258 ; Khurram starts for the Deccan, 281 ; Jahāngīr leaves Ajmer, 282 ; the Surat factors dispatch a ship to Persia, 290 ; Roe quits Ajmer, 300 ; sends to Ispahān a draft of concessions desired from the Shāh, 334 ; his interview with Khusrau, 342 ; Khurram seizes the presents on their way to court, 344 ; these are sent to

LIST OF CONTENTS

Jahāngīr, 346 ; Māndu reached, 353 ; the Persian ambassador departs, 363 ; two Dutch ships wrecked near Damān, 368 ; Khusrau released and offered Nūr Mahal's daughter, 369 ; the birthday festivities, 378 ; Khurram enters Māndu in triumph, 385 ; news of Pring's fleet, 387 ; Roe conciliates Āsaf Khān, 395 ; Jahāngīr leaves Māndu, 404 ; Steel and his projects, 405 ; Roe is entertained by Āsaf Khān, 410 ; he reaches Ahmadābād, 422 ; dispute with Khurram regarding the presents, 425 ; reception of a Dutch embassy, 427.

LETTERS

1615 : To the Governor of Surat (15 Oct.), 54 ; to the Viceroy of Goa (20 Oct.), 57 ; to the East India Company (24 Nov.), 72.

1616 : To Lord Carew (17 Jan.), 88 ; to Sir Thomas Smythe (24 Jan.), 95 ; to the Company (25 Jan.), 98 ; to the Company (29 Jan.), 101 ; to King James (29 Jan.), 102 ; to the Archbishop of Canterbury (29 Jan.), 104 ; to the Company (14 Feb.), 110 ; to the King of Persia (14 Feb.), 114 ; to Lord Southampton (15 Feb.), 115 ; to Sir Thomas Smythe (15 Feb.), 116 ; to Prince Khurram (4 March), 121 ; to Āsaf Khān ([7] April), 139 ; to the Surat factors (26 April), 146 ; to Āsaf Khān (1 June), 163 ; to the Surat factors (19 June), 176 ; to Prince Khurram (13 July), 185 ; to Capt. Pepwell (15 Oct.), 253 ; to Prince Charles (30 Oct.), 269 ; to the Archbishop of Canterbury (30 Oct.), 271 ; to the Company (24 Nov.), 301 ; to Sir Thomas Smythe (27 Nov.), 312 ; to Sir Ralph Winwood (30 Nov.), 316 ; to the Company (1 Dec.), 319 ; to Capt. Pepwell (30 Dec.), 330.

1617 : To William Robbins (7 or 17 Jan.), 335 ; to Sir Thomas Smythe (16 Jan.), 337 ; to Nicholas Bangham (1 April), 359 ; to the Surat factors (22 May), 364 ; to Nicholas Bangham (21 June), 366 ; to the same (1 July), 367 ; to the Surat factors (1 July), 367 ; to Francis Fetiplace (20 July), 368 ; to Libby Chapman (21 Aug.), 370 ; to William Robbins (21 Aug.), 371 ; to Capt. Pring (30 Aug.), 373 ; to the Surat factors (30 Aug.), 377 ; to Capt. Pring (29 Sept.), 383 ; to the Surat factors (29 Sept.), 385 ; to Nicholas Bangham (3 Oct.), 386 ; to Thomas Kerridge (4 Oct.), 386 ; to Capt. Pring (5 Oct.), 389 ; to Thomas Kerridge (5 Oct.), 393 ; to the Surat factors (8 Oct.), 396 ; to the same (11 Oct.), 398 ; to Thomas Kerridge (21 Oct.), 402 ; to the same (3 Nov.), 409 ; to the Surat factors (8 Nov.), 411 ; to Capt. Pring (8 Nov.), 413 ; to Thomas Kerridge (2 Dec.), 414 ; to the Surat factors (6 Dec.), 416 ; to the same (18 Dec.), 422.

1618 : To Thomas Kerridge (— Feb.), 430 : to the Company (14 Feb.), 432 ; to Capt. Pring (14 Feb.), 460 ; to King James (15 Feb.), 463 ; to Sir Thomas Smythe

LIST OF CONTENTS

(16 Feb.), 466 ; to Capt. Pring (10 March), 469 ; to the Surat factors (26 April), 471 ; the *farmān* for Khwāja Arab's house (Aug.), 474 ; negotiations with Khurram (Aug.), 475.

1619 : To the Governor of Mohka (16 Feb.), 483 ; the Surat factors to the Company (12 March), 484 ; Roe to the President at Bantam (11 May), 486 ; to the Company (29 Aug.), 488.

APPENDICES - - - - - - - - - 489

A. Geographical account of the Mogul's territories, 489 ; note on the map, 497.

B. Letter from King James to Jahāngīr (1615), 502 ; and to Roe (4 Feb. 1617), 503 ; Jahāngīr to King James (20 Feb. 1618), 504; another (8 Aug. 1618), 506.

INDEX - - - - - - - - - - - 509

ILLUSTRATIONS

SIR THOMAS ROE - - - - - - - *Frontispiece*	
From the painting in the National Portrait Gallery after M. J. Miereveldt.	
	to face page
MAP OF ROE'S ROUTES - - - - - - -	66
Excluding the later visit to Burhānpur.	
BURHĀNPUR CASTLE - - - - - - - -	68
From a photograph by Mr. B. K. Parry, I.C.S.	
ROE'S QUARTERS AT BURHĀNPUR - - - - -	70
From a photograph by Mr. B. K. Parry, I.C.S.	
THE CITY OF AJMER - - - - - - - -	84
From a photograph by the editor.	
JAHĀNGĪR AND PRINCE KHURRAM - - - - -	176
From an engraving in *Purchas His Pilgrimes* (see *infra*, p. lxxviii).	
THE REV. EDWARD TERRY - - - - - -	216
From his *Voyage to East India* (1655).	
THE FORT GATEWAY AT AJMER - - - - - -	282
From a photograph furnished by Sir John Marshall, C.I.E.	
ROE'S SUPPOSED DWELLING AT MĀNDU - - - - -	354
From a photograph furnished by Sir John Marshall, C.I.E.	
BAFFIN'S MAP OF INDIA - - - - - - -	496
From a copy in the British Museum.	
THE SEAL OF THE GREAT MOGUL - - - - -	508
From *Purchas His Pilgrimes*.	

FULLER TITLES OF THE CHIEF AUTHORITIES QUOTED

Āīn-i-Akbari. Translated by H. Blochmann and Col. Jarrett. 3 vols. Calcutta, 1878, 1891, 1894.
Baffin, William, the Voyages of. Edited by Sir Clements Markham. Hakluyt Society, 1880.
Beni Prasad. *History of Jahāngīr.* London, 1922.
Bernier, François, the Travels of. Translated by Archibald Constable. 2nd edition. London, 1914.
Bocarro, Antonio. *Decada XIII.* Lisbon, 1876.
Calendar of State Papers, East Indies, 1513-1616, and 1617-21. By W. N. Sainsbury. 2 vols. London, 1862, 1870.
Carew, Lord, Letters of, to Sir Thomas Roe, 1615-17. Edited by John Maclean. Camden Society. 1860.
Cocks, Richard, the Diary of. Edited by Sir E. M. Thompson. 2 vols. Hakluyt Society, 1882.
Della Valle, Pietro, the Travels of. Translated and edited by Edward Grey. 2 vols. Hakluyt Society, 1891.
Douglas, James. *Bombay and Western India.* London, 1893.
Du Jarric, P. *Thesaurus Rerum Indicarum.* 3 vols. Cologne. 1615.
Early Travels in India, 1583-1619. Edited by William Foster. London, 1921.
English Factories in India, 1618-29. By William Foster. 3 vols. London, 1906-09.
Faria y Sousa, Manoel. *Asia Portuguesa.* Translated by John Stevens. 3 vols. London, 1694-95.
First Letter Book of the East India Company, 1600-19. Edited by Sir George Birdwood and William Foster. London, 1893.
History of India as told by its own Historians. By Sir H. M. Elliot and J. Dowson. 8 vols. London, 1867-77.
Hobson-Jobson. By Col. Yule and A. C. Burnell. 2nd edition. London, 1903.
Jourdain, John, the Journal of. Edited by William Foster. Hakluyt Society, 1905.

FULLER TITLES OF CHIEF AUTHORITIES

Lancaster, Sir James, the Voyages of. Edited by Sir Clements Markham. Hakluyt Society, 1877.
Letters Received by the East India Company from its Servants in the East, 1602-17. Edited by F. C. Danvers and William Foster. 6 vols. London, 1896-1902.
Linschoten, J. H. van, the Voyage of. Translated and edited by A. C. Burnell and P. A. Tiele. 2 vols. Hakluyt Society, 1884.
Memoirs of the Emperor Jahāngīr (Tūzuk-i-Jahāngīri). Translated by A. Rogers and edited by H. Beveridge. 2 vols. London, 1909, 1914.
Monserrate, Anthony. *Mongolicae Legationis Commentarius.* Edited by the Rev. H. Hosten. Memoirs of the Bengal Asiatic Society, vol. iii. No. 9. Calcutta, 1914.
Mundy, Peter, the Travels of. Edited by Sir R. Temple. Hakluyt Society, 1907, 1914.
Ovington, Rev. John. *Voyage to Suratt.* London, 1696.
Pelsaert, Francisco, the Remonstrantie of (Jahāngīr's India). Translated by W. H. Moreland, C.S.I., C.I.E. and P. Geyl, Litt.D. Cambridge, 1925.
Purchas His Pilgrimes. London, 1625.
Sykes, Sir P. M. *History of Persia.* 2 vols. London, 1915.
Tavernier, J. B., the Travels in India of. Translated by V. Ball. 2 vols. London, 1889.
Terpstra, Dr. H. *De Opkomst der Westerkwartieren van de Oost-Indische Compagnie.* 's Gravenhage, 1918.
Terry, Rev. Edward. *A Voyage to East India.* London, 1655.
Valentyn, François. *Beschryving van Oud en Nieuw Oost-Indiën.* 5 vols. Doordrecht and Amsterdam, 1724-26.
Van den Broecke, Pieter. *Op sijne Reysen.* Amsterdam, 1648.

INTRODUCTION

TOWARD the end of this present yeere 1614, viz. in the beginning of January, His Majesty, at the request of the East India Company, sent Sir Thomas Roe, Knight, ambassadour to the Great Maghoore, whome some corruptly call Mogall . . . unto whome this ambassadour had commission to make and contract a league between His Majesty and his subjects for commerce and traffique in his dominions, and to procure and establish a factory for our nation in sundry parts of his dominions, as well seaports as inland townes, with other instructions yet undiscovered. Hee is the first that ever was imployed in this hie nature to any of those so farre remote easterne princes. (*Stow's Annals, continued by Edmond Howes*, 1615, p. 945.)

WHY should King James have thought it necessary to employ the cumbrous machinery of an embassy in order to secure the admission of English merchants to the dominions of the Mughal monarch who ruled over the greater part of India? And how did it come about that the East India Company—so jealous of royal interference, and so averse from spending money for which no immediate return was likely to be forthcoming—in this instance besought the King to send out such an ambassador at its expense?

The answer is twofold. In the first place, this appeared to be the only satisfactory way of overcoming the difficulties caused by the claim of the Portuguese to a monopoly of the trade by sea between Europe and the East Indies. It was true that the English had never admitted the validity of that claim, and in despite of it had opened up trade at Surat in 1608. But the Portuguese had attacked the Company's ships engaged in this traffic, and were doing their best, by threats and persuasions, to induce the 'Great Mogul' to exclude the English from his country. Remonstrances at Madrid (Philip

III. being at that time ruler of Portugal as well as of Spain) would have been useless, and the most promising course appeared to be to secure by treaty with the Indian monarch the right of English merchants to participate in the trade of his country and obtain for them his protection. The Portuguese authorities would then, it was hoped, think twice before provoking two powerful sovereigns by renewing their attacks.

A further reason is to be found in the necessary conditions of a trade of this nature. Experience had shown that the only satisfactory method was to carry on the commerce by establishing 'factories,' *i.e.* small colonies of merchants residing regularly in the country. This had been for centuries the established practice in such cases—as witness the Hanse factories in London and Bergen—and English trade in the Levant was conducted in that manner. For a ship to call at a port, sell her cargo and purchase a fresh one was a difficult and unremunerative proceeding, especially in the case of India. European articles were in small demand; while on the other hand the products of the country, such as calicoes and indigo, were mostly manufactured to order and could only be collected slowly (unless at a ruinous cost). Moreover, a flying visit of this kind would inevitably result in lowering the prices of the goods imported and raising those of the goods exported, since the local merchants would have the visitors at their mercy. It was requisite, therefore, to leave factors to sell the goods brought by one fleet and to provide cargoes for the next; and the position of those merchants was an all-important point. They could not claim as a right the protection enjoyed by the subjects of the state in which they found themselves; and without some special convention they and the valuable goods entrusted to their care were likely to become the prey of the local officials, whose tenure was always precarious and who were eager to fill their pockets at the expense of the foreigners. A formal agreement, securing to the newcomers the right to administer justice among themselves, to pay only reasonable customs duties, and so forth, was therefore a necessity. Such a concession the English merchants had long been endeavouring to secure from the Great Mogul, but without a satisfactory result; and it was hoped that an ambassador from their king would succeed where they had failed, and would be able to place the relations between the two nations on a stable and lasting foundation.

In passing, we may note the fact that a promise of such an embassy had been made about nine years before, albeit without any authority, by John Mildenhall, an English merchant who had made his way overland to the court of the Emperor Akbar and had demanded for his fellow countrymen access to the trade of India. The Jesuit missionaries at Agra, who were the spokesmen of the Portuguese, thereupon asserted that the English were 'all theeves' (for not unnaturally the subjects of King Philip regarded the exploits of Drake and his compeers as sheer piracy) and that, while they might pretend at first to be peaceful traders, they would soon throw off the mask and seize some of the Emperor's ports. Akbar and his advisers, conscious of the superiority of the Europeans at sea, were manifestly disturbed by this suggestion, and still more by the prospect of the commerce of Western India being impeded by conflicts between the English and the Portuguese. Mildenhall countered by declaring that it was the intention of his sovereign to do as she had done in the case of Turkey, namely, to send an ambassador to reside at Akbar's court, where he would of course be a hostage for the good behaviour of his compatriots; and he added significantly that it was Her Majesty's practice to change her ambassadors from time to time, and to send valuable presents on each occasion. Thus reassured, we are told, Akbar made no further difficulty in granting Mildenhall's demands.[1]

On his return to England Mildenhall found that the East India Company, which had had nothing to do with his mission and disputed the value of the concessions he had obtained, had already dispatched ships to open up trade with the Mughal ports in Western India, and that William Hawkins, the captain of one of these, had been instructed to proceed to Agra with a present and a letter from King James to the Emperor, soliciting the grant of trading privileges. Hawkins's vessel reached Surat in August, 1608, and, although the Company had directed him to call himself a 'messenger' merely, he boldly announced

[1] *Early Travels in India*, pp. 48-59.

himself as an ambassador from the King of England—a pretension to which plausibility was lent by the fact that the royal letter spoke of 'this bearer our servant.' In such capacity he proceeded to the capital and was graciously received by the new Emperor, Jahāngīr, who had been present at Mildenhall's final interview with Akbar, and probably looked upon the coming of Hawkins as a fulfilment of the pledge then given. He demanded to know whether the newcomer intended to remain ; and upon Hawkins replying that he hoped to return to England shortly with a reply to his master's missive, the Emperor declared his meaning to be that Hawkins should stay until another ambassador arrived to take his place. As this proposal was coupled with a promise of generous treatment of the ambassador himself and of concessions to his fellow countrymen, Hawkins agreed to remain, although (as he estimated) the result might be his detention at the Mughal court for ' halfe a doozen yeeres.' However, his own indiscretions, Portuguese intrigues, and remonstrances from the merchants of Gujarāt (intimidated by the threats of the Viceroy of Goa) weakened the Englishman's position, and in November, 1611, he quitted the court and took refuge on board a fleet which had arrived at Surat under the command of Sir Henry Middleton. The latter, having failed to induce the local authorities to permit the establishment of an English factory, broke off relations and departed for the Red Sea, where he retaliated by detaining a number of ships from Gujarāt until they paid a heavy ransom. This demonstration that the English could do Indian trade as much damage as the Portuguese had a great effect ; and when, in September, 1612, Thomas Best reached Surat with another fleet, all unaware of Middleton's proceedings, he was received with a show of cordiality and was able to negotiate an agreement with the local authorities for the establishment of a factory at Surat. One of the articles of this agreement provided for the residence at court of an English ambassador ; and this clause shows that Best and his advisers recognized the necessity of having such a representative, if only to secure the redress of grievances. The Portuguese, hoping by a decisive stroke to crush the intruders and intimidate the Gujarāt officials, sent a squadron to attack the English ships ;

but the result was a victory for the latter that immensely raised English prestige and made it safe to leave at Surat a small colony of merchants under Thomas Aldworth. Soon after Best's departure Paul Canning was dispatched to Agra with a present for the Emperor and another royal letter ; and upon his death, shortly after his arrival, another factor, Thomas Kerridge, was sent from Surat (June, 1613) to take his place. He in turn was superseded (Feb., 1615) by William Edwards, who carried with him a particularly handsome present and yet another letter from King James. All three, however, in turn found themselves disregarded, inasmuch as it was well understood at court that, for all their pretences, they were merely merchants. Edwards wrote to the Governor of the Company in Dec., 1614 (*O.C.* 219) : ' the necessity of residence with the King . . . is such as cannot bee avoyded ; and hee to bee a man sent imediately from our King, for that the title of a merchant is of them despised . . . as by experience in Paule Canning and Thomas Kerredge, who, while they profest to belong to our King and of his followers, they were gracious in the eies of the King and nobles, but afterward were much neglected.' In a similar strain another factor wrote in the following month (*O.C.* 224) that Edwards must of necessity pretend to be an ambassador, ' for he which shall hold correspondancey with the Kinge muste be suche a one and no merchante (unlesse covertlye), for there pride is suche that they scorne them, making no more reaconing of them then of banyans, whome they hold little better then slaves.'

It is true that these letters had not reached the hands of the ' Committees ' (as the Directors of the Company were then called) at the time when the dispatch of a real ambassador was decided upon ; but the views of the factors were sufficiently known from the report made by Best upon his return to London (June, 1614). His glowing account of the prospects of the trade and of the agreement he had concluded for its prosecution, confirmed the Committees in their determination to push matters vigorously. Already, in the preceding February, a fleet of four ships had been dispatched to Surat under the experienced leadership of Nicholas Downton ; and it was decided to prepare a fresh expedition to follow about

Christmastide. William Keeling, who had taken part in the First Voyage and had commanded the Third, was engaged as the 'General' or leader of the new fleet, with the famous *Dragon* as his flagship; to Christopher Newport, of Virginia fame, the successful chief of the Twelfth Voyage, was assigned the *Lion*; Walter Peyton, who had been master of Newport's ship in that Voyage, was promoted to the charge of the *Expedition*; while Christopher Harris was appointed to command the *Peppercorn*.

The fleet was the finest and best-equipped that had yet been sent out by the Company. It had a leader who was second to none in all the qualifications for command and who, moreover, was invested with powers such as had never been conferred upon any of his predecessors. But it was to enjoy a still greater distinction, for it was to carry out, as the factors in India so ardently desired, an ambassador from King James himself. On 7 September, 1614, when the preparations for the dispatch of the fleet were in full swing, the topic was broached by the Governor (Sir Thomas Smythe) to the assembled 'Committees.'

Because there is and wilbe occasion of employinge one of extraordinarye parts to reside att Agra to prevent any plotts that may be wrought by the Jesuits to circumvent our trade, Mr. Governor recomended to their serious considerations the sufficiencye of Sir Thomas Rowe, a gentleman well knowne unto them all to bee of a pregnant understandinge, well spoken, learned, industrious, and of a comelie personage, and one of whome there are greate hopes that hee may worke much good for the Company. Some were of opinion that yt were rather fitt to have a meere marchannt to reside there, and that the buysines is not yet ripe to entertayne such a person, untill they have heard from Captaine Downton howe the estate of their buysines doth stand. But yt was againe supposed by others that there is noe such necessitie of a marchannt there, butt rather of one that hath beene practisde in State buysines, as Sir Thomas Rowe hath beene, and that, yf all bee well, he will be fitt to be aboute the Emperour to procure and confirme such articles and priviledges as may bee most beneficiall; or yf ought should have happened otherwise, yet he wilbe necessary to goe up to the Grand Magore to require a perfect and absolute setlinge, which yf he shall not bee able to effect, then there wilbe just cause and grounde to proceede against the Magore as they did formerlye; which will give good satisfaction to this State, when yt shall bee knowne thatt all faire and peaceable meanes have beene used to effect a quiett and peacable trade.

The question was brought up again at a meeting held on 4 October. Some opposition was then manifested, on the ground that the expense would be greater than any probable benefit would recompense, and that a royal ambassador might give trouble by asserting a right to control the Company's goods and servants.

Butt yt was awnsweared contrarilie that necessitie enforceth to have one there to awnsweare any matters thatt may bee objected and prevent all plotts and conspiracyes that wilbee attempted by the Jesuites to subvert our trade; and that, haveinge one nowe there, as they have contynuallie had, the chardge will nott be found to bee much differinge betwixt that which hath beene and which shall bee, althoughe the qualitie of the personn thatt is in question is like to promise much more hereafter then could bee formerlie expected; neither is there such cause of doubt thatt he should comand their goods, whenas he shall bee limitted by his comission and satisfied before his goinge howe farre his authoritie shall stretch, neither to have power over their servants nor goods, whoe shalbe farr remote from the place of his residence; and Captaine Keelinge haveinge the commannd of their marchandize, shall neither himselfe, nor those whome he shall leave as principall factours in any place, yeald to any other comandinge power, yf yt should bee attempted; supposinge the gentleman nowe in question to bee farre from the desire of such thoughts to seeke dishonorablie any extraordinary gaine unto himselfe. And therefore, seeinge all princes that have commerce each with other have their embassadours, it will be necessary to have His Majestie moved to bee pleased to have one likewise; and none soe fitt in their opinions as Sir Thomas Rowe, beinge a gentleman of civell behaviour, of good bredinge, personage, and very good parts, able to awnsweare any matters whatsoever, and of good understandinge to propound and settle any priviledges for the good of this Companie; and hath gyven good satisfaction in one particuler which was somewhatt doubted, concerninge private trade, wherein he protested neither to offend himselfe nor suffer yt in others, soe farre as ytt shall rest in him, butt will give knowledge thereof, yf he cannott of himselfe hinder the same.

It was stated that Roe had offered to procure sureties in 10,000*l.* for his good behaviour, and had hinted that he would be satisfied with 500*l.* or 600*l.* a year as salary, the Company providing a chaplain, a doctor, a secretary, a cook, and two personal attendants.

Butt annother doubt arysinge whether yt will be fitt to have such a personn for their embassador, or a marchannte rather, leaste tyme may worke to have such an one putt upon them by His Majestie whoe may bringe to passe those things which are nowe soe much doubted, it was awnsweared that experience had approved many times in the like cases howe that His Majestie would never send any butt such as they that were interested had made choise of and approved. And after sundrie objections and awnsweares propounded, it was generallie conceyved very fittinge and necessarie to have one of good partes to reside there, and were of opinion that none could bee found in all respects better qualified for that purpose then Sir Thomas Rowe, whose employment wilbee necessarie, yf the trade bee setled, to capitulate and confirme some certaine and large conditions; or otherwise that by his wisdome hee might conferre withe the Grand Mogore, perswade and settle a trade upon good tearmes, if yt bee possible, and soe putt yt on againe, yf casuallie yt should bee broken off. Which reasons swayinge att present, they were all desyred to keepe the matter (and whatsoever had beene delyvered) private to themselves, and to consider thereof against their next meeteinge upon Fryday to delyver their opinions and resolutions therein.

Accordingly at the next meeting (7 October) the consideration of the matter was resumed, and this time a decision was reached.

The former reasons were againe reiterated and amplyfied, and all inconvenyences and objections fullie considered and argued; and the question beinge thereupon putt, whether they thought yt fittinge and necessary to have an embassadour of extraordinarye countenance and respect to be sent with the next shipps at Christmas next, it was resolvd of by erection of hannds as most necessary. But then entringe into consideration of the person, Sir John Brooke was nominated as a gentleman well qualified for the said employment, butt the estate of his bodie much doubted, beeinge of a weake constitution; as alsoe one Mr. Bailie. Butt none were esteemed soe fittinge for that service as Sir Thomas Roe, yf he may bee had; and therefore desyred Mr. Governor to treate with him, and lefte yt to his wisdome to husband the buysines as well as he might, and to take notice of his demands, that this Courte may consider of the same.

It is evident that the candidature of Roe was favoured by Sir Thomas Smythe; and the following pages will show that

INTRODUCTION

the results amply justified his choice. Roe was in the prime of life, and was well fitted by education and experience to fill the post thus offered to him. His commanding presence and dignified bearing were useful qualifications for a mission to an Eastern court; while in the still more important matters of judgement and tact he was equally well equipped. Sprung from a noted city family, he combined the shrewdness, readiness of resource, and business ability which had raised his ancestors to fortune, with the culture and experience obtained by a varied training in most favourable circumstances. Of his earlier life there is not much to record. He was born at Leyton in 1580, the son of Robert Roe,[1] and grandson of Sir Thomas Roe (lord mayor in 1568). In 1593 he was entered at Magdalen College, Oxford. His father died while Roe was still a minor, and his mother married into the Berkeley family.[2] Probably by the influence of his new relatives, after spending some time ' in one of the Inns of Court [3] or in France or both ' (Wood's *Athenæ*), he was made an Esquire of the Body to Queen Elizabeth. Her Majesty's death did not hinder his advancement at court, for two years later he was knighted by her successor. The young courtier formed close friendships with Prince Henry and his sister Elizabeth (afterwards Electress Palatine and titular Queen of Bohemia); both seem to have been much attached to Roe, and in after-years the unhappy princess kept up a constant and intimate correspondence with ' Honest Tom ' (as she called him), and profited much by his devoted attention to her interests. Under the patronage of the Prince, Roe sought experience of the adventurous sort which was then in fashion. Equipping, with the aid of friends (including the Earl of Southampton and Sir Walter Ralegh), a couple of pinnaces, he set sail in February, 1610, on a voyage

[1] Robert Roe was the fourth son of Sir Thomas Roe, the eldest being John, who married a daughter of Secretary Wilson.

[2] Her maiden name was Eleanor Antingham, and she married as her second husband Sir Robert Berkeley of Stoke (Glos.). Her daughter by her first marriage, Mary Roe, espoused Richard Berkeley, the grandson of Sir Robert through his first wife. See the *Visitation of Gloucestershire*, 1623 (Harleian Society), p. 8.

[3] In Foster's *Alumni Oxonienses* (vol. iii. p. 1272), Roe is stated to have been entered as a student in the Middle Temple in 1597.

of discovery to Guiana, in the course of which he is said to have penetrated three hundred miles up the little-known river of the Amazons, and to have examined the coast from the mouth of that river to the Orinoco, reaching England again in July, 1611.[1] Soon, however, a cloud came over his fortunes. The Prince, from whose favour he might have hoped for much, died in November, 1612 ; and a few months later the Princess's marriage took away his other patron. Though Roe had influential friends at court—as evidenced in his correspondence from India—they were apparently unable to help him to obtain a post worthy of his abilities. After spending some months on the Continent, he resolved to enter public life ; and in the ' Addled Parliament ' of 1614 he sat as member for Tamworth. But though ' he was one of those men who, if James had been well advised, would have been the very first to be selected for high office,'[2] his enlightened views were little likely to commend themselves to that monarch ; and thus left with no prospect at home of reconciling his loyalty and affection for the royal family with his duty to the nation, it was to foreign service alone that Roe could look for a career of usefulness.

There were other reasons why he was glad to accept employment of this nature. His fortune, which was probably in the first instance but moderate, seems to have been by this time seriously impaired. ' I esteeme it an infinite mercy of God,' he wrote later in a depressed mood from India,[3] ' that when I had fully ended and wasted my patrimony and saw no way but scorne (the reward of folly), before I suffred disgrace Hee undertooke mee, and, beeing as it were new borne, Hee restored mee to a new inheritance and sett mee right, for I doubt not but to equall my wastes.' Further, he had contracted a secret marriage with a lady of good social position (see p. 223 *n*): a step which made it all the more prudent for him to take a post which offered a comfortable salary, together with a chance

[1] Howes' continuation of Stow's *Annals*, p. 946 ; J. A. Williamson's *English Colonies in Guiana*, p. 52 ; and V. T. Harlow's *W. Indies and Guiana*, p. lxix.

[2] Dr. Gardiner, in his *History of England* (ed. 1889), vol. ii. p. 311.

[3] Brit. Mus. *Harl. MS.* 1576, f. 225.

INTRODUCTION xxiii

of displaying his diplomatic talents and of thus recommending himself to the notice of the government.

The offer of the East India Company came, therefore, in good season; and no difficulty was experienced in arriving at an agreement. Roe's salary was fixed at six hundred pounds a year, of which one half was to be paid to him in India, and the rest to be put into the Company's stock. Out of the first year's salary, however, a sum of 500 marks (afterwards increased to 400*l*.) was advanced to enable the ambassador 'to satisfie som debts which he oweth abroad'; a similar amount was given him 'to furnishe him forth to sea'; while in addition 100*l*. was lent for the purchase of plate for his table. Except a chaplain and a chirurgeon, whom the Company provided at the cost of 50*l*. and 24*l*. per annum respectively, Roe was to engage his own retinue, receiving for their wages an allowance of 100*l*. a year, with a grant of 30*l*. towards the cost of their liveries. Diet and other household expenses were to be charged to the Company, unless the Great Mogul should make an allowance for this purpose. Finally, Roe was strictly bound to forbear all private trade himself, and to hinder it as much as possible in others; also to abstain from interference with the Company's factors in matters of merchandise.[1]

The royal sanction was readily given, King James approving both the Company's choice of an ambassador and the arrangements made for his mission; 'houldinge yt a good ground for him to worke upon yf occasion should bee to treate with the Spanyard concerninge the East Indies, or else with the Flemyngs.' Roe was accordingly furnished with letters of credence, a royal missive to the Great Mogul, and detailed instructions for his guidance. The latter, it may be mentioned, included directions as to the reply he was to give if asked why the Portuguese aggressions in Asia were not actively resented; and also a recommendation to impress upon the Asiatic monarch, 'by way of discourse,' the greatness of King James

[1] The agreement has been printed in *The First Letter Book* (p. 446) and again in the first edition of the present work. In January, 1615, a further advance of 100*l*. was made to Roe on account of his second year's salary.

and the naval strength of his kingdom, which ' maketh Us even a terrour to all other nations ; concluding all with this happines, that Wee be not onelie absolutelie obeyed but universally beloved and admyred of all our people.'[1]

The importance attached by Roe to the maintenance of the dignity of his position is shown by his lavish expenditure on apparel in his outfit (*Add. MS.* 6115, f. 280). One suit, consisting of a scarlet cloak and hose, with a crimson satin doublet, all trimmed with gold lace, cost him 73*l*. 7*s*. 6*d*. ; another of cloth, lined with sea-green velvet, with a doublet of ash-colour, was priced at 43*l*. ; while his outlay for other articles of attire was in proportion. Besides this, he spent 47*l*. on plate, and 12*l*. on liveries, beyond the Company's allowance for these items ; he bought a bed for use on the voyage, which with the necessary appurtenances cost him 29*l*. ; and he also provided himself with a viol, presumably to while away the hours at sea. On reaching Surat, he bought from Captain Keeling a suit of ' branchd grogram in flowers ' for 14*l*., and caused another to be made for him of white damask ; while at court he invested in several suits of carnation and sea-green, of olive and crimson, of cloth of gold mingled with green, of cloth of silver with a cloak lined with purple ; and so on through a long catalogue.

All being ready, on 2 Feb., 1615, Roe embarked with fifteen followers in the *Lion* at Tilbury Hope.[2] Some time was spent in the Downs, and again at Portland, waiting for a wind, so that it was 6 March before they lost sight of the Lizard. The six months' voyage to Surat was uneventful, and to Roe exceedingly tedious. Apparently, in order to satisfy some of the

---

[1] The royal commission is entered on the *Charter Roll* (*Chancery*) 217 (m. 17). It has been printed in Rymer's *Fœdera* (vol. xvi. pp. 775-6), and in the first edition of the present work. The King's instructions are also given in the latter volume, from a copy in the Public Record Office (*C.O.* 77, vol. i. No. 44). There is an abstract of them among the Carte MSS. (No. 103, f. 282) in the Bodleian Library. The Company's instructions are not extant. According to a note among the Bodleian manuscripts (*Carte* 103, f. 289) Roe also took with him a scroll on which was emblazoned his pedigree.

[2] Peyton's Journal (Brit. Mus. *Add. MS.* 19276 ; and *Purchas His Pilgrimes*, vol. i. p. 528).

INTRODUCTION

wiseacres of the Court of Committees, the commanders had been warned not to allow Roe to encroach upon their authority, and he found himself, therefore, excluded carefully from their deliberations. He could not help resenting this suspicious attitude, and he was consequently in a critical mood for the greater part of the voyage. The situation was, in fact, a delicate one ; and with men less tactful than Roe and Keeling it might easily have brought about a quarrel. The latter, however, showed the ambassador every consideration consistent with obedience to his instructions, and Roe acknowledged in handsome terms his correct behaviour.

The ships touched at the Cape, at the Comoro Islands, and at Sokotra. At the first of these stopping-places they fell in with the *Merchant's Hope*, one of the vessels of Downton's fleet of the preceding year, now on her way back from Surat to England with a lading of cotton goods and indigo. She brought news of important events, as well on the Indian coast as at the Mughal court. The most exciting piece of intelligence was that hostilities had broken out between the Indians and the Portuguese. The latter, impatient at their want of success in persuading the Emperor to expel the English from his dominions, had tried to force the pace by seizing a Surat vessel which was returning from the Red Sea with a rich freight. This was done in spite of the fact that the ship was provided with a Portuguese pass, and that Jahāngīr's mother had a large interest in her cargo. Such high-handed behaviour presumed too much upon the patience of the Emperor, who retaliated by imprisoning all the Portuguese in his realm and by dispatching Mukarrab Khān (one of his most trusted officers) to besiege the Portuguese forts on the coast. At this juncture (October, 1614) Downton arrived in Swally Road with his fleet. Mukarrab Khān at once applied to the English commander for his co-operation against the common enemy. His credit was involved in the speedy capture of Damān, on the fortifications of which his clumsy artillery could make no impression ; and he was anxious, therefore, that the English ships should go ' batter the castle.' He was willing to promise, in return, any concessions the English might desire, and he urged with much force that the quarrel was really due to the presence of their vessels. Downton, however, though a capable commander, was naturally diffident in matters of this kind; while his feeble health probably had its influence in preventing him from adopting a bold policy. A refusal was therefore returned to Mukarrab Khān's demand, and Downton made it understood that he should confine himself strictly to standing on the defensive. Mukarrab Khān, indignant at this reply, put for a time every obstacle in the way of the English trade, and made overtures to the Dutch at Masulipatam. Soon, however, the intelligence that the Viceroy of Goa was preparing an armament to attack Surat convinced him of the impolicy of driving away his only friends; and he therefore made Aldworth 'large promises of future good respect,' and paid a visit to Downton, to whom he was very gracious. A fortnight later, a score of small vessels—the advance-guard of the Portuguese flotilla—arrived; and these were followed shortly after (January, 1615) by the Viceroy himself with a formidable array. Mukarrab Khān, intimidated by these forces, and feeling little reliance on English help, made overtures for peace; but fortunately the Viceroy, convinced that victory was within his grasp, rejected the proffered terms as insufficient. The fight that followed has been several times narrated. The English position amongst the sandbanks of the roadstead, though it had many drawbacks, neutralised to some extent the superiority in numbers of the Portuguese. An attempt to carry the *Merchant's Hope* by boarding was repulsed with great loss; and subsequent endeavours to destroy the English vessels by means of fireships were frustrated by Downton's vigilance and adroit manœuvring. Finding at last that he could make no impression upon his opponent's fleet, and not daring to leave his ships exposed to their attacks while he sent his men up the river to attempt Surat, the Viceroy was forced to retire baffled. Downton remained until 2 March, when the fleet set sail: the *Hope* for England, and the rest for Bantam. Meanwhile, William Edwards, the chief of the newly-arrived factors, had been despatched to court with a new letter from King James and a fresh batch of presents, in the hope that, in the altered circumstances, he would succeed in obtaining the formal grant of privileges for which Kerridge had pleaded in vain.

INTRODUCTION xxvii

Such was the intelligence received by Roe at Table Bay. There was little more to learn when the ships cast anchor in Swally Road (18 Sept., 1615). Edwards was still at court, where, owing partly to the Mogul's gratification at the presents he brought and partly to the impression produced by Downton's victory, he had met with a very promising reception. No peace had been concluded, though a preliminary agreement between Mukarrab Khān and a Portuguese representative had been submitted to the Mogul for ratification, and hostilities were for the present suspended. Surat was now nominally under the rule of Prince Khurram, the Emperor's favourite son, who had committed its government and the care of its rising revenues to one of his confidants, named Zūlfakār Khān. The latter, however, was not more favourably inclined towards the English than his predecessors ; while a powerful party at court, including the Prince and Mukarrab Khān, made no secret of their preference for the Portuguese.

There was thus ample scope for the abilities of the ambassador, whose difficulties commenced from the moment of his landing. He had wisely determined to take a high tone from the first, and to insist upon being received with the respect due to his office. This was the more necessary, as hitherto the English representatives had made no attempt to assert their dignity ; indeed, the latest, Edwards, had ' suffered blowes of the porters, base peons, and beene thrust out by them with much scorne by head and shoulders, without seeking satisfaction, and . . . carried himselfe with such complacency that hath bredd a low reputation of our nation ' (p. 96). Small wonder was it that upon the announcement of the arrival of yet another ' ambassador,' making high claim to respect, the officials ' laughd one upon another ' (p. 30), or that the Governor of Surat felt himself at liberty to flout the new-comer and rifle the merchants' goods at his pleasure, regardless of protests and threats. Finding that no offer was made to bribe him into civility, he threw manifold obstacles in the way of the ambassador, and employed every artifice to humiliate and embarrass him. The story of the contest between the two furnishes most amusing reading. The victory rested with the Englishman, whose cool and resolute fence proved more than a match for the oriental cunning of his adversary ; and when Roe set out on his journey to the court, the Governor humbly desired his friendship, and offered him anything he would demand.

The situation of the English had, in fact, been changed by Roe's arrival in a way that completely justified the dispatch of the embassy. Never, perhaps, were his countrymen so near expulsion from this, their only foothold in the Mughal dominions—and expulsion would have meant reprisals which might well have made an irreparable breach. The draft treaty which was being pressed upon Jahāngīr by the advocates of the Portuguese stipulated for the absolute exclusion of the English from all parts of his empire, and directions to that effect had already been sent to Surat. This *farmān* was followed in the middle of October by one from the Prince, ordering ' that the English should dischardge one ship and have a monthes staye in trade, but no residences in the towne ' ; and although it was afterwards found expedient to disavow these instructions, there can be no doubt that they were issued, and would in other circumstances have been obeyed. Roe, nothing daunted, resolved to hasten his journey to court, and to ascertain from the Emperor himself whether he was disposed to meet the reasonable demands of the English. If not, Roe would ' returne to our ships with expedition, having advertised the Mogull that as he was lord of his owne land and might doe his pleasure, and had forsaken the amytie of a prince who had desired yt in faire and honorable tearmes, for the Portugalls who made him tributary, to his eternall dishonor, so he would fynd by experience the King my master would be lord of all these seas and ports to the prejudice of his subjects, in spight of those in whom he now trusted ' (p. 56). Fortunately, this extreme measure was not required. The news that a real ambassador from the English king had arrived with presents roused the curiosity and cupidity of Jahāngīr himself, and a letter of reproof to the Governor was followed by a safe-conduct for Roe, ' in all things very favorable (except chardges),' which made his opponent look ' very blancke ' and enabled the ambassador to quit Surat in triumph.

Of Roe's arrival, his contest with the Governor, and his journey as far as Burhānpur, we have an independent

INTRODUCTION xxix

account by a Dutch merchant whose narrative has recently been printed by Dr. H. Terpstra in his *De Opkomst der Westerkwartieren van de Oost-Indische Compagnie* (1918). To explain his presence in Surat it is necessary to go back to the beginning of Dutch intercourse with Western India. The first attempt to open up trade was made by two merchants named De Wolff and Lafer, who voyaged thither from Achin in 1602. They met with a friendly reception ; but, no further supplies arriving, they left in the following year and made their way to the Malabar coast, where they were seized by the Portuguese, taken to Goa, and put to death. The next venture was in 1606, when David van Deynsen and two companions started a fresh factory in Surat. The two juniors died, and a dispute with a Portuguese trader obliged Van Deynsen to proceed to the Khānkhānān's headquarters at Burhānpur. Whilst there, he learnt that the Portuguese had secured a monopoly of the trade at Surat, with a promise that Van Deynsen, should he return thither, would be surrendered to them. In despair he shot himself ; and his effects were taken possession of by the Mughal authorities at Burhānpur and Surat. The latter, however, fearing lest reprisals should be made on the Gujarāti shipping, wrote to the Dutch at Masulipatam, offering to deliver the goods to anyone who might be sent to receive them. No one was desirous of undertaking so doubtful and dangerous a mission ; and so the matter was allowed to rest until the offer was renewed in 1613 by the Shāhbandar of Surat. Some correspondence followed, which resulted in fresh promises from the Mughal authorities, who were desirous of Dutch support in their hostilities with the Portuguese ; and it was then decided to dispatch a couple of factors overland, with the double object of recovering the money and goods left by Van Deynsen and of exploring the possibilities of trade. Accordingly Pieter Gillis van Ravesteyn and Hendrik Adriaensen started from Masulipatam in April 1615 and, journeying by way of Hyderābād and Aurangābād, reached their destination in June. They found the situation changed by the negotiations that were going on for the conclusion of peace with the Portuguese ; and before long it was made clear to them that no settled factory would be allowed without the express permission of the Emperor, to obtain which it would be necessary for them to make a journey to court. The recovery of Van Deynsen's effects proved by no means an easy task, for, now that Dutch aid was no longer a matter of solicitude, those concerned were unwilling to disgorge. With great difficulty Van Ravesteyn obtained a part of what was due; while for the rest he was referred to the Khānkhānān at Burhānpur.

In his journal, which Dr. Terpstra has printed in full, Van Ravesteyn records the arrival of Roe, on whom he waited as soon as the ambassador came to Surat. Roe received him kindly, told him some Europe news, and then complained of the Governor's behaviour in detaining his baggage. The Dutchman bears strong testimony to the tyrannous conduct of Zūlfakār Khān, and says that his overbearing and avaricious ways made him detested by the whole community. Finding that nothing more could be obtained at Surat, Van Ravesteyn and his companion resolved to take advantage of the ambassador's protection by making the first part of their return journey with his party. They accordingly travelled in his company as far as Burhānpur. There they remained about three weeks; and then, having procured what they could from the Khānkhānān, they resumed their journey to Masulipatam, which was reached towards the end of January, 1616. In a report sent home in March, 1616, Van Ravesteyn advised against any further attempt being made to trade at Surat, in the face of Portuguese opposition. However, as we shall see, the Director-General Koen had already dispatched a vessel thither; and later Van Ravesteyn himself was to pay a second visit to those parts and renew his acquaintance with the English ambassador.

Roe arrived at Ajmer on 23 Dec., 1615, the journey having taken close upon two months. On his way up country, he paid a visit at Burhānpur to Sultān Parwīz, the Mogul's second son, who was nominally in command of the army operating against the forces of the Deccan kings; and from him Roe obtained a *farmān* authorising the English to establish a factory in that city. The journey was made in much discomfort. At Burhānpur fever laid hold of the ambassador, and shortly after his departure thence, for two nights his life was despaired of by his dismayed attendants. Even when he had reached the court, for a whole week he lay prostrate ; and it was not until 10 Jan., 1616, that he was able to present himself at the *darbār*.[1]

The monarch to whom he was now introduced is known to history by the high-sounding title of Jahāngīr (' World-Grasper,' or ' Conqueror of the World '). He had been on the throne of Hindustān a little more than ten years, having succeeded his father, the great Akbar, in 1605. Some characteristics were common to both father and son—the love of hunting and other sports, the painstaking administration of justice, the considerate bearing towards strangers—but in other respects there was a great contrast between them. Of Akbar's administrative ability, as of his military skill, Jahāngīr had not a trace. Both monarchs interested themselves in religious discussions ; but while Akbar had been actuated by a sincere desire to find a faith which should reconcile the clashing tenets of the creeds around him—' a temple neither pagod, mosque, nor church '— Jahāngīr, though even in drink he would ' dispute of the lawes of Moses, Jesus and Mahomett,' felt but a languid interest in such questions, and his tolerance was the outcome not of reason but of indifference. What in the father had been the eager workings of a mind desirous of collecting and utilising information of all kinds, became in the son a childish curiosity which (as evinced in his diary) found as much satisfaction in counting the number of cups of wine he drank as in hearing of the weightiest matters of state. But, on the whole, despite his drunkenness, his occasional lapses into cruelty, his weak-minded submission to the influence of his wife and of his favourite son, the portrait of Jahāngīr drawn by Roe is not unfavourable. He was uniformly kind and courteous to the ambassador ; and his gracious behaviour on this occasion greatly pleased and encouraged Roe, who notes exultantly

[1] This illness was but the forerunner of many others that afflicted him during his stay in India, and the many vexations of his mission were seriously aggravated by this constant ill-health. Few more melancholy sentences were ever written than that quoted on p. 302 : ' I was not borne to a life smooth and easy ; all my actions have beene mingled with crosses and rubbs, that I might rather say I wrestled then walked toward my grave.'

that he was treated ' with more favour and outward grace . . . then ever was sheowed to any ambassador, eyther of the Turke or Persian, or other whatsoever.' It is evident that the Emperor was favourably impressed by Roe's demeanour; and, indeed, his attitude during the whole period of the latter's stay in the country showed his personal esteem and liking for the ambassador, combined, it must be owned, with a total indifference to the objects of his mission.

But however well-disposed the monarch himself might be, Roe soon found that there were other persons to be reckoned with whose good-will it was not so easy to secure. The ' Conqueror of the World ' was the slave of a woman—his consort, Nūr Mahal, or Nūr Jahān, as she was afterwards styled. Her father, the Itimād-uddaula, and her brother, Āsaf Khān, had a large share in the administration of affairs; while her niece (Āsaf Khān's daughter) was the wife of Sultān Khurram, the Mogul's favourite son, who afterwards succeeded to the throne under the title of Shāh Jahān. All these personages were at this time in close alliance, their special aim being to strengthen the Prince's influence and advance his interests against those of his elder brothers—Sultān Khusrau, who since his rebellion (1606) had been kept a close prisoner, and Sultān Parwīz, who (as already stated) was nominally in command of the army in the Deccan. Unfortunately, Roe did not at first perceive, or else failed to estimate correctly, the strength of the power behind the throne. Confident in the good-will of the monarch himself, he hoped to override, if necessary, all opposition; and the parsimony exercised by the Company in his stock of presents, contrasting with the lavish supply sent with his predecessor, effectually prevented him from making friends in the only way friends could be made at the Mughal court. Even for the Emperor Roe had to draw upon his own slender store, and he was absolutely destitute of presents fit to be offered to the Queen, or sufficient to satisfy the inordinate expectations of her brother.[1]

[1] ' Asaph Chan did expect some great present for him selfe and the Queene, as I understood ; and as he is the cheefest man with the Kyng, soe is he in faction with Sultan Coronne (who hath married his daughter), and Normall the beloved wife of the Kyng is sister to

INTRODUCTION

To the Prince he paid a visit of compliment and delivered a present, though ' not in the name of His Majestie, it beeing too meane ' ; but at the first interview he hinted an intention of appealing to the Emperor if speedy satisfaction were not given for the wrongs suffered at Surat. The veiled threat was hardly likely to be palatable to the Prince, whose ' proud nature ' is especially noted by Roe, and whose prepossession against the English mission had probably been increased by the representations of Zūlfakār Khān and the complaints from the Surat officials, not only of the loss of trade caused by the exclusion of the Portuguese, but also of the riotous behaviour of the English seamen.

For the present, however, no animosity was shown, and Roe set about his negotiations with great hope of success. One of the earliest objects of his solicitude had been the attitude of the Portuguese. As long as such attacks as those of 1612 and 1615 were possible, it was necessary to keep the whole of the English fleet at Surat for one ship's lading, at an expense of time and money which seriously reduced the profits of the trade. Could Roe have had his way, the challenge of the past year at Swally would have been answered at Goa, for ' the offensive,' he wrote to the Company, ' is both the nobler and the safer part ' (p. 79). But his present errand was one of peace, and he had therefore, while still at Surat, addressed a letter to the Viceroy (couched, it is true, in somewhat imperious terms) offering him ' comprisure ' in the intended treaty with

Asaph Chan. So they are lincked togeather, governe the Kyng, and carry busines that no complaynt should be made wherby the Kyng might be angry with Sultan Coronne.'—*Roe to the Company,* 25 Jan., 1616 (*Add. MS.* 6115, f. 70).

' For presents, I have none, or so meane that they are woorse then none ; so that I have resolved to give none, for the last years liberalitye and provision of the Company was such . . . as I can no way equall. Therfore I answer all the great ones : I come from kyng to kyng, not to present every man, but to demand justice for the injuryes and insolencyes offered His Majesties subjects.'—*Roe to Keeling,* 13 Jan., 1616 (*Add. MS.* 6115, f. 65).

In an earlier letter (1 Jan., 1616 : *ibid.*), Roe told Keeling that he had sent Āsaf Khān ' a ringe . . . to make aquayntance (not as a present, but in love),' but it had been returned ' as too poore of valew ; yett did the Kings stone cutter rate it at 400 *rupyes.*'

the Mogul, and threatening reprisals if the Portuguese persisted in their hostility. The letter was ignored ; but gradually the question lost its urgency. The conclusion of peace (in a very informal fashion) between the natives and the Portuguese and the resumption of commerce dissipated Roe's dream of joint action against the Viceroy's forces ; the latter, crippled by want of supplies from home, attacked in the West by the Persians, in the East by the Dutch, could initiate no vigorous action against the intruders at Surat ; while the fact that King James had so far extended his protection to his subjects' trade as to send an ambassador to India may also have deterred the authorities at Goa from giving cause for complaints at Madrid which might prove embarrassing. The English had gained all that was pressingly wanted, when they were no longer actively molested. For past offences, they revenged themselves on the Portuguese shipping whenever an opportunity occurred ; and perhaps they were not altogether sorry that ' the warr was left open for both at sea ' (p. 74), since thus a legitimate excuse was provided for prize-taking.

As already stated, the authorities at Goa made no response to Roe's peremptory summons ; but he had still to feel their influence at court. At his first interview with the Prince, the latter had promised him ' a *firmaen* for Surat effectually ' ; when, however, the document was received, it was found to be contingent on Roe's signature of an undertaking to allow the Portuguese vessels to trade at that port without molestation. To this the ambassador refused to agree, partly because he feared a treacherous attack if the Portuguese vessels were allowed to ride among the English, and partly because he deemed it dishonouring to give such an undertaking unless a similar assurance was required from the Viceroy. To the refusal it was answered he ' should then have no *firmaen* for Suratt ' ; and an appeal to the good offices of Āsaf Khān led to the discovery that he was ' the author of this device and an earnest disputer for the reasonablenes therof.' Roe was for a while irresolute as to his best course of action ; but after waiting some time, and making several ineffectual attempts to obtain his desire, he determined to bring the matter to the notice of the Emperor. An opportunity was afforded by the festival of

INTRODUCTION

the *Nauroz*, at which Roe (12 March) presented, from his private store, a gold chain, with an emerald seal, enclosed in a crystal box inlaid with gold—a curiosity which gave great pleasure to the Mogul. The following evening an opening occurred for making his grievance known, and of this he at once took advantage. The result was not altogether fortunate. A preliminary conversation, regarding the further curiosities which the English could bring, excited Jahāngīr's cupidity, and on hearing the ambassador's vague references to wrongs which, if unremedied, would force them to quit the trade, he ' grew soddenly into cholor, pressing to know who had wronged us, with such show of fury that I was loath to follow yt.' Roe attempted to appease him by saying (through his bungling interpreter) that he would seek justice from the Prince ; but Jahāngīr conceived that he was accusing the latter, and, calling for his son, rated him soundly in the presence of the court. With the aid of a Persian nobleman, Roe succeeded in making his meaning clear, and an animated discussion then took place between him and ' the Portugalls side,' in which (he says) ' I explaynd my selfe fully concerning them ; and . . . wee wear very warme.' At last Āsaf Khān interposed to quiet the dispute, and it was agreed that the ambassador should submit his demands in writing, ' and if they were found reasonable the King would firme [*i.e.* sign] them.'

This arrangement opened the way to a proposal by which Roe hoped to place the position of his countrymen on a lasting basis, and at the same time to avoid these dangerous controversies with the Prince, by obtaining a general concession, which would apply to Surat as to any other ports where the English might settle, and which, as emanating from the Mogul himself, could not be overridden by any lesser authority. *Farmāns*, however favourable, were of little use ; they were partial in their application, and were liable to be contradicted at any moment by fresh commands. What the ambassador desired was something of a more permanent nature —a solemn treaty between his royal master and the Great Mogul, securing definite privileges to the English merchants, and binding ' the high and mighty King of India ' to the due and faithful performance of its conditions. Such a treaty—

intended, in fact, to be on a par with the 'capitulations' obtained by the European nations in Turkey—Roe now drew up and presented for consideration. It provided for the access of the English to all ports belonging to the Great Mogul, including those of Bengal and Sind, and the passage of their goods without payment of any duty beyond the usual customs; they were to be allowed to buy and sell freely, to rent factories, to hire boats and carts, and to buy provisions at the usual rates; while other articles were directed against the confiscation of the effects of deceased factors, the obnoxious claim to search the persons of the merchants on going ashore, the opening of presents intended for the court, delays in the customhouse, and other similar abuses. On the part of the English, Roe was willing to engage that they should not molest the ships of other nations, 'except the enemyes of the said English, or any other that shall seeke to injure them,' and that their factors, while residing ashore, should 'behave them selves peaceably and civilly'; that they should do their best to procure rarities for the Great Mogul, and should furnish him (upon payment) with any goods or 'furniture of warr' that he could reasonably desire; and that they should assist him against 'any enemy to the common peace.' The Portuguese were to be admitted to 'enter into the said peace and leauge,' should they be willing; but if they did not do so within six months, the English were to be allowed to treat them as enemies and make war upon them at sea 'without any offence to the said great King of India.'

This scheme for 'a good and perfect love, leauge, and peace to endure for ever' was referred by the Mogul to Āsaf Khān, through whom all business relating to the English had to pass. After some demur, he appeared to approve the draft, at least with some verbal amendments; and meeting the English envoy one day at the *darbār*, he told him that the articles were 'ready for the seale.'

Meanwhile fresh matter for controversy had arrived in the shape of the long-expected particulars from Surat of the sums extorted by the local officials, especially by the Governor, Zūlfakār Khān, who had been recalled to court in consequence of Roe's complaints, but 'with our goods extorted by force

[had] made his peace.' These statements were sent to Āsaf Khān, who as usual promised complete satisfaction. Seeing, however, no sign of progress, Roe took the Prince ' some powrfull wyne and in the strength therof desired justice.' He received ' an open promise for effectuall satisfaction ' upon all points, except the infliction of personal punishment on the Governor, a demand which he found it would be wiser to forgo ; and so he went home ' well content with this, it beeing the best morning that ever wee had in India.' Within a few days the Prince had signed two *farmāns*, authorizing the residence of the English at Surat and their free passage inland, and ordering redress for the abuses they had suffered. These Roe gladly received, and dispatched to Surat.

Matters went on quietly for another month, which was passed for the most part in negotiations over the sum claimed by Roe from Zūlfakār Khān in repayment of his exactions. After much haggling, the latter offered 17,000 *mahmudis* in full discharge : but Roe, acting on the information supplied to him from Surat, rejected this as insufficient. Later on he was mortified to discover that the account sent up by the factors was incorrect, and that the amount offered in settlement was after all a reasonable one. No opportunity was lost, either, of pressing Āsaf Khān for the signature of Roe's ' articles from the King, which were of most consequence ' : but the minister, while full of promises and artful excuses, seemed determined to delay matters indefinitely.

Soon Roe's prospects grew still more gloomy. The Emperor, finding that no more presents were forthcoming, had lost interest in the demands of his foreign visitor ; the Prince, already irritated by the way in which his favourite was being pursued, was still more angered by some scenes at court over an English runaway, in which he had been entirely discomfited ; and, to crown all, some Portuguese merchants, who had arrived ' with many rarietyes to sell the King and with rich presents from the Vizeroy of Goa,' had made handsome gifts to Āsaf Khān and other influential persons, and were consequently in high favour. The English ' were for a tyme eclipsed,' and the attitude of the courtiers towards the new-comers gave Roe food for deep reflection. The Portuguese, he noted, ' were sought after by every body, wheras they [the Indians] seeme to buy our comodityes for almes. ... Only for a little feare we were entertayned; but for our trade, or any thing wee bring, not att all respected.' On 1 June he was informed by a message from Āsaf Khān that, upon the complaint of the Prince, the Emperor had forbidden him to present himself at court; and hints were not wanting that some of the Prince's turbulent soldiery might take occasion to revenge his open braving of their chief. Nothing daunted, Roe assumed a careless attitude. The threat of violence he treated with scorn; while to Āsaf Khān's offers of help, provided he would compound with Zūlfakār Khān, he replied that he would not 'give away the Companyes monny for good lookes: the world was wyde enough: we gott not soe much by this trade as that wee would buy it with too much injurye'; he would await the King's answer a few days longer, 'and accordingly eyther resolve of longer residence or prepare to retyre my selfe and my nation toward our port to seeke better entertaynment.'

Roe was, in fact, seriously considering the advisability of thus bringing matters to a decisive issue, when the solution of the deadlock came from an unexpected quarter. Mukarrab Khān, hitherto an enemy of the English, thinking he saw a chance of currying favour with them 'in hope of the first sight of raretyes from England,' took an opportunity of telling the Mogul the reason why the English envoy came no more to court. Jahāngīr promptly denied having issued any order for his exclusion, and authorized Mukarrab Khān to inform him to that effect. Roe's new friend was most anxious that he should rely upon him rather than upon Āsaf Khān; but the ambassador, knowing the power of the latter, judged it unwise to break with him, and accordingly accepted with seeming cordiality the assurances of friendship which Āsaf Khān made to him on hearing of Mukarrab Khān's overtures. The mourning caused by the death of a favourite granddaughter of the Mogul delayed Roe's audience, but on 25 June he presented himself at court, and 'was received by the King after the ould manner, no difference, without taking any notice of my absence.' Negotiations were resumed, all the more urgently because Zūlfakār Khān was soon to depart with the

Prince for the Deccan war. By 9 July an agreement had been reached ; but this was followed by fresh evasions, and it was not until 5 August that Roe was able to record that ' this long and troublesome busines is finished.' The full amount demanded had not been obtained, but the loss was trifling ; and to have forced the Prince's favourite to disgorge his exactions was a salutary warning to other governors. The Prince seemed to have forgotten his resentment, and treated the ambassador with civility. Even the ' propositions for priviledges ' were said to have been acceded to ; and a fresh proposal from Roe that the English should pay a yearly sum of Rs. 12,000 in satisfaction of all customs due from them at Surat was courteously debated, though in the end it was allowed to drop, as the two sides could not agree upon the amount to be paid. From Jahāngīr himself he ' never received so much grace and favour . . . as at this tyme ; which all men took notice off and accordingly altered their fashions toward ' him ; while Āsaf Khān was full of ' complements of frendship and love.'

A characteristic incident lightens the pages of the journal at this point. Roe had presented to Jahāngīr a choice miniature, painted by Isaac Oliver, which gave him ' extreame content,' and, ' confident that noe man in India could equall yt,' the ambassador had agreed to a wager that he would be able to distinguish it from any copies the court painters could produce. When, however, the matter came to the test, he found that the native artists had succeeded beyond expectation, and it was only with difficulty that he was able ' to discerne which was which.' The Emperor was ' very merry and joyfull, and craked [*i.e.* boasted] like a northern man.' He insisted on the ambassador presenting the painter with a suitable reward; offered Roe his choice of the copies that had been made, ' to showe in England wee are not soe unskillfull as yow esteeme us';[1] and, as a further mark of favour, gave orders for a portrait of himself to be made for the ambassador.

August brought fresh matter for the exercise of Roe's

[1] Roe was evidently much impressed by the skill of the artists employed by the Emperor. ' In that arte of liminge,' he wrote, ' his płynters woorke miracles.'

diplomacy, for news came tnat a Dutch ship had arrived at Surat, and that her crew spoke of further vessels expected from Holland. It was clearly to the interest of the English to get rid of these troublesome competitors, 'who would both outpresent, outbribe, and outbuy us in all things'; yet Roe was unwilling, for many reasons, to show open hostility, more especially as the arguments he had used against the Portuguese monopoly would then be turned against himself. Ingeniously, if somewhat disingenuously, he endeavoured to compass his object by instilling into the minds of Āsaf Khān and the Prince a suspicion that the real object of the Dutch was to plunder native shipping in revenge for the injuries previously sustained at Surat and Burhānpur : that in any case they would be disorderly and unruly, 'so that if His Highnes could be quiettly ridd of them, it were a happines and ease to him.' The intrigue was not entirely successful. The fear that, if repulsed, the Dutch would retaliate by capturing the ships then due from the Red Sea induced the local authorities to permit them to leave a few factors, with a stock of merchandise, at Surat, 'untill the Princes answere and resolution were knowne'; and the footing thus obtained was successfully maintained. In the spring of 1617 two ships were dispatched from Bantam to Surat, under the command of Pieter van den Broecke, with Van Ravesteyn as his principal coadjutor. Both vessels were wrecked on the Indian coast, but the survivors succeeded in reaching Surat. As the English refused to give them passages to Bantam, the bulk of them, under Van den Broecke, marched overland to Masulipatam, Van Ravesteyn being left at Surat in charge of the factory. In January, 1618, as related in the text, he waited upon Jahāngīr and Prince Khurram at Ahmadābād, and obtained from the latter a grant of privileges ' upon as good tearmes almost as wee ' (pp. 427, 435).

Five months had now passed since Roe had presented for consideration his proposed treaty. He had made every effort to obtain its ratification, yet no answer had been returned. Urged to action by the approach of the new fleet from England, he resolved to wait no longer for this general concession, but to secure at least a temporary grant from the Prince, ' whose port wee were att, and with whom was our greatest busines.' His overtures were well received. Stipulating only that 'whatsoever toyes came to bee sould might be first showed to him,' the Prince agreed to all the privileges demanded, and a *farmān* embodying these was ordered to be drawn and sealed without delay. Thus immediate necessities were provided for, and the incoming fleet might safely land their goods and drive their trade without fear of the hindrances and abuses which their predecessors had suffered.

Meanwhile, renewed tokens of the Mogul's esteem had roused fresh hopes in Roe's breast. At the beginning of September, Jahāngīr celebrated his birthday with great pomp. With his usual considerateness he had ordered that the English envoy should be invited to witness the ceremony of weighing the monarch against gold and other things; but, owing to a mistake of the messenger, Roe attended at the wrong time, 'and soe missed the sight.' In the evening, however, after he had retired to rest, he was sent for in great haste. A few days previously, he had incautiously shown the Emperor's painter, 'for the arts sake,' a miniature he had, depicting—if we guess rightly—the lady whom he had espoused prior to his departure from England. The news had reached Jahāngīr's ears, and he was all agog to see the miniature, thinking, probably, that it had been purposely kept from his sight lest he should expect to be presented with it. Roe found him 'sitting crosse leggd on a little throne, all cladd in diamonds, pearles and rubyes . . . his nobilitye about him in their best equipage, whom hee commanded to drinck froliquely, severall wynes standing by in great flagons.' The miniature was no sooner seen than coveted, and the ambassador, after a faint resistance, was forced to present it. He was then asked to join in celebrating the anniversary, and, after he had pledged the monarch in some wine, was invited to accept the gold cup, with cover and stand, in which it had been served. Jahāngīr's gracious demeanour on this occasion encouraged Roe to press Āsaf Khān for the signature of the desired 'articles,' 'assuring him His Majestie could give mee no present so acceptable'; and Āsaf Khān promised to meet his wishes without delay.

Two days later the answer arrived; but it was far from

being the one he expected. 'I received my articles back from Asaph Chan, who tooke now att last many exceptions, and margined them with his pen in most insolent sort, scorning that any man should article att all ; saying it was sufficient for mee to receive a *firmaen* from the Prince, who was lord of Suratt, and, for lycence to trade at any other port, of Bengala or Syndu, it should never be granted ; but in conclusion pretended the length and forme to be such as would offend the King. Some articles hee consented too, and to them, beeing reducd to the forme of a *firmaen*, hee would procure yt sealed.' This reply appears to have taken Roe by surprise ; yet, after all, there was small cause for astonishment. Quite apart from the fact that an engagement of the kind desired was quite repugnant to oriental ideas of sovereignty,[1] there were other reasons which placed it out of the question. As Roe at once saw, the main objection was that the articles were so drawn 'that I should nott much neede the Prince, and if wee disliked wee might refuse his goverment.' It was a point of honour with Khurram that his administration of Surat should not be interfered with ; and he and his supporters were resolved that nothing should be granted which would in any way lessen his authority. As for the English demand for leave to frequent other ports, this, it was feared, would involve a diminution of the customs of Surat ; and it threatened, besides, to extend to Bengal and Sind the dissensions between the rival European nations which had already worked so much mischief in Gujarāt. Perhaps, too, we may add a further consideration—that it was held to be derogatory that the Emperor should sign a treaty with the representative of an obscure and distant country, especially on matters relating almost entirely to trade.

[1] 'The Mogol,' says Terry (p. 387), ' sometimes by his *firmauns* or letters patent will grant some particular things unto single or divers persons and presently after will contradict those grants by other letters, excusing himself thus : that he is a great and an absolute king, and therefore must not be tied unto any thing ; which if he were, he said that he was a slave, and not a free man. Yet what he promised was usually enjoyed, although he would not be tied to a certain performance of his promise. Therefore, there can be no dealing with this king upon very sure terms, who will say and unsay, promise and deny.'

INTRODUCTION

'Neyther will this overgrowne eliphant,' wrote the ambassador bitterly, ' descend to article or bynde him selfe reciprocally to any prince upon termes of equalety, but only by way of favour admitt our stay so long as it either likes him or those that governe him' (*Letter to the English Ambassador at Constantinople*, 21 Aug., 1617 : *Add. MS.* 6115, f. 207). Indeed, there is nothing more striking to a present-day reader than the indifference towards Europeans displayed by the Emperor and his ministers. Jahāngīr's memoirs, while duly chronicling the arrival of missions from Persia and other neighbouring countries, and minutely noting many trivial details, make no direct allusion to the English ambassador. Though the Emperor himself was courteous and considerate, his son did not conceal his contempt for the foreign traders ; while Āsaf Khān's masterful insolence—as here exemplified—was equally hard to endure. In point of fact, to the sovereign of Hindustān there were only two other monarchs who could even pretend to an equality with himself—the Persian Shāh, and the still more distant ruler of Constantinople and its dependencies. The kings of the Deccan may be left out of the account, for they were looked upon as little more than revolted vassals of the throne of Delhi. That the Franks should send an ambassador to the imperial court was by no means unwelcome as a tribute to its splendour and fame, but that they should seriously claim to treat on terms of equality was not to be thought of. Moreover, it must not be forgotten that the Portuguese and their agents had systematically belittled the English monarch and his representatives ; and, thanks to them, it was perfectly well understood at the Court that Roe was working in the interests of a handful of traders—a profession which the Mughals held in great contempt ; and, had there been any doubt in the matter, it would have been dissipated by the continual representations which the ambassador's position forced him to make to secure the payment of debts due to the merchants. Bearing these considerations in mind, we shall have little difficulty in comprehending the reasons of Roe's failure. He had, indeed, been plainly warned by Āsaf Khān, only eight days after he had presented them, that his demands were unreasonable and could not be signed ' ; but his confidence in the Emperor's favour had buoyed him up with hopes of success. For a time the minister—partly on account of Jahāngīr's partiality towards his visitor, partly in hopes of personal profit—seems to have avoided undeceiving him ; and, with all the cunning of oriental statecraft, he repeatedly led the ambassador to believe that his demands were on the point of being granted. Now, at last, when apparently Roe had brought himself to solicit the desired privileges from the Prince, Āsaf Khān endeavoured to clench the matter by plainly showing him that only in that quarter could his desires be obtained, and that his only course was to ' wholy depend ' on the favour of Khurram.

For a moment, Roe was at a loss what to do. Though filled with anger at Āsaf Khān's duplicity, he ' durst not yet leave him, nor take notice of his falshood.' He felt that he ' had a woolfe by the eares ' ; and that there was no alternative but submission, at least for the present. Pretending to be unaware of the true reasons of the minister's behaviour, he ' seemed only to apprehend his dislike of the lenght and phrase.' So he re-drew his demands—not, be it noted, in the form of a treaty, but in that of a *farmān* to be accorded by the King— in shorter and more general terms ; omitting, too, all mention of the Portuguese. But all was to no purpose. Āsaf Khān returned answer ' that absolutly hee would procure nothing sealed that any way concerned the Princes goverment : that I should only expect from him what wee desired, whose *firmaens* were sufficient.' Temporarily, at all events, it was necessary to be content with the Prince's grant, which met immediate needs. For a general concession, Roe notes, ' I am resolved to use the Prince, and doubt not to effect that by him which him selfe hath crossed and resisted.'

For the present, therefore, the English envoy was forced to fall back on the *rôle* of spectator ; and certainly there was no lack of interesting sights. All the city was in a stir at the prospect of the early removal of the court. Sultān Parwīz, whose want of success against the Deccan forces had led to his recall, approached Ajmer only to be ordered to Bengal in disgrace, after a vain attempt (frustrated by Nūr Mahal) to see his father in the hope of reconciliation ; and Prince Khurram was preparing with all pomp to take his place. The destination of the Emperor himself was kept a profound secret, but it was guessed, and (as the event proved) guessed correctly, that his intention was to move southwards to Māndu to countenance his son's operations in the Deccan. In the early part of October, Abdullah Khān, the late Viceroy of Gujarāt, arrived at court as a prisoner ' in counterfait humiliation,' but was pardoned and taken again into favour at the intercession of the Prince, to whom his military abilities promised to be of assistance. On the same day came two ambassadors from the Deccan princes to treat of peace, at the instigation (it was rumoured) of the Mughal general, who had no wish to see Khurram take command of his forces. Jahāngīr, however, referred them to his son, who, anxious that he should not lose ' the honor of finishing that warr,' refused to listen to any overtures until he had taken the field. To set the seal upon the Emperor's exaltation of Khurram at the expense of his brothers, the unfortunate Khusrau, after a little difficulty, was made over to the custody of Āsaf Khān—a transfer which was looked upon as a presage of his speedy death. Shortly afterwards, an ambassador from Persia arrived in great state, with an equipage and an array of presents beside which those brought by Roe seemed indescribably scanty and mean. The English envoy consoled himself, however, with the reflection that the new-comer did not experience so favourable a reception, and ' had in nothing more grace, in many things not so much' as he had had. In himself the Persian ' appeared rather a jester or jugler then a person of any gravety, running up and downe,' when presenting his master's gifts, ' and acting all his woords like a mimick player.' His servility much disgusted Roe, but it pleased Jahāngīr, who gave him 20,000 rupees to defray his expenses, and treated him with great favour.

In the meantime, news had arrived that the English fleet, under the command of Captain Pepwell, had cast anchor at Swally. On the way out, a return blow had been dealt at the Portuguese for their attacks upon Best and Downton. Near the Comoro Islands a large carrack bound for Goa was overtaken and drawn into a conflict. After a hot fight, in which the English commander, Captain Joseph, was slain and his successor (Pepwell) dangerously wounded, the Portuguese vessel ran ashore, whereupon her crew abandoned and burnt her. This news Roe lost no time in conveying to the Emperor, who seemed to rejoice at the English victory ' and to applaud the valor of our nation, but fell off to : what hath the King sent mee ? ' Roe assured him that ' many curious toyes ' had been brought for presentation to His Majesty, and asked to be furnished with letters ' for the comming of these presents without search, and for the good usadg of our people.' Jahāngīr replied that ' the port was his sonns,' but he directed the latter to give the requisite orders, and Khurram ' professed and promised . . . all reasonable content.' ' This,' commented the ambassador, ' is the strength of new presents.'

One incident should not be omitted. The letters newly received directed Roe to obtain, if possible, the cession of a safe port with permission to fortify. Upon his arrival he had concurred in the advantage of such a plan (p. 73), but a year's experience had made him change his opinion. He was ' sure of refusall,' and was equally confident ' that to be denyed yt is for our advantage.' Still, he felt bound not only to prefer the request but to do so in the way most likely to procure a compliance with it. He addressed himself, therefore, to the Prince, pretending a fear that the Portuguese would retaliate upon both English and natives for their late disaster, and offering, if the grant were made, to undertake the naval defence of the coast and of the Red Sea traffic. As he expected, his proposal was instantly rejected. Khurram ' answered with scorne that his father nor hee needed not our assistance : he ment not warr with the Portugall for our sakes, neyther would ever deliver any fort to us ' (p. 250) ; and when Roe attempted to prefer the same request to the Emperor, Āsaf Khān absolutely refused to put the matter to his master.

Writing to the Company about this time (p. 301), Roe reviewed his year's work and its results. ' For the settling your trafique here,' he said, ' I doubt not to effect any reasonable desier. My creditt is sufficient with the King, and your force will alway bynd him to constancy. . . . Articles of treaty on equall tearmes I cannot effect ; want of presents disgraced mee ; but yet by peices I have gotten as much as I desird at once. I have recovered all bribes, extortions, debts made and taken before my tyme till this day; or at least an honorable composition. But when I deliver the next guifts to the Mogoll, in the Princes absence, I will sett on a new for a formall contract. . . . I will settle your trade here secure with the King, and reduce it to order, if I may be heard.' But, this done, it would be unnecessary to keep an English representative at court. 'An ambassador lives not in fitt honor,' he wrote; 'I could sooner dye then be subject to the slaverye the Persian is content with. A meaner agent would among these proud Moores better effect your busines. . . . I have moderated it according to my discretion, but with a swolne hart'; and a native agent at a salary of a thousand rupees a yea , with a subordinate at Surat, would ' effect all.' Projects of ayding the Mogoll or waffing [*i.e.* convoying] his subjects into the Redd Sea,' of obtaining the grant of a fortified port, and of increasing the number of English settlements, were set aside as impracticable; 'it is not number of ports, factoryes, and residences that will profitt yow; they will encrease chardge, but not recompence it.' Against an extravagant and aggressive policy he solemnly warned the Company: 'A warr and traffque are incompatible. By my consent, yow shall no way engage your selves but at sea, where yow are like to gayne as often as to loose. It is the beggaring of the Portugall, notwithstanding his many rich residences and territoryes, that hee keepes souldiers that spends it; yet his garrisons are meane. He never profited by the Indyes, since hee defended them. Observe this well. It hath beene also the error of the Dutch, who seeke plantation heere by the swoord. They turne a woonderfull stocke, they proule in all places, they posses some of the best; yet ther dead payes consume all the gayne. Lett this bee received as a rule that if yow will profitt, seeke it at sea, and in quiett trade; for without controversy it is an error to affect garrisons and land warrs in India.'

In the beginning of November, Jahāngīr with great pomp left Ajmer, and Roe, after a short delay, followed him. At first, Agra seemed to be the objective; but after a time the Emperor turned suddenly south, and, hunting as he went, pushed 'thorowgh woods and over mountayns' to Māndu,

where stood the ruins of the old capital of Mālwa. From this
point of vantage, on a range of hills overlooking the Narbadā
valley, he could watch over and countenance the operations
of Khurram, whose headquarters were at Burhānpur, ninety
miles away to the south-east. Early in March they reached
this desolate spot, and remained there until late in October.
Roe was fortunate enough to secure eligible quarters in a
deserted mosque, and, having discovered a spring of water
near, was far better off than most of his fellow-travellers.
Amongst the camp-followers, however, the distress was very
great ; and the ambassador says emphatically that ' there was
not a misery nor punishment which either the want of government
or the naturall disposition of the clime gave us not.'

Meanwhile, after much delay, the presents brought by the
1616 fleet had been despatched from Surat under the charge
of the Rev. Edward Terry, who was to fill the vacancy caused
by the death of the chaplain whom Roe had brought out with
him. On the way to the royal camp, the party met the Prince
proceeding to Burhānpur. The latter demanded to be shown
the presents they were carrying to his father, but this was
firmly refused. Finding he could not prevail, and receiving
an order from his father (to whom Roe had at once complained)
not to touch the presents, he sent them under escort to the
imperial camp, where Jahāngīr, unable to restrain his cupidity,
opened the packages and appropriated their contents before
Roe could appear on the scene. The nicknacks provided for
the Prince and the Queen, the reserve stock of presents, even
a hat intended for Roe, and some velvets and silks sent up for
sale at court—all had gone. Roe was extremely angry, and
the interview which followed between the greedy monarch and
the mortified ambassador is described in one of the most
entertaining passages of the journal (p. 346). The Emperor
promised everything that could be wished if he might only be
allowed to retain his new acquisitions ; and he was so lavish
in his protestations that Roe consoled himself with the reflection
that perhaps after all he was ' happely robbd.' In any case,
he was saved a journey he had promised to make to the Prince's
camp ; for the presents intended for Khurram had been seized
with the rest, and Jahāngīr, unwilling to disgorge any part of

INTRODUCTION

his booty, declared the visit unnecessary and wrote to his son to excuse it.

The summer and autumn of 1617 passed away without the occurrence of any incident of special importance. At the beginning of September Roe enjoyed the spectacle (which he had missed the previous year) of the splendour of the Emperor's birthday celebrations; and his description of these festivities is one of the best known passages in his journal. The Deccan princes came to terms with the Prince, who returned in triumph to Māndu at the beginning of October. He was received with extravagant marks of favour by his doting father; honours were showered upon him, including the title of Shāh Jahān, by which he was ever after known; and his ascendancy over the Emperor seemed for a time to be complete. This boded ill for English hopes; for the Prince maintained his former attitude of arrogant enmity. Roe himself had been looking forward to a speedy return to his native country; his health was bad, and he could not but feel that his efforts were being wasted. 'My master hath written most gratiously,' he wrote (*Add. MS.* 6115, f. 273), 'but I pine here while others are in the wayes of preferment.' The 1617 fleet, however, which, under the command of Captain Martin Pring, arrived in September, brought an entreaty from the Company that he would remain another year, and Roe, unwilling to go home without better results than had yet been obtained, consented.

He was not without hopes that he would, after all, procure is desires owing to a fresh change in the political kaleidoscope. The alliance between Nūr Mahal and Shāh Jahān had been weakening for some time; and the former, jealous, it may be, of the increasing power of the latter, had made advances first to Prince Khusrau and then to Prince Shahryār, who, on his elder brother's refusal of her overtures, became her son-in-law by marrying her daughter by her former husband. In these circumstances, neither Nūr Mahal herself nor her obedient henchman Āsaf Khān saw any reason for continuing their unfriendly attitude towards the dispenser of good things from the West. Roe was quick to notice this opportunity, and at once resolved to take advantage of it. A fine pearl, which the factors of the newly-arrived fleet had smuggled up to the ambassador, was secretly sold to Āsaf Khān at considerably less than its cost ;[1] and by this and other favours of a similar nature, the minister and his sister were completely won over to the English side. By the mediation of Āsaf Khān, an interview took place between Roe and the Prince, in which the ambassador was treated with some show of kindness ; and his new friend also undertook to obtain for him not only a *farmān* for Bengal (which he had previously solicited in vain), but also ' a generall command and grant of free priviledges ' in all the Mughal dominions. Hopes were also held out that the Prince, who was about to take up the government of Gujarāt, would surrender, among other *jāgīrs*, that of Surat ; and Āsaf Khān would then apply for its grant to himself and ' make Englishmen content and happy.' In the sequel, however, these fresh promises of the minister proved as untrustworthy as his previous ones.

Towards the close of October, 1617, Jahāngīr struck his camp at Māndu and bent his steps towards Ahmadābād, the capital of Gujarāt. Roe, who, during the later stages of the march, had posted on in advance, reached that city on 15 December. As before, the presents from England, which it had been his special object to secure, became a bone of contention between him and the Prince. They had been sealed at Surat with the latter's seal, in order to make sure that they should not be opened except with his cognisance. Roe waited twenty days for the necessary permission ; and this not arriving, he boldly cut the seals and took possession of the goods. It was a great affront, as the courtiers told him ; and Āsaf Khān, though he seems to have assented beforehand, shrank from supporting the offender. The Prince complained vehemently, and Roe found himself virtually under arrest. For the first time the Mogul spoke roughly to his visitor, ' set on it an angrie countenance : told mee I had broken my word : that he would trust me no more.' The ambassador bore the storm unflinchingly, saying that he had done no wrong, and that if he had seemed to act offensively it had been done in ignorance. Before long, the Prince grew cool again, ' offered

[1] See p. 424. Roe is generally stated to have *given* the pearl to Āsaf Khān ; but this is a mistake.

INTRODUCTION

his friendship, and wee were all reconciled fully, and promises too large'; and the distribution of the presents sealed the reconciliation. On the following day the Prince received the ambassador with all courtesy, gave him a handsome cloak, and 'promised to be the protector of our nation in all things.' In the middle of February, 1618, Roe made his yearly report to the Company (p. 432). By this time he had abandoned all hopes of securing the signature of a formal treaty; but he trusted to obtain all that was practically necessary. 'Yow can never expect to trade here upon capitulations that shalbe permanent. Wee must serve the tyme. Some now I have gotten, but by way of *firmaens* and promise from the Kynge. All the goverment depends upon the present will, where appetite only governs the lords of the kingdome. But their justice is generallie good to strangers; they are not rigorous, except in scearching for things to please, and what trouble wee have is for hope of them, and by our owne disorders.' 'You shalbe sure,' he added emphatically, ' of as much priviledge as any stranger, and right when the subject dares not plead his.' With the Prince, now all-powerful ('his father growes dull and suffers him to write all commands and to governe all his kingdomes') the ambassador was on much better terms. The policy of 'adventuring the feircnes of his wrath' had answered so well that Roe was resolved, if necessary, to push matters boldly to an issue. It was useless to attempt to win the friendship of the Indians by kindly treatment; 'they are weary of us. . . . Wee have empoverished the ports and wounded all their trades'; the only dependence was upon 'the same ground that wee began, and by which wee subsist, feare.' 'Assure yow,' he wrote, 'I knowe these people are best treated with the swoord in one hand and caducean in the other'; and if his demands were not complied with to his satisfaction, he intended to seize the Indian shipping ' and make those conditions bee offered which now I seeke with despayre.'

Fortunately, it was not in the end found necessary to push matters to extremity; but at the time the adoption of a vigorous policy seemed the more necessary, as Roe feared that the Dutch might 'doe it first and then hee wilbe the brave man.' The prospect of their competition at Surat Roe viewed with indignation and apprehension; 'They wrong yow in all parts,' he said, ' and grow to insuffrable insolencies. . . . Yow must speedelye looke to this maggat; els wee talke of the Portugall, but these will eate a woorme in your sides. . . . If they keepe yow out of the Molluccoes by force, I would beat them from Suratt to requite it.' As regards their Portuguese rivals, there was not much to report. Father Corsi, the Jesuit at court, had made some efforts to accommodate matters; and Roe, who knew that ' want of a peace with them . . . makes all these trades of Indya and hopes of Persia heavy and dangerous to the undertakers' (p. 465), was willing, and even anxious, to conclude an arrangement if it could be done without loss of dignity, and with any assurance of permanence. The deputation of a Portuguese officer to Ahmadābād ' to congratulate in the name of the King of Spayne,' appeared to afford an opportunity; but the Mogul refused to receive the envoy, ' principally because his presents were not of great valew.' Apparently Roe, some time in 1618, made overtures by letter to the Viceroy of Goa by the intermediary of a German[1]; but 'the successe answered not expectacion.' Of this incident we know nothing except from a reference which occurs in a letter from Surat of 10 Dec., 1619 (*English Factories, 1618-21*, p. 159).

The diary having now come to an end, we are left dependent upon a few letters for information regarding the last year of Roe's stay in India. In February, 1618, the Emperor started for Māndu, on his way to Agra. Roe took a different route, by way of Broach and Burhānpur; but before he could reach Māndu, he learnt that Jahāngīr had abandoned the journey and had returned to Ahmadābād. Thither the ambassador also returned, arriving about the beginning of May. In the same month an outbreak of disease in that city caused much alarm; with the exception of Roe himself, all the members of the English party took the infection, and seven died in little more than a week. In August, preparations commenced for a fresh departure of the Emperor for Agra. Roe, ' infinitely

---

[1] George Krieger, whom Von Poser met at Bījāpur in 1622 (*Imperial and Asiatic Quarterly Review*, vol. xxix. p. 99).

INTRODUCTION   liii

weary of this unprofitable imployment,' had no wish to accompany him ; his continued presence at court could do no good, and the ships which were to carry him home would shortly be arriving. He therefore took formal leave of the monarch to whom he had been accredited, receiving from him a letter to King James full of compliments and assurances of good usage of the English, and also a general *farmān* ' for our reception and continuation in his domynnyons,' the exact terms of which are unknown (p. 484); also a number of presents for his sovereign. He then addressed himself to the Prince, who, it will be remembered, was Viceroy of Gujarāt, in order to procure a special *farmān* for Surat. Fresh quarrels had occurred between the Indians and the Portuguese. In the end these were amicably settled ; but meanwhile Roe endeavoured to make use of the opportunity by offering to protect the Gujarāti shipping in return for the concessions desired. These demands were kept strictly within the bounds of moderation ; in Roe's own words (p. 477) : ' after almost three yeares experience of the pride and falshood of these people, that attended only advantage and were governed by privat interest and appetite, I was forced to relinquish many poynts often insisted upon, when I could gett nothing, and to make offer of these few as the most necessarie to settle a trade, and which might give the least offence and might pass with ease, leaving the rest to the generall order of the Kyng.' Even then he did not obtain all his demands ; but at last, after a vigorous contest and the usual attempt to deceive him with an incomplete and ambiguously worded *farmān*, he procured a grant which was reasonably satisfactory, though to effect this it was necessary to threaten vigorous action by the fleet expected shortly. The Prince's amity towards the English was publicly acknowledged : in case of an attack by the Portuguese, the local authorities were ordered to assist them with boats or any other requisites : they were to be allowed to trade freely, and former abuses in the levying of customs were not to be repeated: jewels were to be admitted free of duty : no tolls were to be levied on goods passing to or from the port : the factors were to be permitted, under certain restrictions, to hire any house they pleased for a factory : liberty was given them to govern themselves according to their own religion and laws, and any refugee was to be surrendered, even if he had embraced Islām ; while the ever-recurring difficulty about presents was provided against. Liberty to buy or build a permanent dwelling was, however, obstinately refused ; and a determined attempt was made to limit the number of Englishmen permitted to wear arms in the city. On the latter point Roe was determined not to yield ; and partly by threats, and partly by giving a written undertaking ' that during the abode of the English at Suratt they shall do no wrong or hurt to any,' he at last obtained the withdrawal of the obnoxious clause.

This grant procured, towards the close of September, 1618, the ambassador took his departure for Surat, where four months were spent awaiting the completion of the lading of the ships. At length all was in readiness, and on 17 Feb., 1619, the fleet put to sea, Roe himself being on board the *Anne*. At the Cape he learned that negotiations were proceeding in London for a settlement of the differences between the English and Dutch Companies ; and he thereupon wrote to Bantam earnestly deprecating any further hostilities. Towards the end of August the *Anne* reached Plymouth, and a fortnight later she anchored in the Downs, where the ambassador was met by his wife and a number of friends. Proceeding by coach to Gravesend, he was there received by the Deputy and many of the ' Committees ' of the East India Company and was brought by water to the Tower Wharf with all ceremony, and then escorted to Alderman Halliday's house, which had been lent to the Company for the purpose. On Friday, 24 September, Roe, attended by the Governor and ' Committees,' was received in audience by King James at Whitehall ; and we learn from one of John Chamberlain's gossipping letters (*Dom. State Papers*, Jac. I. vol. cx. No. 94) that the ambassador had another interview with His Majesty a few days later at Hampton Court and presented him with ' two antelopes, a straunge and bewtifull kind of red deare, a rich tent, rare carpets, certain umbrellaes, and such like trinckets from the Great Mogul.' This done, Roe's mission was at an end, and ' My Lord Ambassador ' became once more a private individual.

He had still to make his report to his actual employers, the

INTRODUCTION lv

East India Company; and on 6 October he attended a court meeting for that purpose. He first ' gave to understand in what a desperate case he found the factoryes at Surat, Amadavaz, and elswher in the Mogores countrye : proclamations out against them to prohibite them of all trade and to depart the land, which at his coming to court he caused to be revokt, and procured *fermaens* to commaund their acceptaunce and frendly entertaynment, proving against the Prince himself that those things had bene done without aucthoritye from the King and by wicked subornation to have overthrowne the trade of the English ; assuring the Company that now, by a faire and gentle course held and good correspondencie and observation of the Governour in some reasonable sort, they may have as faire a passage of their buysines as can be expected or desired.' Next he dwelt upon the hopeful prospects of the trade he had opened up for them with the Red Sea ports, and urged its vigorous prosecution. ' Lastly, he made knowne that he recovered all the extortions which had bene exacted by sundry unjust governours that yeare and the yeare before, and had left all matters in a good, setled, and peaceable course, drawing out 21 articles, most of which he procured the King to confirme, and got sundry *firmaens* graunted for friggots to be delyvered furnisht to the English for ther defence against the Portugalls (who, as was delyvered, were preparing an *armado* against the English), together with many other priviledges which he thought as much in generall as he could expect or desire ; and recovered all debts, leaving none in the countrye but only one of a *Banyan* who was the Kings prisoner (and yet for him he hath the Kings promise to force him to pay the said debt or else to delyver the partie dead or alive unto their hands).' Further, he handed to the ' Committees ' details of their stock remaining in India, of the debts outstanding, and the investments ordered at his departure. Other interviews followed, in which Roe's proceedings in the Company's business were more closely examined and his accounts (from which it appeared that his ' expence of housekeping ' during his stay in India averaged only 250*l.* or 260*l.* a year) were scrutinized ; and in the end the Court recorded that, ' having duelie weighed his carriage and behaviour from the begining till this present, they estemed him a very worthie gentleman that hath husbanded things excedinglye well and very moderate in his expences, and one that by his modestie, honestie, and integritye hath given good satisfaction.'

The question of a fitting reward for the ambassador's services now came up for decision. It had been hoped that the Great Mogul's liberality to his visitor would relieve the Company of any expenditure on this score ; but it had been always understood that, in the event of this expectation being disappointed, the charge would fall upon Roe's employers. The matter was debated on 12 November, and a proposal was made to give him 2000*l*. ; however, more frugal counsels prevailed, and finally Roe was desired to accept 1500*l*., with an assurance that they held it ' too little compared with his deserts, but their smal retournes pleaded partlye their excuse.' At the same time a hint was thrown out that the Court would gladly avail themselves of his advice in future and would make some further allowance for any such assistance. Roe was evidently disappointed, for in a letter of thanks read at the next meeting he enlarged upon his services and asked that, ' if they will make him one of their bodie, they affourd him meanes wherby to mantayne himself amongst them without thinking of any other course.' It was thereupon decided to make him an extra ' Committee,' with an allowance of 200*l*. until the next election : to refund him a sum of 152*l*. 3*s*. 2*d*. for presents given by him in India out of his own stock: and to convert into a gift the loan of 100*l*. made to him at his going out for the provision of plate.[1]

Though his embassy had come to an end, Roe continued to maintain close relations with the East India Company. In Nov., 1619, he was asked whether he would proceed to Bantam in supreme charge of the Company's settlements in the East ; but, while thanking them for the offer and professing his willingness to accept, ' if the necessitye of their occations did require it,' he desired ' a breathing tyme ' before going into a further exile. In the following month he offered 400*l*. towards

[1] The foregoing quotations are all taken from the Court Minutes. The passages in which they occur were given in full in the previous edition.

INTRODUCTION

the proposed almshouse for persons maimed in the Company's service, *i.e.* the one afterwards started at Poplar. In January, 1620, he suggested that a royal letter should be procured in reply to the one from Jahāngīr which he had brought home; and a draft which he had prepared was accordingly ordered to be engrossed for signature. His membership of the Court of Committees and his special allowance were continued until the summer of 1621, when he was not proposed for re-election, possibly because he was about to proceed to Constantinople as ambassador. The stoppage of the allowance came as a surprise to him, for, as he told the Court on 3 August, 1621, he understood that this had been given to him as a pension, and on the strength of it he had invested in the current joint stock and could not immediately meet the liability. He begged that he might be allowed until Christmas to find the 300*l.* still due, and this was agreed to; but a further request, that the Company should purchase his holding in the old joint stock, was refused, on the ground that the 'genneralitie' had disapproved of such transactions. Roe then asked that as, owing to 'his intended imployment and the encrease of his familie [*i.e.* household], he shalbe driven also to larger lodgings, he should want three peeces of their vellvett embroydered hangings, to add unto five of the same kind which he had allready bought, and three of their Persian carpetts,' they would either bestow them upon him or allow him to ' take them upp uppon stock.' The Court very willingly made him a present of the goods, ' assuring him that, howsoever the Companie was so unhappy as to loose the imployment of so well a deserving gentleman, yet their loves should follow him, and therefore desired the continuaunce of his good affection to the Company; which he freely promised, and tooke very thankefullie the curtisie now donn him.' Roe did not forget his promise; and both during his embassy at Constantinople and in after years, his advice and assistance were always at the service of the body which had given him 'his first public employment,' by sending him to represent England at the court of the Great Mogul.

In endeavouring to estimate the results of this memorable embassy, the question naturally arises how far Roe had accomplished the task which he had been sent out to perform?

Most writers have been content to answer vaguely that he obtained valuable concessions, without specifying either their nature or their extent. Bruce, however, the Company's historiographer, goes a step further. He gives a summary of the ' articles ' printed on p. 134, and says that soon after the ambassador's arrival he procured the signatures of Jahāngīr and Khurram to this ' phirmaund or treaty between the Mogul and the English nation ' ; all further troubles Bruce puts down to the contumacy of the Governor of Surat, who (he says) refused to carry out the agreement entered into by his sovereign (*Annals of the East India Company*, vol. i. pp. 176, 185, 203). How far this is from the truth the foregoing summary will show. Roe himself was studiously moderate in his statements as to his success, and chose rather to put in the forefront of his achievements the successful initiation of trade in the Red Sea. Yet, after all, he had effected a great deal ; and where he had failed the failure was due to causes which were quite beyond his control. At his arrival he had found the English in a precarious position : threatened by the Portuguese, plundered by the native officials, and in imminent danger of expulsion owing to the ill-will of Prince Khurram. Local feeling, which had been for a time in their favour, was now against them, for their active competition injured the trade of the native merchants, while the unruliness of the sailors of the fleet, together with the troubles caused by the hostilities between the Portuguese and the English, estranged the great body of the inhabitants. The coming of the ambassador stemmed the tide of reaction ; it shifted the principal area of contention to the court, where local feelings had little influence, and where, if ' the King and Prince and great men . . . are pleased, the crie off a million of subjects would not bee heard ' (p. 450) ; the provincial authorities were restrained from acts of oppression by fear of representations at headquarters ; and thus time was given for the English to root themselves firmly in the country and to accustom the natives to their presence. By the time Roe left India, this had been accomplished ; all danger from the Portuguese appeared to have passed away ; concessions had been obtained, which he judged to be on the whole satisfactory ; and a good understanding had been established with the court. All this was largely due to Roe's energy and skill, and to the favourable impression he had made upon Jahāngīr and his son. It was indeed fortunate for the future of English influence in India, that while the Portuguese interests were in the charge merely of an ecclesiastic, amiable and clever though he was, England had for her representative one who was not only an able diplomatist, suave and ready, but also a man of resolute character, prepared indeed to yield in small matters, but firm as steel and utterly regardless of consequences where the honour of his king and nation was concerned. Jahāngīr and Shāh Jahān, with all their faults, could and did appreciate such qualities, and English prestige, already growing by the victories obtained over the Portuguese, was raised to a high pitch by Roe's gallant bearing and indomitable will. 'There can be,' wrote Terry (p. 388), ' no dealing with this King upon very sure terms, who will say and unsay, promise and deny. Yet we Englishmen did not at all suffer by that inconstancy of his, but there found a free trade, a peaceable residence, and a very good esteem with that king and people ; and much the better (as I conceive) by reason of the prudence of my Lord Ambassador, who was there (in some sense) like Joseph in the court of Pharaoh, for whose sake all his nation there seemed to fare the better.'

The value to the historical student of Roe's observations has been generally recognised. From no other English source can be obtained so full an account of the events of the time at the Mughal court : the desultory war in the Deccan : the impending troubles in regard to the succession : the waning of the hopes cherished by the partisans of Khusrau and Parwīz, and the rise to all but supreme power of Khurram, strengthened at first by the steady support of Nūr Mahal and her family. Of all the principal personages concerned (except, of course, the Queen, whom Roe never saw) we have vivid portraits : of the amiable but weak Jahāngīr : of his unfortunate eldest son, whose long captivity and reported excellencies excited great pity in the breast of the ambassador : of the drunken and worthless Parwīz : of Āsaf Khān, avaricious, crafty, and unscrupulous : and finally of Khurram (Shāh Jahān), the coming emperor, who, cold and haughty, moves through Roe's pages with a magnificence that suits well the future master-builder of Agra and Delhi. With welcome minuteness, Roe portrays Jahāngīr's mode of living, both at Ajmer, where the functions of government were discharged with the same state as at Agra, and on the march, when all unnecessary parade was abandoned and sport was the order of the day. The splendours of the birthday reception, the vast yet orderly army that followed the Emperor, the wealth of the royal treasury, astonished Roe. But he was too shrewd to allow this pomp and glitter to blind him to the real state of the country, and he brings out clearly in his journal and letters the darker shades of the picture— the poverty and misery of the peasant, the general unrest and insecurity, the corruption and inefficiency of the local governors, and the looseness of the imperial control. He saw clearly, too, the forces which were making for disintegration; and though ' the tyme when all in these kingdomes wilbe in combustion ' was not so near as he imagined, yet it was only postponed by the force of character of Shāh Jahān and his still more capable son. All these things are noted by one whose position gave him exceptional advantages for exercising his powers of observation, and the result is a picture of ' Mogolls India ' of supreme interest and importance.

There are many other attractive topics in Roe's journal and letters, but over most of them we must not linger. Two, however, bulk so largely in his pages, and are in themselves so important, that it is impossible to pass them by. These are the attempts made, largely under Roe's direction, to open up commerce, first in the dominions of the Shāh of Persia, and secondly at the Turkish ports in the Red Sea.

Shāh Abbās of Persia, at the instigation probably of the famous adventurers, Anthony and Robert Sherley, had long been desirous of opening up communication with one or other of the Christian powers, partly in the hope of obtaining assistance in his perennial war against the Turks, but principally with the idea of finding purchasers for the silk of his country, the export of which (a royal monopoly) he was desirous of diverting from its usual channel through the dominions of his enemy. With this end in view, he had, in 1608, despatched Robert Sherley to Europe as his ambassador. Travelling

INTRODUCTION

through Russia, Germany, and Italy, Sherley reached Madrid, where he did his best to induce Philip III. (who, it will be remembered, was King of Portugal as well as of Spain) to enter into an arrangement by which the silk trade would be diverted to Ormus or some neighbouring port on the Persian Gulf. His proposals, however, were coldly received ; and in disgust he crossed to England, and in October, 1611, presented himself to King James at Hampton Court. Here also nothing came of his negotiations. The East India merchants were not to be persuaded : ' the way is long and dangerous,' it was said : ' the trade uncertain and must quite cut off our traffic with the Turk ' ; and insinuations were not wanting that Sherley had no valid commission to pledge his master to so far-reaching a scheme. At the bidding of King James a ship was prepared to carry back the ambassador, which landed him, in September, 1613, at Lahrībandar ; and thence he proceeded overland to Persia by way of Ajmer, where he paid a visit to Jahāngīr. Roe, it may be noted, had been present at the conferences which had been held in London upon Sherley's proposals ; had heard both his arguments and the merchants' objections ; and had formed his own opinion as to Sherley's character and the feasibility of his plans.[1]

The next move was made by the factors at Surat. Induced mainly by the favourable report of trade prospects given by Richard Steel, who had crossed Persia from Aleppo in the preceding summer, they, in November, 1614, determined to dispatch representatives to make investigations and to obtain the grant of privileges for trade. Steel himself and a factor named Crowder were chosen for this task. They reached Ispahān in September, 1615, and found there Sherley, to whom they carried letters soliciting his assistance. He was on the point of starting on a second mission to Spain, to make a fresh attempt to induce the King to accept the offers of the Shāh ; but, with some reluctance, he procured for them three identical

[1] ' I understand that busines well, beeing present at all Sheirlyes offers to His Majestie, who never would speake of bringing downe silke under halfe mony and such a quantetye ' (*Roe to Surat Factors*, 19 June, 1616 : *Add. MS.* 6115, f. 105). In the same letter he says of Sherley, ' as hee is dishonest, soe is hee subtile.'

farmāns, ordering the governors of seaport towns to receive and assist any English vessels that might present themselves. One of these was sent to Jask (the port represented as most suitable for their purpose), Steel carried a second overland to England, and Crowder, as arranged before their departure, returned with the third to India, to report their proceedings to the agent at Surat.

Letters written by the two envoys, announcing their success and the hopes they had formed of a lucrative trade, reached Ajmer on 10 Feb., 1616, addressed to Aldworth and Edwards. As the former was dead and the latter had left for England, these letters were opened by Roe, who lost no time in apprising the Company of their contents, at the same time giving his own views on the matter. The *farmān* which had been procured he thought 'of no consequence,' as no trade worth speaking of was to be had upon the coast and it was not to be expected that the Shāh would send down his silk until a formal agreement had been arrived at. To Roe it seemed that the dominant factor of the situation was Sherley's fresh mission to Europe. Already the Portuguese had an immense advantage in their possession of Ormus; and if the trade monopoly which he was empowered to offer to Philip were accepted (and Roe felt certain it would be) all efforts of the English to obtain a footing would be unavailing. The only hope lay either in defeating Sherley's negotiations at Madrid, or in effecting some amicable arrangement by which both nations should share in the trade. For the present, all that Roe considered it advisable to do was to write a respectful remonstrance to the Shāh, pointing out the perils of allowing the Portuguese to become masters of his coast, and urging him to establish a free port and to throw open the trade to all comers. This done, and the letter forwarded to the care of William Robbins, an Englishman resident in Ispahān, Roe turned his attention to other matters until further news should come from England.

Quite another view, however, was taken at Surat. The ambassador's action in opening and dealing with the letters from their delegates was warmly resented by Kerridge and his colleagues; while his disparaging remarks upon the results of the expensive mission which they had set on foot could not but

INTRODUCTION

be felt as a rebuke. The question of trade with Persia was, they considered, a matter purely commercial, and therefore outside Roe's province ; and as soon as Pepwell's fleet brought in a further supply of men and goods (including a further supply of broadcloth, for which it was hopeless to expect a sale in India), a consultation was held at which it was decided that a ship should be sent to Jask to test the value of the Shāh's *farmān*, and to procure, if possible, whatever further concessions were necessary. Edward Connock, the chief merchant of the new fleet, undertook the management of this mission, and sailed in the *James* early in November, 1616.

Roe was exceedingly angry when he found out what had been done. Not only had his authority been ignored, but his counsels had been treated with contempt. Both publicly to the Company, and privately to its Governor, he complained bitterly of the behaviour of the factors : ' Yow may now see their hast,' he wrote, ' and lack of respect to mee.' Personal feeling, however, was never allowed by him to injure the public service ; and however much he felt inclined to throw upon the factors the responsibility for further action, he determined to do what he could to set matters straight. ' If I left them as they are, it were just,' he said, ' but I am to account to yow, and therfore . . . I will looke out to mend their faults, and, like patient Job, pray and sacrifice for them, as he did for his sonnes whiles they banquetted.' His hand had been forced by the dispatch of the *James*, and with Connock already on his way to the Persian Court, inaction was impossible. After consulting the Shāh's ambassador at Ajmer, and enlisting his advocacy, he wrote again to Ispahān. The ship which had been sent, he told Robbins, was ' but to trye and settle our enterteynment,' and he hoped the Shāh ' will not judge us by this beginning ' : if the necessary privileges were granted (a draft of which he enclosed) ' wee will then roundly and duly fullfill his desire.' Roe strongly urged Robbins to endeavour to obtain the required concessions ; and concluded by intimating that possibly he himself would receive by the next fleet instructions to proceed to Persia and bring matters to a conclusion. As will be seen from p. 76, he had tentatively offered in November, 1615, to undertake the task, should this be deemed desirable by the authorities in London.

Meanwhile the Company at home, though of course unaware of the despatch of Connock to Jask, had had the advantages of the trade urged upon them by Steel, and had received Roe's first letter on the subject. After due deliberation and an interview with the Lords of the Council, they decided to go forward in the matter, though cautiously, in view of the risks and the large capital required, much of which, it was feared, would have to be sent in specie. Their instructions to Roe directed him to make careful inquiry into the prospects of trade, and, if satisfied, to dispatch a fit person to conclude, upon certain conditions, the requisite agreement with the Shāh. With these instructions came a letter from King James, approving of the measures already taken by Roe and authorising him to sign a treaty with the Persian monarch.

These letters, brought by Pring's fleet in the autumn of 1617, settled satisfactorily the question of control. It was now open to Roe, if he chose, to disavow Kerridge's nominee (of whose character he had grave suspicions), and either to make one of the other factors in Persia his representative or to dispatch someone from India to take charge of the negotiations. But, having carried his point, he acted with his usual moderation and good sense. The question whether a ship should be sent to Jask to obtain news of the previous year's mission he left to Pring and Kerridge to decide; but in case they should determine to do so, he forwarded a commission and instructions empowering Connock and his fellows to undertake the necessary negotiations with the Shāh. His personal intervention in the negotiations he judged unnecessary.

The *Bee* was accordingly dispatched to the Gulf, and from the intelligence she brought back in January, 1618, supplemented by letters which arrived overland a few weeks later, Roe learned what had taken place since the landing of Connock and his companions in December, 1616. From Jask the factors had made their way to Shirāz, whence their leader pushed on to Ispahān. On his arrival (May, 1617) he found that the Shāh was with the army on the Turkish border, and thither he determined to follow him; but first he made friends with

Robbins, who handed over to him all the papers he had received from Roe, including the draft articles intended for presentation to the Shāh. Accompanied by Robbins and a factor named Tracy, Connock set out for the court about the beginning of July. They were well received by the Shāh, in spite of the efforts of a friar who was acting in the interests of Spain; and the English envoy obtained without difficulty the grant for which he asked.[1] With this he returned to Ispahān, and thence started for the coast, to meet the shipping which he expected would be sent towards the close of the year. But sickness had laid hold of him, as of most of his comrades, and he died at a village near Jask on 24 Dec., 1617. The concessions he had obtained did not cover all the points mentioned in the Company's instructions lately received; and this rendered it necessary that fresh negotiations should be undertaken. On the return of the *Bee*, therefore, Roe drew up fresh directions for Thomas Barker (who was now the head of the factory in Persia) and Edward Monnox, empowering them to conclude and sign a fresh contract. These he had intended to send by the *Anne*, which was to call at Jask on her way to Mokha; but this course was found to be impracticable. To the Company he wrote that, although, if the trade could be managed without a great export of specie, ' it is the best trade of all India and will yeild yow most certeyne profitt,' yet he could see ' no way sure but a composition in Spayne,' and were this effected there would be no need of any special bargain with the Shāh.

On the arrival of the 1618 fleet Roe despatched the *Expedition* to Jask with a further supply of goods; but she brought back news that was far from satisfactory. The factors were quarrelling violently among themselves (' of all those I saw, wrote the master of the ship, ' one cannot give thother a good worde '); Barker had been to court, but had failed to obtain any further concessions; the Shāh had been forced by the Turks to a disadvantageous peace, and schemes for a monopoly of the silk trade, either to the English or the Portu-

---

[1] No copy of this grant can be found among the contemporary English records at the India Office. See, however, *Letters Received*, vol. vi. p. 293.

guese, had had perforce to be laid aside; he had expressed his willingness, however, to exchange silk for any quantity of goods the English might bring, though he would not sign any formal contract. Thus matters stood at the time of Roe's departure, and thus he was forced to leave them. The results obtained had by no means answered the sanguine expectations which had first been formed; yet he saw no reason to despair. There appeared to be a reasonable probability of finding in Persia a fresh outlet for English goods—a point which he regarded as of vital importance, for India itself could absorb but a small quantity—while silk was in Europe a most profitable commodity. The *Anne*, in which he returned, carried home a quantity of Persian silk which was sold at a high price; and estimates then laid before the Company (*Court Minutes*, 9 Nov., 1619) placed the profit to be made at from 50 to 90 per cent. per annum.

The trade to Persia, though a matter in which Roe took the closest interest, had practically been initiated by the Surat factors, of whose proceedings he could not always approve. There was, however, another development of the Company's commerce—that to Mokha—in which the position was reversed, Roe urging and carrying it through, while Kerridge and his companions somewhat unwillingly acquiesced. Long before the English flag had waved in Indian waters, the merchants of Cambay and Surat had carried on a profitable intercourse with the Red Sea ports. Not only was the pilgrim traffic large and important, but it was accompanied by a lucrative interchange of products. Merchants from Aleppo and Cairo bought eagerly all Eastern commodities, and paid for them partly in European goods, but mostly in gold and silver. The latter circumstance was, in Roe's eyes, a special recommendation. As already noted, the demand in India for English goods was comparatively small, and hence the trade involved a heavy drain of silver from home—a drain which had already seriously alarmed the economists of the time, and had excited an outcry against the Company. Roe, who honestly thought the export of silver from Europe a great evil, saw in the Red Sea trade a means of mitigating it. Let a ship be yearly sent, he argued, from Surat to the Red Sea ports, and she would not only get rid of some English goods which would not otherwise be sold, but in return for these and for spices, calicoes, etc., she would bring back specie enough to help materially towards lading the ships for home. And, besides this, the move would have a powerful political effect; for the Red Sea trade was the principal dependence of the Gujarāt merchants. Roe was sanguine that they would be glad either to freight goods in the English vessels, or at least to pay for the protection afforded by their company; and in any case the power which the latter would possess of taking the Indian junks at their pleasure would be a powerful lever for securing proper treatment at Surat and elsewhere. To those who objected the treachery of which Sir Henry Middleton had been the victim when he visited Mokha on a similar errand in 1610, Roe replied that that was due to a misunderstanding; and he pointed to the success of the Dutch, who had since made a lucrative voyage to Mokha and had experienced satisfactory treatment. The *Anne* was accordingly fitted out and dispatched on 17 March, 1618, in company with a Surat junk. In September she returned, with a favourable account of her reception, and *farmāns* and letters encouraging a renewal of the enterprise; and to reply to those letters and to dispatch his answer by a fresh ship, the *Lion*, was one of the last of Roe's acts before leaving Surat. How much Roe hoped from this commerce will be seen from his report to the Company on his return; and, although, perhaps, he had not made sufficient allowance for the resentment which was sure to be aroused at Surat by this unwelcome competition with the native merchants, he is certainly entitled to count to his credit the establishment of what afterwards became an important branch of the Company's commerce.

The period of his employment in India was for Roe only the commencement of a long and honourable career. It would carry us too far to detail his subsequent history, nor should it be necessary in the case of one who played so important a part in the politics of his time. After a short period of service in Parliament, he was again sent (1621) on a mission to the East, this time to the Ottoman Porte. At Constantinople he repeated the success he had obtained in India, by restoring English prestige and placing English commerce on a sounder footing; while his influence at the Porte secured the conclusion of a treaty between Turkey and Poland, and the rejection of proposals from Spain which he judged inimical to English interests. Another result of his embassy was the presentation to King James, by Roe's friend the Greek Patriarch, of the celebrated *Codex Alexandrinus*, which is now one of the glories of the British Museum. His success was, in fact, too complete for his own convenience; for in spite of his appeals to be allowed to return, his tenure of office was prolonged, and it was not until the spring of 1628 that he obtained his release. His next employment (June, 1629) was the negotiation of a truce between Sweden and Poland. This he successfully accomplished; and his intercourse with Gustavus Adolphus bore further fruit in the following year in that monarch's appearance in Germany as champion of the Protestant faith. Meanwhile, Roe had been warmly received on his return by his own sovereign, who presented him with a gold medal as a token of his approval; and when, early in 1632, the death occurred of his old friend Carleton (created Viscount Dorchester in 1626), Roe looked forward with some confidence to the vacant secretaryship. His opinions, however, were far too liberal to please King Charles and his advisers, and the post was given to Laud's friend, Windebank. Bitterly disappointed, Roe withdrew into the country, and for the next few years lived in retirement. In January, 1637, a tardy recognition of his services was made in his appointment to the Chancellorship of the Order of the Garter, to which a year later a pension was added. At the congress for peace negotiations which sat successively at Hamburg, Ratisbon, and Vienna, Roe represented England, and he is said to have made such an impression upon the Emperor that the latter exclaimed: 'I have met with many gallant persons of many nations, but I scarce ever met with an *ambassador* till now.' In June, 1640, he was sworn of the Privy Council, and in the same year he re-entered Parliament as one of the members for Oxford University. A fresh mission to Germany, however, prevented him for some time from taking a very active part in the deliberations of the Commons; and when he was once more free to devote himself to parliamentary duties, events rapidly led up to a crisis which placed him in a position of great difficulty. Whatever his convictions, he could not fight against his sovereign, the son of his old master, the brother of his dearly-loved patrons ; and in July, 1643, he obtained permission from the Commons to retire to Bath for the improvement of his health. This was almost his last journey. In the words of Anthony à Wood, ' at length this worthy person Sir Thomas Roe did after all his voyages and ramblings take a little breath ; but soon after, seeing how untowardly things went between the King and his Parliament, did willingly surrender it to Him that first gave it, on the 6th day of November in 1644, and two days after that his body was buried privately in the church at Woodford, near to Wansted in Essex ' (*Athenæ*, ed. Bliss, vol. iii. p. 114). An admirable Latin epitaph was written by Dr. Gerard Langbaine for inscription on his tomb, but, though Roe's widow survived him over thirty years, no monument was erected over his remains ; and now, the church having been rebuilt and enlarged in 1815-16, even the spot where they lie is uncertain. Nor has this omission been entirely made good by the more lasting memorial which can flow from the pen of the historian. Of late years, however, some efforts have been made to do justice to his memory, notably by Dr. Samuel Gardiner ; but we still await a proper biography which will give to Roe's merits their due meed of praise.

How great those merits were may be shown by the testimonies of three writers of a later day, and with these we may fitly take our leave of him. Carte, the historian, after reading through Roe's papers, wrote in March, 1737 : ' I cannot sufficiently admire his rare abilities, judgement, and integrity, his extraordinary sagacity in discovering the views and designs of those with whom he treated, and his admirable dexterity in guarding against their measures and bringing them over to his purpose. Wise, experienced, penetrating and knowing, he was never to be surprized or deceived, and though no minister ever had greater difficulties to struggle with or was employed by a court that had less power to support him, yet he supported all his employments with dignity and came out of them with reputation and honour. In all the honest arts of negociation he had few equalls, (I dare say) no superiors' (Brit. Mus. *Add. MS.* 6190, f. 34). More than half-a-century before, David Lloyd had written in his *State Worthies* (London, 1670), pp. 1036-37 : 'Sir Thomas Roe understood the dispositions of men so exactly, could suit their humours so fitly, observe opportunities and seasons of actions so punctually, keep correspondence so warily, wade through difficulties so handsomly, wave the pinch of a business so dexterously, contrive interests so suitably, that he was advised with concerning the most important affairs of the kingdoms he resided in abroad, and admitted of the Privy Council while he lived at home ; where his speech against the debasing of the coyn at the Council-table will last as long as there is *reason of state* in the world : his settlement of trade as long as this is an island : and his Eastern MSS. as long as there are books to furnish libraries, or libraries to preserve books.' And finally we may quote the testimony of Anthony à Wood : ' Those that knew him well have said that there was nothing wanting in him towards the accomplishment of a scholar, gentleman, or courtier ; that also, as he was learned, so was he a great encourager and promoter of learning and learned men. His spirit was generous and public, and his heart faithful to his prince. He was a great statesman, as good a commonwealth's man and as sound a Christian as our nation hath had in many ages ' (*Athenæ*, ed. Bliss, vol. iii. p. 113).

It may be of interest to endeavour, before concluding, to trace the history of Roe's manuscripts and to note briefly the bibliography of his journal. On the first of these two points, we have unfortunately but scanty evidence to go by. The original notes, we may suppose, were jotted down roughly from day to day, possibly on loose sheets, which would naturally be destroyed when they had served their purpose. The next step would be to have a fair copy made for the ambassador's use ; and this seems to have been done in folio volumes, of which there must have been at least two (cf. p. 345). The first, containing the diary and letters to 11 February, 1617, and further letters to 9 October of the same year,[1] has survived,

[1] Roe refers to this volume on p. 432.

and forms the basis of the present text ; the remaining volume or volumes have disappeared. The first volume reappears for a short time at the beginning of the eighteenth century, when the editor of Churchill's *Voyages* (1704) republished Roe's journal ' with considerable additions . . . taken from his own original manuscript.'[1] It is true that he refers also to ' a vast multitude ' of letters ' still preserved in *two volumes*,' and this might appear to imply that he had seen not only the first but also the missing second volume. An examination of his text, however, shows that for events subsequent to February, 1617, he depends entirely on Purchas's version of the journal ; he goes no further than Purchas, and says that the rest is lost ; and the letters he gives are all contained in the extant volume. A possible explanation is that the latter was at that time in two separate books, which were afterwards bound together.

From this date all trace of the MS. is lost for another century. In March, 1737, Richardson the novelist tendered to the newly-founded Society for the Encouragement of Learning the ' original papers and letters of Sir Thomas Roe,' offering to bear part of the expense of publishing them ;[2] but it is expressly noted by Carte the historian (who was asked to report upon them) that ' there is nothing therein about his embassy to the Great Mogul, but two letters of that Emperor and King James's instructions and letters of credance to Sir Thomas Rowe,' with three letters from King James, the Archbishop of Canterbury, and Secretary Winwood, all relating to the proposed trade with Persia, together with four long letters from the Earl of Totnes, giving Europe news.[3] At last, however,

[1] The reference is vague, but the identification is rendered tolerably certain by the fact that, in the entry for 3 Nov., 1615, where our two extant MSS. differ, Churchill's version follows the wrong reading in *Add. MS.* 6115.

[2] The correspondence is in the British Museum collection (*Add. MS.* 6190). The papers offered by Richardson were to have been published in five volumes, but the scheme failed for want of support after the appearance, in 1740, of the first volume, which dealt with Roe's negotiations at Constantinople.

[3] Most of these are now in the Public Record Office. The newsletters from Lord Carew (he was not created Earl of Totnes until ten years later) were edited for the Camden Society by Mr. Maclean in 1860.

the volume came again to light, and found a final resting-place in our great national collection. In a letter dated 4 January, 1817, the Rev. J. Coltman, of Beverley Minster, without saying how he became possessed of it, presented it to the British Museum, where it is known as *Add. MS.* 6115. It is a thick volume of about 288 folios, beautifully written in a neat, clerkly hand,[1] and is in excellent preservation.

Besides the fair copy made for his own use, Roe had others prepared from time to time to send to England. To Lord Carew, for instance, he sent, in January, 1616, a copy extending to the date of his arrival at Burhānpur (p. 88), and later on a further portion. Neither of these is extant. To the Company he sent regular batches as the opportunity occurred. The dispatch of several of these we can trace. Thus, one portion was sent home with Roe's letter of 24 November, 1615 (see p. 72); another, continuing the story to 19 November, 1616, went a year later (p. 302); and a third was dispatched in the middle of February, 1618 (p. 432). The portion for the concluding year of his embassy Roe would naturally take home with him, having no opportunity of sending it before, except perhaps by the uncertain route overland. Whether this last portion got beyond the stage of rough notes,[2] and if so, whether Roe ever delivered a fair copy to the Company, cannot now be determined; but it is plain that the copy, if it existed, had gone astray before Purchas came upon the scene.

It was in 1622 that the reverend geographer, in search of materials for his *Hakluytus Posthumus : or Purchas His Pilgrimes*, applied to the Company for permission to use their collection of logs, and especially Roe's journal.[3] He could not

[1] A comparison of the writing shows that the scribe was Edward Heynes, Roe's secretary (see p. 424 *n*). Some corrections, however, appear to have been made by the ambassador himself.

[2] It is quite possible that it did not, at all events while Roe remained in India. Even before Heynes's departure for Mokha, the ambassador could 'find him woorke day and night' (cf. also p. 432), and after the loss of his services Roe had a difficulty even in keeping copies of his letters (p. 473).

[3] From Purchas's statement that he copied most of the letters he gives 'from Sir Thomas Roes owne booke,' it might be inferred that he had had access to the ambassador's private copy. It seems more

INTRODUCTION lxxiii

have seen, however, more than the three sections which we have already described as having been sent home in 1616-18, for he expressly states that he could find nothing later than 22 January, 1618. He had inquired diligently for the rest, ' but neither with the Honourable Company nor elsewhere could learne of it.' This points strongly to the correctness of our surmise that Roe brought home the fourth section only in rough, and never found the opportunity to have it fairly copied for the Company, or perhaps for himself.

The three sections which the Company did receive have long since vanished from their records. Bruce does not appear to have seen them when compiling his *Annals*, early in the last century. If we mistake not, however, the first of the three is now in the British Museum. *Add. MS.* 19277, purchased in 1852 at the Arley Castle sale, is a contemporary transcript of the diary from the beginning to the departure from Burhānpur ; and both the character and handwriting of the marginal abstracts subsequently added, and the manner in which the volume is labelled, leave little doubt that the manuscript formed at one time part of the Company's records. The second section (Nov. 1615-Nov. 1616) appears also to have been in that collection a century ago, though it has since disappeared. A ' catalogue of damaged papers,' compiled at the East India House in 1822 and still preserved at the India Office, contains the following entry : ' 1616. Journal of Sir Thomas Roe at the Court of the Mogul. This fragment has

probable, however, that he is referring to the transcript from Roe's letterbook which was made over to the Company, as distinguished from the original letters ; and this theory is supported by the fact that (as will be seen from p. 274) in a case where Roe's ' owne booke ' has a wrong figure, Purchas gives the right one.

At the time of Roe's handing in his papers, he suggested that they should be kept together in a special chest, and orders were given that this should be done (*Court Minutes*, 28 Sept., 1619). In 1629 Roe borrowed for a time the Company's copies, possibly because his own were not in London. This appears from the following entry in the Court Minutes of 4 Feb., 1629 : ' Sir Thomas moved the Court that Mr. Ellam may be enordred to lend him for a short time certaine journalls of his owne and bookes of the coppies of letters, because he hath at present speciall occasion to use them. The Court was content that Mr. Ellam should lend them to Sir Thomas accordinglie.'

not an entire leaf. The volume is mutilated from the outward edge half through most of the pages.' The fate of the document is not recorded; but we may surmise that, when the collection was rearranged a few years subsequent to 1822, this particular paper was destroyed as useless. The same fate seems to have befallen another document entered in the same catalogue, viz. : ' 1615-16. Household expences of Sir Thomas Roe at Agra (*sic*) and Ajimere.'

As we have seen, it was in *Purchas his Pilgrimes* (vol. i. p. 535) that Roe's journal, with a few letters or portions of letters, was first given to the world ; and practically it is this version which has formed the basis of all succeeding accounts of the embassy. It is therefore all the more to be regretted that the materials available were handled in such an unsatisfactory manner. When one remembers the difficulties, monetary and otherwise, under which the reverend geographer laboured, and the inestimable service he rendered by placing on record so much that would otherwise have perished, one is little inclined to join in the sweeping condemnation often passed upon him. But it must be confessed that his editing of this particular journal is a very bad piece of work. That he should cut it down to a third or less was perhaps to be expected, in view of the restrictions of space imposed by his general plan ; but that, while leaving untouched many trivialities (such as ' the copy is registered,' when he does not print the letter in question), he should excise passages vital to the comprehension of others which were allowed to stand : that his dates should often be wrong : and that the carelessness of his copyist (or his printer) should be allowed to make nonsense of important passages, will scarcely admit of excuse. However, as we have said, the difficulties in which his work was produced may be pleaded in his defence, and we must at least be grateful to him for having preserved for us extracts from nearly a full year of the journal (1617-18), for which no manuscript account is now available.

Purchas's collection contained also (vol. ii. p. 1464) some notes by the Rev. Edward Terry, who had acted as Roe's chaplain during the greater part of his embassy ; and these (which have recently been reprinted in *Early Travels in India*, 1583-1619, pp. 288-332) were subsequently expanded into a small volume, which was published in 1655. In the following year a Dutch version of Roe's account, translated from Purchas, was published at Amsterdam in a small quarto of 126 pages, embellished with four quaint copperplates. The next appearance of the diary was in the first volume of Thevenot's *Divers Voyages Curieux* (1663), where it is stated to have been translated ' du Recüeil Anglois de Purchas.' The editor has added a few notes, an extract from *Purchas his Pilgrimage*, three letters (also from Purchas), and Roe's geographical description of India, with the map. In 1705 was published *Navigantium atque Itinerantium Bibliotheca ; or a Compleat Collection of Voyages and Travels*, by John Harris. In this (vol. i. book ii. ch. xxx.) is given an inaccurate and much compressed paraphrase of Roe's journal, derived from Purchas. Great liberties are taken with the text, some of it being incorporated with Peyton's journal in ch. xxviii., and other portions amalgamated with extracts from Terry and others to form ch. xxxi. In Harris's second edition (1744) the narrative is entirely suppressed, and in lieu of it a short account of its contents is given in a chapter containing a general history of the Company's trade.

Meanwhile an attempt had been made to produce an entirely new edition. Having somehow procured, as already related, the first volume of Roe's own MS. copy, Messrs. Awnsham and John Churchill in 1704 made the journal a special feature of the first volume of their *Collection of Voyages and Travels*. Roe's work, said the preface, had already appeared in part, but ' now he comes abroad again with considerable additions, not foisted in, but taken from his own original manuscript, which it is likely Purchas had not, but some imperfect copy of it. It is true, the additions are not great in bulk . . . but they are valuable for the subject. . . . In fine, here is all that is valuable of Sir Thomas Roe, and nothing that may cloy the reader.' These are brave words, but the performance is far from bearing out the promise. ' After an attentive comparison of these two former editions,' wrote a subsequent editor (Robert Kerr), ' it obviously appears that the edition by Purchas, in 1625, is in general more circumstantial and more satisfactory than that of Churchill . . . notwithstanding its superior pretensions'; and this verdict is entirely borne out by an examination of the latter. It is a veritable piece of hack-work, performed in most careless fashion. The additions are chiefly the dates of Roe's arrival at or departure from various places, though a few incidents are recorded which had been passed over by Purchas. On the other hand, the omissions (of which nothing is said in the preface) are numerous and important. The events at Surat are told in eleven short lines; Roe's reception at court is said to have been 'very favourable, but needs not particularizing'; and all details of commercial matters and of Roe's negotiations are omitted. By these means the bulk of the narrative has been reduced to less than one-half of that of Purchas's version. The spelling has been modernised, and, not content with this, the editor has taken upon himself the task of improving Roe's diction. In the earlier portion of the work scarcely a sentence escapes alteration; but later on the editor's energy flags and changes are much less numerous. Dates are frequently given incorrectly, and the editor's knowledge is displayed by changing the Mogul's 'shash' (*i.e.* turban-cloth) into 'staff.' Four letters of Roe's, written all before November, 1616, his geographical account of India, and a note of presents asked for by him, are also included in the volume.

It is unnecessary to trouble the reader with a detailed account of subsequent versions, since they are all reproductions, more or less complete, of Purchas or Churchill. It may suffice to mention that the journal appears in the collections of the Abbé Prévost (*Histoire Générale des Voyages*, Amsterdam edition, vol. xiii.), Schwabe (*Allgemeine Historie der Reisen*, 1747, etc., vol. xi.), Knox (*New Collection of Voyages*, 1767, vol. vi.), Pinkerton (*General Collection of Voyages*, 1808-14, vol. viii.), Kerr (*General History and Collection of Voyages*, 1811-24, vol. ix.), and Laharpe (*Abrégé de l'Histoire Générale des Voyages* [Prévost's], 1816, vol. iv.). Finally, in our own day, Purchas's version of the journal appeared in serial form, under the care of the late Mr. Talboys Wheeler, in the Calcutta *Englishman*; and a small impression of this edition was issued in book form a few years later (1873), together with Dr. Fryer's *New Account of East India*, by Messrs Trübner and Co.

INTRODUCTION lxxvii

The present work, as already mentioned, is based upon the only portion of Roe's own copy which has survived, viz., *Add. MS.* 6115, in the British Museum collection. This has been given in full, whereas previous editors have printed only about one third of it. A diligent search having failed to discover the rest of the journal in any known collection, it has been necessary, when the manuscript comes to an end, to fall back upon the mutilated version of Purchas, which carries on the narrative to 22 January, 1618. For the remaining year of Roe's stay in India, we are almost entirely dependent upon his letters and such scraps of information as can be gathered from contemporary documents. In the journal have been interspersed a number of the more important of Roe's letters. It was impossible, within the space available, to include all that are extant; nor was this necessary, for many either deal with matters of detail which have now lost their interest, or else repeat what has been said elsewhere. For the same reasons it has been judged advisable to cut down most of the letters for which we have been able to find room. Each letter has, however, been carefully examined, and it is believed that nothing of real importance has been omitted. In many cases, passages for which room has not been found in the text have been utilised in the notes or in this introduction. *Add. MS.* 19277—the other contemporary copy of Roe's manuscript, to which we have already alluded—has, of course, been collated (so far as it goes) with our text, and in a few cases its readings have been followed in preference to those of the principal manuscript. Where, also, two or more contemporary copies of the letters exist, these have been carefully compared, and any differences of importance noted.

Before concluding, a few words may be said concerning two of the illustrations of the present edition. The portrait of Roe which forms the frontispiece is from a painting now in the National Portrait Gallery, having been acquired early in 1904. This is regarded by the authorities as merely a copy of an original portrait by Michiel Jansz Miereveldt, the fate of which is unknown, though at the time when it was engraved by George Vertue for *The Negotiations of Sir Thomas Roe in his Embassy to the Ottoman Porte* (1740), it was in the possession

lxxviii THE EMBASSY OF SIR THOMAS ROE

of the Hon. Wills Hill, whose father, Viscount Hillsborough, had married into the Roe family. The date of its execution is not known; but since Roe is depicted in his robes as Chancellor of the Garter, it cannot have been earlier than 1637. At the base of the picture is inscribed *Te colui, Virtus, ut rem: sed nomen inane es*. This gloomy motto (which we may suppose to have been chosen by Roe himself) is possibly derived from Bacon (*Advancement of Learning*, ed. Wright, p. 248). It may be traced back to Plutarch (*De Superstitione*, ed. Hutten, vol. viii. p. 54) and to Dion Cassius (ed. Sturzius, vol. ii. p. 564), who in turn seems to have got it *ex incerto Tragico*.

The second illustration to which attention may specially be drawn is that representing the Emperor and his son Khurram, with an attendant. This is reproduced from a woodcut in *Purchas His Pilgrimes* (vol. ii. p. 1474), where it appears in connection with Terry's account of his Indian experiences. From the use of the plural ('Indian copies') in the inscription at the top, as well as on general grounds, it may be inferred that the English engraver combined for the purpose two, if not three, separate miniatures, though the Persian inscription which he copied along the bottom can only have appeared on the portrait of Jahāngīr himself. From that inscription we learn that the original artist was no other than the celebrated Hindu painter, Manohar Dās. Apart from this, the chief interest of the picture (unsuspected at the time of its reproduction in the former edition) lies in the fact that the said Persian writing undoubtedly represents an autograph inscription on the original by the Emperor's own hand. Its interpretation is not free from difficulty, owing to the English engraver's want of familiarity with the script; and in the first edition I gave, on good authority, a rendering which made the inscription appear to be the signature of the Indian artist. This version was at once challenged by Mr. (afterwards Sir) Arthur Wollaston, who, in a note contributed to the *Journal of the Royal Asiatic Society* for January, 1900, gave reasons for thinking that the inscription had come from the pen of the Emperor himself. Other scholars joined in the discussion. Almost all admitted the correctness of this conclusion, though there was some difference of opinion as to the

INTRODUCTION

exact wording; and the late Mr. William Irvine clenched the matter by referring (*ibid.*, April, 1903, p. 370) to an admitted autograph of Jahāngīr's (*ibid.*, vol. 39, pt. i. p. 271), which presented the same characteristics.

As to the actual wording, the best version appears to be that given me by the late Syed Ali Bilgrami, which runs as follows: *Sanah* 1[0]26, *dar shahr-i-Māndū. Rāqimuhu Manohar. Dar sinn-i-panjāh sālagī būdam.* In English this reads: *The year 1026, in the town of Māndu. Painted by Manohar. I was in my fiftieth year.*

Now A.H. 1026 was practically the same as A.D. 1617; Jahāngīr's fiftieth (lunar) year ran from March 1617 to March 1618; and we know that he was at Māndu from March to Oct. 1617. The conclusion is that he gave the miniature to Roe on some occasion during the latter period and, probably at the ambassador's request, added his autograph. Obviously this could not have been the portrait presented on 17 Aug., 1616 (p. 214); and it must therefore have been a subsequent gift, of which we have no record—an omission easily accounted for by the fact that of this portion of the diary we have only the extracts made by Purchas. The latter, by the way, nowhere refers to the illustration he gives, nor says how he obtained the loan of the original miniatures. As to this, we can only conjecture that they were presented by Roe on his return to Prince Charles, whose taste for such things is well known. As shown in *Early Travels in India* (p. 289), there is some reason for thinking that Purchas obtained from the Prince the manuscript of Terry's narrative; and it is permissible to infer that he procured from the same source the loan of the miniatures which he used for its illustration.

THE JOURNAL OF SIR THOMAS ROE.[1]

(Brit. Museum : *Add. MS.* 6115.)

1614[-15], *March* 6.—This day wee lost sight of the Lizard, and begann our course for the Cape of Good Hope.

1615, *March* 26.—On this day in the morning wee saw the mayne of Barbery, making that for Fortaventura,[2] and then stood away S.W. by S. till noone, and saw land N.W. for the Canarye 8 leauges off ; then wee steerd S.S.W. all night.

***March* 27.**—At 6 in the morning Cape Bugador bare E. by S. 4 leaugs off ; wherby wee found 30 leagues error in westerly way. This cape lyeth in 26 lattitude, 353° 50′ longitude, differing from the meridian of the Lizard 6° 10′ by Mercators projection, but I suppose it is layd 20 leagues to much to the E., the Canarye Islands in the same error.[3] The land to the sowthward trendeth S.S.W. ; for steering S.W. by S. I could

---

[1] The 'table of course,' which occupies the first nine pages of the manuscript and shows in tabular form the course, variation, latitude, etc. from 6 March to 17 September, has been omitted, as containing nothing of general importance. It may be consulted in Churchill's *Collection of Voyages*, 1704, vol. i. The 'observations according to the table of course,' which immediately follow it, have also been omitted, but will be found in the previous edition.

[2] One of the Canary Islands. The *Expedition* nearly ran ashore, having 'muche adoe to perceave the land, being but lowe,' and the coast being wrongly laid in the charts (Peyton's Journal : Brit. Mus. *Add. MS.* 19276).

[3] Cape Bojador is about 9° 17′ W. from the meridian of the Lizard. Roe is therefore right as to its incorrect position in the chart referred to. The latter was probably one of 'the platts of John Danyells making (being Mercators projection),' which Peyton used, and censured as unreliable. Cf. also the journal of the Eleventh Voyage in *Purchas* (vol. i. p. 486).

not cleare the land in 24 howers. So that when, on the 26 day, wee tooke our selves to bee betweene the island[s], we were betweene the mayne and Forteventura, a sandy shoure, 16 fadome, 4 leagues off; and steering that day 6 howers S.W. by S. we could only discerne land in the topp for the Canarye. Wheras, had wee bene with the islands, we should with that course from Forteventura have shott faire out by the Canarye. The 27th at noone the mayne bearing E. in 26° five leaugs off, wee shaped our course. . . .

April 5.—This day the sunne was in our zenith, crossing the paralell at midnight.

April 10.—This night we meett the turnados next hand in 2°; the wynd at E. with a terrible gust of raine for two howers.

April 12.—This day a counsell was held, wherin a captain complayned against his master; the playntiffe was satisfied, the accused advanced, the inocent punished, all pleased. . . .[1]

April 14.—This night I passd the line; Cape de Golinus,[2] the next [*i.e.* nearest] land, bearing N.N.E. half E. 158 leaugs off. . . .

May 2.—This day the sowth tropique.

May 3.—The *Magillan* cloudes [3] first appeare, and they keepe their course with the Polar Starrs about the Pole, alway equidistant, 11 or 12° the most sowthermost. They are streamy and glaring, whyte, like the *Galaxia* [*i.e.* the Milky Way]. . . .

June 5.—Pengyn [4] Island at one in the morning four leagues E. This day at nine a clocke I came to anchor in the bay of Soldania in five fadom water, from Pengyn bearing E. four

[1] 'This daye Tho. Barwicke, maister of the *Peppercorne*, was displaced, or raither removed (upon complainte made against him by his captaine) into the shipp *Lyon*, and Jno. Curtis removed into the *Peppercorne* in his roome' (Peyton's Journal). See also *Letters Received*, vol. ii. pp. 184, 185, ete.

[2] Probably a Cabo das Gallinhas. Several old maps have a Rio das Gallinhas just north of Cape Mount, in Liberia.

[3] Three small nebulæ in the southern part of the heavens.

[4] Now Robben Island. The bay of Soldania is of course Table Bay, not the modern Saldanha Bay.

leagues. . . . In comminge in it is better to hale in with the sowth then the north shoare, for the flatts and sands and breaches of Pengyn.

The 4th of June I was by reckoning 28 leagues off 33° 35'; soe that, the wynd standing, I did expect to be near land the first night watch. Most of our fleete, all except John Hatch,[1] who keept the same manner of reckoning, havinge looked for land two and three days before; their accounts out. Besides, they made sure to see it within 12 howers after the variation was lessened to one degree, but this alsoe deceived them and is an error. I was open and confident on my dead reckoninge, the rather because the longitude of the Cape by Mercators projection is rectefyed in 28° 30' from the meridian of the Lizard, and is, I suppose, truly projected; and though the variation be an excellent evidence in the whole course of nearing land, yet it delivereth no other certainty but warninge to looke out, for it lessens not in the same proportion near land, but by a much slower; for which I could give a perspicuous reason, but to learge for this place. Nor can any judgment att all be made to 20 leaugs therby that shalbe infallible, the magneticall amplitude being soe difficult to observe truly, by the shipps motion and the needles quicknes, that a degree is scarce an error. This consideration made me confident that wee should see noe land untill the 5th day early in the morning. The wynd at N.N.W. and fresh, wee steering E. to the sowthward, at one aclock after midnight the Admirall[2] tacked, and sawe land faier bye, and heaving the dipsall[3] we had 35 fadome. Standing off, in two glasses we deepned to 60 fadom. Nowe to this hower from noone the 4th day we had runn 27 leaugs, and my reckoning was the day before 28 leauges; soe that in tyme I faild not an hower, in distance but one leauge, if wee had not stoode off in the night. At breake of day the 5th day we stood in, and sawe Pengwin

[1] Master's mate on the *Lion*. We shall hear of him again later.

[2] At this period the commander of a fleet was usually called the *General*, while the ship which carried his flag was the *Admiral*; cf. Drake's *World Encompassed*, p. 8: 'the admirall, wherein our generall himself went.'

[3] The deep-sea-line, for sounding.

Island east, and steering away S.E. for the baye came to anchor....[1]

Soldanya is, as I suppose, an island,[2] on the sowth end wherof is the Cape of Good Hope, devided from the mayne by a deepe bay on the S.E. side and due E. by a river which wee discerne upon the Table.[3] The land is fructfull, bearing short thicke grasse. The mayne is devided with most high and steepe rocky mountaynes, covered with snow, and unaccessable, except it be scearched by the river of Dulce [*i.e.* the Sweet River], which doubtlesse is veary great, falling into the bay on the E. syde. There is on the island 5 or 600 people, the most barberous in the world, eating carrione, wearing the gutts of sheepe about their necks for health, and rubbing their heads (curled like negroos) with dung of beasts and durte. They have noe other cloathing then beastes skins wrapt on their shoulders, the skinne next the body in heate, in could the heairy syde. Theyr howses are but one matt concaved like an oven, into which they creepe, and turne them about as the wynde chainges, for they have no doores to keepe it out. They have lefte their stealinge by trading with us, and by signes make showe their harte is good. They knowe noe kind of God or religion. The ayer and water is veary wholsome, and both of them subtile and searching. There is on the island bulls, cowes, antelops, babones, mowles of great bignes, fezants, partriches, larcks, wildgeese, ducks, pascer flamingos, and many others. On Pengwyn there is a foule soe called that goes upright, his winges without feathers hanging downe like sleves faced with whyte ; they fley not, but walk in pathes and keepe their divisions and quarters orderly ; they are a strange

[1] Here follows a long excursus on the course taken in making for the Cape, Roe considering that the pilots were wrong. It can be consulted, if desired, in the previous edition.

[2] The Cape peninsula has this appearance from the sea, and is so represented in old maps. But ' island ' was often used in the sense of ' peninsula.'

[3] During the stay of the ships, Roe spent some time on land, one of the five tents erected being set aside for his use (Peyton's Journal). A summary of a letter from one of the factors mentions that while at the Cape Roe set up a pillar with an inscription of his embassy (*Letters Received*, vol. ii. p. 184).

fowle, or rather a *miscelanius* creator of beast, bird, and fishe, but most of birde, confuting that difinition of man to be *Animall bipes implunæ*,[1] which is nearer to a discription of this creature. The comodities here are, first, reasonable refreshing with cattell (soe that a season be chosen when they are not leane, a month after the sunn is departed from them northward); *Nangin* [2] rootes; arras,[3] if our merchants be not deceived; and I doe strongly suppose that I found a rocke yeelding quicksilver and virmillion,[4] the stone being spotted all without with a most pure redd coulor, equall to any paynting, and that will come off upon paper or other fitt matter; by the description of John Acosta [5] it cannot fayle to be the same; it is alsoe veary heavie, full of marquisate and minnerall apperannces. The Table, or high rocke soe called, by a streight lyne from the water syde is ii853 foote high.[6] The bay is full of whales and seales; the Dutch have fished on Pengwyn for them. The lattitud is 33° 45′; the longitude 28° 30′ from the Lizard; the variation doubtfull whyther to the east or west, but my opinion is that the variation is west 30ᵐ; the cause of variation beeing in the mayne, as apperes evidently by the many lynes and changes towards the Cape E. and after westerly. If any shipping (having tym enough) fall but 100 leaugs more to the north with the mayne (which may

[1] The well-known definition of man (ζῶον δίπουν ἄπτερον) ascribed to Plato—'that unfeathered two-legged thing,' as Dryden renders it.

[2] *Nangin* or *ningin* appears to be the Japanese name for a plant identical with, or allied to, the Chinese *ginseng*, a medicinal root highly esteemed in the East as a restorative, and hence possessing a considerable commercial value. For searches made for it at the Cape in this and other voyages see *Letters Received*, vol. v. p. 18.

[3] Orris root. Several varieties of *Iris* are found at the Cape.

[4] On the strength of Roe's opinion, '30 or 40 lbs.' were sent home in the *Hope* 'for a trial' (*O.C.*, No. 187). As nothing more is said on the subject, it is probable that the results were unsatisfactory.

[5] *The Natural and Moral History of the Indies* (Hakluyt Soc. ed.), p. 214. 'John' is a mistake (probably due to the original copyist) for 'Joseph.'

[6] Meaning 2,853 feet. Such a mixture of Roman and Arabic numerals, though rare, is not unexampled. Purchas prints it as 11,853, and Herbert follows him in this error. The height is really about 3,550 feet.

be done with saftye, no wynds forbidding it), I assure myselfe they shall have good trade for cattle and other comodities, and may by leaving some men discover the land, and perhaps gett knowledge of the people that trade with the Spaniards on the east syde in 21° for gould, after the manner of the Moores in Barbery to Gago.[1] These lefte at the Cape [2] will goe no further, but attend opportunity of passage ; and thear can

[1] See *The Historie of Barbary*, by Ro. C. (London, 1609), sig. K 3.

[2] The reference is to the ' condemned men from Newgate,' whom the Company, as a charitable deed, had begged of the King upon the understanding that they would be left at the Cape. This anticipation of the transportation system (which was not unusual in voyages of the period) was attended by very poor success. In two letters to Sir Thomas Smythe, Roe pointed out the mischievous influence exercised by these malefactors upon the crews of the ships, and the futility of expecting that they would either settle at the Cape or make any attempt to discover the interior ; and, when the time came for quitting the Bay, he protested warmly against their abandonment. Keeling, however, considered that he had no option : though as a courtesy to the ambassador he spared two, one of whom, named Duffield, was taken into Roe's service, and rewarded his benefactor, upon their return to England, by absconding with some of his plate. The remaining ten were set ashore, with a few provisions and tools ; and Cross, a former yeoman of the royal guard, who had been sentenced to death for killing several men in duels, was, with their consent, constituted the captain. Shortly after, one man was killed and two were wounded in a skirmish with the natives ; whereupon the *Hope*, before departing, gave them four muskets and a boat, in order that they might find a safe dwelling-place upon Penguin Island. Eight months later, the *New Year's Gift*, on her homeward voyage, took off three of the survivors ; and the rest are said to have found a passage in a Portuguese ship. The three brought back to England deserted in the Downs, ' took a purse ' within three hours, were captured, and ordered for execution on their old sentence.

Three more condemned men were carried out in the fleet of 1616. On reaching the Cape and learning the fate of their predecessors, they besought the commander on their knees to hang them outright rather than leave them. He refused to depart from his instructions, and they were put ashore accordingly ; but the *Swan*, the last ship of his fleet to leave the bay, took them on board and carried them to Bantam. The experiment seems then to have been abandoned. (See Terry's *Voyage* ; Court Minutes and Dodsworth's Journal, in I. O. Records ; Peyton's Journal, *ut supra* ; Pring's narrative in *Purchas*, vol. i. p. 631.)

doe noe great good, beeing amounge the basest banished people, that knowe nothing savoring of man, nor are no other way men, but as they speak and walke like men.

June 17.—This night the *Hope* [1] came to an anchor in the bay from Suratt, laden with indicoes.

June 20.—Wee weighed at 4 in the morning, the wynd at E.S.E., and ... proceeded towards Santa Lawrance [*i.e.* Madagascar].

June 25.—Wee sawe the land, which I suppose was Cape Fernoso, N. by E. ... I alwayes made 2 or 3° more variation then all the fleete, for my needle beeing touched afresh once in 10 dayes I suppose it was more animated and fixed then those that beeing long touchd must daylie somwhat weaken; the needles I touchd for others performing the same difference.

July 8.—I was a shore by reckoning on Santa Lawrance in 22° 30′ latitude, 51° 10′ longitude, the fleete having by account looked for land 24 howers; but we could not make the Cape Augustine, the wynd hanginge off the land. But wee found that wee were hindered of eastering by the first currents at Cape des Agullas 50 leaugs, and by the current setting after to the north we made more N. way then wee could alowe, and by consequence lesse E., the current setting N.N.W. between the latitude of 30 and longitude of 46, and the lattitude 24 and longitude 29 [39 ?]. For we wanted, as I suppose, 20 leaugs off Saint Lawrance, notwithstanding wee had runn over him 80 leaugs. But of this I dare affirme on good reason, that the Cape Augustine must be layed in the E. 40 leaugs more then it is in Mercators plott, being there in 51° 10′, truly in 53°. The land alsoe at the foote of Affrica is more in longitude then it lyeth for. Seeing in three dayes we could not gett into the land, and beeing put to the N., the 12th day, the wynd at N.E., we stood away for Molalia [*i.e.* Mohilla], judging my selfe to be 20 leaugs from Saint Lawrance

---

[1] The *Merchants' Hope*, one of the vessels of Downton's fleet of the preceding year. 'June 17, aryved the shipp *Hope* homeward; in her Mr. Dodsworthe, by whome wee understood at lardge the many injuryes and abuses offred our nation at Suratt by the Portugalls, and howe their malitious projects and fyre devises weare with Gods assistance withstood' (Peyton's Journal).

W. in 21° 10′. It is necessary to see the Cape of Augustine, to correct the errors of the currents, else hee that shall shape his course by reckoninge may be deceived in longitude 50 or 60 leaugs, which is veary daingerous because of the shoales of Judia [1] near 21, and the currents soe variable that it wilbe hard to conjecture on which hand yow leave them. Therfore I advise (if weather be faier at the Cape of Good Hope) to make Aracifo [2] in 33° 30′; so yow shall correct the fierst currents. Then to runn large away E. neare to the longitude of the island before yow hale to the north, for yow will rayse apace both by the current and variation, into the latitude of Cape Augustine. If it be foule weather getting about the Cape of Good Hope, stand into 37° before yow hale to the east; and then runn in a paralell, or little to the N., aloweing by conjecture for the currents, but not soe much as if yow stood nearer into the shoare, wher they are more violent, but are soone lost in the sea. From Cape Augustine a N.W. by N. course will goe cleare both of the shoales of Judia and the shoales of Saint Lawrance in 20°. These shoales are bould, and, as a Pilott of Magadoxa tould me [see p. 13], have fine shoalinge 12 and 15 fadome to the shoare. I thinke I lefte Judia 20 leaugs W., because at Molalia my reckoninge came well out.

July 21.—At two in the afternoone wee made lande N.E. by N. 7 leaugs off, taking it for Molalia, in 12° 57′; and stood in with it till 5 at night, when wee sawe another island bearing N.W. by W., the true Molalia, which beare N. of us at noone (when we made Juanny for it) both by my reckoning and the truth. Then standing W. off and W. by S. till 7 in the morning the 22th, seeing Molalia playn N.N.W. we stood away N.W. and N. about the west ende of the island, and came to anchor on the north syde in a little bay in 24 fadome water, the poynt to the west having a ledge of rocks W.S.W. and the other poynt E. by S., the soundings veary deepe as wee came alonge the shoare unto the roade.

[1] The *Bassas da Judia* of the Portuguese charts, now known as the Europa Shoals.

[2] Cape Recife, near Port Elizabeth.

Molalia is one of the four islands of Comory,[1] Angazesia, Juanny, and Mayotta beinge the other three. They lye E. and W. near in a paralell one of a nother, except Angazesia, which lyeth somwhat more N. ; Molalia in 12° 20′ sowth lattitude, in the same meridian with Cape Augustine, the variatione being 16° 40′. Angazesia bears from it by the compasse N. by W. 7 leaugs off, the sowerthmost[2] end in a 11° 55′, extending it selfe north to a 11° 6′, as I observed within 5 leaugs therof, bearing sowth from me. It is the highest land I ever sawe, inhabited by Moores trading with the mayne and the other three easteren islands with their cattle and fructs for callicoes or other linnen to cover them. It is governd by ten petty kings, and is sufficiently fruictfull of kine, faire goates, cocors, orrenges, and lemons. They made us fiers as we passed by, being desierous of trade at the first hand, which nowe they fetch by cannoes at Molalia, whear our ships ride. They are helde a falce and an unfaythfull people, having betrayd some of Sir James Lancasters men long sithence,[3] but nowe, havinge experience of us at other islands, I doubt not they would regayne theyr creditts.

Juanny lyes from Molalia east, and Mayotta in the same course. The coast betweene them is every way bould. These three islands are veary full of good refreeshings, but principally Mayotta, as I was enformed by the Arabs trading in Molalia ; and the Dutch stoppe thear. The next in goodnes is Juanny, whear lives an ould woeman Sultanness of them all, to whom they repayre for justice, both in civill and criminall causes. Molalia hath on yt three Subsultans, childeren of the ould woeman, two men, one daughter, who governe severall parts of the island. The Sultan in whose quarter we anchored hath such authoritye that his subjects dare not sell a nutt untill leave obtayned. To which end Captaine Keeling[4] sent four

---

[1] The Comoro group, consisting of Angaziya (Great Comoro), Johanna, Mayotta, Mohilla, and a number of small islands.

[2] ' Furthermost ' in *Purchas*, where the succeeding sentence is with equal carelessness turned into ' extending itselfe North eleven degrees sixe minutes.'

[3] In 1591. See *Voyages of Sir James Lancaster*, pp. 6, 26.

[4] William Keeling, the ' General ' of the fleet. He was at some time or other Groom of the Chamber to King James, probably before

boates to his towne, desiringe libertye to trade ; wher they were received by a governor or rather an admirall or commander of the porte, lyeing some four leauges to the eastward of our roade, where, havinge obtained leave to come a shoare, we landed some 40 men with Captaine Newport.[1] The Governor he entered the Company's service. In their employment he was captain, first of the *Susan* and then of the *Hector*, in the First Voyage, and held the chief command in the Third. He was now going out with a special commission to pass from port to port in the Indies, and regulate the Company's affairs in all the factories. As he was to remain five years abroad, he had pleaded very hard to take his wife with him. For a short time the Committees were inclined to agree, but finally they determined to refuse the request. At the last moment, however, they found that he had secretly smuggled his wife aboard, and it was only on a threat of dismissal that he was induced to leave her behind. Writing from the Cape, he implored the Company to send her out to him ; and as this was not done, he hurried home in 1616. By 1618 he had been appointed captain of Cowes Castle ; in September of the following year he died, and was buried at Carisbrook, at the early age of forty-two. His quaint epitaph, still to be seen in the church there, calls him ' a merchant fortunate, a captain bould, a courtier gracious ' ; and that he was a man of real merit and capacity is evident from the terms in which Roe speaks of him. Although there was a coolness between them at first, this left no real hostility ; and, writing to Pepwell on 30 Dec. 1616, Roe says emphatically that Keeling ' did use his authoritye with more moderation and better judgment and integritye then most men would, and will not be easely matchd for sufficiency every way, and did as well deserve the trust as any, I beleeve, they [the Company] can ever employ.'

[1] Christopher Newport, captain of Roe's ship, the *Lion*. It had first been intended that he should command the fleet, and he was by no means pleased to find Keeling placed above him. He had had a distinguished career. In 1592 he swept the Spanish possessions in the West Indies, and ended by assisting to capture the great carrack *Madre de Deos* ; later he made five voyages to the New World, and shared with Somers in the re-discovery of the Bermudas. His first voyage in the service of the East India Company was in January 1613, when he carried out Sir Robert Sherley in the *Expedition* to Lahrībandar, went on to Bantam for a cargo of pepper, and was back in England by July 1614, a record passage (' I thinke,' wrote one of the Company's factors a little later, alluding to an old superstition, ' Captain Newport . . . carryeth a fly in a box with him '). His next voyage was the one in which we now find him engaged. Returning with the *Lion* in the autumn of 1616, he was

THE COMORO ISLANDS

they found sitting upon a matt of strawe, under the side of a junck which was a building, accompaned with about 50 men. His aparell was a mantell of blew and red lynen wrapte about him to his knees, his leggs and feete bare : on his head a close cape of checker woork. The enterpreters were certaine Magadoxians, that spake Arabicque and broken Portuguese. Captaine Newport; presenting him with a peece [*i.e.* musket] and a swoord blade from Captain Keeling, received a welcome ; and [the Governour] commanded 4 bullocks to be returned in requitall, and with gravitie enough entertayned them, gevinge free libertye to buy and sell and signifiinge soe much by a messenger to the inhabitance round about, and promised to send downe his owne cattle ; but professed he had noe power to compell or make price for others, but lefte the trade open to everie mans will. He sent for cocore nutts to give the company, himself chaweing bittle [betel] and lyme of burnt oystershells with a kernell of a nutt called arracca [areca], like an ackorne. It bytts in the mouth, avoydes rume, cooles the head, strengthens the teeth, and is all their phisicke ; it makes one unused to it giddy, and makes a mans spittle redd, and in tyme coullers the teeth, which is esteemed a beawty. This is usd by all men howerly. From the Governor they were leadd to a carpenters howse, a cheefe man of that towne ; the howse builte of lyme and stone, playstered with morter or whyt lime, lowe, and little, roofte with rafters of woode covered with cocor leaves, the outsides watled with canes. They are keept cleanly and their poore houshould stuff neate, their gardens pald with canes, enclosinge some tobacco and plantan trees. For dinner a boorde was sett upon tressells covered with a fine new matt ; benches of stone about yt likwise covered, on which they scatt. First water was brought to everie man in a cocor shell, powered out into a wooden platter, and in steed of a towell the rinds of cocor. Then was sett boyld rise and rosted plantens, upon the rice

sent with a fresh ship to Bantam, and reached that port on the 15th August, 1617. He died not long after, but the exact date is not known. There is a good notice of him in the *Dictionary of National Biography* ; and a few additional particulars of his home life will be found in *Stepney Registers*, p. 25 *n*.

quarters of henns and peeces of goate broyld. After grace said, they fell to their meate, with bread made of cuscus, beaten and mingled with honny and soe fryed, and palmeto wyne and cocor milke for drinke. I sent a gentellman and my chaplen [1] to see the Sultan himselfe, who lives three miles up in the land from Fambone [Fumbuni], the towne of the Governor ; but they found him by chance there. He used them curteously and made them dyne with him, differing little from the former entertaynment, only the Governor and all others gave him much respect, kissing his hand. His name is Sultan Amar-Adell,[2] akinne to Mahomette [*i.e.* a *sharīf*], not unlike to be descended of such an imposturous race ; his cloathes not unlike the Governors but somwhat better stuffe ; his manners differing much, being with lesse gravitie and state ; somwhat a light foole, and veary hastie to be druncke with wyne carried by the English. The other Vize-Sultan his brother, in whose quarter we wear not, I sawe, being come downe to our roade with three slaves to trade. Hee brought a certifficate from Captain Sayers that hee had usd the English well in his dominion.[3] He is as well *Xeriff* [*sharīf*] as Sultan, which is high Preist. Hee keept a kinde of state in place, but otherwise a poore bearefooted roauge. He offered to trade for quicksilver, and being asked what quantitie he would buy, replyed, to 4 or 5 rialls of eight. When this marchandice faild him, hee fell to begginge of shooes ; then I left him.

All the people are strickt Mahometans, observing much of the old lawe, and at this tyme, beeing the preparation to their *Ramdam* [*i.e.* the month of *Ramazān*], or Lent, unwilling to drink wyne. They are veary jelous to lett their weomen or

[1] The Rev. John Hall. Little is known of him, except that he came from Petersfield in Hampshire ; matriculated at Oxford (Magdalen Hall) in July, 1596, at the age of seventeen ; became a fellow of Corpus Christi College in 1600 ; and graduated M.A. in 1604 and B.D. in 1613 (Foster's *Alumni Oxonienses*, Clark's *Register*, and Terry's *Voyage*). His death at Ajmer is recorded on a later page. Roe told the Company, on Nov. 24, 1616, that Hall was ' one of the best and quietest and humblest men that ever I knew.'

[2] Probably Umar-bin-Ādil (see *Letters Received*, vol. vi. p. 271).

[3] Eighth Voyage (1611-14). See Saris's narrative in *Purchas*, vol. i. p. 336.

moschees[1] be seene ; of which wee had experiance by an alarum of one of their preists, who espied one of ours comming toward a village, who shutt up all the woemen, and cried out if we came neare them or their church they would kill us ; but by the authoritie of the *Xeriff*, the stone [*i.e.* lustful] preist was appeased and suffered it with more patience. Many of them speake and writt the Arabique in a fair character, and some few Portuguese, trading to Mosombique in junks of 40 touns made of cocor, sowed in steed of pinns, cawked, tackled, and wholly fitted, victualed, and fraighted with that universall tree.

Here our fleete refreshed with oxen and cowes, smale as two-yeareling but good flesh, with goates veary fatt and large, Arabian sheepe, henns, cocors, orenges, lemons, lymes in great abundance, which we bought for callicoes, hollands or other lynnen, sword blads, and rialls of eight ; and their fruicts for glasses, knives, and trifles. Whatsoever is bought for mony is bought dearest.

Here was in trade a junke of Madagascar [2] with slaves. The pilott of the junke, called Malim-Abrimme,[3] spake Portiguse, and toulde me on the sowth side of St. Lawrance ther was store of amber greese, and cokar of the sea.[4] Hee was skillfull in the coast and in the lyeing and bearing of lands

[1] Mosques (from the Arabic *masjid*, probably through the Spanish *mezquita*). The English form was originally dissyllabic, as is here shown ; its present-day pronunciation being due to the misleading influence of other words ending in -que. The English translation (1669) of Olearius's account of the Holstein embassy to Persia gives throughout the form ' mosquey.'

[2] ' From Gangamora in Madagascar ' (Peyton's Journal).

[3] See p. 11. *Malim* is the Arabic *mu'allim*, the ' instructor,' hence the pilot or sailing master of a vessel. Peyton mentions this man as ' one of theis pylotts named Bram (which is as muche to saye Abram),' and says that he tried hard to persuade the English commander to send one of the ships to the eastern coast of Africa, offering his own services as pilot. A consultation was held, at which this proposal found some support ; but in the end it was judged unwise to divide the fleet, as they might need all their force to repel a Portuguese attack at Surat, and time would not allow of the whole fleet going round by that coast.

[4] Coco-de-mer.

both in course and distance. Hee had a good partchment carde, lyned and graduated orderly, which I sent to see. He founde faulte with many things in my carde at sight, which I mended by his direction, and with reason; as the distaunce from Socatra from the mayne, and razinge quite out certaine islands to the sowthward of Molalia, affirming thear are non such. His cuntrie lyes from 1° 50′ to 4°, the port in 2° 10′ N. latitude; governed by one king. Hee assured me of trade enough at his porte to loade one ship with marfil,[1] ambre, and *tinta roxa*.[2] He promised to bring me his plott and soundings and a sample of *tinta roxa*; but some other cause diverted him that hee would come no more at me, notwithstanding I dealt liberally with him, in present and in promises. To the sowth of Magadoxo all the ports are governed by Moorish petty kings, even to Mosambique. He perswaded me that wee might in many places trade for gould and silver; that in Magadoxo the howses roofes were guilt, and that they had gould in sand and mingled with earth, which they esteeme not; off the inland hee knew little, only naming some places or regions between Magadoxo and Prester Jhon, as Odola, Maheza, Rehamy, and Gala;[3] of which Odela and Gala are *Chapharrs*, which signifieth misbelevers (I knowe not whether he means Gentiles or Christians,[4] using the same promiscuously as well to Prester Jhon as to other Gentiles). Off Prester Jhon he knoweth noe more then that he is a great prince and a *Capharr*. From Magadoxo to Cambaya he was expert. His brother, who came with him to me, was in fight against the *Hope*,[5] in a Portugall shipp pressed from Damon, in which 45 were slayne; more he knewe not, but that 3 shipps

[1] Ivory (Sp. *marfil*).

[2] Probably orchilla weed, a lichen which grows on rocks and trees near the sea-coast, and yields a purple dye.

[3] These are unrecognisable; though perhaps Odola is the 'Adel' of Alvarez (part of Somaliland), and Gala the land of the Galla tribes. By Prester John is meant Abyssinia, which was by that time generally recognised as the realm of this mysterious potentate.

[4] Of course he meant *both*. To Muhammadans all outside Islam are *Kafirs*.

[5] See p. 7 *n*. The reports of the capture of Chaul, etc., proved to be untrue.

were burned and the rest runne away. Hee said the King of Dabull tooke courage on this victory and surprised Chaul, Damon and other the Portugalls port townes and was marching to Goa : that the Portugalls was in great distresse of victualls. I hoped to have stored my selfe with more discourse from him, but I was, I knowe not howe, prevented. It were tyme well bestowed to see this coast, and I spake to some of it ; but it fared the woorse for the father.

The road of Molalia lyes in 12° 10′, and for the first six dayes the current setts two leauges a watch S.W., the moone increasinge. At the full, we wounde up N.E. the other way ; but veary easily, for the most parte riding upon the current. The Magadoxians made some absurdly beleeve that the current sett 15 dayes one waye, and 15 another, and 15 dayes still ; which, because of the first six dayes it sett S.W. and after wee wounde up N.E., it begott the opinione of a wonder. Butt the current setts constantly S.W., and before the full of the moone it had such power on the ebbe and flood that wee never wound up ; but at the full moone and springe tydes we rode upon the floud against the current, it runninge under and the tyde above, highinge 16 foote water, and the ebbe wynding back with the current ; soe that the supposed chainge of the current was only strong tydes at the full moone overcomminge it above. For at sea, when the springe was past, I found the same current, and though we weare sett to the eastward the first day wee weighed, and to the westward the next, the cause was the eddies off Juanny one day and Angazesia the other ; but being clear of them, it sett his dew course, that I raised little and did westward much.

August 2.—Wee weighed from Molalia and stood our course for Socatra. . . .

August 10.—In the morning we repast the equinoctiall.

August 14.—In the morning wee saw the coast of Magadoxo in 4° N. latitude 4 leagues off ; sounding had 18 fadome of lowe land, whyte sandye bankes. Then wee stood off E.N.E. The difference of longitude betweene the mayne and Molalia in Mercators projection agreeing with our account and alsoe by course, havinge found the longitude of Cape Saint Augustine and Molalia to be one, I conclude that Saint Lawrance ought to be layde to the E. 39 or 40 leaugs, according to my first opinion, and all the coast of the mayne, beeing broader then it is layde in the carde, must be also sett in proportion to the eastward : because the distance of longitude is right from one to the other, though all their longit[udes] falce in themselves. From Molalia to fall with Cape de Bussos [1] N.N.E. ¼ E. way is the best course, it beeinge necessarie to see the mayne aboute the latitude. In this course since wee lost the westerly current at Angazesia I found none or very little, contrary to all jornalls. Our marriners in this course are off as many opinions as poynts in the compasse, both for currents, distances, and bearings, according to compasse or variation. But I observed the truth in the later end of this S.W. monsone ; which, I confesse, may alter in the hart of a contrary monzon, the settlednes of the wynd causing much chainge in currents of which noe rule can be geven.

August 16.—At eight in the morning, having stood N.E. from 6 to make the mayne, we heaved the dipsall and had no ground. At seven a clock at night, standing in still with much wynd, wee had suddenly whyte water as whyte as milke, soe that wee could not discerne the flory of the sea.[2] Fearing we were near land, we heaved and had noe ground at 70 fadome ; and by and by, discerning a black miste on our lee bowe, they cried out ' land ! ' bringing the shipp too, to stand off east. A new alarume of land a head and on both bowes ; this made much confusion amoung us with all the babell language of the sea, stumbling almost a boord one a nother with more danger then of rocks. But it vanished like a mist, and wee stood of N.E. 18 leaugs till four in the morning, and then stood in againe N.W. 19 leaugs, with a high sea and much wynd. This night wee crost the paralell of the sunne northward.

August 17.—At noone we made Cape Guardefuy, 8 leaugs

[1] Dos Baixos, *i.e.* Ras Awath.

[2] The phenomenon was probably due to the presence of animalculæ. ' Flory ' is no doubt ' flurry,' *i.e.* the agitation of the sea breaking over rocks, as they expected to find. Saris, in his diary, 1611-13 (I.O. Marine Records, xiv.), speaking of a shoal, says : ' you shall see the sea *flur* one it yf there be anye wynd.'

off west, being the cape of the enterance of the Red Sea. At this hower I was 5 leaugs ashoare upon the mayne,[1] some others keeping me company; the rest out of reckoning, fearing wee could not fetch the mayne till we should overshoote Socatra....[2] But the right and surest course is to fall with the mayne in 4° and soe to stand alonge the shoare within 7 or 8 leaugs, soe to see the land once in four howers if yow please. The coast is bould, as the Magadoxian pilott did assure me. From Cape Alabana in 11° to Cape Guardafuy in 12° the land lyes N. and S. Yow may ride under the cape, and bringe a high sandie clifte sowth east and the northwardmost land yow can see N.W. by W. by the compasse, in 12 fadome water, faier whyte sandy grounde. The poynte bearing W.S.W. as we stood in is a downeright sharpe rocke with two notches making a baye, lyeing in W.S.W. Thence it ryseth round and higher land and lyes away toward the Red Sea N.W. ½ W. by the compass. We ... anchored in 12 fadome, in a little baye, wher we stayed the 18th day and sawe some people in turbants, but they would not come near us. Ashoare ther was a tombe of whyte stone with a pillar at each end, neare the water syde, in a sandy baye.[3] The latitude is 11° 55′, the variation 17°.

August 19.—At 3 in the morning we wayed and steered for Abdalacora [4] E. and E. by S. and E.S.E., having the sea on our starboord side, 17° variation, making an E. by N. waye 15 leaugs, and then we sawe Abdalacora E. by N. 3 leaugs off, lyeing 12° 20′ the bodye of the island. Upon the west poynt there lyes a daingerous ledge of rocks. The true course and distance from Cape Guardefuy to Abdalacora being E. by N. 18 leaugs. From the wester end therof N.N.E. by the

---

[1] By reckoning.   [2] Here Roe criticises the course followed.

[3] 'Our boats went ashoare with saynes to take some fishe and to speake with the contry people, whearof 10 or 12 came downe, but (they soe fearfull of us) would not come near, but made signes for one of our menn to come to them. Soe wee onlye tooke a fewe freshe fish and retorned abourd, not speaking with them. We could not diserne any howsen or place of habitacon neare to the sea side; yet theare was a monument built of a reasonable height, of lyme and stone, whearunder, as it semed, was enterred some great mann late deceased' (Peyton's Journal, p. 18).

[4] Abd-el-Kuri, between C. Guardafui and Sokotra.

compasse, 4 leaugs off, ther lyes a smale island,[1] showeing three whyte bankes. We stood alonge to the eastward end of this island from the west end, lowe ragged barren land but showeing higher and higher till we saw two high hills toward the eastward end. About the middle theroff there are fine sandy bayes and I suppose good riding, we having had in the openings 12 and 14 fadome water, sandy ground. But the *Dragon* standing off we stood alongest till they tooke in all their sayles, and had an anchor a pike, but it seemes could gett no ground ; and supposing shee intended to anchor, the fleete loofte up close aboord the shoare under the eastermost high land, wher wee had ground in 18 fadome, shelly and foule. But all our anchors tript, soe that wee were putt off twice apeece, except the *Dragon*, whose anchor when shee came into us helde by a rocke, and wee stood it off and on, with much foule weather all that night. But in the morninge, having loste sight one of a nother, and beeing putt to leeward of the island, wee steered away E.S.E. at six a clock the 20th day.

By eight wee had sight of the *Pepercorne*, who had shippt a sea into her mainetopp, and filld her betweene the decks that shee was in great perill. By nine we sawe the *Expedition* alsoe ahead, steering for Socatra, a mightie sea on our starboord side. The variation and all allowed, wee made our way E. ¾ N. ten leaugs, being to the northward of Abdalacora in the morninge, when we stood off three leaugs, the wynd at S. by W. At twelve at noone wee sawe the W. end of Socatra E. by the compasse 3 leaugs off ; soe that the true course and distance betweene them is E.N.E. 13 leaugs. From the W. end of Socatra 2 leaugs off N.W. by N. there showes a rock like a saile or a ruyned church. At 5 of the clock in the afternoone we anchored in the seconnd baye [2] from the W. end of the island, wher we rode in 6 fadome water, grosse sand, and brought the poynts the one east the other west, being a mightie highe cliffe. This is in 12° 50′, variation 17° 50′. At 8 at night the wynd powred downe the hills with such violence that we drove into 15 fadome, our anchor beinge broken, and

---

[1] One of the two islands called ' The Brothers.'

[2] Peyton calls it the road of Galencia, *i.e.* Gollonsir.

having lett fall another our cable broke, and then wee were forced to bend our sheate anchor and lett it goe, and ride by a whole shott [*i.e.* two cables spliced], having strooke all our yeards and topmasts. We had much adoe to ride it out, havinge a wyndward shoar within a mile, but soe much wynd till morning as noe ould seaman in our fleete ever sawe or felt.

August 21.—This day at four in the afternoone the Admirall [*i.e.* the *Dragon*] came into the roade with soe much wynd that shee splitt her foresaile, wherby shee was putt to lewward, and anchored in a baye at the east end of the bay wee rodd in, against lowe whyte sand hills in 19 fadome water ; shee having stayed at Abdala [cora] the 20th day, hopinge we had been able to recover againe the island.

August 22.—We weyed with much adoe, having had the same violence of wynd the night past as wee had the first night, and came to anchor in the little baye by the Admirall in 13 fadome water, sandye ground ; where we rode at ease this night, the wynd being dispersed by the lesser hills and valey betweene us and the high land. Here we spake one with a nother and bemoned our losses, the Admirall having spent a mayne and a fore course, and bent a sheate anchor streight out ; we brake an anchor and a cable and bent a nother, and almost wore asunder a wholle shott ; the *Peppercorne* lost 3 anchors and 2 cables and fretted another ; the *Expedition* lost two cables and anchors ; for both at Abdalacora and these high lands of Socatra the wynds power down with such impetuousnes and the ground soe rockye, that I advise all men to forbeare to anchor under them ; for if they be putt from their anchors in the night, they shall fall soe farr to leward that they cannot recover the island but must loose company. But if night or weather force them to anchor, lett them choose to ride where some lower land breakes the violence of the wynde from the hills. Wee rodd in the seconnd quarter of the encreasing moone, which rose then above the horizon about 12 at noone and sett at midnight, at which tym these wynds beginn to rage soe long as shee is under the earth, and rising againe it becomes temperate. The moone is a great ladie of weather in these parts and requires much observation.

August 23.—We weyed togeather, and came to anchor afore Tamara [*i.e.* Tamarīda], the kings towne, bringinge the lowe poynte to the east of the high sandy hill without itt E. by N., in 10 fadome water, a mile from the towne. Here the Sultan sent us woord the wynds were from the hills soe forceable that we should hardly ride, but advised us to goe to Baya Delicia [Delishi], two leaugs to the East, where he would meete us. It is a veary good roade, deservinge the name of delightfull for the peaceablenes thereoff in respect of others. It is a valley of much lower hills, betweene the water and the raggid mountaines of Tamara. . . . The ground is whyte sand but rockye ; soe that yow must crotch or boye your cables.[1]

August 24.—We came to anchor by nine in the morninge in Baya Delicia, where the Sultan mett us with all his pompe.

Socatra is an island in the mouth of the Red Sea, called anciently Dioscuria or Dioscorida [Dioscorides], standing in 12° 55′ ; governed by a Sultan called Amar-ben-Seid [Amr-bin-Saīd], borne in the island, the sonne of the king of Fartaque in Arabia Fœlix, called Sultan Seid-ben-Seid [Saīd-bin-Saīd], who was Sultan of Socotra in the tyme of his grandfather, as this shalbe king after his father of Fartacque, and his sonne lefte at Socatra.[2] The kingdom of Fartacque lies from 15° to 18° alonge the coast of Arabia, and to the north to the mountayns. Hee is at peace with the Turke (who houlds all Arabia in tribute, except this cuntrie) on this condition to send 5000 menn in ayde of the Turke, if he requir it, to be paid by the Turke, without other acknowledgment. Thear lyes neare the sea a petty king about Dofar,[3] with whom he dare not meddle, being in the grandsigniors protection. This is the relation of Amar-Ben-Seid of Socatra. The Sultan of Socatra mett our fleete with 300 or there abouts, havinge sett up a tent at Baya Delecia. He rode upon a horse, and three of his cheife servants

---

[1] To keep them from rubbing.

[2] By Fartāk is meant the petty kingdom of Kishin in Southern Arabia, the chief town of which (bearing the same name) is about 470 miles north-east of Aden. Sokotra has long been a dependency of Kishin, and its local governor (under the British) is still a member of the ruling family of that kingdom.

[3] Hāfah, on the Arabian coast, a little to the west of Murbāt.

on two horses and one camell, the people marching before and behinde him, shouttinge after the Turkish manner, with two guards, one of souldiers which are his cuntrimen, and 12 of his privat guard, hiered Gusaratts, some with Turkish bowes, some with pistolls, some with musketts, all with good swoords. He had a few kettell drums and one trumpett. When the Generall went ashoar, he received him with state and curtesie. Hee is a subtile man, of good understanding, as appeares by his goverment and divers answers. He raignes soe absolutely that noe man can sell any thing but him selfe. His people sitt aboute him with great respect; his officers standing by, who take account of trade, and receive and paye. His clothes are of Suratt stuffs, after the Arabs manner, with a cassocke of wrought velvett, red and whytt, and a nother the ground gould, a very good turbant, but barefooted. Every night at sunne sett they stand or kneele all toward the sunn and pray, the *Xeriff* throweinge water on their heads. Their religion is Mahometan. The kings towne of Tamara is built of lyme and stone whyted over, battled and pinnacled, the howses being flatt at the top. It showes faire in the road, but when one is there, is but poore. Mr. Boughton [1] borrowed the Kings horse, and obtayned leave to see his house, the King sendinge a *Sheck* [shaikh] with him. Hee found it not answerable to the apperances, yet such as an ordinary gentellman might make a shifte with in England. His lower roomes were usd as warehowses, one as a wardrope, wher hung along the walls some changes of robes and 25 bookes of their law, religion,

[1] Humphrey Boughton, 'one of His Majesties pentioners,' applied to the Company in Dec. 1614 for leave to go in the fleet as a passenger, 'his desire beeinge to spend some tyme and his owne meanes in travalinge into remote kingdomes.' His request was at first refused; but afterwards, finding that he was determined to go if necessary in a Dutch ship, and fearing, too, that he would carry the matter to the King, the Court decided to accede to the application, and room was accordingly found for him on the *Peppercorn*. A further motive for granting his request was that he proposed to make his way to China, and it was thought that ' yf a lettre may be procured from His Majestie unto the Emperor of China . . . good use may bee made thereof.' The letter seems to have been obtained, but Boughton was not destined to make use of it, for he died at Burhānpur, within two months of his landing at Surat.

story, and saints lives (of which I could obteyne non); but above noe man may come, to see his wifes, which are three, nor other weomen (but the ordinary are seene in the townes, with their ears full of silver rings). In the church the preist was at service, butt seeing Mr. Boughton take out his watch hee soone finished, and came and woondred. Ther was provided three henns for their dinner with rise, and for drink water and cohu,[1] blake liquor taken as hotte as may be endured. At his returne the King in complement said hee had seene a poore place, but desired him to accept it. Ther is a castell four square on a hill a mile from Tamara, but hee could not gett licence to see it. The people are of four sorts: Arabs his cuntrimen, who it seemes are his strength, and such as are not the ancient inhabitans but come in with the conquest of his ancestors, and these obey him and dare not speake without lycence (as apeared when one seemed of quallity spake, he asked him how he durst open his mouth in his presence), but aproching kisse his hand. A seconnd sort are slaves who, when they come to him, kisse his foote, and these doe all his worke and make his aloese. A theird sort are, as I suppose, the ould inhabitants of the country (but not the eldest) called Bedwynes [Bedawīn], the same which other historians have called Jacobites, Christians that have longe dwelt there; with these he hath had a warr (as the Arabs report), and dwell in the mountayns, very populus, but are now at peace, on condition to live quietly, and to breed their children Mahometans; which I perceive they doe not, having noe manner of conservation [conversation?] with the Arabs. The reason why I take them to be the ould Jacobite Christians mentioned by Maginus,[2] Purchase,[3] and others, is because Mr. Boughton sawe an ould church of theirs in the way to Tamara, left desolate, the doore shutt but only tyde. Beeing desierous to enter yt, the *Shecke* his guide tould him it was full of spiritts; yet hee adventured in, and found an alter with images and a crosse upon yt, which he brought out. Then the *Shecke* tould him they were a people of a nother religion, but very loath to have them much enquired

[1] Coffee (Arabic *kahwa*).
[2] Giovanni Antonio Magini, the Paduan geographer (1556-1618).
[3] See the second edition (1614) of the *Pilgrimage*, p. 708.

after ; as I suspect (knoweing them to be a kind of Christians) doubting wee would eyther wish them better, or not suffer them to be oppressed. The four[th] sortt are a savage people, poore, leane, naked, with long hayer, eating nothing but rootes, hidinge in bushes, conversing with none, afrayd of all, without howses, and almost as savadge as beasts ; and by conjecture the true ancient naturalls of this island.

This island is very mountaynous and barren ; havinge some beefes, goates and sheepe, a few dates and oranges, a little rice, and nothing else for sustenance. Of comodytie they have aleos, which is the juyce of a leave like sempervive [*i.e.* the house-leek]. They make a poore cloth of their woole for the slaves. The King had sanguis draconis and indico of Lahor, but held it deare ; many small civitt catts and civitt. All is either the Kings, or passes his hands and price. He hath a handsome gally and junke of Suratt, with marriners that serve him to transport his goods for wages by the yeare. The King hath some knowledge of Prester John, confessing him the greatest prince in the world, above the Turke and Persian, givinge faire reasons for his opinione. Hee hath amonge his slaves divers Abbassines. Hearing our hoeboyes in the Generalls boate, he asked if they were the Psalms of David ; and beeing answered ' yes,' he replied it was the invention of the Divell, who did invent yt for King David, who before praysed God with his lipps and hart in devotion, but after it was lefte to senclesse instruments. They burye their dead all in tombes, and have in great reverance the monuments of their saints, wherof there have been many, but of most account Seidy-Hachim [Sīdī Hāshim], buried at Tamara, who being slaine 100 years since by the Portugalls once inhabiting here,[1] apperes to them, and warnes them of dangers to ensue. They impute the violence of wyndes to his walking, and have him in wonderfull reverance. I never went ashoar, not knoweing what entertainment I should find in respect of the qualety I bare ; but gleand up the most probable reports. If I had gone my selfe, and conferd with the King, or could have spoken with any of his people of understanding, I had enquired further to satisfie the

[1] Sokotra was subdued by Albuquerque in 1507, but the Portuguese garrison was withdrawn four years later.

curious. But all the interpreters followed the Generall, that I had noe oportunitie. The Generall delivered him a lettre from the King, which hee received with soe much seeming content as if hee knewe himselfe not worthy such a favour; and alsoe a present from the Company, for which he returnd 10 beefes, 30 goates, and 20 hens, and at his departure some perticular presents, which I understand not their qualitye.

Seeing by many experiences the wynds are in August soe violent about Abdalacora, Socatra, and betweene them and the Cape Guardfue.... Therefore I give my advice that the fleete stop not at all outwarde bound at Socatra; but, from Molalia having made Cape Guardafuy and there rested a convenient tyme for refreshing, or attending the later end of the monthsone if it be soone in the yeare, shape theyr course right for Suratt. If it be objected that they shall want their usuall refreshings, I answer: At Socatra the victualls is both carrion and as deare as in England, goodnes considered, the water farr to fetch and dangerous, soe that everie fleete hath lost some men in rowling it downe a streame full of deepe holes; at Cape Guardafuy yow shall ride at ease, and without doubt trade plentifully and cheape, and fishe at pleasure; and though wee made noe experience of trade, yet we sawe people in turbants and clothed, who assuredly if we had stayd mought have beenn drawne to bringe downe cattle, for not farr to the west of that place Sir Henry Middleton and some other ships had excellent goats and sheepe for trifles, as both his journall [1] and Mr. Barrett [*i.e.* Barwick] of his owne experience have enformed mee.

When the fleete is arived at Suratt, the shipp appoynted to returne must have her lading provided ready, that shee may not staye past December to keepe the other shipps to attend her safety, which they must doe or expose her to the Portugalls; and soe they may stand off to sea, and she come for Socatra with the N.E. monsone, when the season is calme, and shee may ride by a hazer [*i.e.* hawser], and buy aloes both oulder, dryer, and cheaper, for out of doubt (if it were insisted upon) they would be had for halfe mony, halfe goods. My reason is grounded on this experience, that although this

[1] See *Purchas*, vol. i. p. 260; *Letters Received*, vol. i. p. 57.

yeare the King said hee would have all mony, yet after he had sould for mony, he bought swoord blads at great rates with the same monny and divers other comodities. And besides, all the cloth he and his people weare are stuffs and callicoes of Suratt, which Guseratts bring, and fetch his monny. Therfor I see noe reason why hee should not as well take them of us, with halfe mony, for his goods as of them for all mony. He is understanding enough and frendly to our nation, and wilbe drawne unto this course upon the former reasons; if not, yet hee will honestly part with mony for swoords, stuffs, and some two or three peeces of silverd velvetts, or such trifles as may be fitted in England, for he bought two watches at great rates. He hath all the yeare alioes ready, and in great quantityes. Our earnestnes hinders our owne markett. By this course yow shall save the hazard of a whole fleete to stop, in the violence of weather, for that one ship with noe hazard may dispatch, returning in that monsone before the wynd and riding at Tamara roade smooth and calme; from thence to Molalia for refreshing, and soe to the Cape; wherby men shall come in health and in sommer upon our coaste; for our late returnes, few refreshings (by reason of hast) kills up our men, hazards your goods, and discreditts the voyadge.

August 31.—At night we weighed and stood off our course for Suratt.

September 13.—This night I was by reckoning from the W. end of Diu 6 leaugs off, it bearing E. ⅓ N. We sounded, and had 36 fadome, oazy ground. Then wee shortned saile till midnight, sounding every two howers; and, shoalinge easily, at midnight we lay a trye.

September 14.—At fower in the morning we sett saile and stood N.E. by N. to make the land of Diu, which by 6 we sawe, a round homock 6 leaugs off. . . .

September 15.—We steerd away E.S.E. for the mayne, everie two howers sounding. . . . Then wee bare up into 10 fadome and came to anchor, resolving to ride all night. . . .

September 16.—At 6 in the morning at the first of ebb we weighed and turnd out S.W. . . . At 3 a clock in the afternoone we sawe the land, beeing hidden before in a fogg, bearing from E. by S. to E.N.E. along, 8 leaugs off; wherby wee found we were gott about the eastermoste sands into the channell betweene that and the mayne. Then we weighed with the rest of the floud and stood away S.E., making by reason of the variation and the floud an E. way some 3 leaugs ; and then, the Ebb being come and little wynd, we came to anchor in the same depth 20 fadom water, soft ground ; Damon [Damān] bearing E.N.E. 5 leaugs off, and the poynt of the sand W.N.W. and from Damon W. by S., in the latitude of 20° 25′. . . .[1]

September 17.—At noone we weighed with the floud ; . . . it being spent we came to anchor in 13 fadome, 6 leaugs shortt of Suratt.

The land at Damon is high. To the sowthward ther is a round hill much higher ; to the northward somewhat lower land then Damon, showeing divers round hommocks ; and the most northerwardmost high land seene is somwhat ragged, with little copped hills upon it, and betweene it and the water lowe land, the trees seeminge to stand in the sea. The towne of Damon showes three whyte towers or castells.

September 18.—In the morning at flood we weighed and stood N.N.E. some three howers along the coaste, being all lowe land, discerning only the trees and some juncks and frigetts standing in, and came to anchor in 9 fadom water, 3 leaugs shortt of the barr of Suratt, bearing N.E. Our deepths were from 13 fadom, 12, 11, 10, and 9.

At noone with the flood wee stood away N.N.E. along the shoare 9 and 10 fadame water, some 3 leaugs to seaward of the river of Suratt. On the sowthside theroff in a tufft of trees ther stands a whyte house like a tower, from whence discerning Swally,[2] edginge in as the channell laye, we had 15, 16, and 17 fadom, and beeing shott a litle to the northward we came to anchor in 8 fadom water, soft ground, close by the edge of a sand. The *Pepercorne* and *Expedition*, beeing two cables lenght ahead, anchored in 6 fadom. At lowe water the *Peppercorne*, being somewhat nearer, came aground, but tooke noe hurtt. It highes here 3 fadom flood.

[1] Here follows a paragraph on the best course for reaching Surat from Diu.

[2] A roadstead situated a few miles north of the mouth of the Tāpti River. The English ships usually anchored here, as the river entrance was too shallow to permit of large vessels entering it.

ARRIVAL AT SWALLY

September 19.—In the morninge a frigatt came to the W. of us, which we supposing it had benn a Portugalls spie, made some fewe shott to fetch her in; but shee stood away for Cambaya, beinge one of the cuntrie. At 8 a clocke we mand our fower long boates, and sent ashoare, wher wee found ready one Bidolph [1] a factor, and one Robart [2] that had lived long with the Portugalls. They came presently aboord the Generall, and after to me, relating that ther was not one Portingall frigatt on the coast, but that they labored a peace with the Mogull on condition to bannish the English, but had yet effected nothing; the new Viceroy unheard of at Goa; some of the factors sicke, and Mr. Edwards [3] above with the King, but noe newes of extreordinarie favoure; Mochrebchan [4] removed to the court, and a new governor for the Prince [5] sent

[1] William Biddulph, who had gone out with Captain Best in 1612. Keeling placed him in charge of the factory at court, and he was consequently with Roe nearly the whole of the latter's stay in the country. He returned to England in 1623. Roe thought him 'faithfull . . . but a little opiniastre, and of good ordinary abilitye.'

[2] Possibly this was the 'R. Carelesse' mentioned by Finch (*Early Travels in India*, p. 127).

[3] William Edwards, the English representative at the Mogul court, had been sent out in Downton's fleet (1614) as cape merchant. On his arrival at Surat he was dispatched to court as the English representative, but, though painstaking and conscientious, he was not at all a success in that position. The factors complained of his dilatoriness, while his mild character induced him to put up with slights in a way which by no means smoothed the path of his energetic successor. After Roe's arrival at Ajmer, Edwards proceeded to Surat, where he was censured by the other factors in consultation, and sent home in disgrace. There is no further record of him.

[4] Mukarrab Khān, who, as the superintendent of the customs at Surat and Cambay, had been the persistent enemy of the English. His name was Shaikh Hasan, and the title by which he is always known was given him for his skill in surgery. Jahāngīr in his memoirs has many references to him. As mentioned later, he was made Governor of Gujarāt, and retained that post until displaced by Prince Khurram. Mukarrab Khān then received the government of Bihār, whence, three years later, he was transferred to that of Agra. He was pensioned off at the beginning of Shāh Jahān's reign, and died some years later at the age of ninety.

[5] Prince Khurram, third and favourite son of Jahāngīr, and afterwards the Emperor Shāh Jahān.

to Suratt, for whose mayntaynance that province is lately dessigned ; he bears a faire countenance to the English, but effects little. Ther was noe lading come downe for a ship, nor any newes of those gone up to provid yt ; but Bidolph tould me in 15 dayes they could provide to lade one ship with indico—his performance I knowe not.

September 20.—In the morning the Generall dispatched Bidolph ashoare with a lettre signed by the Generall to the Governor of Suratt, to signifie my arrivall ; the coppie I keepe in my boock.[1] At two a cloke wee weighed, having sounded the barr 3 foote at lowe water, and with the last quarter ebb stood back two mile to the edge of the barr, and somwhat nearer the land, and came to anchor at 5 fadom and a halfe at lowe water, bringing the lowe smooth poynte with the two highe palmeto trees S. by E. and the northwardmost land showeing like an island N.N.E.

September 21.—The Generall sent ashoare, but had no returne. The *Expedition* gott over the barr.

September 22.—A messenger came from the Governor of Suratt with answer of the lettre, a complement that I should be welcome, and if I would dessigne the daye he would send 30 horse for my traine, and his commanders to meette me, and in all things studdie to give me that contentment his power or the means of the place did affoord ; and if the merchants could find a howse emptie, he would command it for me. But because hee offered me none, I sent to take one.

September 23.—I sent ashoare about my house, and with a complement to the Governor this message, that, understanding the custome of the Kings officers to scearch everie

[1] See f. 56 of the MS. It announces that in consequence of the friendly reception of former messengers and the agreement made with Captain Best, the King of England, ' for the better establishment and confirmation of the said happy amytie and love ' has sent a ' nobleman of his Court and Chamber, with letters of credence and rich presents . . . authorised with full commission under the Great Seale of England and firma of His Majestie as his Ambassador as well to congratulate the said mighty King the Great Mogull as to propound, treate, and conclude of sundry matters of consequence ' ; and it gives notice that the envoy proposes to land and repair to some town of rest (having been long at sea) until the pleasure of the Emperor is known as to his journey to the Court.

thing that came ashoare, even to the pocketts of mens cloathes on their backs, for custome, I, beeing an ambassador from a mightie King, did expect to have all things appertayninge to my selfe and my followers free by priviledg; givinge him the woord of one of my qualetye that there should not be landed under that protection one penny woorth of marchandize, and that if any such affront were offered me, I would returne to the ships, untill I had order from the King his master.

This day I dispatched a lettre to Mr. Edwards at Adjumere, the Mogulls Court, which the Generall signed with me; the coppie wherof I keepe.[1]

September 24.—Answer was returned that it was the custome of this cuntrie that nothing could passe but by the custome house, and thear to be se[e]arched; but, because they would doe me as much favour as they could answere, the Governor would send an officer to the waterside to take note of those things belonging to me and seale them, and they should goe without stopp to my house, wher the Customer should come and visitt them, but not in the nature of a search, but only to be able to answere they had seene what I landed; for my selfe and my followers, they should be free from all offer of affront. After some dispute with the messenger, I yeeilded to yt, and returned answer that on the morow, the 25, I would land my chests, and on the 26 come ashoare in expectation of the horses and company offered and the honorable reception promised by the Governor.

September 25.—I landed my chests and provitions, with directions to suffer them to be sealed, but not opened; and to deliver them at my house and to prepare yt next day. This day came a handsome frigatt from Cambaya with a principall servant of the Governors aboord the Generall, and with complements of frendship and desire of trade to theyr towne as a head citty. He gave the Generall a present of sweetmeates and some fewe stuffs in the name of the Governor, and desiring to buy some rarietyes or toyes for theyr master, especially enquiring for English swyne for the Mogull, in which

---

[1] See f. 56 of the MS. It announces Roe's arrival and directs Edwards to acquaint the Emperor therewith.

beast hee takes infinite delight, having had two from one
ship the last yeare ;[1] telling the Generall he should find the
new Governor of Suratt a clowne and a frend of our enemyes,
but that if wee would make our residence at Cambaya we
should receive notable content. The Generall tould them ther
was an embassador sent by the King of England, that was
the next morning to land, a man of qualetye : and untill
he sawe what reception he should fynd, and how theyr busines
stood with the factory, with the principalls wheroff he had not
spoken, he could resolve nothing ; but in other complements
gave them content. At this name of an ambassador they
laughd one upon a nother ; it beeing become ridiculous, so
many having assumed that title, and not performed the offices ;
and though the Generall did endeavour to make them better
understand yt, they would not, and so did never offer to visitt
me. Besides, when the Generall dealt with the *makadow*
[*mukaddum* : headman] of Swally (a frend to the English)
that they must not esteeme me in the qualetye of my fore-
runners, with all the right he could doe to honor His Majestie,
yet he when he was ashore answered he could not tell, nor any
else, but that I might be an imposture as well as the rest ; and
this was dayly objected unto us, even from the cheefe of Suratt.
I mention these only to lett the Company understand how
meanly an embassador was esteemed at my landing ; howe
they subjected them selves to all searches and barbarous
customes, and became sutors to the governors and great men,
who, as appears by the discourse following, sufficiently understand the rights belonging to that qualetye ; and that therfore,
if it seeme to any that shall heare of my first carriadge that I
was eyther too stiff, to punctuall, too high, or to prodigall,
lett them consider I was to repayre a ruynd house and to make
streight that which was crooked. If I had beene the first
that ever landed under that title, I would have done noe less ;
and I best know that see yt, these men triumphe over such as
yeeld, and are humble enough when they are held up. The
Kings honor was engaged more deeply then I did expect, and

---

[1] Van Ravesteyn (Terpstra, p. 208) reported that Jahāngīr,
'though circumcised [*i.e.* a Muhammadan], goes every morning to
visit two hogs recently presented to him by the English.'

I was resolved eyther to rectifye all or lay my life and fortune both on the ground.

September 26.—A sine beeing made from land that the Suratts were come ready to receive me, I landed, accompanyed with the Generall and the captaines and the principall merchannts ; the Generall having first sent 100 shott by Captaine Harris to make me a court of guard, and the shipps in their best equipage giving me their ordinance as I passed ; with his trumpetts and musique ahead my boate in the best manner he could, which I only signify for acknowledgment unto him.[1] At my landing, the cheefe officers of Suratt with about 30 companions wer sitting under an open tent upon good carpetts, in grave order. Comming almost to them and they not rising, I stayd and sent them woord I would not come farthur if they satte still ; wherupon they all rose, and I entered the tent and went streight up and tooke my place in the middest of them, turning my face toward the Generall and the English, who stood right before us. They by an enterpretor bade me welcome with a long complement, which was payd in the same mettle. And I added to yt that the Kings Majestie, having received assurance from the Great Mogull of the good affection borne to His Majestie and our nation, and under confidence of the *firma* [2] sent by Captain Best, to receive his ambassador in the behalfe of the merchants trading in his dominions, had sent me with full commission as his ambassador, as well to congratulate the happy frendship begunn betweene too soe mighty princes and their subjects, as also to assure a readines in the Kings Majestie on his part to continew the same inviolably ; and to propound unto the Great Mogull many other

[1] 'The Lorde Ambassador landed, being accompanied by the Generall, captains, and merchants of the fleet on shoare, for His Lordshipps better grace ; alsoe fower score menn in armes with shott and pyke redye ordred upon the sand in rancks against his landing for guard, and 48 peeces great ordnance discharged from our fleete ; this daye our shipps weare all hansomlye fitted with their waistclothies, ensignes, flaggs, pendents and streamers' (Peyton's Journal, p. 29). Before landing, Roe distributed 30 *l.* among the officers and crew of the ship (f. 280 of the MS.).

[2] This word is familiar as signifying an order, patent, or passport (Pers. *farmān*). As noted in *Hobson-Jobson*, Roe sometimes writes it *firma*, as if suggestive of the Italian for 'signature.'

matters of great consequence, both for the mayntenance and
securitye of the leauge already treated on, and for the mutuall
good of the subjects of both the kings : that I did receive yt
as an assurance of the good affection of the Great Mogull
and off his commanders and ministers in these parts that they
did soe much honor the King my master to meete me in so
respective manner, and furnish mee with horses to theyre
towne, for which I gave them thancks, and did not doubt
that my comming would prove benificiall and acceptable to
them : and that I was ready to take horse and accompany
them to Suratt, to repose my selfe untill I could be prepared
to advance toward the court. Then they begann a new tune,
that I would be pleasd to be content that all my company
might be searched, according to the custome of the cuntrye.
I replyed it was strange to me to heare any motion from them
contrary to the promise of the Governor, wherupon only I sett
my foote ashore : that I was the ambassador of a mightie
and free Prince : that I would never dishonnor my master so
much, whose person I bare, as to subject my selfe to so much
slavery : I would engage my honor (which I esteemed as
my life) that no follower of myne had the worth of a *pice* of
trade or marchandice : and that in Europe and most parts
of Asia all ambassadors and theyr traynes were so far priviledged as not to be subject to common and barbarous usage :
that seeing I found so little assurance in that woord which had
drawne me ashoare, I would retyre to the ships, to attend the
Mogulls pleasure : for that I could not answere it with my
head to loose the right and freedome due to the embassador
of a Christian king. They answered it was also more then the
Governor could avow to let them passe unsearched : it was a
great curtesy don to my person, and sufficient acknowledgment
of me, all others pretending my place having never had so
much honor : [1] that it was absolutely the custome of this
cuntrie, and they could not breake it. I replyed : I had
thought that they had understood that free kyngs and theyre

[1] Edwards and his company had had to submit to this indignity
the previous year, being ' verie familyarlye searched all of us to the
bottom of our pocketts, and nearer too, modestlie to speake yt '
(Dodsworth's MS. narrative.—I.O. Records).

ambassadors had beene above ordinary customes ; which since they would not take notice off, I would not perswade them to breake theyrs, and I was resolved I would not dishonor my selfe ; but I would send to the Great Mogull and attend His Majesties answere : that I hoped they had come to entertayne and honor me, not to enslave and entangle me with barbarous customes. And so after much dispute I turnd about and departed to our boates. Then by the mediation of messengers they offered that I should choose to my self five persons, whom I would, that in honor of me should goe free ; and that they only would for a cerimony sake lay theyr hands about the rest, not as to search but to embrace them. So I landed againe and repeating the offer by my interpretor, that I was content they should lay theyr hands upon my servants, not with intent to search but to embrace, calling to wittnes the Generall, what were my conditions, they intend not to search but to embrace. They desired me not to take yt in ill part that they did not yeild in all my desire ; that they would signifie to the Great Mogull I would not yeild to that custome they claymed, and that they did it in honor there, that they might send before to the officers of Suratt that all ceremonyes were ended ; because, if the Governor should insist upon yt when I came to Suratt, it would be more dishonor to returne or suffer it publiquely, and that this would prevent farther question. Wherupon I called five of my company to stand behynd me, expecting what they would doe to the rest; but seeing them stand still, I asked if all were done, that wee might goe to horse. They answered they were ready. Soe taking leave of the Generall and all the rest, accompanied with Mr. Boughton, Mr. Barkley [1] and four other merchants, I tooke horse with all my followers ; the Suratts keeping me company. When I was about halfe way, they sent to me that I would call three or four of the better sort to ryde with me, and that they would follow in order, and that after them my men might come in rancke, pretending to enter the towne in this fashion. I, doubting nothing, appoynted yt soe, and called three or four

---

[1] George Berkeley, afterwards President at Bantam, where he died in March, 1617. His travels in Eastern Europe are chronicled in Purchas's third volume (pp. 625, 631).

S.T.R.   C

to me, and one of the principall of them to ride with me, every man observinge this order, and some distance betweene me and the Suratts, and betweene the Suratts and my servants. They were about 50 horse and 200 foote, and all my company were 23. On the suddeyne, I being before, they stayd, and under pretence of drinck called my men, who wisely came, and beeing among them, they tooke houlde of their horses and offered by force to search them. Mr. Wallis breaking out came up after me, and tould me this treachery; wheron I turnd my horse, and with all speed rode backe to them, I confess too angry. When I came up, I layd my hand on my swoord, and my men breake throwgh and came about me. Then I asked what they entended by soe base treachery: I was free landed, and I would die soe, and if any of them durst touch any belonging to me, I bade him speake and shew himselfe. Then they desired me not to take yt in ill part: it was done in frendship. I called for a case of pistolls and, hanging them at my saddle, I replyed those were my frends, in them I would trust: that they had dealt treacherously with me, and soe I did esteeme them. They desiered me to goe on: that all was mistaken. I answered I would returne to the ships, but that they would basely suppose it to bee feare: therfore I would goe on to seeke justice; but tould them they should not mingle with my trayne: I tooke them for enemyes to the King my master, that soe sought my dishonor; but that eyther they or I would goe before and the other follow, for if any came among myne they should expect the entertaynment of one that was highly offended. It were much vanety to say in what a feare the best of them were, beeing so many; but the truth is not ashamed. So we rode on, in severall troupes, they before. On the way they stayd all in a shade, and called to me as I passed, but I did not looke towards them. Then they sent after, desiring me to eate a plantine, which I refused, with answer: untill I had satisfaction for the affront done my servants, I would not receive any thing as curtesye. They replyed they had searched none, and did mean only to excecute the ceremony agreed on at the tent, without farther purpose of injurye. So I tooke this for answere and left them at theyr refreshing, till I came to the water syde over against the towne. But noe boates would carrie me untill they arrived. At last they came, and with many good woords did assure me they had no purpose to injure mee ; that they only entended to doe what I yeeilded too, there in privat, that they might certifie all was finished, least the officers of the custome howse (that knew no civility) should stay me at the enterance of the towne ; and perswaded me to be yet content withall. I answered I was ever equall with my woorde, and that though they taught me to breake my woord, it was a lesson I scornd to learne : but I would be a wittnes of theyr fashion, least they under coulor of ceremony did use villany. Soe I entered a boate with the officers and called five to mee, Mr. Boughton, my chaplain, and three servants ; who came in free. The rest stood to enter after this ceremony of embracing. The first that came they playnly, insteed of embracing, offered to feele his pocketts without ; whereat I rose and sayd I would not endure yt ; and in extreame cholar telling them it was a custome to be usd to rouges and theeves and not to free men : I was resolved not to returne to my cuntry with shame : I would rather dye there with honor. Wherupon they lett all of them come to me without more woords ; and smiling desired me to be appeased, seeing I was satisfyed in all. So soone as I was putt off, they tempted me a new (knowing I could not now goe back) : I must goe see the Governor, before I went to my house. I answered I was weary and unfitt for visitation. They tould me it was the custome and I could not refuse yt. Then I saw how every way they besett me. I sayd playnly I would not nor could be compelled : that in all their dealings ther was new falshood : I was resolved : they could not but under trust have cercumvented me : that I durst not answere visiting the Governor untill he had visitted mee : that I doubted not he, bceing borne a Persian, understood the right due unto mee : if not, yet I would rather returne then loose it. In this dispute we arrived att the stayres to enter the towne, wheras [wher was ?] the Governors brother with many attendants to conduct me to the castle. But, after some few woordes betweene them, he bad me welcome, and desiered me to take my rest in my howse this night : that to morrow would be fitter for ceremony. I gladly and shortly accepted yt, and tooke horse, the sackbotts of the towne goeing before and many following me. I gott my house, resolving it should be my castle ; but, comming in, I found, contrary to all faith, that my necessaries sent before were kept at the custome house, and would not be delivered without search. Whereupon I sent to the Governor that it was strange to me to receive soe many discourtesyes after his woord past, but that I doubted not he would upon better advise give me content the next day, it beeing to late at present : I only desired my bed and such provisions as I could not want [*i.e.* could not do without]. Which was granted, and a message withall that on the morrow I should receive the rest without delay. Soe I was satisfyed with hope, and ended a wearisome day.[1]

September 27.—I sent to the custome house for my stuff, but it was refused me, except I would concent it should be

[1] Terry (p. 173) mentions an incident of this day to which Roe makes no allusion. It may be quoted as an example of the disorderliness amongst the English subordinates which was a constant cause of friction with the authorities at almost every port frequented by the Company's ships. 'When my Lord Ambassador at first arrived at Surat, it so was, that an English cook he carried with him, the very first day of his comming thither, found a way to an Armenian Christians house, who sold wine in that place, they call Armenian wine. . . . The cook had his head quickly over-freighted with it, and then staggering homeward, in his way met the Governors brother of Surat, as he was riding to his house ; the cook made a stand, staying himself up upon his sword and scabbard, and cry'd out to the Governours brother : *Now thou heathen dog.* He not understanding his foul language replyed civilly in his own : *Ca-ca-ta* [*kyā kahtā*], which signifies : What sayest thou ? The cook answered him with his sword and scabbard, with which he stroock at him, but was immediatly seised on by his followers, and by them disarm'd and carried to prison. The ambassador had present intelligence of the misbehaviour of his drunken servant, and immediatly sent word unto the Governours brother that he was not come thither to patronize any disorderly person, and therefore desir'd him to do with him what he pleased ; upon which he presently sent him home, not doing him the least hurt. But before I leave this storie, it will not be amiss to enquire who was the *heathen dog* at this time, whether the debaucht drunken cook who call'd himself a Christian, or that sober and temperate Mahometan who was thus affronted.'

opened there. I answered I would never agree to any condition contrary to the priviledge I claymed as my right and contrary to that conclusion I made before my landing: I was a stranger to such doublings: but that I was resolved to lett them rott there, and not be farthur behoulding to him, but would dispatch a messenger to the Great Mogull of the faythlesse dealing and barbarous usage of me, beeing ambassador to a mightie King in leauge with him, and come a far journy upon his royall woord: and that they should farther forbeare to putt new devices upon me: I would not be wrought on upon any pretence. Hee [*i.e.* the Governor] sent me woord I should take my course. Within an hower he sent me a messenger to perswade me to come visitt him, and that then he would bring me to my house and do me all honor, and all my desires should be fullfilled. I replyed it was too late to offer me curtesyes, especially under pretence of dishonoring my master: that it was the custome of Europe to visitt those of my qualety first, and that I durst not breake yt in penaltye of my head, haveinge expresse command from my master to mayntayne the honor of a free king, and to visitt none but such as first did that respect due to His Majestie: and that therfore I would never doe yt. He returnd me answere it was the custome of this cuntry that all embassadors did first come to the governors, and that he was servant to a great king as well as I: that no man could be a better man than he, exept he were made so by his master: that all other that pretended to be embassadors before me did not only come, but sue to the governors, had their personns and goods publiquely searched, which had not beene done to me, nor should not be offered to the provisions remayning if I would see him: and that hee was no way inferior to any former governor. I replyed: for the customes of embassadors to visitt governors I did know the contrary by the Persian; and that I did beleeve he did never receive any at this port, nor ever from a Christian King; and hee beeing governor for the Prince (as yet a subject), I could not thinck he wronged himselfe to visitt me that did represent the person of a King: but my businesse here was not to dispute titles: I was not sent to him, and therfore would not see him: for the prescedents of former men, they were noe rules to me that was a full ambassador, and they, though sent by the King, yet were but agents to prepare my way and to negotiate in the behalfe of the Honourable Company : but because I did desire to give him all reasonable satisfaction, if he would honor my master so much as to see me and give me welcome, I would showe him my commission under the great seale of England, and his masters *firma* conditioning to recieve an ambassador with all due respect, which I had in keeping, and under confidence wheroff the King had sent me : wherby he might receive assurance it was no disparagement to him : and the next day I would visitt him in requitall, which I could alsoe hardly answere, before I had presented my selfe before his master : but if hee were not purposed, I would not perswade him to breake his pretended custome, and desiered him not to expect that I would disobey and dishonor my master : but leaving ceremonyes apart, I did looke for, according to his promise, my provisions detayned in the custome house. Then hee sent me answere he would not nor durst see me first, but that, if I would come to him, he would come forth of his house and receive me in the place of audience : if not, I must be contented to have my chests searched. I answered : I card not for them : the breach of his woord was enough : but to visitt him in his place of audience was a proposition most obsurd : it was as much as I would doe to his master. But because these ceremonyes should not hinder our businesse, I said, if he would meete me in an indifferent place a horsebacke, wher neyther might be before other, I would condescend, and soe neyther of us should wronge his master, though in that he brake all rule of curtesie : if not, I desired him to trouble me with no more articles : I was resolved to keepe my howse and expect his masters answer to the affronts done to me. Thus we wore out the day and yt rested. Wherupon hee commanded none in the towne to sell us any thing but victualls, and imprisoned some that did ; Mr. Barkley and the merchants, thincking this night to returne to the ships, could not be suffered, nor any from them to come to us. This made me somewhat jealous [*i.e.* suspicious] of treachery, but breake not my sleepe.

September 28.—In the morning the merchants went to aske leave to depart ; beeing warned by me to make no motion concerning me, but to gett aboord and I would trye it out with him. But they were delayed till after dinner, [the Governor] basely begging of presents that he did expect, and withall sayd : your embassador lookes I should visitt him ; what jewell or diamond will he give me ? and so, only provoking guifts, dismised them. After noone they sollicited him againe, and in answere of his desire of presents sayd the first sent him, beeing small, was only at their first arrivall : but that there was entended a better present for him, but it was kept untill they saw what entertaynment he would give the Kings ambassador, and could not be delivered untill hee had received better satisfaction, who was so farr from seeking to buy his favour that he had commanded not to deliver yt on such conditions : and that presents were given of curtesy, not off duty, and to expect any from the embassador, they had commandement to say he came not as a sutor, and he should expect no more from him then he deserved. Wherupon, after some consultation and woords betweene him and other of the Kings officers, that he could not answere his usage of me, and it was in vayne to expect more, they saw my resolutions, he gave leave for my chests to be brought to my howse sealed, and to bee seene there according to our first agrement ; and licenced all English to returne to the ships ; and sent the Cheefe Customer, his brother and some others, to visitt my provisions. But, it beeing late, they would stay but openinge two or three that I had most use off. I saw them at their departure, and only spake of the injuryes somewhat roughly ; which they excused and tooke their leave. This night the merchannts returned to the Generall ; who was glad to heare any newes of us, beeing very doubtfull, seeing none in two dayes could passe betweene us. I wrote him to stand out, for I was resolved to bring these people to a better understanding or to perish in yt ; but I left yt to him whether hee would send him a present or no, seeing it was intimated that, after I had my provisions according to promise and was content, he should have one ; but in no case to deliver any in my cause or to buy me better usage.

September 29.—The morning passd without farther entercourse; only the people were still forbidden trade with us. In the evening came his brother with the principall of the towne to visitt the rest of my goods; which havinge almost finished, they desiered to speak with me. I sent for them up; and, beeing sate, they tould me the Governor sent them to desire me not to be afrayd nor sad for any thing past: ther was no harme intended me: that I should command any thing in the towne: and what was done was but for the mayntenance of their ancient priviledges; with a multitude of complements. I answered: I thancked the Governor and them for any thing I could call a curtesye, but of these good woords I saw small effects: for feare, I esteemed them so just as not to betray their masters fayth, but I could better tell how to be angry for these discurtesies then to feare any thing in his power: and for their priviledges, they were to be excersiced on ordinary persons, and not upon my qualety. They made many excuses and professions of all love and respect to me, saying they had three yeares beene stoppd up by the Portugalls, who were robbers, for our sakes; and that, hearing the Governor of Cambaya had sent a frigatt to entreat trade, they came to me to advertise me that the Cambayan was a frend to the Portugall and labored a peace: that they were our ancient frends and would remayne soe, and desired me to forgett all things past and to be a means that no goods might goe for Cambaya, but be landed at theyr towne: it beeing now the Princes port, wee should dishonor yt if we sought other trade: who should be our frend and protector in that cuntrye, and that we should have all good content from them. I replyed: these were good woordes, but they came from desire of proffitt and not from good harts: for the Portugales, it might soe come to passe that eyther a peace might be made on all parts, and theyr ports open by our means, or at least they should not be injuryed in our presence: that the King my master had much sence of the injuryes offered his subjects and his allyes for theyr sake, and I had instructions concerning yt for theyr good: and bade them remember that our fleete in the last yeare defended their frontire, the Vizeroy purposing to take Suratt; and soe in generall tearmes gave them content. For the trade to Cambaya, I said it was true the Governor desiered the remove of trade, but nothing was yet done: if I sawe effects of these promises, we weare not soe unconstant to forsake ould frends to seeke new: we honored the port for the Princes sake, whose favour the Company would study to meritt: but that if they would not give such dispatch and such price as others would, it was unreasonable for me to motion to the General, who had to doe with the landing and sale of goods: but if they would perform these conditions, or such other as the General should propound, I would write to him, who would doe nothing without my consent in yt; in the mean tyme I desired the commandement not to sell us necessaryes might be recalled, in sine of faythfull meaning; which was promised. Then I offered them drincke, which they refused, beeing *Ramdam*, but sayd after it was finished they would come daylie and sitt and eate with me. I tould them I would give no presente, seeing it begett an ill custome: but if they had seene any trifles of myne, as knives or such, which they liked, I would bestow them willingly. They said it was theyr parts first to presente me, and therfore would take noething; and so wee parted.

September 30.—In the morning they returned with new complements, telling me the prohibition was withdrawn: that all my desires should be accomplished; and that the Governor would visitt me after dinner, and at night goe to the ships to conclude in all things with the General: iterating theyr feare we should trade with the Cambayans, and urdging me to dispatch a lettre to the General that I had received content, and to perswade him to land all his goods at this port; which I promised to doe as farr as it concernd mee, having the night before given the General advise of their faire offers and usage of me, and that (though then I had noe knowledge that the Governor would visitt me) I would not ceremony should hinder busines; for I beeing resolved not to see him, lost no honor, and so had as much contentment as I did now expect. Wherupon he sent him a good present in his name, that was delivered him about noone this day. This made him thinck, as I suppose, he needed not looke after mee: from the other place came benefitt; and so changd his purpose, not to visitt me, but to goe right out to Swally. But receiving advertisement of yt, I sent presently to him, to tell him: if hee would ride twelve mile to visitt the General and neglect me, that was the Kings ambassador, it was so great an affront that I tooke yt woorse then any other thing: therfore I desired him to advise better, for the General could not nor would receive him, having so neglected his master, and that I had sent a post to him to signifye so much; which I had done, and received from the General very woorthy and respectfull satisfaction. Then answere was returned at 4 a clocke he would come to me, desiering all might be forgotten: his usage to come should wittnesse for his hart toward me. In the evening he came, very well accompanyed and in good equipage after the manner of the country, clothed in linnen and Persian cloth of gould very rich.[1] I mett him at the doore, and soe ledd him in. He, goeing rudely like a horse forward, gott before me; which thincking he did on purpose, I crossed the way and was at the stayers foote before him; and so telling him I would lead him in, a servant of his puld me and said I might not goe before the Governor; but the Governor thrust him back and followed me. When we were sett in the chamber, he begann with many complements of welcome and excuse of any discurtesie past; which I received with thancks that he did me the honor at last to visitt me, desiering him not to esteeme it pryd, that I insisted on such tearmes with him: that as a privatt man I would alway be ready to meete him or prevent him in any curtesye, but in the place and qualetye I now held I could not have done yt without dishonering and disobeying my master, whose expresse chardge was that I should preserve the rights of an embassador and

[1] The Governor of Surat, who now appears in person on the scene, was originally a body-servant of Prince Khurram, named Muhammad Beg. Despatched to court with the news of the submission of Amar Singh, the Udaipur Rānā, he received from the delighted emperor a handsome present and the title of Zūlfakār Khān, by which he is always designated in the present work. On the Prince receiving the government of Surat, he sent Zūlfakār Khān thither as his deputy. The date of his arrival at Surat was 4 Aug. 1615 (Terpstra, p. 184).

visitt no subject until I had presented my selfe before the
Great Mogull, except such as, having the Mogulls authoritye,
did first show that respect toward His Majestie and curtesye
toward me that was due. He replyed I [had] done like my
selfe in yt, and as a good servant ought : he did esteeme
me the more for obeying my master and standing for his
honor : and desiered me to excuse the latenes of his visitation :
he did [not ?] know me : but he was now there to doe me
any service. Upon this I gave him thankes, and, to better
satisfye him I was the person I did pretend, I called for my
commission, and having causd yt to be delivered me with
great reverance, I rose and kyssed yt and showed yt. He
tooke yt with much respect, and rising put yt to his head ;
and veiwing it well, delivered yt back. Then I called for the
Mogulls *firma*, and tould them upon that confidence I was
come among them, not doubting of any thing but faire usage,
since therein the Mogull had given his royall woord that hee
would receive an ambassador from the King of England with
all due respect, with many other priviledges granted to the
merchants ; and with a ceremony I delivered yt him. He rose
up and layd yt on his head, and read yt, allowed every woord ;
which finished, they all rose and badde me welcome with one
voyce. So I putt it up with my commission. Then he began
to speake of the Portugalls and of the lose they [*i.e.* the people
of Surat] susteyned by the barring up of their trade, which
yet they were content with for our sakes : that he was theyr
enemye ; and much to this purpose. I replyed in generall
termes, that I did not doubt all these quarrells should be well
accomodated : however, wee would remayne theyre frends
and protectors while our shipping was here : that when hee
and I mett in more privat manner (which I doubted not this
frendship would occasion) I would discourse and open to him
some propositions concerning that busines which would give
him content. He seemd pleasd with this ; and continued to
perswade me (as his messenger had done) to hinder any trade
with the Cambayan, urdging the dishonor of the Princes port,
to whom he would write in all things to countenance our
nation. He sayd hee had received a lettre from the Governor
of Cambaya, expostulating with him how he durst trade with

the English or receive them, seeing he had made an agreement with the Portugall : advising him not to suffer us to land our goods : that he was a great frend of the Portugall and a dishonest base man : that he had returned answer here was an ambassador come to the Mogull from the King of England : that hee could not deny him welcome and safety, beeing a qualetye priviledged even amonge enemyes : concerning any peace with the Portugalls, he knew not of any, nor would take any notice but from his owne master. I replyed he should not doubt any unconstancy in us to our ould frends : if they continued so, we English knew what did appertayne to kings and princes, and therfore in honor of his master wee would be veary wary to doe him any affront, provided he like a carefull servant did give us no just occasion : for the Governor of Cambaya, I knew not his affection but by outward complement of inviting us : if he were the Portugalls frend, and they our enemyes, we card for neyther : but if he had made peace for the Portugall without prejudice of us, it greevd me not : the cuntry was lardge enough for both ; but if he made peace to banish us, we would trade in spite of the Portugall and all his frends, even at Goa and Ormus. For the ill language he gave the Cambayan, I could have requited him with the like commendations received of him ; but they are both false alike and attend only present gayne, and are constantly a frend to that only. Soe, urdging me to write a lettre to the Generall (which I did), he tould me it was late, and excused his goeing away, for that night he went toward Swally : at his returne, we should be no longer strangers; and thus tooke his leave. I offered him the doore, which he accepted, desiering me to goe no farthar ; and in the same manner at the stayres ; but I brought him to my gate, wher we parted.

October 1.—The Governor was with the Generall, wher, mutuall ceremonyes and curtesies beeing past, the Generall procured him to sine too certaine conditions concerning the landing of our goods ; the particulars I know not. This day came lettres from the factory at Amadavaz[1] to the General. The contents I know not, only a clause or two that concerned mee.

[1] Probably the letter, dated 26 Sept., to be found in *Add. MS.* 9366, f. 6. In it Kerridge desired that Roe should be warned that

October 2.—The Governor returned by day: signifying some discontent that he had no present of the Generall at Swally for the Prince, whose port the shipps now ryde in.

October 3.—In the morning I sent the Governor woord that I would come visitt him at evening: but that beeing yet unfurnished with horse, I would accept of his offer of halfe a sckore of his. He returned answer they should not fayle to attend me. At evening he sent me woord it was an unlucky hower for us both and desired me to deferr till the next day. But faling into speach of presents with the messenger I first sent, I causd it to be tould him he must not expect any from me in that kynd : presents were for sutors : but having knowledg that he had a desire to have some such strong water as was in a chest of myne (which hee offered to stay at the custome house before our frendship, to which I then answered I would rather send my servants to break them before his face then to give any in that sort, but receiving them with curtesie, I would att any tyme give him some); therfore I had now a case for him, if he would accept them as a trifle betweene frends. He returned me many thancks and sayd he expected no present at all from me : if I sent him any thing in love, he would receive it soe : if nothing, he would not take yt in discurtesye. Upon this civill answere I sent him a small case of bottles given me by the Generall of the Companyes for that use ; and with it a very lardge fayre mapp of the world (cost in England as I take yt 3*li*.); which he accepted with all kyndnes, and asked if I had such a nother for the Great Mogull, making more estimation of yt then off all other presents.

October 4.—I expected his horses, but they came not. This day I sent a letter to Amadavaz, in answere to some clauses in theyre lettre to the Generall. The copy is registred [*not in the MS.*].

' the articles agreed upon by Captayne Best were never signed by the Kinge, otherwise then by a generall *firmaen* without knowledge of the particulers, and, those (the governours) that signed them beinge dead, are of small valliditye.' Hence, no doubt, Roe's efforts to induce Zūlfakār Khān to confirm these articles, as at least a temporary security for the trade of the English.

October 5.—The Governor received a lettre from the King; which meeting it with all respect, this ceremony and joy tooke up the day.

October 6.—The Governor of the Custome House came to visitt me, perswading me to see the Governor, that all frendship might followe for our mutuall good. I replyed that it had not beene my faulte : that I had two dayes expected his horses, beeing yet unfurnished : that I had no sute to him but curtesie, which if he were not as willing to accept as I to offer, I did not meane to thrust yt upon him. Wherupon he offered me his horses, which I refused, saying if the Governor had a mynd to see me, he would furnish me to yt. For this curtesy I sent him sixe fayre knives and two quarter mappes, which he accepted gratefully. This day I sent a lettre to Mr. Edwardes to signifye my purpose of hasting to the court, desiring his stay there for many resons specifyed. The coppy is registred [*at f.* 57 *of the MS.*].

October 7.—The Governor sent in the morning to offer me horses ; which I accepted. At night they came, but not so many as I expected. But beeing loth to occasion any distast, I went with such company as I could, having woord he was at his house attending me. But passing by the custome house, they calld and tould me he was their, moyling among our cloth, and desiered me to come in. I answered : I had not so used him : I did expect more civilitye, but I would now take occasion to visitt the feilds ; and soe rode toward them. Which he hearing came a back way suddenly into his howse, and sent after me to entreat me to returne : that he was ready to doe me all honor ; which I did. And beeing come into his court, I was brought into a tent wher were all the principall of the towne, but not the Governor. They bad me welcome, desiering me to sitt. I asked for the Governor. They tould me he had beene busy in the custome house and was shifting him selfe, desiering me to staye a little : he would presently come. I answered : this was an incivilyetye I understood not : that I mett him at my gate : if I had suspected soe little manners, I would have spared my labour : but that the King of Englands embassador scorned to attend any subject. Soe I went out toward my horse ; which the Governor seeing sent to desire me, rather then to take yt in ill part, to come into the roome wher he was shifting, that I might see it was noe excuse; and one of his men offered to pull me; wherat I layd my hand on my swoord and bad him not touch me: I knewe my way; and soe went to the gate. The Governor, seeing yt, followed after in hast and overtooke me unready, desiring me to pardon him: it was done out of negligence and no ill purpose. So, with some replyes on both sides, I went in. He offered me to sitt on the carpetts, but I tould him I could not stoope; wheratt hee sent for two chayres, and soe we sate. He began his ould tune of curtesy and complement, to which I replyed alike. But I tould him hee was a souldier and did not understand what losse of tyme was to merchants in such delayes as he dayly gave: that I had only to propound two things to him, which if he did performe it would give me some testemony he was our frend: that I desiered not to be his enemie: that I came to offer love: that I wish[t] rather make good report of him at the court then have cause to complayne, which, if many reformations were not, I should be enforced too. He replyed all my demands should be effected. I demanded that the 13 articles signed by the former governor to Captain Best might be signed by him: and that, since he seemed not to know them, I had caused [them] to be reduced into the Persian, which beeing almost in all poynts broken, I required his confirmation for the future: secondly, that, in his absence out of towne which was spoken off, order might be left with the Kings officers who were of sufficient trust, that our busines might goe forward, and not abyde the delay of his returne; both which hee promised on the woord of a man of honor. I tould him souldiers and men of honor esteemed theyr woord above theyr life, and desiered he would remember what he sayd. He vowed it should be performed. He desiered me to entreat the Generall to lett him have three fine cloathes to send to the King, for which hee would pay ready mony. I answered I had not to doe in yt, but I would write in his behalfe, assuring him for mony he might receive any content. Then he asked when I would sett forward to the court, and perswaded me to hasten, to prevent the Portugall. I tould him : within ten dayes : that I was a stranger and could not be suddenly provided for so great a journy. Hee tould me I should have his assistance. I thanked him, and replyed I did expect no more then what the lawes of nations cast upon me, securitye and safe conduct in his goverment. He answered that he was bound unto, but he would send divers gentelmen to bring me to the King, who would give me brave welcome and rich presents. I thancked him for his offer, and accepted yt : that I doubted not the King would receive me like the ambassador of a mightie Prince, his frend: that the bountyes of kings wear ever to be accepted gratefully : but that I expected no reward : I served a master was able to recompence mee. Soe giving me two pines,[1] with a long speech of the dayntenes, which I bade a servant take, telling him I knew the fruict veary well, I took my leave. He brought me to the tent doore, and some of the rest to my horse.

October 8.—The Governor sent to desire he might see the coach and virginalls for the King. I answered him it was not the custome to have kings presents veiwed, yet I was content to give him any satisfaction : that he should be welcome.

October 9.—In the morning he came to my house ; and when he was in the lower roome I came downe, and setting him and his officers in chayres I gave him the 13 articles [he] promised to subscribe. He refused yt, answering he durst not, I beeing goeing to the King : but when I was there I should have better conditions. I pressed him with his woord, with the *firma* of the Kings relating to them and confirming them, with many arguments ; but not prevayling, I tould him I could expecte no fayth from him that card so little for any vow : I should be forced to complayne of him, for which I was sorry, but now hee had them in the Persian and knew them, if he would there give his fayth they should be executed in forme as they were granted, and that, if any of our factors came to complayne of the breach of any, he would speedily doe

---

[1] The pineapple had been introduced into India by the Portuguese some years before. Jahāngīr (*Memoirs*, vol. i. pp. 5, 350) refers to this fruit as being grown in the European ports, though he adds that it was being cultivated with success at Agra and in Bengal.

justice, I would take it as some content; which he agayne vowed, and many with him, and upon yt gave me his hand; which I was forced to accept off, but will not owe him his falsenes. I complaynd that poore men could not be suffered to carry a little stuffe aboord for cloathing our people; to which he promised reformation, and to content me in all things I would require. Soe I gave him some toyes he fancyed; and showed the virginalls, which he much misliked not. Then he asked for the coach. I tould him it was in a warehouse: if he pleased he might goe in. Soe he rose and asked me if I would goe with him. I tould him I had seene yt often; which I did because I would not bring him out, having learnd the discurtesie of him. When hee saw yt, he scornd yt and sayd it was little and poore: that wee bought ill velvett of the Chinoyes [Chinese] and sent it his master in coaches. From thence hee tooke horse. At night he discovered him selfe more playnly, telling the factors his present was little: that the Portugalls in one frigatt gave more: that they should not land any more goods untill he had a present from the Generall to content him: that all other ports had made peace with the Portugall: hee had only received us: that hee had commandement to dismisse us, and that for my sake, who was an ambassador (with other good woords), he suffered them to remayne in the towne: but that resolvedly ther should be no trade without a better present. Soe base are our conditions in this port and subject to soe many slaveryes, such as noe free hart can endure, that I doe resolve eyther to establish a trade on free conditions or to doe my best to dissolve yt. For noe profitt can be a good pennyworth at soe much dishonor; the person of every man landing loccked up and searched like a theefe; sometymes two dayes before leave can be had for any man to passe the river; a poore bottle of wyne sent to the sick deteyned; and every trifle ransacked and taken away, with unsufferable insolencyes.

October 10.—The Governor went to the *alfandica* [custom house: Port. *alfandega*], shares our cloth, takes whatsoever he pleaseth, and finally steales one by a base convayance out of a wyndowe, while a broyle was purposely made to amase all men; yet barrs not trade absolutly, but forbidds cloth and lead to be landed untill the swoords, strong waters, and looking glasses and such lighter comodityes come to his eye, that he may satisfye his ravenous avarice or poverty. This day arrived Jhon Browne [1] from Amadavaz with the ill newes of Mr. Aldwoorth's death [2] by the way; who had long beene sicke, and now, desirous to doe his last service, three dayes journy onward to Suratt performed yt. What other newes he brought of the affayres of the busines I am a stranger too; only, wheras ther was doubt made at Amadavaze that, if Mr. Aldwoorth had died there, the Governor would make seysure of all goods in his hands (having lately practized yt

[1] John Brown, a factor who had come out in Downton's fleet in 1614, and had been sent up to court with Edwards. Early in 1616 he was placed in charge of the Ahmadābād factory, a post which he held until his death in April, 1620. The ambassador always spoke well of him, describing him as 'a very honest fellow, and nimble and industrious and valiant'; but Brown made an ill return, for after Roe's departure from India he wrote a letter to the Company, so full of invective against the ambassador that it drew upon him the sharp censure of his employers (Court Minutes, 28 Sept. and 1 Oct., 1619). In one of Coryat's letters will be found some facetious verses addressed to him by Brown.

[2] Thomas Aldworth, the first English agent at Surat. When Keeling's fleet arrived, he was lying dangerously ill at Ahmadābād, 'more like an anothomy then a man'; and fearing that if he died the governor would avail himself of the pretext to seize all the goods of the English, the factors (as narrated in the text) despatched an urgent message to Ajmer for a special *farmān* to protect them. A day before it arrived, however, Aldworth, fearing to remain longer, and anxious to get down to the coast, caused himself to be carried out of the city on the road to Surat; but the hand of death was upon him, and on the following day (4 Oct., 1615) he expired, at the little village of Nariād, in Kaira district (*Add. MS.* 9366, f. 9). Kerridge, lamenting his death to Brown, who had been Aldworth's companion on the fatal journey, expressed a hope that he had been interred in such a manner that his body might be afterwards transported to Ahmadābād, 'that som memorye may be of him to succeeding tymes' (*Ibid.* f. 10); but the idea was never realised. The want of a tombstone was probably due in part to the fact that, as mentioned in a letter from the Surat factors, 31 July, 1616 (I.O. Records: Surat Letter-book, p. 62) 'the costom hath bine to interr our dead at the Companies charge, but the tombe or any extraordinaryes are to bee paid out of their owne meanes'; and Aldworth's friends were not wealthy enough to spend money in erecting a monument in a distant land.

upon an Armenian merchant, and both enquiring suspitiously after his recovery and command not to depart the towne without leave; and further, a plummer dyeing there about the same tyme, the officers came to enquire his estate, and beeing tould he was a servant and a poore man were satisfied, yet with their brokers *scrito* [1] in testemony), the factors very discreetly despatched away for the court to procure the Mogulls *firma* in prevention, which was granted and returned with expedition, remayning yet at Amadavaz for securytye of the goods under Mr. Aldwoorths chardge, but the coppy was sent downe by Jhon Browne; which I demanded and I was answered he had sent yt the Generall. Jhon Browne, desiring to goe to the ships, could not be suffered. I sent to the Governor a message about yt. His Lordship was in his *seralia*.[2]

October 11.—In the morning leave was obteyned for him with much adoe. At night arrived one Young,[3] a youth of Mr. Aldwoorths, with his masters goods, and a German that had served him.[4]

October 12.—Came to the custome house all the provisions for presents and other necessaryes for my journy and residence at Agra; but were not suffered to be landed, to theyr great spoyle. The factors all gone to the Generall to a councell. I sett downe all my greavances and complaynts in writing, and all my demands, with my full resolution in both cases of refusall or content; and caused them to be translated into the Persian in two coppies.

October 13.—In the morning, my provisions all remayning in the custome house and the merchants returned, I sent

---

[1] Attestation, note, or list (Ital. *scritto*, a writing). This word, often anglicised as *screet*, was no doubt brought into use, like many other mercantile terms, by the factors engaged in the Mediterranean trade.

[2] More familiar in the Italian form, *serraglio*.

[3] John Young, afterwards made a factor.

[4] His Christian name was Jacob; his surname is unknown. He was for some time a slave in Turkey, having been captured in the wars in Hungary. Escaping, he made his way to Goa and thence in May, 1613, to Surat, where Aldworth engaged him (*Letters Received*, vol. i. pp. 299, 304).

them with one coppy of them to the Governor, keeping the other to showe the Mogull howe fayrely I required justice and howe unwilling I was to be forced to complayne. The coppy in English is registred.[1] This frighted him so. farr as he asked who could witnesse the accusations theyr layd against him; and so redelivered presently all the cloathes in his hand except five, for which hee gave payment by the custome. For the stolen cloth, it was alsoe acknowledged, and order to clear all the goods landed. For my provisions he would see them at the *alfandica*, and what was for the King should passe, what for other uses should paye and passe. But he would not come any more into my howse; saying he only was our frend: that we traded by his licence: that he had received his Kings command to dismisse us.[2] Whereto it was answered: we did trade by virtue of the Kings *firma*, and not by him; if he had received warrant to dismise us, lett him proclayme and puplish yt: they would all depart. Thus it rested.

October 14.—He without my consent searched all thoose chests sent me in the custome house and tooke whatsoever pleased him in a most imperious sort, whipping a servant of the English almost to death for speaking, and using the merchants like his slaves. Wherupon I sent to them to come away and leave all to him, protesting I would never receive his leavings, and unlesse I might have them sent home entyre and undiminished in any part, I would depart the towne, though without fitt presents yet full of just complaynts.

To day came one Chrabchan[3] (that was Deputy Governor

---

[1] The draft (in Roe's own hand) is in the I.O. Records (*O.C.*, No. 298). It enumerates the various abuses, and demands redress, especially the delivery of the articles intended for presents, and the provision of means to transport them to the court. The document will be found in full at p. 182 of *Letters Received*, vol. iii.

[2] This seems to have been the case. Van Ravesteyn says that on 8 Sept., 1615, the Governor received a *farmān* from the King, declaring that an agreement had been reached with the Portuguese and ordering that the English should not be allowed a settled residence in Surat, though their ships might trade there during the monsoon (Terpstra, p. 188).

[3] Possibly this is meant for Kharrāb Khān. He is also called (f. 276) 'Chrab-Beacke' (Kharrāb Beg).

when this Zulphephar Chan arrived) to visitt me ; and after many curtesyes propounded and unhappy counsells against the Governor, offered to give me six horses, woorth 400*li*., and all meanes to furnish me for my journy, perswading me to receive none of my goods, but to goe up and complayne : tould me of injuryes done to him ; and desired I would take his petition. I knew him not, and, though jealous of his extreame offers, yet I thanckd him : that I could not receive so great an obligation of a stranger, of whom I had not deserved and to whom I had nothing to recompence in that kind : for his petition, I came betweene princes and durst not meddle in busines betweene the subjects of another king, nor betweene him and his subjects ; and so desired to be excused. He replyed it would be a great grace to him if I would accept his horses ; and then offered me one (that I desired to buy, but was prised 100*li*.) with much importunitye ; saying, if I lived to come back from Agra, he could not loose by any curtesye done me : and since I would not undertake his petition, that I would suffer a servant of his to goe in my company, for he durst not send for feare of the Governors tyranny but at such an oportunity. His horse I refused, and for his servant I said I would not forbidd any man the passage in my trayne, but I would neyther take notice of him nor of his busines. So we departed. This man is truly an enemy of the Governors, and the best frend the English have here.

Mr. Aldwoorthes roome was broken up, and his accounts, bookes, and goods taken by inventory and possessed by Mr. Barkeley.

October 15.—The *Ramdam* finished, ther was held a great feast and triumphe in Suratt, the Governor with all the principall men, near 1000 brave horse, excersicing to shoote on horse back at a ball on a high pole. The Judge of the *Alfandica* came to invite me, offering me his horses both for that day and up to Agra, telling me it was recompence enough to lett the Mogull know he had done yt : encouraging me to complayne with much vehemency. I refused to see sports or to receive too great a tye. He is a frend to the English and often viseted me. Within an hower the Governor sent to invyte me, an oliphant to ride upon with footemen with flaggs and pendants, and some horse and gentellmen to accompany mee. I answered I was no baby to be abused one day, and pleased with a pageant the next: he had a nother account to make with me before I could receive any curtesy. So they departed.

October 16.—My goods remayning still in his hands, I sent a lettre, which was written the former day but could not be delivered for the triumphe, wherin I playnly defied him as an enemy; I repeated all his abuses, and lett him know my purpose to leave all behynd me and seeke justice of the King. The coppy is registred in English and Persian, as I did all things that passed betweene us, that I might show the Mogull the fayre course I held to bring him to reason without complayning. His answere stood most upon denyalls; offering the Kings presents free, but of others he would have a share and I should pay custome. So I prepare to be gone without them.

To the Governor of Surat.
(*Add. MS.* 6115, f. 58.[1])

15 October, 1615.

The injuryes yow have offered mee, contrary to the fayth given by your King, to all civilitye and law of nations, beeing a free ambassador, and contrary to your owne honor and promise, forceth me to send yow woord I am resolved not to endure yt. I come hither not to begg, nor doe nor suffer injurye. I serve a King that is able to revenge what soever is dared to be done against his subjects. I am come under assurance of the Great Mogulls *firma* and lettre sent unto the King of England my master, promising all love and frendship to him, and therfore I am confident that no man dare presume to wrong mee. Under which confidence I lett yow knowe that, without seeking farther frendship from yow, that have ransacked my chests, taken by violence the presents sent your Kyng, cruelly whipt a servant of the merchaunts for doeing his duty, abused with contempt all the English, notwithstanding they have both sought in good sort your favour and have sundry tymes presented yow: and to leave all in your hands, to goe with speede and desire justice against yow, that

[1] There is another copy of this letter in the India Office Records (*O.C.*, No. 303). This has been printed in vol. iii. of *Letters Received* (p. 196).

yow may appeare to answere before your King to my face for these wrongs ; when I doubt not (so great fame I heare of the royall disposition of His Majestie) to have honorable and speedy redresse. I am sorry for nothing but that ever I vouchsafed to send yow any remembrance of mee, of whom in love yow might have received any thing ; but by this course of me nor my nation I am resolved yow shall never gett one pice ; assuring yow I am better resolved to dye upon an enemye then to flatter him, and for such I give yow notice to take me untill your master hath done me justice.

October 17.—I wrote in the Generalls name to the same purpose and sent yt by Captain Harris, who was then with mee. (The coppy is alsoe registred.[1]) He gave faire woords and promised all things should be dispatchd, but nothing was effected ; yet desiring Captain Harris to make him and me frends, repeating to him the refusing of his oliphant and my not comminge to his howse.

October 18.—I entreated Captain Harris to returne with a civill message to him, which he tooke in good part. At which instant came a lettre from the Prince, which hee read thear. The contents were, that the English should dischardge one ship and have a monthes staye in trade, but no residences in the towne.[2] Wherat the Governor perswaded to land no more goods, and gave order to take up all that was come to the custome house ; desiering that I might hasten to procure a residence here, or otherwise wee must depart. He would yet doe nothing to farther me ; but delivered some few of the things I desiered, but sealed and directed to the Mogull. The chests sent a shoare, wherout I was to choose such presents as should lye bye to serve all occasions, were deteyned. Wherupon, our residence here standing on so fickle tearmes, I resolved to goe up with more hast and lesse carriadge, with only presents for one or two audiences, in which if I could procure fitt conditions for our stay and securitye for our farther trade, I would signifye I had left many things behynd by reason of the doubts cast into me by the Princes lettre : desiring both the *firma* to such articles as I had propounded, and a warrant for the passing up of all such things as I would send for without

[1] Not in the MS.

[2] This is confirmed by Van Ravesteyn (Terpstra, p. 193).

the impeachment [*i.e.* hindrance] of the Governor. In refusall, I did purpose to returne to our ships with expedition, having advertised the Mogull that as he was lord of his owne land and might doe his pleasure, and had forsaken the amytie of a Prince who had desired yt in fayre and honorable tearmes, for the Portugalls who made him tributary, to his eternall dishonor, so he would fynd by experience the King my master would be lord of all these seas and ports to the prejudice of his subjects, in spight of those in whom he now trusted and should not dare to releev them. To this purpose I wrote the Generall, with my opinion and resolution at lardge ; and sent the merchaunts aboord to conferr of these businesses and to deliver me in writing all their demands and greavances. At Captain Harris parting with the Governor, he was veary kynd, sending the Generall a very good present, and giving him a nother of good valew.

October 19.—All the merchants beeing at the fleete, nothing was done at the custome howse. I received advise by a Persian whom I used, that the souldiors of Damon and Chaule and the land of the Portugalls were drawne downe to Goa, under coulor of sending a fleete for the releefe of Ormus, from which the Persian had taken all supplyes : that the new Viceroy was arrived with three caricks.[1] Wheron, doubting whether the preparation might be divulged for Ormus but fale upon our fleete, I wrote a lettre to the Viceroy signifying our desire of peaceable trade without theyr prejudice, His Majestie[s] resolution to mayntayne his subjects in theyr honest course of trafique, and offer of comprisure in the treaty now negotiated with the Mogull and to endeavour to procure an open free trade on all sydes ; which I sent in Portugall and English, limitting a tyme for answer. The coppy is registred.

[1] This was a mistake. There was no change of Viceroys between 1612 and 1617, when the Conde de Redondo replaced Don Jeronimo de Azevedo.

To the Viceroy of Goa.
(*Add. MS.* 6115, f. 58.[1])

Most Illustrious Lord,

The injuryes Your Excellence or your predecessors have offered to the subjects of the high and mighty Prince, the King of England, my royall master, by assalting them in theyr peacable course of trade, contrarye to the amytie and leauge of both our soveraynes, although by the asistance of God yow have received shame and confusion in your unchristian attempts, yet I have commandement to admonish yow, like the subject of a Prince at peace with my master, to desist from undertaking that which can bring foorth no other effect but warr and revenge and shedding of Christian blood. And because it can not bee supposed yow have done thus unwoorthely without having mistaken the entent of our comming into these parts, I have command from His Majestie to signifie to yow, as His Majesties embassador resident at Madrill hath done there, that the English entend nothing but free trade, open by the lawes of nations to all men, wherof in these terretoryes of the Mogull and other neighbouring princes there is enough for both, if avarice doe not blynd all reason in Your Excellence. It is not the purpose of the English to roote out or hinder your trade, but to continew theyr owne in frendship, and wilbe ready as Christians to doe yow any curtesye or assist Your Excellence or nation in any want. Neither doe they desire, if Your Excellence have any custome, revenewe, or gabell [*i.e.* impost] from the merchants subject to the Mogull trading at sea, to take it from yow or otherwise impeach your receipt therof. That it is strange that the two mightie princes our masters and theyr subjects beeing freends and in free commerce one with a nother, Your Excellence should dare to infring yt; wishing Your Excellence to remember what the wronges offered by your nation did cost yow, how many millions, both of men and crownes, in the dayes of the blessed and famous Queene Elizabeth, the same force and spiritt still living in our nation; advising yow to give more reverent tearmes of the Majestie of a Christian Kyng then your barbarous miscelaneous people have used in these parts. To which purpose having now in frendly manner admonished Your Excellence, as befitts the honor of a Prince tender of his royall woord, I am to give yow farther notice that His Majestie is resolved to maynteyne his subjects in their honest indeavours, in spight of any enemyes; and to that purpose hath sent me,

---

[1] There is another copy in the I.O. Records (*O.C.*, No. 303), but it presents no variation. It is printed in *Letters Received*, vol. iii. (p. 197).

beeing a gentellman of his privy chamber and a souldiar, his ambassador to the Greatt Mogull, with full power and authorytye to conclude a leauge and frendship betweene theyr Majesties and theyr subjects for ever, bynding himselfe by his royall woord to maynteyne and fullfill whatsoever I his embassador shall conclude with the Great Mogull, to the securytye of theyr subjects. Into which leauge I have command to offer Your Excellence comprisure ; letting yow knowe I am ready to goe for Adsmere, wher I will attend your answer 40 dayes, and, in case of refusall or silence, which I will understand a refusall, I will proceede to such conclusions as I shall in my judgment thincke conduceable to the ends for which I am imployed ; assuring Your Excellence, if yow continew in this course, the Kings Majestie will not only give protection in the way of defence, but grant his lettres of prisall free to all his subjects to make war upon yow in all parts of the Indyes, a thing infinitely desiered and dayly sued for to His Majestie, wherby yow shall not be able to looke out at your ports, much lesse to attempt to injure us. But, hoping yow will have more consideration, I require your answere within the tyme prefixed, and so I committ yow to Gods protection.

Your frend or enemye at your owne choyce,
D. THO. ROE,
Ambassador of the Majestie of England.[1]

Suratt, October 20, 1615, stil. vet.

October 20.—A lettre came from the King, but not once named the English, as my intelligence enformed me ; but concernd the injuryes of a merchant wroongd by the Governor.

October 21.—I rode early with Captain Peyton, Mr. Bonner [2] and others, to the Tancke [see p. 90] to take the ayre ; and

---

[1] As will be seen later, no reply was made to this letter. The factors at Surat, in a note dated 3 May, 1616, informed Roe that the messenger had returned about four days previously ; at first (he reported) he was promised an answer, but after waiting three months, and being refused admittance to the Viceroy, he judged it best to make his way back to Surat. In July, 1616, Richard Cocks wrote to another factor in Japan that, in default of a reply, Roe had ' pronounced open warrs against the Portingals in the East Indies with fire and sword in the name of the Kings Majestie of England' (*O.C.*, No. 377) ; but this story, though apparently accepted as correct in the preface to the *Calendar of State Papers* (*E. Indies*), 1513-1616, is quite baseless.

[2] This was Thomas Bonner, who, on the way out, had been promoted to the post of master of the *Expedition*. He died at Tiku (Sumatra) on 20 July, 1616, and was buried on a small island near

returned on purpose by a greene, wher usually the Governor is at his excercise, to observe his countenance, because Captain Harris tould me hee desired a frendship. When I came there, he left his play at balle on horsbacke [1] and came toward me. I stayed his comming up. After salutations, and asking of my horses and why I used not his, to which I answered I had these at my command from a good frend, Chrabbeckcan,[2] he desired me to see theyr excersice a horsebacke, which I accepted off. Wherupon hee sent for his bowes, and with divers others passed many carrers [3] shooting backward at a marke on the ground, and after at an eastreadge [*i.e.* ostrich] eggshell on the top of a May pole. Then hee tooke his peece [*i.e.* gun] and did the like, and after with lances, counterfeyting a chase and at the full speed of theyr horses, full of varietye, beeing veary active and manly sports; which finished, he desired me to honor him to see his house. I was so willing to close with him for the furtherance of our business that I was entreated to doe yt, though I knew I should find in my reception nothing to content me. For, after theyr rude manner, at his court gate he alighted and went in in a hurry; soe that I stayed a pretty whyle and entered with the English alone. When I came neare, he mett me and led me up into a howse of pleasure, where wee sate, discoursing of the warr, armes, and customes of these parts. Then Captain Peyton tould him the Generall had sent him a present in requitall of a former; and soe delivering the parcells, he tooke two things and with infinite scorne cast the rest away, saying thoose hee tooke as a token

that port. Three years later was buried in the same spot, 'so neere as could be ghessed,' the body of his brother Robert Bonner, the leader of the 1618 fleet. He had died at Tiku on 9 Oct., 1619, of wounds received in fighting the Dutch when they attacked and captured, amongst others, his vessel, the *Dragon*, Lancaster's old flag-ship.

[1] The modern 'polo,' which (under the name of *chaugān*) was the favourite pastime of Akbar.

[2] See p. 52. Evidently Roe had consented to make temporary use of the horses proffered by Kharrāb Khān.

[3] This was the technical phrase for running the charge in a tournament or attack.

but not as a present, repeating the valew of his. This I mention that yow may know theyr custome, at least this man. So I returned to demand my goods, to repeate the discurtesyes, but I wanted no fayre promises and excuses. Asking when I departed, I replyed: in two dayes; wherat the merchannts desired leave to pass up some cloth in my company, which hee flattly refused, turning to me, swearing by his head and beard he had expresse order to the contrary, and to suffer us only to unlade one ship in a month, and after to depart; and except I could dispeed and procure longer tyme, he must obey it. I answered him roughly that we card not, yet I could not beleeve his master was so unconstant. Soe I tooke my leave; butt at night could get nothing from the custome howse.

October 22.—Having advised that, seeing now in five weekes we hard not one woord of Mr. Edwards, woondring that these changes would be at court without his pryvitye, and that I could not goe on my journy with any expedition, desierous to have some newes from above and to take my provisions with me, I resolved to addresse my complaynt by post to Mr. Edwards to deliver to the Mogull in my name. The merchannts acquaynting the Generall speedily therof, who wrote his lettre to Mr. Edwards, as I suppose, of complaynt; and it beeing sent to Suratt, the merchants dispeeded it away without my knowledge, or once asking me if I would write; which I tooke in veary ill part, having received many neglects by reason that all obedience and obsequiousnes was given him [*i.e.* Keeling] who could pleasur them, and it was published among them I had nothing to doe with them. Yet within one hower I sent a post after yt, with my instructions to Mr. Edwards how to proceed and how far for our present redresse here, and to dispeed yt to the factory; letting him know, since I was arrived, all the wrongs of the Kings subjects concerned me and that I should answer for them, and that therfore in my name he ought to proceed; which I doubt not he will effect. The coppie therof is registred [*at f.* 59 *of the MS.*]. The Generall sent four of the factors for Baroch and Amadavaz[1] by a new way from the ships, the Governor suffering none to passe from Suratt.

[1] To provide a cargo for the ship intended to be sent home.

October 23.—I sent two merchants to the Governor to demand those things which he deteyned. He answered hee [*sic*. I ?] might be gone to night if I would, but I should have nothing, bidding them tend their owne busines : that they had but 15 dayes to staye. At night the Generall writte me woord of the misfortune at Adsmere, which hee received from Amadavaz by way of apologye in the excuse of one Mitford, that had stabbd Mr. Edwards at a consultation for some woords used ; which the Generall very rightly conceived a great offence and dispatchd lettres to Adsmere. But I, not knowing the contents, but wrighting [weighing ?] the offence to be of a high nature, dishonorable to His Majestie, whose ambassador Edwards pretended to be, and prejudiciall to the busines now in hand on fickle tearmes, I thought it fitt that, to avoyde the scandall, some part of justice and reparation should beginn where the offence was most scandalous, and therfore wrote to Mr. Edwards to cause him to be layd in irons in his house untill I came up ;[1] purposing after examination to send him publiquely bound as prisoner to the fleete, with the true coppy of the cause on both parts. For if authoritye have abused it selfe, though it be free from revenge by those that are subordinat, yet it must answere to a higher authoritye, or all bands of goverment are dissolved.

October 24.—The Governor, beeing gone a hunting, gave order for my dispatch ; but nothing was effected. The cause of this change was the goeing of some boates to Baroch, beeing afrayd to loose our trade ; wherby he betrayd his lyes of command for our departure.

October 25.—I laded my goodes, thincking the order was sufficient, but ther came some presently from the custome house and would new search them, which I was angry at and would not suffer. Wherupon they beate one of the wagoners at my dore and would have carried the cheefe to be whiped ; whom I tooke into my house and gave him protection, and

---

[1] The letter is given at f. 60 of the MS. The brawl was found to have been a very slight affair, and no serious notice was taken of it. Mitford went home in the *Globe* in March, 1617 ; and in May of the following year the Company presented him with one hundred nobles in recognition of his services.

bad them be gone ; but they offering by force to search my
chests that were laded, [I] showed them a swoord in a nother
mans hand that stood by, and tould them they abused us
enough at the custome house : if they presumed yt here, I
would recompence yt. Wherat they departed and wrote to
the Governor that I drew a swoord and beate them ; and
tooke this occasion not to execute the Governors command
for my dispatch. Withall I sent speedely to the Generall,
desiering him that one ship might ryde out, as if wee meant
to seeke other trade ; a thinge which only awed them, and
tooke good effect. For the Governor returning at night, I sent
him woord howe I was abused by the officers of the custome
house, and he in theyr reports made that I drew a swoord.
He sent presently Abram Chan,[1] the cheefe man in the towne
and our frend, to tell me he had punished them for lying and
misdeameanor toward me, and was sorry I did not beate them
in earnest : that on the morow Abram Chan should come and
dispatch me with his passe and lettre to the Prince and that
he would present me with a horse and furniture. I thanked
him, desiering expedition and no other present. Abram Chan
tould me hee never durst visitt me before, nor meddle in my
busines, the Governor beeing soe unconstant ; but now he
had leave, and gave me his woord it should be effected. Thus
I stood delayed in hope and doubt. Within an hower came
a lettre from the King, which was received with great solem-
nytye. The contents I could not learne : but by the effect
it was in our behalfe and some checke to the Governor. For hee
speedily, though it was late, sent for Mr. Bangham [2] and

[1] Ibrāhīm Khān, who was appointed shortly afterwards Governor
of Surat, chiefly, it would seem, because he was favourably disposed
towards the English. But, after some experience of him, Roe
declared him ' good, but soe easy that he does no good ; wee are not
less afflicted with a block then before with a storck ' (O.C., No. 558).

[2] Nicholas Bangham, originally a joiner, was left at Surat by the
Hector, returning to England with Best in 1614. In recognition of
his services he was given a hundred pounds, made a factor, and
admitted to the freedom of the Company. He was appointed to
proceed with Roe to India in the capacity of steward, to control his
household expenses ; but the ambassador, when he heard of this
arrangement, remonstrated so strongly with Keeling that the idea
was given up. Bangham was made cape merchant at Burhānpur

made Abram Chan deale with him to appease me and all the English, protesting we should have all good usage, and gave leave to goe and carry our goods up or any wher without stopp. He was very sadd, which is a signe that the lettre was some reprehension; for otherwise the custome is, upon the receipt of any thing from the King, to drincke and be veary frolicke. As yet we had not one woord from Mr. Edwards, havinge beene in the roads six weakes. At night was a proclamation made, giving leave for boates to carry over the lead and teeth [*i.e.* elephants' tusks], which had now layne in the sunne a month at the water syde, and were cleft and spoyld: which was next day performed.

October 26.—I expected all day, but could not procure any thing; nor any answere nor leave to loade my chests.

October 27.—Abram Chan came with a multitude of officers, and brought the Governors seale and sealed the Kings presents, counted my chests, and gave a warrant to carry them; and withall brought such things as the Governor had left [1] to my house, of which I tooke some; and promised whatsoever was in the Governors hands should be delivered the next day. I answered: I could not accept of these, to have the other deteyned. He sayd all should be brought, except two basens which the Governor had sent the Prince. I replyed they were taken from mee, and I would demand them at court, and give as I sawe fitt. He desired me to be content with soe smalle a matter. The Governor sent me a horse to give mee, entreating to speake well of him to the King. I answered: for his horse, I would not receive him, but caused the bringer to returne yt: that [if?] I found my selfe yet at last well dealt with, and liberty for the merchants to transport their goods freely, I would make such report of him as became a frend: but otherwise I would doe my dutie to my master and the service

---

instead, and held that post until the spring of 1618, when he went home in the *Bull*. He came out again in 1621, and served till early in 1624, when he returned finally to England. Roe spoke very favourably of him in a letter to the Company: ' though hee bee not a bredd merchant, hee hath a good head, learns aptly, and is of a judgement not rash nor peremptorye, and is your best linguist.'

[1] *Add. MS.* 19277 has ' kept.'

to my countrymen for which I was imployed. Abram Chan importuned me to accept of the horse. I answered: the Governor would take yt as an ingagement to speake well of him, and ingratitude in the contrary: that I came not to be brybed, neyther would I leave any tye on mee, that it should not bee free, if any lettre of complaynt came after mee, to doe my nation right against his injuryes: and that therfore ther was no other way to deale with me but by usinge the merchants well, both in theyr bodyes and goods. And so, receivinge many promises, they and theyr horse returned.

October 28.—I laded most of my provisions, expecting the rest from the Governor; but nothing came nor any answere.

October 29.—I sent my carts before, expecting those things deteyned; but with so small hope that I resolved to goe without them. Within an hower came Abram Chan with most of the things taken by the Governor, and a warrant for my departure. When I demanded the remaynder, he desiered to be excused: that hee [*i.e.* the Governor] knew not when hee tooke them but that they were the merchannts, and offered to paye for them: but hee had sent them to Prince, beeing some seven or eight basons, French and other sorts. I answered: I would challendge them at court, and complayne of the violence.

October 30.—Many messages past about leave for cloth and swoords to goe up with mee, but none could be obteyned; so I prepared to be gone. As I was ready, came a lettre or *firmaen* from the Mogull to me, staying (according to the custome) without the towne to be mett by us. I sent the merchants, who brought it to me, beeing procured by Mr. Edwards, with his lettre; it conteyned a command to all governors of provinces or townes to attend me with sufficient guard and not to meddle with any thing was myne; and in all things very favorable, except chardges, which was left unmentioned. When I had read yt, beeing ready to goe to horse, hearing the Governor and all the towne were assembled in an open space, I rode that way, and showed the Governor my lettre; wherat he was very blancke, desiring my frendship, and offered me anything I would demand. I answered it was now too late: I only came to lett him see the King had a better estimation of ambassadors and theyre qualetye then he, that had so ransacked mee : but I did not desire his ruyne : if he would yet give content to the merchannts, I would make the best of soe ill usage. He bad aske any thing. I demanded leave for twelve carts to goe up with goods at their pleasure ; which hee refused. Then I tould him I saw he would doe nothing of curtesye : it was but losse of a little tyme : I would procure it in dispight of him ; desiring to know his reason why, contrarye to his woord, he kept our people and goods prisoners. He gave none, but sayd for my sake five carts should have leave. Though I scorned this answere, yet since it was some helpe toward dispatch I seemed content. He demanded if I were frends. I sayd untill I heard new complaynts, which I expected howerly, [I] was ; and that I required his *chop* [1] for the five carts presently, for I would stay for them the morrow at my tents. He promised, and I departed foure *course* [2] from Suratt to Cumaria [Khumbāriā], expecting the merchannts. At my goeing I had no guard from him ; having before hyred such guard as by councell of all your factors, and such other necessary men as was requisite (having five sicke men in my trayne and few perfect) to Bramport [Burhānpur], where I hope for some ease of my great chardge. Yet I will prove I have in no thing taken so many nor so much as the factors thought requisite. At my goeing I was perswaded to give in the custome house, because I had all theyr assistance and paynes in these broyles with the Governor, and to others that had broked [*i.e.* negotiated] in my affayres, and to the Governors under servants, as porters, wayters and *peons* [messengers].

October 31.—I rested in expectation of the merchannts and goods which were to goe up ; but at night I received lettres that the Governor would not hould his woord, except he might have 30 clothes at his owne rates ; wherat I sent him woord I was free of all promise of frendship, it beeing

[1] A seal-impression (Hind. *chhāp*), and hence also the document thus authenticated.

[2] The usual measure of distance in India. Later Roe makes the *kos* two miles, but adds that the *kos* of the interior is longer than that of the coast districts.

given upon the last condition, which hee had dishonarably falsefyed.

November 1.—I went 11 English mile to a village,[1] lying alway in my tents. Hither Abram Chan sent me a bullocke to carry water, fitted with sckinns, a cammell, with two tents and some hens. I tooke his meate and some sckinns; beeing provided of all necessaryes, I returned the rest, haveing nothing of valew to give in requitall; which his men were hardly enforced too. This man showed me both most affection and most honor in all his actions.

November 2.—To Biarat [Viāra] 21 mile.[2] This towne hath a walled castle, beeing [in] the border of the kingdome of Guzaratt subject to the Mogull; belonging to Abram Chan, by whose order I had a guard of horse watched about my tent all the night.

November 3.—I entered the kingdome of Pardaffsha,[3] a Gentile lord of the hills, subject to none; and lodged in the feilds at 15 miles end. His cheefe cytty is called Mugher.[4] He lives in a castell in the mountains.

[1] Van Ravesteyn, who (as already mentioned) accompanied Roe as far as Burhānpur, gives in his journal (Terpstra, *op. cit.*, p. 194) the names of several places to which the ambassador refers but vaguely. From this source we learn that the village was Mota.

[2] Roe followed the ordinary route from Surat to Burhānpur, described by Finch, Jourdain, Mundy, and other travellers. Van Ravesteyn states that this day they rested on the way at ' Croda,' *i.e.* Karod, on the left bank of the Tāpti.

[3] Partāb Shāh, the ruler of Bāglān, a mountainous district of considerable extent, represented to-day by the Bāglān and Kalvan sub-divisions of Nāsik district. Akbar had attempted to reduce it, but had failed; Partāb Shāh, however, subsequently acknowledged the overlordship of Jahāngīr, and the kingdom was finally conquered by Aurangzeb. The chief's headquarters were at Jaitāpur, near Mulher Fort (Roe's Mugher). According to Van Ravesteyn, the midday halt was made at ' Carckga ' (5 *kos*), and in the evening they reached ' Criali ' (another 5 *kos*). Neither name is found on modern maps; but the former is evidently the ' Curka ' of Finch and the ' Kerkoa ' of Tavernier.

[4] This is the reading of *Add. MS.* 19277. The version in *Add. MS.* 6115 is ' nie a cheefe cytty '; but this is obviously wrong, as Mulher is more than twenty miles away.

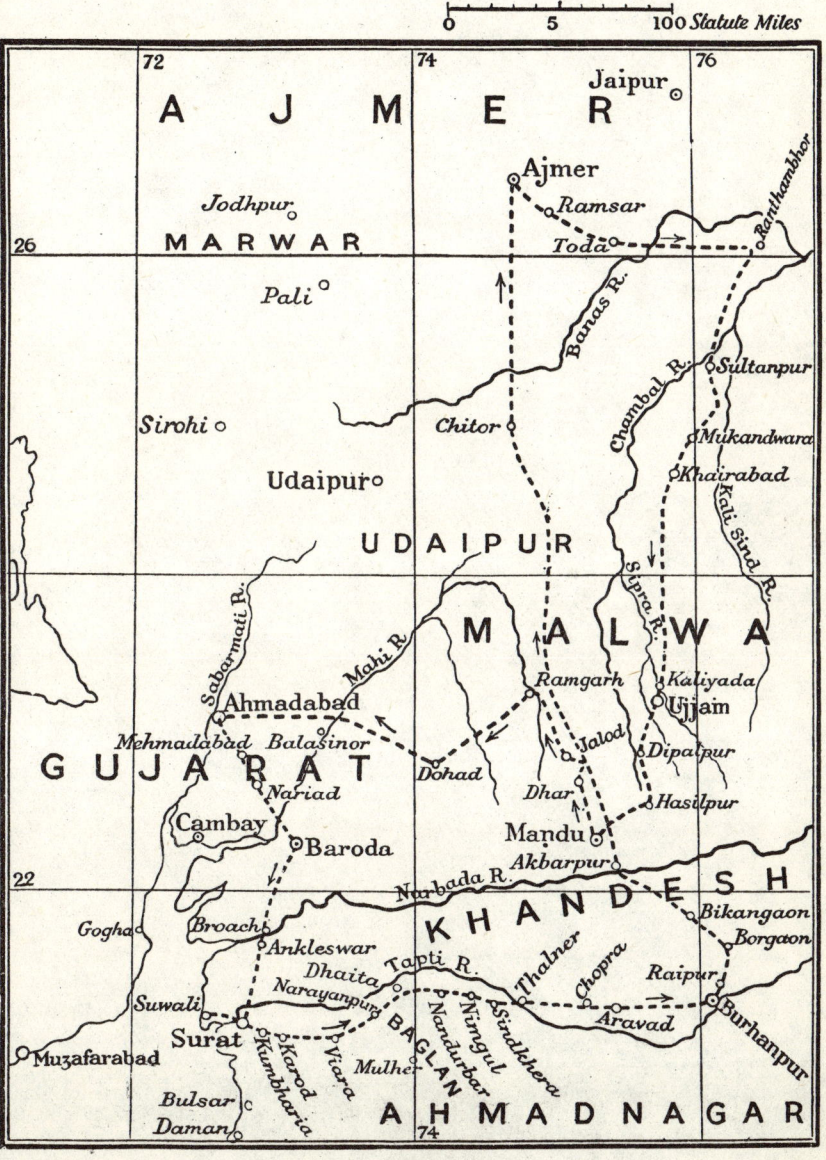

ROE'S ROUTES

November 4.—9 mile. Rocky way, by a village called Narampora [Nārāyanpur].

November 5.—15 mile. In the feilds [dyning by Dytat].[1]

November 6.—20 miles to Nunderpar [Nandurbār], a citty of the kingdom of Bramport, subject to the Mogull; having passed a corner of the kingdome of Pardasha.[2] Here I gott first bread since my comming from Suratt; for though the cuntry be plentifull, especially of cattle, by reason of the *Banians*,[3] that will kyll nothing, inhabiting all over, yet by the same reason they would sell us none; and bread they make not, but dow cakes. I mett in one day 10,000 bullocks in one troupe laden with corne, and most days others, but lesse; which showes the pleanty.

November 7.—18 mile to Nimgull [Nimgul].

November 8.—15 mile to Sinchelly [Sindkhera].

November 9.—15 mile to Tolnere [Thālner].

November 10.—18 mile to Chapre [Chopra]. Here, having pitchd my tents without the towne according to my custome, the Kings officers came and tould me that there were 200 theeves in the hills and I could not lye without great danger, perswading me to pitch within the towne. I answered I was not afrayd: if they came I would leave some of them on the ground for them in the morning, and that now I would not stirr. They replyed they could not answere it to the Mogull if any thing happened unto me; but if I would stay without, they desired a dischardge in writting that they had warned mee. I tould them I was resolved not to moove, but, if the dainger were soe important, I required a better guard to watch with mee; which was granted, and the Governor with the other officers came out with 30 horse and 20 shott and watched all night. In the morning they brought me to their precinctes; to whom I gave a small present, and reward to the souldiers.

---

[1] Added from *Add. MS.* 19277. 'Dytat' is Dhāita, on the Sarpini River.

[2] 'Departed, and midday rested at Badora [Bhadwār], five *kos*. This is the last place in the kingdom of Pardasscha. Came in the evening to Nasabar . . . another six *kos*' (Van Ravesteyn).

[3] The well-known term for Hindu traders, often extended by the early travellers to all persons professing the Hindu religion.

November 11.—8 mile to Arawd [Arāvad]. Hence I sent Mr. Shalebanck [Salbank] to Bramport with the Kings *firma*, to *Channa Channa* the Governor, to see what comoditye I could procure for my furtherance.

November 12.—18 mile.[1] *November* 13.[2]—18 [3] mile.

November 14.—15 mile. I arived at Brampore,[4] being by my conjecture 223 mile from Suratt [5] and the course wholy east : a miserable and barron country, the townes and villages all built of mudd, soe that ther is not a house for a man to rest in. This day at Batharport [Bahādurpur], a village two mile short of Brampore, is the stoore house of ordinance. I saw divers of brasse, but generally to shortt and too wyde bored. Betwen that and Brampore I was mett by the *Cuttwall*,[6] well accompanied and 16 coullers carried before them. He brought me to the *saralya* [7] wher I was apoynted to lodg (where at the

[1] According to Van Ravesteyn the day's march was one of 14 *kos*, through ' Bevel ' (Yāval) to ' Hinguna ' (Hingona).

[2] ' This morning betimes we departed, and we ended our march at Ravel [Rāver], being 12 *kos*. On the way we were attended by two headmen of two villages ; but we imagined that this was in hope of a reward from the ambassador rather than out of courtesy or for any respect towards his *farmān* ' (Van Ravesteyn).

[3] *Add. MS.* 19277 has ' 15.'

[4] Burhānpur, on the northern bank of the Tāpti, in the Nimār district of the Central Provinces. It is now a place of small importance, but was at the time of Roe's visit the seat of the Mughal administration of the Deccan, and the headquarters of the army. The citadel, called the *Lāl Kila*, or Red Fort, which was probably the scene of Roe's presentation to Prince Parwīz, is still in existence, though much dilapidated.

For the topographical notes on Burhānpur utilized in the following pages, I am indebted to Messrs. A. K. Smith and B. K. Parry, both of the Indian Civil Service. The photographs here reproduced were taken by the latter gentleman.

[5] Roe's estimate is a fairly close one. When Colonel Goddard passed along the same route (in the reverse direction), in the course of his celebrated march across India (1779), his surveyors made the distance from Burhānpur to Surat 237¾ miles (MS. in I.O. Map Room).

[6] The *Kotwāl*, or native official who had the general superintendence of the city, especially as regards police functions.

[7] The caravansary (Pers. *karwān-sarāi*) or public lodging-house for travellers and their pack-animals. The one to which Roe was

BURHANPUR CASTLE

gate hee tooke his leave), beeing a handsome frunt of stone, but when I entered I had four chambers alotted me like ovens, ₁oe bigger, round at the topp, made of brick in a wall syde. This trubled me ; but my tents were my refuge, and I sent the *Cuttwall* woord I would depart the towne, scorninge soe meane usadge. He desiered me to be content untill morning. Here lives Sultan Pervies,[1] the kings seconnd sonne, houlding the state and custome of his father ; and the *Channa Channa*,[2] being the greatest subject of the Mogull, generall of his armies,

taken was evidently the *Akbari-sarāi* (near the Fort), which is still standing. Mr. Parry has sent me a copy of the Persian inscription over the main gate, which shows that the *sarāi* was completed in 1027 A.H. (1617-18) ; but the name implies that the building was in existence before that time, and (as will be seen) it answers exactly to Roe's description.

In a letter to Keeling (f. 65 of the MS.) Roe says : ' As soone as I was arrived in the *seraglia*, when I expected good lodging, I was allotted by the *Cuttwall* four roomes (the rest full of strangers), each of them in a walle, no bigger then ovens and in that shape, round at the tope, no light but the doore, and so little that the goods of two carts would fill them all. I had 20 persons (some sicke), all the presents, the cases of bottles, my owne chests, to unlade and bestow safe in this narrow compasse ; my selfe to lodge, my preacher, and some others unfitt to lye in the open ayre in a bare court.' Whilst trying to arrange for an equitable distribution of the small accommodation available, the ambassador learned to his annoyance that Boughton had taken possession of one of the four rooms, filling it with his own belongings. He was asked to admit some other members of the party, but rudely refused. Roe resented this behaviour at the time ; but in a few days he and Boughton ' were as good frends as ever.'

[1] Parwīz, who, as Roe states, was nominally in command of the army operating against the Deccan princes. He died at Burhānpur in 1626.

[2] Khān-khānān (Khan of Khans), a title usually given to the officer who acted as commander-in-chief. The individual here referred to was Mīrza Abdurrahīm, son of Bairām Khān, Akbar's celebrated general. He had been given the title for reconquering Gujarāt ; and later he distinguished himself in several campaigns, especially in the subjugation of Sind. For some time he was a strong partisan of Prince Khurram, though afterwards he deserted him for Parwīz. His death occurred at Delhi in 1627, at the age of seventy-two. Captain Hawkins, while on his way up to Agra in 1609, had an interview with the Khān-khānān at Burhānpur and was given by him ' his most kind letter of favour to the King, which avayled much.'

whereof 40,000 horse are with nim. The Prince hath the name and state, but the *Chan* governs all.[1]

November 15.—I removed into a handsome garden and sett up my tentts with some of my people, leaveing the rest with my goods at the *saralia* ; where the *Cuttwale* came to visitt me and excuse my lodging, protesting it was the best in the towne, which after I found true ; the wholle citty (which is veary great) being all builte of mudd baser then any cottage, except the Princes howse, the *Chan Channas*, and some few others.

November 16, 17.—I rested, and sent about my carriadges, only receiving twenty dishes of meat, drest after their country manner, sent me in covered platters by the *Cutwall* for a present.

November 18.—For many considerations, as well to see the fashiones of the court as to content the Prince (who desired yt, and I was lothe to distast him, because ther was sume purpose of erecting a factory in the towne, and I found by experience swoord blades were well sould in the armie), I went to visitt the Prince, and carried him a present. I was brought in by the *Cuttwall*. At the outward courte wear about 100 horsemen armed, being gentellmen that attend the princes sitting out to salute him, making a lane of each side. In the inward courte he satte, high in a gallerie that went round, with a cannipe over him and a carpett before him, in great but barborous state.[2] Comming toward him thorowgh a lane of people, an officer came and brought me woord I must touch the ground with my head, and my hatt off. I answered: I came in honnor to see the Prince and was free from the custome

---

[1] Kerridge, in a letter to Roe from Ahmadābād, 21 Oct., 1615 (Brit. Mus. *Add. MS.* 9366, f. 19) warned him that he must visit Prince Parwīz, 'whose cappacitye beinge weake and he geven to womanish pleasures, ther is no hope either of honnour or content from him.... He supplieth the place in name only ... the *Chan Chan* in matters of consequence ther ordereth all, esteemed for nobillitye, honnour and valor to be the cheifest of the land.'

[2] The scene of Roe's reception was probably the *Diwān-i-ām*, in the Fort. It is now in ruins. Mr. Parry writes : 'the walls of the side rooms are still intact, but the terrace has disappeared ; on the walls are the remains of old paintings in square panels.'

ROE'S QUARTERS AT BURHANPUR

of servants. Soe I passed on, till I came to a place rayled in right under him, with an assent of three steeps, wher I made him reverance, and he bowed his bodye ; and soe went within yt, wher stood round by the sid[e]s all the great men of the towne with their hands before them like slaves. The place was covered over head with a rich cannapie, and under neath all carpetts. To discribe it rightly, it was like a great stage, and the Prince satt above, as the mock kings doth thear. When I was entered, I knewe not where to be placed, but went right and stood before him, wher there is an assent of thre steeps, upon which stands his secretary to deliver what is sayd or given. Breifly I tould him, being an ambassador from the King of England to his father and passing bye, I could not but in honor visitt him. He replied I was veary wellcome, and asked me many questions of the King, to which I replied as I thought fitt. But standing in that manner belowe, I demanded lycence to come up and stand by him. Hee answered: if the King of Persia or the Great Turke wher there, it might not be admitted. I replyed that I must be excused, for I doubted not hee would come downe and meete them at his gate ; but I desiered noe more priviledg then the ambassadors off such princes had, to whom I held my selfe equale. Hee protested I had that, and should in all things. Then I demanded a chaier, but I was answered noe man ever satt in that place ; but I was desiered, as a curtesye, to ease my selfe against a pillor covered above with silver, that held up his cannapie. Then I moved him for his favour for an English factory to be resident in the towne ; which he willingly granted and gave present order to the *Buxy*[1] to drawe a *firma*, both for their comming up and for their residence. I alsoe desiered his authoritye for carriadges for the Kings presents ; which he gave in chardge to the *Cuttwall*. Then I gave him my presents, which hee tooke in good part ; and after some other questions, he said: to give me content, although I might not come up wher hee satt, hee would goe into another place, wher I should come unto him. But one of my presents was a case of bottles, which tooke him up by the way ; and after I had

[1] Paymaster (Hind. *bakhshī*), generally a military paymaster.

stayd a while I hard hee was drunck,[1] and one of his officers came to me in his name with an excuse, desiering me to goe home and to take some other tyme to returne to visitt him. This night I took my feevor.

November 19.—I sent to the *Chan Channa* a smale present, but would not visitt him (expecting it from him), nor utterly disrespect him in regard of our factory. He received it with great curtesie and promised all frendship to the English. This night Mr. Boughton sickned.

November 20-24.—Being veary sick, I intended nothing but to gett the *firma* promised and carriadges to be gone from thence; wher in the one the *Buxy*, and in the other the *Cutwall*, did most manifestly abuse me, and I could find no reamedye. In this tyme the Prince, taking knowledg of my sicknes, sent one day his swoord bearer and a nother day his chamberline to visitt me, to whom I complaynd, and had promises to noe effect.

To the East India Company.
(*Add. MS*. 6115, f. 60.)

Brampore, 24 November, 1615.

What hath passed in my journy by sea to Suratt, wher by Gods mercy I arrived the 20th of September with your whole fleete in safety and extraordinary health, I hope yow expect no more from me then I could collect by circumstances and the outward face of what was resolved in councell, to all which I was a stranger, no man ever acquaynting me with any proposition or conclusion. For outward things, our course, my opinion, and such like, I refer yow to a journall sent herewith, which I pray accept in good part; and though it be long, and I, as yow suppose, a young marriner, yet yow shall fynd some cautions very necessary for yow. . . . What course I tooke at my landing the journall will relate, and how every day was spent at Suratt; in this lettre yow may expect nothing but my poore councell and judgment of this trade, and the managing therof; wherin it seems to me yow never have had any true enformation. First, for liberty of your people, I found them all in absolute servitude, so as no privat man, much lesse a nation, could endure. And though, when ther was no busines (as at our comming) it seemd not so

---

[1] Parwiz's addiction to liquor (the hereditary vice of the Mughal imperial family) is well known.

tyrannous, and that the former Governors were somewhat better, yet I have enformed my selfe off all, and it was ever servile and base, since Captain Best had a ship under his lee. And take this generall rule : it is the custome to change the governors here every yeare, and some tyme the rule of the province (as now it belongs to the Prince) ; that new humors must be dayly fedd ; and presents are here expected as due as the Kings customes, and not such as yow will send, but as they will choose. Besides, unlesse the peace may be made with the Portugall (which I have endeavored), the roade is unsafe at Swally, and yow must alway maynteyne a fleete four monthes for the safety of one ship. By water in boates ther is no possibility to transport your goods, the river beeing under command of the frigatts ;[1] and to carry them 12 mile by land[2] is an infinite chardge, trouble, and decay of many things. Soe that, to conclud, if a better could be procurd, Suratt is no residence for your factory ; or, if it must be, yow must send a pinnace of 80 tunns with 12 peices, that may goe over the barr of Suratt and carry your owne goods to the key, safe from frigatts and other dangers. Your goods, when it is come in carts, lyes ten or twelve dayes at the water side before leave cann be obtayned for boates to transport them. I entend for better securitye to motion the giving yow an ould towne called Maladafar,[3] into which your ships may come with six fadome water and anchor under the forte ; yea, they may harbor at all tymes in a storme and ride without the woormes as smooth as in Theames. The charge wilbe maynteyning 150 men in garrison and reedefying the ruyns. So yow shall command your owne, and rent your customes, or perhaps obteyne them free. But because I have no commission from yow to engage my woord to yt, I will only conditionally secure it for yow at your pleasure. For the chardge (beside the slavery yow shall ever be subject too, in a place soe remote from justice) I will prove it shalbe saved in one yeare, in carts, guards, bribes, and most tyrrannus customes. And when yow have footing in his country, yow shall alway treat of new conditions with more advantage. Cambaya nor Baroch your ships cannot come neare but that still yow are under the danger of the Portugalls and the robberye of theyr frigatts ; and of this be resolved, they will by fire or some meanes execute theyr purpose, and you shall never be secure.

[1] *I.e.* the Portuguese frigates. The term was at this time applied to shallow, undecked boats, carrying one gun in the bows. They were very useful in the shoal waters of that coast.

[2] From the beach at Swally to the city of Surat.

[3] Muzafarābād or Jafarābād, on the Kāthiāwār coast, about 30 miles N.E. of Diu.

A truce, rather than a peace, with the Mogull is newly procured by the Portugall payeing three *leeks* [1] of *rupias* for the ship taken, and licence to goe to the Red Sea signed. This newes I mett on the way; a Moore comming from court with 300 followers, sent to Meca, going to Suratt to take shipping, where three shipps have order to make ready this yeare without theyr ancient tribute to the Portugall. He had store of indico with him. I demanded what conditions concerning the English this peace did conteyne. An Armenian Christian merchaunt tould me the Mogull had answered he could not put out the English, beeing powerfull at sea, but he lefte it to the Portugalls to doe what they pleased and to endure likewise theyr fortune.[2] So that the warr is left open for both at sea, and wee must woorke and stand upon our owne safety. The Portugall mannaginge this peace bought presently as much indico as laded 180 bullocks, and are now comming downe with yt. I hear they have geven a great rate. But if eyther at Suratt or Baroch yow may have peace with the Portugall, or Gods blessing to defend your selves, and the Kinges *firmaes*

[1] ' A *leecke* [lakh] is 100,000 rupees ; a rupea is 2*s*. 3*d*. starling ' (marginal note).

[2] On 7 June, 1615 (N.S.), by the mediation of the Jesuit Xavier, Mukarrab Khān and Gonçalo Pinto da Fonseca had signed a preliminary treaty of peace, which it was agreed should be submitted to the Great Mogul and the Viceroy respectively for ratification within fifty days. Amongst other things, it provided that the English should be expelled from Surat, and in future they, as well as the Dutch, should be excluded from the territories of the Mogul ; if the fleet from England should arrive and refuse to leave, the Portuguese were to be permitted to land guns for the purpose of driving them out of the pool of Swally ; the Portuguese effects which had been confiscated were to be restored, after deducting 70,000 *xerafins* as compensation for the merchandise seized by the Portuguese, and the latter were to present a ship to the Queen-Mother in lieu of the one they had burnt at Gogo ; further, the Viceroy was for two years to grant free passes for two ships to go from Surat to the Red Sea, in addition to the ordinary yearly grant for one vessel (Bocarro's *Decada XIII*, c. 88 ; Faria y Sousa's *Asia Portuguesa* (Stevens' trans.), vol. iii. c. 6 ; Biker's *Tratados*, vol. i. p. 189).

The particulars given by the Portuguese historians are so vague that an impression has been created that the treaty was actually completed ; but this was not the case. Although the Portuguese Viceroy signified his approval, the Mogul, as stated above, refused to ratify it. This is clearly shown by Kerridge's letters from Ahmadābād now in the British Museum (*Add. MS.* 9366). Writing on 26 July, 1615, he speaks scornfully of ' Macrobchans Maye games in Cambaya, setting a Portingall on an ellephant and in a manner

for your good usadge, yet I say, except eyther yow rent the customes or keepe in pay a Mogull, who shall have commission from the King to arbitrate and negotiate your busines at your port, yow can never be free men, nor have your goods without searches, bribes, ill debts, and a thousand other insolencyes offered your people. A nother insufferable inconvenience I fynd in your trade, and a faulte in your factors in them [*sic*] that a ships lading is not provided against the arrivall of your fleete, ready at your porte, wherby long stay and huddling of busines may be prevented. Besides, I see by experience every trifle at Suratt is twice the price it was att before the ships came in; and this yeare ther was not bought a pound of goods toward lading when we came to anchor. In the trade, that all your goods come by land long journyes at your chardg, both for carts, *peons*, guardes and such trach; wheras I suppose some residence may be had upon some river that may ease most of yt; of which I will enforme my selfe, and endeavour yt. But according to such relations as I have gotten, the River of Syndu [1] were most comodious of all others, to which

publishinge a peace with them upon incertayne and base conditions (therby to blinde the Kinge)'; a little later he repeats intelligence received from Edwards at Ajmer, of ' Macrobchans cominge to the courte and acquainting the Kinge with the peace concluded, which consulted upon was greatly disliked both by the Kinge and nobillity; wherof the Jesuistes havinge intelligence, they petitioned for the Kings answere, who sayde that when the Viceroy had made restitution for all the goodes taken from his subjects he then would hearken to conditions of peace and that otherwise ther could be no conclusion'; on 24 Sept. Edwards sent a further message that the composition ' is farther of nowe then ever, for that it is resolved that the Vicereye of Goa cann make no peace with this people, the English remayning in the country, except by espetiall order from the Kinge of Spaine, and that of our expultion he hath no feare'; and later still (25 October) Kerridge says that Edwards has written that ' the expected peace with the Portingalls is confidently broken of.' These extracts, together with what is stated above, show that the proposed treaty was never formally concluded, and that in lieu thereof the Portuguese had to be content with a simple cessation of hostilities, though a show of compliance with their desires was made by issuing the *farmāns* mentioned on pp. 52, 55. It is probable that, in the later stages of the negotiations, the news of the arrival of an English ambassador with a fresh batch of presents had no small share in deterring the Mogul from agreeing to expel his compatriots.

[1] The ' Rio de Diul Sinde ' of Linschoten and Mercator had not hitherto been identified with the Indus. Diul-Sind was the name given by the Portuguese to Lahrībandar, the port of Tatta in the Indus delta.

from Lahor any thing may passe by water; besides, the cuntry is more healthy and plentiffull in indico and comodytyes fitt for England then these parts, the Portugall having great ladings yearly from thence. Further, if yow may procure the Port Jasques [*i.e.* Jask] in Persia, the places are neighboring and a countenance one to a nother; or, if not, yet many comodytyes of Persia will there be found, by reason the river comes from far within land, navigable with boates, and is truely the mouth of the famous Indus, and not that discribed by cosmographers faling into the Baye of Cambaya. And since I am fallen upon Persia, breefly ther is no such place for the benefitt of our nation to settle a trade for venting cloth and buying silke, and for good justice toward all men. And if no greate quantety at first (beeing the south parts) will away, wherby yow may returne from thence one ship: yet it may be taken in the way, and what yow vent may be sould for silkes (which are very vendible here) or ready mony, wherby these parts may be furnished and the exportation of monyes saved from England. Somewhat hath beene done in this, but to no great purpose, because all the hopes given were before the returne of Sir Robert Sheirly. Since two merchants have beene dispatched to court. . . . I purpose to send to Hispan [Ispahān] with all expedition, as well to enforme my selfe off all possibilitye as to procure your securytye and welcome to Cape Jasques, if yow please to accept yt; and after, if I may receive a commission from His Majestie, by your procurement, to treat farthar with him, or to goe to his court and meete your shipping at Cape Jasques, I doubt not to settle yow such a meanes for vent of cloth as yow shall well esteeme of yt.

Ther passeth yearly caravans from Agra to Cambalu,[1] which stands in a could part and may also vent much cloth for mony, the cuntrye beeing exceeding rich and the court near the sea, upon a navigable river; and seeing yow send to Japan, it is not many dayes wyde of yt. I entend to procure the Mogull to write in our behalfe and to know if he [*i.e.* the Chinese monarch] wilbe pleased to give yow leave to send a ships lading of cloth yearly unto him. . . .

The presents yow have this yeare sent are extremely despised by those [who] have seene them; the lyning of the coach and cover of the virginalls scorned, beeing velvett of these parts and faded to a base tawny; the knives little and meane, soe that I am enforced to new furnish the case of my owne store; all those guilte glasses on paste, and the others in leather cases with handles, are soe mean, besids so ill packt, that noe man will except of them of guift, nor buy; they are rotten with mould on the outside and decayed within. And ther is not any thing for to drive out the yeare with presents, nor any

[1] Cambalu ('seat of Cathaian Can') was of course Peking.

busines to be effected without them ; for Mr. Edwards wrote me that it is neyther person, qualetye, commission that will distinguish an ambassador of higher quality then my predecessors, but only presents ; for which I am woorst furnished, having nothing at all. The other things so decayed, as your guilded looking glasses, unglued, unfoyled, and fallen a peeices (and here no man taught to mend them) ; the burning glasses and prospectives [*i.e.* telescopes] such as no man hath face to offer to give, much less to sell, such as I can buy for sixe peence a peice ; your pictures not all woorth one penny ; and finnally, such error in the chooyce of all things, as I thincke no man ever heard of the place that was of councell. Here are nothing esteemed but of the best sorts : good cloth and fine, and rich pictures, they comming out of Italy over land and from Ormus ; soe that they laugh at us for such as wee bring. And doubtlesse they understand them as well as wee ; and what they want in knowledge they are enformed by the Jesuites and others, that in emulation of us provide them of the best at any rates. Soe that for my welcome, if it depend on presents (as I am enformed), I have smale encouragment, and shalbe ashamed to present in the Kyngs name (beeing really his embassador) things soe meane, yea, woorse then former messengers have had ; the Mogull doubtlesse making judgment of what His Majestie is by what he sends. . . .

I can say little of the estate of your busines ; only it is kept in the brest of some few men, and your jelousy to give mee any authorytye of your busines or factors hath disabled me to looke into many things that should have redounded to your profitt. I know not what suspect yow had that I would eyther abuse them or your stocke ; but yow were deceived to my great ease and your owne disadvantage, it beeing so divuldged here (as I thincke, by your expresse command, or for some other vayne end) that I have nothing to doe with the merchants nor their busines, nor that they neede make mee no account of any thing ; wherby, if I but fynd just fault or give honest councell, the meanest can say it concerns not me : I have not to doe with them. I write not this that I desire myne owne trouble or others ill will, but that I may be dischardged of any blame if all goe not soe well as it should or that I cannot enforme yow of such things as want of creditt here keepes from me. . . . Yet I cannot stand by and see yow abused ; and shall talke bigg, though I have no power to reforme. If the Generall keepe not good eyes (which I doubt not, he beeing every way a very able man) yow shalbe sufficiently abused in privat trade ; for this I know, that many of the meanest, and unde the degrees of factors, brought ashore 100*li.*, 80*li.*, and few under 50*li.*, which went liberally for callicoes and the like. . . .

... Yow may thincke that I have broken your order in desiring the Generall to pay me 200*li*. beforehand, on my second yeares wages now currant ; because he frugally for yow made curious of yt, and yet curteously, when he saw reason, did yt for mee. I desire to make this apologie for him : I did not thincke yow held it reasonable I should land and goe a great journy without one penny in my purse for my privatt use ; for yow all knew I carried none ; that yow gave mee and lent mee, I protest I disbursed, with additions of myne owne, for my preperation ; and I never ment to make use of any of that allowed for my chardge for my particular, but to receive yt and expend yt and give an account of yt apart to a penny. ...

Besides, I have required that my servants halfe yeares wages behynd may be payed here the first yeare, for els they must goe naked, and I am not able to supply all wants. What is 50*li*. for 15 men—about 3*li*. apeice, a poore allowance for such as must attend mee ; and it is not 50*li*. more then yow give me that dischardges theyr wages ; [1] so far I am from gayne. ...

... For my extraordinarye expence of goeing to Court and dyett, I have undertaken the carriadge of the presents and your servants sent with them (wherof the coach is extreame cumbersome) and received 1,000 royalls of eight ... wherof yow shall receive by my first from Adgmere a just accompt. ... I landed at Suratt, where I was esteemed an imposture like my predecessors (for the Jesuits dive deepe into your secretts and blaze them) ; two before having taken the title of ambassador, Mr. Hawkins and Mr. Edwards,[2] but so that they have almost made yt ridiculous to come under that qualetye. I speake not to disgrace Mr. Edwards, of whom I heare nothing but well, as a marchaunt ; but he hath not so understood what he assumed as to doe yt any honor. I was enforced for honor and to repayre His Majesties and your reputation to give somwhat extraordinary, yet not as I would if I had a good

---

[1] 'Servants wages paid in the countrie more then the Companyes allowance—112*l*. 10*s*.' (MS., f. 280).

[2] 'I heare Mr. Edwards disavowes it' (marginal note by Roe). Edwards had been specially cautioned by the Company not to assume the title, and had consequently resolved to describe himself merely as a messenger from the English King (see *Letters Received*, vol. ii. p. xix). On the other hand, Kerridge (letter to Roe, 10 Oct., 1615, *Add. MS*. 9366, f. 12) distinctly asserted that ' Mr. Edwards in his landinge for the reputation of our buisines assumed the title and qualletye [of ambassador] and in that nature was presented unto the Kinge and so hath continewed in indifferent good esteeme, notwithstanding his course of frugall livinge hath somthinge impayred the reputacion of so honourable an employment.'

purse ; which I have helped many wayes more then by yours, and often with myne owne. It is better to build from the ground then to reedefy a rotten house. . . .

Only I lett yow for conclusion know the estate of the Portugall in all these parts. By the disgust of the Persian ; [by] the small good will of the Mogull, enforced by necessytye that his people may goe to sea, who else is weary of him ; which if they might effect by any other way (for which purpose I have beene motioned to have shipping arrive here quarterly, and so some would be here alway) he would assist to turne him from his coast : by the Dutch plantation below him, and the disreputation of his beeing twise beaten by us, he is on veary ill tearmes and with a little helpe would be utterly broken heare. But His Majestie must be dealt with. It is good pollycye of state to sett foote on him now he is falling, and if I had authoritye to treate roundly with the Persian and to engage any helpe to the Mogull by sea, I could dissolve him quite in these parts. Or if this may not be convenient to enterprice, yet if yow will give him one good blow, which yow have power and reason to doe, whensoever yow will send sixe good ships togither for this place, under colour of safe conduct of those to returne hence, and so to take theyr course for the sowthward, they may ride in the roade and enforme them selves dayly of the comminge in of the gallions for Goa, which arive alsoe in September, and lade in December for Lisbone. The *peons* of Suratt may and will goe to Goa for 30s. and bringe weekly advise when they beginn to lade ; for they halfe lade within the barr, under the fort, and then come out to take in the rest ; where they ryde unfitted for any defence, halfe their men ashoare with frigatts to fill them ; and then four of your ships may way and bee with them in so many dayes, and take what they please, almost without shooting a shootte, lade themselves, and fire them ; and one prosperous assault upon them would more disharten them, bring them to better termes (when they sawe your resolution to prosequute them), give you more reputation and good booty, then twenty repulses ever in your owne defence. It is a rule in warr : the offensive is both the nobler and the safer part. They make this use of your sparing them : that their king dares doe any affront to yow, because the King of England is a tributarye ; but that yow dare not attempt them, but only defend your goods, least the King of Portugal should punish His Majestie for such bouldnes at home.

It is thought requisite that yow seeke trade in the terretoryes of the Mogull in Bengale. I will enforme myselfe of the fittest port and procure a *firma* for residence of your factors. . . .

Since my arrivall at Bramport, beeing the 14 of November 1615, I visited the Prince ; which I rather did because ther was a purpose to settle a factory ther. . . . I am hear visited by Gods hand with a terrible feaver, now sixe dayes, and brought veary weake ; abused in my carriadges, notwithstanding the Prince gave order for me, and the Kings *firma*. The *Cuttwall* tooke my mony and made price as he pleased ; and when I sawe his abuse, I sought abroad, but none would stirr without his leave. So that my chardge is above my expectation, but I must suffer it, as I doe manyfould and infinite abuses, this beeing a generall character : every man will promise any thing, but to this hower I never found one man that ever held his woord in any one thing without beeing followed and sued too sixe dayes togither—no answere but ' to-morowe.' Notwithstanding, I will goe one in this weake estate, not able to walke two turnes in my tent, and divers of my men in the same case : that yow shall see I will rather venture to end my life honestly, in performing my dutie. . . . The cuntrye is all slavish. In this towne of Bramport, the ancient and cheefe cytty, except the castle and some fewe ill howses of commanders, your swyne lye better then any man ; and what I endure I best knowe. . . .

November 25.—Mr. Boughton dyed,[1] and I buried him by leave early the next morning.

November 26.—Being enforced to take the *Cutwalls* price, I laded.

November 27.—In much weaknes, beeing carried in a *pallankie*,[2] I parted Brampore, and lodged that night at Raypora [Raīpur], 3 *course* off.

November 28.—15 *course* to Burgome [Borgāon]. This day I lost my carriadges, and all my company. Beeing very sicke, I hastened away in my *palenkie* to Burgome ; but they not beeing able to follow, we were afrayd one of another. I was without tent or provision, and gott into a little open house,[3] and soe rested in my *palenkie*. I sent away a *peon*, who before morning returned with newes of one another.

November 29.—My carriadges and company came to me ; and I rested this day, beeing soe sick as at night I was past sence and given over for dead ; but God raysed mee.

[1] According to Van Ravesteyn he had been ill for three days.

[2] Hind. *pālki*, a litter. The form in which Roe uses the word is nearer the original than the more usual ' palankin,' which bears traces of its derivation through the Portuguese.

[3] A *choultry*, or resting-place for travellers.

ON THE WAY TO AJMER

November 30.—In the morning came a *firman* from Sultan Pervies for our entended factory at Brampore; which I dispeeded backe to Surat. At noone I remooved 7 *course*.

December 1.—10 *course* to Bicangome [Bikangāon].

December 2.—7 *course*. *December* 3.—5 *course*.

December 4.—To Ecbarpur,[1] 11 *course*. It stands on a goodly river, falling into the sea nere Baroch [Broach], and is doubtles navigable.

December 5.—Spent in passing the river called Narbodah, being forced to unlade.

December 6.—8 *course*; lodging in a wood, not farr from the Kings famous castle of Mandoa [Māndu], which stands on a steepe hill, walled round in circuit 14 *course*. The castle is faire and of woonderfull greatnes.

December 7.—10 *course*. *December* 8.—8 *course*.

December 9.—10 *course*. *December* 10.—12 *course*.

December 11.—16 *course*. *December* 12.—14 *course*.

December 13.—6 *course*.

December 14.—I rested to drye my tents and ease my selfe and company.

December 15.—6 *course*. *December* 16.—6 *course*.

December 17.—12 *course*. Hence I sent Mr. Shalbancke[2] to Adsmere to prepare for mee.

---

[1] Akbarpur, where there is a ford over the Narbadā, a few miles S. of Māndu.

[2] Joseph Salbank, the oldest servant the Company had in India—' the almond tre,' he wrote to them, ' hath displaied his white blossoms upon my head ever since I was admitted into your service.' Roe describes him as ' a very playne ould man, hardy to travell and thrifty, and for having beene often in the country fitt to receive some pension at home rather then wages abroad.' He was one of the original subscribers upon the establishment of the Company, and went out to the East as purser of the *Susan* in the First Voyage. Next he took part in the disastrous Fourth Voyage. With others of the crew of the shipwrecked *Ascension*, he made his way to Agra, whence he started home overland in company with Covert. At Bagdad they heard that Sir Henry Middleton was in the Red Sea, whereupon Salbank set out to join him. On the road, however, he learned that Middleton was a prisoner in the hands of the Turks, and consequently determined to make for Sokotra in the hope of finding some English shipping there; but he fell into the hands of the Portuguese, who carried him by way of Muskat and Ormus

S.T.R. F

December 18.—5 *course* to Cytor,[1] an ancient cytty, ruined, on a hill, but so that it appears a toombe of woonderfull magnificence. Ther stands above 100 churches, all of carved stone, many fayre towers and lanthornes cutt thorowgh, many pillars and innumerable houses; but no one inhabitant. Ther is but one ascent to the hill, it beeing præcipitious, sloping up, cutt out of the rocke, having four gates in the ascent, before one arrive at the citty gate, which is magnificent. The hill is in compasse at the top about 8 *course*, and at the S.W. end a goodly ould castle. I lodged by a poore village at the foote of the hill. This citty stands in the country of one Ranna,[2] a Prince newly subdued by this King, or rather bought to confesse tribute. The citty was woone by Ecbar-sha, father to this Mogull. Ranna is rightly descended from Porus, that valient Indian overcome by Alexander, soe that I take this citty to have beene one of the ancient seates of Porus; though Dely, much farther N., bee reported to have beene the cheefest, famooues now only in ruynes.[3] Neere that stands a pillar erected by Alexander the Conqueror, with a Gricke [4] inscription. The present Mogull and his ancestors, descendants of Tamberlan, have brought all the ancient cyttyes to ruine, having dispeopled them and forbidden reparation. I know

to Goa, and so to Lisbon, whence he returned to England. In 1613 e went out as chief merchant in the *Expedition* (Twelfth Voyage); and he had now come to India for the third time in the fleet which brought out Roe. He was chiefly employed at Agra, where (as will be seen later) he ran considerable risks from the plague epidemic. In 1618 he was employed as chief merchant in the voyage to the Red Sea, and was again sent thither in 1619 and 1622. He was drowned in the oversetting of the *Whale* in March, 1623.

[1] Chitor, the ancient capital of Mewār. After its capture by Akbar in 1568, its temples and palaces were dismantled and all symbols of regality taken away. Udi Singh, the Mewār Rānā, retreated to Udaipur, and founded there a new capital.

[2] Amar Singh, Udi Singh's grandson. He had been reduced to submission in 1613-14 by an army under Prince Khurram and Mahābat Khān.

[3] This refers, of course, to Firozābād (Old Delhi).

[4] 'Great' in *Purchas* (as originally in the MS.). For an account of this pillar see *Early Travels in India*, p. 248.

not out of what reason, unlesse they would have nothing remembred of greatnes beyond theyr beginnings, as if theyr famely and the world were coevalls.

December 19.—12 *course. December 20.*—10 *course.*
December 21.—10 *course.*
December 22.—9 *course.* At noone Mr. Edwards the agent mett me, accompanied with the famous unwearied walker Tho. Coryatt (who on foote had passed most of Europe and Asya, and was now arrived in India, beeing but the beginning of his purposed travells)[1] and some other Christians resident in Adsmere. I lodged in the feilds, Mr. Edwards having sett up his tents and provided for mee.

[1] Coryat's own account of his overland journey to India and his experiences there will be found in *Early Travels*, pp. 234-87.

Chronicling Roe's arrival in India, he speaks of him as his 'deare friend'; but the ambassador, who was keenly sensitive to anything likely to lower English prestige, seems to have been little pleased to renew their acquaintance in such circumstances. He wrote, however, good-humouredly enough, to Lord Pembroke (14 February, 1616), of 'Thom Coryatt ... whom the fates have sent hither to ease mee, and now lives in my house. He came heither afoote, hath past by Constantanople, Jerusalem, Bethlem, Damascus, and breefly thorowgh all the Turkes territory, seene every post and pillar, observed every tombe, visited the monuments of Troy, Persia, and this kings dominion, all afoote, with most unwearied leggs, and is now for Samarcand in Tartarya to kisse Tamberlans tombe, from thence to Susa, and to Prester Jhac in Ethiopia, wher he will see the Hill Amara, all afoote, and so foote it to Odcombe. His notes are already to great for portage, some left at Aleppo, some at Hispan—enough to make any stationer an alderman that shall but serve the printer with paper. And his excercise here or recreation is making or reapeating orations, principally of my lady Hartford.' Peyton, in his Journal, records that Coryat welcomed Roe to Ajmer in 'a long, eloquent oration.'

In September, 1616, when the English factory was about to be broken up, upon the intended departure of the Mogul, Coryat left for Agra. He had first, to Roe's annoyance, taken opportunity to address an oration (in Persian) to the Emperor, who threw him a hundred rupees. Reproved by the ambassador for this action, as tending 'to the dishonour of our nation, that one of our countrey should present himselfe in that beggerly and poore fashion to the King, out of an insinuating humour, to crave money of him,' Coryat answered (according to his own account) 'in that stout and resolute manner ... that he was contented to cease nibling at me.'

December 23.—I arrived at Adsmere [1] (10 *course*), comming in privatly in the evening, beeing not able to sitt upp. From Brampore toward Adsmere, for six dayes my course was much westerly or N.W. to compasse the hills, but after due north, or so that the bearing from one another is next hand N. by W. and S. by E.; the distance 209 *courses*, which I judge about 418 miles English, the *courses* beeing longer then toward the sea.

December 24-30.—I kept my bed and was not able to stirr, but sent my excuses to the King.

December 31.—This night the King, impatient of my delay and eager on his presents, suspecting I was not so ill as I pretended, sent a gentellman with a wyld hogg to mee for a present, which hee kylld in hunting; and chardged him to see mee, so that I was forced to admitt him into my chamber, wher he saw my weaknes and gave satisfaction to the King.

January 1-4, 1615-16.—I began to recover and sitt up.

January 5.—Mr. Edwards departed for Suratt.[2]

January 6-9.—I prepared to see the King.

January 10.—I went to court at four in the evening to the *durbar*,[3] which is the place wher the Mogull sitts out daylie,

---

[1] Ajmer, 230 miles S.W. of Delhi and 48 miles from Jaipur in the same direction, had been a favourite abode of Akbar, who found it both a charming residence and a convenient centre for his operations in Rājputāna. Jahāngīr had made it his headquarters during the war with the Udaipur Rānā, and had been there over two years at the date of Roe's arrival.

[2] After a farewell audience of the Emperor. As Edwards had nothing to present, Roe furnished him for this purpose with a ' mapp of the world, bought in Antwerpe, as great as the side of a roome, cost 40*s*.' (Roe's Accounts, f. 277 of the MS.).

[3] In Douglas's *Bombay and Western India* (vol. i. p. 305) was given a coloured drawing from an old painting at Jaipur which, in the author's opinion, represented the Emperor Jahāngīr giving audience to Sir Thomas Roe. Such an interpretation, however, appears exceedingly doubtful, for the figure pointed out as Roe is not only very unlike him in appearance, but occupies quite a subordinate position in the picture. Moreover, the costume and weapons are Indian, whereas we know from Terry (p. 218) that Roe and his suite wore always English dress. ' For my lord ambassadour and his company, we all kept to our English habits, made as light

THE CITY OF AJMER

to entertayne strangers, to receive petitions and presents, to give commands, to see and to bee seene. To digresse a little from my reception, and declare the customes of the court, will enlighten the future discourse. The King hath no man but eunuchs that comes within the lodgings or retyring roomes of his house : his weomen watch within, and guard him with manly weapons. They doe justice on upon another for offences. He comes every morning to a wyndow, called the *jarruco*,[1] looking into a playne before his gate, and showes him selfe to the common people. At noone hee returns thither and sitts some howers to see the fight of eliphants and willd beasts ; under him within a rayle attend the men of rancke ; from whence hee retiers to sleepe among his woemen. At afternoone he returnes to the *durbar* before mentioned. At eight, after supper, he comes downe to the *guzelcan*,[2] a faire court, wher in the middest is a throune erected of free stone wherein he sitts, but some tymes below in a chayre ; to which are none admitted but of great qualetye, and few of those without leave ; wher he discourses of all matters with much

and coole as possibly we could have them ; his wayters in red taffata cloakes, guarded with green taffata, which they alwayes wore when they went abroad with him ; myself in a long black cassock.' We must therefore take leave to doubt the correctness of the ascription, especially as no such claim was put forward when the picture was first brought to notice in the *Journal of Indian Art*, No. 25 (1889). It may be added that in Lady Wantage's collection, exhibited at South Kensington in 1917, there is a painting, entitled ' Jahāngīr inspecting a golden image,' which resembles this one in every detail, save that the image referred to is included.

While on this subject attention may be called to the fact that Peter Mundy, when at Agra in 1631-33, saw in the Moti Bāgh of the palace a portrait of Roe, apparently in the form of a fresco (*Travels*, vol. ii. p. 215).

[1] The *jharokha*, or ' interview-window,' which Roe describes at greater length later. The royal headquarters were at the fort, now called the Magazine, on the city side of which there is a window answering to Roe's description.

[2] *Ghusl-khāna*, ' bath-room,' hence ' private apartment ' (privy chamber). Professor Jadunath Sarkar states that the use of this term for the hall of private audience arose from the fact that the apartment used by Akbar for this purpose was next to his bath-room.

affabilitye.[1] Ther is noe busines done with him concerning
the state, goverment, disposition of warr or peace, but at
one of these two last places, wher it is publiquely propounded,
and resolved, and soe registred ; which, if it were woorth the
curiosytye, might bee seene for two shillings, but the common
basse people knew as much as the councell, and the newes
every day is the Kings new resolutions, tossed and censured
by every rascall. This course is unchangeable, except sicknes
or drinck prevent yt ; which must be known, for, as all his
subjects are slaves, so is he in a kynd of reciprocall bondage,
for he is tyed to observe these howres and customes so precisely
that, if hee were unseene one day and noe sufficient reason
rendred, the people would mutinie ; two dayes noe reason can
excuse, but that he must consent to open his doores and bee

[1] Compare Terry's account (p. 389) : ' First, early in the morning,
at that very time the sun begins to appear above the horizon, he
appears unto his people in a place very like unto one of our balconies,
made in his houses or pavilions for his morning appearance, directly
opposite to the East, about seven or eight foot high from the ground ;
against which time a very great number of his people, especially
of the greater sort, who desire as often as they can to appear in his
eye, assemble there together, to give him the *Salam*, or good morning,
crying all out, as soon as they see their King, with a loud voice,
Padsha Salamet, which signifies, *live O great King*, or *O great King,
health and life*. . . . At noon he shows himself in another place
like the former, on the south-side ; and a little before sun-set, in
a like place, on the west-side of his house or tent ; but as soon as
the sun forsakes the hemisphear, he leaves his people, ushered in
and out with drums and winde instruments, and the peoples acclama-
tions. . . . And between seven and nine of the clock at night, he
sits within his house or tent more privately, in a spacious place
called his *goozalcan*, or bathing house, made bright like day by
abundance of lights ; and here the King sits mounted upon a
stately throne ; where his nobles, and such as are favoured by him,
stand about him ; others find admittance to, but by special leave
from his guard, who cause every one that enters that place to breath
upon them, and if they imagine that any have drunk wine, they
keep him out. At this time my lord ambassadour made his usual
addresses to him, and I often waited on him thither, and it was a
good time to do business with that King, who then was for the most
part very pleasant, and full of talk unto those which were round
him, and so continued till he fell asleep (oft times by drinking), and
then all assembled immediately quitted the place, beside those
which were his trusted servants, who by turns watched his person.'

seene by some to satisfye others. On Tuesday at the *jarruco* he sitts in judgment, never refusing the poorest mans complaynt; where hee heares with patience both parts, and some tymes sees with too much delight in blood the excecution done by his eliphants. *Illi meruere : sed quid tu ut adesses ?* [1]

At the *durbar* I was led right before him, at the enterance of an outward rayle, where mett mee two principall noble slaves to conduct mee nearer. I had required before my going leave to use the customes of my country; which was freely granted, soe that I would performe them punctually. When I entred within the first rayle I made a reverance; entering in the inward rayle a nother; and when I came under the King a theird. The place is a great court, whither resort all sorts of people. The King sitts in a little gallery over head; ambassidors, the great men and strangers of qualety within the inmost rayle under him, raysed from the ground, covered with canopyes of velvet and silke, under foote layd with good carpetts; the meaner men representing gentry within the first rayle, the people without in a base court, but soe that all may see the King. This sitting out hath soe much affinitye with a theatre—the manner of the king in his gallery; the great men lifted on a stage as actors; the vulgar below gazing on—that an easy description will informe of the place and fashion. The King prevented [*i.e.* forestalled] my dull enterpreter, bidding me welcome as to the brother of my master. I delivered His Majesties lettre, translated; and after my commission, wheron hee looked curiously; after, my presents, which were well received. He asked some questions, and with a seeming care of my health, offering me his phisitions, and advising mee to keepe my house till I had recovered strength; and if in the interim I needed any thing, I should freely send to him, and obteyne my desiers. He dismissed me with more favour and outward grace (if by the Christians I were not flattered) then ever was sheowed to any ambassador, eyther of the Turke or Persian, or other whatsoever.

---

[1] This may be freely rendered: 'Doubtless they have merited their punishment; but why should you be present?' As pointed out by Mr. E. Bensly, it is an adaptation of a passage in Seneca's *Epistles* (vii. 5).

January 12.—Hee sent a gentellman for my commission to show his queene[1] the seale; which he kept one night, and returned yt with such care that the bringer durst not deliver it but to my owne hands.

January 14.—I sent to the Prince Sultan Coronne,[2] his third sonne by byrth but first in favour, that I determined to visitt him, not doubting he would use me with due respect; for I was enformed he was enemy to all Christians, and therfore feared some affront. He answered I should be welcome, and receive the same content I had from his father. Hee is lord of Suratt, our cheefe residence, and his favour important for us.

January 15-21.—These days I stirrd not abroad, the King and Prince beeing often a hunting; from whom I received two wild hoggs, part of theyr quarry.

To Lord Carew.[3]

Asmere, the Court of the Mogoll,
January 17, 1615[-16].

My Lord,

Only for promise, which is an honest debt, I send Your Lordship a journall till my arrivall at Brampore, a citie of houses made of mudde, where one of the Kings sonnes keepeth his court. He is called Perveys. I had need to write an apologie for it, there being nothing of worth, nothing memorable, and yet not my fault; but I had rather trust your

---

[1] It is scarcely necessary to recall the romantic story of Nūr Mahal (better known by her later title of Nūr Jahān)—her marriage to Shīr Afgan, his assassination, and her subsequent union with the emperor, who had already been attracted to her before her first marriage. At this period her influence over her husband was so unbounded that she practically ruled the empire, and Roe soon found out the error he had made in not seeking to conciliate her and her partisans.

[2] Prince Khurram, afterwards Shāh Jahān.

[3] This letter is not in the MS., and consequently is here printed from Purchas's work (vol. i. p. 581), where it is introduced with a note that it was found 'amongst Master Hakluyt his papers.' Purchas purposely omits the name of the person to whom it was addressed, but that this was Lord Carew is evident from the latter's reply (see *Letters of Lord Carew*, p. 27). Carew also mentions the receipt of a letter from Roe dated at the Cape, and another which, together with a further portion of Roe's journal, reached him on 28 Sept., 1617 (*Ibid.* pp. 27, 122).

noblenesse, then trouble you with excuses ; and so descend to a more universall description of the state and customes of the land.

They have no written law. The King by his owne word ruleth, and his governours of provinces by that authoritie. Once a week he sitteth in judgement patiently, and giveth sentence for crimes capitall and civill. He is every mans heire when he dyeth ; which maketh him rich, and the countrey so evill builded. The great men about him are not borne noble, but favourites raised ; to whom hee giveth (if it be true) wonderfull meanes. They are reckoned by horses ; that is to say ; coronels of twelve thousand horses, which is the greatest (whereof are foure, besides his sonnes and wife) : so descending to twentie horses. Not that any of these are bound to keepe or raise any at all ; but the King assigneth them so much land as is bound to maintaine so many horses as a rent, each horse at five and twentie pounds sterling by the yeere ; which is an incredible revenue given away, so many (that is, almost all but the ploughmen, artificers, and tradesmen in townes) living upon it. But as they die, and must needs gather, so it returneth to the King like rivers to the sea, both of those he gave to, and of those that have gained by their owne industry. But for the most part he leaveth the widowes and children their horses, stuffe, and some other stocke, and then putteth them into a signiory, if the fathers were of sixe or seven thousand horses, perhaps of a thousand or five hundred ; and so setteth them to begin the world anew, and advanceth them as they deserve of him. They all rise by presenting him ; which they strive to doe both richly and rarely, some giving a hundred thousand pounds in jewels at a time.

He hath one beloved wife among foure, that wholly governeth him. He received lately a present from the King of Bisampore,[1] to obtaine peace (whose ambassador knocked his head three times against the ground) of six and thirtie elephants, of two whereof the chaines and all tackles were of beaten gold, to the weight of foure hundred pounds, two of silver, of the same fashion, the rest of copper ; fiftie horses richly furnished, and ten *leckes* of *rupias* in jewels, great pearles, and balasse rubies. Everie *lecke* is an hundred thousand *rupias*, every *rupia* two shillings sixe pence sterling ;[2] so tenne *leckes* is a million of *rupias*.

[1] Bījāpur. Roe evidently had this account from Coryat, who was an eye-witness (see *Early Travels in India*, p. 250). Jahāngīr's own account will be found in his *Memoirs* (vol. i. p. 298).

[2] 'Some say two shillings, some two shillings three pence.'—Note by Purchas. Roe seems often to take the former figure.

His territorie is farre greater then the Persians, and almost equall, if not as great as, the Turkes. His meanes of money, by revenue, custome of presents, and inheriting all mens goods, above both. His countrey lyeth west to Sinde, and so stretcheth to Candahar, and to the mountaines of Taurus north; to the east as farre as the utmost parts of Bengala, and the borders of Ganges; and south to Decan. It is two thousand miles square at the least, but hath many pettie Kings within, that are tributaries.

The true descended heire of Porus, that was overcome by Alexander, called Ranna, is lately conquered, more by composition then force; the King having rather bought him then wonne him, and hereby no way augmented his revenue, but given a great pension to him. His countrey I crossed, betweene this towne of Asmere and Brampore, Cetor having beene anciently the chiefe towne, and surely [*i.e.* securely] standing on an hill, steepe as a rocke, some fifteene miles about, that is all walled; the citie within but with one ascent, and five admirable gates in the ascent, all ruined and no person dwelling. But there stand an hundred *muschees*,[1] many lanternes, and such reverend and brave reliques of imagerie and carved workes, that few or hardly any where can be equalled. In generall, all the old cities are beaten downe, by what policie I understand not; but the King seeketh the ruine of any thing not begunne by his ancestors, so that all the land hath not an house fit for a cottager, but in such cities as he favoureth. Surat is best builded of any; and in old time they in these parts made mightie workes, which every day decay. At Surat there is a tanke for water of free-stone, in a polygon forme, of above an hundred sides, every side eight and twenty yards; it hath staires on every side for men to descend, and many stopes[2] for horses. It is a wonderous worke, both for the hugenesse and for the brave building.[3]

I have now on the court to touch, and mine entertainment. The King never used any ambassadour with so much respect; without any dispute giving mee leave to use mine owne customes, not requiring that of me, which he useth of the Persian. He presented me with a welcome before I spake, and said the King and he were brothers, with many other courteous words. I having bin sicke, he offered me physitians. He tooke the presents in good part, and was so fond of the coach, that at night in his court he got into it, and made two or three

---

[1] Hindu temples, he should say, not mosques.

[2] Stoops, *i.e.* descents or slopes.

[3] The celebrated Gopi-talão, or Gopi-pond, so called from the name of the person at whose expense it was formed. It has long been dry, and is now used as a garden.

of my men draw him a little in it. He is very affable, and of a cheerefull countenance, without pride. Three times a day hee sitteth out in three places : once, to see his elephants and beasts fight, about noone ; after, from foure to five or sixe, to entertaine all that visit him ; at night, from nine till mid-night, with all his great men, but none else, where he is below with them, in all familiaritie. I visited him in the second of these, where I found him in a court, set above like a King in a play, and all his nobles and my selfe below on a stage covered with carpets—a just theater ; with no great state, but the canopies over his head, and two standing on the heads of two wooden elephants, to beat away flies. They weare nothing but calicoes, but are ever attendant.

The great men ride in traines, some two hundred, some five hundred, foot-men following them, and foure or five banners carried before them, and an hundred or two hundred horses after them. This is all their pride. They keepe their horses most delicately, fed with butter [*i.e. ghi*] and sugar ; and though they be not very great, yet they are of delicate shape, both of Persia, Arabs, and of this land.

I have one observation more to make of the falsenesse of our maps, both of Mercator and all others, and their ignorance in this countrey. First, the famous River Indus doth not emptie himselfe into the sea at Cambaya as his chiefe mouth, but at Sinde.[1] My reason is : Lahor stands upon Indus, from whence to Sinde it is navigable, to Cambaya not so. Lahor in the maps is also falsely set downe, it lying north from Surat above a thousand miles.[2] The citie where the Kings ordinarie residence is, Agra, not described at all ; but it standeth north north-east from Surat on a river that fals into Ganges. But the King now resideth in a base old citie, wherein is no house but of mudde, not so great as a cottage on Hownslo-heath ; only himselfe hath one of stone. His Lords live in tents, and I have suddenly built to my mudde wals, upon canes, a doozen thatched roomes. This towne is short of Agra ten daies journey, two hundred miles, which standeth from hence north north-east. This place is from Bramport north foure hundred and fiftie miles ; Bramport from Surat east about two hundred miles. The latitude neere five and twentie degrees.[3]

Thus, My Lord, I have said some-what, but to little purpose. I forget not some bookes for yow ; but load-stones heere are none. They are in the farre east countries. Neither is there

---

[1] Della Valle points out the same error (*Travels*, Hakluyt Soc. ed., vol. i. p. 63).

[2] The distance in a straight line is about 750 miles.

[3] The true latitude of Ajmer is 26° 27′ 10″ N.

any correspondence with China. To Persia, and so to Aleppo, there goe caravans ; to Cathaya none.

Heere is no newes but of Persia. The King hath taken away water and reliefe from Ormus, and banished the Portugals his territories. He hath lately over-runne the poore Georgians with fire and sword ; and, being of an unquiet nature, intendeth the conquest of the Uzbiques,[1] a nation between Samarchand and him, which he aymes at. He lately strucke off his sonnes head with his owne hand.[2] Hee is favoured and feared of the Mogoll, as being lord of the more warlike nation ; for these are more then halfe *Bramanes*, whose religion is not to kill a louse byting them, and the Mogolls are an effeminate people. So that the Turke the last yeere sending on ambassage to entreate him not to assist the Persian, hee gave him very harsh entertainment ; made his *salem* to the ground ; and, as soone as he was dismissed, sent the Persian ten *leckes* of *rupias*.[3]

I shall be glad to doe Your Lordship service in England ; for this is the dullest, basest place that ever I saw, and maketh me weary of speaking of it. Therefore if yow be also weary of reading, I am glad. I shall desire Your Lordship to let Master Hackwell [4] reade the journall ; for I promised him one, but I had not leasure to write it.

And so, with all respect and little ceremonie, I hope to returne to doe yow better services. In the meane time to live a miserable life, though with abundance and state enough ; yet I want the conversation and presence of those friends I love and honour ; in which number Your Lordship hath made me presume to esteeme yow and to account my selfe

Your Lordships humble friend, to doe yow service,

THOMAS ROE.

January 22.—I visited the Prince, who at nine in the morning sitts out in the same manner as his father, to dispatch

[1] The Uzbeg Tartars.

[2] Prince Safī Mīrza, the Shāh's eldest son. When Jahāngīr received the Persian envoy (as described later), he inquired the reason for this act. The ambassador excused it on the ground that unless he had been thus prevented, the prince would certainly have slain his father (*Memoirs*, vol. i. p. 338). The murder was really carried out by a slave (*Ibid.* p. 294, and Sykes's *History of Persia*, vol. ii. p. 267).

[3] This Turkish embassy is not mentioned in Jahāngīr's *Memoirs*.

[4] William Hakewill (1574-1655), the legal antiquary. Carew (*Letters*, pp. 106, 107) refers to him as ' your olld acquayntance Mr. Hackwell, the lawyer,' and mentions his having married a niece of Bacon.

his busines and to be seene of his followers. He is proud naturally, and I feard my entertaynment. But on some occasion he not resolving to come out, when he heard of my arrivall, sent a principal officer to meete mee, who conducted mee into a good roome (never before done to any), and entertayning me with discourse of our own bussines halfe an hower untill the Prince was ready; who came abroad on purpose, and used me better then his promise. I delivered him a present, such as I had, but not in the name of His Majestie, it beeing too meane; but excused it that the King could not take knowledge of his beeing lord of Suratt, so lately conferrd on him, but hereafter I doubted not His Majestie would send to him according to his woorth: this was the respect of the merchants, who humbly recommended themselves to his favour and protection. He received all in very good part; and after opening of some greavances and injuries suffered at Suratt by us from his Governors, of which, for respect to him, I had forborne to complayne to the King off, he promised mee speedy and effectuall justice, and to confirme our securytye by any propositions I should offer; professing to be ignorant of any thing past, but what hee had received by Asaph Chan [1] delivered by mee; especially of any command to dismisse us,[2] which the Governor had falsly coyned and for which he should dearly answer. Soe he dismissed mee full of hope to rectifye the decayed estate of our reputation, with promise of a *firmaen* for Suratt effectually.

[1] Mīrzā Abūl Hasan, better known by his title of Āsaf Khān. He held a strong position at court, as son of the prime minister, elder brother of Nūr Mahal, and father of Prince Khurram's favourite wife, Mumtāz Mahal. When the prince came to the throne as Shāh Jahān, Āsaf Khān was advanced to high dignities; and he died (1641) in possession of great wealth. His eldest son was Shāista Khān, who, as Governor of Bengal, came into collision with the English settlers at Hūgli.

[2] See pp. 55, 60. After Roe's departure the Governor had forced the General and others to give an undertaking in writing 'for clearing the cuntry after the expiration of one yeare to come, sayeing it was the great Mugolls pleasure to be soe ordred; yett not anye wayes denying us free trade, but enjoyned us not to make any residence of aboad longer then our shipps were theare' (Peyton's Journal, f. 34).

January 24.—I went to the *durbar* to visitt the King, who, seeing mee afarr off, beckned with his hand, giving signe I should not staye the cerimony of asking leave, but come up to him; where hee appoynted me a place above all other men, which I after thought fitt to mayntayne.[1] I gave him a small present,[2] it beeing the custome when any body hath busines to give somewhat, and those that cannot come neare to speake send in or hould up their guift, which hee eccepts, bee it but a *rupie*, and demands their bussines. The same course hee held with mee. Having looked curiously and asked many questions of my present, he demanded what I required of him. I answered: justice: that, on the assurance of His Majesties *firmaen* sent into England, the King my master had not only given leave to many of his subjects to come a dangerous voyadge with their goods, but had sent mee to congratulate the amytye so happely begunne betweene two soe mighty nations, and to confirme the same: but that I found the English seated at Amadavas [Ahmadābād] enjuryed by the Governor in their persons and goods, fined, exacted upon, and kept as prisoners: that at everie towne new customes were taken of our goods passing to the port, contrarie to all justice and the former articles of trade.[3] To which hee answered hee was sorry; it should be amended; and presently gave order for two *firmanes* very effectually according to my desire to be signed, one to the Governor of Amadavaz to restore mony exacted from Mr. Kerridge,[4] and to use the English with all

[1] The exact position of each dignitary was minutely regulated (see *Āīn-i-Akbari*, vol. i. p. 160).

[2] A 'clock and two other trifles' (*Letter to E.I. Co.*, 25 Jan., 1616; reproduced in part at p. 98).

[3] Roe had consulted Āsaf Khān, who had 'encouraged him to complayne,' Ahmadābād 'beeing absolute under the King.'

[4] Thomas Kerridge, who in the following month (18 Feb., 1616) was chosen agent at Surat in succession to Aldworth. He had gone out with Best in 1612, and had spent some time at court after the death of Canning. On Edwards's arrival, Kerridge moved down to Ahmadābād to provide indigo for the lading of the fleet. His letters from that city, and later from Surat, will be found in Brit. Mus. Add. MS. 9366. As will be seen, his imperious temper led to much friction between him and Roe, and though the latter acknowledged

favour; the other to release all customes required on any pretence on the way, or if any had beene taken to repay it; of his owne accord wishing mee that, if these gave not speedy remedy, I should renew my complaynt against the disobeyour, and hee should be sent for to answere there. And soe hee dismissed mee.

To Sir Thomas Smythe.
(*Add. MS.* 6115, f. 69.)

Adsmere, 24 January, 1615[-16].

... Some things, as fitter to be more privat, I have reserved for your consideration, and in some loath to complayne to publiquely. I confesse it is very necessary that the commanders of your fleets have full authoritye to governe those in theyr chardge and to punnish offenders; but yow know not to what height it riseth as soone as it looseth sight of land. Some experience I have in this commander; yet I thincke him as sufficient and discreet as any yow can imploy; but so absolute (I speake not of him alone) that the woord of a Generall is law eaven agaynst your commissions, and a woord against them is the undooing of theyr fortune that have the miscry to lett it fall; for every woord is carried (the Kyng hath no such spyes). Yet I must say truth: Captain Keeling, for any thing concerning him selfe, hath showed much generosyty in free remitting, and useth the Company very fayrely. But this is one great inconvenience, that they have absolute power to place and displace, eaven your cape merchaunts that

his opponent to be 'quick and sufficient,' he held that he had 'too much heate and opinion of abilitye.'

Kerridge resigned his post in April, 1621, and returned to England; but came out again in the same capacity in March, 1625, and served until April, 1628. After his return he was elected a 'Committee' of the Company, and held that position almost continually till his death at the end of 1657 or the beginning of 1658.

The wrongs complained of in the text are detailed in Kerridge's letters mentioned above. At Ahmadābād, a dispute with a native merchant over some indigo led to their broker being beaten and imprisoned. Kerridge himself was beaten; and in addition was fined on the pretext that he had defrauded the Governor of the estate of Aldworth, who was alleged to have died in the town and to have been carried forth by the English to escape the confiscation of his goods. When the English merchandise was ready to start for Surat the Governor demanded four per cent. duty, though at last he accepted one and a half per cent., and a bribe of a hundred rupees.

have served many years. It makes all men almost adore them, and depend on them for theyr fortune. But that which is most inconvenient for the Company is, the cape merchaunt, if he be honest, he must be severe, and looke into the actions of all your factoryes, punish and take away privat trade; which must necessarily bring him into hatred, and the factors knoweing every yeare a power comes able to displace him, they band all agaynst him, despise his authority, crosse his commands, hinder your busines, and *una voce* provide complaynts, some just, some false, against the ships arrivall, and by many meanes, if the Generall be not upright, wynn him to theyr ends. This is partly the case of Mr. Edwards; though I cannot excuse him in all things layd to his chardge, as managing your pressents for privat benefitt, and some what about the indico, for which hee pretends good amends. . . . The factoryes heere are extreeme weake, and some in theyr accounts abuse yow and fetch up theyr owne expence. Here is no profitt for mee that I can honestly seecke, and the cuntry is most base, and the wayes for me to tread in so foule that I am enforced to seek new. I am tould that Mr. Edwards hath beene so loath to complayne or displease that, having taken on him a high qualety, hath suffered blowes of the porters, base *peons*, and beene thrust out by them with much scorne by head and shoulders, without seeking satisfaction; and that he hath carried himselfe with such complacency that hath bredd a low reputation of our nation, much to my prejudice that follow. . . . I am resolved to sett it right and upon good ground (not rashly), or to leave this service only to an agent, that may give and creepe and suffer any thing, both for yow and for himselfe. When I returne, I desire I maye command the ship. It goes agaynst my stomack (that am very moderat) to be denyed a candle, or a draught of bere, of a steward without asking the cap[tains] leave; whom yet, I must say, usd me well; but lov'd I should know his authoryty, and then denyed me nothing. . . . I desire to have my share of sack layd in in strong beare; wyne agrees not with mee. I am able yet to send yow no present; which, though yow expect not, I owe. I hoped to have sent yow a carpett; but I must first lay out at Lahor to entercept those of Persia. Here all are taken up for the Kyng. . . . If God give me life, I will ever acknowledg your favour at home, wher I can doe yow better service then in this place; hoping yow wilbe a means that in the yeare 1617 or 1618 I maye returne; this cuntry neyther promising profitt nor agreeing with my disposition of mynd or body. One of those years will finish four years service, the other five . . . I have had seven could agues, two fevers, since my beeing at Bramport. . . .

January 25-30.—I made my dispatches for England, and wrote earnestly to the factory at Suratt for a particular of the Governors debts, exactions and injuryes ;[1] and solicited the *firmaens* promised, of which the Prince sent by his officers one for Suratt, but withall articles for mee to signe very dishonorable, wherin amonge others [2] it was required that I should firme [*i.e.* sign] a peace and safe conduct to the Portugalls shipps and frigotts to come safely to Suratt, without any accord, promise or counter securytye of peace on their parts; which I utterly refused, but made offer that for the Princes sake I was content to give the Viceroy of Goa six monthes liberty to enter into leauge, and to open the ports. But the present writing was required to be sealed; wherby, besyds the folly and dishonor, they might under coullor of frendship have rode amonge our fleete with boates laden with fire woorkes to have taken advantage. So, as I absolutely rejected the motion, I was answered I should then have no *firmaen* for Suratt. Soe it rested two dayes. I, supposinge the fault only in the Princes officers, sent to Aasaph Chan, to complayne of the unequalle demands of Sultan Carronne and that the *firmaen* promised beeing sealed was deteyned from mee, contrarye to all the Prinnces faire woords and his owne assurances of the justice; but insteed of releefe I found Asaph Chan the author of this device and an earnest disputer for the reasonablenes therof; and soe returned me a round answer, that unlesse I would signe the one I should not have the other. This awaked me. I saw now the faction, but was irresolute what to doe. Asaph Chan was a broken reede; the Prince governed by him; the King was my only refuge, from whom I was sure of justice if I complaynd, but I feard I should drawe upon me the hate of Normall the beloved queene, ante to Sultan Corrons wife, sister of Asaph Chan, whose daughter the Prince married, and all that powrfull faction, against whom, though I might once prevayle, yet the advantage of tyme, language, and oportunitye, the power of a wife, a sonne, and a favorite, would produce revenge. Soe

---

[1] This had been asked for by the Prince at the late interview.

[2] For these articles see Roe's letter to the Company of 29 Jan., 1616 (p. 101).

that I resolved to temporize, and to see if I could remove Asaph Chan from his opinion, and then all would follow; if not, to take a desperate remedy, when I saw all other wayes were desperat.

To the East India Company.
(I.O. Records : *O.C.* No. 335.[1])

Adsmere, 25 January, 1615[-16].

... I arrived at Adsmere with a new ague that tooke me in the way. I was mett by Mr. Edwards and the English of this factory one dayes journy; who had fitted (with as much conveniency as the place will affoord) his house for mee. I was so farr from beeing able to present my selfe before the King that I could not stand, but was lifted eaven to my bedd; of which I advised the King, and hereby had good leysure to repayre many things decayed in the coach, and to advise of somwhat else. It pleasd him to send a gentleman to see mee, with two wyld hoggs, within a weeke (I thincke to satisfie himselfe of my delay); after, hee was well content I should take leysure. Within six dayes my two agues forsooke me; and by the 10th of January I recovered so much strength as to sitt on a horse; and, having demanded leave, presented my self to the King.... After many complements, I usd some woords to him, delivering His Majesties lettre and showing my commission, the coppy wherof (I meane the lettre) I then alsoe delivered in Persian; after that, your presents, to say, the coach, the virginalls, the knives, a scarfe all richly imbrodred, and a rich swoord of myne owne.... He sitting in his state could not well descerne the coach, but sent many to see yt, and caused the musitian to play on the virginalls there, which gave him good content.[2] ... At night, hee having

---

[1] There is a copy of this letter in *Add. MS.* 6115, f. 70, and another in the *Duplicate O.C.* series at the India Office. The latter has some marginal comments which are obviously of later date, and it must therefore have been sent home in a subsequent packet. The necessity of economising space has led to the omission, in this and the succeeding letters, of particulars already related in the journal, etc. The present letter is given at full length in *Letters Received*, vol. iv. (p. 9).

[2] Of the coach and coachman, see the entry under 2 Nov., 1616. The musician was a Thomas Armstrong. The Mogul soon got tired of him, and dismissed him with a present of 96 rupees. With this he made his way down to Surat, and there obtained permission to embark in Pepwell's fleet for Bantam (*Letters Received*, vol. iv. p. 289, and vol. v. p. 89). He was dead by Oct. 1618.

stayd the coachman and musitian, he came downe into a court, gott into the coach, into every corner, and causd it to be drawne about by them. Then he sent to me, though ten a clock at night, for a servant to tye on his scarfe and swoorde[1] the English fashion; in which he tooke so great pryde that he marched up and downe, draweing yt and flourishing, and since hath never beene seene without yt. Soe that in conclusion he accepted your presents well; but after the English were come away he asked the Jesuyte[2] whether the King of England were a great Kyng, that sent presents of so small valewe, and that he looked for some jewells. To this purpose was I often felt by some, before I sawe him, whither I had brought jewells or no. But raretyes please as well, and if yow were furnished yearly from Francford, wher are all knacks and new devises, 100 *li.* would goe farther then 500 *li.* layd out in England, and here better acceptable.... Ther is nothing more welcome here, nor ever saw I man soe enamord of drincke as both the King and Prince are of redd wyne, wherof the Governor of Suratt sent up some pottle. Ever since, the Kyng hath sollicited for more. I thinck four or five handsome cases of that wyne wilbe more welcome then the richest jewell in Cheapesyde. Pictures, lardge, on cloth, the frames in peeces; but they must be good, and for varyetye some story, with many faces, for single to the life hath beene more usuall. If the Queene must be presented (which I will not advise too, and doe purpose, as well out of necessytye as judgment, to breake this custome of daylye bribing) fine needle woorke toyes, fayre bone lace, cuttwoorke,[3] and some handsome wrought wastcote, sweetbaggs or cabinetts, wilbe most convenient.... I would add any faire China bedsteeds; or cabinets or truncks of Japan are here rich presents. Lately the King of Bisampore sent his ambassador with 36 elephants, two with all their chaines of wrought beaten gould, two of silver, the rest brasse, and 40 rich furnished horses, with jewells to the valew of 10 *lecks* of *rupias*; yet withall he sent China wares and one figure of christall, which the King accepted more then that masse of wealth....

Further, besides the ill president of giving, this place is

---

[1] These had been substituted by Roe for some scarlet cloth which he judged unfit to be presented. The sword, says Salbank, in a letter to the Company (*O.C.*, No. 568), 'did yeeld such surpassing content unto him that for the [space of ?] a moneth or more scarce did he come to any publique shewe without the sword hard by him.'

[2] Francesco Corsi, an account of whom is given later.

[3] 'Bone lace' was lace knitted with bone bobbins upon a pattern marked by pins. 'Cutwork' was the openwork embroidery in lace then so much in fashion.

either made, or of it selfe unfitt for an ambassador. I speak against my self, but I will enforme truth; for though they understand the qualetye, yet they have much adoe to understand the priviledges which that qualetye with us doth require, the rather because they have ever beene sought too humbly and they expect as much of mee; but they shalbe deceived. I stand upon my selfe, and yet fynd good effects of yt. But if I cannot change the ill customes begunn, and sett the busines upright, without base creeping and bribing (which one years experience will show), then I shall roundly advise yow, as the best course, never to send an ambass[ador] more hither; both because he may not dishonorably attend at theyr doores, nor suffer such affronts as they barbarously often use, without injury to the King; and if he cannot be righted, his discontent will prejudice your busines. Besides, the chardge which yow are att, in maynteyning him, bestowed in presents (if that course must be proceeded in) will effect more then his countenance; and an agent may with no dishonor sue and goe to theyr houses. For were yt here, as in other parts, that after an ambass[ador] had moved the King, his secretary or some other might sollicite the busines, it were somwhat; but here a man must goe him selfe, be refused at the doores, wayte on base persons, and undergoe a thowsand indignytyes unfitt for a qualety that represents a Kings person. But of this, one years experience will make a full tryall; and I am resolved to proove what another course will doe. Another terrible inconvenience I suffer: want of an interpreter. For the brokars here will not speake but what shall please; yea, they would alter the Kings lettre because his name was before the Mogulls, which I would not allowe. But if we had one of our owne nation, that were of understanding and could in good termes deliver himselfe, I could effect more then ever I shall by these, that speake, not what I command, but what they conceive is fitt, by example of others that have ever sought to content and not to contest; which is here very needfull, and woorkes as well as phisique. And at this present, when I had commission to propose and draw what I please, I can doe nothing; an Armenian that usd to write in Persian (for soe are all that passeth the King) beeing absent. . . .

Everything is as deare here as in London. A small sheepe will cost three *rup.* and a halfe; the stable is veary deare; *peons* a custome (and necessary) of great chardge. . . . I have spent of my owne 200 *li.* at least. Cloathes and stuffes are here twice as deare as in Cheapesyde, if they be not pintadoes [*i.e.* chintzes] or stripd bald taffeties. Good silkes cost 10 *rup.* theyr *cobda*,[1] and meane cloth of gould 35 and 40 *rup.*

---

[1] A cubit or ell (Port. *covado*). It varied in length, not only with the locality, but also with the material it was used to measure.

a *cobda*. And seeing I have gone this course, I must beare yt out with some countenance of bravery ; which is myne owne chardge, but it will leave me never a penny. When you see what I have done, I must referr my selfe to yow, for I expect nothing from the King. I had not presents to fee those about him ; or if I had, to that end I would not bestowe them. . . .

To the East India Company.
(*Add. MS*. 6115, f. 77.)

Adsmere, 29 Jan. 1615[-16].

Since the sealing of my last, some stop is fallen in my court busines, wherby I discover the feare they have of the Portugall ; they incurring (for our sakes, as they pretend) the same danger in sending to the Redd Sea which they sought to avoyd by givinge us trade. They are very giddy in theyr resolutions whom they shall entertayne, and will resolve upon the stronger. They would fayne have peace on all sides ; but the Portugall will never conclude, and keepe yt, while we remayne here, nor till he be rooted out. A discourse was reaveld to me that the new Governor of Suratt offered to use the English so as they should never returne, but was answerd theyr ports must then never be open and theyr sea townes in continuall danger ; but these are but discourses. The busines at the court is betweene Sultan Caronne and me. I having proposed certayne articles for our future good, and procurd his *firma* written and sealed, he sent me three articles, on my behalfe to signe, or else he would not deliver, nor signe the rest of my demands. The first was that the Portugall frigotts might come safe to Suratt Roade without molestation ; to which I answered I thought it hard that His Highnes should desire to bynd our hands and leave loose our enemyes, that wee must fight when he was strong, and not revenge yt at the same advantage ; but if he would be pleased to attend an answer from Goa (wherin I offered the Portugalls peace, that the sea might be open to all), or give me his *firma* in theyr behalfe and I would signe yt : otherwise not. The second was that we should build no house of strength in Suratt, for that it seemes they feare shaddowes ; to this I agreed. The third was that all presents should come untouchd to mee or my predecessor [successor ?], but what soever was to be sould should be opened in the *alfandica*, and if the Princes servants could agree of price, they should pay ready mony ; if not, it should be sealed and sent to mee, and the Prince and I should agree heere. To this I answered I would consent for any goods of the Company, with this provision, that I would make no bargayne, but he must agree with the factors. Thus it stands dead ; but I shall turne the streame, I doubt not. This is a Jesuiticall bone cast in over night, for every thing was ready to passe the seales without any interruption. . . .

To the Kings Majestie.
(*Add. MS.* 6115, f. 76.)

Adsmer, 29 January, 1615[-16].

May it please Your Majestie,
That I have the honor to be calld Your Majesties Ambassador me thinckes requires out of the nature of the place, at least embouldens mee, to send Your Majestie these humble lines ; otherwise the importance of what I can write is not woorth one the least pause or interruption of Your Majesties higher meditations. To relate the customes of this cuntry, the state of the court or their goverment, were fitter to beguile the wearines of the way (like a tale) at Your Majesties stirrop then for a discourse in earnest. Fame hath done much for the glory of this place. Yet it cannot be denyed that this King is one of the mightyest Princes in Asia, as well in extent of territory as in revenew ; equall to the Turke, far exceeding the Persian. But the goverment so uncertayne, without written law, without policye, the customes mingled with barbarisme, religions infinite, the buildings of mudd (except the Kings howses and some few other) : that eaven this greatnes and wealth that I admired in England (reserving due reverence to the persons of Kyngs) is here, wher I see yt, almost contemptible, and turnes myne eyes with infinite longings to see Your Majesties face and happines. . . .[1]

The trade here will doubtlesse in tyme bee very profitable for Your Majesties kingdomes, and may vent much cloth ; but as yet our condition and usadge is so bad (notwithstandinge fayre woords) that will require much patience to suffer, much industry to sett upright. They feare the Portugall, they feare us, and betweene both patch up a frendship ; but in hart (if we were of force) more unsound to them then us. The Portugall professing here himselfe enemy to Your Majesties subjects, speaking unreverently and falsly of Your Majesties estate and greatnes with many bragging insolencyes, having twice with a great *armado* assaulted us and by Gods assistance repulst, and beeing twice well beaten, hath so lessened his reputation (which was his strength) that his utter ruyne were an easy woorke. The Dutch hath planted below Goa, the seat of the Viceroy, and beaten him in late sea fights, and dayly wynns ground upon him ; and our trade hath soe deminished his returns that not halfe the gallions that were usually laden in

---

[1] The description of Roe's reception is omitted, as it contains nothing fresh.

these parts are sett out, and those doe little more then defray chardge. The King of Persia hath distressed Ormus, that the Portugalls are retyred to the castle, which is in great want, all releefe from the mayne beeing taken away and the residers in his whole dominion (of that nation) banished. Doubtlesse hee would putt it into the hands of the English, for his want of shipping. They are in all this quarter in theyr wane, and might, while they are swimming for life, easily be suncke: a matter of great consequence, as well to abate the pride of the Spanish empire as to cutt off one master vayne of their wealth. And it hath beene observed *malum omen*, when any kingdome having risen suddenly to an unwildy height, that one eminent limme, like a pinnacle of a tower, hath fallen off. If Your Majestie were pleased to grant by your gratious commissions leave for the East Indya Company to assault as well as defend only (it beeing the nobler part of a warr, to which we are bound whensoever the enemy is stronge), it would strike such a terror and give such reputation to our cause as would almost decide the contention for this trade at once, and stopp theyr mouthes from bragging that, for offending the King of Spayne, we dare not assayle, only we defend ourselves, which every living creature would doe.

Doubting much exclamation hath come to Your Majesties eares that the Company transports great summes, above their licence, to doe Your Majestie service by enforming truth if it had beene so, or to free them if falsly accused, I have searched the invoice of every ship and do deliver it, on that credditt which I had rather dye then abuse to Your Majestie, that this fleete had but 43572 royalls sterling mony (somwhat above 10000 *li.*), beeing not a theird of the cloth and other goods.

The Persian Kyng hath lately with fire and swoord wasted and subdued the poore free Georgian Christians, and with his owne arme strooke off his eldest sonnes head. Revenge is like to follow; the Turke preparing to enter his country with terrible hostilitye by the way of Bagdatt.

If Your Majestie but pardon my presumption and errors, which will vanish before the brightnes of your wisdome, I am acquitted of the fault, because I have spoken with sincerity, though perhaps without judgment. I humbly desire Your Majestie to beleefe I would despise 100 lifes to your humble service, which seeing my pilgrimage interrupts, I will in my dayly vowes and meditations to Almighty God supplicat a long, glorious and happy raygne among your subjects, and that, having fullfild much tyme, yow may reigne for ever in the kingdom of eternitye.

Your Majesties most loyall subject
and humble servant,
THO. ROE.

To the Lord Bishop of Canterbury.[1]
(*Add. MS.* 6115, f. 74.)

Adsmere, 29 January, 1615[-16].

May it please Your Grace,

Places farr remote, having somwhat of woonder in the distance, cause much expectation in them selves of strange matter among the vulgar, such as I supposing they should have subject of woorthy and lardge discourse. But these are unlike the starrs, that seeme lesse the farther off. Heere the remotenes is the greatnes, and to maynteyne the ancyent priviledge of travellers, they have beene so far alchymists as multiplication, some ground, some spiritt, to quicken the body of their monstrous relations.

Wher I shall beginn, what I shall say woorthy one of Your Graces vacancyes from great affayres, I know not. To undertake a cosmographicall description were a labor not unwoorthy of tyme, but not proportionall to a lettre ; Ortelius, Mercator, Atlas, nor any understanding any truth herein. Yet for the maynnes of the error, I will observe that the famous river Indus doth not powre him selfe into the sea by the bay of Cambaya, but far westward, at Sindu. For from Lahor, standing 1000 myle north, into the mayne upon Indus, it is navigable to Syndu ; to Cambaya not, but certayne byestreames begotten by the seasons of rayne make mightie inundations, which have cherished the error. All the rest is as false, both in bearing, distance, longitude and latitude, as that ; but the correction here incomprehensible. The true latitude of this place 25 d. $\frac{1}{2}$.

A discription of the land, customes, and manners, with other accidents, are fitter for wynter nights. They are eyther ordinary, or mingled with much barbarisme. Lawes they have none written. The Kyngs judgment bynds, who sitts and gives sentence with much patience, once weakly, both in capitall and criminall causes ; wher some tymes he sees the execution done by his eliphants, with two much delight in blood. His governors of provinces rule by his *firmanes*, which is a breefe lettre authorising them. They take life and goods at pleasure.

---

[1] Printed by Purchas in his first volume, p. 582, but with an incorrect date (27 Jan.), and without any indication of the person to whom it was addressed. Much of it has been omitted here, as repeating what has already been said in the letters to Carew and others. Abbot's reply, dated 20 Jan., 1617, is among the State Papers at the Record Office. It will be remembered that the Archbishop was brother to Sir Maurice Abbot, the Deputy-Governor of the Company and a friend of Roe.

Many religions, and in them many sects ; *Moores* or *Mahumetans* adhering to Aly [1] (such is the King) ; *Banians* or *Pithagorians*, for the transmigration (and therfore will not kyll the vermyne that bytes them), who often buy many dayes respite in charety from kylling any flesh att all, in such a province or cytty ; *Gentills* of sundry idolatryes, theyr wives adorning the pyle, and entring the funerall fyres with great joy and honor.... The buildings are all base, of mudd, one story high, except in Suratt, wher are some stone houses ; but (I know not by what polycye) the King seekes the ruyne of all the ancient cyttyes, which were bravly built and now lye desolate and ruynd. His owne houses are of stone, both in good forme and fayre ; but his great men build not (for want of inheritance), but, as farr as I have yet seene, live in tents, or houses woorse then a cottager. Yet where the King affects, as at Agra, because it is a cytty erected by him,[2] the buildings are (as is reported) fayre and of carved stone. In revenu doubtlesse he exceeds eyther Turke or Persian or any Easterene prince. The summs I dare not name ; but the reason. All the land is his ; no man hath a foote. He maynteynes by rents, given of signoryes counted by horses, all that are not mechanique ; and the revenews given to some are a German princes estate. Secondly, all men ryse to greater and greater seignoryes, as they rise in favour, which is only gotten by frequent presents, both rich and rare. Lastly, he heyres all mens goods that dye, as well those that gayned by industry (as merchants) as those that lived by him ; and takes all theyr mony, leaves the widdow and daughters what he pleaseth, gives the sonnes some little seignorye and putts them anew to the world, whose fathers dye woorth two or three millions....

All the polycye of his state is to keepe the greatest about him, or to pay them afar off liberally. No counsell, but every officer answers to the King apart his duty.

Hee is of countenance cheerfull, and not proud in nature, but by habitt and custome ; for at nights he is veary affable, and full of gentle conversation....

Never were such oportunytyes to dischardge the Portugall from all these coastes.... We have now twice beaten a great *armado* with few shipps, an *armado* that was appoynted *por castigar los hereticos Ingleses* (the woords of one Father to a nother), and after to punish the Mogull for enterteyning us ;

---

[1] Shīas, the Muhammadans who upheld the claims of Ali and his descendants to be the true successors to the Caliphate. The Mughals, however, belonged to the Sunni sect, which opposed this view. The statement in the text regarding Jahāngīr must not be pressed beyond a general reference to his heterodoxy.

[2] This is of course an error.

so that he hath lost more in reputation (which was his strength) then in substance. But if His Majestie would condescend that wee should assault them, as they doe us, it would utterly breake them, it beeing both the nobler and safer part of a warr (to which wee are subject at theyr pleasurs) then to defend always. Besides, they make this use in reports of us, that the King of England is so afrayd of the King of Portugall that he dares not warrant an assault, but only to defend. What they say of the Kyng and our nation is so slanderous that *periit sua mole*.[1]

Further east, the Dutch hath taken many townes, and playes the mole better then he; and hath beaten him in many sea conflicts. He is declining on all sydes, and a little weyght on his head now layd by us would sincke him. It is a matter of great consequence for future tymes; and, though I have no hope, I propound yt to Your Grace to make what use seemes best to your wisedome. I have reward enough if I have pardon for my talketivnes; but it is obedience to Your Grace, and not presumption, whose wisedome and sinceryty I did ever honor, and to whom I shalbe happy to be tyed

In all humble services,
THO. ROE.

January 31.—Hojay Nassan, the new designed Governor of Suratt,[2] came to visit mee and to excuse him selfe of an accusation made to me against him; with whom for his manifould protestations I contracted a frendship.

February 1.—Seeing noe effect in the Kings promise for Amadavaz and the rubbs geven in that of Suratt, I went

[1] This seems to be an imperfect recollection of Horace's *mole ruit sua*.

[2] Khwāja Nizām had been Governor some time before, and was well acquainted with all that had taken place there regarding the English. His appointment in supersession of Zūlfakār Khān was mentioned in Roe's letter to the Company of 25 January, also his overtures to the ambassador : ' he was our ould enemy and feares my oposition.' The interview here referred to is thus described by Roe in a subsequent letter, dated 14 Feb., 1616 : — ' In my last I advised yow of the small hope wee might conceive of Hoyja Nassan, the new farmer, rather then Governor, of Suratt, by some discourse he usd of wearying us by little and little ; upon which I sent him a message that it was strange he would threaten a nation licensed by the authorytye of his soveraynge before he was warme in his seate : that he was ould, and should be wiser : he knew us better then any other, that we traded peacably and fayrly : that if by his folly he

to visitt Asaph Chan, who received me unmannerlye. But my busines closed myne eyes, that I entred into discourse of my employment in generall, and assured him I came not hither to be abused. I desired him to remember that by his advice I had refrayned to complayne to the King of the passadges of Suratt, and that my respect to the Prince yet deteyned mee, but that I could not long endure; that if I were enforced to yt, the fault was his, for which, though I should be sorry, yet I was free from blame. After some discourse he begann to change, and to encline to mee so farr, that I should have the *firmaen* as I desiered ; only he required my woord that, if the King wrote to Goa to signifye the justnes of my demands (which was only free and quiett trade, and protection from injury), and could procure the Viceroy to enter into the leauge, that I would attend the answere and receive them, to which I agreed ; and in the interim he promised me redresse in all particulars ; and if the Portugall refused, that then I should draw what articles I would for our nation, and hee would procur them to be signed. On these tearmes we parted, with seeming content and complements on both parts.

February 2.—Asaph Chan sent me the two *firmaens* for Amadavaz, which he had kept sealed a weeke with coulorable delayes.

gave us occasion to doe other and brake the peace, the misery would light on him, for neyther should his port be open to goe out nor any suffered to come in, nor his head secure, no, not in his castle. To which he answerd he had never usd any woords agaynst us, and that he was our frend and would on the morowgh come and satisfie mee more at lardge ; which he performed, denying by his God the woords accused off, vowing all respect to our nation, and protesting that I should be Governor of Suratt and command the towne, he only would bee my deputy ; with many complements, offering suertyes for his fidelitye. We became great frends and enterchangeably made sundry professions, on my part ever with reservation that if he wrongd the English in his authorytye, no respect could withhould mee from prosequuting him like an enemy.'

As a matter of fact, Khwāja Nizām did not go to Surat as Governor, Ibrāhīm Khān (see p. 62) being appointed to that post. In the duplicate copy of *O.C.* 335 (see p. 98), a marginal note by Roe states that the former ' refusd the Princes conditions.'

February 3.—Samuel Peirce was sent me from Agra, that had robbd the cash at Amadavaz.[1] The mony was seized by the Governor.

February 4.—I procured Asaph Cans lettre for the monny, which was delivered to the English.

February 5.—I dispatched an expresse to Amadavaz with the *firmaens* for Mr. Kerridge.[2]

February 6-9.—The King sent me a hynd, as tall as a horse but veary leane.

February 10.—I received lettres from Mr. Crowder and Steele, employed into Persia, directed to Mr. Edwards and the factory, which I opened.[3]

February 12.—At night Asaph Chan sent in great hast to desire mee to come speake with him, using the Kings name to quicken mee. I went and on the way mett divers messengers, which made me woonder at the hast and suspect some great change. When I came I found him writing (as hee pretended) for the King, desiering me to stay in an outward roome among sutors and servants; which I did a while, much against my stomack. But presently went by his supper, which he mente to eate with his frends while I attended.

[1] The incident is described in Kerridge's letters (*Add. MS.* 9366). In the previous December, Pierce had presented himself at the house in which the English were living in Sarkhej, near Ahmadābād, pretending that he had been sent by Keeling with letters which he was to carry to Agra, but had been robbed of them on his way. Finding that the factors were suspicious, and had sent to Surat to inquire into the truth of his story, he broke open the trunk of the cashier while the latter was changing his stockings, took out a sum of over four hundred rupees, and decamped. Apparently he had been captured by the *kotwāl* with the money still in his possession.

[2] Under this date is a mysterious entry in Roe's accounts: 'Sent to Normall the Queene, having occasion to use her favour to deliver something in secrett to the King, one of the looking glasses, with guilt past images of [on ?] the sydes.'

[3] See the introduction. Crowder arrived a little later, and handed over his papers to Roe. The Surat factors were much displeased with him for this, and later on the ambassador had to interfere to shield him against their resentment. Roe describes him as 'a gentle, quiett, and sufficient fellow, fittest to follow court busines, of faire language and behaviour, and well profited in Persian.'

When I sawe it, I rose up full of just indignation, and departed his house, sending only this message, that if his greatnes were no more then his manners he durst not use me soe : that I was an ambassador from a mighty and free prince, and in that qualety his better, and scorned to attend his banquetings : that I judgd it want of civilitye and barberisme, rather then a purposed affront and therfore would forgive him without complayning to the King : but that if here after wee were to meete, I would expect he should better remember him selfe, and know mee : and if he had any message now from the King, hee might send it by my servant. To this hee answered not a woord, but layed his finger on his mouth, a signe that he had erred ; and tould my messenger that the Prince had sent me the *firmaen* desired for Suratt, but withall the securitye for the Portugall to be firmed by mee : and that a servant of the Princes was there ready to deliver one and receive the other. My interpreter, knoweing my resolution, answered hee was sure I would not accept any *firmaen* on soe dishonorable conditions, to give our enemyes peace, when they could not make warr, and to leave them at liberty when they were better able. So Asaph Chan seemed to app[r]ove the reason, and desired the Princes servant to moove him to send it without any conditions, and dismissed myne.

February 18.—I dispatched an expresse for Hispan in Persia with lettres for the Sophy [1] and a packett into England, directed first to one William Robbins [2] (servant to Arnold Lulls), and after to the ambassador at Constantinople, or the consull of Aleppo.

[1] The title by which the King of Persia was generally known to Europeans. It is derived from *Sūfī* or *Safī*, the family name of the reigning dynasty. The monarch here referred to is the famous Shāh Abbās (1585-1629).

[2] An English jeweller, who had found his way to Ispahān, and had there obtained profitable employment. When, later on, Connock and other English factors arrived, he was of considerable service to them in their efforts to obtain privileges from the Shāh. He was admitted into the Company's service in May, 1619, but died a few months after. His linguistic attainments are praised in Roe's letter to Smythe of 27 Nov., 1616 (see later).

To the East India Company.
(*Add. MS.* 6115, f. 81.)

14 Feb., 1615[-16].

Since my last of the 25th and 29 of January, sent by Captaine Newport, in the later of which I made known to yow some difference betweene the Prince and mee concerning the Portugalls, I have received these inclosed from Persia, though not directed to mee by name, yet as I thought necessary for me to open, yow having, to my knowledge, no cape merchant in the country. . . . I have by two wayes over land dispeeded with all expidition these and theyr coppy : not only that yow may know what they conteyne, but to give my judgment of the busines, how it is, to what ends, by what means, and, if it be possible, which way this new resolution may be diverted, for Mr. Steele hath not (in myne opinion) seene farr into the misterye, if (as he writes) he beleeves he hath procured for yow a trade. His owne desire to doe yt may blind his judgment. . . . You shall fynd here among these a fayr command to the governors of Jassques [1] and other sea ports, if any English ships arrive, to give them trade and entreat them frendly, and in the severall lettres many clauses that a trade is procured yow, that ther is hope yow shall have licence to fortefye, and a great opinion of the excellency of the woorke done, flattering themselves, wheras the whole scope and marrow of the relation is quite contrary ; and it seemes to me, by these very lettres that promise trade, almost impossibilitye of obteyning yt. For thus much I collect out of the history, which, agreeing with other circumstances known to me heere, is doubtlesse truth, that, before any intelligence of the Turks purpose of invasion, the Persian for many reasons was resolved against the Portugalls to open his owne way to sea and to keepe his gulph free for all nations and to dischardge yt of the Portugall bondage, and to this purpose tooke Bandell,[2] theyr foort on the mayne, distressd the iland by cutting off

[1] Jask. The *farmān* is printed in *Purchas*, vol. i. p. 519.

[2] See pp. 92, 103. The reference is to the capture of the Portuguese fort at Gombroon, established there in 1612 to secure provisions and water for their settlement at Ormus. In the letter to King James (see p. 113 *n*) Roe says that the Shāh 'put to the swoord 70, and carryed 55 prisoners.' After its capture it was entirely destroyed by the Persians, who, however, built a larger fort near the site of the old one. From this period dates the rise of Gombroon or Bandar Abbās, as the new settlement came to be called—a rise much accelerated by the capture of Ormus in 1622. 'Bandell' is of course 'Bandar,' 'the port.' Faria y Sousa speaks of this place as 'el puerto de Bandel' (vol. iii. p. 241).

provisions, and sett a day of exile to all the residers in his land.[1] But this cloud from Turky threatning a storme on every side, when hee had sett that noble project afoote, diverted him wholy to attend his owne safety and to weaken his enemy, resolving for the present upon his ould course, to waste his borders that the Turke might fynd no forradge, and to forbidd all caravans or merchants passadge into Turky. In this exigent arived Sir Robert Sheirley and was welcommed like one that brought some new hopes or remydye. He, that was to make his fortune by imployment and to mayntayne his credit by new projects, finding the Emperor in trouble and irresolute, the Portugalls in disgrace and neede, tuned the ould string of some way diverting the whole trade of Persia from Turky; and beeing assured that the King of Spayne would for many reasons accept of yt, solicited by the friars, men of his owne faith,[2] he offered to procure that, conditionally the Spaniard might receive all the silkes and have leave to refortefye Bandell and some other ports, the King to send royally every yeare a fleete which should both bring ready mony for most part and for the rest should serve him with spyces, pepper, Indian lynnen, and such comodities: that the Emperor should not doubt his fortefying, for it would be easy for him to turne them out if he procurd peace from the Turke: in the mean tyme they were his fittest allyes, because they were ever ennimyes to the Turke. This is the resolution, and to this purpose hath Sir Robert procured him selfe an imployment into Spayne, wher I doubt not hee wilbe veary wellcome. It needes be no question wheither the Spaniard will accept off this offer. First, it will add to the Kings coffers 1,000,000 of crownes yearly. Secondly, it will occasion him to send good fleetes into these coasts, which will not be idle. Therdly, it will recover him all his reputation, that was eaven sick to death in this quarter, for the disgusts of Persia and the danger of Ormus was like a plauge sore in his syde. Lastly, the Mogull, who harkens after him [i.e. the Shāh] and his proceed-

---

[1] In his letter to King James, Roe adds that the Shāh had further refused to give audience to 'a Spanish ambassador who had attended a yeare.' He is apparently referring to Don Garcia de Silva e Figueroa, who had reached Goa in the autumn of 1614 as ambassador from the King of Spain and Portugal to the Persian monarch. An account of this embassy will be found at p. xv of *Letters Received*, vol. v.; and from this it will be seen that the envoy did not arrive in Persia until the autumn of 1617 and did not reach the court until the following June. Possibly, however, Roe merely meant that the Shāh had refused to authorise the coming of the ambassador to his country.

[2] Sherley was a Roman Catholic.

ings and will judge, first by the peace made, after by the number of shipps that will hant this coast, that it wilbe wisedome to follow the example and entyrely embrace the Spaniard. Now to the command granted by the Persian in behalfe of our nation, it is of no consequence, for who would doubt that he would refuse us leave to trade? But what conditions are there to deliver silke, or to receive us only, such as are sent into Spayne? Sir Robert Shirly could not, beeing an English man, refuse to procure that that was even due by common equetye and to which the Persian was inclinable, and as yet it were folley to reject us, beeing not assured of the Spaniard; but he hath discovered playnly his hart a nother way, and knowes that if his embassadge succed in Spayne, this command will fall of yt selfe, for that all is conditioned to the Spaniard, and the coast given him, and then we must obteyne leave of him, not of the Persian. That he hath a message to the King of England I beleeve is a colour to deceive these the easier; for how dares, or with what face can hee see his soveraynge, to whom and to whose kingdomes he hath done soe ill offices? That he will breake off with the Kyng of Spayne and come for England, if Sir Thomas Smith hould intelligence with him, is a meere mockery, for that is beyond his commission, or at least a nother string to his bow if the Spaniard refusse. No, he hath a *discalsadoe* [1] Portugall for his confessor and hee knowes that the start in this busines wynns yt, and is sure of great reward from the Spaniard for him selfe; and eaven this, were ther no other, makes me suspect his affection, that to wynne tyme of Steele, least hee should arrive in Christendome before him, he hath taken Robinns the English man with him toward Ormus, who is become keeper of the commands, and without whose presence it seemes Steele cannot dispatch; which him selfe sees, though somwhat darkley. The consequence of this is very important, eaven for His Majesties estate, for yt will add both wealth and creditt to that nation, that I can never beleeve wilbe our frend longer then whyle their owne wants constreyne them. It wilbe very dangerous for your trade here, in respect that your enemy wilbecome your strong neighbour, wheras he was languishing and wearing to nothing. Therfore, if it be possible, yow must seeke some prevention. For my part I have ventured to write to the Persian kyng my opinion of his resolution and enlightned him with some better understanding of the Spaniards nature and qualety, wher they gett footing, and to

---

[1] Barefooted (Ital. *discalsato*). The ecclesiastic was no doubt a 'discalsed Carmelite,' and is probably to be identified with the 'Carmelite friar,' who later opposed the efforts of Barker to obtain privileges from the Shāh (*Cal. S.P., E. Indies*, 1617-21, p. 303).

lett him see he may vent his silkes and all the comodytyes of his country at better rates, if he erect a free mart in some coast towne for all nations, then to be bound to the Spaniard, who will creepe the first yeare and insult the next; offering our selves to trade with him royally, if hee wilbe pleased to stay his resolution of delivering him selfe into the wardship of the Spaniard. The coppy of which at lardge is herein enclosed.

I can doe yow no further service but adventure my poore advise what you should doe in England, if by this lettre or Mr. Steele[s] intelligence this Spanish negotiation come to yow before Sir Robert Sheirleys arrivall in Spaine (which wilbe in July 1616[1]), to sollicite His Majestie to command his embassador resident there to woorke him to propound a peace in those seas between the English and Spaniards, and so to offer the dessigning of a free place for trade, pretending that, if the Spaniard should have yt alone, the seas would never be quiett: that the English would infest the coast, and nothing but warr would ensue: wheras there was comodytye enough for both, and with more profitt on both sydes then eyther to defend or gayne yt by a warr. And though I doubt not but Sir Robert Sheirley usd the woords, of quitting Spayne and comming for England, to abuse Mr. Steele, yet he may be taken in his owne nett, and they may serve to be urdged to him in His Majestics name as a promise. Though this take no great effect, nor that I beleeve eyther the Spaniard will agree to peace nor Sir Robert Sheirly effectually and cordially move yt, yet by the negotiation he shall loose some tyme and you may send two ships upon the coast and gett this start, to offer your selves first, really there, wherby yow shall engage the Emperor, eaven in good nature, to be willing to make conditions for yow; but to expect any trade (as I signifyed in my last lettres), except it be royally undertaken, that the Persian may be sure of full vent, is a vayne hope. Yow may range the coast one yeare, and make a saving voyadge, but fynd little silke, which growes above,[2] nor vent much cloth, which is comoditye only fitt for the remotest parts, neyther doe I perceive by Steele that much will vent at all; but his advise is good, that if yow only serve them with pepper and Indian comodytye great profitt will arise.

I have breefly acquaynted His Majestie and the Lords with the busines and my poore opinion.[3] If I have beene two busy

[1] In the letter to King James, referred to below, Roe states that Sherley embarked at Ormus for Spain, with his wife and many followers, at the end of January, 1616.

[2] Up in the country (in the districts bordering the Caspian Sea).

[3] See *Add. MS.* 6115, f. 78 *et seq.* The letter to King James has not been reproduced, as it is largely a repetition of what Roe had

I hope yow wilbe mediators for mee, that have erred out of blind zeale to doe my country service. If any alterations happen, I will spend yow some mony to advise you over land, but not as others have done. Yow will fynd a dear reckoning of Mr. Steeles employment; and, if I durst take such liberty, I could procure yow camells loads of *firmaens* to no purpose. . . .

To the King of Persia.[1]
(*Add. MS.* 6115, f. 84.)

14 Feb. 1615[-16].

Most magnificent and highly descended Emperor,

The respect Your Majestie hath mutually borne and received from the King of England my royall master, whose ambassador I unwoorthely am to the great King of India, hath encouraged me to send Your Highnes these my poore advises, not presuming to councell Your Majestie, but, in honor of your most royall vertues, not to be wanting to doe yow any service.

I received lately your most gratious command to your Governor of Jasques to entertayne the trafique of our nation with frendship and amitye; for which in the name of my master I render condigne thanckes. But with the same I fynd Your Majestie hath sent into Spayne to offer and contract for all your silkes and comodytyes, with instructions to give leave to fortefye, wheras Your Majestie had otherwise nobly purposed (as fame reported) to free your gulph of slavery and to keepe it open for all nations (a resolution woorthy of your greatnes); which if it be soe, then, notwithstanding your Majesties command, wee must eyther aske leave of the Spaniard (which wee scorne) or else force our way by armes, which will hynder the speedy vent of your silkes, seeing all trades only flourish by peace. Therfore, if Your Majestie tye your selfe to the Portugall or Spaniard, it wilbe both as prejudiciall to your estate in future tyme as was the way of Turky, and far more dishonorable, for that hee will never thancke Your Majestie for that which hee thinks necessitye or his owne witt procured; and, when he is in possession, he will use it with such insolency as will not beseeme a monarque to endure. Besides, if Your

said concerning Persia in his letter to the Company. The other letters are to the Secretary of State (Sir Ralph Winwood), the Lord Treasurer (Lord Thomas Howard, Earl of Suffolk), the Lord Chamberlain (the Earl of Somerset), Lord Pembroke (see p. 83 *n*), the Archbishop of Canterbury, and Lord Southampton. Only the last of these seems to call for reproduction.

[1] This was enclosed in a letter to William Robbins, who was asked to get it translated and present it to the Shāh on Roe's behalf.

Majestie be perswaded you can make use of him for a tyme and, when yow are returned victorious over the Turke, yow can turne him out at pleasure, Your Majestie may fynd the woorke more difficult then now yow consider; the fortifications of Europe, where the sea is open and too frend, are not easely rased. But if Your Majestie were pleased to cleare your coast and the sea of that bondage it hath beene long in, and be lord of your owne, erecting a free mart in some convenient port under the command of your ordinance, publishing to all nations they should trade securely, and thither send all the silkes and comodytyes of your several kingdomes, Your Majestie should effect with honor the dessigne of weakening your enemy the Turke, and be engaged to none, but all the world would seeke yow, and your subjects should passe theyr goods for mony or any other comodytye that eyther Europe or the East doth afford. There would bee the English, Spanish, French, Venetian, and all that had meanes of shipping, envying one a nother and only raysing the price, to Your Majesties profitt.

This I have thought fitt to offer to Your Majesties consideration, my respect commanding me to tell yow that single councells have single force; which I submit to Your Majesties judgment, hoping Your Majestie will so restrayne your conditions with the Spaniard that your favour to us become not uselesse, and we enforced to trade with them by the bullett, as they have unprosperously given us cause. Praying to the Creator of heaven and earth to give yow victory on your enemyes and renown in your life and posterytye,

To doe Your Majestie service,
THO. ROE,
Ambassador for His Majestie of England.

TO THE EARL OF SOUTHAMPTON.[1]
(Add. MS. 6115, f. 88.)

My Lord, Adsmere, 15 Feb., 1615[-16].

Since my arrivall in this country, I have had but one month of health and that mingled with many relapses, and am now your poor servant scarce a crowes dinner. . . . But what have I to doe with any descriptions, when the Fates have provided me an historiographer as fitt for yt as Zenophon for Cyrus or Homer for Achilles—the unwearied Coriatt, who now is in my howse, and hath not left a pillar nor tombe nor ould charactar [*i.e.* inscription] unobserved almost

---

[1] Henry Wriothesley, Earl of Southampton, the friend of Essex, and (according to some critics) the 'W. H.' of Shakespeare's sonnets.

in all Asia ; and is now goeing to Samercand in Tartary, from thence to Prester Jhon in Africke ; and hath written more volumes then leaves in his last Venetian travell, wherin he houlds still the correspondence of goeing on foote. He is already, or wilbe shortly, the greatest traveller doubtlesse of the woorld. . . .

I thought all India a China shop,[1] and that I should furnish all my frends with rarietyes ; but this is not that part. Here are almost no civill arts, but such as straggling Christians have lately taught ; only good carpetts and fine lawne, all comodityes of bulke, wherby I can make noe proffitt but publiquely ; muske, amber, cyvitt, diamonds, as deare as in England ; no pearle but taken for the King, who is invaleweable in jewells.

But I am not alone cossened in this hope, but in the Kings liberallitye. He alowes me nothing but a house of mudd, which I was enforced to build halfe ; yet is it as good as any favoryte of 100,000 *li*. per annum dwells in, for, no man having inheritance, no man will build. . . . Yet though I live in such a house, perhaps many wayes in more state and with many more servants then any ambassador in Europe, such is the custome here, to be carryed in a bedd all richly furnished on mens backes up and downe ; though it needs not, for here are the finest horses that I ever sawe, of gennett size and infinite store, besides guards and footmen, of which only I keepe 24. But this my expected liberallitye fayling makes all tedious and loathsome ; for though the King hath often sent to me, yet this bounty is only expressed in whyld hoggs.

Yow expect no ceremony, and I have learnd none here, but I am ever, and will dye soe,

Your Lordships most affectionate servant,

THO. ROE.

Give me leave to present my humble service to my lady, my Lady Penel[ope],[2] my little lady mistress, for whom I wilbe provided with presents.

TO SIR THOMAS SMYTHE.
(*Add. MS.* 6115, f. 84.)

Adsmere, 15 Feb. 1615[-16].

It wilbe superfluous to repeate any of the newes or my opinion of Persia, being most principally submitted to your judgment in my other lettre. All exhortations to stirr yow up to prevent yt and to uphould our creditt in these parts to

---

[1] A reference to the 'China houses' (*Silent Woman*, 1, i.) in London, where porcelain and other curiosities were sold.

[2] Lord Southampton's eldest daughter, wife of Sir William Spencer.

yow, who are, not of this only but off all active trades and discoveryes, the life and soule, were to light the sunne to rise. What then is lefte mee but to discourse or communicatte my privat thoughts, which are soe heavy in this monestary, and wha: I could say so lately uttered in my last (by Captain Newport) that all is now eyther dullnes or repetition. . . . Wee must have for our perfect health and better constitution of your affayers here effectuall and materiall conditions, wheron only to relye, and not patch up abuses by *firmaens*, like a boddy maynteyned by phisique. And I knowe they all fear I should bee open and playne to the King, who yet knowes not that ever wee were discontented, but what hee hath lately discovered in mee, but without complaynt. If they had beene used these last years with civil stiffnes, it had not beene thus perplexed now, for they desire to keepe that greatnes over your minister here that they have had, which I will not be subject too, and they feare my breaking out, which only effects that little I doe. So that, if with this way it had beene my good fortune to have had presents in any proportion to Mr. Edwards, now and then to have sweetned busines (which now allwayes goes roughly on), I should have brought them to a veary gentle rayne and easy goverment. Now both the labor and hazard of all lyes upon mee. I writte not this to endeare my service, but for evident truth ; for I have eaven stript my selfe of all my best, eaven wearing implements, to stopp gapps ; and yet noe man hath presented mee with any thing but hoggs flesh, goates and sheepe, no, not the valewe of one *pice* ; and I wow to God I spend myne owne so freely that I am next doore to a begger, only to uphould myne honnor and port I ought to beare. I hope the Company will have some consideration, and send me somewhat to repayre those wants, in a swoord and hangers, hatts, or such like ; not that I entend not to be payd at my returne for any thing I have parted from to their use, but because I make no price, I take no mony here to diminish theyr stock (which all men else doe that sell them), nor convert them to myne owne profitt (which I could have done to unreasonable gayne), but referr my selfe wholy to them, when they shall judge all togither. The King, seeing me weare a French plush, called in England muff (it is at foure pounds a yeard, if it be good), made Asaphe Chan feele if it were silke ; who, being resolved, extreamly desired to send for two or three peices for the King (carnation, light purple, or greene, or watched [*i.e.* blue]). I tould him it was too late : that the ships were gone. He urged me to send over land : that the King should be at the chardg. I tould him it was dear, and the price. He sayd the Kyng would give any. I referr it to yow. I feare, if it were here, they would not make you profitt. Yet I promised one peice of carnation. . . . I for

myne owne sake must pray for your health and life ; but not
for that only, but because I would live to requite your favour
toward mee ; which now must be used in helping mee home,
for this place will not make mee rich, and to be poore is no
dishonesty. Fower years in all is a lardge prentiship for one
of 34 years ould. I referr now my fortunes into your hands.
You have, as it were, taken them upon you, and are my civill
father. . . . [PS.] Sir, yow appoynted in some of your
commissions the discoverie of Syndu, in which nothing hath
beene done. But that of all things I am afrayd to be bould
with the Companyes purse (which others more freely and to
less purpose doe), I would not only send thither ould Shalbancke, who is most fitt for travell, but alsoe, least before yow
receive any advice concerning Persia, your shipps should
touch next yeare at Port Jasques, to prepare a wellcome at
the port and to give them information of the estate or alterations of the place. For Tarturia or Cambalew, I hav spoken
with a Turke, who assures mee they have no trade but for
rhubarb, and the sea is not discoverable over land.

February 19.—I went to repay the visitt of Hoja Nazon, who
entertayned me with very good respect, very good woords, and
very good meate.

February 21.—Having now long attended with patience and
found no effect in the Princes promises for a command for
Suratt, nor any answere resolute that I should have none,
Asaph Chan consenting that the conditions demanded should
be relinguished, I went to visitt the Prince at his sitting out ;
not knoweing whether this jugling might bee without his
knowledge (for I received his pleasure by others), or if it were
his owne, yet I would once more prove him and dispute my
owne cause, that, if I were enforced to complayne, I might be
fully blamlesse of any disrespect toward him. When I came
nere, whether by the Princes command to prove if I would
yeild, or by ignorance of his servants of the liberty I had
obteyned and used before, one of them stayed mee, and made
signes that I should make the reverence of the country called
teselim.[1] I rejected him with some mislike, and went on untill

[1] ' The salutation of *taslīm* consists in placing the back of the right
hand on the ground and then raising it gently till the person stands
erect, when he puts the palm of his hand upon the crown of his head :
which pleasing manner of saluting signifies that he is ready to give
himself as an offering ' (*Āīn-i-Akbari*, vol. i. p. 158).

I came to the asscent of the inmost rayle right before the
Prince, whom I saluted after my owne manner, and offering to
goe up, I was stopped and showed a bye entrance, at which
the meaner sorte comes in. The Prince seeing all this, and
not correcting yt, I turnd about to depart; wherat hee called,
and the way was open for mee to take and choose my place.
When I was entered, I bad my interpreter tell the Prince I
came thither in honor of him and to visitt him, expecting that
I should have beene welcome, but the usage of his servants
made me doubt yt: that if my comminge discontented him,
I could with more ease keepe my house. He answered I was
very welcome; wherat I made a reverance, and one of his
principalls, not content with that, came and pulld me to make
teselim, whom I thrust from mee with open scorne; wherat
the Prince smiled, and commanded to lett me use my libertye.
Then I presented him with a few toyes after the custome,
and demanded the *firmaen* long promised mee. He answered
it was signed, and calld to know whye yt was deteyned. Soe
presently it was sent for, and answered I had refused to firme
the conditions required by the Prince and sent with yt; wherat
the Prince said it was there ready: if I would seale the one,
I should have the other. I replyed: I would not; and gave
my reasons. Then hee fell off from that to complaynts of the
unrulines of the English at Suratt, of their drincking and
quarreling in the streets, and draweing swoords in the custome
house. I answered: I knew not, nor could excuse it: only
I knew the abuses offered them might provoke some beyond
reason and patience: but that I hoped the rest was not true.
Then hee calld for a lettre to showe mee wittnessing yt. I
demanded whose it was. He sayd the Governors. I answered
then I would give no creditt to yt, for that he was a veryer
drunckard then any English in Suratt, and for his untruth he
had often belyed the King and the Prince himselfe, as I would
prove to his face when he came to answere. The Prince
demanded why hee should write yt if yt were not true. I
answered: to excuse, by accusing others, his owne villanous
insolencyes: that if he had beene woorthy to have governed
a province, he should have taken those who were so disorderly
and have punished them, and done justice to the honest and

sober: but that hee made a pretence, for the fault of a drunckard, to abuse the innocent. It was replyed that it was for my sake it was forborne. I answered: I renounced giving protection to such as were unwoorthy of yt :[1] I came to defend my countrymen that were civill and honest in their rightfull causes, and was as desirous to punish outrages as to maynteyne sobryety: and for any privat frendshipp or respect to mee, the Governor had used none, nor I was other to him then a professed enemy. Wheratt the Prince asked if I would writte to Suratt to restraine the abuses and drunckennes of our people, and if no warning of myne could prevayle, if I would not be displeased that punishment might be inflicted on those taken in the offence. This motion savored so much reason I could not refuse it; only I putt in this caution, that, as I consented to punish the notorious offender, so the honest and sober might have protection and justice; and on this condition I promised to writt. He demanded when, for he would send the lettre post to prevent more disorders and complaynts. I answered: to morow. And so this discourse ended. The Prince converting him selfe to some others, I called to him to know his resolute answer for the *firmaen*, for that was my principall errand, which if hee refused mee, I knewe my wayes. He replyed: for the busines of the Portugall he was satisfied: that hee would send it to Asaph Chan, and what hee liked should content him; and desiered me to require on the morrowe an answer from him, and withall called for yt and delivered it to a gentellman to carry it presently with that command, that, if he liked it, it should be delivered to me.

This night the King sent mee a mighty elke kylld in hunting, reasonable ranck meate.

February 22.—I sent according to my promise a lettre for Suratt, the coppy wherof is registred.[2]

February 23-26.—I sent dayly to Asaph Chan; but he was sicke and I could have no answere.

[1] Cf. p. 36 *n*. This was rather a dangerous concession, for the English attached impor... he exclusive right of punishing the evil-doings of their con... and later on this was one of the privileges contended for ... the ambassador.

[2] At f. 90 of the MS. It repeats the complaints and desires that steps be taken to prevent such disorders.

February 27.—The King and Prince went a hunting journy 12 *course* off, that his house might be fitted against the *Norose* [see p. 125], which began the first newe moone in March.

Marche 1.—I rodde to see a house of pleasure of the Kings, given him by Asaph Chan, two miles from Adsmere, but betweene two mighty rockes so defended from the sunn that it scarce any way sees it; the foundation cutt out of them and some roomes, the rest of freestone; a handsome little garden with fine fountaynes; two great tanckes, one 30 stepps above another; the way to it inaccessable, but for one or two in front, and that very steepe and stony; a place of much melancholy delight and securitye, only beeing accompanyed with wild peacokes, turtles, foule, and munkyes, that inhabitt the rocks hanging every way over yt.[1]

March 2.—I receved answere from Asaph Chan resolute that hee had sent to the Prince, and could not obteyne no order for the delivery of the *firmaen*, without I would signe the articles. The Jesuite had much poysoned Asaph Chan, in whom was the fault, and I resolved to startle him.

March 4.—I wrote a lettre to the Prince as round and peremptory as was the refusall made mee, and sent it after where he was in progresse. The coppy is registred.

To Sultan Caronne.
(*Add. MS.* 6115, f. 91.)

Most Noble Prince,   4th March, 1615[·16].

It seemes to mee that Your Highnes is weary of the English at Suratt, or else yow would not refuse to deliver me a *firmaen* for their saftye and good usage, but upon dishonorable conditions and such as I cannot answer. Therfore I desire Your Highnes to give me a playne answer, which I require in the name of the King of England, beinge a frend and confederatt of your most royall father; for, if Your Highnes be resolved that

---

[1] This spot, known as the fountain of Hāfiz Jamāl (the name of the daughter of the saint Muīnuddīn), was a favourite resort of Jahāngīr. It lies at the back of the Tāragarh hill; and the fountains and tanks are now in a ruinous condition. The Emperor in his *Memoirs* (vol. i. p. 269) describes the palace which was erected there by his orders and called the *Chashma-i-Nūr*, or 'fountain of light.' He says nothing about Āsaf Khān in this connexion.

they shall have noe better justice then they have had, my master is likewise resolved not to have his subjects live where they shalbe injured, but we will seeke some other residence, wher wee shalbe better wellcome. For the losses and injuries suffered by your last Governor, your princly woord is already past for satisfaction. In all which, without Your Highnes ayde, I shalbe enforced to complayne to the King, for which I am sorry. I hope yow will excuse my bouldnes, because I doe performe but my dutie. And soe I committ Your Highnes to God. THE ENGLISH AMBASSADOR.

March 5.—Mochrebchane, governor in the Kings absence, and Haja Nassan, with some others, came of their owne accord to visitt mee, having sent woord that they would dine with mee. I entertained them as I was able, to theyr content, but kept as much state in myne owne house as was used towards me by others;[1] but wee exchanged many complements, Mochrebchan excusing himselfe of all things past, professing he knewe not the English, but that now he was theyr servant. So wee parted very good frends; and I gave him at his goeing six glasses guilt.

March 6.—The Prince sent his principall officer to Adsmere to give me content, fearing I would complaine; which hee desiered mee to forbeare and that I should have satisfaction in my desiers, justice for what was passed, and amends in the future. Soe hee propounded three other articles to me, leaving out that of the Portugall, and sent them in Persian desiring me to signe those to his master, and I should have the *firmaen* delivered upon receipt of yt. When I had gott them translated, though in substance there was nothing which I might not assent unto, they beeing rather frivolous then dangerous for mee or materiall for the Prince, yet in the woording and forme ther was somthing I misliked, wherin they might, if they had so much cunning, by hard construction

[1] From Terry's account (p. 211) we get a glimpse of Roe's household arrangements. 'My Lord Ambassador (he says) observed not that uneasy way [*i.e.* the native fashion] of sitting at his meat, but in his own house had tables and chayres &c. Served he was altogether in plate and had an English and an Indian cook to dress his dyet, which was very plentifull and cheap likewise; so that by reason of the great variety of provisions there, his weekly account for his housekeeping came but to little.'

bynd mee to some inconvenience, and restraine the merchants of full liberty. Therfore I drew them anew according to my owne mynd, altering those clauses and reserving the substances, and, to avoyd more messages too and fro, I sealed them, and sent them with this answere, that the articles propounded to mee were suspitiously expressed: that I only had made them playne and keept the substance; which I had there signed and sent, wherof if he would accept, I desired the *firmaen*, and that resolutely: I would loose no more tyme in treatyes nor firme any other. Both he and Asaph Chan read them, and answered they liked them well: that the alterations were not prejudiciall to their meaning; and soe delivered the *firmaen*; which that night I gott translated, that I might know what I had laboured for. This day I sent the secretary [1] a present, but it is not his custome to receive any thing.

March 7.—I found the *firmaen* very effectually reapeating my complaynts, mentioning the injuryes in particular, and commanding all manner of redresse; but in the end a conditionall clause poysoninge all the rest, that which I had so often refused, that the Portugalls should have free liberty to come to Suratt at his pleasure, and that wee should not molest them, take their goods nor persons, without any promise or intimation that they should not offend nor assayle us. Now to grant them peace in a roade of another prince wher they are equally licenced with us may seeme reasonable; but I knew the purpose of the Portugall and the instrument of this device, and that the Prince was abused and sawe not the disadvantage. First, if they had liberty to trade, they would use yt only to hynder ours; secondly, they would lye with 100 frigatts, under colour of this peace, and take the first advantage to fier or assault our fleete, which is not to be avoyded, if they obteyne this liberty to mingle amonge us; lastly, though the Prince explaynd him selfe in woordes that

---

[1] Mulla Shukrullah Shīrāzi, the Prince's *diwān* or steward. Roe often refers to him by his title of Afzal Khān, which was given to him by Jahāngīr when he accompanied to court the emissaries of the Rānā of Udaipur. In the succeeding reign he rose to high office, and died at Lahore in January, 1639.

he ment we should not molest them except they begann the quarrell and in our owne defence, yet when a mischeefe had beefallen us too late, of whom should wee have sought satisfaction? The Prince had not undertaken; the Viceroy had not signed any instrument of peace; only an Italian poore Jesuite had enformed the Prince the Portugall would be quiett —a brave securitye! Besides the folly and dishonnor, to appeare so eager of a peace, as if wee feard them, as to take it on any weake base, or rather on no conditions. These considerations enforced me to refuse and send it backe; desiering to have that clause strooke out, or else the fraud was evident, and I would never accept of yt. A day was demanded to give answer.

March 8.—I sent for a resolution, and received yt: that that clause must remayne or I should not have none. I gave order, suspecting the tricke, to redemand the articles signed by mee (but could not gett them, nor was the matter great, but for forme sake); and alsoe to pronounce as well my resolution that I mente never to seeke farther after yt, never to accept yt, or any other, on ill conditions: that I knew my way to seeke assured remedye: that I was sorry I had so long forborne yt.

March 9.—The King being returnd, the preparation for the *Norose* made all men soe busy that I had no oportunyte to doe myne, but purposed to prepare the King by visitations and presents to heare my demands with the first oportunitye. But I had no enterpreter, the brokar not daring to speake any thing that would displease Asaph Chan, nor would hee in any thing deliver mee truly to the King. Soe I sought out a third, an Italian jeweller, a Protestant, that useth much liberty with his toung, and in whom the King takes often delight to heare him rayle at the Jesuits and theyr factions;[1] who undertooke to say all I would deliver him.

[1] This Italian was known as John Veronese. For his services as interpreter he received a knife and a bottle of strong waters (Roe's accounts). Later, he angered Roe by abetting the runaway Jones; and shortly after he was dismissed from the King's service and ordered out of the country. Father Hosten has suggested that he should be identified with Jeronimo Veroneo, the reputed designer of the Tāj; but, apart from the difference in name, it is certain that the latter was not a Protestant.

March 10.—This day arrived our cloth and goods to Adsmere; having beene long on the way, to the great prejudice in the sale.[1]

March 11.—The *Norose*[2] begann in the eveninge. It is a custome of solemnizing the new yeare, yet the ceremonye beginns the first new moone after it, which this yeare fell togeither. It is kept in imitation of the Persians feast and signifyes in that language nine dayės, for that anciently it endurd no longer, but now it is doubled. The manner is: ther is erected a throne fower foote from the ground, in the *durbar* court, from the back wherof to the place wher the King comes out, a square of 56 paces long and 43 broad was rayled in, and covered over with faire semianes[3] or canopyes of cloth of gould, silke, or velvett, joyned together and susteyned with canes so covered. At the upper end were sett out the pictures of the King of England, the Queene, my lady Elizabeth,[4] the Countesse[s] of Sommersett[5] and

---

[1] Roe had written on 22 Feb. (*MS.* f. 90) to Biddulph, who was in charge of the caravan, to hasten his arrival. In the letter he said that a warehouse had been provided for the goods in the ambassador's dwelling, with a separate entrance; while 'for dyett yow will be content with myne.' Roe explained that he had judged it inadvisable to build another house for Biddulph, since 'it is daylie sayd here the King will away toward Decan.'

[2] The *Nau-roz*, 'New (Year's) Day,' a feast instituted by Akbar in imitation of the Persians. 'It commences on the day when the sun in his splendour moves to Aries, and lasts till the 19th day of the month. Two days of this period are considered great festivals, when much money and numerous other things are given away as presents: the first day of the month of *Farwardīn* and the 19th, which is the time of the *Sharaf*' (*Aīn-i-Akbari*, vol. i. p. 276).

Terry and Mandelslo follow Roe in his mistake as to the meaning of the term. The error is corrected in Thevenot.

The account in the text should be compared with that in the *Memoirs* (vol. i. p. 317). The latter, however, indicates the date as March 10 (O.S.).

[3] Pers. *shāmiyāna*, a canopy or awning.

[4] The Princess Elizabeth, King James's only daughter.

[5] The notorious Frances Howard, the divorced wife of the Earl of Essex, lately married to James's favourite, Lord Somerset, on which occasion the East India Company presented a piece of plate. At the time her portrait was decking the Mogul's feast, she and her husband were awaiting their trial for murdering Sir Thomas Overbury.

Salisbury,[1] and of a cittizens wife of London; below them a nother of Sir Thomas Smyth,[2] Governor of the East India Company. Under foote it is layd with good Persian carpetts of great lardgnes. Into which place come all the men of qualetye to attend the King, except some fewe that are within a little rayle right before the throne to receive his commands. Within this square ther were sett out for showe many little howses (one of silver) and some other curiosityes of price. The Prince Sultan Coronne had at the lefte syde a pavilion, the supporters wherof were covered with silver (as were some of those also neare the Kings throne). The forme therof was square; the matter wood, inlayd with mother of pearle, borne up with fower pillars and covered with cloth of gould about the edge. Overhead, like a valence, was a nett fringe of good pearle, upon which hundg downe pomegranetts, apples, peares, and such fruicts of gould, but hollow. Within yt the King sate on cushions, very rich in pearles and jewells. Round about the court before the throne the principall men had erected tents, which encompassed the court, and lined them with velvett, damask and taffety ordinaryly, some few with cloth of gould, wherin they retyred and sett to show all theyr wealth; for anciently the Kings were used to goe to every tent and there take what pleased them, but now it is changed, the King sitting to receive what new years guifts are brought to him. He comes abroad at the usuall hower of the *durbar*, and retyres with the same. Here are offered to him, by all sorts, great guiftes; though not equall to report, yet incredible enough; and at the end of this feast the King, in recompence of the presents received, advanceth some and addeth to theyr entertaynment some horse at his pleasure.

March 12.—I went to visitt the King and was brought right before him, expecting a present, which I delivered to

[1] Lady Somerset's elder sister, Catherine, who had married Robert Cecil's only son, William.

[2] This had been brought out by Edwards, who wrote to Smythe that the court painters had confessed their inability to imitate it, and that consequently it was much prized by the Mogul (*Letters Received*, vol. ii. p. 246).

his extraordinary content.[1] So he appoynted I should bee directed within the rayle, to stand by him; but I, beeing not suffered to step up upon the rising on which the throne stood, could see little, the rayle beeing high and doubled with carpetts. But I had leysure to veiw the inward roome and the bewty therof; which I confesse was rich, but of so divers peices and so unsuteable that it was rather patched then glorious, as if it seemed to strive to show all, like a ladie that with her plate sett on a cupboord her imbrodered slippers. This eveninge was the sonne of Ranna, his new tributary,[2] brought before him, with much ceremony, kneeling three tymes and knocking his head on the ground. He was sent by his father with a present and was brought within the little rayle, the King embracing him by the head. His guift was an Indian voyder[3] full of silver, upon yt a carved silver dish

---

[1] A purse which cost in England 24s., containing 'a little boxe of cristall, made by arte like a rubie, and cutt into the stone in curious workes, which was all inameld and inlayde with fine gould. Soe rare a peece was never seene in India, as can wittnes all your servants resident at Adsmere. I can sett noe price, because it was geven me; but I could have sould it for a thousand rupees, and was enformed that had it beene knowne how highlye the King esteemed it, I mought have had 5000 rupees. The King the same night sent for all the Christians, and others his owne subjects, artificers in gould and stone, to demand if ever they sawe such woorke or howe it could be wrought; who generallie confessed they never sawe such arte, nor could tell how to goe about it, whereat the King sent me woord he esteemed it above a diamonde geven him that day of 6000$li.$ price. .... Within the boxe (which I presented to keepe the jewells in which others gave him) I putt a chain of gould of double lincks veary small, wheratt was hanged a whyte emrald cutt in the forme of a seale, and therein engraved, no bigger then a penny, a Cupid drawing his bowe, with this motto *Guardes*: being a curiositie not easilie matched, and esteemed by the King for exellent woorke. The stone was unsett, pendent and veary lardge, above halfe an inch in length. The gould wayed 46s. .... There being noe man in London, much lesse here, that can enamell upon stone, and therfore I knowe not what it [the box] coste; and the seale stone uncutt, I bought in the West Indies, and had it pollished and carved in London; it cost noe great matter rough.'—Roe's Accounts (*Add. MS.* 6115, f. 277).

[2] Karan, eldest son of Amar Singh, Rāṇā of Udaipur.

[3] '*Voiders*, great broad dishes, to carry away the remains from a meat-table' (*Dunton's Ladies' Dictionary*, 1694). In the *Memoirs*

full of gould. Soe he was ledd toward the Prince. Some eliphants were showed, and some whoores [*i.e.* nautch-girls] did sing and dance. *Sic transit gloria mundi.*

March 13.—At night I went to the *Gussel Chan*, wher is best oportunitye to doe busines, and tooke with mee the Italyan; determining to walke no longer in darkenes, but to prove the King, beeing in all other wayes delayed and refused. I was sent for in with my ould brokar, but my enterpreter was kept out, Asaph Chan mistrusting I would utter more then hee was willing to heare. When I came to the King, he appoynted me a place to stand just before him, and sent to aske me many questions aboute the King of England and of the present I gave the day before; to some of which I answered, but at last I sayd my enterpreter was keept out: I could speake no Portugall, and soe wanted means to satisfie His Majestie. Whereat (much against Asaph Chans desire) he was admitted. I bad him tell the King I desired to speake to him. He answered: willingly. Wherat Asaph Chans sonne-in-law [1] pulld him [*i.e.* the interpreter] by force away and that faction hedgd the King so that I could scarce see him nor the other approach him. So I commanded the Italian to speake alowd that I craved audience of the King; wherat the King called me, and they made me way. Asaph Chan stood on one side of my interpreter and I on the other; I to enforme him in myne owne cause, hee to awe him with wincking and jogging. I bad him say that I had now beene here two monthes, wherof more then one was passed in sicknes, the other in complements, and nothing effected toward the end for which my master had employed mee, which was to conclude a firme and constant love and peace betweene Their Majesties and to establish a fayre and secure trade and residence

(vol. i. p. 317) Karan's offering is stated as 100 [gold] mohurs, 1000 rupees, an elephant with fittings, and four horses. It also places the date at the 5th *Farwardīn,* which appears to correspond with March 15 (O.S.).

[1] Possibly the Mīrza Beg mentioned in *Letters Received* (vol. iv. p. 330) as having married Asaf Khān's daughter (see also Roe's letter at f. 125 of the MS.). His father was Amānat Khān, Governor of Cambay, who is on this account called later the brother-in-law of Āsaf Khān.

for my countrymen. He answered that was already granted. I replyed it was true, but it depended yet on so slight a thredd, on so weake conditions, that, beeing of such importance, it required an agreement cleare in all poynts, and a more formall and authentique confirmation then it had by ordinarie *firmaens*, which were temporarye commands and respected accordingly. He asked mee what presents wee would bring him. I answered the leauge was yet new and very weake: that many curiosityes were to be found in our country of rare price and estimation, which the King would send and the merchannts seeke out in all parts of the world, if they were once made secure of a quiett trade and protection on honorable conditions, having beene heeretofore many wayes wronged. He asked what kynd of curiosityes those were I mentioned, whether I ment jewells and rich stones. I answered no: that we did not thinck them fitt presents to send back, which were brought first from these parts, wherof hee was cheefe lord: that wee esteemed them common here and of much more price with us: but that we sought to fynd such things for His Majestie as were rare here and unseene, as excellent artifices in paynting, carving, cutting, enamelling, figures in brasse, copper, or stone, rich embroderyes, stuffs of gould and silver. He sayd it was very well: but that hee desiered an English horse. I answered it was impossible by sea, and by land the Turke would not suffer passadge. He replyed that hee thought it not impossible by sea. I tould him the dangers of stormes and varietye of weather would prove yt. He answered: if six were putt into a shipp, one might live; and though it came leane, he would fatt yt. I replyed I was confident it could not bee in soe long a voyadge, but that for His Majesties satisfaction I would write to advise of his request. So he asked what was it then I demanded. I sayd: that hee would bee pleased to signe certaine reasonable conditions which I had conceived for the confirmation of the leauge and for the securitye of our nation and their quiett trade, for that they had beene often wronged and could not continue on such termes: which I forbeare to complayn off, hoping by faire means to procure amendment. At this woord Asaph Chan offered to pull my interpreter; but I held him, suffering him only to wincke and make unprofitable signes.

The King hereatt grew soddenly into cholor, pressing to know who had wronged us, with such show of fury that I was loath to follow yt; and speaking in broken Spanish to my interpreter to answere that with what was past I would not trouble His Majestie but would seeke justice of his sonne the Prince, of whose favour I doubted not, the King, not attending my interpreter but hearing his sonnes name, conceived I had accused him, saying *mio filio, mio filio*, and called for him; who came in great feare, humbling him selfe. Asaph Chan trembled, and all of them were amazd. The King chidd the Prince roundly, and hee excused him selfe; but I, perceivinge the Kings error, made him (by means of a Persian Prince [1] offering him selfe to enterprett, because my Italian spoke better Turkish then Persian; the Prince both) understand the mistaking, and so appeased him, saying I did no way accuse the Prince, but would in causes past in his goverment appeale to him for justice; which the King commanded he should doe effectually. The Prince for his justification tould the King he had offered me a *firmaen*, and that I had refused yt. Demanding the reason, I answered: I humbly thanckd him, but hee knew it conteyned a condition which I could not accept off, and that farther I did desire to propound our owne demands, wherin I would conteyne all the desires of my master at once, that I might not daylye trouble them with complaynts; and wherin I would reciprocally bynd my soverayne to mutuall offices of frendship, and his subjects to any such conditions as His Majestie would reasonably propound, wherof I would make an offer; which beeing drawne tripertite, His Majestie I hoped would signe the one, the Prince the other, and in my masters behalfe I would firme the third. The King pressed to know the conditions I refused in the Princes *firmaen*, which I recited; and soe wee fell into earnest dispute, and some heate. Mocrebchan enterposing sayd hee was the Portugalls advocate, speaking slightly of us, that the King should never signe any article against them. I answered:

[1] 'Meermera, a Persian nobleman nere of bloud to the Sophy and lately fledd upon the death of the Prince for safety to this court' (Roe's accounts). This was Mīr Mīrān, an account of whom is given in Jahāngīr's *Memoirs*, vol. i. p. 305.

I propound none against them, but in our owne just defence, and I did not take him for such a frend to them. The Jesuite and all the Portugalls side fell in, in soe much that I explaynd my selfe fully concerning them; and as I offered a conditionall peace, so I sett their frendship at a mean rate and their hatered or force at lesse. The King answered my demands were just, resolution noble, and bad me propound. Asaph Chan, that stood mute all this discourse, and desiered to end it, least it breake out againe (for wee wear very warme), enterposed that if wee talked all night it would come to this issue: that I should drawe my demands in writting and present them, and if they were found reasonable the King would firme them; to which the King replyed yes, and I desiered his sonne would doe the like, who answered hee would. Soe the King rose. But I calling to him he turnd about, and I bad my enterpreter say that I came the day before to see His Majestie and his greatnes and the ceremonyes of this feast: that I was placed behynd him, I confesed with honor, but I could not see abroad, and that therfore I desired His Majestie to lycence me to stand up by his throne; wherat hee commanded Asaph Chan to lett me choose my owne place.

March 14.—In the morning I sent a messenger to Asaph Chan, least he or the Prince mought mistake mee, by the Kings mistakings, that I had complayned against them; which as I did not, so it was not yet in my purpose; only I was willing to lett them see I did not so depend on Asaph Chan, by whose mouth I used to doe my busines, but that if he continued his manner of never delivering what I sayd, but what he pleasd, I could fynd another way. My message was to cleare any such doubt if it remayned, or if not, to entreat him that he would soften the Prince in my demands concerning Suratt. He answered neyther the Prince nor he had any reason to suspect my purpose was to complayne of them: that the error was evident enough: for his part he had ever had the love of the English, and would endeavour to continew yt.

March 15.—The King sent me a tame sheepe new shorne with his owne hand, so fatt that it had not leane to eate halfe. At evening I went to the *Norose* and demanded of Asaph Chan a place. Hee bad me choose; so I went within the rayle, and stood on the right hand of the Kynge upon the rising of the throne; the Prince and young Ranna on the other syde. So that I sawe what was to be seene: presents, elephants, horses, and many whoores.

March 16-22.—I prepared my demands perfect and in the Persian toong. My course was by way of articles, to make provision for our securitye and peace and to prevent all such abuses as the former yeare had given me experience of; that I might doe all at once, and not trouble the King with new motions and complaynts. I projected to have divers coppies signed togither and to send two to every factory, one to be proclaymed and after sett up in some publique place, the other for the merchants for dayly use.

March 23.—The King condemned a Mogull on suspition of felony, and beeing loath to execute him, both in regard of his person, the goodliest man I ever saw in Indya, and that the evidence were not cleare, hee sent him to mee by the officers in irons for a slave, or to dispose of him at my pleasure. This is esteemed a high favour, for which I returnd thancks: that in England we had no slaves, neyther was it lawfull to make the image of God fellow to a beast: but that I would use him as a servant, and if his good behaviour merited yt, would give him libertye. This His Majestie tooke in very good part.

1616, *March* 26.—I went to the *Gusell Channe*; and delivering the King a present of picturs,[1] I offered up my articles to His Majesties consideration. Asaph Chan tooke and opened them, and finding them somwhat long he found fault; to which I answered they were no longer then the many late abuses required; which I thinck made him doubt they conteyned complaynts. So, showing them the King, they were referrd to him, with promise if they stood with his honor they should be sealed, and I should expect my answere from Asaph Chan. He stept to the Prince and togither reading one or two, finding they were not accusations, he came to mee and promised mee all favour; only hee stuck at the length. But here fell a crosse. I keeping the place which I first tooke,

---

[1] 'The fower pickturs of the fower eliments' (Roe's accounts).

alone and out of ranck which the Kings subjects observe, a place dessigned mee by the King, the place given to Sir Robert Sheirly,[1] and indeed above all his subjects, Asaphe Chan sent mee a message to goe downe and stand by the doore among the Kings servants. I answered: if the King commanded, I knew what I had to doe, but to stirr for any other I would not. He sent againe that it was not the custome for any to stand alone: that I should goe backe in the ranck of noble men. I replyed: I was a stranger and ignorant of their customes, but I was not ignorant that I was a Kings ambassador, and not of the qualety of servants; that His Majestie had placed mee and saw mee now: if I did amisse hee was fittest to find faulte: if it were his pleasure I should goe home, I was ready, but one foote back I would not: and that I expected from him rather additions of grace then discurtesies. Then hee sent an officer to fright mee, but I went so much higher and nearer the King; and standing awhile without molestation, alone and every bodyes eyes cast upon mee, I saw place wherin stood only the Prince and young Ranna by the King, to which I went, resolvinge, if I must rancke, I would rancke with the best. This angred Asaph Chan woorse, who ever sought to woorke me to the humilitye of my predecessors, and to an absolute dependance and obedience on his will. So that, stepping to the Prince, he desiered him to complayne of mee, as of a great insolencey to approach him; which hee did willingly. The King asked why I went from my first place. Asaph Chan replyed that hee had sent to mee to take ranck with the noble men, and made mee move. The King answered: then hee hath done well; what had any man to doe to displace him? Was it not in my sight? What harme does hee? Hee comes to see me; and with such reprehension commanding them to lett me use my discretion. Soe I stood in peace, but with Asaph Chans displeasure.

[1] On his visit to India in 1613-14.

The Coppie of my Demands follow.[1]

Articles of amitye, commerce, and entercourse, betweene the two most high and mighty Kings, the Great Mogull, King of India, and the King of Great Brittane, France, and Irland, concluded on by the said Great Mogull on his part, and in the behalfe of the King of Great Brittane by Sir Thomas Roe, knight, his ambassador for that purpose authorised.

1 First, it is concluded on both parts that ther shalbe a good and perfect love, leauge, and peace to endure for ever betwixt the said mighty Princes, their subjects, and dominions.

2 Secondly, it is concluded and agreed unto by the said high and mighty King of India on his part, which by this writting he doth promise and to all the world declare, that the subjects of the most renowned King of Great Brittane shall come freely without any prohibition to any of the ports or havens in the dominions of the said King of India, as well in Bengala and Syndu as in the lordship of Suratt, with their ships and other vessells, and so arrived may quietly, safely, and peaceably land theyr goods, and for their mony shall have liberty to hire a convenient house, wherein they may remayne, freely to sell, buy, or otherwise transport their goods into the mayne at their pleasurs.

3 Theirdly, it is concluded, that when any ships of the said English shall arrive at any port, the Governor of the place or cheefe citty adjoyning shall publish three severall dayes this agreement, to the end that all men may freely sell at the shore any provision of victualls and releefe and may alsoe goe aboord the ships, trade and buy at their pleasurs, and may freely furnish the said English at the ordinary rates of the Kings subjects with boates, cartes, and other provision of carriadge at their pleasurs without any prohibition, as well at the sea syde as at the rivers; in which the English have lately susteyned great losse.

4 Fowerthly, it is agreed that the persons of English merchants nor theyr servants shall not be searched, nor dispightfully used, but that comminge to the *alfandica* they shall show what necessaryes they bring with them and what mony for expence, which shalbe free unto them from any violence or force of the Governor or other officer, and free of any custome, soe that it exceed not 10 rialls of eight [2] in goods or mony.

5 Fiftly, it is agred that what presents soever are sent by the most mighty King of Great Brittayne, or the Company of Merchants, unto the said great King of India, or for any such

[1] There is a copy of this document in Pepwell's Letter-book, preserved among the I.O. Records. It presents no material difference.

[2] The rial of eight was worth about 4s. 6d. in English money.

use, shall not be touched, opened, nor meddled with by the Governor or any officer what soever; but only beeing marked with their seale shalbe delivered without delay to be sent to court unto the English embassador or agent there resident, that hee may according to directions deliver them unto the said mighty King; wherin the English have beene heretofore much wronged.

6 Sixtly, it is concluded that the goods of the said English merchants landed at any port within the domminions of the King of India shalbe dispeeded to their howse without lett or hinderance and shall not be stayed on any pretence above one day and night in the *alfandica*, to take notice of the number and markes, and soe shall be ther sealed and within six dayes after opened and rated at the house of the said merchants by the officers of the custome, at reasonable prices, and not exacted upon as heretofore.

7 Seventhly, it is agreed that no Governor nor any other officer shall presume to take by force any trifles from poore privat men at their pleasures, but shall suffer them to make price of their owne, and soe paye for yt. Neyther shall the Governor, nor any other officer, by force and without the consent of the merchants take into his house or custody any of the goods so landed, under pretence of servinge the King, nor for his owne use, untill such prises and dayes of payment be agreed on as shall give content to both sides.

8 Eightly, it is concluded that for any goods so landed and agreed for, having dischardged the duties of the port, the said English shall have free liberty to sell to any person, wherin the Governor shall not hinder them, nor force them to agree at his price; or otherwise it shalbe lawfull to convoy and send them to any other their factory without any hinderance or other dutie required in any place as they shall passe, the duty of the port beeing dischardged, wherof the Judg of the *Alfandica* shall give certificatt.

9 Ninthly, it is agreed that what goods soever the English shall buy in any part of the dominions of the said mighty King of India shall passe safely and freely toward their port without any enterruption or force or exaction of convoyes, other then such as them selves shall thinck requisitt, or requiring any custome or duty on the way untill they arrive at their port; wher it shalbe lawfull for them, paying the duties of the port only, according to agreement, to ship theyr said goods without the hinderance or delay of any whatsoever.

10 Tenthly, it is concluded that what goods soever shalbe soe brought downe to any port, shall not be agayne opened by the officers of the port, the English showeing a certificat from the Governors and officers where the said goods were bought, of the numbers, qualeties, and conditions of the said goods.

11 Eleventhly, it is concluded, if any of the said English shall dye in any part of these dominions, ther shalbe no confiscation of any mony or goods in his custodye, but both those and all other debts shall remayne to the factors surviving ; and if all the said factors shall happen to dye, in any of their residences, the officer of the towne shall take notice upon register of all such monyes, goods, bookes, bills, and papers as shalbe found in their house ; which beeing sealed up shalbe delivered to the English at their request.

12 Twelftly, it is agreed that no custome be exacted for victualls during the abode of the ships at any port.

13 Thertine, it is agreed that the servants of the said English shall not be punished, beaten, nor misused for doeing but their duties, whether they be English or Indians ; wherby they have not dared to speake when they have beene commanded.

14 Lastly, it is concluded that in the breach of any of these articles and conclusions by any Governor or officer, and upon any other just occasion, the most mighty King wilbe pleased to give his severall *firmanes* for speedy justice and redresse in all such injuryes ; and upon neglect therof, to give condigne punishment to the offendors. And alsoe to *chop* divers coppyes of this agreement, to be sent by the English ambassador as well to the King of Great Brittaine for his full assurance of the amitye and leauge concluded, as into divers parts of the dominions of the said mighty King of India, to the end that all his officers may without excuse take notice of his command.

It is farther agreed and concluded by the sayd ambassador, on the behalfe of the most mighty King of Great Brittaine, that all the shipps and forces of the said English arriving in any port or coast of the dominions of the said Great Mogull shall suffer all merchannts to passe and repasse quietly with their ships and goods in peace, except the enemyes of the said English, or any other that shall seeke to injure them ; and that all the factors of the English residing in any citty upon the land shall behave them selves peaceably and civilly like merchants, without offering wrong to any person what soever.

Secondly, it is agreed that they shall bring and furnish the said mighty King with all the rarietyes yearly that they can find and with any other goods or furniture of warr which the said King shall reasonablie desire at indifferent [*i.e.* fair] prices, and that they shall not conceale any rarietyes or goods whatsoever (the presents only excepted), but shall make offer to the Governors of the ports wher they arive, for the use of the said King, for which the Governor shall agree for the price and pay for them to theyr content. And if it shall happen that such prices cannot be agreed upon, that then the Governor shall not take them by force, but shall sett his *chop* upon them, and so deliver them to the factors, to be transported to the court, wher they shalbe showed the said King, and agreed for by the factors there resident. But if the said goods appertaine to any privat man, that is to depart with the said ships, then the said Governor shall pay for them at the delivery, or otherwise restore them to the owner.

Therdly, it is concluded that the said English shall pay the custome agreed on at the porte, to say, three per cento and a half for goods reasonably rated, and two per cento for rialls of eight;[1] for which upon certiffcate they shall pay no other custome in any towne wher they shall passe their said goods.

Fowerthly, it is agreed that the said English shall in all things be ready to pleasure and assist the said mighty King and his subjects against any enemy to the common peace, as it becomes the subjects of kings mutually in leauge and confederacy one with another.

Fynally, wheras the Portugalls have, contrary to the lawe of nations, sought by severall assaults to molest the quiett trade of the said English, and have declared them selves theyre enemies and to keepe in subjection the subjects of the said great King of India, notwithstanding the said mighty King of Great Brittaine, beeing a frend to peace and justice, hath given commission to his said ambassador to conclude and comprehend the said Portugalls in the said peace and frendshipe, to the end that trade and commerce might be open and free to all nations, to the great honor, security and proffitt of the said great King of India and his subjects; wherof he the said ambassador by his lettres to the Viceroy of Goa hath made offer, and the said embassador doth farther promise that if, by the means of the said great King or Prince, the said Viceroy (having showed good authoritye from the King of Portugall) will in the space of six monthes enter into the said peace and leauge, he wilbe reddy to accept therof; and in case of refusall it shalbe lawfull for the said English on the seas as well to chastice the stubbornes of an obstinat enemie to peace, as alsoe to requite any robberyes made by them, in taking any of their shipps, boates, or goods, without any offence to the said great King of India.

To all which articles and conclusions all the foresaid mighty Princes have sett their *chops*, and doe promise faythfull performance on all parts on their royall woords.

March 27-31.—I attended Asaph Channs answere, but could not obteyne yt.

The King was feasted at Asaph Channs house, Normall, the Prince, and many attending. From the Kings house to his were velvetts and silkes sowed and layd underfoote an

---

[1] These were the usual rates at Surat (both for imports and exports) for foreigners' goods. Natives paid only 2½ per cent.

English mile, but rouled up as the King passed ; much talked of, but most ridiculously. They reported the feast and present cost 6 *lecks* of *rupias*, which is starling 60,000*li*. ; the particulars [*blank in MS.*] [1]

April 1.—The King went a hunting. At his returne he sent me two willd hogges by a gentellman : that they were kylld by his owne hand, and many favourable complements ; which gladded mee, that His Majestie I perceived was not incensed against mee.

April 3.—I received answer from Asaph Chan that my demands were unreasonable and could not be signed, without mention in what clause or part. This I tooke but as a brave, knoweing the King had not seene them ; or else to drawe a bribe, to which, eaven to base and sordidnes, he is most open. So I resolved to trye by faire meanes, and if there were noe remedie, to appeale to the King for a more indifferent judge.

April 4.—I sent Asaph Chan a lettre expostulating some unkindnesses and the particulars which he misliked in the articles : offering all tearmes of frendship, if I might have yt on free conditions. The coppy is registred.[2]

April 5.—I received answer that he had ever beene a frend to the English, and would so continew to mee if I would follow his councell : that Mocrebchan and others desired that wee should be banished, but that hee withstood yt ; excusing himselfe for sending to mee to take another place, that hee knew not the customes of England ; of the articles not one woord. At night I received lettres from Suratt with the particulars soe long desired of the Governors publique and

[1] The following is Jahāngīr's account, under a date corresponding to March 28 : ' I went to the house of Āsaf Khān, and his offering was presented to me there. From the palace to his house was a distance of about a *kos*. For half the distance he had laid down under foot velvet woven with gold and gold brocade and plain velvet, such that its valûe was represented to me as 10,000 rupees. I passed that day until midnight at his house with the ladies. The offerings he had prepared were laid before me in detail. Jewels, jewelled ornaments, and things of gold and beautiful cloth stuffs, things of the value of 114,000 rupees, four horses, and one camel were approved of ' (*Memoirs*, vol. i. p. 319).

[2] At f. 93 of the MS. It is sufficiently summarized in the text.

privat abuses, which were soe intollerable that never any Christians endured the like from open enemyes. Though these came somwhat late, Zulphekcarcon beeing arrived at court and with our goods extorted by force made his peace, much to my prejudice who had threatned him before his comming and now was silent for want of them, yet I resolved to prosecuute my course, but as warely as I could, taking occasion upon Asaph Chans answere to pretend that I had forborne complayning for respect to the Prince and attended to doe nothing without his advise, which by lettre I requird.

April 7.—I wrote to Asaph Chan about Zulphekcarcon and the abuses of Suratt,[1] sending in Persian a generall complaynt of the personall injuryes to the English and their goods, and with yt three particulars : one of the Companyes goods taken by force from the factors, and of the robberies of privatt men, of his bribes and extortion ; the second, of the goods yet remayning in the custome house deteyned by the judg, with his extortions ; the third, the numbers of presents given voluntarilye to procure his favour, wherby it might appeare wee had not merited the least of his tyrannyes. Asaph Chan read them all in the presence of my messenger and answered that if hee might receive certayne knowledg whether the custome were dischardged or not, that soe much might be deducted toward satisfaction ; the rest, he [Zūlfakār Khān] should bee enforced to pay ; and hee would procure the Princes order for justice in the wrongs for example in tymes to come, and alsoe give us a dischardge for the goods deteyned in the *alfandica*, with restitution of the bribes, and liberty to sell or transport at pleasure ; with many promises of frendship to the English.

To Āsaf Khān.
(*Add. MS.* 6115, f. 93.)

[ ] Aperill, 1616.

Noble Lord, I receive your answere in good part, and am ready to joyne in all offices of love toward yow. Two things only I cannot forbeare to signifie : that the honnor and qualety

---

[1] See the documents printed at pp. 78-85 of *Letters Received*, vol. iv.

of an ambassador is not ruled by the customes of England, but the consent of all the world. He represents the person of a kyng, and the Great Turke soe receves him. Therfore I would not be measured by those that were here before mee, beeing messengers and merchaunts, that came to prepare my way. I would not yow should esteeme it pride I insist on my right; for, if my lord the King know that I dishonor him, it will cost my life. Wheras yow say that I should follow your advise, I am most willing to embrace yt, so long as yt stands with my honor and the good of my cuntrimen. For those that perswade the King to turne out the English, I feare them not. His Majestie is a gratious and just prince, famous for wisdome and benignitye toward strangers; and His Majestie will fynd in the end they are ill councellers and traytors to his peace. But I will say that it were better for us to bee turnd out then to endure the slaveryes, robberyes, and injuryes that this last yeare have beene inflicted on us. And because yow shall perceive that I am ready to take your councell and to doe nothing without your knowledge, and may find the respect I beare the Prince Sultan Corronne, I have sent yow a breefe of the injuryes, bribes, extortions, and debts of Zulpheckcarcon, which are soe villanous and intollerable that no free nation may endure them. And wheras yow thought my articles long and unreasonable, now yow may see whether the abuses suffered require not more. I knowe the King will doe me justice, if I present my petition with these just accusations; but because His Majestie may be angry with the Prince, and for love to yow, I desire first to acquaynt yow with yt, trusting by your advise and favour to find redresse and to gett payement, wherin I will doe nothing without yow. All the presents he hath given the Kyng and the Prince are taken by force from us; soe that I must seeke justice. For, if I should for any respect forbeare, the merchants here would complayne to the King of England, and hee would take my head. Soe, not doubting but yow will take to your consideration both our manifold abuses and the redresse, I committ yow to the great God.

April 8.—Mr. Bidolph returnd with my answer that I knew not whether the customes were payd or not, but that I did desire he [Zūlfakār Khān] might answere and satisfie here for the goods taken by him perforce: that however ther remayned in the *alfandica* sufficient to dischardge the Kings dues, which we prayd warrant to receive upon satisfaction. He answered it was all reason, and that on the morow he would enforme the Prince and cause the mony extorted to be restored, the debts payd, and a command sent to Suratt for the release and liberty of the goods, the customes beeing dischardged ; and if the Prince refused, he would assist mee in seeking justice of the King.

April 10.—I sent to Asaph Chan ; who answered he had delivered my severall papers to the Prince, who had sent them to Zulphekcarcon that hee might peruse them, and whatsoever was due should be payd. He was also new writting the articles by me demanded with his owne hand, saying some woordš were not well placed by my translator : that he would mend them, and procure it signed. This night came the second *caphila* [*kāfila* : caravan] from Suratt with cloth, sent by [1] a Dutchman new tooke up and a boye that was stewards mate in the *Lyon* ; who had beene 62 dayes on the way, to the prejudice of sale, great expence and losse of the Company to employ so ignorant and carelesse fellowes. I received by this *cafala* three cases of bottles of alegant [2] (the cases ould and woorth nothing), and advise from Mr. Kerridge of all busines at Suratt.

April 11-13.—The King went to Hafaz Gemall [see p. 121 *n*] a hunting, and I could not follow, for a flux [*i.e.* dysentery] that hung on mee. Late at night the King returned.

April 14.—I went to the *durbar* and presented the King one case of allegant, which hee tooke very gladly. This was the first tyme I saw Asaph Chan after the unkindnes taken at the *Guzel Chan* ; who, to prevent any woords, used mee with more curtesy then usuall, and tould mee the articles were ready for the seale, and all other my demands should bee fulfilld. This day your cape merchannt at Adsmere dispatched a supply of cloth and factors to Agra ; which I urged a month sooner, but could not prevayle, though the yeare were farr spent.

April 16.—I went to visitt the Prince Sultan Caronne ; for though Asaph Chan had undertaken the busines, yet I feard hee was slow and perhaps the Prince did expect so much observance from mee as to speake to him in myne owne cause.

---

[1] Under the charge of. The English lad was probably William Partridge, while the ' Dutchman ' was the Jacob of p. 51.

[2] A Spanish wine, then much esteemed ; so called from its place of origin (Alicante).

So I tooke some powrfull wyne and in the strength therof desired justice against Zulphekcarcon, offering my four papers of severall accusations. The Prince seemed at first discontent, and answered only : his debts should be payd out of the custome due, when hee had confessd them. I replyed that was not all I desiered nor enough in that poynt : for first, I knew him so false he would never confesse them, if that would avoyd it : next, I expected restitution of bribes, a warrant to deliver the goods deteyned in custome house, liberty to transport at our pleasure, a declaration that the Governor had belyed the King and the Prince in publishing our banishment, and a conformation of our residence, with justice for all personall injuries to the example of future tymes ; which if it were refused mee here, I would appeale to the King, without abusing my selfe with farther hopes. Only I desiered the Prince to doe me this favour, to receive the papers and to read them him selfe ; for our injuries were of soe high a nature and soe unsupportable that I did assure my selfe of speedy redresse from a prince full of honor, when he rightly understood them ; which I knew yet were delivered to him with all favour for my adversary. He sayd that Zulpheckcarcon should be sent for to answer to the particulars. But some replyed yt would be to late, his house beeing farr off ; wherat I seeing the *Buxy* of Suratt in presence, an honest man and a frend to us, I tould the Prince, for the wronges and forces used to us, his servant the *Buxy* [was ?] present, who could give both testemony for mee and satisfaction ; who speaking as far as he durst, the Prince sent for his secretary [see p. 123] and bad him take my papers, read them diligently, and examine Zulpheckcarcon, and make warrant that what bribes, extortions, debts, eyther he or the Judge of the *alfandica* had taken (against whom the complaynt was joyntly) should be deducted out of the custome ; if it sufficed not, the remayner should be here payd : that our goods should be delivered and our abode confirmed, with protection from wrong. In a woord I had an open promise for effectuall satisfaction in all my desiers, except only some exemplary justice upon his person ; which when I urged, the secretary answered that the Judg of the *alfandica* should be dischardged of his place for his corruption towards us, and

that the warrante was passed the seale for his appearance, for
that the Prince had beene enformed by Asaph Chan of as much
as I could say; and for my assurance in what he had there
commanded, he desiered me to take his woord it should bee
effected to my full content in every poynt with all expedition:
that he was sorry and ashamed of the injustice wee had endured; and that hee would ever doe his endevour for our
content. This is hee that almost only will never receive guifte
nor present. When I could obteyne noe more, I was well
content with this; it beeing the best morning that ever wee
had in India.

April 18.—Aganor [Āgha Nūr), the *Cutwall* of Agra, invited
him selfe to breakfaste. He is one of our best frends, very
rich, and defends our nation from all injuryes in Agra.[1]

I sent to Socorola, the Princes secretary, to sollicite the
firmaen. Hee answered he had drawn yt according to my
desire in every clause; only it could not be sealed untill the
debts demanded by us weere agreed unto by Zulpheckcarcon,
who was then gone with Sultan Caronne to Hafaz Geamal;
but that two dayes after, if I would send any to meete Zulpheckcarcon or his *Buxy*, the debts should bee accorded and
all dispatched.

April 19.—Mirza, my neighbour and brother-in-law to the
King, came to visit mee and stayd dynner, but would not eate.
He beggd every thing, but I pleasd him with a feather, three
or four paper picturs, and an ould pare of spurrs.

April 20.—I sent according to appoyntment to meete
Zulpheckcarcon at Sacarollaes; but neyther hee nor any
from him would appeare. Soe he desiered those deputed by

[1] In Roe's list of presents occurs the following account of this
gentleman's behaviour on the occasion: 'I gave him according to
the custome two knives, one of amber and one of jett, cost x*s*., and
a pare of tables of ebonie and eliphants tooth, worth 30*s*. Then hee
desired mee to give his brother a pare of knives, which I did, of
vi*s*. price. After that hee desired some greater knives, and I sheewd
him fower, which hee tooke every one, without restooring the former.
Though this was somewhat unmannerly, yet I was content, because
hee is one of the best frends wee have in India and did keepe the
English house from being taken from them in Agra' (*Add. MS.*
6115, f. 278).

mee to come agayne on the morow, and he would take order they should not loose more labour.

April 21.—They returned, and Zulpheckcarcons steward mett them at the secretaryes, who tooke great paynes to accord the accounts, and with all indifferency and justice assisted them in theyr demands ; but no conclusion could be made, the steward almost absolutly denying every particular, and for some few confessed would not consent to the price demanded. So that concerning the debts it was resolved to write to Suratt to examine witnesses and to make proofe, and upon certifficat wee should here be payd. But this course seemed to mee tedious and delatorye ; so that I resolved of a nother way, receiving at present a *firman* for the goods deteyned in the custome house, and wheras Zulpheckcarcon had devuldged that a *firmaen* was granted for our banishment, it was playnly declared a lye, and command given to entertayne and use the English with all favour, authorising not only their residence but transport and free trade at their pleasurs. Concerning other particular injuries complaynd off long before, for which I was offered a *firmaen* very effectuall, but for a clause concerning the Portugalls I had refused it : it was now new drawen, that article left out, and offered mee, beeing more lardge and ample in many poynts for our redresse ;[1] which I alsoe thanckfullie accepted, resolving to take what I could, and after to seeke remedy for the rest ; but with that was sent the three articles signed by me long before, requiring a fourth that for all armes, as swoords, peices, and such, [they ?] should remayne in the custome house and be sould there, with some other frivolous motions ; which I rejecting

[1] From Roe's letter of 19 June, 1616 (f. 102 of the MS.) it appears that the *farmān* ordered that no goods should be taken, even for the King's use, without payment of ready money : that the English were to be permitted to sell at their pleasure without molestation ; and that their goods were to be allowed free passage to their ships. One clause directed that they should be suffered to hire a house, but not to build one : a prohibition which Roe confesses was due to his motion to Āsaf Khān for a place to fortify—a course to which the Prince would never consent. Another stipulation was that the factors should show all imported novelties to the Customer, for purchase on the King's behalf.

absolutly, it was delivered without yt, and the former articles alsoe forgotten to be remanded. For my demand of justice against the parsonall wrongs offered to our nation, I was answered that Zulpheckcarcon did recriminat and complaine as much against theyr extreame drunckennes, ryott, quarreling and drawing their swoords in the *alfandica* against the Kings officers, and that therfore I was to sett one against other and seeke to mend both in tyme to come : or, if I would not, that then the Prince would expect that justice were likwise done upon such as had offended. I knew to my shame this accusation true and so demurrd of my resolution to prosecute against his person, beeing a favoritt of the Princes, untill I had satisfaction in my other demands ; it being free for me to renew it at my best advantage. Now I had many sutes a foote and durst not venture to have all my desiers at once or none.

April 23.[1]—I sent to Sacarolla this proposition : to give me another *firmaen*, directed to Abram Chan, to examine our account at Suratt (wher, if any proofe could be made, the wittnesses were) and, for as much as should be made manifest, to give warrant to be deducted out of the custome ; for first to send downe to examine wittnesses, to expect answer, and after to attend payment, when in the meane tyme we were forced to cleare the custome, or suffer our goods to lye and take losse, I thought unreasonable. He answered he had labored for us, and had drawen him [Zūlfakār Khān] to confesse most part, to the summe of 14 or 15,000 *mamo*[*odies*] ; [2] so that he was resolved he had all the rest, and therfore would putt him to sweare to every particular by the Princes head, which was as much as could be done in the case of any subject ; and when he had answered, wee should receive a *firmaen* for all togither. Further he sayd that 700 and odd ryalls of eight specifyed in our bill to rest in the custome house was sent to the Prince in specie, for which we should have warrant.

April 25.—Seeing this could not be effected with expedition,

[1] Shakespeare's death-day.

[2] The *mahmūdi* was a Gujarāt coin which circulated extensively in Western India. Terry calls it 'about twelve pence sterling ' ; Peyton says it equalled 30 *pice*, of which 33½ were equivalent to an English shilling.

S.T.R. K

I sent downe the two *firmaens* received to Suratt,[1] with advise how I would proceede in the busines, giving warning to arme themselves with what proofe could be made against that which Zulpheckcarcon should here forsware

To the Factors at Surat.
(*Add. MS.* 6115, f. 93.)

26 April, 1616.

Yow may thinck I have forgotten to write, so teadious uncertaintyes having shutt up all occasion. . . . Nowe I will give yow particular answers to all the parts of your lettres, as also some generall advises and observations of myne owne. . . . I am very glad to here your opinione that this trade were better dissolved then continewed on soe base termes ; which I have freely both professed to the King, the Prince, and those lords that meddle in our busines, and will eyther reduce it to some better oonstitution or withdrawe yt. . . . For other wrongs, the *firmaen* herewith is somwhat more then yow have had, though not according to my entent, for I have undertaken a more generall course, to cure the whole disease and not dayly to apply plasters of ordinary *firmaens* (which are regarded as long as they are reading) ; but in the meane tyme make this use of them to serve the present ; which yow shall better effect, if yow stand confident on my resolution to prosecute every injury to satisfaction or to depart the countrye. . . .

The continuinge of this trade consists principally on two poynts : our good reception and priviledges to be obteyned and performed to us here : and the vent of our owne comodityes. Without the one, wee cannot abyde with honor ; without the other wee will not, to no proffitt. For our reception and priviledges they stand on doubtfull tearmes and will runne the chaunce of fortune. For the King respects us very well and is ready to grant all reasonable demands ; but this affection is forced and not naturall, and therfore noe permanent nor assured ground to build on. The Prince dislikes us, and though he favour no Christian, yet the Portugall most, and hath pleaded for him (under pretence of more profitt to his port, disdainfully asking what wee bring, but cloth and knives). Now this disposition is naturall, like to continew and in tyme upon all advantages to woorke or weare out his fathers better opinione, which is att best but feare and temporising ; for if ever the Portugall can give us one blowe, wee are lost here. . . . For our second foundation of our residence in these parts, the

---

[1] Also a letter to Ibrāhīm Khān, the Governor (MS., f. 96), desiring him to assist the English factors.

venting of our owne comodytye, though I have no sckill in particular merchandize, yet I universally discerne they will sooner and faster weaken us here then the want of priviledges, for I see no comoditye that will prove staple and certaynly vendable, able to returne a ship yearly. Our cloth will not off in many yeares ; here I am perswaded twenty will not sell ; the King is glutted with the last, and no man reguards it. Swoords are woorse ; lead and teeth, if they will vent, yet will they lade faster out then home. For one yeare gould or silvered velvetts, grogrames, chamletts and silk stuffs may serve us, but constantly noething. So that my opinion is, breefly, seeing our state cannot beare the exportation of mony, except some new trade can be discovered from the East to serve this kingdome, it must fall to ground by the weaknes of itts owne leggs.[1] . . . Ther remaynes only two things : that

[1] This letter initiated an interesting correspondence on the prospects of the trade and the drain of silver from Europe which it entailed. Writing on the 26th of the following month, Kerridge and his colleagues agreed that the English trade was tolerated rather than desired, for more profit was derived from that with the Portuguese, and moreover the competition of the English in the trade with Java and Sumatra was a great grievance to the merchants of Surat. ' Soe that, as our entertaynment was in a manner forced, our privilidges and good usadge (if at all, as wee feare) must accordingly bee obtayned and continued.' As regards the prospects of the commerce, the factors took a more cheerful view than Roe. They considered that the sale of lead, tin, broadcloth, etc., would be fairly constant. ' And though all these should faile, the commodities of this country may have such currant vent in some of our neighbour lands as will produce more ready coyne then the Company shall neede to send heyther to supplie this trade ' (*Letters Received*, vol. iv. p. 314). Roe returned to the subject on 19 June (MS., f. 104) :• ' Without mony this trade will fall, which is one motive not to be too base to hould it up. That these comodityes will vent for silver in other countryes our neighbors is no answere ; for this [*silver*] comes not out of England which is now sent, and wee are as well members of Europe as citizens of England, which is but one lymne, and if the whole growe poore wee beare our proportion. But the losse is more particular ; for if wee did not send mony this way, the merchant, who often sould for mony, gott more by returning it in specie very often then by investing it ; and so it came to the Kings mynt, which now cryes like a hungry belly against this trade.' The factors replied (23 July) with some spirit (*op. cit.*, p. 325) that the interests of England ought to be studied rather than those of the Continental nations ; and that, if the East India trade did not exist, an equal amount of silver would be sent to Turkey for the purchase of similar goods. Moreover, they pointed out that all the

tryall be made of some cloth toward Lahor and downe into Bengala, which is your care; secondly, the discovery of Syndu, which the Company much desire and is very requisite; for this roade of Swally is no place of securitye for our shipping, if the Portugall persist our enemy. . . . Therfore I purpose, as soone as I gett my articles sealed, to send Shalbanck over land for discovery of the port, the depth of the barr, and comoditye of the river, which I know is navigable from Lahor, and will much ease the convayance of our goods, if wee settle that way. From thence hee offers to goe by frigott to Jasques, to prepare the place, if our ships should putt in as they passe in August. . . .

silver landed at Surat that season amounted only to about 4,000*l.*, whereas the goods sent home in the *Lion* totalled four times that sum, the difference having been provided from the proceeds of English goods. The customs on the *Lion's* cargo would, they averred, give a profit to the King's treasury far outweighing the loss caused by the silver not being available for mintage. Roe, in a further letter of 20 August (MS., f. 114), rejoined with some asperity that he 'doubted not but that the King may gayne in customes wher the common wealth doth loose; that England might profitt by Europes detriment. But I proposed a generall care, wherin if the Dutch and Portugall fayle in their duties, it doth not follow yow should err in your judgment. . . . However yow esteeme that little losse, the Parliament of England, which is the spiritt and soule of the wisedome of England, more valewes 10,000*li.* mony in regard of substantiall wealth then 100,000 in estimation in China dishes, silkes, spices, dyes and trash, that consume in one yeare, the fuell of yearely pride and gluttony; for in the neede or perill of the commonwealth none of these will sett out a fleete to sea nor pay an army. And if their authorytye prevaile with yow, know, if the last [*The* 'Addled Parliament' (1614), *in which Roe had sat as member for Tamworth*] had proceeded, they had limited both this and the Turkish Company, supposing the crye of the Kings mynt to be as mournfull a hearing as if the liver, the fountayne of blood, should complayne in a naturall body. For they consider not like yow that more profitt came to the Kings coffers by customes of East India goods then would arise by all the mony that is transported; but they regarded that so much mony in England were more esteemable then all that goods to the common wealth, for that what soever comes in by customes is the Kings owne and is payd by the mony already in the land, but the silver that comes to the mynt is as it were new begotten and added to the stocke of the kingdome, and is the property of divers men, beeing enfranchised and naturalized by the Kings stampe and impression.'

It will be noticed that the factors, in defending the export of silver from England, took the line of argument adopted five years later by Thomas Mun in his *Discourse of Trade* (1621).

April 26.—I received intelligence that the Prince caused one of his servants at the *durbar* to aske the King why he used so good countenance to the English that for their cause the Portugalls were barred the port of Suratt, who brought more proffitt to the King, as many ballaces,[1] pearles, and jewells, wheras the English came only to seeke proffitt with cloth, swoords, and knives of little estimation. The King answered only: it was true, but who could mend yt?[2] Hereby the Princes good affection was manifest, and I had faire warning to be watchfull and to study to preserve ourselves in the Kings grace, in which only wee were safe; but I resolved to take notice of this and to make proofe if I could settle a better opinion in the Prince of our nation.

April 27.—I advised Asaph Chan what had passd concerning Zulpheckcarcon; who returned me that I should not abate one *pice*.

April 28.—I sent to Socarolla, who answered that Zulpheckcarcon had beene putt to sweare according to promise to the particulars unconfessed, and that hee had craved three dayes to call all his people to account what had beene taken without his knowledge or not in his memorie, which was granted; and that the *firmaen* for the 700 riall of eight and the debts confessed was ready, but, to end it togeather, it was deteyned untill the expiration of this tyme, when wee should have satisfaction in all.

April 29.—I roade to visitt Asaph Chan in the morning, but hee was asleepe. At night I went to the *durbar* about my articles from the King, which were of most consequence. Asaph Chan, after many complements excusing his sluggishnes, desiered me to take no care for them: he would gett them signed, and send them: that he tooke so to hart our busines that I might rest secure, and that he needed no other remembrancer then his affection to mee. This overmuch kindnes

[1] The balass ruby, really a rose-red spinel.

[2] Roe refers to this incident in a letter to Surat of 19 June, 1616 (f. 102 of the MS.), saying that the Prince alleged that the customs of Surat were diminished and the merchants impoverished by the discouragement of Portuguese trade. Roe adds that when he himself hinted at his withdrawal if not satisfied, Jahāngīr merely said: 'if I would bee gone, I might; if stay, I should bee welcome'

was suspitious to mee, but I seemed to beeleve it sincere. So I desired him to tell the King I had some wyne left, which, beginning to be hard, I durst not present, not knoweing how hee liked yt, but if it were agreable to His Majestie, I would send it to the *Guzell Chan*; which he accepted, and I performed.

April 30.—I sent to Socorolla; who answered hee would make a warrant for the payment of as much as was confessed, which should bee ready on the morowe.

At night Etiman-Dowlett,[1] father of Asaph Chan and Normall, sent me a basquett of muske-millons with this complement, that they came from the hands of the Queene his daughter, whose servant was the bearer.

May 1.—I sollicited Socorolla for the warrant for our debt; but insteed therof received that Zulpheckcarcon had not swoorne to all particulars demanded, beeing loath to venture perjurye, and therfore would on the morowe send Hoja Nasson to my house to agree on every poynt, and soe eyther pay mee ready mony at Adsmere or by bill of exchange at Suratt at my choyce.

May 3.—I received lettres from the factory of Amadavaz that, because they had demanded the 500 rupies taken from them, by virtue of the Kings command sent them, the Governor, Abdella Chan,[2] beeing returned from the armie in Decan, sent the *Cuttwall* to take theyr howse perforce for one of his trayne. They resisted, and craved releefe.

May 4.—I went to Asaph Chan to acquaynt him with this affront and desiered his councell, pretending I was unwilling to complayne to the King and provoke his indignation against a great man who had contemned His Majesties *firmaen*, that commanded all sort of good usage to our nation; both because I would not on every slight occasion trouble His Majestie, nor

---

[1] Itimād-uddaula (Ghiyās Beg). After his daughter's marriage to Jahāngīr, he was made Wazīr of the kingdom, but he does not seem to have taken an active part in the administration.

[2] Abdullah Khān, Fīrūz Jang, governor of Gujarāt, who had just prosecuted an unsuccessful campaign against the Dekhan kings. As will be seen, he was soon after recalled to court in disgrace, but was pardoned through the influence of Prince Khurram. He was a strong partisan of the latter, and took a prominent part in his rebellion.

willingly draw on me the hate of the nobilitye (who would all partake against a stranger), if I could by any faire way procure remedye and enjoy our libertyes with good liking. He gave me great thancks, and assured mee hee would see my redresse should be speedy and effectuall : that therfore hee desired mee to forbeare, according to my proposition : that hee would write on the morrow to Abdella Chan and to two other frends he had there, who should be solicitors for the English ; and that if after that he contineued to injure us, he would cause him to be sent for, and to answere yt to the King. With this I rested content. About my articles he sayd they were in some places obscure : that he had cleard them to the King and would procure them signed : that he was never lyar nor of a double hart : that I should find him so ready to doe my nation any service, as our cause were his owne. Only hee sayd wee brought not so curious toyes for the King as did the Portugall ; to which I answered fully, and to give him proofe I desiered a *scrite* in what sorts the King would most delight ; which hee promised, naming for the present, picturs in brasse, the coullors layd in, especially a basson and ewre of such woork, some coulored French muff or plush, some good cloth of gould and silver, some sutes of arras in great imagery and fine, a saddle and feild caparison, but above all an English horse ; and for our cloth the finest sort, wherof the King would buy quantetyes. I replyed that the Company could hardly venture upon cloth of high price and the richest clothes of gould, unlesse they were sure of vent : for toyes, they would furnish the King of guift, but miattres of great chardge theyr gaynes would not beare : but if he would sett downe the particulars and quantetyes and prices, and give the Kings *chop* that they should be taken off and payd for, I would promise his desire should be satisfied fully ; which he sayd he would enforme the King. Hee drew the swoord I wore, and with extraordinarie commendations provoked mee to say it was at his service. He answered hee was no man of complement : that to take a swoord from soe good a frend was held unluckye. I replyed the excuse was not strong enough against the affection with which it was offered : that with us one frend gave a nother a swoord when he was to use yt.

He sayd small perswasions would serve from mee: that he would use yt at my service; and with more complements then any Parisian tooke yt. He invited mee to dinner some dayes after (but naming none), where he promised to be merry and drinck wyne with me as a curtesye. So I took leave. About two howers after he sent his steward with 20 musk-mellons for his first present. Doubtlesse they suppose our felicitye lyes in the palate, for all that ever I received was eateable and drinckable—yet no *aurum potabile*.

May 5.—In the morning came a Mogull merchant from Hoja Nasson to desier a peace, offering to bring Zulpheckcarcon to my howse and to make eaven the accounts, and to pay the mony here or at Suratt. I replyed I was ready to forgive some injuries, but his abusing my master would alway stand betweene us untill he made amends: for the debts I desird him to dine with mee on the morow, when I would be ready to make my demands; which hee promised. At night I sent to Asaph Chan for the three promised lettres. Hee answered the procurator of Abdela Chan was newly arrived at court, with whom he had beene so round that he doubted not of good satisfaction to the English: that he was to returne in few dayes: that it had beene his watch,[1] which hindered him for performance of his promise, which hee would presently fullfill: desiring to send for them in the morning. This day I received lettres from Agra complayning of theyr house; but they had it rent free and it was lardg, and I held it not fitt to trouble the King unnecessarilye.

May 6.—Came Hoyja Nasson to account for Zulpheckcarcons debt. After some particulars read, for want of one to write on their sides, he desird that some English might early on the morow come to his howse, wher should meete a *scrivano*[2] and finish that busines, and that ready mony should be delivered or bills to Suratt at choyse; to which I agreed, and dessigned Mr. Bidolph and Fettiplace[3] to attend

[1] The nobles were required to take turn in mounting guard.

[2] A scrivener or writer (Port. *escrivão*).

[3] Francis Fetiplace appears to have arrived at Surat in Downton's fleet. He was at Ajmer till the autumn of 1616, when he proceeded to Agra, returning to the royal camp a few months later. He died

yt. This day I dispatched for Amadavaz three lettres from Asaph Chan, one to the Governor, Abdela Chan, the other to his brother, Zudgar Chan,[1] the third to Abbal the *Buxy*, signifing both the Kings pleasure for the good entreatment of the English and his owne desire and favour on their part, perswading to suffer them abyde in their house and to use theyr trade with freedome ; for that otherwise complaynts would be addressd to the King by the ambassador, to whom His Majestie had promised speedy justice. I wrote also to Abdela Chan in fayre tearmes to procure him my frend, knowing the easeyest is the safest way : but withall letting him know I must performe my duty, if he neglected his. The coppy is registred.

May 7.—Hoya Nasson could not attend our account.

May 8.—They mett and the *scrivane* of Zulpheckcarcon was present. They charged him by particulars, wherof some he denied. The conclusion was that Hoya Nassan would goe to him and showe him our demands and perswade him to pay us if not, wee should on the morowe receive a resolute answere To day I received lettres from Amadavaz that the Englis were removed out of their howse by the Governors order, but without force ; in which they were too hastie, for they wrot to me for redresse, which I sent within two dayes,[3] and the would not attend an answere, to the great losse of the Compan

May 9.—Hoya Nassan returned this answere : that Zu pheckcarcon had confessed many particulars denied by h *scrivano*, and the rest hee doubted not but hee would pay, f that hee desiered peace and frendship with mee ; and that two dayes it should be finished. At noone the late *Buxy*

at Agra in May, 1621. Roe praised him as 'a plodding fellow, ve honest and religious, a good accountant, industrious, and stout.'

[1] Khwāja Yādgār, on whom Jahāngīr had in 1613 conferred t title of Sardār Khān.

[2] See f. 98 of the MS. A letter from Roe to the factors at Ahma ābād is given on the preceding folio.

[3] On 9 May (see f. 99 of the MS.). In the letter the factors w told to bid the Governor ' enquire of the successe of Zulpheckcar and the Judg of the *alfandica* at Suratt, both which are removed their abuses to us : that the Prince hath entreated me not to l the King know of yt, who swore that hee would putt them under feete of elyphants that wrongd us.'

Suratt came to visitt me, one well favored by the Prince; with whome, knoweing the qualetye of our injuries, having beene an eye wittnesse, I had some conferance about Zulpheckcarcon, in whose behalfe hee spake to make agreement. I tould him in conclusion that I would be noe longer delayed: if in two dayes Zulpheckcarcon did not ingenuously confesse the injuries and debts, and give me satisfaction, I would acquaynt the King not only with his villany toward us but with the oppressions of his subjects, his robberies, and all his tiranney excersised in his goverment, and in particular of the forcing the house of the Governor of Gundivee [1] and taking all his goods and drowening his mother, keeping him in a dungion to prevent complaynts. He promised mee his endevour to end all in the prefixed tyme.

At night the King sent me a woeman slave, servant to Normall, who for some offence was putt away. I was loath to receive her, it beeing midnight; but the officers would take noe refusall, having command to deliver her to my selfe, that I was enforced to lett one come into my bed side with her; and soe received her, a grave woeman of 40 years. I demanded her fault. The officer answered the King bad him assure me she was honest, only shee had offended the woeman. The particulars shee after tould me. For that night I was forced to lodge her in my dininge roome, and early in the morninge I sent to Asaph Chan to give the King thancks, but that a woeman was unfitt for my house: that shee had some frends on whom I would bestowe her, if it might not bee displeasing to the King, shee having beene soe neare his person.

This night I was encompassed with fier, it having begune on three sydes; one wherof was soe vehement that it consumed many thousand howses. Wee were all at our doore ready to shift, for wee had beene [2] forced to loose all our goods. Ther were burnt in one house 14 woemen and some men, and many others otherwere. My house Mr. Edwards builte all of strawe sides and tops,[3] so that it neither kept out wynd, dust, nor

[1] Gandevi, 28 miles S.E. of Surat, now in Baroda territory.
[2] Should have been.
[3] Probably of bamboo or some kind of reed; such buildings are common in India. Roe had added some rooms (see p. 91).

rayne, to our infinite discomoditye, and wee were nightly afrayed of our lives, the fiers being soe common that to my remembrance no night did escape without some, and soe terrible in the wynds that, all the streets beeing of straw howses and many places grasse, hay, corne, and wood piles, that there hath beene no possibility to come neare, it licking up all eaven to the townes end. It had beene thrice within a quayts [*i.e.* quoit's] cast of my house, but the wynd favored, or else we had lost all. Soe that, beeing prest by the merchannts, whose goods were utterly lost if the fier took us, and for our securitie, having scarce had one night of rest, and finding by myne owne experiance I could build sufficient roomes of bricke and lome fier free every way for lesse mony the[n] Mr. Edwards his steward spent in straw, I resolved to pull all downe, which I did in one day; and in ten after I had finished seven good roomes, wherby the English shall now bee sufficiently howsed for 20 years, with some reparation by reason of the violent raynes, and secure both in theyr goods and persons.

May 10.—Asaph Chan sent me woord that, by reason the woeman sent by the King had beene neare the King and Queene and putt away in cholar, he wished me not to give her libertie before hee had spoken with the King; giving me thancks for my respect towards His Majestie in sending before I delivered her.[1]

May 12.—I received answer that hee would send a *Banian* for her, and keepe her untill the King might forgive or dispose her; for I was in trouble with her, but had placed her in a servants house that was married. This night Hoya Nassan sent woord I should know a resolution concerning the debts of Zulpheckcarcon on the morrowe. This day I dispatchd an advise to Suratt.[2]

May 13.—I received answer that hee had labored in the busines and had drawne him to agree to pay 17 thousand *mamodoes*, which was all hee could doe, and desiered mee to accept it. It was 2900 lesse then the bill sent of the publique

[1] In a letter to Surat a month later, Roe humorously summed up the tokens he had received of the king's liberality as consisting of 'hoggs flesh, deare, a theefe, and a whore.'

[2] The letter is given on f. 99 of the MS.

and privat debt; but in consideration some things were overrated, both on the Companyes behalfe as alsoe of privat mens, and that the losse was not very great, every man beeing to beare a part, I sent Mr. Bidolph to see if [in] this offer the 750 rialls acknowledged by the Prince and the bribe of the Judge of the *alfandica* were not comprehended, but that those should be payd apart; then I gave him order to make a finall end, knoweing it better to loose somewhat then wholy to draw the Princes indignation toward us, who much desiered an end of this question; but withall I bad him make tryall to advance as much more as could be gotten without open warr. He returned with answere that all was comprehended in this offer, and that I must give a generall acquittance for any further demand, for that hee [Zūlfakār Khān] had taken on him to satisfie the royalls of eight and to cleare all questions, and that if I would not accept of this I should seek remedie; if I showed papers he had papers to answer them (thus confident he bare himselfe on the Prince); and that hee did offer to pay what wee could prove, which was not halfe, beeing taken on the way, in the boate, and in the towne without any order. At evening I sent the Princes secretarie woord of this answer: that I was resolved to complayne to the King: and that, having attended soe long for respect only of the Prince, I hoped hee would not be displeased. He answered hee would acquaynt the Prince what I said: for his owne parte he would no longer diswade mee from seekin justice. I sent alsoe to Asaph Chan to the same effect, and to lett him know that he should not bee seene in the busines to displease the Prince, but that I would deliver my complaynt in writing my selfe: I only desiered his favorable good woord to the King in our behalfe. He gave me many thancks for this respect toward him, but hee entreated mee for his sake to forbeare a few dayes: that hee would speake with the Prince and Zulpheckcarcon and procure an end. Hee desiered I would not stand for two or three thousand *mamodoes*, for the Princes sake and his: that other wayes it should not bee lost: that he spake this for love, knoweing the Princes affection to Zulpheckarcon and his unreaconsilable disposition: that wee should never have quiett at Suratt whilest hee was lord therof, without daylie complaynts to the King, which would much prejudice us, to sett the father against the sonne, and give great advantage to our enemyes. He sent a servant for my woeman and I was very glad to returne my present.

May 15.—I sent Asaph Chan an antidote for poyson,[1] giving thancks for his free dealing and favour, and, that he should see what power eyther the Prince or him selfe had to command mee, I would venture beyound my authoritye to give away that which was non of myne owne, and that, if hee pleased to spend one hower to hear us both, he should be judge and decide the difference. He replyed he would not meddle in that kinde, the Prince beeing in a sorte a party, for he had most of the goods ; but he assured me he had dealt the night before very effectually with the Prince, and that hee had not received any other then a generall answere : that the next day, if he could procure it, hee would send me a resolution : if I hard not from him in four dayes, then I should understand he could doe noe good ; and bad me make readye a petition in the name of the merchannts to the King, and hee would give mee all my [*sic*] assistance.

May 16.—I dispatched a lettre to the Governor of Agra,[2]

[1] Probably a bezoar-stone ; they were ' much used in India against all poyson and other diseases ' (Linschoten, vol. ii. p. 143), and thence derived their name (Pers. *pādzār*). In April, 1617, Roe asked Bangham to procure for him a few of these stones, adding some particulars which are sufficiently interesting for quotation : ' For Bezars,' he says, ' ther are three sorts ; the best are of Persia, others from Malacca, the last of Masolapatan and Bengala. . . . The best . . . are a blackish greene of Persia. . . . The prices in England are about 3*li*. an ounce ; if the stones be great and whole they are woorth 5*li*. . . . To avoid counterfaytes . . . with a very hot needles poynt peck them. If it make noe signe, they are not false ; if the nedle enter or burne them, they are made ones. The best triall of the virtue is to lay them in buffles milke, and the best will turne it like runnett and those are rich.' Roe himself seems to have been rather sceptical of their efficacy, at least in ordinary diseases ; for when, in 1624, the Queen of Bohemia commissioned him to procure some for her, he wrote that ' Sir Thomas Smyth is alway furnished plentifully, yet they will not cure his gowt.'

[2] See f. 99 of the MS. From an entry on a later page, we learn that the brother's name was Muhammad . Husain, and that the transaction had been managed by Robert Young.

concerning a debt oweing by his brother, to see if with faire woords I could procure it, having soe many of that kinde that would cloye the King; and this some tymes proves the best and is ever the easiest way. This eveninge the King went to Pocora,[1] four *course* off Adsmere, a village of the *Bannians* wher they resort for devotion, full of their pagods and other gentilitiall impietyes. When they have any solemnitye, he useth to visitt it for sport.

May 21.—The King returned from Pocora.

May 22.—I went to the *durbar* to visitt the King and to desier his authoritie to have one Jones, a youth that was runn away from me to an Italian and protected him selfe under the name of the King, to the infamy of our nation.[2] The King gave order for his deliverie; but the Prince, who ever wayted oportunitye to disgrace our nation, for the cause of his favoritte Zulpheckcarcon (with whom I was newly broken off from conference, and had sent the Prince woord I would noe longer forbeare openinge my cause to the King), mooved the King in privatt to send for the youth first; which at the *Guselcann* he did. And the Prince giving him countenance, he rayled to my face with most virulent malice, desiering the King to save his life; so the King resolved not to deliver him to mee, but to send him prisoner to Suratt. But the Prince, to brave mee, beggd him for his servant, the fellow having quite renownced his countrie. The King gave him to the Prince, notwithstanding any reasons I could alleadge. Soe the Prince presently gave him 150 *rupies* and the pay of two horse, and forbad mee to meddle with him.

May 23.—At night my man came and fell at my feete, asking pardon for his lyeing and madnes, and offered to submitt him-

---

[1] Pushkar, where there is a celebrated temple to Brahma (see Tod's *Rajasthan*, ed. 1920, vol. ii. p. 892). It is still a great place of pilgrimage.

[2] In a letter to Masulipatam (see later), Roe stated that Jones 'departed my house without consent and lived a life scandalous both to myne and my nations honor, from which when I sought to withdrawe him by force and to punish him exemplarily, hee fell to woorse, abusing both His Majestie, my selfe, and all his countrimen' (*Letters Received*, vol. iv. p. 144).

The Italian referred to was John Veronese, of whom see p. 124.

selfe in any kind. I tould him I would not now keepe him prisoner: he was the Princes servant: but that before I could give him any answere, he should make me publique satisfaction as farr as he was able. This day I received lettres from one Lucas[1] at Mesolapatan concerning merchanntes affaires; which I understood not, and delivered them to Bidolph to be sent to Suratt.

May 24.—Jones made means to come to the *Guzelchan* and ther asked pardon of the King for his lyes, denieing every woord he had spoken to have beene done to protect him selfe from mee, whom hee had offended; desiering the King to send for mee, that hee might there aske my pardon. The King was well pleased; but the Prince fell into a great rage.

May 25.—I went to the *Guzellcan*, where after many protestations of the King that hee never beleeved him: that hee was a villayne: yet that hee could doe noe lesse but protect him, having cast him selfe into his mercy, the youth was sent for, who on his knees asked me forgivenes and on his oath swore to the King that he had in every particular belied mee; which hee professed to doe voluntarie, for that hee never durst returne to his countrie. The King chid him a little and tould me, he nor any good man ever beleved him. But the Prince grew so angry that, moevinge him with many questions to stand to his first woords, which hee refusing was bid begone; and the Prince, publiquely calling for him againe, bad him most basely returne him the 150 *rupies* delivered him, for that hee gave it to mayntayne him against mee; which seeing he went from, he would have his mony; which the fellow promised; but he would have it presently and so sent an under treasurer with him to the house wher he was lodged, for into myne I would not suffer him to come.[2]

[1] Lucas Antheunis. He and another Dutchman, Pieter Floris, were the leaders of the Company's seventh voyage (1611), which was especially intended to open up trade on the Coromandel coast, and at Patani and Siam. He had reached Masulipatam from Patani towards the end of 1615. His letter is printed at p. 28 of vol. iv. of *Letters Received*.

[2] Jones had been recommended to Roe by Lord Carew, who, on learning of his behaviour, expressed extreme vexation and regretted that the 'monstrous wretche . . . was nott hanged by the Kinge or

May 26.—I sent to Asaph Chan, the tyme being expiered about Zulpheckcarcon, having promised to doe noething without him ; which promise necessitie urged me too, for that I am tyed to this inconvenience, that my linguist may never speake to the King but only to Asaph Chan, who is appoynted sollicitor for our nation ; soe that I can doe nothing without him, neyther will he ever deliver but what hee pleaseth. I sent him woord my petition was ready : I only attended his answere. He returned mee that I should forbeare yet a few dayes : that hee would see mee payd, or pay it himselfe. I urdged a day, which hee would not sett ; for, said he, if I misse one, you will count me a promise breaker ; but that I should take his woord hee would see the mony satisfyed.

May 27.—I went to the *durbar*, wher the King used me with extraordinary favour ; but the first woord hee asked when any English shipps would come. I answered : about fower monthes. Then he demanded what presents they would bring. I named arras and pictures in brasse. He asked for doggs. I tould him I doubted not but hee should bee furnished alsoe this fleete. So he seemed content.

I alsoe sent to Asaph Chan in the morning about the debt,

---

you when his fillthenesse and treasons towards you were manifested ' (*Letters of Lord Carew*, p. 122). How much Roe was angered by being braved in the face of the court by one of his own followers is shown by the pains he took to secure the punishment of the culprit, who was now desirous of quitting the country. To send him prisoner to Surat was out of the question, as the ambassador had ' promised the King otherwise ' ; so Roe stooped to gain his ends by a trick. He persuaded Jones to make his way overland to Masulipatam with the idea of getting a passage by a Dutch ship ; then, to secure his capture, an order on the English factory for 25*l*. was given him, and directions were secretly sent to the factors to seize him when he should present it ; should he be suspicious and abstain from claiming the money, he was to be inveigled aboard an English ship ' under pretence of merriment,' and sent home. Antheunis duly carried out his instructions, and Jones reached London a prisoner in October, 1618, and was at once committed to Newgate. On 20 Jan. and 16 March following, he petitioned the Privy Council for release on bail (*Cal. Dom. State Papers*), but, upon a representation from the East India Company, it was determined to leave him where he was until Roe's return. His subsequent fate is unknown.

but hee answered hee would not meddle farther in yt: the Prince he would not loose for us. So at the *durbar* I expostulated with him about this answere: that I only depended on him: and now contrarie to his promise to be rejected, I thought it very unjust. I desiered him to deale playnly, for I [he?] knew I was able to deliver the King my complaynts at any tyme in writing without him, which I was resolved to doe: wherin I would lett the King know both our wrongs and how little meanes wee had to seeke redresse, by reason no man would speake for us: which when I had done, I must referr it to His Majesties justice, and I was dischardged of my dutie to my master. He answered that I was willfull and impatient: that he could not loose the Prince: that I was a stranger and knew not the pace of this court nor the King soe well as hee: that if I would use him, I must follow his councell, which if I would doe, hee was ready to assist mee: if I thought my owne wayes better, then hee would no way meddle. Soe I tould him I had alway depended on his advise and deferred my complaynt for his sake four monthes: that I had sent the Prince woord I would complayne was not without his consent, having prefixed me a tyme when I should be free to doe soe, which was expired. So we agreed that I should come to his house within a day or two, and ther conclude what was to bee done in this busines; promising to perfect all my demands, if I would have patience. Thus I was enforced to seeme content, because I had noe way to seeke remedie; for presents I had none, and the King never takes any request to hart except it come accompaned, and will in playne tearmes demand yt; which advantage the Prince takes, urdging the Portugalls bringing of jewells, ballests, and pearles, with much disgrace to our English comodytye.

May 28.—Ther came divers Portugalls merchannts from Goa with many rarietyes to sell the King and with rich presents from the Vizeroy of Goa. This is yearly theyr custome at this season to bring goods, and so to goe for Agra and invest in indico. While these presents are fresh, the English are lesse respected.

May 29.—The Portugalls went before the King with a present, and a ballas ruby to sell that weighed, as was reported,

13 *tole*, two *tole* and a half being an ounce.[1] They demanded five *lecks* of *rupies*, but the King offered but one. Asaph Chan is also theyr sollicitor, to whom they gave a present of stones. They had divers rubies, ballaces, emrallds, and jewells sett to sell; which so much contented the King and his great men that we were for a tyme eclipsed. The Prince and the Jesuite fell out about presenting them; which the Prince desiered, but it was promised before to Asaph Chan. Concerning the Portugalls creditt here, I ever made my judgment by report, but now experience showes me the difference made betweene us and them; for they were sought after by every body, wheras they seeme to buy our comodityes for almes. Besides, their neighborhood and advantage to hinder that trade into the Red Sea is ever more ready then ours to doe harme, because they are settled. So that only for a little feare we were entertayned; but, for our trade, or any thing wee bring, not att all respected.

May 31.—I went to Asaph Chan to visitt him, but hee was sick of a fever, or rather of the Portugalls, from whom he daylie expected new guifts, and enterteyned them with all kindnes. So I resolved to write, which the next day I did. The coppy is regestred.

[1] More exactly, the *tola* was about 187·5 grains troy. This would make the weight of the ruby a little over 5 ounces troy.

On 10 Sept. (f. 118 of the MS.) the ambassador wrote: 'The merchaunts sent hither yearely from Goa have sould their jewells, made mony in a mounth, and gone up to Agra to invest yt. The principall is returned with a ballax ruby unsould, which hee helde at seven *leckes* of *rupias*.'

The ruby reached Jahāngīr's treasury after all, being presented to him in Oct., 1617, by Mahābat Khān, who bought it at Burhānpur for 100,000 rupees. The Emperor, who records its previous offer to him, says that the price then demanded was two *lakhs*, but that his jewellers only valued the ruby at 80,000 rupees. He gives the weight at the more reasonable figure of 11 *miskāls* (about 800 grains, or $1\frac{2}{3}$ oz. troy) (*Memoirs*, vol. i. p. 394).

To Āsaf Khān.
(*Add. MS.* 6115, f. 100.)

Adsmere, the [*blank*].

I was yesternight at your howse to see Your Lordship and to speak with yow ; but your porter would not lett me in (but said Your Lordship was sicke), contrary to your promise at the *durbar* and contrary to the noblenes of your selfe, who are ever curteous to all strangers, and especially to our nation. I hoped I should have had no more distast from yow in that kind. My busines to Your Lordship was to give yow satisfaction in that yow said I would not follow your advise ; wherin Your Lordship doth wholy mistake mee. I have ever so much esteemed your frendship that I have neglected all other means of seeking justice, only relyeing on your councell and favour ; for I have forborne four monthes to complayne of Zulpheckcarcon, who owes the merchaunts five and twenty thowsand mamo[odies], nineteene thowsand nine hundred for himselfe, and 750 rialls of eight taken by force in mony and given the Prince. Your Lordship knowes that I have remitted it into your hands, wholy trusting to your promises, upon which I must yet relye, because yow ought to bee so noble as not to goe from your woord. Concerning the desier I had to clear my honor before the King, yow have no reason to blame mee, neyther did I yt but with your knowledg. I was willing to speak to the King by my interpreter, because I knew the Prince was not my frend (without any desart) and I thought he would take it ill of Your Lordship to speake for me. Therfore what I did was for respect and love ; yow did mistake it to be done of neglect toward yow. I pray Your Lordship hould a more constant opinion of my love toward yow. Yow shall find in the end that I am your true frend and will deserve better, both of His Majestie and yow, then any stranger. I therfore pray yow take here my promise that in all things I wilbe ready to give yow that content is fitting (my masters honor preserved) ; desiering Your Lordship to send me your opinion what course yow will have me take about the debt. Zulpheckcarcon is obstinat and will not pay yt, and it is tyme for the merchants to provide for our next ships, which wilbe here within four mounthes with many raretyes and rich presents for the King. Hoping yow wilbe alsoe pleased to remember the articles of securitye for our better usage which Your Lordship hath promised mee ; else I shall not dare to suffer any goods to be landed, to be so abused by the Governors as Your Lordship knowes wee have beene. Thus relyeing in these two poynts on Your Lordships frendship, I committ yow to the great God.

June 1.—I sent my lettre, but withall I had received advise that the King gave order I should not come at court. So that with my lettre I sent to knowe the truth and reason. Asaph Chan read my lettre and made this answer : that it was true the King had soe commanded : the cause was for certaine woords I gave the Prince when I was with the King about Jones my runnaway : therfore the Prince had intreated of the King to give me no more audience : but that if I would accept of the 17,000 *mamod*[*ies*] offered by Zulpheckcarcon and clear all demands of the Prince and him, he would bring me to the King and I should have all right and favour due unto me ; for to presse the Prince for mony hee could not, for that hee had not to pay his souldiers, beeing now ready to goe for the warrs of Decan ; with whom Zulpheckcarcon went, and when hee was gone it would bee hard to gett any thing, and therfore hee councelled me to accept of this offer and make peace on all parts. This motion was somewhat strange ; but I saw what was the purpose by the offer of peace ; not any thing I had sayd to the Prince, but that I tould Asaph Chan I could deliver my complaynts without him at the *durbar*, if hee forsooke us ; which the Prince prevented by hindering my comming. And now was all way shutt up to write or speak to the King ; only Abdalasan [1] offered me his frendship, which I yet reserved, with due respect. I considered what pretence could be taken from any woords spoken to the Prince, which were only these, of which I will never repent : I tould the Prince I was a Kings ambassador, and that I thought it stood not with his honor to protect a villayne against mee, considering what I was the King his father had my masters lettre to testefye : but that that was not all the discurtesy I and my nation received from him. Then hee chardged me that I drew my swoord on a servant of his, into whose hands he had delivered my man within the court ; which the King demanded of me if it were true. I answered : noe. He said his sonne tould him soe. I replyed :

[1] Later, Roe describes him as commander of the troops in the royal camp, and paymaster-general. This identifies him with Khwāja Abūl Hasan, whose appointment as one of the paymasters of the royal household is recorded at p. 260 of the *Memoirs* (vol. i.).

notwithstanding, I would mayntayne the contrarie and for noe mans woord would forsake truth : that I was bredd in a civill court, and knewe better what became me. So the man was called, and some others that reported it, and it was prooved a lye ; wherat the Prince was both ashamed and extreame angerye. This beeing all that passed, my innocence made me confident ; for though Asaph Chan to fright me sent me woord of this complaynt of the Prince some few dayes past, wishing me to take care : we were but a few, and might be soone subject to mischeefe ; to which I answered the accusation was false, and that for any force I was resolved I could not loose my blood in a better cause. These, I say, considered, and the case now standing on so desperate tearmes, I sent this answere : that I gave him thancks for his offer to bring me to the King, but that I was not so desierous as to doe that beseemed me not : if His Majestie did command us out of the countrie, wee were ready to goe : yet to showe how willing I was to content the Prince, though I had naught to doe with the merchannts mony nor awthority to compound to their losse, yet seeing hee pretended the Prince wanted mony, if he would give me his *firmaen* to deduct the 750 royalls of eight received in mony out of the custome this yeare, if it were not all payd, or, if it were, out of the next customes if goods came a shoore, or ells to pay yt in Suratt at four months end, I would accept of Zulpheckarcons offer and make an end of this busines with the losse of 2,900 *mamod[ies]*, which was more then I could answere : if the Prince would not doe this, I must doe my best to acquaint the King both with our wronges and the true cause of complaynt against mee wherby His Majestie refused mee audience, only to hinder me in seeking justice : and soe departe the cuntrye.

June 2.

June 3.—I received answere that hee would move the Prince to pay that mony : if Zulpheckcarcon had confessed 17,000 *mamod[ies]* of his owne debt, it should bee performed : he desiered me to have patience : that he would make the Prince and mee frends, and that the King should send for mee with more honor then ever, if I would end this controversy.

June 4.—I returned answer that I would be sent for before I would come, neyther would I ever come upon ill conditions to loose our mony : that I expected, if I came, some declaration from the King of better respect, for the worlds satisfaction ; to accord with the Prince I was ready, and if he could accuse mee of any disrespect toward him, I would make such amends as was fitt for us both : if not, I hoped His Highnes would not expect I should give away the Companyes monny for good lookes : the world was wyde enough : we gott not soe much by this trade as that wee would buy it with too much injurye: the Mogull had promised the King of England that his sonne should be our protector,[1] which I doubted not but hee would bee upon better experience : but that I would attend his answere some few dayes, and accordingly eyther resolve of longer residence or prepare to retyre my selfe and my nation toward our port to seeke better entertaynment.

June 5.—The Princes child dyed,[2] wherat the King tooke great greefe, so that he came not abroad, neyther the Prince nor any other great man. Soe that noe busines could be proceeded in.

June 6-8.—The King remooved to the Princes house, for that the child died in his, and came not abroad ; but gave leave for divers to visitt him. It was reported he would keep in at the Princes eight dayes, at Etemon Doulatt eight dayes, at Hafaz Gemal eight, at Pocora eight, and then returne to his custome.

June 9.—Mochrebchan sent a *Banian* to my house with this message : that the night before he had watched with the King, and took occasione to aske why the English embassador came not to visitt him. He answered hee knewe not. Wherat hee replyed hee hard I was much discontent. The King

[1] See the letter brought to England in 1616 by Steel (*First Letter-book,* p. 478 ; *Letters Received,* vol. iii. p. 284).

[2] ' A daughter of Shāh Jahān, whom Jahāngīr had brought up and loved more than his own life ' (Elliot and Dowson's *History,* vol. vi. p. 450). The chronicler goes on to say that this sad event happened on a Wednesday ; and that for this reason and the fact that the Emperor Akbar had died on the same day of the week, Jahāngīr ever after disliked Wednesdays. See also the account in the *Memoirs* (vol. i. p. 326).

demanded the reason : that hee had ever used mee with more respect then any stranger, and never given me any cause. To which hee answered that it was reported in the towne, and tould the ambassador, that His Majestie had given order that hee should not come at court nor have any more audience ; to which the King replyed it was veary falce : he never gave such order, nor knew not of any such, nor any occasion : that if I would come to him I should be as wellcome as ever, and no man should dare to stay or forbidd mee. Soe hee demanded of the King if His Majestie were pleased he should send me this message ; which hee commanded him to doe. This was strange to mee, that any body should presume to forbidd me entrance without the Kings knowledge, though I well sawe by Asaph Chan it was Zulpheckcarcons busines that putt this trick upon mee, by the Princes order and Asaph Chans connivence in the Kings name. But withall I feard some trick in this or mistaking in the message, for that I never made meanes to Mochrebchan, but had rather refused it ; neyther did I suppose him for many reasons our frend. So I resolved the next morning to send Mr. Bidolph to him to understand more certaintye.

June 10.—Mr. Bidolp went to Mochrebchan with complements of thancks for soe undeserved a favour ;[1] but that I well understood not the *Banian*, but desiered to bee enformed from him of this passage. He began all the discourse, adding many good woords that hee spake of mee : that I came from myne owne country to see His Majestie, and that it was very unjust without cause to refuse me admittance to His Majesties presence ; wherat he said the King was very angry and calld Asaph Chan, demanding if hee had given such order, who protested no, that hee never heard of yt (yet it was hee that sent mee woord it was true). So His Majestie gave me order (sayd hee) to bring the embassador to him, whensoever he desird to come, and to send woord that I had beene abused, for he never had any thought to refuse seeing mee. So that whensoever I would visitt the King (which hee perswaded

[1] As an acknowledgment of Mukarrab Khān's assistance, Roe presented him with ' 13 pictures of Christ and the 12 Apostells,' which had cost in England eightpence apiece (Roe's accounts).

me too, for His Majestie would take it kindly, though hee came not out), if I would send to his house he would goe and bring mee to him, and no man should dare to stopp mee. When I was fully resolved of the truth, I yet stayed from accepting this offer; for beeing upon new termes of frendship with the Prince and Asaph Chan, and pretending only to rely on him, I feard, if I tooke a nother way, they would become more virulent enemyes then ever; and this kindness of Mochrebchans was but a flash, or, if it continued, he had not power to effect all my busines; it was Asaph Chan whom I must wholy recover, and that faction, or stand on fickle tearmes. So I resolved to trie him fully and clearly before I forsooke him; that I might justly say he left me first, and in my greatest necessitye. This day Zulpheckcarcon, beeing by when this passd publiquely betweene the King and Mochrebchan concerning mee, and, as I suppose, seeing now that I could not be kept from the King with any trick, and fearing this would exasperate me to take up the first oportunitie of complaynt, came to Abrams the Dutchman [1] and offered frendship, sayeing the account was finished and that hee was ready to pay the 17,000 *mamod[ies]* offered for him selfe and his followers: and that the 750 royalls of eight were the Princes debt, which hee would pay: so that he knew no cause why wee should not be freends. I requested the merchants to goe speake with him, and that, if hee were constant to this offer, I would accept it and finish all broyles untill I had gotten better footing.

A warrant under my hand geven to the merchants how they should deale with Zulpheckcarcon about his debte.

First, I would have demanded of Zulpheckcarcon in generall what his offer is concerning the finishing of the account and paying the debt. If hee offer the 17,000 *m.* for all, comprising the Princes [debt?] and the 3 cloaths ½ newly mentioned, then breake off all speech and utterly refuse yt. If he offer

[1] 'A Dutchman from Antwerp, called Abraham de Duyts, a diamond polisher, a great friend of the Sultan Khurram, in whose service he was' (*Hague Transcripts*, at I.O.: series i. vol. iii. No. 96). From a statement by Jourdain (*Journal*, p. 153) it appears that this Dutchman was the stepfather of the Armenian lady who became in succession Mrs. Hawkins and Mrs. Towerson.

FURTHER NEGOTIATIONS

the 17,000 *m.* for the rest of the goods and require only a dischardge for them, giving a note of his hand that the 750 royalls is the Princes debt, for which hee will eyther gett payment here or procure a dischardge for so much in the custome at Suratt, or else to remayne answerable, then yow shall accept yt. When yow are agreed of the summe and come to speake of the manner of payment, for which somme I would the agreement were in writting if it could bee procurd and signed by him, then yow may lett him know that yow understand that three cloths and a halfe were delivered to such at Suratt, and that it shalbe at his choyse whether hee will pay for them here or to give yow his lettre to the debtor there that hee hath not satisfyed for yt, but that hee doth chardge it upon them, requiring theyr present payment and giving yow such a note or mentioning it in the quittance received, and then so much rateably shalbe abated here of the summe agreed on : of these two propositions [I ?] only desire that yow will presse him to a resolute answer, that I may understand from him selfe his purpose, that I may accordingly proceed in the prosequution of justice.

June 11.—I sent to Asaph Chan what message I had receved from Mochrebchan, but that I could not chainge my frends, though I would acknowledg it a great curtesie from the other, beeing both undeserved and voluntary : desiering him to beeleeve the truth, that I had not made any meanes to Mochrebchan to doe yt, but had only relyed on him, which hee might easily bee assured off by demanding him : that if hee pleased to lay asyde all jealousy and to accomodate the difference betweene the Prince and mee, whose favour I especially desiered, and to continew the protection of our nation, I was not so fickle to take every occasion to forsake him, who had beene our ancient and best frend : and that I would attend a day or two that hee might bring me to the King, that no notice might be taken of any discontent betweene us, which would perhaps, if the King asked the reason of this chang, call many matters in question that were better passed over on all sides : desiering him to deale soe faierly as to send me his resolution, assuring him I would remayne his frend till hee did to openly reject mee.

June 12.—Mochrebchan sent to mee to know if I would goe see the King ; but for that hee was yet in the Princes howse, I would not affront[1] him, attending untill I had answere from Asaph Chan, whom I must not loose if I would stand here. Besides, I determined, before I went to him, to know whether any fitt reconciliation could bee effected beetweene the Prince and mee, and that I might have satisfaction from Zulpheckcarcon without complaynt, first using all faire means that were honest and became my masters ambassador to make smooth my way; which when I could not effect, I resolved to fly to a very round complaynt, both of our publique wrongs and robberies committed upon us by the Governor, the Princes maynteyning him in yt, and Asaph Chans negligence and falshood for the Princes sake; and lastly I would discover the trick putt on mee to keepe mee from court, to this end only, that I should not seeke justice; which I would desier very roundly of the King, or lycence to depart with all my nation. This night I received lettres from Suratt[2] of the receipt of the *firmaens* sent downe, which for a few days useth to prevaile, and gott our goods from the Customer and procured an agreement on all particulars; some difference in price, which was referrd to Abram Chan, the Governor, then absent, our very good frend. In this lettre I received great encouragment to putt the King to tryall for an absolute reformation and for new priviledges, or to breake off the trade, the oportunitye beeing very good, for that many ships were expected from the Red Sea this season and soe wee might dispute our cause with advantage. I confesse, if it were myne owne privat cause, I would never endure halfe those injuryes wee have suffered; they are insupportable; the Prince beeing soe proud, and in such esteeme with his father, that nothing but chasteninge can humble him. But I serve for a publique cause, wher are divers dispositions to please, divers opinions to satisfye, and I know not how it wilbe construed that I dissolve that which was never tyed; all the factors here seeming discontent, and write resolutly, but if

[1] Meet. In *Hamlet* (iii. 1) the King arranges that the Prince, 'as't were by accident, may here affront Ophelia.'

[2] Dated 26 May, 1616 (*Factory Records*: *Surat*, vol. 84, pt. i. f. 36). The greater part of this letter is printed in *Letters Received*, vol. iv. p. 307.

this councell did not please in England, I can not tell whether they would change advise, and cast all on mee, *more vulgi, suum quisque flagitium aliis objectantes.*[1] This is one of those councells that cannot bee praysed untill they bee acted; so that necessitye shall compell mee, and then it will justefye mee. But this I dare affirme, if their ships be taken but once in four years, ther shall come more cleare gayne, without losse of honor, then will advance in seaven years by trade; and nothing is unjust in retribution and returne of the injuryes done unto us.

Ther is a resolution taken that Sultan Caronne shall goe to the Decan warres[2] and the day prefixed, having consulted all the *Bramans*.[3] Prince Parvis is called home, whom it is reported wrote his father that, if hee would send his elder brother,[4] hee would obey, but to dishonor him by imploying this, he would first fall on him and after finish the warr. All the capptayens, as *Channa Chana*, Mahobet Chan,[5] Chan John,[6]

[1] 'In the fashion of the vulgar, each one imputing to others his own transgression.'—Tacitus, *Hist.*, ii. 44.

[2] See the *Memoirs*, vol. i. p. 329.

[3] *I.e.* Brahman astrologers, of whom there were always many at court.

[4] Sultān Khusrau.

[5] Mahābat Khān (Zamāna Beg) is a familiar figure in the history of the times. Son of a Kābuli named Ghayūr Beg, he had been a personal attendant of Jahāngīr when Prince, and upon the latter's accession he was made paymaster of the royal household. He rose steadily in the emperor's favour, and Roe specially notes (see pp. 178, 192) how highly he was regarded. When, in 1623, Shāh Jahān rebelled against his father, the conduct of the war was entrusted to Mahābat Khān, who brought it to a successful conclusion. Soon after (1626), the intrigues of the empress threatening his ruin, he seized the person of Jahāngīr and held him prisoner for a considerable period. He then allied himself with his former opponent, Shāh Jahān, who in a short time succeeded to the throne. Subsequently, Mahābat Khān was entrusted with the government of the Dekhan. He died in 1634.

[6] Khān Jahān Lodi, who was, like Mahābat Khān, of Afghān origin, held important commands, and at the time of the death of Prince Parwīz had charge of the troops in the Dekhan. Distrusting Shāh Jahān's intentions towards him, he rebelled in 1629, and allied himself with the King of Ahmadnagar; but the confederates were defeated, and Khān Jahān slain, in January, 1631.

refuse to stay if this tyrant come to command, so well he is beloved. It is true all men awe him more then the King, now that hee is to receive the armie. The King cannot bee remooved from his resolution to send him : so that his sodeyne departure 22 dayes from this present must hasten mee to finish this busines and to know a resolution ; for after his departure, with his minione Zulpheckcarcon, ther is no hope to recover a penny, nor any justice against him.

June 13.—I received lettres from Amadavaz, signifying that the course I tooke with the Governor by Asaph Chans lettre had soe farr prevayled that the 500 *rupies* was at sight payd, all manner of frendship offered, a new house or whatsoever was wanting. Concerning the *firmaen* sent for restitution of custome taken the year past at Cambaya and Barooch, they are offered that of Baroch back, and all kyndnes from the Governor of Cambaya, promising to take such order next yeare as shall prevent all unkyndnes. I answered this packett [1] and advised to accept it, though never so little : the example of restitution was more then the mony.

June 14, 15.—The King yet kept at the Princes howse.

June 16.—The merchannts went according to my order to Zulpheckcarcon ; wher, after much dispute too and fro and many complaynts of unkindnes against mee, in conclusion hee denyed to pay 17,000 *ma.* promised, making new reckonings that the Prince had this, others that, and for his owne debt remaynd but 3,000 *m.* : but to finish for all and to have a generall realease, hee offered 12,000 *m.*, objecting still the 1,000 *m.* of Mr. Sadlers account,[2] without naminge for what : or else to stay the comming up of the Judge of the Customehouse, and so to pay whatsoever he would say was taken. But this delay I durst not abide, for that his departure was soddeine. Now in my last advise from Suratt they confesse Mr. Sadlers debt was mistaken (yet they chardge some

[1] See f. 101 of the MS.

[2] Richard Sadler was entertained in January, 1614, went out in Downton's fleet, and was appointed a junior factor at Surat. It would seem that he had died before this date, and no one could supply particulars of his claim, which was evidently for a matter of private trade.

260 *rup.* by particular for trifles) : and concerning the 750 rialls formerly charged to the custome house, and beeing confessed by the Princes officers to bee received here, I, as was reason, ever demanded restitution ; but in this second they write that they have come to account with the Customer and are agreed on all particulars, without once mentioning the royalls. So that I concluded that mony was found in the custome house and I had wrongfully demanded it, though without faulte, by Socorallas mistaking. So I knew not what to say in this uncertainty ; yet I had rather aske to much then too little ; therfore they still demand it. Zulpheckcarcon answered hee never tooke that mony away, but that it rested still in the custome howse, and were not those sent the Prince ; but beating this question, at last hee said those royalls sent up were 2,000 *m.* paid in royalls to him for licence to transport up our two caravans of cloth, hereby confessing the bribes playnly ; and upon examination wee found the summs to agree, no more beeing received : which, seeing that I heard not one word from Suratt of the 750 royalls, I resolved that my opinion was true that the mony was found and allowed below ; so that I gave over that clayme, and fell to a reckoninge apart of goods only chardged to Zulpheckcarcon, which beeing 19,900 *ma.* and Mr. Saddlers 800 [sic] mistaken : his offer of 17,000 *ma.*, considering price of cloth insisted on, and many trifles of privat mens hard too prove, and the necessitye of a peace with the Prince, they offered him a generall acquittance for the mony by him agreed on. But hee then as absolutely refusd it ; yet some tymes hee was content, sometyme not, soe that noe conclusion could bee made. But he desiered a new reckoning and to pay his owne and assigne under his hand who should pay the remayner. This was a tedious course, to seeke our mony from divers men, and they as absolutely refusd yt : all was taken by his authoritye, and wee would seeke no further. This was the error of the first account sent up, for had not the 750 royalls beene charged and Mr. Sadlers 1,000 *m.* (both mistaken), I had accepted his first offer of 17,000 *ma.* with little losse, and finished all long since with good will, and had avoyeded much trouble and the Princes displeasur ; but seeing one stood doubtfull, the other

directly charged, I could not yeild to loose 6 or 7,000 *m.*; for I could not have one *pice* without a generall quittance, as well agaynst the Prince as the Governor and all under him. But yet hee seemed very desierous of frendship, taking much unkindnes at mee for bitternes against him. They answered: hee deserved it, for his violence used to our nation: but that which I tooke woorst was his slight and base woordes given of my King, my lord and master. He replyed: he spake not ill of him, but, as was the custome of this countrye, hee only magnifyed his owne: for his hard usage and discurtesyes to our nation, hee sware he had expresse order from the Prince in four severall *firmaens*, not only to doe all hee did, but to turne us out and suffer us no trade. They answered they could never beleve yt, for that they were in presence when I demanded of the Prince if it were true (for that it was so published at Suratt) and hee forswoore it openly, giving it under his hand and seale that it was a lye. He replyed with many oathes it was true, and to satisfye their incredulitye and to dischardge himselfe, he asked if they would beleve the *firmaens*: so hee sent for them, and caused one to bee read before our interpretor, wher the Prince gave express order not to suffer our goods to passe out of towne but to keepe them in the custome howse, and ther to give leave to sell, and when they had traded, to command all aboord and to depart, forbidding any longer residence, and that if any thing came downe not traded for in towne hee should not suffer it to goe aboord; with many other clauses of vexation and wrong to be done us. Now, sayd hee, you see my innocence, and that I executed my commission with favour. They answered it could not be denyed, but that now the Prince had given mee a *firmaen* for our residence, justice, and good reception. It is true, said hee, yet shall the next Governor use yow woorse, for, whatsoever the ambassador can procure outwardly, the Governor should have advise underhand how to execute his masters will; which I know well. But, said hee, I am sorry for any thing is past, and if your ambassador will make frendship and force me to pay no more then due, I will endeavour to reconcile him and your nation to the Prince. They answered I was ready to embrace peace, but would not give away the Companies mony. He replyed 3 or 4,000 *m.* would not make us rich nor him poore. But of this his weaknes, to discover his masters secreetts and the Princes double and underhand basenes, I will make good advantage off if wee come not to composition. Now is evidently seene the miscery of our estate and the Princes faith. Who can bee secure, or resolve wisely, when outwardly wee shall have fayre woords, *firmaens* and all desird, and in secreett advise to wrong and abuse us ?

June 17.—I sent both to Hoja Nazzan, who had finished the account for both and had offered the 17,000 *ma.* in his name, and to Mochrebchan, before whom the Governor was content to pay it : to lett them know for the Princes sake and peace I was ready to accept the offer made, but that Zulpheckcarcon was started backe and would not pay it : that if they would tye him to his woord, I was content to be the looser : if not, I would goe instantly with full complaynt to the King ; wherin hee would wrong his master, whose name would come in question many wayes. Hoja Nassan answered : he should not flye from his woord : though hee had not confessed by particular so much debt, yet in grose he was content to pay it, and soe this day hee would meete our merchants there and procure his *chop*. This day the King remooved to Asaph Chans to moorne there.

June 18.—Mochrebchan sent to me to come to court : that my longer absence would bee ill taken : that His Majestie did expect mee : and that hee which would effect any busines with the King must bestow some labor in visiting him. For Zulpheckcarcon, hee answered that hee was agreed to pay us 17,000 *ma.*, and that hee was a base fellow to refuse it : that hee would compell him to satisfye us, or pay it him selfe and tell the King that hee did it on the others woord, and soe take the debt upon him. Asaph Chan returned me answere of my last message : that hee was most reddy to doe mee or my nation any curtesye, as he had ever : that on the morrow the King went to Havaz Jemall and returned the next day, when he would send to mee to come to his house and goe with mee to the King, and that all matters past should bee forgotten : wishing mee to take no notice that my absence was any other then voluntary: desiering me to beleeve he had twenty tymes more creditt and affection to doe my busines then Mochrebchan: that the next day he would himselfe carry me to the Prince and fully reconcile us, and so accord all differences that I should proceed in my busines without crosses or lett, and that I should have reformation in all my pretences: advising mee to accept of Zulpheckcarcons offer, and that for a little losse I should not breake off, now that all matters were so neare composed: and so desiering me not to hould him in jealousy, for hee was ever as much my frend as he durst declare against the Prince.

The King commanded one of his brothers sonnes,[1] who was made a Christian in pollicye to bring him into hatred with the people, to goe strike a lyon on the head, which was brought before the King; but hee beeing afrayd refusd yt. Soe the King bad his youngest sonne [2] to goe touch the lyon; who did so without any harme. Wheratt the King tooke occasion to send his nephew away to a prisson were hee is never like to see day light.

June 19.—The King remooved the Prince and all the court to Havas Gemall.

To the Factors at Surat.[3]
(*Add. MS.* 6115, f. 102.)

Adsmere, 19 June, 1616.

... It was our misfortune that this goverment is fallen into the Princes hands, who hates all Christians, and principally

---

[1] The sons of Prince Dāniyāl; see *Early Travels in India* (pp. 86, 147, 162), Bernier (p. 287), and Roe's letter to the Archbishop of Canterbury, 30 Oct., 1616 (given later). Which of the three princes is here intended is not clear; but it was probably Bāyasanghar, since the other two were married to a daughter and granddaughter of Jahāngīr respectively.

[2] Prince Shahryār, who was now about eleven years of age. Probably the lion had been tamed. Tavernier (vol. i. p. 80) describes the process. Terry mentions (p. 197) that a tame lion was kept at court: 'The Mogol, at my being there, had a very great lion (I often saw) which went up and down amongst the people that frequented his court, gently as a dog and never did hurt, only he had some keepers which did continually wayt upon him.'

[3] Other portions of this long letter are quoted in various notes.

JAHANGIR AND PRINCE KHURRAM

mee, for that I have not yeilded to all his insolencyes but insisted on my rights.... His faction is strong, and now more then ever. The King, dotinge on his supposed valor, hath resolved to send him to Decan, and disgracefully calls home Sultan Parvies; all men fawning on this idoll. Asaph Chan eyther dares not or will not open his mouth against him, and that notwithstanding all his promises of assistance.... Concerning my retyring to Suratt upon my next refusall ... I will wade very warely into this depth, and endeavour by all fayre meanes that are honest and becomming my qualetye to soder up these breaches and to leave it in no woorse estate then I found it, which yet wilbe a patchd and sickly constitution, apt to fall dayly into deadly diseases. I confesse my hart riseth against this resolution; but that I wilbe able to answere all objections, eyther of ignorance or malice, and say necessitye compelld mee and must beare me out.... This resolution must be taken by generall consent and advise, for I shalbe loath to undergoe it alone.... This I desire may be debated, and your conclusion sent in writting, according to which I will bend my actions as farr as I am able.... As touching all conditions past, the progresse wherof yow have clearly informed mee in, I have often urged, and have received answere ever that the goverment is now in the Prince, who will not be tyed to any thing done by his predesessors, and expects that wee take all new conditions from him; judging himselfe affronted if I but seeke to the King in any thing, as if wee were his subjects without right of appeale; and I as much scorne to be sutor to him, that tooke exception at my first lettre that it began not with the stile of a petition....

June 20.—The merchannts went to Socarolloes, before whom they were referrd to make agreement and conclusion with Zulpheckcarcon: but hee was gone with his master. His *scrivano* mett, who answered hee was that day to goe after him, to bring eyther his *chop* to Hoja Nasson for soe much to receive in Suratt, or ready mony. So that I hope this quarrell is at an end.

June 21.—I dispatched lettres to Bramport to Mahobet Chan [1] to desire a command to his lieutennant at Baroch to give our merchants entertaynment and trade at his port and to suffer them to hiere a house for their residence, and to procure his favour for them in dooing them justice and right; also I signifyed that his officers had the last yeare exacted certayne mony at the passadge of our goods to Suratt, which

[1] See f. 109 of the MS.

was not due ; for which I craved restitution, and redresse for tymes to come. This I did, for that I knew not to what inconvenience the Prince might drive us by his underhand dealing, for though now I was in hope to make a frendship with him (who was lost long before my arrivall), yet I could not discerne his hart and had experience of his falshood ; and therfore would prepare a retrayt in necessitye. Besides I knew that any such doubt or report would startle him ;[1] for though he would that wee were wholy banished, yet hee would not that wee quitted his port and seated soe neare him, wherby he should have no profitt by us, and yet the Portugall equally hindered. Lastly, if ther may bee found any roade for our ships, the place is fitter, in respect that all the cloth and cotten yearne sent home is bought there, besides carriadges from thence to Suratt, and all other comodities sent from above passe that towne ; so that both the way to our ships and the duties of Baroch would bee saved ; and, which is noe small respect, the Governor is not only a frend to our nation but a man full of honor and liberallity, scorning all base gettings and of all men in most high favour with the King, beeing his only minion [*i.e.* favourite] ; in whose presence Asaph Chan is but a shaddow.[2] The solicitation of this I committed to Mr. Banghame.[3]

June 23.—The King returned to his house, and sate out according to his usual custome.

[1] With this end in view, Roe had desired the factors at Surat to make a show of moving to Broach. They accordingly informed the Governor and others that this was their intention. However, nobody believed them, although ' for respect ' a hope was expressed that they would not think of removing. Later on, Kerridge, with the help of an English sailor, sounded the river at Broach, and found it very shallow and treacherous. Any anchorage there would be much exposed to wind, and the surrounding district seemed to them very barren and sparsely inhabited. This report satisfied Roe that the proposed change was impracticable.

[2] Kerridge, writing to the Company in March, 1615 (*O.C.*, No. 270), said much the same about Mahābat Khān, characterising him as ' the Kings greatest mynyon and of longest contynuance, of greatest powre and lybertye of all the nobyllyty.'

[3] Bangham was cape merchant at Burhānpur, where Mahābat Khān then was. Roe's letter to the latter is given at f. 108 of the MS.

June 24.—Asaph Chan sent to me to come to the King; but I refusd that day, except I might have a *chop* to all porters, or some officer sent to conduct mee, least any affront should be offered by base people. This day I received from Hoja Nassan a particular of 17,000 *m.* agreed on by Zulpheckcarcon, wherof part of the debt was the Princes, part others. Soe I sent to know what order I should have for the mony. Zulpheckcarcons *scrivano* answered that I should not trouble my selfe further : that hee had order for my satisfaction, and was procuring the Princes *chop* for his part, which had passd two seales, and was collecting the rest, and that he would finish it all in a few dayes.

The Prince had a sonne borne ;[1] and now beeing preparing for this warr, all mens eyes were on him, eyther for flattery, gayne, or envy, non for love. He received 20 *lecks* of *rupies* toward his chardge (200,000*li.* starling), and began to deale mony liberally. But notwithstanding this show of his fathers affection and greatnes, a Chan perswaded the King that the voyadge would be dangerous in respect of the Prince Parvis, whose honor was soe wounded that he would not returne without revenge. The King replyed : lett them fight : I am well content ; and hee that prooves him selfe the better captaine shall pursue the warr.

June 25.—Asaph Chan sent one of his cheife servants to the court gate to attend mee ; but I had resolved I would bee sent for. So hee, perceiving I stayd long, doubted that I would not come, causd him to come a foote in hast to fetch mee. So I went and was received by the King after the ould manner, no difference, without taking any notice of my absence. The Prince bowed him selfe. And soe I stayd His Majesties goeing in without farthar speech. Asaph Chan and divers others saluted mee, and I returnd.

June 26.—I sent to Asaph Chan that, as I was at an agreement with Zulpheckcarcon, payment only wanted, which was most materiall : that therfore if hee would accord all other matters with the Prince, I was ready to visitt him. I heard noe answere.

[1] Shuja, his second son. See the account given in the *Memoirs* (vol. i. p. 328).

June 27.—I went to visitt Mochrebchan, to thancke him for his voluntary kindnes. Wee had long speech. The effect was hee sought to withdrawe mee from Asaph Chan, offering to doe all my busines, in hope of the first sight of raretyes from England ; telling me that it was Asaph Chan that putt that tricke upon mee, for when the King called him to know who had forbidd mee the court, he answered he knew not inded : that hee had given order I should not enter the *guzelchan* without especiall leave, for that it was His Majesties privacye, wher were none admitted but those that were his nearest servants, and for that His Majestie often did use to drincke there, to be barbd,[1] and such other businesses as were unfitt for strangers to see : and that the Persian ambassadors never came without sending a day before : but that other order hee never gave, nor knew of any. I answered that I did accept his love in the highest degree : that Asaph Chan was as jealous of me for his sake, but that I could not absolutely quitt him first : both the articles I demanded were referrd to him and remayned in his hand, so that I was tyed to him ; and also, I knew well that, if he had no affection to doe mee good, yet hee had power to crose mee : that I was resolved to procure and hould every bodyes love, and not to runne my selfe into open factions : though in my hart and inward affections I could make difference of frends, as I did of him, from whom I had found so free and noble kindnes. But really I trusted neither ; the one was sower, eager of bribes, proud and knew his owne strength, the other fickle, flattering, and loved to have his power beleeved to be more then it was ; but neyther card for us longer then some end of their owne enticed them. Soe I playd at their game, held correspondence with both, and resolved to use both as long as I could, and to quitt him (when I must needs) that could doe mee least good. He asked mee what then he should doe for mee. I answered : continew his affection to our nation : and for my particular, I desird him to remember my service to His Majestie, and to recommend our cause in generall termes, and to signifye to His Majestie that I well sawe our ignorance in tymes past of what comodityes were fitt for His

[1] ' Barb ' is the verb. now obsolete, from which ' barber ' is derived.

Majestie had made our trade fastidious [*i.e.* distasteful], but that if I knew His Majesties mynd he should see how able wee were to serve him. He replyed hee would doe it; but withall he said wee brought too much cloth and ill swoords and almost nothing else: that every body was weary of yt; that hee advised wee should forbeare two or three yeares, and insteed therof, seeing our ships went to China [1] and Japan, to bring all the raretyes of those parts (which were more acceptable here then gould), and from our countrie the best cloth of tissue and richest stuffs of silke, gould, and silver that wee had, but especially good quantety of arras for hangings, saying that the King would buy for a *leeck* or two of *rupies*, and every great man in proportion. And this, I thinck, is true, and would serve for two years. I replyed wee considered this, but the merchannts sought proffitt: that those things were deare with us, and the chardg of bringing halfe as much as the goods: and that wee feared fewe would come to the price, for that our best cloths of gould and tissue were woorth 100 *rupies* a *cobde* [see p. 100] with us, and soe meaner to 40 *rupies*, and ther was arras from 20 *rupies* to 150 *rupies* a sticke (much about a *cobdee*): so that, if I should advise of such things, they would answer I had little skyll in those matters; but that if His Majestie would make a bill of what sorts and conditions he desired, and what quantetye and what rates, and sett his *chop* to it that hee would take yt, and such other great men as desired the like, I would send into England and might then wright with confidence; and I doubted not but His Majesties will should bee in all things accomplished. He answered he would acquaynt him with my motion, which would highly content him, and cause a bill to bee made and sealed; and for his part hee would give me a nother. Wee had some speech about the Prince, whom hee rayled at freely: that hee never went to him, nor had power to doe mee kyndnes there: but that, when he was departed, hee could not harme mee. I answered: as long [as] hee had the goverment of Suratt, his favour was as consequent to us almost as His Majesties, and

[1] The English had not yet opened a direct trade with China; they, however, procured Chinese products from the junks that frequented Bantam, Patani, and other ports.

that I had had a bitter experience of his affection, notwithstanding his faire pretences, besides the bearing up of Zulpheckcarcon. Hee replyed hee knew it well, and would shortly tell mee how it should bee remedyed : for Zulpheckcarcon, hee desired mee not to stir nor send after soe base a fellow : that in four dayes hee would see the mony paid. Wee exchanged many complements and many professions. At last hee prest upon mee too bottles of muske, that were sent him for a present from his goverment, held above 100 ounces, woorth 500*li.*, with much importunitye ; but I refusd too great an obligation, least for that cause I should bee tyed to him to the prejudice of the Company, for hee would expect some recompence. I cannot bragg of this follie, but it is a vice that few in my place are guiltie off ; but I had resolved, rich or poore, to doe nothing unwoorthy the honor of my master nor the good name of an honest man. The King this evening went to Havas Jemall.

June 29.—At night the King returned.

June 30.—I went to visitt Abdala Hassan, from whom I had received a former kindnes unexpected [see p. 164], for that wee were mere strangers. This observance I was enforced too, partly by gratitude, but principally by necessitye. *Obsequium amicos parit.*[1] I needed them, and to the markett I could not goe (for all are to be sould) for want of guifts. Yet hee is noe taker, and I tooke knowledge of yt, to his joy. Hee offered me much kindnes, eyther to speake to the King or deliver any wrighting. I accepted of yt generally, but at first would not engage him into busines, beeing yet dependant on Asaph Chan. He answered they were all one, and that I could not keepe a better way. I replyed I had not much to aske the King: my principall busines (which I had in command from His Majestic my soverayne) was the procuring better priviledges for the continuance of love and commerce betweene both nations, which demands had long remaynd in Asaph Chans hands, to whom they were referrd : if I had answere of that, my busines after would passe with more ease, for that, if it pleasd the King to seale, confirme and publish those articles, I presumd

---

[1] 'Obsequiousness procures friends' : a well-known quotation from Terence (*Andriae*, 1, i. 41).

no man would dare to infringe them, and that our merchannts should trade securely, free from violence and injurye; and then I should have no cause to offend any by complaynt, and should have little els to doe but to wayt on the King and visitt my frends: if His Majestie utterly refusd them and the alliance and leauge of the King of England, I had noe more to doe but to returne unto my countrie: I had dischardged my dutie. Hee answered I should not feare but that the King would continew a frend to His Majestie and our nation, and that noe reasonable demand would bee refused mee. I replyed I had expected long and saw fewe effects, and what had passed last yeare at Suratt and in many parts I was sencible off: but that for some respects I would not violently pursue just complaynts. Hee said hee understood mee: that the Prince was sorrie for what was past. Demanding if Zulpheckcarcon had payd his mony, I answered no: wee were agreed (to our losse), mony only wanted. He said hee would that night acquaynt the Prince and procure present payment. He is captaine of all the souldiers entertayned at court, and treasurer to all armyes. He entertayned me curteously, with few complements but much civilitye. Wee sate to see his souldiers shoote in bowes and pieces. Most of them with a single bullett did hitt the marke, beeing a hand breadth in a butt. Wee had some discourse of our use of such weapons; and soe I departed.

July 2.—I went to visitt the King and to move him about our articles, if oportunitye favoured. He only bowed him selfe at my comming, and was poseest with much busines, for that the Princes goeing for Decan was altered, at least deferrd. He had gott mony to pay his debts, and his warr was ended.

July 5.—I sent to Asaph Chan to know a resolution concerning my demands, and upon what tearmes I stood with the Prince, for that I knew, if he remaynd our enemye, Suratt would bee no port for us: that our shipps were ready in three monthes to arrive: that it concernd mee to know whertoo I should trust, for unlesse I might have our residence confirmed and those priviledges granted which I had demanded, and eyther assurance of frendship or at least justice from the Prince, I must take my leave. He replyed hee would that night speake with the Prince, and in four dayes answer mee absolutely.

July 7.—He sent me woord that concerning my propositions for priviledges and the Kings command for redresse in all our former injuryes, that that day or the morrow he would deliver it to the scale : they were accorded too [*i.e.* to] amply, and in few dayes I should have them : that he had conferrd with the Prince, who was very willing to bee our frend ; and if I would come to him, I should be very wellcome, and what soever I could require reasonably at his hands should bee performed.

July 9.—I went to visitt the Prince, but sent before ; who returned I should bee very welcome. He expected a present, but when none appeard, hee proceeded to business ; and supposing I would iterat Zulpheckcarcons delayes openly, his officer Socarolla came to mee and said for the Princes part of the debt wee should have a *chopp* for Suratt whensoever I would send, and that Zulpheckcarcons remayner should bee payd ready mony by order from him. So that if the merchannts will follow the getting it in (in wnich their is little done), they may bee satisfied ; for my part is ended. I have made agreement and devided the debt, and procured order for payment, but cannot runn up and downe to *Banians* and officers, in whose hands now it rests.

July 10.—I received advise from Agra that not one *cobde* of cloth would sell but at veary lowe rates ; they lay the faulte on the last yeares sales ; for swoords no man would looke on them, and hydes not at the price they cost in England. Concerning the debt of the Governors brother left by Mr. Young, they first sollicited it, but could not procure a penny ; then they made use of my lettre mentioned to the Governor, who sent presently to command satisfaction. Mr. Shalbanck was imployed to him, beeing a daies journy out of towne. Ther hee [*i.e.* the debtor] pretends Mr. Browne offered him abatement, or els that hee would retourne some cloth. So that Mr. Shalbancke finished with him with the losse of about 90 *rupies* ; for which hee excuses himselfe upon Browne and upon their neede, that, having not sould one penny woorth of goods in three mounths, they had not mony lefte to pay horsemeat ; for that before his comming he had command from mee for example sake not to doe yt. If I had the assistance of one honest sufficient man, that loved the Companyes profitt better then their owne ease or pleasure, or had had that authoritie over them which was requisite, or that it had not beene published to them that I had none, I would have caused many things to have had a nother face.

July 11.—I received from Amadavaz the long expected wyne; one runlett three quarters full, conteyning six gallons and one glase, the other runlett was leaked. It was sowred with long keeping; yet it came fittly for my new reconcilements, and will serve turne.

July 12.—I sent to the *guzelchan* one case of aligant. It was somewhat sower, yet soe much in request that it was received with good acceptance. I sent such excuse with yt as was requisite.

July 13.—In the morning I sent Sultan Carronne three bottles of aligant, and a lettre concerning the Portugalls, the differences betweene our trade and theirs, and to procure all the customes in and out to farme for the Companyes use. The coppie is registred. The Prince caused (as is the barbarous custome, all busines passing in publique) the lettre to bee twice read by his secretary, and often interrupted it with speech to him; in the end sent woord that at night, when hee came downe, hee would read it him selfe and consider yt, and that I should receive answere from Merze Socoralla.

To Sultan Caronne.[1]
(*Add. MS.* 6115, f. 96.)

Most Royall Prince,   1st Maye, 1616.

I cannot but confesse and acknowledge the great justice yow have done our nation in the debts and extortions of Zulpheckcarcon, wherof I will speedily advise my lord the most

---

[1] Copies of this letter, in English and Persian, are among the I.O. Records (*O.C.*, Nos. 360-1), and the former has been printed in *Letters Received*, vol. iv. (p. 101). The Persian copy is endorsed by Roe 'copy of my lettre to the Prince, 1 May, 1616.' As this date appears on all the copies, it is evidently not a slip; but it seems equally clear that the above is the letter which was presented to the Prince on 13 July. We must therefore suppose that this endeavour to 'settle a better opinion in the Prince of our nation' was written

mighty King of England, that His Majestie may render Your Highnes condigne thanckes and that your fame and renowne may be knowne in all parts. But I cannot but greeve when I consider that Your Highnes good opinion and grace toward us is averted by some misfortune or misinformation, which by many cercumstances is manifested to mee, principally in that favour Your Highnes hath declared to the Portugall, our enemyes. Butt if Your Highnes were pleased to regard the differance betweene our proceedings and theires, that wee only desire open trade for all nations, to the enriching of Your Highnes kingdomes and the advancing of your customes, wheras they have ever sought to keepe in subjection your subjects, suffering none to trafique but them selves and exacting dutyes for licence to passe upon your seas, contrary to all honor and justice, calling their king in Europe King of India. In proofe wherof our readines to embrace peace and their obstinacy in yt is sufficient wittnes; though theyr force is no way terrible to us, that are so poowrfull in shipping that all Europe is not able to equall His Majestie therin. And if Your Highnes suppose that the Portugall hath or would bring eyther more raretyes or more profitt to your port, I dare affirme Your Highnes hath received wrong enformation. First, for curious and rare toyes, we have better meanes to furnish Your Highnes then any other, our kingdome abounding with all arts and our shipping trading into all the world; wherby there is nothing under the sunne which wee are not able to bring, if we knew Your Highnes pleasure, what yow did most affect; wherof whensoever yow shall please to give a writing, yow shall have experience of our readines to doe yow service. Secondly, for profitt, our kingdome is naturally the most fructfull in Europe and the most abundant in all sorts of armes, cloth, and what soever is necessary for mans use; besides which, Your Highnes I suppose knowes not wee yeerly bring into your port in ready mony 50,000 rialls [1] of eight, for which wee only carry away callicoes and indicoes, to the enriching of Your Highnes kingdomes with silver. And that Your Highnes may better perceive what profitt doth arise by our trade at Suratt, and that hereafter we may not bee vexed by officers at the *alfandica*, wherby we shalbe enforced to

on 1 May, but that its delivery was postponed, probably on account of the renewed hopes of an amicable arrangement with Zūlfakār Khān. The difference in tone between this and Roe's previous letter to the Prince (p. 121) is significant.

[1] There is probably some exaggeration here. On Roe's own testimony (p. 103), Keeling's fleet had brought but 43,572 rials, and this was for Bantam as well as Surat. According to the factors (p. 148 *n*), only about 20,000 rials were landed at the latter place.

trouble Your Highnes with daylie complaynts, wee are desierous to rent our customes of Your Highnes, both in and out, and will yearly pay Your Highnes at one payment 12,000 *rupies* for our sayd customes, so that Your Highnes wilbe pleased to dischargde us of all other duties and troubles ; which I suppose is a farr greater summe then ever your officers made yow any account. And in all mattres wherin Your Highnes shall command, yow shall fynd our nation most ready to obey yow, and my selfe in particular will not omitt all occasion to doe yow service, wherin I doubt not I could some wayes give Your Highnes content, if I had oportunitye to speake with yow. Your Highnes noble nature will excuse my bouldnes, and that I wayte not on yow my selfe, for that for want of language I could not so well expresse my desires as by writing. The great Creator of heaven and earth blesse yow and multiply on your head all felicitye and honor.

To doe yow service,
THO. ROE
the English Ambassador.

At night I went to the *durbarr* to visitt the King. So soone as I came in, hee sent Asaph Chan to mee; that he heard I had in my house an excellent paynter, and desiered hee might see some of his woorke. I replyed, according to truth, that ther was none but a young man, a merchant, that for his excercise did with a pen draw some figures, but very meanly, far from the arte of painting. The King replyed that I should not feare that hee would take any man from mee by force: that hee would neyther doe me injurie nor suffer any other ; and prayed that hee might see that man and his woorke, whatsoever it was. I replied I had no such doubte of His Majestie, and for his satisfaction I would bring him to the *guzellchan* with such toyes as hee had, which perhapes was an eliphant, or a deare, or such like in paper. At this answere the King bowed him selfe ; and returnd that if I desiered an eliphant or the figure or any other thing in his cuntrie, I should not buy it nor seeke any other way but to him : that what soever I had a minde too, hee would give mee: and that I should freely speake to him, for he was my frend. I made a reverence and answered that I humblie thanckd His Majestie: eliphants were of no use to mee, neyther was it the custome of my nation, especially of my place, to aske any thing : if His Majestie gave mee but the woorth of a *rupy*, I would receive it and esteeme it as a marke of his favour. He replyed that hee knewe not what I desiered : that ther were some things in his countrie rare in myne, and that I should not make daynty to speake to him, for hee would give mee such things as should bee most wellcome : and that I should bee cherfull, for that hee was a frend to our nation and to mee, and would protect us from any injurye ; but desiered that I would that night come to the *guzellchan* with the youth that paynted and his pickturs. So Asaph Chan wishd mee to send home to fetch him to his howse ; whither if I would goe and stay with him untill the King came abroad I should bee veary wellcome ; which I promised. I never received so much grace and favour from the King as at this tyme ; which all men tooke notice off, and accordingly altered their fashions toward mee. Especially it hapned well that the Jesuite was made interpreter of all this by the Kings appoyntment.

When the King rose, I went to Asaph Chans house (having sent for Mr. Hewes,[1] the supposed paynter), Asaph Chan beeing gone somwhat before. I found him satt on a poore tarras in the ayre on a sheete with other great men. His porters stayed mee at the doore at my entrance ; so that as soone as I came to him I said I was come according to his request and did often desire to visitt him, but his servants stopped mee as if I were a sutor : I entreated him to reforme it, for that it was a discurtesye to one of my place. He called his steward and master porter, and commanded them that, if I came my selfe, no man should presume to stay mee but lett me passe into him, and that all my servants at all tymes should bee brought into a roome to sitt downe, and that his house should ever bee free for them. So I satt, and for complement acknowledged the favour the King had done mee so publiquely to proceed from good reports made by him of me and our nation, which wee would with all

---

[1] Robert Hughes. He was admitted a factor in Nov., 1614, and went out in the same fleet as Roe. In 1617 he was sent to Agra ; and later still (1620-21) was one of the pioneers who opened up trade at Patna, where Mukarrab Khān, who was then governor, treated the English factors with great cordiality. Hughes seems to have died in 1622 or 1623.

due respect endeavour to requite. He replied he was ever my frend in his particular, but that the Kings good opinion and favour to mee proceeded from his owne good disposition. I answered: seeing he was so modest not to take it upon him and so refuse the thancks, yet I desiered him that hee would use this oportunitye and season of His Majesties gratiousnes to moove at night the sealing of our priviledges, for that our ships were ready to arrive, and if they found no alteration they would land no goods, and I should bee reputed very negligent in my dutie, to my utter disgrace and ruine in my masters favour, who would not lay the fault on any other nor beeleve any excuse, having received such assurance of love from the Great Mogull by his last lettres; and that I had a pickture of a frend of myne that I esteemed very much, and was for curiositye rare, which I would give His Majestie as a present, seeing hee so much affected that art;[1] assuring my selfe he never saw any equall to it, neyther was any thing more esteemed of mee. He answered it was not good to move yt publiquely, it might bring forth opposition and dispute: but that I should relye on him: hee would see them sealed speedely: that the Kings consent was already passd by referrence to him: but for the picture he desird I would send for yt presently, that hee might see it, and present it to the King (so nothing in this kynd once named is lett slipd, and I was engaged to my guift). I sent for yt and astonishd him, hee seeming to take extreame content, eaven to admiration; assuring mee it would bee the most welcome guift I ever presented. Suddenly hee rose (the King beeing come out) and desiered me to staye there: that hee would goe to the King and send for mee, leaving mee musique and company. Within halfe an hower two of the Kings servants came for mee; and after some speech with Mr. Hewes, wherin hee was satisfied, Asaph Chan asked mee for my little picture and presented it to the King. Hee tooke extreame content, showeing it to everie man neare him; at last sent for his cheefe paynter, demanding his opinion. The foole answered he could make as good. Wherat the King turned to mee,

[1] Jahāngīr considered himself a connoisseur in such matters; see the *Memoirs*, vol. ii. p. 20.

saying : my man sayth he can do the like and as well as this : what say yow ? I replyed : I knew the contrarie. But if hee doe, said he, what will yow say ? I answered : I would give 10,000 *rupies* for such a coppy of his hand, for I knowe non in Europe but the same master can performe it.[1] Nay, said the King, I will call four paynters, my cheefe woorke men, and what will yow give mee if they make one so like, that yow shall not knowe your owne ? I replyed : I had nothing of valewe to give His Majestie, but at the arivall of the ships I would give the best rarety I could procure. He answered : that was long : but what wager would I lay in the mean tyme ? I replyed : I knew not what to offer in wager to so great a Prince, nor became it me to name it; but if His Majestie were pleasd, I would lay any in my power to pay. Why, said hee, if yow will not lay with mee, lay with the paynter. I answered : no, sir, as I am unfitt to contend with Your Majestie, so your paynter is no equall match for mee : but I will wager with Asaph Chan or Abdalazan or any of your lords. So he commanded Asaph Chan, who offered 5,000 *rupies*. I replyed I was content, but mony was no honourable bett, especially among frends : but I would lay a good horse. Soe the match was agreed on ; but Asaph Chan recanted in privat.

After, the King fell to drincking of our allegant, givinge tasts to divers, and then sent for a full bottle, and drincking one cup, sent it to mee : that it beegan to sower soe fast it would be spoyld before hee could drincke all, and that I had none. So hee turnd to sleepe ; the candles were poppd out, and I groppd my way out of doores.

This day a gentellwoeman of Normalls was taken in the Kings house in some action with an eunuch. Another capon that loved her kylld him. The poore woeman was sett up to the armepitts in the earth hard ramed, her feete tyde to a stake, to abyde three dayes and two nights without any

[1] From Roe's accounts (*Add. MS.* 6115, f. 276) we learn that the painter thus characterised was Isaac Oliver, the celebrated miniaturist (1551-1617) ; that the painting was a ' smale limned picture of a woeman ' ; and that it cost in England 6*l*., and would have sold in India for 150 rupees.

sustenance, her head and armes bare, exposed to the sunns violence: if shee died not in that tyme, she should bee pardoned.[1] The eunuch was condemned to the cliphants. This damsell yeelded in pearle, jewells, and ready mony 160,000 *rupias*.

July 14.—I sent Asaph Chan a bottle of wyne, putting him in mynd to dispatch the sealing of our priviledges. Hee called to his secretarie for them, and promised to send them seald with expedition.

July 15.—I sent to Zulpheckcarcon for mony. He desired that I would forbeare six dayes; for that his mony and the Princes was ready, but for som goods delivered to others ther was difference: that hee had sent to Suratt for testemony against such as denyed, and wee should bee cleared withall togither. I gave order to Mr. Fettiplace to returne that I was content to forbeare tenn dayes for mony: but that I desiered he would firme the agreement in generall with his hand and seale, that I might be secure from any new cavells; which hee promised to doe the next day.

July 16.—I could not gett the brokar to goe; by whose negligence all our busines was deferrd and delayd. I had not power to dismisse him, though hee did more hinder us then all other letts togither; neyther had the merchannts any will, for I mooved it often. So that I can doe no more. He offereth his bill for the mony, and that is a warrant for the Princes part, if they will fetch it; if not, I am blamelesse.

July 18.—I went to the *durbar* to visitt the King, but could not yet gett a dispatch of my demands.

July 19.—I sent to Socoralla for the Princes answer to my lettre concerning the farme of coustomes. Hee said that it was referrd to Asaph Chan and him: that they must meete and conferr about yt, and then I should receive yt. At evening I sent to Asaph Chan, desiering him to favour my request for renting the Princes dues at Suratt, it beeing referrd to him and

---

[1] Terry (p. 407) relates the same or a similar incident. According to his story, the fault the woman had committed was kissing the eunuch: the latter was cut to pieces in her sight: and she lived a day and a half, 'crying out most lamentably, while she was able to speak, in her language, as the Shunamites childe did in his (2 King. 4): *Ah, my head! my head!*; which horrid execution, or rather murder, was acted near our house.'

Socorolla ; in which by a speedie answer hee should doe mee curtesie, that I might tymely advise therof to Suratt. He promised that hee would that night consult about yt and give me all assistance, and for my other busines in his hand it should bee ready in two dayes. Thus I was fedd with hopes and delayes to no effect.

July 22.—I received lettres from Bramport in answer of those to Mahobet Chan, who at first [*i.e.* at once] granted my desier, making his *firmaen* to Baroch most effectuall, to receive our nation and to give them a house near the Governor : strictly commanding no man to molest them by sea or land, nor to take any custome of them or any way trouble them under colour therof : finally that they might buy, sell, and transport any comoditye at their pleasurs without any molestation : concluding that they should expect to heare no other from him and therfore they should be carefull in execution. I received with yt a lettre from himselfe (which was more civilitye then all the Indyes yeelded mee), full of curtesye and humanitie and great respect, protesting his desier to give me content and that what I had demanded I should make no doubt of performance : and if I had any other occasion to use him, hee desiered me to write and it should bee performed. The coppies are woorthy the seeing for the rarenes of the phrase. The *firmaen* I caused to be sent to Suratt.[1] So that Baroch is provided for a good retraite from the Princes injuryes, and the custome given, wherby 1,500*li.* per annum wilbe saved, besides all manner of searches and extortions. For the performance of this no man maketh any doubt, for that all men confesse that hee neither careth for the Prince, and soe feareth not,[2] nor needeth any man ; beeing the only beloved man of the King, and second person in his dominions, and in all his life soe liberall of his pursse and honorable of his woord that hee hath engrossed good reports from all others. And concerning custome, the King takes none ; the Governors

---

[1] The original letter from Mahābat Khān is among the I.O. Records (*O.C.*, No. 380). A translation of it is given at p. 141 of *Letters Received*, vol. iv., followed by an English version of the *farmān*.

[2] Kerridge wrote (23 July, 1616), that Mahābat Khān hated the Prince and his favourite, Zūlfakār Khān.

make it their proffitt; which hee professeth to scorne that hee should abuse the liberty of the Kings ports.

July 23.—I wrote to Mahobett Chan complements and thancks,[1] and sent away lettres to Mesolapatan concerning a factory at Bengala.[2] At night I solicited Asaph Chan for my

[1] The letter is copied at f. 112 of the MS.

[2] In answer to the letter received by Roe on 23 May. Roe's original letter is now among the I.O. Records (*O.C.*, No. 382), and there is also a copy in *Add. MS.* 6115 (f. 113). It is printed at p. 143 of *Letters Received*, vol. iv. In it he says that he ' was requested to procure a *firmaen* or command for Bengala, it beeing supposed that some shipping would be this yeare directed theither'; but that, finding *farmāns* of little use, he is waiting for the conclusion of the proposed treaty, of which a copy shall be forwarded in due course to Masulipatam, ready for any English ship that may be sent to Bengal.

Roe had already suggested to the Surat factors that an attempt should be made overland to open up trade with Bengal, ' so desiered by the Company and impressed into me by Captain Keeling,' and also with Lahore and Sind; but Kerridge and his companions doubted whether they would sell much cloth in Lahore, and pointed out the risk in Sind from the Portuguese settled at Lahrībandar. 'Bengalla gennerally,' they wrote, ' is a whott country, the moste of the inhabitants very poore Gentiles, and upon the sea coaste, where there is any hope of bennefitt, the Duch and Portingales have trade; wherby wee conceave that the transportation by land theither wilbe more hazardous and chargable then the bennefitt by the sale of a smale quantety can answer' (*Surat Letters*, 26 May, 1616). To this the ambassador retorted: ' that Bengala should bee poore I see no reason; it feedes this countrie with wheate and rise; it sends sugar to all India; it hath the finest cloth and pintadoes, musck, civitt and amber, [besides] almost all raretyes from thence by trade from Pegu. . . . If wee keepe Jasques in our hopes, wee must plant at Syndu and unite our forces; they wilbe els too farr distant to assist one a nother; and it is the fittest place of all these dominions, considered in yt selfe, for our residence. The number of Portugalls residing is a good argument for us to seeke it; it is a signe ther is good dooing. An abby was ever a token of a rich seoyle, and store of crowes of plenty of carrion. . . . It is to bee understood wee must fire them out and maynteyne our trade at the pikes end' (*Add. MS.* 6115, ff. 102-108). The factors replied that they were still unconvinced, but would agree to the venture if Roe would take the responsibility (*Letters Received*, vol. iv. p. 327). Upon this the ambassador ceased to urge the proposal; and so the matter rested for a time. In writing to the Company (2 November, 1616), the factors merely said that the suggested voyage to

articles. His answere was short: tary a whyle; which I understand not.

July 25.—I sent to Zulpheckcarcon at the Princes. He desiered the merchannts to come to his house and hee would dispatch them.

July 26.—I sollicited Sacarolla for the Princes answer. He replied that Asaph Chan and hee had not mett, and that I must move him to yt, for that else it would bee forgotten.

July 28.—I went to the *durbar* to visitt the King, who referrd me to Asaph Chan, with whome I went home and with all earnestnes pressed the dispatch of my demands and that hee would meete Sacarolla about the farme of our customes. He answered me with many complements of frendship and love, but delayed mee with sentences [1] and morality: that kings were to be attended, and that things must come from them of their owne mynde, without importunitye: that patience would bring all to passe. I answered I had worne out all my store with so tedious delayes, and that, if I had not depended on his promise, I would have some way at least procured a refusall and so departed: but that I hoped he would effect yt, for that the King my master would impute the faulte to my negligence and I durst hardly see his face without a better account of that committed to mee. He replied I must not use such speeches, for the King could not blame me for any thing out of my power: that hee knewe the mynds of kings were in Gods hands only, and no man could rule them but Himself: that hee spake not this with any purpose that I should not have them, but to give me content, least I should with impatience mistake his good meaning and

'Port Pequeno' could not be made for want of small ships 'fitting that purpose.' Porto Pequeno, by the way, was the term originally given by the Portuguese to Sātgāon, on the Hūgli river, in contradistinction to Porto Grand or Chittagong. It seems, however, that the English factors meant by the former appellation the town of Hūgli, which had by this time ousted Sātgāon as the seat of Portuguese trade in those parts. De Laet (p. 50) identifies 'Porto Piqueno' with 'Ugeli.'

[1] Adages or aphorisms (Lat. *sententiæ*). Ben Jonson, in his *Discoveries*, complains of the fondness of Terence and some of the Greek poets for 'the sticking in of sentences.'

affection towards mee. I answered I was free from jelousy of him, but if I were more importunate now, the comming of the ships enforced mee : that I was resolved noe goods should be landed untill I had some better assurance of our usage. Hee said all was past and that these articles I should have, but that the kingdome of Suratt was wholie in the Princes power : the King would doe nothing to prejudice his authority : that I should visitt the Prince and give him a present, and make frends among his servants, for from him I must expect my best reamedy and our quiett residence. I answered I had no presents untill their arrivall : that all other means I used to procure the favour of the Prince, and the assistance of those neare him, but it became not mee to seeke to every body in that which was a free demand of leauge betweene princes, which I thought they should as readily accept as the King of England should offer yt. Concerning the farme of customes hee promised to send for Socorolla and give me answere. Many faire woords were cast away on both parts, and so I returned only with new promises.

July 31.—I went to visitt the Prince ; and, because I would have occasion to speake, as well as to follow Asaph Chans advise, I presented him a very delicate peice scrued, with a fier loock, made in Leige, that would carrie poynt blanck as farr as a muskett and weighed not 4 *li*.[1] He saw first all the qualetyes, and after, as I suppose, sent for Zulpheckcarcon, whom I had not seen since his arrivall at Adsmere. When hee came, the Prince poynted him to mee ; wherat hee came and saluted mee. My enterpreter was called for, and hee asked mee why I was angry with him. I replied the cause was publique : for many injuries offered our nation, and for yet deferring any honest satisfaction. Hee replied with protestation that hee was my frend : that what hee had done was by commandement ; poynting to the Prince confidently and carelessly, ther, saith hee, is hee that did it : but for his owne affection he swoore hee would doe me any service, and that I should not refuse to bee his frend : that hee would feast mee, and make any recompence, for that was not his owne faulte. I replyed that as long as the busines stood unfinished

[1] *I.e.* four lb. It ' cost in Leige 52*s*.'—Roe's accounts.

I could not accept nor embrace his frendship : hee had daylie promised to seale the agreement, and made the merchanntes attend in vayne, which I tooke in great scorne. He answered if that were all betweene us, that I should send this day : it should bee signed and the mony paied : that hee cared not for such trifles : to doe me service hee would doe a thousand tymes more, soe that I would bee reconciled. I answered : when I saw his performance I would readylie embrace him, and both visitt him and invitte him to mee : and that if his harte were answerable to his professiones, hee should for amends of past wronges moove the Prince to a better opinion of our nation, and procure for us such priviledges as hee in his owne experience best knew were necessary for us : this performed and our reckonings evened, I was very ready to exchange any curtesy with him. Hee replied : if I would come oftner to the Prince, he would effect all my busines and use his best creditt ; and soe wee parted. The Prince harkened to this discourse, and many of the principalls were gathered about us, supposing wee would have chidd, or at least expecting some better sport then wee made them (for they delight in contraversies as a pastime), but his faire woords prevented yt. This obsarvance I made of him, that hee seemes to bee a free and good naturd man, for that hee confidently avowed the fault in his master, and seemed as it were to scorne to have done such outrages of his owne disposition ; and his professions appeared harty, his carriadge to the Prince carelesse and familiar, unlike all other men. At afternoone I desiered Mr. Fettiplace and Jadowe[1] to goe make experience of his promises.

August 1.—Mr. Fettiplace went to Zulpheckcarcon for his *scrito* for our mony according to agreement ; but hee refused to seale it, under pretence that hee would first collect the mony from divers that had parte of the goods, and for his owne hee gave a bill to receive 3,500 *m.* of Abram Chan ; but would not tye himselfe to answer other mens debts.

August 2.—I wrote to Asaph Chan eyther to procure the seale to my demands before the ships arrivall, with all the reasons I could urdge, or to deale soe nobly as to give me a

[1] Jādu, the factors' Indian broker.

reasolute answere; and to meete Mirze Socorolla about the farme.[1] The coppy is registred.[2] Hee returned: for my articles they should bee sealed without delay, but that by the negligence of his servant they were mislayed, else they had bene finished, and required a nother coppy: for the farme of customes, hee would advise thereon and doe me all frendship;[3] but in plaine termes hee beggd a rich present for the Prince.

August 5.—I seeing how Zulpheckcarcon, notwithstanding all promises, used us, I resolved I would trye the uttmost and bee no farther abused with delaies. Soe that I tooke the occasion of his watch day at the Princes, where hee must needs bee, and ther publiquely to demand satisfaction before his face and lett His Highnes know with what evasions my long patience had bene tyred. But before I went in, I sent Jaddow to signifie the intent of my comminge; whereatt hee entreated mee not to complaine nor speake of yt for that day, and if I would trust him soe farr as to forbeare untill the Princes goeing in, hee would returne with mee, and give me full satisfaction. So that I ventured once more, not for his sake, but for that I knewe it would not bee a wellcome motion to the Prince that was soe unpleasing to his minion. When the Prince rose and departed, I, that never thought my selfe suer of soe uncertaine a man, desiered Merzie Socorolla to heare the conditions agreed on, and lett him know that at Zulpheckcarcons entreaty and promise to finish it now, I had that day forborne complaint, desiering [him] to wittnes to the Prince, if I were enforced, the just cause of greevances I received by his daylie falshood; repeating the debt, the abatement, and my desier, with the others promise. With much adoe I gott him to confesse the sumes, but then, beeing free for four or five daies and having now escaped mee, hee sought all means to deferr giving his *scrito* for the whole, which

---

[1] Of the Surat customs.

[2] See f. 114 of the MS. The letter is, however, dated 31 July.

[3] In a letter to Pepwell of 10 September, 1616, Roe says that his offer was accepted in principle. No actual arrangement, however, was made, as they failed to come to terms; see the letter to the Company, 14 February, 1618 (*infra*).

was that I insisted on. Breefly, after many disputes Socorolla tould him plainly it was dishonest to putt us off to any other, seeing hee tooke our goods, however hee bestowed them : for the Princes part, it was given as a present : but that if hee would doe as hee ought, give me content by his bill for the whole debte and take it upon him selfe, that hee would move the Prince to pay as much as hee had received, and soe farr ease him : if not, hee would hinder him all in his power and assist mee next daye to complayne. Divers others councelled him and perswaded him ; soe at last he gave his woord publiquely, desiering me to goe with him to the court of guard, wher hee sate, and I should have my desier. Socorolla intreated mee to doe soe and finish yt ; and for the mony hee promised to see it performed. When wee were sate, hee offered mee presents and much kind usage. I desiered a dispatch of that I staied for, and before I could accept of none. Soe hee drewe the bill him selfe, and sealed in the presents of divers and read it to our interpreter and Mr. Bidolph, who said it was well and sufficient ; wherat wee tooke hands. And pressing mee to take a gould *shash* [*i.e.* turban-cloth] I answered wee were but newly frends : when I saw any constancy in his carriadge and the mony paid, I would bee more free with him, yet I would receive no obligation. Thus this long and troublesome busines is finished ; in which I was so farr from any sistance of justice that I got the disfavour of him that should have been my judge, and Asaph Chan my procurator could find noe other means of reconcilment but by agreement with my enemie. Yet the losse is not great or none to the Company, for it is in their powers to make shares, more beeing recovered then their debt by 300 *m*. or therabouts ; and in theirs not only all things at their owne rates, but the 2,000 *m*. given is comprised and restored (which was almost a shame to demand, beeing called a guift) ; and I shall desier those that deale in the busines not [to] ease them selves in their dispatches, soe gently parting with mony, and cast the burthen and envy on mee to recover it. What paines and adventurs I ran, what I bare shutting myne eyes and ears against many ill usages, I best know, that soe often felt nature and honor repine and object a stupid patience.

This night the King sent four or five messengers for mee to [come to] the *guzelchan*, but the first mistaking his arrand and my owne indisposition deferrd my goeing.

August 6.—I was sent for to the *durbar*. The busines was about a picture I had lately given the King, and was confident that noe man in India could equall yt. So soone as I came, hee asked mee what I would give the paynter that had made a coppy soe like it that I should not knowe myne owne. I answered : a painters reward—50 *rupies*. The King replied his painter was a *cavallero*,[1] and that too smalle a guift ; to which I answered I gave my picture with a good hart, esteeming it rare, and ment not to make comparisons or wagers : if his servant had done as well, and would not accept of my guifte, His Majestie was most fitt to reward him. Soe with many passages of jests, mirth and brages concerning the arts of his countrie, hee fell to aske mee questions : how often I dranck a day, and how much and what ? What in England ? What beere was ? How made ? and whether I could make it heere ? in all which I satisfied his great demands of state. He concluded that I should come to the *guzelchan*, and then I should see the picturs. At night hee sent for mee, beeing hastie to triumph in his woorkman, and shewed me six pictures, five made by his man, all pasted on [2] one table, so like that I was by candle light troubled to discerne which was which ; I confesse beyond all expectation ; yet I showed myne owne and the differences, which were in arte apparant, but not to be juged by a common eye. But for that at first sight I knew it not, hee was very merry and joyfull and craked [3] like a northern man. I gave him way and content, praysing his mans arte. Now, saith hee, what say yow ? I replied I saw His Majestie needed noe picture from our country. But, saieth hee, what

---

[1] A gentleman—a term Jahāngīr had doubtless learned from the Portuguese.

[2] Purchas has ' in one table,' as if using the word in the sense (then not uncommon) of ' picture.' Evidently the six were fastened (slightly, for the Mogul detached one afterwards) upon some flat surface, probably of thin board.

[3] Boasted. ' Then is she mortal borne, howso ye *crake* ' (*Faerie Queene*, Bk. vii. c. 7, st. 50).

will yow give the painter ? I answered : seeing hee had soe farr excelled my opinione of him, I would double my liberalitye, and that, if hee came to my house, I would give him 100 *rupies* to buy a nagg ; which the King tooke kindly, but answered hee should accept no mony, but some other guifte ; which I promised. The King asked : what ? I said it was referrable to my discretion. So hee answered it was true ; yet desiered I would name yt. I replyed a good swoord, or pistoll, or picture ; wherat the King answered : yow confesse hee is a good woorkman : send for him home, and showe him such toyes as yow have and lett him choose one ; in requitall wherof yow shall choose any of these coppies to showe in England wee are not so unskillfull as yow esteeme us. Soe hee pressed mee to choose one ; which I did. The King, wrapping it up in paper and putting it up in a table booke [1] of myne, delivered yt with much joye and exultation of his mans supposed victory.[2] Wherat I showed him a picture I had of His Majestie farr infearior to the woorke I now sawe, which caused mee to judg of all other by that which was delivered mee as the best. He asked me where I had it ? I tould him. Why, said hee, doe yow buy any such things ? Have not I the best, and have

[1] Note-book.

[2] The following is Terry's hearsay account (p. 135) of this incident, which, it will be noticed, is incorrect in some particulars : ' It happened that my Lord Ambassadour visiting the Mogol on a time, as he did often, he presented him with a curious neat small oval picture done to the life in England. The Mogol was much pleased with it, but told the Ambassadour withall, that happily he supposed that there was never a one in his countrey that could do so well in that curious art ; and then offered to wager with him a *leck* of *roopies* (a sum which amounted to no less then 10,000*l*. sterling) that in a few dayes he would have two coppies made by that presented to him, so like that the Ambassadour should not know his own. He refused the great wager, but told the King he would adventure his judgment on it. Two coppies taken from that originall were within few dayes after made and brought and laid before the Ambassadour in the presence of the King ; the Ambassadour viewing them long, either out of courtship to please the King, or else unable to make a difference 'twixt the pictures, being all exquisitly done, took one of them which was new made for that which he had formerly presented, and did after profess that he did not flatter, but mistake in that choise.'

I not tould yow I will give yow what soever you desiered ? I thancked His Majestie, but that I held it not civilitie to trouble him in such trifles, especially as a begger. Hee replied it was noe shame to aske of him, and bad mee speake at all tymes freely ; pressing mee to aske some what. I answered I would not choose my guifte : what soever came from His Majesties hands I would receive as a marke of honor. He replied : if you desier my picture, I will give you one for your selfe or for your King. I answered if His Majestie would send the King one, I would gladly carrie yt, and knewe His Majestie would take it frendly and esteem it much : but that since His Majestie had embouldned mee, I would desier one for my selfe, which I would keepe and leave to my posterity as an ensigne of His Majesties favour. Hee replied : your King doth not desier one, but yow doe : therfore yow shall have it ; and soe gave present order for the making. Then hee turnd to rest, and wee were blindfold dismissed.

August 8.—I received lettres from Agra, which signifie that indico is like to bee at good rates and cheape : cloth sells not att all ; hides for losse. Concerninge the debt of Mahamett Hassine left by Robert Young [see pp. 157, 184], upon my lettre the Governour wrote to him to pay it ; who refusing, he sent for his officers and hard the cause and judged the debt dewe to the English, and gave sentence for payment. Yet ther was after abated about 90 *rupies*, of which Mr. Crowther frees him selfe.

August 9.—This empty day of other busines envites mee by the strangenes of the action to mention breefly a sentence of the King and execution accordingly. 100 theeves were brought chayned before him and accused. Without farther ceremony, as in all such cases is the custome, the King bad carry them away and lett the cheefe be torne with doggs, kyll the rest. This was all the processe and forme. The prisoners were devided to severall quarters of the towne, and openly in some street, as in one by my howse, wher 12 doggs tare the princepall ; and 13 of his fellowes, having their hands tyde downe to their feete, had their necks cutt with a swoord, but not quite off, and so left naked, bloody, and stincking to every mans vew and incomodytie.

August 10.—I received lettres from Amadavaz ; with which a copy newly arrived, from Mr. Kerridg to Jhon Browne, concerning a Dutch shipp of 300 tunns at ankar at the barr of Swaly.[1] She had been at Ba[n]tam, and laden with south comodities, had dischardged most part at Moha in the Redd Sea, wher shee tooke *chickenes* [2] and royalls for her goods, and with about 100 tunns of spices and that mony came to Suratt, pretending to seeke trade. Her people seemed not willingly to disclose their purpose, but that they expected a fleete from Holland and would ryde untill the season, and accordinly declare. Her arrivall, it seemes, made our factors at Suratt much afrayd, eyther of their purpose to doe some spoyle on the coast in revenge of certeine debts oweing, or of settling a factory in India, wher they would both outpresent, outbribe, and outbuy us in all things ; ether of which would be very prejudiciall to our proceedings, especially if they should robb Sultan Caronns ship expected this season in returne from Moha. So that although I had not advise particularly addressed to mee (of which I woonder) [3] and this comming casually, yet I

---

[1] This was the *Nassau*, commanded by Pieter van den Broecke. She reached the mouth of the Tāpti on 23 July, 1616.

[2] The Venetian gold ducat (*zecchino, cecchino,* or *sequin*). It was long current on the shores of India, and was held to be worth about four rupees. For an interesting note on the subject see *Hobson-Jobson*.

[3] The Surat factors sent off the intelligence on 26 July, but their letter did not reach Roe until 14 August. It is printed at p. 320 of *Letters Received*, vol. iv. (cf. also p. 278). In it they stated that the ship left Bantam in the previous September, and, capturing on her way a Portuguese vessel laden with cinnamon, entered the Red Sea and anchored at Mokha ; after disposing of most of her lading to great profit, her commander, encouraged by some Gujarāti merchants, determined to visit Surat, after spending the monsoon at Sokotra ; failing, however, to fetch that island, he was forced to proceed, in spite of the danger of approaching the Indian coast at this season. The governor, wrote Kerridge, was afraid either to entertain the Dutch or to drive them away, and so was temporising : he had refused them a house, though he offered to buy their cargo at current rates ; and he was trying to frighten them away by representing their danger of shipwreck or of attack from Portuguese vessels. The English, it seems, entertained the Dutch merchants hospitably, but were evidently alarmed by the prospect of com-

went to visitt the King and enformed him of all my jealousyes [*i.e.* suspicions], which were noe other then to begett some in him. Hee enquired what this shipp brought? which I declared according to relation: what the fleete was like to bring? If they intended trade? Or, if they were men of warr, upon whom the storme were most probable to fall? I answered that for their trade they could bring nothing but easterne comodityes, from China or the islands, for that their owne land yeilded nothing fitt for these parts, but that they lived upon transport of forraigne goods, and seeking new trades, gayning by all nations that needed others and had not use of shipping: but that they most affected a footing in these parts, and some hould and retrayt, both for the keeping in awe of those with whom they traded, and for a security for them selves from all violence or unconstancy, which course they had held in all parts to the south and east where they had any recourse, building forts for defence of them selves, wherby by little and little they became masters of the port,[1] wherof at Mesolapatan was a neighbouring example: but I thought if they came as men of warr, they would not attempt any thing on this coast, especially in presence of our fleete, which wee expected as soone as they could arive, nor in any place where

petition from this quarter; and Kerridge expressed a strong hope that the expected fleet from England would drive them away, 'for such,' he said, ' is their practice against the English wher or whensoever they have power to effect it.' Roe's reply, however, was: ' concerning the Hollander I have received instruction from England how to deale—not by force, as yow intended '; and, although he spared no pains to secure their dismissal, he was careful to avoid all show of hostility.

For a fuller account the narrative of the Dutch commander, Pieter van den Broecke, published at Amsterdam in 1648, should be consulted. Therein he expressly says that ' the English did their best with presents and bribes to cause our departure '; and in his letter to the Directors at Amsterdam describing his voyage (I.O. Records: *Hague Transcripts*, series i. vol. ii. No. 78) he specifies the amount thus given as 800 rials. He also mentions that there was an English ambassador at court with a large train of from twenty-five to thirty men.

[1] Roe's drift will be easily perceived. He knew how distasteful the idea was of any European power getting a footing in the Mogul's dominions.

wee had residence, for reverence to His Majestie the King of England, to whom they did owe eaven that liberty wherby they molested others : but rather they would prosecute their mortall quarrell against the Portugalls, eyther at Damon, Chaul, or perhaps at the head, Goa it selfe, for that if they came with such intent, they would doe somwhat woorthy their labour. The King was somewhat troubled at my relation ; but, as if all things were to little to concerne such mightines, it passed away without any resolution.

August 11.—I visited Asaph Chan, and cast new doubts into his head, pretending service and much affection to the Prince : that, because the Hollanders were in leauge with the English, I would not speake that openly to the King which I had reason to feare in behalfe of the Prince, whose shipps were now abroad, to whom all the coast was now subject : therfore I had reserved matter of most consequence for His Highnes, wherin if hee would bee pleased to heare mee and to follow my advise, I would perhaps prevent that which would both trouble and dishonor him : in all which, seeing it proceeded out of an earnest seale to doe His Highnes service, I hoped hee would judge of my good meaning and purpose, not according to events, which were subject to casualties, which had often more force in execution of councells then the wisest and most advised reasons. He gave mee great thancks for my care and love to them, desiering me to goe on the morowe to the Prince, whom hee would prepare that eveninge for a conferance with mee ; withall admonishing mee (with deepe protestations that he spake it with the like affection and love to mee that he saw I carried toward them by tymely warning) that I should by all meanes indeavour to prevent that the Dutch should neither robb the Princes ships nor spoyle the coast, for that it would bee very ill taken of the King and dangerous for us, in respect that he had often hard that they were a nation, though not subject, yett some way dependant upon the King of England. I answered : though I had no reason to doubt the Kings justice and wisdome in discerning and doeing right, yet hee might see that I had their safety already in my care, which made mee so farr wade into the busines almost against our frends : yet the love of justice compelled me to yt, for that wee were frends to the Dutch, but not to any of their unlawfull attempts : that I could by noe means answer, nor by any equitye be required to yt, for what they should doe at sea : but after the arrivall of our fleete, or where wee were seated, I supposed they would offer no violence, and to that end I would both use my creditt and authoritye, and also give such dayly advise and intelligence as came to mee : and that for prevention of what might happen at sea, I would deliver my opinione to the Prince. Now though these doubts which I sowed (especially of any enterprice on the coast) were not so urgent as I pretended, yet they served my turne for many purposes; first, to imprint in the Prince an opinion of my desier to doe him service and good affection of our nation toward him, and hereby to procure a more familiarytie of discourse ; secondly, I would under that pretence lay such rubbs in the Hollanders way as should not easely bee remooved, a matter of no small consequence to this trade, by whose admittance wee were utterly lost; at least I would so farr norish jealousy as to keepe them from any footing ; lastly, and which is not of least use, I would tell my owne tale in the Hollanders person, seeing it is necessarie that the Prince know how wee wilbe revenged if we continew to bee misused, and yet not convenient that I deliver so much playnly, as our business now stands. Asaph Chan seemed greatly pleased, assuring mee of favour from the King to our nation and of very gratfull reception from the Prince of my endeavours ; wherat I tooke occasion to tell him how little encouragment I had yet received, especially in the delay of those articles propounded in the name of my master, which was a busines most concerned mee and was the only siment to joyne the affections of both nations to avoyed and disperce all jealousyes, wherby a perfect leauge and a kind of naturall love would growe by continuall trafique, commerce, and entercourse one with another. He answered it was his faulte, but that ther was tyme enough, it beeing six weekes to the shipps arrivall, before which I could make little use of yt : but that if hee had any honor in him, I should receive them sealed within three days, and that what soever else lay in him to doe mee or my nation service I should command. I answered in the same mettle of obedience ; but to shorten complements hee said wee should bee brothers, and that the title should bee sufficient to expresse all profession.

August 12.—I went to the Princes, to whom (as if I had reserved the secrett and misterie of the busines only for him) I desired what I delivered might bee privately ; which was done. First, I tould him I had great reason to suspect that the Dutch fleete expected had some ill purpose, by the carriadge of the shipp arived, who offered to land no goods but dealt closely, reserving their resolution untill the comming of their fellowes, pretending that they entended a factory ; which if they did, they would unlade and not venture to ride in soe terrible a roade open to the sea upon a lee shoare, a thing strange and with us held impossible, that any shipp could gett in from the westward in this season, much lesse bide at anchor the force of wynds ordinarye untill the change of the monson : but for prevention, I understood they desired to bring their ship, was which drew but 12 foote water, over the barr and to ride in the river, yet without command of any fort ;[1] which gave mee the more suspition, for shee would bee master of the river, and goe out at pleasure ; but that which did almost confirme mee that assuredly they ment to surprise His Hignes ships was that about tenn years since the Hollanders had a factorie at Suratt where all their merchannts died, leavinge much goods and mony in their house ; which beeing veiwed and taken by inventorie, *Channa Channa* and divers great men devided and tooke amonge them, yet sending lettres to Mesolapatan of the particulars, offering to repay it all to any that should bring lawfull authoritie to receive it ; wherupon this last yeare the Hollanders sent over land two principall merchannts from Mesolapatan to Suratt, hoping to have found such justice as their promise pretended, but contrary they were beaten and ill used, recovering scarcly their chardge and some indico that was kept unsould, but for the mayne of the mony it was pretended to be in the hands of *Channa Channa* and other great men. These merchants thus baffalled at Suratt resolved to trie the utmost by faier meanes, and desiered leave of mee to goe in my company to Brampore ; wher beeing, as they pretended, refused audience and all satisfaction, they

[1] Out of the reach of the guns of any fort.

returned to Mesolapatan, but first reavealing to mee their intents: that they feared this refusall before they undertooke the voyadge, but yet to bee free from all scandall they had made tryall: but that it was resolved the yeare following (which is this present) there should come a fleete to the port of Suratt, wher, if satisfaction had beene made, they would trade; but finding the contrarie, with some ships they would shutt up the river and with others range too and againe and surprise all that came out of the Redd Sea and all other trading on the coast; all which considered, and that this shipp desiers to come over the barr, I had great reason to suspect that now that was in execution which was so long threatned: that this shipp should stopp the entrance to safety while the others tooke the booety; the rather because the Hollanders were soe incensed at the insolencyes offered them, and that they were a people strong at sea and revengefull, and would neyther forgett to [nor?] pardon injurye. I put His Highnes in mynd how easy it was to take his shipps and all others trading into the Redd Sea, and what losse it would bee to him and to all his subjects to have the trade either shutt up or to expose his goods to yearly and certaine danger: that therfore His Highnes should well advise how those were entreated that, beeing too strong in shipping, were so able to requite all injuryes.[1] Hee gave mee many thancks, with much profession of his gratitude for my good affection showed him in this intelligence; but withall was much troubled, desiering me to give him some councell what to doe and how to behave himselfe at present, and to avoyd the danger of his ships. I answered I was very unfitt to give him advise, being so naturally pregnant, haveing so many wise men about him: but, seeing hee so pleased to command, I would venture my opinione and referr it to his judgement to execute according to his wisdome: that hee should write to the leiutenant at Suratt to give them all good woords, but if it were possible (under pretence of care of their safety) to fright them from comming over the barr with the many shelffs, sands and dangers of the river, and then His Highnes should bee sure they would either away for feare

[1] In all this Roe was 'telling his own tale in the Hollander's person.'

of the weather, and not returne untill the season of change, when I hoped our ships would be arrived to doe him service and to prevent any injury : or, if they resolved to ride it out, it was 100 to one they would be cast away, and soe the question ended. But if no perswation could prevaile but that they would over the barr, then the Leiutennant should perswade them to bring the ship up to the towne, under pretence of better riding and more convenience of refreshing (which may else be refused them) and so draw them under the command of the castle, wherby they could not depart without leave, and if their fellowes had done any thing at sea this would bee a good pawne to redeeme yt. But because it is easier and wiselier done to prevent mischeefe then to redresse it or punish yt, His Highnes might send a post over land to Syndu in six dayes, and thence send an advisall frigott to his shipps to give warning to looke out for a fleete and to keepe in sight of land, so that if such bee discovered, they may shift under some fort or gett into Syndu : and that after, if the fleete arrive at Suratt peaceably and desier satisfaction and trade, His Highnes in honor would I doubt not cause them to have justice, but for trade I must referr it to his wisdome. Only thus much I would signifie : they would bee very unruly ashore, disorderly, especially by drincke, and that, if any justice were done in such case, they would make it a quarrell, beeing desierous of any occasion, for that accept they might command here (which would not befitt his greatnes) as they did in all other their residences, they professe them selves they shall gaine more by stealing in one yeare then by trading in many : so that if His Highnes could be quiettly ridd of them, it were a happines and ease to him. But, however, if His Highnes saw cause to entertaine them, I hoped it should noe way bee in our prejudice, who had beene priviledged many years by his father, and were most ready to doe him service. Hee answered mee they should noe way disadvantage us : that in all that I had delivered he would follow my councell and would not resolve anything concerning the Hollanders without my advise ; desiering me to continew to enforme him, and hee would apply him selfe wholy according to such instructions as hee should receive of mee ; with many promises, good woords, and complements. So that I have arrived at one of my proposed ends, and am in a faire course to all ; but successes are subject to the chance of circumstances, and the mynds of princes alter with tyme, or are overswayd with passions and some tymes bought with too easy a price.[1]

Here I mooved Mirze Socorollo for the Princes resolution for so much of Zulph[eckcarcons] debt as hee chardged the Prince withall, for that Mr. Bidolph the day before had showed him his hand and seale for the whole, wherin was mentioned to be oweing by His Highnes 5,500 *m.*, and hee desiered to show the bill to the Prince and to know his pleasure. He answered he had moved the Prince and had order for so much, and would eyther pay it on the morrow or give warrant to receive so much at Suratt ; and for 3,500 *m.* [for ?] which Zulpheckcarcon had previously given his bill to Abram Chan, hee would write his lettre to command the delivery, which made 9,000 in all ; the remainder, which was to bee payd by Zulpheckcarcon, hee would see performed at the arrivall of the Judg of the Custome House, who was dayly expected.

I am loath to omitt any curtesie done me—I had so fewe— and because this was one of the greatest and for the manner new and from a person of so great qualety, I cannot in gratitude but confesse it. His name is Gemal-din-Ussin,[2] a man of 70 yeares, Vizeroy of Patan and lord of four cittyes in Bengala, one that hath beene often embassador, and of more understanding and curtesye then all his countriemen, and to be esteemed hospitable and a receiver of strangers, not secrettly

---

[1] All mention of the arrival of the Dutch and Roe's action thereupon was suppressed by Purchas, doubtless in accordance with his expressed intention of recording as little as possible of the bickerings that, at that time when he wrote, were fast envenoming the relations between the English and the Dutch. In the same fashion he omits the entries under the 26th and 27th of this month.

[2] Mīr Jamāl-uddīn Husain. He had served Akbar in various military and political capacities, and under Jahāngīr had risen to high rank. He had been recently employed on an embassy to Bījāpur, and on his return had been dignified with the title of Azud-uddaula, or 'Arm of the State.' He was at this time *Sūbadār* of Patna or Bihār, but was shortly afterwards transferred to Mālwa ; in 1621 he was pensioned, and amused himself with the compilation of a Persian dictionary, which he presented to the emperor two years later.

S.T.R.

ambitious. Hee often made meanes that I would come to his howse ; which at last I did, and was received with extraordinary familiarity and kindnes ; offering me a *leeck* of *rupias* and such other curtesyes so great that they beespake their owne refusall. His favour with the King, his creditt, his councell, all was offered that could fullfill complements. And this I must confesse that from a person reverent in yeares it seemed more cordiall ; and for in some discourse speaking so playnly of his fellowes in court truthes in myne owne experience, I resolved hee was a good natured and right harted ould man. He tould mee much of the customes of this countrie, of their servitude, of their want of lawes, of the encrease of this empire, wherin hee had served three Princes in grace and favour (of which tymes hee showed mee a booke or annall of all memorable actions, which hee had daylie committed to record and had nowe composed them into a historye, the copy wherof hee offered mee, if I could procure it translated [1]), concerning the Kings revenew and the manner of raysing it, besides confiscations, guifts, and cuttings upon great men : that the goverment of every province did yearly pay a rent, as for his goverment of Patan only hee gave the King 11 *leecks* of *rupies* [2] (the *rupe* starling is two shillings two pence) : all other profitts were his, wherin hee had regall authoritye to take what hee list, which was esteemed at 5,000 horse, the pay of everie one at 200 *rupies* by yeare, wherof hee keept 1500 and was alowed the surplase as dead pay. Besides this, the King gave him of pension 1,000 *rup.* a day and some smaller goverments ; yet hee assured mee ther were divers that had double his enter-

[1] Lord Carew, in his letter to Roe in January, 1618, expressed a hope that the ambassador would find some means of procuring a translation of this work. In response to an enquiry, the late Dr. Ethé kindly informed me that the work is not included in any collection of Persian books or manuscripts known to him ; but he added that there was in the Royal Library, Berlin, a short collection of memoirs by Mīr Jamāl-uddin Husain, which may possibly have been extracted from it.

[2] This appears to be the net contribution to the royal exchequer, after deducting all expenses of administration. For particulars of the various provincial subsidies see Thomas's *Revenue Resources of the Mughal Empire*, where this passage is quoted (p. 24 *n.*).

taynment, and above 20 equall. Hee praysed the good Prophet Jesus and his lawes, and was full of very delightfull and fruictfull discourse. This visitt was past some few dayes, and I thought that his curtesye had beene at an end, but this day hee had borowed of the King his house and garden of pleasure Havaz Gemall [see p. 121], a mile out of towne, to feast mee in ; and over night earnestly inviting mee, I promised to come. At midnight he went him self and carried his tents and all furnitur and fitted up a place by the tancke side very handsomly. In the morning [1] I went. At my comming hee came to meete mee and with extraordinary civilitye carried me into his roome prepared, wher hee had some company and 100 servants attending two of his sonnes (being a father to 30). Hee entertayned mee with showeing the Kings little closetts and retyring roomes, which were paynted with antique, and in some panes [*i.e.* panels] copyes of the French kings and other Christian princes ; wanting no courtship : that he was a poore man, slave to the King : that hee desiered I should receive some content, and that therfore hee had drawen mee to a slight banquett, to eate bread and salte togeither to seale a frendshipp, which he desiered mee to accept : that ther were many great men able to showe mee more curtesye, but they were proud and falce : wishing mee to trust to none, for that if I had businesess to the King of any weight, eyther concerning the Portugalls or any other, they would never deliver truth who were my enterpreters, but only what eyther pleased them selves or would content in the relation : that therfore I should never be rightly understood, nor effect my busines without abuse, nor never clearly know my estate, untill I had an Englishman that could speake Persian, and that might deliver my mynd without passing the toong of a nother ; which the King would grant mee if I could fynd any, for that hee had conceived a good opinion of mee, and the last night at the *gusselchan*, having brought before him the jewells of Sheck Ferid,[2] Governor of Lahor, lately dead, hee remembred

[1] August 12. Roe carried, as a small present, two pairs of gloves that had cost in England 4*s*. (Roe's accounts).

[2] Shaikh Farīd Bukhāri. He had rendered important services in quelling Khusrau's rebellion, and had been rewarded with the

me of him selfe, and seeing a pickture of his owne that pleased him, hee delivered it to Asaph Chan, commanding him to send it mee to weare for his sake ; with many woords of favour towards mee, which would make all the great men respect mee. In this tyme came in dinner ; soe sitting on carpetts a cloth was layed and divers banquetting sett before us ; and the like a little apart for the gentellmen that companied him, to whom hee went to eat, they houlding it a kynd of uncleannes to mingle with us. Wherat I tould him hee promised wee should eate bread and salt togither : that without his company I had little appetite. Soe hee rose and sate by mee, and wee fell roundly to our victualls. The substance was made dishes of divers sorts, reasons, amonds, pistachoes and fruict. Dinner ended, hee playd at chesse, and I walked. Returning, after some discourse I offered to take my leave. Hee answered he had entreated me to come to eate : that what was passed was a collation : that I must not depart till I had supped ; which I easely agreed too. About an hower after cam to visitt him the ambassador of one of the Decan kings,[1] whom hee presented to mee, using him with civilitye, but in a much inferiour manner in respect of his fashion toward mee. Hee asked me if His Majestie my master would not take in scorne the offer of service from so poore a man, and if hee would vouchsafe to accept of a present from a stranger : for that hee would send a gentellman with mee to kysse His Majesties hands and to see our countrye. I answered him as became civilitye and good manners. So he sent for one presently and questioned him if hee would venture the journy, who seeming willing hee presented to mee, and said hee would provide some toyes of the cuntrye for His Majestie and send him in my company. By the manner this seemed to me to be earnest. While wee

command of 5,000 horse and the title of Murtaza Khān. Subsequently he was appointed Viceroy of Gujarāt, but was recalled in 1609 on account of oppressions committed by his subordinates. He was then appointed to the post mentioned in the text, viz. Viceroy of the Punjāb, and died while on an expedition against Kāngra (*Memoirs*, vol. i. p. 324).

[1] Probably one of the ambassadors from Bījāpur mentioned at p. 335 of the *Memoirs* (vol. i.).

thus spent tyme our supper came, two cloths beeing spread as in the morning, and before me and my chaplayne and one merchant were sett divers dishes of salletts and meate rost, fryed, boyld, and divers rises. He desiered to be excused: that it was their manner to eate among them selves: his countrymen would take it ill if hee eate not with them. So hee and his guests, I and my company sollaced our selves with a good refreshing. The meate was not amisse, but the attendance and order much better, his servants beeing very diligent and respectfull. Hee gave me for a present, as is the manner when one is envited, five cases of sugar candy dressed with muscke, and one lofe of most fine sugar white as snow, about 50 *li.* weight:[1] desiering mee to accept of 100 of such against my goeing. Which, sayd he, yow refuse of mee, thincking I am poore, but it costs me nothing: it is made in my goverment and comes gratis to mee. I answered hee had too far already obliged me: that I would not refuse his curtesye when I was ready to depart. Hee replyed hee might be then unfurnished, and therfore desired I would nowe speake, that hee might not loose his offer and labour too. Thus, professing him selfe my father and I his sonne, with complements I tooke my leave.

August 14.—I received lettres from Suratt,[2] beeing nothing but a bundell of contradictions to what soever motion I made in my opinion for the advancement of the Companys affayres; wherin I saw they tooke more pleasure to argue then to excecute, and to shewe their witt and authoritye then to yeild to any thing not of their owne propounding, their reasons beeing a mist of errors; with which they sent a formall resolution of councell to abyde the injuryes and not to dissolve the factorye, presupposing neyther restitution of extortions, reparation of wronges, payment of debt, nor confirmation of priviledges, contrary to their owne motions severally made, which beegatt the question, which they now interpreted they intended that the Princes shipps should be taken, and I att

---

[1] 'Spent in the howse-keeping' (Roe's accounts).

[2] Printed (with a few omissions) at p. 320 of vol. iv. of *Letters Received*. Roe is somewhat severe on the factors, whose letter is not quite so unreasonable as is here implied.

court; but that indiscret motion I could not tast. With these I received a confirmation of the Hollanders arrivall, with their opinions to have me procure their disgrace (wherby I was sure they would seeke revenge, and the blame and hazard lye on us) or els to consent that the expected Generall should beate them out, contrary to that profession I ever made, in comparison of the Portugall, that wee sought open and free trade without purpose to wrong any. What was fitt to be done I had not neglected before this advise, and found no reason to alter it. Want of power saved mee much labour, but disadvantaged much our busines.

August 16.—I sent to Asaph Chan for my promised articles. Hee swore by his god I should receive them that night or the morrow.

August 17.—I went to visitt the King; who, as soone as I came in, called to his woemen and reached out a picture of him selfe sett in gould hanging at a wire gould chaine, with one pendant foule pearle; which hee delivered to Asaph Chan, warning him not to demand any reverence of mee other then such as I would willingly give; it beeing the custome, when soever hee bestowes any thing, the receiver kneeles downe and putts his head to the ground [1] (which hath beene exacted of the embassadors of Persia). So Asaph Chan came to mee, and I offered to take it in my hand; but hee made signe to putt of my hatt, and then putt it about my neck, leading mee right before the King. I understood not his purpose, but doubted hee would require the custome of the country called *Size-da*; but I was resolved rather to deliver up my present. Hee made signe to mee to give the King thancks, which I did after my owne custome. Wheratt some officers called mee to *Size-da*, but the King answered no, no, in Persian. So with many gratious woords sent mee, I returned to my place. Yow may now judg the Kings liberallitye. This guift was not woorth in all 30 *li.*; [2] yet it was five tymes as good as any

---

[1] The *sijdah*, or prostration.

[2] In a letter to the factors at Ahmadābād, Roe speaks of it as worth 'not above 600 rupees'; and in one to Surat he reckons its value at about 500 or 600 rupees. This is double the value here assigned.

hee gives in that kynd, and held for an especiall favour, for that all the great men that weare the Kings image (which none may doe but to whom it is given) receive no other then a meddall of gould as bigg as six pence,[1] with a little chayne of four inches to fasten it on their heads ; which at their owne chardg some sett with stones or garnishe with pendant pearles..

August 18.—I received a warrant from the Prince for 5,500 *ma.*, part of Zulpheck[carcons] debt.

August 19.—Gemal-din-Ussin (who invited mee to Havaz Gemall), beeing newly made Governor of Syndu,[2] came to mee to dinner, with two sonns and two other gentellmen and about 100 servants. Hee eate some banqueting stuff made in my house by a Moore cooke, but would not tuch such meate as I had provided of my owne fashion, though his appetite was very good; a kynd of superstition forbidding him. But hee desired mee that four or five dishes might bee sent to his house, such as hee would choose, beeing all backd meates which hee had never seene, and that hee would dine on them in privatt ; which was accordingly don. And soe, offering us the town of Syndu and all other curtesyes in his power, hee made hast to fill his belly. I gave him a small present according to custome.[3]

[1] These appear to be the ' portrait-coins . . . in the nature of medals or presentation pieces ' referred to in Dr. Stanley Lane-Poole's *Moghul Emperors and their Coins*, p. lxxx.

[2] That this is an error (as also the mention of ' Syndu ' below) is shown by an entry in Roe's accounts (f. 278) under date of 5 Sept., where Jamāl-uddīn is spoken of as ' made newly Governor of *Seringe* ' (*i.e.* Sironj). This is corroborated by a passage in Jahāngīr's *Memoirs* (vol. i. p. 333), recording Jamāl-uddīn's departure to take up his new post, and referring to him as ' a *jagirdār* in the province of Mālwa ' (such, Mr. Beveridge tells me, is the correct rendering of the Persian text).

Roe refers to him again later, in a letter to the Surat factors (f. 137) : ' At Bramporee the cloth of Sering, which in fine[ne]s exeeds all the kingdome, is to be bought. The Governor is my frend and offered mee (yea, importuned mee) to take creditt for 40,000 *rup.*, to be payd in English goods, such as hee would name, at the ships returne ; which offer I surrender to the Company to make use off.'

[3] A book containing 48 sheets of pictures, ' beeing the whole historie of our Saviour Christ,' which cost in England 24*s*. (Roe's accounts).

This day soddenly dyed, to my great greife and discomfort, my minister, Mr. Hall, a man of a most gentle and mild nature, religious and of unspotted life. Hee had beene ill but five dayes, and that but easely. In the morning he had walked abroad, and lay downe in a garden on the wett earth, supposing him selfe in no danger. At noone hee eate with very good appetite. In two howers after he dyed. Thus it pleased God to lay a great affliction on mee and my famely for our sinnes, taking from us the meanes of His blessed woord and sacraments for our neglect off so heavenly benifitts; which was to mee (God knowes my hart) the heaviest punishment I did feele or feare in this country.[1] Gods will be done. My houshould was sickly, my cooke new dead, and I had as little joy or consolation as I beleive any ever had; noe comfort, no conversation, no such dispatch in my busines as might give me creditt or content, no such entertaynment as my qualetye required nor which might have appeasd and made other inconveniences tollerable, no hope of profitt in myne owne estate. This was all that made me live : a resolution to performe with an honest hart all I had undertaken, according to my power, comitting my selfe wholy to my Creator.

August 20.—I dispatched answer to Suratt,[2] with bills of

[1] The ambassador wrote at once to Surat for another chaplain. 'Heere I cannot live the life of an atheist; lett mee desire yow to endeavour my supply, for I will not abyde in this place destitute of the comfort of Gods woord and heavenly sacraments.' The post was offered to Mr. Leske (who had come out in the same fleet as Roe and had remained at Surat as chaplain), but he was unwilling to accept it. So the matter remained in abeyance until the arrival of Pepwell's fleet with two young ministers on board. 'The graver of them,' wrote the Surat factors to Roe (26 September, 1616), 'about 25 yeares of age, is called Edward Terry; was a fellowe of Corpus Christi Colledg in Oxford. He is verry desirous to staye in the countrye and . . . would willingly imbrace your Lordshipps service. The Generall hath spoken to me in his behalfe and geven him fayre comendations.' Thus it was to the occurrence of the vacancy at this time that we owe the *Voyage to East India*. Terry belonged, not to Corpus Christi, but to Christ Church. He matriculated there on 1 July, 1608, at the age of 18; took his degree in Nov. 1611; and proceeded M.A. in July 1614.

[2] The letter is given at f. 114 of the MS. Part of it has already been quoted on p. 148.

THE REV. EDWARD TERRY

9,000 *ma.* of Zulpheck[carcons] debt and a copy of his agreement, to showe such as hee charged with part of the goods, though hee now stood bound for all; with these I sent the Persians *firmaen* for Jasques [see p. 110] and copyes of all the proceedings therin (to bee ready att the arrivall of our fleete, if occasion required them), advise about Barooch, the Dutch, and all necessary busines.

This day and the night past, fell a storme of rayne called the *oliphant*,[1] usuall at goeing out of the raynes, but for the greatnes very extraordinarye; wherby ther rann such streames into the tanck, whose head is made of stone, in show extreamly strong, but the water was soe growne that it bracke over in one place and ther came an alarum and suddeyne feare that itt would give way and drowne all that part of the towne wher I dwelt;[2] in soe much that the Prince and all his woemen forsooke their house; my next neighbour carried away his wife and his goods on his eliphants and cammells to fly to the hillssyde; all men had their horses ready at their doores to save their lives. So that wee were much frighted, and satt up till midnight, for that wee had no helpe but to flye our selves and loose all our goods, for it was reported that it would runne higher then the topp of my house by three foote and carry al away, beeing poore mudd buildings (14 years past a terreble experience having showed the violence); the foote of the tanck beeing levell with our dwelling and the water extreame great and deepe, so that the topp was much higher then my house, which stood in the bottome in the course of the water, every ordinarie raine making such a current at my doore that it runne not swifter in the arches of London

---

[1] This seasonal storm is often mentioned by early travellers (see Yule's *Hobson-Jobson*). The name is the Portuguese *eléphante*, a translation of the Hind. *hathiya*, *i.e.* the 13th lunar asterism.

[2] The tank referred to seems to be the Āna Sāgar, which has a stone *band* or embankment; and the camp in which the ambassador and the bulk of Jahāngīr's retinue and troops resided was probably situated between that lake and the city. In 1904 I was told that the site of Roe's dwelling was still pointed out at Ajmer, but the statement appears to have been incorrect, as Mr. L. W. Reynolds, C.I.E., the Commissioner, and Mr. Har Bilas Sardar have been unable to find any foundation for it.

Bridge and is for some howers impassible by horse or man. But God otherwise disposed it in His mercy. The King caused a sluce to bee cutt in the night to ease the water a nother way. Yet the very rayne had washed downe a great part of the walls of my house, and soe weakened itt all by divers breaches in, that I feared the fall more then the flood, and was soe moyld [*i.e.* softened] with durt and water that I could scarce lye drye or safe ; soe that I must bee enforced to be at new chardge in reparation. Thus were wee every way afflicted— fires, smokes, floodes, stormes, heate, dust, flyes, and no temperate or quiett season.

August 22.—I received from the Prince a nother warrant for 5,500 *ma.* formerly mentioned ; for that the first, it seemes, was not sufficient.

August 24.—I visited the King at the *durbarr*, and there demanded of Asaph Chan the sealing of the priviledges long granted by the King and by him deferrd. I got his oath to receive them on the morninge.

August 26.—I went to the Prince to know the resolution of the Hollanders receptions ; wher I found it was resolved that, by reason of the expectation of the ships from the Redd Sea, content should bee given them in trade, but as yet no factorye nor house of residence granted, other then a ware house for the landing of their goods.

August 27.—I went to Asaph Chans, but he was among his woemen and came not that day abroad. I caused him to bee watched at night by Jaddowe, who tould him I had beene at his house and that if I received any more delayes I should bee enforced to complayne. Hee excused himselfe with com- plements enough that hee was very sorry ; commanding Jaddowe to lett him know over night whensoever I resolved to com to him, and desiering him to satisfie me, for that on Sunday, when hee spake with his sister Normall, the seale should bee given.

This day I received advise from Suratt that noe end could bee made with the Customer for cloth rated, yet no desire to complaine, for that the Governor had promised to arbitrate the busines ; and that a sayler of a frigott from Socatra reported that the English fleete was there arived with four shipps and one pinnase, the men sicke and weake :[1] that the Governor of Suratt offered the Hollander arrived at the barr to buy all his goods by the great [*i.e.* wholesale] and soe to dismisse him ; which hee refused, requiring to bee received on all the same conditions and priviledges which the English enjoyed. To which was answered that hee durst not consent to that without warrant, the English havinge obteyned theire residence by sute ; but to give them content they offered them a house to remayne in and to land their goods, and leave to trade untill the Princes answere and resolution were knowne, on this condition that, if His Highnes would not conscent, they should depart upon the first warning, eyther in their owne shipp or, if shee wear gone, in the first passadg to the sowthward. The conditions accepted, the Hollanders came over the barr at Swally and there moored, resolving to ride yt all weathers, and landed goods daylie ; pretending that hee would only this yeare buy cloth and comodityes for the sowthward, and be gonne with his shipp within 20 dayes, for that hee feared the Portugalls and had noe desier to bee found there by us, but that, if hee could obteyne licence, hee would leave some merchant in the towne.[2] With these lettres I received one from the Governor of Suratt, promising mee all frendship.

August 29.—The King went to Havaz Jemall, and so a hunting. Ther was taken a resolution to remoove to Mandoe [Māndu], a castell neere Bramport [Burhānpur], wher is no towne ; for that Sultan Parvis, beeing come from the warr in disgrace, and beeing with his trayne neare Adsmere, the King commanded him to Bengale, excusing himselfe to bee

[1] The fleet of 1616, of which see later. The report was false, for the ships did not touch at Sokotra.

[2] The desired permission was granted, for fear that otherwise the Dutch would retaliate on the native shipping. A stock of merchandise was accordingly landed and placed in the charge of a factor (Wouter Heuten) with three assistants, and the *Nassau* sailed for Bantam on 30 August. They had bought little at Surat, as they found calicoes there to be dearer than in Java (*Factory Records, Surat*, vol. 84, part i. ff. 69, 73 ; *Letters Received*, vol. iv. p. 339 ; *Hague Transcripts*, series i. vol. ii. No. 78 ; Van den Broecke, *Op sijne Reysen*, already quoted).

seene; and soe, having dispatched him without such incomodytie as was feared would arise if the two brothers mett, he entended himselfe to settle Sultan Caronne in the warrs of Decan; to which all the cheefest were soe contrary that the King feared to send him downe (as was the resolution some monthes past), and therfore dissembled it untill the other Prince were withdrawne and hee established by his owne countenance, comming so neare as Mandoa; which remoove, if it proceed, will putt us to extreame trouble and cost, for that wee must build a new house, both for our selves and goods, the castell standing on a hill without any other buildings neare yt.

August 30.—The King returned in the night, and about 11 a clock sent mee a very fatt wild boare, and so great that hee desiered the tusks back; with this messadge that he kyld it with his owne hand, and that therfor I should eate it merrilye and make good cheare. This occasion Jaddowe, that was sent for to the King to bring yt, tooke to tell Asaph Chan that I desiered to visitt him on the morow, and hoped to receive from his hands the priviledges granted by the King. He answered hee could not dispatch them so soone, but that they should on Sunday be sealed; and that he was loath to see me untill he had given me content.

August 31.—I went to the *durbar* to visitt the King; and there I acquaynted Asaph Chan with the newes I had received of our fleete at Socatra; that therfore in all probabilytyes they might by that day bee arrived at Suratt: that his long delay had much hindered our busines, for that I was resolved neyther presents nor goods should be landed before I had received them.[1] Hee acquaynted the King with the comming of our fleete, but with no complaynt against him selfe; protesting on the morrowe I should bee dispatched.

This day I received advise from Agra; wher no cloth, no comoditye would vent, insomuch that factory spent moore then they tooke, and is needlesse untill the season of investing; but I had no power to save you many a thousand *rupies*.

September 1.—I sent for my priviledges, but receiving a nother excuse of the Kings nativitye and a great feast for

---

[1] The required concession of privileges from the King.

two dayes, I resolved I was abused, and so tooke this way to serve the present necessitye : I went to the Prince, whose port wee were att and with whom was our greatest busines, for what priviledges soever I obteyned without his favour wee should still bee subject to vexation and injury ; I acquaynted him with the nearenes of our fleete, desiering his command for their entertaynment and good usadge, and that hee would grant us such priviledges as I would propound, or els I was resolved not to dischardge there. Hee began roundly : that the former yeare he had beene neglected : that hee had chosen that goverment only for the ports sake, and yet every body, eaven his owne men, were served before him, which hee tooke in ill part : but if I would undertake to him that what soever toyes [*i.e.* curiosities] came to bee sould might be first showed to him, hee would grant mee my full desiers and give such order that no man should in any sort molest us, promising to take nothing from us, only to satisfye his curiositye : and to that end hee would give mee a *firmaen* that whatsoever I would send for should come untouched, unseene to my hands, soe that I would bringe them before him. I replyed concerning his fathers presents, and such others. Hee agreed to all reason, and requiring mee to give him under my hand on the morrow my promises and demands and hee would confirme them, so that I should find him our best frend ; soe with very good usadges I departed. The promise and condicions I drew the sam day and putt them into Persian for the morrowe.

September 2.

This day was the birth of the King and solemnized as a great feast, wherin the King is weighed against some jewells, gould, silver, stuffs of goulde [and ?] silver, silke, butter, rice, frute, and many other things, of every sort a little, which is given to the *Bramini*.[1] To this solemnitye the King commanded Asaph Chan to send for mee, who so doeing appoynted mee to come to the place wher the King sitts out at *durbarr*, and there I should bee sent for in. But the messenger mistaking, I went not untill *durbarr* tyme ; and soe missed the sight.

[1] See the account given in the following year. Jahāngīr was weighed on both his lunar and his solar birthdays. The ceremony on the present occasion is described on p. 332 of vol. i. of his *Memoirs*.

But being there before the King came out, as soone as hee spyed mee, hee sent to knowe the reason why I came not in, hee having geven order. I answered according to the error; but hee was extreame angry and chydd Asaph Chan publiquely. He was so rich in jewells that I must confesse I never saw togither so unvaluable wealth. The tyme was spent in bringing of his greatest eliphants before him, some of which, beeing lord eliphants, had their chaynes, bells, and furniture of gould and silver, attended with many guilt banners and flaggs, and eight or ten eliphants wayting on him, clothed in gould, silke, and silver. Thus passed about twelve companyes most richly furnished, the first having all the plates on his head and breast sett with rubyes and emralds, beeing a beast of a woonderfull stature and beauty. They all bowed downe befor the King, making reverence very handsomly, and was a showe as woorthy as I ever saw any of beasts only. The keepers of every chefe eliphant gave a present. So, with gratious complements to mee, he rose and went in.

At night about ten of the clock hee sent for mee. I was abedd. The message was: hee hard I had a picture which I had not showed him, desiering mee to come to him and bring yt; and if I would not give it him, yet that hee might see yt and take coppyes for his wives. I rose and carryed yt with mee. When I came in, I found him sitting crosse leggd on a little throne, all cladd in diamonds, pearles, and rubyes; before him a table of gould, on yt about 50 peeces of gould plate, sett all with stones, some very great and extreamly rich, some of lesse valew, but all of them almost covered with small stones; his nobilitye about him in their best equipage, whom hee commanded to drinck froliquely, severall wynes standing by in great flagons. When I came neare him, hee asked for the picture. I showed him two. Hee seemed astonished at one of them; and demanded whose it was. I answered a frend of myne that was dead. Hee asked mee if I would give it him. I replyed that I esteemed it more then any thing I possessed, because it was the image of one that I loved dearly and could never recover: but that if His Majestie would pardon mee my fancy and accept of the other, which was a French picture but excellent woorke, I would most willingly give it him. Hee sent me thancks, but that it was that only picture hee desiered, and loved as well as I, and that, if I would give it him, hee would better esteeme of it then the richest jewell in his house. I answered I was not soe in love with any thing that I would refuse to content His Majestie: I was extreame glad to doe him service, and if I could give him a better demonstration of my affection, which was my hart to doe him service, I was ready to present it to him. At which hee bowed to mee and replyed it was sufficient that I had given it: that hee confessed hee never sawe so much arte, so much bewty, and conjured mee to tell him truly whither ever such a woeman lived. I assuered him ther did one live that this did resemble in all things but perfection, and was now dead.[1] He returned mee that hee tooke my

[1] The identity of the lady thus referred to is an interesting question. Roe's description of her is so lover-like that one may presume her to have been no other than his lately-wedded wife. She was a daughter of Sir Thomas Cave, of Stanford in Northamptonshire, and had been married in 1610 to Sir George Beeston (Nichol's *Leicester*, vol. iv. p. 352). The date of her subsequent marriage to Roe I have not been able to discover, but probably it was just before his departure for India. As first shewn by a passage in one of Carew's letters (p. 79), pointed out by Dr. S. Lane-Poole, the marriage was kept a secret; and this, together with the fact that she had a pension from the Exchequer of 200*l*. a year in her own right (Brit. Mus. *Harl. MS.* 2039, f. 179), explains why Roe made no provision for any payment to her from his salary during his absence. In a letter (undated, but apparently written towards the end of 1616) Roe refers to their separation and the embarrassing position in which his wife was placed. 'My absence was a fault, but wee tooke one another on condition.... If her mother and all her freindes persecute her for my sake, her constant vertue will bee more honoured and I bound to a stricter gratitude. If I retorne, they may repent it.... Though I cannot make her a durty jointure, shee may live as comfortably, as free from want or its companion, scorne, as any of her bloud.' He begs his (unknown) correspondent to visit her and her uncle, 'to whose discretion I have referrd her and the revealing of the mariage' (*Harl. MS.* 1576, f. 225). The resolution to keep the matter secret would also account for the ambassador's diplomatic statement that the original of the miniature 'was now dead.' In one of his letters to Sir Thomas Smythe (who was doubtless in his confidence) he asks that 'my lady' may have her choice of some quilts after Smythe has made his own selection; and letters in the British Museum (*Egerton MS.* 2086, f. 45, and *Harl. MS.* 1576, *ut*

willingnes very kindly, but that, seeing I had soe freely
given him that I esteemed so much, hee would not robb
mee of yt: only hee would show yt his ladyes and cause his
woorkmen to make him five coppyes, and if I knew myne
owne I should have yt. I answered I had freely and willingly
given it and was extreamly gladd of His Majesties acceptance.
He replyed hee would not take yt: that hee loved mee the
better for lovinge the remembrance of my frende, and knew
what an injurye it was to take it from mee; by noe means
hee would not keepe yt, but only take copyes, and with his
owne hand hee would returne yt, and his wives should weare
them; for indeed in that arte of limninge his paynters woorke
miracles. The other, beeing in oyle, he liked not. Then
he sent me woord it was his byrth day and that all men did
make merry, and to aske if I would drinck with them. I
answered: what soever His Majestie commanded: I wished
him many prosperous dayes, and that this ceremonye might
bee renewed 100 years. Hee asked mee what wyne, whether
of the grape or made, whither strong or small. I replyed:
what hee commanded, hoping hee would not command to
much nor too strong. So hee called for a cupp of gould of

supra) show that Roe received a packet from her by the 1616 fleet,
entrusted to the care of William Methwold. These are the only
references to her which I have been able to discover during the
period of the embassy. By the time of Roe's return all necessity
for concealment had evidently disappeared; for (as will be seen
later) his wife met him on landing, and accompanied him to town.
They were never again separated. She shared his long exile at
Constantinople, and her intrepid behaviour during a sharp engagement with Algerine pirates on the return voyage is proudly related
by her husband, whose references to her are always charged with
the tenderest feeling. How much she was to him cannot be better
shown than by the words of his will: ' here I take my last leave of
her, my most faithful, loving, and discreet companion in all the
troubles and infirmities of my life, beseeching God that we may meet
in the joys of heaven; and I desire that my whole will may be
interpreted for her best advantage, for I am not otherwise able but
with love to requite her merits to me.' Lady Roe survived her
husband over thirty years, dying in December, 1675: she left
special instructions that she was to be buried by his side, ' in as
private a manner as he was '; and they rest together in that nameless
grave in Woodford Church.

mingled wyne, halfe of the grape, halfe artificiall, and dranck, causing it to bee fylld and sent it by one of his nobles to mee with this message: that I should drinck it twice, thrice, four or five tymes off for his sake, and accept of the cupp and apurtenances as a present. I dranck a little, but it was more strong then ever I tasted, so that it made mee sneese; wherat hee laughed and called for reasons, almonds, and sliced lemons, which were brought mee on a plate of gould, and hee bad mee eate and drinck what I would, and no more. Soe then I made reverence for my present after myne owne manner, though Asaph Chan would have caused mee kneele, and knocke my head against the grownd; but His Majestie best accepted what I did. The cupp was of gould, sett all over with small turkyes and rubies, the cover of the same sett with great turquises, rubyes and emralds in woorks, and a dish suteable to sett the cupp upon. The valew I know not, because the stones are many of them small, and the greater, which are also many, are not all cleane, but they are in number about 2,000 and in gould about 20 oz.[1] Thus hee made frolique, and sent mee woord hee more esteemed mee then ever any Francke; and demanded if I were mery at eating the wild bore sent mee

---

[1] In a letter of 10 Sept. (see p. 232 n) Roe says that the present was 'wrought all with flowers sett with rubies, turqueses, and emralds, in number 2110, beeing two pound weight; the valew I cannot judge, because many of the stones are foule.' The presentation cost the ambassador 36 'Ganger' (*i.e. Jahāngīri*) rupees, which he had to give to 'the Kings porters and wayters of the *gussell chan*' (Accounts, f. 278 of the MS.).

Terry (p. 397) mentions the presentation, and takes occasion to reprehend the Mogul's niggardliness. 'unto my Lord Ambassadour, whom he ever used with very much respect, and would moreover often ask him why he did not desire some good and great gifts at his hands, he being a great King, and able to give it: the Ambassadour would reply that he came not thither to beg any thing of him: all that he desired was that his countrey-men, the English, might have a free and safe and peaceable trade in his dominions. The Mogol would answer that he was bound in honour to afford them that, we coming from the furthermost parts of the world to trade there; and would often bid the Ambassadour to ask something for himself; who to this would answer that, if that King knew not better to give, then he knew to ask, he must have nothing from him. Upon these terms they continually both stood; so that in conclusion the

a few dayes before ? How I dresd it ? What I dranck ? and such complements : that I should want nothing in his land; which his publique and many graces I found presently in the fashion of all his nobilitye. Then hee threw about to those that stood below two chargers [*i.e.* large dishes] of new *rupyes*, and among us two chargers of hollow almonds of gould and silver mingled ; but I would not scramble as did his great men ; for I saw his sonne tooke up none. Then hee gave *shashes* of gould and girdles to all the musitians and wayters and to many others. So drincking and commanding others, His Majestie and all his lords became the finest men I ever saw, of a thowsand humors. But his sonne, Asaph Chan, and some two ould men, and the late king of Candahor [1] and my selfe forbare. When he could not hould up his head, hee lay downe to sleepe and wee all departed. At goeing out I mooved Asaph Chan for dispatch of my priviledges, assuring him His Majestie cou d give mee no present so acceptable ; if hee pleased not to dispatch mee, which I doubted not if it lay in his power, but that some other hinderance was in my way, I would on the morrow moove the King. Hee desiered mee not to doe soe, for the King loved mee and had given order for yt : that the preparation of this feast had hindered him, but that now hee would send it mee, and doe mee all service.

September 3.—I went to the Prince and delivered the

Ambassadour had no gift from him, but that before mentioned [the cup and stand], besides an horse or two, and sometimes a vest, or upper garment, made of slight cloath of gold, which the Mogol would first put upon his own back, and then give it to the Ambassadour. But the Mogol (if he had so pleased) might have bestowed on him some great princely gift, and found no greater misse of it, than there would be of a glasse of water taken out of a great fountain. Yet although the Mogol had such infinite treasures, yet he could finde room to store up more still ; the desires of a covetous heart being so unsatiable, as that it never knows when it hath enough ; being like a bottomlesse purse, that can never be fill'd, for the more it hath, the more still it covets.'

[1] Mīrza Rustam, a Persian prince (grandson of Shāh Ismāīl of Persia), who, finding his position at Kandahār precarious, had in 1593 made over the city to Akbar, receiving in exchange the *sūbah* of Mūltān and other dignities. Kandahār was recovered by the Persians in 1621.

conditions demanded on my part, and withall a breefe of what I required in his *firmaen* ; to all which hee agreed. I gave him for a present a silver watch very small,[1] which hee tooke kyndly ; but tould mee the pictures I showed his father the night before, if I had given him, hee would have better accepted then any thing ; demanding if I had no more. I answered they were toyes, only valewable in my fancy, which I never purposed to give, nor esteemed them woorthy presents for Princes : but that, showeing them for the arts sake to the paynter, he had enformed the King and so His Majestie had commanded them : that I had but only that which His Majestie had returned, which hee [*sic*] should bee at his service. At night I sent to his secretary for the *firmaen* ; who promised in two dayes to finishe yt.

The Copy of the conditions demanded by the Prince on my part, and therewith what I required of him to be expressed in his Firmae, delivered him as aforsaid.[2]

Most excellent Prince,

Wheras Your Highnes doubts the good respect I and my nation bear Your Excellency, I humbly desire yow to believe that I will doe all my endeavour to give yow content and satisfaction ; and Your Highnes may therto bee perswaded, because the cheefe place of our residence and the port of our ships is in Your Highnes dominion and therfore it is most requisite by all meanes for our owne good to seek your favour. For the tyme past, neyther the most famous King my lord and master could know, nor the merchannts in England, that Your Highnes was the lord of Suratt, it beeing newly given yow ; and therfore I hope Your Highnes will not take any thing in ill part, assuring Your Excellency that His Majestie the King of England will both send Your Highnes very acceptable presents and receive very kyndly your good usage of his subjects, beeing your frend and confederate ; and I also his Ambassador will take care and endeavour to give Your Highnes all due respect, and that what soever I can procure woorthy your seeing shalbe brought before your eyes and bee at your disposing. The goods comming in our fleetes are of three sorts. One are presents sent by my lord and

---

[1] Cost 7*l*. (Roe's Accounts).

[2] There is another copy in the I.O. Records (Pepwell's Letter-book in *Marine Records, Miscell.*, vol. 2). The two are practically identical.

master to the Kings Majestie, your royall father, and to Your
Highnesse ; which I desire Your Highnes wilbe pleased to
grant your *firmaen* that they may bee sealed only by your
officers and soe delivered to the English to bee sent up to mee
unsearched or without violence, beeing the presents of a king,
that I may according to my duty present them to the King
and Your Highnes. Other toyes are sent to mee to give to
our frends heare, and for the merchants to sell ; all which, if
Your Highnes will alsoe give your command that they may be
sealed and sent up, I will truly bring them before Your Highnes
that yow may take your choyce of what soever pleaseth yow ;
and I will send my command to search the ships for all things
that are rare, to present them to yow before any other shall
see them. And wheras some things may bee the goods of
privatt men, which I cannot take away, I will also command
that such be brought before Abram Chan, that hee may buy
them for Your Highnes ; desiering that hee may have order
to pay for them to the owners, who are to depart with the
ships. In all this I give Your Highnes my woord I will
performe it faythfully. The last sort is cloth, quicksilver,
marfill [see p. 14], and other marchandice, for which I desire
Your Highnes command that it may be landed and rated
reasonably, and that it bee not deteyned in the custome house,
to the great losse of the merchants, but, satisfyeing Your
Highnes customes, may have free liberty to sell and transport
yt without trouble ; and that our people may not be misused,
but have leave to passe freely to their ships and to buy fresh
victualls without custome ; wherin I desire Your Highnes to
give your command that the country people may have liberty
to bring meate to sell at Swally, for that after a long voyadge
ther are many sick and weake. And lastly, that Your Highnes
will give command to the Customer to pay for such goods as
hee hath agreed for the last yeare, wherin by his hard usage
the merchants have susteyned great losse. And Your Highnes
shall find both my selfe and all my nation most ready to doe
yow all service.

September 4.—I received my articles back from Asaph Chan,
who tooke now att last many exceptions, and margined
them with his pen in most insolent sort, scorning that any
man should article att all ; saying it was sufficient for mee
to receive a *firmaen* from the Prince, who was lord of Suratt ;
and for lycence to trade at any other port, of Bengala or
Syndu, it should never be granted ; but in conclusion pretended the length and forme to be such as would offend the
King. Some articles hee consented too, and to them, beeing

reduced to the forme of a *firmaen*, hee would procure yt sealed. Now is it easy to judg what vexation it is to trafique with these faythlesse people. Seven mounthes I had promise from weeke to weeke, from day to day, and no exception; but fynding I had so drawne them that I should nott much neede the Prince and if wee disliked wee might refuse his goverment, hee utterly renounced his woord in chollar and rage. I durst not yet leave him nor take notice of his falshood. He that first took him for our sollicitor engaged us into this miserye,[1] knowing him to be the protector of our enemyes and a slave to bribes, which they multiply upon him. But now I had a woolfe by the eares. I seemed only to apprehend his dislike of the lenght and phrase, and sent him a lettre to enterprett mee, and a breefe of the substance of all required on their parts conteyned in generall woords, touching only such particulars as hee liked, and left quite out all the conditions demanded formerly by him of mee; desiering him to putt it in forme, and procure the seale, or to give me leave to receive my owne deniall from the King, and soe to depart the countrie. These I finished in Persian the same day and sent them to him. They are recorded in their order.

The Copy of my new Demands upon refusall of the former Articles, sent this 4th of September, 1616.[2]

Wheras the most famous King of England hath sent his Ambassador to our court with lettres to desire our frendship and to give leave for free trade for all his subjects in all parts of our dominions, which wee take in good part, and are willing to consent unto, wee therfore command all our governors and officers of all our kingdomes to receive the said subjects of the King of England with frendshipp and to suffer them to land their goods in peace, and to assist them with fresh victualls for their mony, without taking any custome for the said victualls;

[1] A hit at Kerridge, who, on going up to court in 1613, had accepted Āsaf Khān's offer of assistance in his business and 'founde him reasonable and honest.' Subsequently, at his own request, Āsaf Khān was allowed to present Edwards to the Mogul, 'yett continewed to be the Portingals agent also' (Kerridge to Roe, 23 July, 1616).

[2] A comparison with another copy (I.O. Records: Pepwell's Letterbook) confirms the material accuracy of this transcript. The covering letter to Āsaf Khān is given at f. 118 of the MS.

and, having soe landed any goods and satisfyed for the duties of the port according to agreement, they may have liberty to sell to any person ; in which the Governor nor any other shall not hinder them, nor force them to sell at a lower price then they shall bee content withall, not taking any things from them without payment. And further wee command that the said English may freely passe and goe with their goods to sell them in any place at their pleasure, and that noe exaction bee taken from them as they passe, having payd their dutyes at the port : and that they alsoe may buy any goods in this country and carry downe and into their ships, without any manner of vexation or payment, but only at their port. And further wee command that such presents as shalbe sent unto us by the King of England shall not bee opened nor searchd by any body, but, having beene sealed by the Governor, shalbe sent to the Ambassador resident at our court to be delivered to us, taking no custome for them. And that, if any English shall dye in any of our dominions, wee command that no confiscation bee made of any of their monyes or goods, but they shall remayne to the factors that are living ; or, if ther bee none alive, the officers of the place of their residence shall take note in writing of all such monyes, goods, boocks, bills of debt, and papers as shalbe found in their house, which beeinge sealed up shalbe delivered to the English at their request. And finally wee command that no manner of injury bee any way offered them : but that they may quicttly buy, sell, trade, and passe up and downe in our dominions without any extortion, payment, or hinderance what soever, but only the duties of the port wher they land or ship their goods. This wee strictly command and chardge, because it is our gratious pleasure to content our frend the King of England, as by our lettres wee have heretofore promised on our royall woord, and therfore wee expect that no man dare to break our said gratious command.

September 5.—Mochrebchan sent to speake with mee ; who reayealed to mee in great frendship that Asaph Chan was our enemy, or at beste a false frend : that hee had faltered with mee in my busines with the King : that hee would undertake yt and effect yt. I gave him thancks and seemed to accept of yt ; but yet I had hope of Asaph Chan, or at least was not cleare of him, because the new demands were in his hand, and I knew his power, but how to trust the other I as little knew. Besides hee was to depart to the government of Amadavaz[1] within ten dayes, and so, when I had declared a

[1] See the *Memoirs* (vol. i. pp. 331, 334).

defection from Asaph Chan, hee would leave mee without any frend. I resolved to bee driven by necessytye.

September 7.—I went to visitt the King.

September 8.—Asaph Chan sent mee that answer that absolutly hee would procure nothing sealed that any way concerned the Princes goverment : that I should only expect from him what wee desired, whose *firmaens* were sufficient. And so reavealed that purpose which hee had long in practice to make us wholy depend on the Prince. Now I had just cause too looke out, and was blamles if I sought new frends when hee had forsaken mee. I resolved to trye the Prince, and to seeme to depend wholy on him ; having sent formerly to his secretary fower clauses to which I demanded his *firmaen* for our present use at Suratt for the fleete expected, which His Highnes had agreed too.

September 10.—I went to the Prince, who cast downe to the secretary the *firmaen* by mee desiered and promised ; so that I hoped I had beene at rest.

September 11.—I received yt, but when I read it, it was in two of the four clauses demanded and promised much different, and one whole branch left out. Soe I returned yt with a round answere I would not accept yt, nor suffer any goods to come a shore. Never man had to doe with soe much pride, covetousnes and falshood. At night I rode to Merze Socorolla, the Princes secretarie, to expostulate the busines and to declare my resolution of departure ; but I found the *firmaen* not such as I was enformed, but conteyning all the clauses required by mee, though in the phrase to my judgment somewhat restrayned ; which hee expounded in the best sence, declaring that it was the Princes entent to satisfie my desier fully, and that it was sufficient. I urdged the obscurnes of some poynts, desiering him, as hee had cleared His Highnes meaning to mee, soe hee would by his lettre to the Governor of Suratt ; which hee granted, principally commanding that the Customer should pay for 50 clothes, which hee had many mounths since bought and now would returne them unto the factors to their extreame losse. In the end hee opened the ould poynt of the Princes desire that I should rely on him, and not crosse him in busines of his goverment with the King, and I should fynd

him a better frend then I expected; and finally gave mee
such satisfaction in all poynts that I was both pleased and in
some hope of good successe; the rather because hee is no
briber, reputed honest, and did undertake on his creditt (to
whom the Prince had referrd all busines) that wee should not
susteyne the loss of one *pice* nor any the least injurye. So
I accepted the *firmaen*, which upon translating I found very
effectuall.

September 12.—I received this lettre from Socorolla to Suratt,
so punctuall and playne in our behalfe, commanding the
Governor to pay all ould debts of Zulpheckcarcons yeare,
and that, if any remaynd there that had not given us content,
the difference should bee examined, the English satisfyed, and
the wrong certefyed to the Prince, that gave mee more confidence. Wherupon I dispeeded the *firmaen* and lettre with
myne owne to Suratt to meete the expected Generall,[1] encouraging him to land his goods bouldly upon such conditions
as I sent unto him, which the Prince had required on my part.
And if I bee not deceived, our busines was never in so probable
a way; because hee that requires conditions to be performed
is more lickely to fullfill his owne then hee that carelessely
leaves all things at liberty, to whom all things are lawfull.
Concerning other priviledges I am resolved to use the Prince,
and doubt not to effect that by him which him selfe hath
crossed and resisted. This day two of our factors [2] went to
Agra to invest some mony. I had no authoritye, but by much
perswasion and dispute I overcome them, for in cash was very
little, and they resolved to linger untill the arrivall of the ships
or receipt of mony for goods sould, which could not bee gotten
in two mounthes, too late to buy goods and send it to Suratt

---

[1] Roe's letter is given at f. 118 of the MS. The India Office has
other copies (*Factory Records*, *Miscell.*, vols. 8, 10, and Pepwell's
Letterbook). In it he says that the Prince 'governs all here by a
faction with weomen, and is soe respected of his father that no
opposition is safe. Yf you have any blanck lettres signed by His
Majestie that I may make use of one to him, it will advantage us
very much, for his pride expects the same complements that are
given to the King; and seeing it hath pleasd His Majestie to write
here to a common governor, it shalbe noe error to descend to this.'

[2] Francis Fetiplace and Robert Young. Coryat accompanied them.

this yeare. I prevayled so farr as to make them understand the losse of tyme, and to take so much mony up of the *sheraffs* [1] for two mounths as was due at Adsmere, to dispeed goods to our port. The interest is not the 100th part of the chardge the Company beare in attending five mounthes with a fleete for the fitting and safety of on ship; and I can proove that this yeare (which was yet most backward) a lading might have beene ready at Suratt by the 30th of September, so that our fleete nede not to have stayed above 20 dayes.[2] So should they have been free from the danger of enemies, that cannot attempt them so suddenly; the ships to the sowthward might proceed in their voyadg, and make quicker returnes for England by a yeare, loosing the season in their abode here; which would gayne and save the Company in the use of their stocke in wages and other expence 20,000 *li*. yearly. This I can prove without any coulor of contradiction. For if 4,000 *li*. had been taken up and employed at Amadavaz and Barooch (whoose broad cloth is fitter for England then *semianoes*,[3] which are false and beaten full of holes) with those monyes made from Suratt and Brampore, and our factors here had two mounthes sooner beene ruled, this had beene accomplished; the debt at Agra, the sales at Adsmere would have payd; what had beene oweing below more then goods sould, it had beene better to have taken so much mony out of the fleete to pay yt, then so much to invest after the arrivall, which course last yeare stayed Captain Keeling five mounths or no ship had been dispatched. And now if I had suffered them to stay the receipt of mony, from Agra nothing had beene done, but the stock had layne dead till another yeare. I know

[1] *Shroffs*, money-changers and bankers.

[2] The Surat factors, however, asserted that at the time in question Agra was the only place where English credit was sufficiently good to enable a loan to be obtained for such a purpose, and there only a small amount could be procured without heavy security. It is easily intelligible that the natives, knowing how precarious the position of the English had been ever since their arrival, should have been unwilling at this time to venture their money, even at a high rate of interest.

[3] A fine cloth, made at Samāna (whence the name), in Patiāla; see *The English Factories*, 1618-21, p. xxi. *n*.

not what blinds your servants. They pretend want of authoritye to take up mony, for no man can plead against the benefitt gott by yt. This error last yeare was more grosse, when Mr. Edwards had in cash almost 4,000 *li.* three months, and invested none untill our arrivall. I did my endeavour to perswade, but yow left mee so little creditt among them that whatsoever I motioned was contradicted, eaven to show their authoritye. This fault I touched to the Generall, and the error of factoryes, for your chardge here is extreame and unne[ce]ssarye. I know your busines may bee effected with more reputation with halfe the chardge and with extreame ease; but this seemes a paradox to your factors, but is such truth that if hee heare mee, or my credit can prevayle, yow shall feele the profitt; and though in this I transgresse your order to meddle in the merchandize, yet I cannot beleeve it is fitt for mee to see yow wronged by weaknes and to say: I know how, but may not help it. It was not your purpose to hurt your selves, but to restrayne mee from wasting your stock; but experience hath manifested I have more saved yt, and sought to husband yt, then all those to whome it was entrusted, sparing eaven my owne allowances and necessaries to advance yours.

September 13.—I went to Mochrebchan, and carried both the first articles and the breefe of them, desiering him to reade them and tell me his opinion, because that Asaph Chan objected that there were many things in them would distast the King; and, if hee found them no way unreasonable nor unfitt, that hee would acquainte the King with my comming to visitt him: that I was much discontent and very sadd; but to proceede to noe particulars, for displeasing the Prince, but in generall to signifye that somwhat was amisse, and soe, recommending our cause to His Majesties favour, to give the King occasion to demand of mee or Asaph Chan the reason of my dislikes. For to engage or accept of Mochreb Chans offer to procure the seale in spight of the other faction, I knew was both vanetye and braggs, without power to effect yt or courage in him to undertake yt; or if such foolhardines for our sakes should posses him to moove the King and to gett yt, yet the Prince would recalle yt; and my new solicitor beeing departed to his goverment, I should be left not only destitute but a declared enemy to those that had most power to hurt mee. All this hee promised.

September 15.—This day the Portugalls house was fiered and burnt downe, not saving their cloathes nor goods nor jewells that remayned unsould ; yet the losse did not amount above 7 or 8,000 *rupias*.

September 16.—I visited the Prince, purposing yet to runne on in a way of seeming dependance on him, untill I heard from our ships and what entertaynment they were like to receive this yeare. I found him sadd, fearing the coming of Sultan Parvis to court, beeing within eight *course* and importuned to kisse his fathers hands, who had granted him,[1] but by the power of Normall was after diswaded and a command sent that the Prince should take his journy right to Benga[l] ; yea, although the King had fallen downe and taken his mistris [2] by the feete to obteyne her leave to see his sonne. The Kings remoove continued, but whither noe man could certainly resolve.

September 17.—I went to the Kings *durbar*, hoping Mochrebchan had given occasion to the King to aske mee some questions, but hee had not spoken ; and Asaph Chan, as soon as the King appeared, departed. Rumor reported that the King commanded him away in displeasure ; but I found no such matter on the morrowe.

September 18.—I sent to Mochrebchan, who returned my papers with his judgment that therin was nothing conteyned at which the King could take exceptione, but that the Prince would fynd his liberty at Suratt therby restreyned : that he had not spoken to the King, but at his taking leave hee would not fayle.

September 19.—Mochrebchan tooke his leave and departed to his tents a *course* out of towne ; soe that I must attend his answere.

---

[1] Writing to the Surat factors on 10 Sept. (f. 122 of the MS.) Roe had said : ' Sultan Parvis is within eight *course*, and hath obteyned leave to see his father, who is like to enterteyne him so well that our young master [Khurram] is blancke at yt.'

[2] Nūr Mahal. Purchas (or his printer) made nonsense of the passage by turning ' mistris ' into ' mother.'

September 23.—I went four *course* after Mochrebchan to take my leave: But hee had not spoken to the King according to promise ; excusing himselfe that, hee beeing to depart and so not able to goe thorough with that hee had begunn, it would rather rayse jelouses then doe good : that at my first comminge I was ill advised to use Asaph Chan, who was knowne to bee the Portugalls frend and had his factors in Goa : [1] but that, since it was not to bee remedyed, hee would commend our cause to his frend Abdala Hassan by lettre, who should effect all our busines to content. This man was both able to doe yt, and uncorrupt. But I feared hee, following no mans busines, would not for our sakes crosse the power of Asaph Chan ; but the others confidence made mee accept of the lettre to keepe by mee, and to use as occasion advised me. And soe, recommending our factory at Amadavaz to his favour,[2] I tooke leave. But yet I stood in feare of my ould frend, to whom if I had never beene engaged, it was at first free for mee and had beene no discourtesye to make my owne choyce, but now to forsake him would doubtlese leave him myne enemy. Our busines for the present standing on good tearmes by my last agreement with the Prince, I determined to rest, and with patience to watch the advantage of many supposed and expected changes, and to temporize withall untill I saw the

[1] In a letter to Roe of 23 July, 1616, Kerridge declared that Āsaf Khān had first brought himself into notice by gratifying the Mogul's eagerness for novelties. ' It hath been his pollicy to favour strangers and, wantinge better meanes, in his first risynge made them instruments of his further grace ; for, knowinge the Kings extraordinarye delight in toyes, acquaintinge himself with the Jesuytes and Portingals (after his sisters admittance to the *sarralya*), he brought their presents, suytes, and them to the Kinge, bargayning for their juells, etc., therby expressinge his abillitye and better parts (till then obscure), which, by his sisters meanes, in short tyme purchased this allyance [with the Prince] and advaunced him to highe offices ' (*Factory Records, Surat*, vol. 84, part i. f. 50).

[2] ' Mochrebchan . . . hath vowed by all his godes,' wrote Roe to the factors at Ahmadābād, ' that yow shalbe as his sonns and no injurie offered yow shalbe unrequited. . . . The Prince hath alsoe entrusted to him a superintendency over Suratt, wherin hee will favour us all hee may. Hee is departed hence in much grace and, in my judgment, with the Kings very good opinion ' (MS., f. 123).

fruict of the Princes promises by the usage of our fleete lookd for, and that the supply of presents were come to my hand; for then both the King is easye and all about him soe slavish to bribes that I knew I could take my choyse of new, or returne with grace to my ould sollicitor; and then upon delivery of a new lettre from the King my master, I would once more present and urdge my generall desires. The Prince I entended cheefely to make sure unto us; but now hee is ready to depart for Decan, and the King some other way; wherby, as hee cannot bee my assistant here, so will hee expect some agent to attend him, and I feare that all presents and whatsoever els is landed shall first be brought to him, while hee is lord of the port; which wilbe both a great inconvenience and disgrace to our goods. But I entend to sound his purpose and maynly to oppose yt, if it runne that way. I am not sent to him, but to the King. Hee would make mee, if not his servant, yet to cast my reguard wholy toward him.

September 24.—I received lettres from Agra, of the rising of indico 5 *rup*[*ies*] in a *maune* [maund], as it always doth at buying tyme; but, seeing the Company was at chardge to keepe a factorie ther all this yeare to no purpose, if they had taken up mony to buy at the best hand and at leysure, besides the dispatch of our shipping they had saved in price eight in the hundreth above the interest. Yet I wished that the merchannts would proceed to investure according to their last purpose.

September 25.—I received lettres from Amadavaz, signifieing their imployments, which will rise to 800 *ch*[*urls*];[1] so that had the mony due here beene taken up and employed in tyme, and at Amadavas but 20,000 *rupias*, to have beene paid out of the ships at arrivall, it is evident that a lading had beene ready by this day at Suratt, and the goods in both parts bought at better rates by ten and twelve in the hundred. This night I went to visitt the King, and was used by Asaph Chan and his father with much false curtesye; but I tooke it for currant pay.

---

[1] The *churl* (bundle, or, as the English factors called it, fardle) was the unit by which indigo was bought and sold.

September 30.—I went to visitt the Prince in the morning, and tooke with mee the bill of Zulpheckcarcons debt, of which 6 or 7,000 *m.* was behinde, and made offer to complayne ; but Mirze Socorolla perswaded mee that, wee beeing now in good termes with the Prince, hee would take it ill to heare more publique exclamations on his servant : that hee had written to Suratt to know what part other men had received of the goods, and upon answer, which hee dayly expected, hee would see us satisfyed. At night I went to the *durbar* to see the King.

October 3.—I received lettres from Agra that indico was risen to such rates that they resolved to buy none, but advised to make over their monyes to Amadavaz. So by neclect of the season the goods is unbought, and before any advise can be made to Amadavaz it wilbe later then the last yeare ; and so if any ship returne, it must stay five mounthes for dispatch. These lettres I answered not, resolving not to meddle further. The faulte is eyther in the commissions that restrayns the cheefes from using oportunitye, or in their want of judgment in apprehending yt.

October 4.—I sent to Asaph Chan complements and to signifye my desire to visitt him ; for the Kings remoove was certayne, and meanes of carriadge so scarce and doubtfull that it was tyme for mee to provide. The Kings journy was a secrett ; much of his goods and woemen were dispatchd for Agra, but the pretence was for Mandoa near Brampore, but nothing certayne. By judgment I gathered that the King would make a countenance that way, as well to settle by his nearnes his sonne, Sultan Coronne, in the warrs of Decan (to whose comming *Chan Channa* and other cheefes stood yet averse, and it was feared that some troubles would ensue), as alsoe to terrifye his enemyes and to force them to some agrement by his approach, which pretented a terrible prosecution of the warrs (which are made only by treachery, perjury, and advantages, without one honorable blow of eyther syde) ; but without any determination to stay (as I conceived by many circumstances), but that if on the way, eyther his sonne were quietly received, or some advantageous peace made, hee would make a turne and spend six monthes in progresse, and settle eyther at Agra or Dely. This was the most probable opinion; which seeing it would be a great chardge to follow, and yet necessity requiring it, beeing the season of our busines, by the ships arrivall and the merchants having great quantetyes of goods on their hands, unlike to sell on the way, and unsafe to stay at Adsmere after the Kings remoovall, I resolved by consultation with Asaph Chan to determine of my selfe and to advise the factorye. Hee answered mee it was the end of their Lent [see p. 12] and Mahometts feast day or their Easter[1] next day; after which solemnitye I should bee welcome.

October 5.—The feast was kept, shooting at a goulden ball on a May pole; but I stirrd not abroad.

October 7.—I visited Asaph Chan, and propounded my attending the King. Hee promised mee camells and carriadge for my mony, and the comoditye of his quarter, but no farther ease. Hee mooved my goeing with the Prince, but I gave him reasons of my refusall. I acquaynted him of the goods and great chardge in the hands of our factors, desiering him to advise mee how to dispose them, for that to remayne here was dangerous, to remoove with the King was an infinite incomoditie and chardge: next, hee would favour mee soe much as to lett me know his opinion of His Majesties settling, and which way hee would take; for then I could send before and build and prepare. He answered: for my selfe, it was fitt I should follow the King, and I should have such comoditye as his servants had, for my mony: but whither the King went, more then toward Mandoa: whither hee would stay ther, or goe forward or returne, and in what place hee would settle, or when, hee protested was shutt in the Kings brest, and that hee could give no answere nor advise for our factors and goods, other then to remoove to some place of retraict untill the Kings resolution were declared. So I prepared my selfe for the progresse, making provision to goe in some reasonable fashion, beeing dayly in the worlds eye; yet with such sparing as was fitt.[2] For these remoove all like princes, with severall

[1] The *Idu'l Fatr* festival.

[2] On 8 Oct. Roe suggested to Fetiplace at Agra that the caravan with goods from that place for Surat should come by way of Ajmer, as he wished to send with it all his spare baggage (f. 124).

shifts of tents that goe before, compassed in with pales of *pintadoes*,[1] which are ready ever two dayes for them. I would doe honestly and thriftely. For the factors, I advised them my opinion was they should with all speed, before carriadge grew deere, send their goods weekly to Agra (which may be done safely with little chardge), and there to abide a resolution ; for to wander with us were very unfitt and unprofitable. The most probable place of the Kings settling was there : that this journy was but a circuit : if ther wanted any cloth at Mandoa, Brampore was nere, which factory could furnish yt : if the King settled there, they might come after at lesse chardge, when provision was made for them. This was my opinion, and I was discharged ; what they entend I knowe not, for they so depend on advise in all matters from their cheefes in Suratt (who in these busines cannot judge, or when they doe, too late), that my woords were of no other then perswations. At night I went to the *guselchan* to the King to offer my attendance on His Majestie in the journy. Hee accepted of yt, but demanded how farr I would goe. I answered : to the worlds end, if His Majestie did. Then hee demanded whither hee went. I replied : I knewe not ; whither so ever hee went I would wayt on him. Hee thancked mee, and gave Asaph Chan order for mee, but what, I knowe not. Lastly, hee asked if I went home this fleete and a new ambassador in my place to come. I answered : I thought not, for I could not returne until I was eyther recald by my master or dismissed by him ; and for any other, I knew the King my master hoped it would bee needlesse to keepe one alway here, not doubting of the frendship and justice of His Majestie. These questions were somewhat extravagant ; but hee had beene very busy with his cupps, and suddenly fell asleepe.

October 8.—I received a lettre from Mr. Kerridge, of the date of the 24th September, 1616, by a *patmar* [*pattamar*, a courier] of the Princes, that our ships were seene on the coast and that hee was ready to passe for Swally.

[1] ' Painted ' cloths, *i.e.* chintzes, which formed the inner lining of the screens. On this system of a double set of tents—still a familiar feature of Indian camp life—see Bernier (p. 359), and the extract from Terry given later.

October 9.—In the morning I received from the Admirall or Judge of all marine causes in Suratt a lettre signifying the arrivall of fower English ships, and therin offering me all his furtherance and assistance in our speedy and faire dispatch; but withall hee gave me advise that wee wanted there a sufficient procurator to follow our busines, which I understood to bee one of that country, for I knew the brokar entertayned by ours was a foole and one that durst not open his mouth with such freedome as often our affayres requird. But because his meaning was somwhat obscure, and might concerne a dislike of the cheefe of the English, for that the woords litterally imported that I should send downe a sober, discret, and grave man for a procurator in our busines to bee indifferent, which might alsoe (meaning a Mogull) on our behalfe [be?] authorised by the King, I wrote to him to expound his entent and accordingly I would follow yt. Wherupon I was of opinion that no man was soe fitt as Jaddow, that remayned here; for the mayne of our busines for dispatch lying at Suratt, and finding it fitt to reduce the factoryes att Adsmere and Agra to one, the brokar there [*i.e.* at Agra] is by report both well knowne and sufficient in all but his honesty (wherin ther is little choyce); but I stayed the resolution for the Admiralls answere. Upon reading this lettre, I went to the Prince to heare what newes hee had received. He acquaynted me that four ships were arrived, but that hee was enformed they ment to trouble and stay the boates of the country; which hee wished mee to looke too, for that I should answer yt. I replyed I knew it was a wrongfull enformation: I was a sufficient pledg, provided that all covenants and promises were kept towards us, and that wee might trade peaceably without any violence or oppression: that perhaps some of our factors might in anger threaten (which I perceive they had done, it agreeing with their advise to stay the Princes ships), but that I would take order to accomodate all to His Highnes content. He answered that on his part all should be performed to our satisfaction, but hee required my persent lettre to the commander of our fleete for good order and quiettnes on our parts, as well in the towne as at sea; which I promised. I sollicited Zulphercarcon for our mony with some sharpnes. Mirze Socorolla gave his woord to pay it in ten dayes.

October 10.—Abdala-Chan, the great Governor of Amadavaz,[1] beeing sent for to court in disgrace for many insolencyes and neglects of the Kings authoritye, and thought that hee would stand on his guard and refuse : yet the Prince Sultan Coronne, whose ambition wrought on every advantage, desirous to oblige so great a man (beeing one of the cheefe captaynes in these kingdomes), prevayld with him on his woord to submitt. So that comming in pilgrams clothes with 40 servants on foote about 60 mile in counterfait humiliation, finished the rest in his *palanckee*, untill hee arrived near the court; but one dayes journy behynde hee had 2000 horse attending. This day hee was brought to the *jarruco* (the publique sitting of the King to see games, and to here complaynts) chayned by the feete, bare foote betweene two noble men. Hee pulld his turbant in his eyes, because hee would see noe man before hee had the happines to behould the Kings face. After reverence made and some few questions, the King forgave him, caused his irons to bee loosed, and clothed in a new vest of cloth of gould, turbant, and girdle according to the custome. The Prince, who entended to build his honor on the warrs of Decan, which his elder brother had left with disgrace and the great commander *Chan-Channa* did not prosper in (which doubtlesse was a practiser with the Decannins, from whom hee received pension[2]),

[1] See p. 150. His exact offence, as appears from the *Memoirs* (vol. i. p. 330), was insulting and imprisoning the official newswriter of the province, who promptly complained to the King. As indicated above, there was some fear that he would not comply with the summons. On 10 Sept. Roe had written (f. 122 of the MS.) : ' Abdala Chan, the Governor of Amadavas, is sent for prisoner. Mochrebchan is ready to be gone in his roome'; and again, on the 26th (f. 123) : 'Abdela Chan yet is feared will not obey, but fly. His feador (Port. *fiador*, a surety] Dionet Chan [Dayānat Khān] is commanded to bring him on perill of his owne heade. Many rumors come daylie of his rising in armes.' However, the offender thought it wise to make his submission, and started for the court on foot until he met Dayānat Khān. His arrival and his interview with the Emperor are mentioned in the *Memoirs* (vol. i. pp. 331, 335, 336).

[2] As here indicated, it was generally reported that the Khān-Khānān was secretly on friendly terms with the enemy against whom he had been sent (see Blochmann's *Āīn-i-Akbari*, vol. i. p. 338).

caused his father to recall *Chan Channa*, who, refusing to
come, desiered the King not to send Sultan Coronne to
that warr, but one of his youngest sonns,[1] about 15 years of
age. This Coronne tooke to hart ; but prosecuting his purpose
of the warr, promised to Abdela Chan the command of the
army under him, by displacing *Chan Channa*.[2] The King,
fearing troubles, and knowing all the ambitions and factions
of this sonne, the discontent of his two elder, the power of
Chan-Channa, was desierous to accomodate all by accepting
a peace and confirming *Chan Channa* in the goverment he held,
and closely to that end wrote a lettre of favour ånd purposed
to send a vest according to the ceremony of reconciliation to
Chan-Channa. But before hee dispatchd it, hee acquaynted
a kinswoeman of his living in the *zereglia* [*i.e. serraglio*] of his
purpose. She, whether false to her frend (wrought by Sultan
Coronne) or out of greatnes of hart to see the top of her famelye
after soe many meritts stand on soe fickle termes, answered
playnly that shee did not beleeve *Chan Channa* would weare
any thing sent from the King, knoweing His Majestie hated
him and had once or twice offered him poyson, which hee
putting in his bosome instead of his mouth had made tryall
off : therfore shee was confident hee would not dare to putt
on his body any thing that came from His Majestie. The
King offered to ware it himselfe before her an hower, and that
shee should write to testefye it. Shee replyed hee would
trust neyther of them both with his life ; but if hee might
live quietly in his command would doe His Majestie true
service. Wheruppon the King altered his purpose and
resolved to proceed in the sending Sultan Coronne, and, to
countenance his reception, would follow after with a nother

---

[1] The Sultāns Jahāndār and Shahryār. As they were both born
a few months before Akbar's death, they could only have been
about eleven years old at this time.

[2] 'Abdala Chan is here forgiven, in extreame grace with the
Prince. For anything I can judge of great men, hee lives in better
fashion, both in his trayne, equipage, and expence, and carries more
sowrnes or gravety in his person then any here. Yow see the justice
of the King. His sonne woorkes all to his owne ends, and setts up
this man agaynst Chan-Channa.' (Roe to the factors at Ahmadābād,
25 October, 1616 : MS., f. 125.)

armie. *Chan Channa*, that discovered the storme, practised with the Decans (who were at his service) to offer termes of peace for a season (fynding noe other way to disolve this clowde that hung over them both), until the King and Prince were departed and settled farther off. To this end came two embassadors this day from the princes of Decan. They brought horses, barde,[1] richly furnished, for presents. At first the King refused to heare them and their guift, but turned them over to his sonne with this answer : if hee would have peace or warr, it was in his breast.[2] The Prince, advanced by this favour and swelling with pride, resolved (though, as I was enformed, the conditions were very honorable and such as the King would have accepted) to goe on the journy, answering hee would treat of no peace untill he were in the feeld with his armie : *Chan-Channa* should not so beguile him of the honor of finishing that warr. The ambitions of this young Prince are open, the common talke of the people ; yet his father suffers all, but entends him not the kingdome ; for Sultan Cursoronne, the eldest brother, is both extreamly beloved and honored of all men, almost adored, and very justly, for his most noble parts ;[3] and this the King knowes and loves, but thincks his liberty would diminish his owne glory, and sees not that this sly youth doth more darken him by ambitious practices then the other could by vertuous actions. Thus hee nourisheth division and emulation betweene the brethren, and putteth such power in the hand of the younger (supposing he can undoe yt at his pleasure) that the wisest foresee a rending and tearing of these kingdomes by division when the King shall pay the debt to nature, and

[1] Provided with horse-armour (see Nares' *Glossary*).

[2] See the *Memoirs*, vol. i. p. 336. The ambassadors came from Ibrāhīm Ādil Shāh II, the King of Bījāpur.

[3] In the same strain James Bickford writes to Sir Thomas Smythe, 4 March, 1617 (*O.C.*, No. 454), that Khusrau is ' best beloved of his father and ever was, though a prisoner, which is more for feare of him then hate to him, he being so generally beloved of all the country and joyned in intimate freindshipp with some of the greatest and most honorable men of the country. Notwithstanding, the Kinge hath sworne that he shall raigne after him ; but dares not give him his libertie for feare of his flying out.'

that all parts wilbe torne and destroyed by a civill warr. The history of this countrye, for the variety of subject and the many practises in the tyme of Ecbarsha [Akbar Shāh], father of this king, by him then Prince, and these later troubles, were not unwoorthy committing to writing; but because they are of so remote parts, many will despise them; because the people are esteemed barberouse, few wil beleve them; therfore I content my selfe with the contemplation, but I could deliver as many rare and cunning passadges of state, subtile evasions, policyes, answers, and adages, as I beleeve for one age would not bee easely equald. Only one that passed lately I cannot omitt, to show wisdome and patience in a father, fayth in a servant, falshood in a brother, impudent bouldnes in a faction that dare attempt any thing, when the highest Majestie gives them liberty beyond eyther the law of their owne condition or the limitts of policye and reason. The Prince Sultan Coronne, Normahall the deare queene, aunt to his wife, Asaph Chan his father-in-law, brother to the Queene, and Etiman Dowlett, father to them both, beeing they that now governe all and dare attempt any thing, resolved it was not possible for them to stand if the Prince Sultan Corsoronne lived, whom the nobilitye loved, and whose delivery or life would punish their ambitions in tyme; therfore practised how to bring him into their power, that poyson might end him. Normahall attempts the King with the false teares of womans bewitching flattery: that Sultan Corsoronne was not safe, nor his aspiring thoughts deposed. The King heares, sooths yt, but would not understand mor then shee delivered playnly. This fayling, they tooke oportunitye of the Kings beeing drunck; the Prince, Eteman Dowlett, and Asaph Chan mooved the King that, for the safety of Sultan Corsoronne and his honor, it were fitter he were in the keeping of his brother, whose companyes would bee pleasing one to the other, and his safety more reguarded then in the hands of a *Rashboote* Gentile (to whome the King had committed him): therfore they humbly desiered His Majestie that he might be delivered into the hands of his deare brother; which the King granted, and so fell asleepe. They thought their owne greatnes such as, bringing the Kings authority, no man durst refuse ; and beeing once in their possession, they would dispute the redelivery. So the same night Asaph-Chan in the name of the King, sent by the Prince, came with a guard to demand and receive Sultan Cursoronne at the hand of Anna Rah,[1] a *Rajah Rashboot* to whom the King had entrusted him. He refuseth to deliver his chardge, with this answere : that he was Sultan Coronns humble servant, but that he had received the Prince his brother from the hands of the King and to no other would deliver him ; that hee should have patience till the morning, when hee would dischardge him selfe to His Majestie, and leave it to his pleasure to dispose off. This answere coold all. In the morning Anna Rah came to the King and acquaynted him with the demand of the Prince, his refusall and answer ; and added His Majestie had given him chardge of his sonne, and made him the commander of 4000 horse, with all which hee would dye at the gate rather then deliver his Prince to the hands of his enemyes : if His Majestie required him, hee was ready to obey his will, but hee would provide for his owne innocency. The King replyed : yow have done honestly, faythfully : yow have answered discretly : continew your purpose and take noe knowledge of any commands : I will not seeme to know this, neyther doe yow stirr farther : hould your fayth, and lett us see how farr they will prosecute yt. The Prince and the faction the next day, finding the King silent, hoping he might forgett what passd in wyne, tooke no notice of the grant nor of the refusall ; but it fell (not without suspition) on both parts. This I insert to this end that yow may beware scattering your goods in divers parts and engaging your stock and servants farr into the countrye ; for the tyme will come when all in these king-domes wilbe in combustion, and a few yeares warr will not decide the inveter.te malice layd up on all parts against a day

[1] This faithful Rājput is mentioned by Jahāngīr in his *Memoirs* as 'one of my close attendants.' His name was originally Anūp Rāy ; but for the bravery he showed in an encounter with a tiger, in which the Emperor's own life was endangered, he received the title of Anīrāi Singh-dalan (*ibid.*, vol. i. p. 185). The incident is mentioned by Finch (*Early Travels*, p. 154), by Jourdain (*Journal*, p. 160), and by Pelsaert (*Jahāngīr's India*, p. 52).

of vengance ;[1] wherin if Sultan Corsoronne prevayle in his right, this kingdome wilbe a sanctuary for Christians, whome he loves and honors, favouring learning, valour, the discipline of warr, and abhorring all covetousnes and discerning the basse customes of taking used by his ancesters and the nobilitye :[2] yf the other wynne, wee shalbe the loosers, for hee is most earnest in his superstition, a hater of all Christians, proud, subtill, false, and barberously tyranous.

Ther is dayly expected an embassador from the Shabas [Shāh Abbās], King of Persia.

October 13.—The King was gone to hunt. I received from Agra that indico was well fallen and that they would proceed to invest. At night the King returned, and sent mee a wild pigg. I received advise [3] of the arrivall of four ships safe at the port of Swally with lettres from England :[4] that they departed the coast the 9 of March 1615 [1616] with six ships, losing company of the *Rose* about the N. Cape by weather : June the 12, 1616, the other five came safely to the bay of Saldania, wher the *Lyon* hoomward bound was ready for a wynd, her commanders and people in health : staying [*blank*] dayes at the roade without newes of the small ship, they dispeeded the *Swan* to Bantam, for effecting the busines, and sett saile for Suratt the 29 with fowre ships, and came to anchor to their

---

[1] The death (of which it was strongly suspected Shāh Jahān was guilty) of Sultān Khusrau in 1622, followed, four years later, by that of Parwīz, averted the fratricidal war here foretold. But the prophecy came true at the close of the reign of Shāh Jahān, who not only saw his sons slaughter one another in the struggle for mastery, but was himself forced to yield his throne to the victor.

[2] It is to be feared that Roe's dislike of Khurram inclined him to credit too easily the reported excellencies of the elder brother. Khusrau's previous behaviour certainly does not bear out the favourable view here expressed.

[3] In a letter from Surat dated 26 Sept. (*Factory Records, Surat*, vol. 84, part i. f. 87).

[4] For an account of the voyage of this, the 1616 fleet, see Terry's book. He gives a spirited description of the fight with the carrack. Among the I.O. Records there is an equally interesting account in a letter from Pepwell to the Company (*Letters Received*, vol. v. p. 140). For the Portuguese version, see Bocarro, pt. ii. ch. clv., and Faria y Sousa, bk. iii. ch. xi.

port the 24th of September, 1616. In their passadge (August 6) neare the Islands of Comora (about 12° 50^m) they had sight of a carrick, burthen 1500 tunne, manned with 600, beeing Admirall of the fleete sent for Goa, bearing the flagg. The *Globe* fetchd her up to wyndward, and after salutations of the sea, the carrick commanded her to leaward, and seconded it with five shott thorowgh her hull, which shee requited with 18, and soe fell off. The Admirall and English fleete comming up demanded satisfaction for the injurye, which was replyed too with scorne ; soe began a fresh fight ; in few shott the commander, Benjamin Joseph,[1] was slayne and, the new established, they continued yt. At the evning shee ran her selfe ashore among the rocks of Angazesia. The fleete anchored short of her to attend the issue, and sent a boate to offer faier warrs, but about midnight shee fired her selfe and burnd all the next morning ; the English sending their boates could not approach, but beleeve that not one man was saved, by circumstances very probable. The new Viceroy for Goa was in this ship,[2] whose resolution was the death of all the others.

October 14.—I sent for the Jesuite and gave him knowledge of what had happened, desiring him to advise yt for Goa : and wheras I had written a lettre to the Viceroy, which his pride pleased not to answere, if hee, beeing a man of the Church and seeing how unprosperously they had begunn a warr with us, would yet admonish them to entertayne those conditions of truce that were honorable for both nations and send commissioners hither, I was ready to treate with them : in the meane tyme to forbare on all parts acts of hostilitye, and to draw and agree on some articles, with the reasons and pretentions on both sydes, to be judged off by our masters, eyther for an open warr or a full peace, at the end of three

---

[1] Of whom see Sir Clements Markham's *William Baffin*, p. 38 *n.* Terry says he was ' for years antient,' and ' had commanded before in sea-fights, which he met withall within the Streights in the Midland Sea.' His successor, Henry Pepwell, was desperately wounded in the fight that followed, but lived to reach Surat and afterwards Bantam, where he succumbed early in 1618.

[2] This was an error, as Roe learned later.

years: but if this course liked him, I required honorable and faythfull dealing and expected to see good authoritye and to receive and give good securitye for mutuall performance, for that I was not to be abused with the ould coulors of a Spanish treaty : if hee refused once more these Christian offers, agreable to the amytye of our most royall masters and their subjects in the parts of Europe, I then professed his obstinacy and pride enforced mee to declare him a breaker and disturber of the comon peace and so would pursue him and his nation as an enemye. This meditation [mediation?] the padre most willingly undertooke, corresponding to his owne desiers and the necessitye of their affayres.[1] For our busines (if it could with honor be obteyned) it were a matter of great ease, both in tyme, chardge, and expence, that wee might with one shipp safely trade on this coast. I hope not in the successe; but I would not the fayling were on my part. Now was the oportunitye to offer with honor, when wee neded it least, and if ever to effect yt in their necessity. I confesse it were the better consayle to pursue them faynting and to follow the victory, but I found here was no disposition in this Prince to breake with them; if hee did, no faith nor constancy, but would make the peace for his owne ends; and without such an ayd by land the woorke was too great for a company; the event of warr uncertayne, the end of our nation peaceable and quiett trade, in the calmes wherof trafique and merchandice only or principally flourished. I went to the Prince with the newes I had received; and because I had found his disposition was to draw my dependance on him, and that hee was ambitious of respect, I was indulgent toward him, and, hoping to take him in his owne netts, I propounded to him certayne offers which I pretended to receive in command from the King my master to deliver to his father, but for respect to His Highnes I addressd my selfe to him, both to acquaynt him with the propositions, to desier his favour, and to obteyne his mediation to present mee to the King at night. He demanded what was my desier. I first delivered him certayne

[1] 'Geven to the Padre the Jesuitt, Azorius and Bellermines woorks, cost in England 5*l*. 15*s*. Hee undertook to treat a peace betweene the Viceroy and mee' (Roe's Accounts: MS., f. 279).

complements sent by my soveraigne to the King : that His Majestie, taking notice of the favour showed to our nation, and that the Portugalls for our sakes robd and abused the subjects of this kingdom, hee was bound in honor to enter into the quarrell and had commanded mee to offer to His Majestie the assistance of our fleete arrived, eyther for the chastising of the common enemy or for the safe conducting of the ships of his dominion into the Redd Sea : and that, though now ther was a truce, yet I thought it my dutie to signifie to His Majestie the affection and honorable care of my master in beeing ready to performe all the offices of a good ally and frend. He answered that with the Portugall he had noe warr : to wefte [*i.e.* convoy] ther fleete was needlesse. I replyed wee had latly had a victory over a carrick which I supposed would draw on desire of revenge and that the Portugalls would bee attempting, if but for our sakes, to doe injury to our frends : that his coast could not bee quiett for our discentions : that therfore, though this instant His Highnes had noe neede, yet if hee would be pleased to give us a river and towne to fortefie in, for a retrayct for our shipping in foule weather, wee would alway keepe such a strength as should secure the coast on all occasions. This was that I aymed at, and that I knew was ill musique ; [1] but I received order, which I obeyed, though I can give reasons that to be denyed yt is for our advantage in my judgment, as our busines stands, and is mistaken by those from whom I receive directions ; and was sure of refusall. Hee answered with scorne that his father nor hee needed not our assistance : he ment not warr with the Portugall for our sakes, neyther would ever deliver any fort to us, to receive his owne at our curtesye : if wee came as merchants we were wellcome : wee had Suratt for our port : wee weare seated in Amadavaz, Brampoore, Baroch, Adsmere, Agra ; and Lahor or any other citty was free for us to abyde, buy, and sell in : what could wee in reason demand more ? I replyed all those places were inland, and at Suratt noe safety for our shipps. Hee returned quick that other port would

---

[1] In his letter of 10 Sept. (see p. 232 *n.*) Roe had said : ' I have endeavored to gett a towne and river to our selves to fortifye in ; but that motion is odious.'

not bee given in that manner, nor the Portugalls never requird yt. I thought to have proceeded, but finding his sharpnes and negligence, I ended. At night I went to the King. I found Asaph-Chan ready to meete mee with smiles and embraces and newes of our ships. New hope of presents made al wayes easye. I desired him first to deliver the complements of my master in forme, as I did in the morning to the Prince, with the same overtures. The King with much more curtesy received them, but begann with the presents. I first mentioned our late fight and victory, which hee seemed to rejoyce in, and to applaud the valor of our nation, but fell off to: what hath the King sent mee? I answered: many tokens of his love and affection: that my master knew hee was lord of the best part of Asia, the richest Prince of the East, that to send His Majestie rich presents were to cast pearls into the sea, the mother and store house of them: that therfore His Majestie thought it unnecessarie, but had presented him with his love, with many curious toyes, which I hoped would give him content. Hee urdged mee to some particulars, which I named. Hee asked for French muff or velvett. I answered my lettres were not arrived: some other was come which hee desiered. Hee enquired for doggs. I tould him some had their fortune in the fight, some dyed, two were preserved for him: at which hee rejoyced; and continued if I could procure him a horse of our great size such as I had described (beeing a rone or Dutch horse) hee would accept it better then a crowne. I replyed: I would doe my indeavour for His Majesties satisfaction, but I feared it could not bee effected. Hee answered: if I would procure on, hee would give mee a *leck* of *rupias*. I desired His Majesties lettre for the comming of these presents without search, and for the good usadg of our people. Hee replyed the port was his sonns, but sent for him and publiquely gave expresse order for what soever I would requier and take on mee,[1] that it should not be searched nor pay custome, but bee dispeeded with expedition safe to my hands, that I might distribute yt at my discretion: that hee should command the good reception of our people, and

[1] *I.e.* all things which Roe would certify to have been sent for presentation.

finally that hee should give mee content in all my desiers. This generally extended not to the grant of a fort, for that clause Asaph-Chan refused to deliver. This chardge was very round and harty in the King, and a grace to mee. The Prince called Asaph-Chan and mee, and there professed and promised before his father and all the court to give mee all reasonable content. This is the strength of new presents.

October 15.—I dispatched for Suratt the generallity of this, and my advises to the commanders; but because I lately sent downe a *firmane* sufficient, I would not retard our busines, but signifyed this grace and favour and, if any thing yet wanted, that in few dayes they should receive this new promised command. The Prince sent mee woord, wittnessed by two lettres from the Judg of the *Alfandica*, that I brake covenant with him: that our people came ashore and by force would passe the custome house, without showeing any goods to the Governor according to my promise: that his officers for feare of his displeasure had suffered them: but required my order in yt. I knew the complaynt was false and to excuse the knavery of the Judg, who had wronged us and, fearing complaynt, began first: yet I advised roundly to the commander and cape merchant, as my lettres will declare.[1] I received from Mesolapatan that Captain Keeling had taken two Portugall barks and a ship, one on the coast of Cochyn, laden with tynn, the other fraighted from Bengala, which hee carried to Bantam:[2] that Sir Robert Sheirly was dismissd with disgrace from Goa, and that hee was on his way overland to Mesolapatan to seeke passadge—unprobable and I beleeve untrue.[3]

[1] The letter to Kerridge is entered at f. 126 of the MS. It has been printed in *Letters Received*, vol. iv. p. 202. In it Roe begged Kerridge to hasten the despatch of the presents, including one for Nūr Mahal. 'The neglect of her last yeare,' he wrote, 'I have felt heavely.' He also made handsome amends for his late reprehension of the factors, assuring them that he was really their friend.

[2] See Peyton's journal in *Purchas*, vol. i. p. 528.

[3] As indeed it was. Sherley remained in Goa until his departure for Lisbon.

To Captain Pepwell.
(*Add. MS.* 6115, f. 125.)

Adsmer, *October* 15*th*, 1616.

Yow are welcome to this port. Gods name be blessed for your safety and protection. I am sorry to heare of the death of the first commander and of your owne maymes and hurts. All the comfort I can give yow they are the marks of honor and the wittnesses of an honest man, such as your employers can never forgett to reward nor your country men to honor. . . . My last lettres . . . will give you some light of our busines here, but Mr. Kerridge still more. The errors are manyfould in past tymes; and I should be glad yow would beeginn to reforme one in your power, of which I received this morning a complaynt from the Prince: the suffering of many people unorderly to goe ashore with their privat goods. . . . Yow have many young gentlemen come, that will not know how to bestow them selves here. The countrie is mistaken. Here are no inns, no chambers to hyre; every man must build a house; and the Companyes, by expresse order, can bee no refuge for them. As many as yow can continew at sea, soe many burthens yow take of myne and the Companyes shoulders. To enter into these warrs is a poore hope. Theyr pay is not like ours. So much trouble, so much servilitye as noe free hart can endure. Besydes, these people are soe proud they despise any arte or forme of warr but their owne. One or two men cannot breake the ancient customes of a nation wedded to their owne discipline. . . . It were fitter for us to contract then enlardge our factoryes. The busines truly understood, two are sufficient for all these dominions—Suratt and the court; perhaps Brampore during the stay of the Prince, but after it will not pay diett. . . . The comodytyes sent are trash. . . . The presents are meane and fewe. . . .

October 16.—I went to Afzul Chan, the Princes secretary, to give him satisfaction in the complaynt; and there opened to him the abuse and falshood, requiring His Highnes lettres according to the Kings order. He tould [me?] he would informe the Prince and drawe us a command to our full content; and that, seeing wee thought the Judg of the *Alfandica* unjust, hee desiered mee to name any one in Suratt to sitt in the custome house to doe us right, and hee should be joyned in commission for our behalfe. I replyed I knew none more upright then Abram Chan, the Governor of the towne, whom hee promised should have such order to meete with the

Customer in the office on our part to moderate the abuses of the other, and that all other our contentments should bee given in chardge to him; that at night, if I sent, I should fynd these ready. Ther, as a secrett to engage the Prince, I tould him of the unicorns horne,[1] which I would not name to the King that His Highnes might buy it for a rarety to bestow

[1] On the 'unicorn's' [*i.e.* rhinoceros's] horn, its supposed efficacy as an antidote for poison, and its consequent value—'worth halfe a city,' says Dekker in *The Guls Horne-booke*—notes will be found in Burnell and Tiele's *Linschoten*, vol. ii. p. 9; Grey's *Della Valle*, vol. i. pp. 5, 7; and Yule's *Marco Polo*, vol. ii. p. 273. Compare also Ovington (*Voyage to Surat*, 1689, p. 267), who says that one of the English Presidents at Surat believed so much in its 'medicinal excellence and singular quality . . . that he exchang'd for a cup made of this horn a large capacious silver bowl of the same bignes.' Fuller, in his *Worthies* (p. 193), speaking of a unicorn's horn, says: 'Amongst the many precious rarities in the Tower, this (as another in Windsor-Castle) was, in my memory, shown to people.' The specimen here referred to failed to find a purchaser. The Prince declined to buy it at the price asked; and it was then offered to Mukarrab Khān for 5,000 rupees. Its supposed virtue the latter 'made tryall of by the lives of a pigeon, goate, and man, which they loosing, itt also lost his esteeme' (Brown to the Company: *The English Factories*, 1618-21, p. 12). Roe was shocked at this callous experiment, and wrote gravely to Brown: 'I hope neyther your consent nor commendation ayded to trye the unicorns horne on a man. But Mochreb-Chan may bee deceived; it may bee true and rare without any such vertue as absolutly and alone to bee an antidote to any poyson. Ther is no such property in the best of the world; and, if it were soe, he knowes one *seare* of yt were woorth more mony then you demanded. But lett him know this from mee (which is true) that wee esteeme it in Europe a great cordiall and good to strengthen the stomack, to cheere and remooue melancholy from the hart, and a preserver against poyson equall to beazer stone; yet it is not expected that beazer alone shall protect a man from a strong poyson. Breefly, besides the rarotye (beeing a jewell kept of all princes) it is usd in all sorts of cordiall phisique to make restorers and strengtheners, with gould, pearle, corall, amber and such; and for virtue is held equall with any. . . .' (*Add. MS.* 6115, f. 200). But Mukarrab Khān was not to be tempted; and Roe therefore directed that the precious horn should be sent on board ship again, with a view to its being despatched to Persia. This intention, however, was not carried out, the horn being sent to Achin, and thence to Bantam, though at neither place could a purchaser be found. Later it fell into the hands of the Dutch, who sold it in Holland for 400*l.*

on his father. I told him of the rich estimation and qualetyes: that it was esteemed among the jewells of princes: but that I had no power to give it, beeing of great valew: that the merchannts made it a secrett and intended not to suffer it come out of the ship, but that for His Highnes content, if hee pleasd to buy it and would give order for mony at Suratt, I would procure his officers should see yt. This I hoped would both sett an extreame appetite on the Prince, to passe it at a high price, and would insinuate an extraordynary desire in mee to doe him service; and if hee reavealed it to the King, I would answere: because it was not in my power to give His Majestie, I was ashamed to name yt, but had mooved the Prince to buy it for his use. For this I had many thancks and complements. His secretary mooved by His Highnes order to procure for him two gunners out of our fleete to serve him in this yeares warrs for good pay, which curtesy hee would take very kindly and requite yt. I promised to effect his desier, and doubted not to procure them of the commander, seeing ordinary ones in that art will exell here.[1] I pressd the clearing of Zulpheckcarcons account; though I knew not what it was, for Mr. Kirridge advised satisfaction of 9000 *m.* for which I sent bills, and that of the 8000 remayning he had received content for two clothes and a halfe, but not how much, nor what rested. Yet I urdged the use of our mony now to employ, and showed his bill: that what was mistaken, wee would bee answerable for; which hee promised Mr. Biddolph this day or the morow. Abdala-Chan came to visitt the Prince, so bravely attended as I have not seene the like. To the gate his drumms and musique a horsback, about 20, made noyse enough, fifty *peons* with white flaggs carried before him, and 200 souldiers well mounted in coates of cloth of gould, velvett, and rich silks, which entered with him in ranck; next his person 40 targiteers [2] in like liveryes. He made humble reverence, and presented a black Arabian horse with furniture studded with flowers of gould, enameld and sett

---

[1] Roe duly transmitted this request to Surat, but no one in the fleet was willing to accept the employment.

[2] Soldiers armed with sword and buckler (targe).

with small stones. The Prince according to custome returned a turbant, a coate, and a gyrdle.

October 17.—The Prince, pursuing his purpose of finishing the Decan warrs by his owne person, and undertaking to give answere to the ambassadors, gives none, but deteynes them untill his approach. But, beeing to depart, he nor his party thought not themselves secure if Sultan Corsoronne remayned in the hands of Anna-rah : that in his absence the King might be reconciled, and by his liberty all the glory and hopes of their faction would vanish and the injury and ambition hardly bee pardoned. They newly assayle the Kinges constancy to deliver up his sonne into the hands of Asaph Chan, as his guardian under Sultan Coronne. They pretend that it will fright *Chan Channa* and the Decanns, when they shall heare that this Prince is soe favoured, who nowe comes to make warr upon them, that the King hath delivered up his eldest sonne, in that as it were the whole kingdome and hope of succession and the present power therof. The King, who had yeeilded him self into the hands of a woman, could not defend his sonne from their practises. Hee either sees not the ambition, or trusts it too farr in confidence of his owne power, and consents : soe that this day hee was delivered up, the souldiers of Anna-rah dischardged, and a supply of Asaph Chans planted about him, with assistannce of 200 of the Princes horse.[1] His sister and divers weomen in the *seraglia* mourne, refuse their meate, crye out of the Kings dotage and crueltye, and professe that if hee dye ther will 100 of his kindred burne for him in memorye of the Kings bloudines to his woorthyest sonne. The King gives fayre woords, protesteth no intent of ill toward the Prince, and promiseth his delivery, and sends Narmahall to appease these enraged ladyes ; but they cursse, threaten, and refuse to see her. The common people all murmer ; they say the King hath not delivered his sonnes but his owne life into the hands of an ambitious prince and a treacherous faction : that Corsoronne cannot perish without scandall to the father or revenge from him : therfore hee must goe first, and after him

[1] ' On the 4th [Ābān] Khusrau, who was in the charge for safekeeping of Anīrāi Singh-dalan, for certain considerations was handed over to Āsaf Khān ' (*Memoirs*, vol. i. p. 336).

his sonne; and so thorough their bloods this youth must mount the royall seate. New hopes are spread of his redelivery, and soone alayed; every man tells newes according to his feares or desires. But the poore prince remaynes in the tygers power, refuseth meate, and requires his father to take his life and not to lett it bee the triumph and delight of his enemyes. The whole court is in a whisper; the nobility sadd; the multitude, like it selfe, full of tumor and noyce, without head or foote; only it rages, but bends it selfe upon noe direct end. The issue is very dangerous; principally for us, for among them it matters not who wynns. Though one have right and much more honor, yet hee is still a Moore, and cannot bee a better prince then his father, who is soe good of disposition that he suffers ill [1] men to governe, which is woorse then to bee ill; for wee were better beare injuryes of princes then of their ministers. So that I may say of this tyme and the constitution of this state as Tacitus did of the empire of Roome, when it was contended for by Otho and Vitellius: *Prope eversum orbem etiam cum de principatu inter bonos certaretur: utrasque impias preces, utraque detestanda vota inter duos quorum bello solum id scires deteriorem fore qu vicissitt.*[2] And although the elder brother is not yet in armes, nor so like (if he prevayle) to tyrannise, yet it is to bee feared, *Rebus secundis eatiam egregios duces insolescere.*[3] I did advise our little common wealth to keepe close and neare togither, to attend the issue, to know no syde, to make few debts, and to

---

[1] Purchas (or his printer) has turned this into 'all,' and has thus entirely altered the sense.

[2] *Hist.*, i. 50. The passage is thus translated by Messrs. Church and Brodribb: 'The world ... was well-nigh turned upside down when the struggle for empire was between worthy competitors, yet the Empire continued to exist after the victories of Caius Julius and Cæsar Augustus; the republic would have continued to exist under Pompey and Brutus. And is it for Otho or for Vitellius that we are now to repair to the temples? Prayers for either would be impious, vows for either a blasphemy, when from their conflict you can only learn that the conqueror must be the worse of the two.' Roe has omitted a portion of the quotation, and has thus to a slight extent obscured the sense.

[3] *Ibid.* ii. 7. 'In the day of success even great leaders grow insolent.'

keepe as few residencyes as the necessitye of their affaires will suffer.

October 18.—I sollicited my new promised *firmaen*, but in these troubles and preperation of remoove I found slow dispatch.

October 19.—The Persian ambassador, Mahomett Roza Beag,[1] about noone came into the towne with a great troup, which were partly sent out by the King to meete him with 100 eliphants and musique, but no man of greater qualetye then the ordinary receiver of all strangers. His owne trayne were about 50 horse, well fitted in coates of cloth of gould, their bowes, quivers, and targets richly garnished, 40 shott, and some 200 ordinary *peons* and attenders on bagage. He was carried to rest in a roome within the Kinges outward court till evening, when he came to the *darbar* before the King; to which ceremony I sent my secretary[2] to observe the fashion. When hee approched, he made at the first rayle three *teselims* [see p. 118] and one *sizeda* [see p. 214] (which is prostrating himselfe and knocking his head against the ground); at the entrance in, the like; and so presented the Shabas his lettre; which the King took with a little motion of his body, asking only: How doth my brother? without title of Majestie; and after some few woords hee was placed in the seaventh rannck against the rayle by the doore, below so many of the Kings servants on both sides, which in my judgment was a most inferiour place for his masters embassador, but that hee well deserved it for dooing that reverence which his predecessores refused, to the dishonor of his prince and the murmer of many of his nation.[3] It is said hee had order from

[1] Muhammad Riza Beg. His reception is thus described in the *Memoirs* (vol. i. p. 336): 'After performing the dues of prostration and salutation, he laid before me the letter he had brought. It was decided that he should produce before me the horses and other presents he had brought with him. The written and verbal messages sent were full of friendship, brotherhood, and sincerity. I gave the ambassador on that same day a jewelled tiara and a dress of honour.'

[2] Edward Heynes, of whom see later.

[3] Kerridge, writing to Roe on 10 October, 1615 (*Add. MS.* 9366, f. 12), says that 'the custom of these princes is not to receave embassadour[s] with such dewe observation and honourable respect

the Sophy to give consent; and therby it is gathered his
message is for some ayde in mony agaynst the Turke, in which
kind he often finds liberall succour; though it bee pretended
hee comes only to treat a peace for the Decanns, whose protection the Shabas taketh to hart, envyeing the encrease of
this empire. The King according to custome gave him a
handsom turbant, a vest of gould, and a girdle; for which
againe hee made three *tesselims* and one *sizeda*, or ground
curtesye. Hee brought for presents three tymes nine horses
of Persia and Arabia (this beeing a ceremonius number among
them), nine mules very fayre and lardg, seven camells laden
with velvett, two sutes of Europe arras (which I suppose was
Venetian hangings of velvett with gould, and not arras), two
chests of Persian hangings, one cabinett rich, 40 musketts,
five clocks, one camell laden with Persian cloth of gould, eight
carpetts of silke, two rubyes ballast, 21 cammells of wyne of
the grape, 14 camells of distilld sweet waters, seven of rose
waters, seven daggers sett with stones, five swoords sett with
stones, seven Venetian looking glasses, but these soe faire, so
rich, that I was ashamed of the relation. These presents were
not delivered now, only a bill of them. His owne furniture
was rich, leading nine spare horses trapped in gould and silver;

as is accostomed in Christendom. For if the Kinge of Persia, who
is the mightiest neighbour to this country, sent a prince of his bloud
in embassage heather, he should allwayes stand and attend in
presence of the Kinge, as if he were his servaunt; and hath only
this priveledg, to geve attendance but when himself shall please
or occasions induce him. Many of them att their first appearinge
stand upon tearmes of honnour, refusing the accostomed obedience
to the Kinge; and one them doth he strive to exact. And others
of them perform it with much submissivenes; with them he is well
pleased. His nature being gentle and debonaire, he exacteth
no such duetye one Christians, but accepteth of their accostomed salutations.' At a later date, the Persians appear to have
received better treatment, for Bernier (p. 120) says that the privileges
of saluting according to the customs of their own country, and of
delivering their letters ' without the intervention of an *Omrah* . . .
belong exclusively to Persian ambassadors,' although they are not
granted, ' even to them, without much hesitation and difficulty.'
Bernier tells an amusing tale (p. 151) of Shāh Jahān's expedient to
force a Persian ambassador to make reverence *à l'Indien*, and the
way in which he was foiled.

about his turbant was wreathed a chayne of pearles, rubies, and turqueses, and three pipes of gould answerable for three spriges of feathers. Yet I caused diligence [diligent?] observance to be made of his reception, and compared it with myne owne, and fynd he had in nothing more grace, in many things not so much ; in ranck far inferiour to that alowed mee, except only his meeting without the towne, which by reason of my sicknes was omitted to be demanded. Neyther did the King receive the Shabas his lettre with such respect as my masters, whom hee called the King of England his brother, the Persian barely brother, without addition (which was an observation of the Jesuits, that understood the language).[1]

October 20.—I received a lettre according to promise, written in the Princes name, commanding the Governor of Suratt and others to sitt with the Judg of the *Alfandica* in our behalfe, repeating the complaynt made by mee and by the Judg against us, and giving order so to dispose of the busines that wee might receive no more discontent, and in that matter full and effectuall ; but concerning the presents, which hee so much desiered to have choyce in, only these woords : and for all presents sett too your seale and send them to court—without naming to which court (which was now seperating) not [nor ?] to whom, but leaving it doubtfull. I suspected it was not right ; wherupon I sent back the lettre to the secretary, with answere that I doubted not His Highnes meaning was faire, according to the order of the King, but, to avoyd all occasion of evasion or error in those who sought all advantage of construction to wrong us, I desiered him in few woords to explayne it for future quiett, expressing the termes that the presents are to be sent unopened to the hands of the ambassador at the court. Hee underwrote the lettre, but with such cunning that it might bee construed both wayes like the ould oracles : concerning presents doe as they will, but lett the Prince loose nothing : if wrong bee offered, doe not suffer yt. Our sollicitor returned it : that it was very well and to my content. Yet I misdoubted fraud, and sent for a translator, who found the

[1] Yet Jahāngīr not only describes the embassy in his *Memoirs*, but gives the Shāh's letter in full ; whereas Roe's mission was not thought worthy of mention.

sence so intricat and doubtfull I could scarse understand the riddle. I only discovered the cunning was to bring them into the Princes hands, as it were by error on the way, who would eyther carve all to himselfe or send some part to the King in my name. This abuse justly enraged mee, both against some of our owne and my linguist that received it soe slightly without reading, and stirrd mee to putt it to triall; wherupon I returned yt: that it was now more obscure then before and woorse for the correction; that if this were all the fruicts of the Kings gracious grant, I should bee compelld to move it anew. The secretarye replyed he durst not transgresse his order, but desired mee to meete him in the morning at the Princes.

October 21.—I went to the Prince and opened my desire to have that clause expounded; at which His Highnes stucke a little, and I perceived the purpose to be as hollow as I imagined. Hee demanded then how hee should have his presents or see such toyes as came up, and mooved mee to goe with him. I replyed I could not doe soe untill I had delivered my masters message and tokens to the King; but that finished, I would my selfe attend His Highnes with his presents, and all such raretyes as came to my hands should bee sent after him. Hee pressd mee to passe my woord; and so I obteyned order for the *firmaen* to my content. His Highnes, looking on a whyte feather in my hatt, demanded if I would give it him. I replyed I would not offer that I had worne, but, if hee pleasd to command it, that or any thing in my power was to serve him and I was highly honored in his acceptance. Hee asked if I had any more. I answered: three or fower of other coulors. He replyed if I would give them all, for that hee was to show his horses and servants to the King within two dayes and that hee wanted some, beeing very rare in these parts. I promised to bring all I had on the morow that His Highnes might take his pleasure. Abdala Chan, in a gallant equipage, both of his person and attendants, in apparell strange and antique, but in these parts *a la soldado*,[1] presented the Prince a white horse, the saddle and furniture of gould enameld, a beast of delicate shape, life, and couradge;

---

[1] Spanish *soldado*, a soldier.

who returned him a swoord, playne, with a belt of leather. Ther were brought before him many others, the hilts of silver, chapes [*i.e.* scabbard-mountings] sett with small stones, and targetts covered with gould velvetts, some paynted and bossed with gould and silver, which hee gave to his servants against this muster; many saddles and furniture of gould, rich sett with stones, of his owne were showed for spare horses, his bootes embrodered, and all other ingredients of bravery. I confesse the expence is woonderfull, and the riches dayly seene invaluable. This night passd it is reported six of the Princes servants came to murther Sultan Cursoronne, but were refused the key by the porter; that the Queene Mother [1] is gone to the King with an overture of all the practice. The truth is uncertayne, and it is daingerous to aske. At evening I went to the *durbar* to visitt the King; wher I mett the Persian embassador with the first muster of his presents. Hee appeared rather a jester or jugler then a person of any gravety, running up and downe, and acting all his woords like a mimick player. Now indeed the *atashckannoe* [2] was become a right stage. Hee delivered the presents with his owne hands, which the King [with] smiles and cherfull countenance and many woords of contentment received. His toong was a great advantage to deliver his owne busines, which hee did with so much flattery and obsequiousnes that it pleasd as much as his guift: ever calling His Majestie King and Commander of the World, forgetting his owne master had a share in yt; and on every little occasion of good acceptation hee made his *tezelims*. When all was delivered for that day, hee prostrated himselfe on the ground, and knocked with his head as if hee would enter in. The guifts were: a fayre quiver for bow and arrowes, delicately embrothered; all sorts of Europian fruicts artificiall in dishes; many other foulding purses and knacks of leather, wrought with needlewoork in coloured silkes; shooes embrodered and stichd; great glasses inlayd in frames; one

[1] Maryam-zamāni. She was one of Akbar's Hindu consorts, being daughter of Rāja Bihāri Mal and sister of Rāja Bhagwān Dās of Jaipur. Her death occurred in 1623.

[2] *Yātish-khāna*, strictly a guard-room, but also used (as here) for an audience-chamber. See Monserrate, p. 645.

square peice of velvett embrodered high with gould in panes, betweene which were Italian picturs wrought in the stuff, which hee sayd was the King and Queene of Venice (which, as I suppose, was the hangings called arras); of these six were given, one only showed; many other *tricanados*[1] of small valew; after, the three nines of horses and mules, which were faire ones; the horses eyther had lost their flesh or bewty, for except one or two I judged them unfitt for to be sent or taken by princes. So he returned with many antique tricks to his place, far inferior to that allowed mee, which was alone and above all subjects (which at first Asaph Chan would have putt mee by, but I maynteyned it as my due). This is but the first act of his presenting. The play will not bee finished in ten dayes. At night I sent to the Princes secretary for my promised writing; but His Highnes was loath to lett the presents passe without ransacking and had changed his mynd, refusing to seale the lettre.

October 22.—I went early to the secretary to know the reason of this inconstancy, and the Princes resolution. He answered I could not have the letter sealed unlesse I would consent to have all opened in the *alfandica*, pretending that the merchannts would pass up jewells and pearles to sell under that coulor. I assured him on my woord they were dearer in England then here: that wee brought none: that I would not countenance any thing under that coulor to abuse the Prince and dishoner my selfe: that I scorned to save petty customes basely: that I gave among the Princes porters dayly more. I urdged the Kings command, his masters promise; but no reason, no importunitye would prevayle against this gredy desier of presents, though in yt hee robbd his father. What will not youth and insolency attempt when it knowes no limitts, when it is advanced beyond the capacitye and law of reason? I replied as peremptorily that I was as resolute not to bee abused: that I would keepe these aboord the shipps untill His Majestie sent for them, and in future tyme I would take order that my master should send no more guifts to be so uncivilly entreated: that it was a busines in which my honor was interested, and for no complacency I would not yeild to

[1] Trinkets or trifles (Span.).

bee riffled with my consent : that these injuryes were so grose that I doubted not the King would have sence of them : in the meane tyme I would prevent their greedy purpose of oppression. So I rose to depart. Hee importuned mee to goe with him to the Prince and move it once more. I replyed I had the Kings order and his masters woord before His Majestie, since his owne command, and all this beeing retracted, I could expect no more but delay and injurye : that I would seeke to the King and no further. But hee pressd mee so far as I yeelded ; and at my comming I delivered him [*i.e.* the Prince] two plumes and two birds of paradice.[1] Hee accepted them easely ; and my busines beeing mooved and my resolution made knowne not to consent to open nor to send them up but by the hands of my servants, att last he yeilded and gave command to the secretary to dispatch mee. At night I went to the *durbar* to observe the ambassador of Persia. I found him standing in his ranncke, and often remooved and sett lower as great men came in. The King once spake to him, and he danced to the tune therof, but gave noe present ; only the King commanded hee should be feasted by the nobles. The tyme was spent in seeing saddles and furniture for the remoove ; of which His Majestie gave some to his followers, it beeing dayly expected to rise ; the Kings tents were out four days since. I sent to the secretarye for my *firmaen*, but hee delayd yt with excuses.

October 23.—I sollicited the grant ; but the Persian dined with him.

October 24.—The King remooved to Havaz Gemall, and called the Persian ambassador ; wher at night hee eate and drancke before the King with the nobilities in the same fashion that I did the birthday ; the difference only was the King gave him for expence 20,000 *rupias*, for which hee made innumerable *teselims* and *sizedaes*, not rising from the ground in good space, which extremely pleased the King and was base but profitable idolatrye. The Prince attending his father, I could gett noe dispatch in my busines. These presents yet were not digested ; all delayes, all fraudes practised to possesse

---

[1] According to Roe's accounts, the two plumes had cost 20*s.* and the birds were worth 60 rupees.

them first. The condition of this people, my sufferings and travell will appeare, I doubt not to the ease of my successors, how to deale with them. I received lettres from Agra, advertising all the factory were disposed away. I advised my opinion it was to no use to follow the court : that it were better to abyde togither untill wee saw where wee should settle : otherwise the chardge would bee infinite. So much I propounded to ours here, but know not their resolution.

October 25.—The King returned at evening, having beene over night farr gone in wyne. Some by chance or malice spake of the merry night past, and that many of the nobilitie dranck wyne, which none may doe but by leave. The King, forgetting his order, demanded who gave it. It was answered : the *Buxy*; for no man dares say it was the King, when hee would only doubt yt. The custome is that when the King drinckes, which is alone, sometyme hee will command that the nobilitye shall drinck after, which if they doe not, is an offence too ; and so every man that takes a cup of wyne of the officer his name is written and he makes *teselem*, though perhaps the Kings eyes are mistye. The King, not remembring his owne command, called the *Buxy* and demanded if he gave the order. He replyed : no (falsly, for hee received it, and by name called such as did drinck with the ambassador) ; wherat the King called for the list and the persons, and fined some one, some two, some three thowsand *rupies*, some lesse, and some that were nearer his person he caused to bee whippd before him, receiving 130 stripes with a most terrible instrument, having at each end of fower cords irons like spur rowells, so that every stroke made fower wounds. When they lay for dead on the ground, hee commanded the standers by to foote them, and after the porters to breake their staves upon them. Thus most cruelly mangled and brused, they were carried out ; of which one dyed in the place. Some would have excused it on the ambassador ; but the King replyed he only bad give him a cupp or too. Though drunckennes be a common and a glorious vice, and an excercise of the Kings, yet it is soe strictly forbidden that no man can enter the *guzelchan*, wher the King sitts, but the porters smell his breath, and, if hee have but tasted wyne, is not suffered to com in ; and, if the reason bee knowne of his absence, hee shall with difficulty skape the whip ; for, if the King once take offence, the father will not speake for the sonne. So the King made the company pay the Persian ambassadors reward.

October 26.—I sent to Socorolla for the *firmaen*. Hee sent mee a copy as ambiquious and fraudulent as the former ; which I refused, and drew the misliked clause my selfe, which I sent back, and was promised that on the morow it should bee sealed.

October 28.—The Kings day of remoove at hand, I sent to Asaph Chan for a warrant for carriadges ; the merchants, having sought all the towne to remoove their goods to Agra, could find none. So I received order, beeing enrolled by His Majestie, upon my offer, for 20 camells, four carts, and two coches at the Kings price ; whereof I disposed as many as the factors needed to their use. But it were an extreame error to omitt a passadge, either of woonderfull basenes in this great monarch or a triall of mee. The King had condemned divers theeves, among which were some boyes. Ther was noe way to save their lives, but to sell them for slaves. His Majestie commanded Asaph Chan to offer two of them to mee for mony, which hee appoynted the *Cuttwall*, that is the Marshall, to doe. My enterpreter made answere (without my knowledg) that Christians kept no slaves : that those the King had given I had freed : and that it was in vayne to propound it to mee. But after of him selfe hee did. I suspected it might be a tryall of mee whether I would give a little mony to save the lives of two childeren, or els I supposed, if it were in earnest, it were noe great losse to doe a good deed ; and, to trye the basenes or scope of this offer, I commanded my enterpreter to returne to Asaph Chan, to tell him hee had acquaynted mee with the motion and his answere ; that I reprehended him for presuming in any case to give my resolution : that my owne reply was, if there were any mony to be payd to save the life of twoo children to those whom they had robbd, or to redeeme them from the law, both for respect to the Kings command and for charetye, I was ready to give it : but I would not buy them as slaves, only pay their ransome and free them : that if hee pleased to know the Kings pleasure that I might give them liberty without offence, I was very willing to doe it. Asaph

Chan replyed I might at myne owne will dispose them : that it was an extraordinarye goodnes ; with many prayses accepted the mony, desiring mee [to] send it to the *Cuttwall* and to use my discretion to the boyes : not once offering to enforme the King, which was one end of my liberallitye. I, that was loath to be cosened, and knew not whither this might bee the profitt of officers or no, resolved to pay the mony, but so as the King should not be ignorant I had more mercy then hee, and that a Christian esteemed the life of a Moore above mony. So I sent a factor and my enterpreter to the *Cuttwall* to acquaynt him with the communications with Asaph Chan and to lett him know, if at night hee would enforme the King that I had offered to redeeme the prisoners for charetyes sake, if after His Majestie would consent to their liberty, I was ready to send him mony : but to buy them as slaves, though but for an hower, I would not : they should never come nor bee manumissed [*i.e.* released from slavery] by mee, but that I desiered His Majestie to pardon them upon my redemption. So I putt them to the test of theire base offer. This mony execeded not ten pound, a poore summe to impose on a stranger, or to be gayned by any king. The *Cuttwall* returned answere that hee would know the Kings pleasure and accordingly advise mee. Some would perswade mee this is one of the Mogols signal favours : to choose out such great men as hee will give occasion to doe good and honorable woorkes, to redeeme prisoners : and that the mony gives satisfaction to the playntiffe robbd, and that those so appoynted by the King to ransome others make *sizeda* as for some benefitt received ; yet I fynd not any honor in a prince to impose it on a stranger, to whom he gives neyther mayntenance nor liberalitye. I went to the *durbar* to see if His Majestie would of himselfe speake to mee, that I might deliver myne owne offer. The *Cuttwall* made many motions, brought in the executioner, who received some command ; but I understood it not, but expect my answere. This day I sent my secretary to visitt the Persian embassador and to give him welcome to this court : that seeing ther had passed many effects of love and amitye betwene our royall masters the King[s] of Great Brittaine and Persia, I had received command to give all respect and due

complements to any of his ministers whersoever I mett them:
and that, it beeing the custome of Europe that the last come
to any place in curtesy is visited of him that hath longer beene
resident, beeing both embassadors of one qualetye, I was
resolved to come my selfe to see him, whensoever I received
notice of his comoditye : when I would also open some busines
to him both for the honor and service of his master : but,
because I knew not the customes of these parts, I had first
sent to advice him that I expected the same good respect
from him toward my soveraigne, and that hee would in like
manner after visitt mee, to whom hee should bee most welcome : and without that assurance on his woord, I durst not
come at all to him. Hee received my message very courteously,
replying hee tooke it for a great honor : that the custome of
this kingdome was that no ambassador did meete or make
acquayntance without the knowledge of the King and leave
obteyned : that hee would move His Majestie on our behalfes
and after both receive mee with all frendship and repay my
curtesy toward him with all good correspondence : that hee
knew Sir Robert Sheirly, and should bee very gladd, if I had
any busines with his master, to convey my lettres or enter
into any other communication or advise therein according to
my directions.

October 29.—I received news of a great plauge at Agra ;[1]
so that I judgd it dangerous to send up the goods into an in-
fected place from whence no comodytye could bee suffered
to passe, and to engage the Companyes servants ; wherupon
I persuaded the factors to remoove the cloth within the walls
of the towne, and that I would desire of the King some secure
place for their rest untill His Majestie were settled.[2] This
course will save much mony and more trouble. The brokar

[1] Further references to this epidemic occur under 25 November
and 15 December, 1616, and 14 January, 1617. See also the accounts
given in the *Memoirs* (vol. i. pp. 330, 442) and in *Letters Received*
(vol. v. p. 198).

[2] In the end William Biddulph accompanied Roe, to recover debts
and take any opportunity of selling goods in the imperial camp ;
Hughes was left at Ajmer with the remaining store ; and Fetiplace
was ordered to join him from Agra (*Letters Received*, vol. iv. p. 288).

offered us a sufficient roome, without danger, the King leaving a good guard for defence of such as could not remoove; soe I resolved upon yt.

To Prince Charles.
(*Add. MS.* 6115, f. 129.)

Adsm[ere], the camp of the Great Mogull, Emp[eror] of India,
30 October, 1616.

Most excellent Prince,

If Your Highnes have any vacancy from better recreations to caste your eies upon one of the greatest theatres of the world, I could take pride in the paynes to relate to Your Highnes many rare varietyes, wherin the goodnes and greatnes of God in sundry operations is manifested, and the divers and irregular dispositions of man (his principall creature) are not unwoorthy some observation. But the woorke would bee eyther to great for the proportion of a lettre, which would require a little history, or, beeing brokenly and by fragments delivered, would be obscure and harsh, both to the understanding and delight. The cosmography and discription of the land, the storye and light of the kings and customes yet made to us, beeing both corrupted, eyther by ignorance or the vanitye of travelers, that love alway to tell things strange and woonderfull rather then true and profitable, I will not offend in any of these to Your Highnes, knoweing I speake to a prince of excellent witt, acute judgment, and entyre sinceretye, a lover of truth (though naked or clothed in raggs); and I am more ambitious of the reputation of honesty in your gratious opinion then of any other vayne and vanishing abilityes. I humbly desier yow will beleeve that all the endeavours of my life shall tend to doe yow faythfull service; and though my present employment affoord me not subject nor means to present usefull matter, wheron yow might excercise your abilityes of nature and education, yet yow wilbe pleased to accept my offers and the preparations of my hart in vowes and meditations to receive your instructions and to obey yow with all duty and integritye. The estate and affection of the Portugalls is first woorthy Your Highnes consideration; who are stronger in reputation then in substance.... Your Highnes cannot take to your care an action more profitable then the suppressing of proud and insolent enemyes, nor more honourable then the protection of those who by free trafique seeke the uniting of remote kingdomes in a necessary frendship and advance His Majesties revenewes. Some generall light of this kingdome,

at least of the customes of the court, will not bee perhaps
unpleasing. The present emperor is descended from Temarlane
the Great. His territorie conteynes the last harvest of Alex-
anders conquests, the dominions of Porus, whose lyne remayens
a tributary prince ; and some other countryes added to yt, on
both sides of Indus, beyond Ganges, in a square at least 2000
myle, some wayes more. The border westward is Persia, east
the Gulph of Bengala, north the mountaynes of Taurus (that
divide him from the Tartars), sowth the kingdomes of Decan
and the Bay of Cambaya. Plentifull in corne and cattle for
mans necessitye : aboundant in wealth and comodityes of
trade for superfluitye. His revenew far above any easteren
monarch knowne : farr above the Turke : incredible if I sawe
not the issues and incomes and could not give a better reason
of yt then report. In jewells (which is one of his felicityes) hee
is the treasury of the world, buyeing all that comes, and
heaping rich stones as if hee would rather build then weare
them. And yet all this greatnes, compared and weighed
judiciously, is like a play, that serves more for delight and to
entertayne the vulgar then for any use. For noe man enters
his house but eunucks ; his weomen are never seene ; his
nobilitye are like counters, placed high and low at his pleasure :
his servants base and barbarous : and all his life as regular as
a clock that stricks at sett howers. For hee comes to bee
seene at a wyndow at sunne rising to all his idolaters ; at
noone to the fight of eliphants and wild beasts ; at evening hee
removes to a theatre under canopyes, wher in a gallery hee
sitts to receive sutes, to see and to bee seene ; wher the great
men on a stage belowe him act their parts, and the vulgar
under them gaze on. The tyme is spent in showeing of
eliphants and horses richly furnished. At night hee descends
into a court ; on a throune hee discourseth and drincketh
with much affabilitye. To this place are none admitted but
with leave and of eminent qualety. This course is infallably
kept, except sicknes prevent yt ; for which alsoe the people
will exact a reason, and endure not long the abscence of their
king. The rest of his motion is inward amoung woemen,
of which sort, though hee keepe a thowsand, yet one governs
him, and wynds him up at her pleasure. His negotiations
are for the most part publique. His religione of his owne
invention ; for hee envyes Mahomett, and wisely sees noe
reason why hee should not bee as great a prophett as hee, and
therfore proffeseth him selfe soe ; and yet finds not (or confesseth not) that they are both imposturs in that kind. Hee
hath found many disciples that flatter or follow him. The
rest are circumcised Mahomatans, and the issue of the con-
querors planted by Temurlane. The naturalls are Gentills,
following sundry idolatryes and worshiping the creaturs of

heaven and earth promiscuously. The severest sect of these are Pythagorians for the opinion of the soules transmigration, and will not kyll any living creature, no, not the virmine that bites them, for feare of disseising the speiritt of some frend departed. All ascribe a kinde of divinitye to the river Ganges, and by infinite troupes visitt it, casting in oblations of gould. Many woemen burne with joye at their husbands funeralls. Finally, all sorts of religions are wellcome and free, for the King is of none. The buildings were anciently magnificent, but ruyned by these new lords, that love noe woorke not done by them selves. Civill arts are borowed from us, and some are genuine, wherin they excell, and expresse great abilityes of nature and invention. They are governed by noe constant lawe, which in all new occasions is received from the Kings mouth, and, farr distant, from his vizeroyes. No man hath proprietye in land nor goods, if hee please to take it; soe that all are slaves. Witchcraft, sorcery, juggling, yea, all cunning that the Divell can teach, is frequent, eaven in the court, wher is wanting noe arte nor wicked subtillty to bee or doe evill; soe that, comparing the vices of some cittyes in Europe, which I once judged the treasuries and sea of synne, I find them sanctuaryes and temples in respect of these. Your Highnes cannot but bee weary to heare of soe much iniquitye; chast eares are defiled with noyse of evill. Yow may blesse God that hath enlightened your royall hart and placd yow as a shining lampe in His Church, wher Hee hath vouchsafed to reveale His truth and glory, and desseigned yow, not only to bee a member, but a principall pillar, guider, and protector of yt. . . . I most humblie crave Your Highnes pardon. I have presumed not to counsaill yow, but to utter the meditations of a bannished man, that honors, loves, serves yow with all fayth, with all integritye: that owes yow, not only by bond of dutye as a prince, but as hayre of those graces and virtues that have renowned your happy brother, all those cleare affections I bare to him, which yow now inherite, with all my poore unwoorthy devotions. . . .

To THE LORD BISHOP OF CANTERBURY.[1]
(*Add. MS.* 6115, f. 130.)

Adsmere, October 30, 1616.
May it please your Grace,
The fraylty of passadge betweene this place and England, especially of my last lettre [see note on p. 114], that wandered over land and rather went upon discovery then busines,

[1] Printed in *Purchas*, vol. i. p. 584, but with many inaccuracies, and without indication of the person to whom it was addressed

adviseth mee to send your Grace transcripts of them. Not
that ther is conteyned any matter woorthy Your Honors
leysure ; but seeing yow commanded me to write, the relation
of one to another will somwhat cleare the whole discourse.
For broken and undependant peices and fragments have little
light in them, lesse pleasure, and no proffitt ; so that hee that
would doe any thing in this matter should write a historie,
and take it somwhat high, to show the beginnings and groweth
of this empire ; what fortunes and what impediments it hath
overcame ; what frendships it hath needed and affected ; the
ambitions and divisions in the present state, that like im-
postumes lye now hidd, but threaten to breake out into the
rending and ruine of the whole by bloody warr ; the practises,
subtiltyes, and carriages of factions and court-secretts, falsly
called wisdome, wherin I assure Your Grace they are pregnant,
and excell in all that art which the Divell can teach them, and
are behynd none in wicked craft, some passadges wherof were
not unwoorthy nor unpleasant to relate ; their religions
suffered by the King, and practised without envy or contention
on any part ; how the Portugalls have crept into this kingdome, and by what corners they gott in ; the enterance of
the Jesuits, their entertaynment, priviledges, practises, ends,
and the growth of their Church, wherof they sing in Europe
so loud prayses and glorious successes ; lastly, the arrivall
of our nation on this coast, their fortunat or blessed victoryes
over their enemyes, that not only sought to possesse these
quarters by them selves, and to forbidd all others that which
Nature had left free (as if God had created the world for them
only), but alsoe to abuse this people, as if they alone were
the sonns of warr, they only trihumph, and that all other
Europeans stroocke sayle to their fortune and valor ; which
now is brought so low in valew, that it is growne into a proverbe
(*one Portugall to three Moores, one Englishman to three Portugalls* [1]), soe that the best foundation of their greatnes is
absolutly mined and blown up ; and our reception here
stands on the same ground from which wee have cast them
downe, which is feare, an honorable but uncertayne base of
so great a chardge—for if either the enemy once prevayle,
or other misfortune happen to us, our wellcome will turne
round with yt ; the profitt and fittnes of this trade for
England (while it may stand), not only respecting the Company
now interessed, but the State, whither the commonwealth
in generall loose or wynn. For often in trafiques privat men
prosper by detriment of the *Republique*, as in all trades that
mayntyne vanetye and sinne. This woorke and method were
woorthy some paynes, and, as [it ?] would require a good

---

[1] Terry (p. 163) quotes this as a saying of Jahāngīr.

judgment and much tyme (both which are wanting to mee), so it would not bee unprofitable to reade, nor without some pleasure to view and meditate the divers operations and woorkes of God, the variable constitutions and dispositions of men and all things under their goverment. But, seeing nature and conveniency have denyed mee abilitye and leysure to sett upon soe great a labor, I have chosen one branch only to treat of to Your Grace, without other meathode then by way of bare relation; which is, the estate of the Church heere, as well Christians as of all other diffused sects of infidells.

But to continew (as in a parenthesis) the advise I gave Your Honor in my last, of our constitution here, and the newes of Persia. Breefly, I stand on very fickle termes, though in extraordinarie grace with the King, who is gentle, soft, and good of disposition; yet on poynts and disputes with an insolent and proud sonne of his, into whose hands hee hath remitted all power, which hee is neyther woorthy nor able to mannage. Hee is lord of our port, and by his folly gives mee much travell [*i.e.* labour]; so sordidly ambitious, that he would not have mee acknowledge his father King, nor make any addresses, nor deliver any presents nor complements of honor, but to him selfe; which I will never yeild too, and so I maynteyne my creditt by confidence on the priviledges of my qualetye and the Kings goodnes. Yet an ambassadour in this court that knowes him selfe, and will not wrong his master, shall oftner wynn enemyes then frends. Their pride endures no tearmes of equaletye, especially wher ther is no other honor nor title but what is measured by expence; so that to maynteyne one that shall in his equipage and life hould proportion with his qualety in this court will cost much more then the profitt of the trade can spare; and hee that lives under it, wrongs his degree, and slides into contempt. I doe my uttmost to hould up with little poore meanes; but my opinion is, a meaner instrument would better effect busines of trafique, that might creepe, and sue, and suffer some affronts, which my ranck may not endure. And I find the King of Spayne would never send any ambassadour hither, out of greatnes, knoweing they are not received with proportionable honour; and with my small experience I could doe the Company better service by my returne, in advise how to governe the whole.

Concerning Persia, the Turke hath only yet made a bravado, and performed little; the passages are stoppd, and the King, drawing his armies into his borders to defende him selfe and finding no great woorke, tooke occasion to take in by force a revolted nation to the east of Babilon. The people are called Coords [*i.e.* Kurds]; how by the ancients, or the true geographicall scituation of their cuntry, I am yet ignorant in.

Sir Robert Shirly, by an ill passadge to Goa, lost the oportunitye of the fleete for Lisbow, and is stayed there another yeare; so that negotiation will not so speedely be advanced as I feared. Wee shall have breath and tyme to woork upon yt, according as it shalbe requisite in the judgment of Your Honors in England, or at least of the merchants, whom it first regardeth. Her is arrived a Persian embassador; with little newes, it beeing nine mounths since his departure from Spahan. .... The King is now ready to march toward Decan; whose armie is commanded by his sonne. And wee with much toyle shall hang in the sckirts. ....[1]

Thus Your Grace hath some touch of our affaires; and I will fall upon my purpose of the Church, with your favour and patience. Before the inundation of Temar the Great, the ninth ancestor of this King, these cuntries were governed by divers petty Gentile [*i.e.* Hindu] Princes, not knoweing any religion, but woorshipped after their severall idolatryes all sorts of creaturs. The descendants of him brought in the knowledg of Mahomett, but imposed it upon none by the law of conquest, leaving consciences at liberty. So that these naturalls, from the circumcision (which came in with the Moores), called them Mogolls or cheefe of the circumcised.[2] Among the Mogolls ther are many strict Mahometans, many that follow Aly, his sonne-in-law, and other new risen prophetts, which have their *xeriffs, mulas* and preists, their mosquies, religious votaries, washings, prayings, and ceremonyes infinite; and for penitenciaryes, no herecye in the world can show so strange examples, nor bragg of such voluntarie povertyes, punishments, sufferings and chastisments as these; all which are esteemed holy men, but of a mingled religion, not upright with their great prophett. The Gentiles are of more sorts, some valiant, good souldiers, drinking wine, eating hoggs flesh, but woorshiping the figure of a beast; some that will not touch that flesh which is not holy by imputation; others that will not eate any thing wherin ever there was any blood, nor kill the vermin that assaulteth them, nor drincke in the cup with those that doe; superstitious in washing, and most earnest in their profession; but all of them ascribe a kind of divinitie to the River Ganges, at which at one season of the yeare 4 or 50,000 [3] meete, and cast in gould and silver for

---

[1] Roe goes on to relate the fight with the Portuguese carrack.

[2] There is, of course, no truth in this fanciful piece of etymology, which is given also by Terry (p. 363) and Salbank (*Letters Received*, vol. v. p. 184).

[3] A slip for 500,000—the number printed by Purchas. Coryat, who was evidently Roe's authority, says 'about foure hundred thousand.'

oblation. In like manner to a piggs head [1] in a church near this citty, and to all living cowes, and to some other beasts and kinds. These have their synogoags and holy men, prophetts, witches, sooth-sayers, and all others the Divells impostures. The *molaes* of Mahomett know somwhat in philosophy and mathematiques, are great astrologers, and can talke of Areistotle, Euclyde, Averroes [*i.e.* Averrhoës] and other authors. The learned toong is Arab.

In this confusion they continued until the tyme of Ecbarsha father of this king, without any noyce of Christian profession who, beeing a prince by nature just and good, inquisitive afte noveltyes, curious of new opinions, and that excelled in man virtues, especially in pietye and reverence toward his parent: called in three Jesuits from Goa, whose cheefe was Jeronim Xavier, a Navarroies.[2] After their arrivall hee heard the reason and dispute, with much content on his and hope c their parts, and caused Xavier to write a booke in defence his profession against both Moores and Gentilles; whic finished, hee read over nightly, causing some part to 1 discussed; and finally granted them his lettre pattents build, to preach, teach, convert, and to use all their rit and ceremonyes, as freely and amply as in Roome, bestowei on them meanes to erect their churches and places of devotic So that in some fewe cittyes they have gotten rather *templ* then *ecclesiam*. In this grant he gave grant to all sorts men to become Christians that would, eaven to his court owne blood, professing it should bee noe cause of disfava from him. Here was a faire beginninge, a forward spr of a leane and barren harvest.[3]

Ecbar-Shae him selfe continued a Mahometan, yet hee be

[1] An image of Vārāha, the boar incarnation of Vishnu.

[2] Jerome Xavier, grandson of a sister of St. Francis Xavier, v out to India in 1581, and at the end of 1594 was despatched from to the Mogul court, where he remained nearly twenty-three ye His influence with Jahāngīr, which was considerable, was of co exerted against the English; and Nicholas Withington, writin Sir Thomas Smythe on 9 November, 1613, said bitterly that Mogul would do nothing against the Portuguese 'soe longe as witch Savier liveth (for soe the Moores themselves terme him), wl is an ould Jesuitt residinge with the Kinge, whom hee much affe (Brit. Mus., *Egerton MS.* 2086). He died at Goa in 1617.

Roe's account of the early Catholic missions is a very conf one, and entirely ignores the work of Aquaviva and his imme successors.

[3] Compare Terry's account (pp. 440 *et seq.*) of the religions of I and of the Jesuits' progress in 'that most acceptable, but I labour of washing Moors.'

to make a breach into the law ; considering that Mahomett was but a man, a king as he was, and therfore reverenced, he thought hee might prove as good a prophett himselfe. This defection of the King spread not farre ; a certayn outward reverence deteyned him, and so hee dyed in the formall profession of his sect. Ghehangier-Sha, his sonne, the present king, beeing the issue of this new fancy, and never circumsised,[1] bread up without any religion at all, continewes so to this hower, and is an athiest. Sometyme hee will make profession of a Moore : but alway observe the hollidayes and doe all ceremonyes with the Gentilles too. Hee is content with all religions ; only hee loves none that changeth. But, falling upon his fathers conceipt, hath dared to enter farther in, and to professe him selfe for the mayne of his religion to be a greater prophett then Mahomett ; and hath formed to him selfe a new law, mingled of all, which many have accepted with such superstition that they will not eate till they have saluted him in the morning, for which purpose hee comes at the sunnes rising to a wyndow open to a great playne before his house, where multitudes attend him ; and when the Moores about him speak of Mahomett, hee will sooth them, but is glad when any one will breake out against him. Of Christ he never utters any woord unreverently, nor any of all these sects, which is a woonderfull secreett woorking of Gods truth, and woorthy observation. Concerning the new planted Christian Church, he confirmed and enlardged all their priviledges, every night for one yeare spending two howers in hearing disputation, often casting out doubtfull woords of his conversion, but to wicked purpose. And, the rather to give some hope, he delivered many youthes into the hands of Francisco Corsy,[2] now resident heere, to teach them to reade and write Portuguse, and to instruct them in humane learning and in the law of Christ. And to that end he kept a schoole

[1] Coryat, who makes the same statement, was possibly Roe's authority for this. Salbank repeats it (*Letters Received*, vol. v. p. 185), but he, no doubt, had it from the same source. The assertion was probably correct, as circumcision, though usual, is not obligatory upon Muhammadans.

[2] The ' Jesuit ' of several preceding entries. The Reverend Father Goldie, S.J., has kindly procured for me an extract from the archives of the Society, in which it is stated that Corsi was a Florentine, born in 1575 ; that he entered the Order in the year 1593, and six years later was sent from Portugal to India, where he lived ordinarily in the household of the Great Mogul : that he bore a high character, and had a talent for mission work ; and that he died at his post on 1 August, 1635 (N.S.). References to him occur also in Father Cordara's history of the Order (pt. vi. tom. i. p. 59), and in the

some yeares, to which the King sent two Princes, his brothers sonnes; who, beeing brought up in the knowledg of God and His Sonne our Blessed Saviour, were solemly babtised in the church of Agra with great pomp, beeing carried first up and downe all the citty on eliphants in triumph; and this by the Kings expresse order, who often would examien them in their progression, and seemed much contented in them. This made many bend toward the same way, doubting His Majesties entention; others, that knew him better, supposed he suffered this in pollicye, to reduce these children into hate among the Moores for their conversion, of whom consisted the strength of his estate; but all men fayling of his purpose, which was thus discovered. When these and some other children were settled, as was thought, in Christian religion, and had learnd some principles therof, as, to marry but one wife, not to be coupled with infidles, the King setts the boyes to demand some

similar work by Father Jouvancy (pt. v. tom. ii. lib. xviii. p. 468). His tomb is still to be seen in the old Roman Catholic cemetery at Agra.

The relations between Roe and Corsi were very amicable; and Terry's account of him, though tinged with professional jealousy, is favourable on the whole. It runs as follows (p. 444): 'Francisco Corsi . . . a Florentine by birth, aged about fifty years, who (if he were indeed what he seemed to be) was a man of a severe life, yet of a fair and an affable disposition; he lived at that court as an agent for the Portugals, and had not onely free access unto that King, but also encouragement and help, by gifts, which he sometimes bestowed on him. When this Jesuit came first to be acquainted with my Lord Ambassadour, he told him that they were both by profession Christians, though there was a vast difference betwixt them in their professing of it: and as he should not go about to reconcile the Ambassadour to them, so he told him that it would be labour in vain if he should attempt to reconcile him to us. Onely he desired that there might be a fair correspondency betwixt them, but no disputes. And further his desire was, that those wide differences 'twixt the Church of Rome and us might not be made there to appear, that Christ might not seem by those differences to be divided amongst men professing Christianity, which might be a very main obstacle and hinderance unto his great design and endeavour, for which he was sent thither, to convert people unto Christianity there: telling my Lord Ambassadour further, that he should be ready to do for him all good offices of love and service there; and so he was. After his first acquaintance, he visited us often, usually once a week. And as those of that Society, in other parts of the world, are very great intelligencers, so was he there, knowing all news which was stirring, and might be had, which he communicated unto us.'

Portugalls wifes of the Jesuitts; who, thincking it only an idle motion of their owne braynes, chyd them, and suspected no more. But that being the end of their conversion, to gett a woeman for the King, and no care taken, the two Princes came to the Jesuits, and surrendred up their crosses and all other rites, professing they would be noe longer Christians, because the King of Portugall sent them no presents nor wives, according as they expected. The Padre, seeing this, began to doubt ther was more in that then the boyes revealed, especially seeing their confidence, that had cast off the awe of pupills; and, examining the matter, had it confessed the King commanded them. They refused to accept the crosses, answering they had been given by His Majesties order, and they would not take notice from boyes of any such surrender; but bad them desier the King to send some of those who by a kynd of order are to deliver all His Majesties commands, whose mouths are by priviledges sufficient authoritye, and then they would accept them; hoping, and knoweing the Kings nature, that hee would not discover him selfe to any of his officers in this poore plott. The boyes returned with this message, which enraged the King. But, beeing desierous to disolve the schoole, and to withdrawe the yowths without noyse, hee bad them call the Jesuitts to the woemens doore, wher by a lady he received the order; and without ever taking any notice since of any thing, his kinsmen recalld, who are now absolute Moores, without any tast of their first fayth; and so the fruict of all these hopes are vanished. And I cannot fynd by good search that ther is one Christian really and orderly converted, nor makes the profession, except some few that have beene babtised for mony, and are maynteyned by the Jesuitts; of which sort ther would bee more, but that they find the deceipt, and cannot endure the burthen. This is the truth of all their bragg and labor, and the full groweth of their Church here.

But, that Your Grace may a little more understand the fashion of this King and the Jesuits proceedings, I will make yow one or two merry and late relations; and either say hee is the most impossible man in the world to be converted, or the most easy; for he loves to heare, and hath so little religion yet, that hee can well abyde to have any derided. Not many dayes since, the Jesuits house and church beeing burned, the crucifex remayned safe; which under hand was given out for a miracle, and much talked off. I, that could be content any use might be made of an accident to enlardg the name of Christ, held my peace. But the Jesuite, suspecting I would not agree to the miracle, disavowed it to mee, and made it a matter of reason why it was not burned; insinnuating that the Moores had caught up this opinion of miracle without his consent or suggestion, though hee confessed hee was glad of the occasion. But the King, who never lett slip any oportunity of newe talke or novelty, calls the Jesuite, and questioneth him of it. He answers ambiguously; wherupon His Majestie demanded if he did not desire to convert him, and, receiving full answere, replyed: Yow speake of your great miracles, and of many done by yow in the name of your prophett; if yow will cast the crucifix and picture of Christ into a fyre before mee, if it burne not, I wil become a Christian. The Jesuite refused the tryall as unjust, answering that God was not tyed to the call of men: that it was a sinne to tempt him: that hee wrought miracles according to his owne councell; but offered to enter the fier himselfe for proofe of his faith; which the King refused. Here arose a great dispute, begunn by the Prince, a most stiff Mahometan and hater of all Christians, that it was reasonable to try our religion by this offer, but withall that, if the crucifix did burne, then that the Jesuit should be obliged to render Moore.[1] Hee urged examples of miracles professed to bee done for lesse purposes then the conversion of soe mightie a king, and, in case of refusall of that triall, spake scornefully of Christ Jesus. The King undertooke the argument, and defended our Saviour to be a prophett, by comparrison of his woorkes with those of their absurd saints, instancing the raysing of the dead, which never any of theirs did. The Prince replyed: to give sight to one naturally borne blind was as great a miracle. This question beeing pressed hotly on both sides, a theird man, to end the contraversie, enterposed that both the father and the sonne had reason for their opinions; for that to rayse a dead body to life must needs bee confessd to be the greatest miracle ever done, but that to give sight to an eye naturally blynd was the same woorke; for that a blind eye was dead, sight beeing the life therof; therfore he that gave sight to a blind eye did as it were rayse it up from death. Thus this discourse ended, and soe in wisdome should I; but that I cannot leave out an apish miracle which was acted before this King, which the Jesuits will not acknowledg nor owne as their practise; only

[1] Terry, in telling this story (p. 448), says that the crucifix was on a pole near the Jesuit's house; and that the Prince's proposal was that, if it did not resist combustion, the Jesuit should be burnt with it. He also says that he himself was at court when the incident happened—another proof that the reverend gentleman's memory is not to be trusted implicitly. Corsi's offer to undergo the ordeal of fire recalls the challenge of the Muhammadan doctors at the court of Akbar to Aquaviva (recorded by Monserrate), and the somewhat similar story related of Father Da Costa by Bernier and Manucci (vol. i. p. 160).

of the truth *de facto* ther is no doubt. A juggler of Bengala (of which craft there are many and rare) brought to the King a great ape, that could, as hee professd, divine and prophesy (and to this beast by some sects is much divinitie ascribed). The King tooke from his finger a ring, and caused it to bee hid under the girdle of one among a dozen other boyes, and bad the ape divine ; who went to the right child, and tooke it out. But His Majestie (somwhat more curious) caused in twelve several papers in Persian lettres to bee written the names of twelve lawgivers, as Moses, Christ, Mahomett, Aly, and others, and, shuffling them in a bagg, bad the beast divine which was the true law ; who, putting in his foote, tooke out that inscribed of Christ. This amazed the King, who, suspecting that the apes master could reade Persian, and might assist him, wrote them anew in court characters,[1] and presented them the second tyme. The ape was constant, found the right, and kissed it. Wherat a principal officer [2] grew angry, telling the King it was some imposture, desiering hee might have leave to make the lotts anew, and offered him selfe to punishment if the ape could beguile him. Hee wrote the names, putting only aleven into the bagg, and kept the other in his hand. The beast searchd, but refusd all. The King commanded to bring one ; the beast tore them in fury, and made signes the true lawgivers name was not among them. The King demanded wher it was ; and hee rann to the nobleman and caught him by the hand in which was the paper inscribed with the name of Christ Jesus. The King was troubled, and keepes the ape. Yet this was acted in publique before thousands ; but wher the abuse was, or whether ther were any, I judg not. Only one of the Jesuits scollers ran to him with open mouth, professing the King had an ape a good Christian. Of this accident the Jesuitts make great account ; to me they slight it, except the truth of the fact, which is not unlike one of their owne games.[3]

[1] *I.e.* an official cypher. ' Court characters are such as he only and his nearer ministers used in mysteries of State, unknowne to all others ' (*Note by Purchas*).

[2] Mahābat Khān, according to Terry ; but it is scarcely likely that he was at court, or Roe would have mentioned him.

[3] Terry (p. 403) relates this incident at length and says that, although he was not present, ' it hath been often confirmed there in its report unto me by divers persons who knew not one another, and were differing in religion ; yet all agreed in the story, and in all the circumstances thereof.' The same tale is to be found in *A True Relation without all Exception of Strange and Admirable Accidents which lately happened in the Kingdome of the Great Magor or Magull* (London, 1622), with the addition that it was averred to be true by

Your Grace will pardon mee all this folly, to interrupt yow with soe much and soe uselesse tattle. I should be glad to remoove wher I might learne and practise better matter. But I cannot repent my journy. It hath made me know my God and my selfe better then ever I should have learned eyther among the pleasure of England. He hath woonderfully showed mee His mercy and taught mee His judgments: His goodnes be glorifyed and magnified for ever.[1] I humbly desire Your Grace to present my name (I dare not say my service) before His Majestie my lord and master. It is enough for mee if I bee not forgotten. I shall never meritt nor aspire the employments of his favour; but I will pay my vowes, and pray for His Majestie, that hee may live a happy and glorious long life to the comfort of his Church, and enjoy the crowne of crownes, prepared by the King of Kings for those that love him. Wherin I have fayled toward Your Honor, or by myne owne weakenes, Your Grace will measure by this rule: *exigitt et postulat amicitia non quod cuique debetur, sed quod quisque efficere potest*;[2] and yow will pardon the assuming so high a woord as frendship, with this enterpretation: *Servus est humilis amicus*;[3] which, as I am bould to professe, I will be ready to demonstrate by obedience to your commands. THOMAS ROE.

November 1.—Sultan Coronne tooke his leave and went to his tents. The King at noone sate out at the *durbar*, where the Prince brought his eliphants, about 600 richly trapped and furnished, and his followers, by estimation 10,000 horse,

Master Edward Terry, who heard it credibly reported, and *had often seen the ape*. This latter statement Terry takes occasion to correct (p. 405).

[1] The extent to which Roe's frequent illnesses had deepened his religious convictions is shown in the undated private letter (Brit. Mus. *Harl. MS.* 1576, f. 225), to which reference has already been made. 'O my deare freind,' he writes, 'that God which some thinke is confined to Europe and onely in the temples made with handes hath mett with mee in the wildernes. I have tasted his displeasure. I knew I was to bee humbled, not by sicknes onely, but by inward affliccions. . . . Hee began with mee in England, but Hee knew it was not a place where I could bee cleansed. I must goe wash in Jordan.'

[2] This quotation (from an unknown source) may be freely rendered: 'Friendship demands not what is actually due, but as much as one is able to effect.'

[3] 'A slave is a humble friend.' The sentiment is Seneca's: 'Servi sunt humiles amici' (*Epist.* 47, s. 1).

many in cloth of gould with hearne top feathers in their turbants, all in galanterie; him selfe in a coate of cloth of silver, embrodered with great pearle and shining in diamonds like a firmamentt. The King embraced him, kissd him, and showed much affection. At his departure hee gave him a swoord, the scaberd all of gould sett with stones, valewed at 100,000 *rup[ees]*, a dagger at 40,000, an eliphant, and two horses, all the furniture of gould sett with stones, and for a close one of the new caroches made in imitation of that sent by His Majestie my master, and commanded the English coachman to drive him to his tents; into which hee ascended, and sate in the middle, the sides open, his cheefest nobles a foote walking by him to his tents about four mile.[1] All the way hee threw quarters of *rupias*, beeing followed with a multitude of people. Hee reachd his hand to the coachman and putt into his hatt about 100 *rupias*.

I could not gett any despatch, neyther heard any newes from Suratt; so that Zulphe[carcon] is departed in our debt for want of an account, which I had often written for. I doubted our *patamars* miscarriage, for it is now 36 dayes since I heard a woord.

November 2.—The King remooved to his tents, with his weomen and all the court, about three mile. I went to attend him. Comming to the pallace, I found him at the *jarruco* wyndow and went up on the scaffold under him, which place, not having seene before, I was glad of the occasion. On two tressells stood two eunuches with long poles hedded with feathers, fanning him. He gave many favours and received many presents. What hee bestowed hee lett downe by a silke stringe rouled on a turning instrument; what was given him, a venerable fatt deformed ould matron, wrinckled and hung with gimbells [2] like an image, pulld up at a hole with such a nother clue. At one syde in a wyndow were his two

---

[1] Cf. the account given in the *Memoirs* (vol. i. p. 338). On this occasion the Prince was given the title of Shāh (Shāh Sultān Khurram).

[2] Gimbals, or gimmals, were rings intertwined or linked together. Cf. Holinshed in *Description of Ireland*, book vi. c. 2: 'truly this argument hangeth togither by verie strange *gimbols*.'

THE FORT GATEWAY AT AJMER

principall wifes, whose curiositye made them breake litle
holes in a grate of reede that hung before yt to gaze on mee.
I saw first their fingers, and after laying their faces close nowe
one eye, now a nother; sometyme I could discerne the full
proportion. They were indifferently white, black hayre
smoothed up; but if I had had no other light, ther diamonds
and pearles had sufficed to show them. When I lookd up
they retyred, and were so merry that I supposed they laughd
at mee. Suddenly the King rose; and wee retyred to the
durbar, and sate on the carpetts attending his comming out.
Not long after hee came and sate about halfe an hower, untill
his ladyes at their doore were ascended their elephants, which
were about 50, all most richly furnished, principally three
with turretts [*i.e.* howdahs] of gould, grates of gould wire
every way to looke out, and canopyes over of cloth of silver.
Then the King descended the stayres with such an acclamation
of ' health to the King ' [*Padshāh salāmat*] as [w]ould have
out cryed cannons. At the stayres foote, wher I mett him, and
shuffled to be next, one brought a mighty carp; another a
dish of white stuff like starch, into which hee putt his finger,
and touched the fish and so rubd it on his forhead, a ceremony
used presaging good fortune. Then a nother came and buckled
on his swoord and buckler, sett all over with great diamonds
and rubyes, the belts of gould suteable. A nother hung on
his quiver with 30 arrowes and his bow in a case, the same
that was presented by the Persian ambassador. On his head
he wore a rich turbant with a plume of herne tops, not many
but long; on one syde hung a ruby unsett, as bigg as a walnutt;
on the other syde a diamond as great; in the middle an emralld
like a hart, much bigger. His shash [see p. 198] was wreathed
about with a chayne of great pearle,[1] rubyes, and diamonds
drild. About his neck hee carried a chaine of most excellent
pearle, three double (so great I never saw); at his elbowes,
armletts sett with diamonds; and on his wrists three rowes
of several sorts. His hands bare, but almost on every finger
a ring; his gloves, which were English, stuck under his girdle;
his coate of cloth of gould without sleeves upon a fine *semian*
[see p. 233] as thin as lawne; on his feete a payre of em-

[1] Here, as elsewhere, ' pearl ' is used as a plural.

brodered buskings with pearle, the toes sharp and turning up. Thus armd and accomodated, hee went to the coach, which attended him with his new English servant, who was clothd as rich as any player and more gaudy, and had trayned four horses, which were trapped and harnassed in gould velvetts. This was the first hee ever sate in, and was made by that sent from England,[1] so like that I knew it not but by the cover,

[1] Jahāngīr mentions in his *Memoirs* (vol. i. p. 340) that he left Ajmer in ' the Frank carriage, which had four horses attached to it.' He goes on to explain that it was the custom for a king going forth to conquest to ride a tusked elephant, if proceeding towards the east, or a horse of one colour, if moving towards the west : if towards the north, a palanquin or litter was used : while if to the south (as in this instance) a cart or car was the proper conveyance.

Of the coach presented by Roe, see p. 98. Terry (p. 385) gives the following particulars of its transformation : ' Amongst many other things, when my Lord Ambassadour first went thither, the Company sent the Mogol an English coach, and harnesse for four horses, and an able coachman to sute and mannage some of his excellent horses, that they might be made fit for that service. The coach they sent was lined within with crimson China velvet ; which when the Mogol took notice of, he told the Ambassadour that he wondred that the King of England would trouble himself so much, as to send unto China for velvet to line a coach for him, in regard that he had been informed that the English King had much better velvet near home, for such or any other uses. And immediately after the Mogol caused that coach to be taken all to pieces, and to have another made by it, for . . . they are a people that will make any new thing by a pattern ; and when his new coach was made according to the pattern, his workmen first putting the English coach together, did so with that they had new made ; then pulling out all the China velvet which was in the English coach, there was in the room thereof put a very rich stuffe, the ground silver, wrought all over in spaces with variety of flowers of silk, excellently well suited for their colours, and cut short like a plush ; and instead of the brasse nails that were first in it, there were nails of silver put in their places. And the coach which his own workmen made was lined and seated likewise with a richer stuffe than the former, the ground of it gold, mingled like the other with silk flowers, and the nails silver and double guilt ; and after having horses and harnesse fitted for both his coaches, he rode sometimes in them, and contracted with the English coachman to serve him, whom he made very fine, by rich vests he gave him. allowing him a very great pension ; besides, he never carried him in any of those coaches, but he gave him the reward of ten pounds at the least ; which had raised the coachman unto a very great estate, had not death pre-

which was a gould Persian velvett. Hee gott into the end ; on each side went two eunuchs that carried small maces of gould sett all over with rubies, with a long bunch of white horse tayle to drive away flyes ; before him went drums, ill trumpetts and loud musique, and many canopyes, quittasolls,[1] and other strange ensignes of majestie, of cloth of gould sett in many places with great rubyes, nine spare horses, the furniture some garnished with rubyes, some with pearle and emralds, some only with studds enameld. The Persian ambassador presented him a horse. Next behynd came three *palenkees* ; the carriages and feete of on plated with gould, sett at the ends with stones, and covered with crimson velvett embrodered with pearle, and a frengg of great pearle hanging in ropes a foote deepe, a border about sett with rubyes and emrallds. A footman carried a foote stoole of gould sett with stones. The other two were covered and lyned only with cloth of gould. Next followed the English coach newly covered and trimed rich, which hee had given the queene Normahall, who rode in yt. After them a third of this cuntry fashion, which me thought was out of countenance ; in that sate his younger sonns. After followed about 20 eliphants royall, spare for his owne ascending, so rich that in stones and furniture that they braved the sunne. Every eliphant had divers flags of cloth of silver, guilt satten, and taffata. His noblemen hee suffered to walke a foot, which I did to the gate and left him. His wives on their eliphants were carried like parrakitoes halfe a mile behynd him. When hee came before the doore wher [h]is eldest sonne [*i.e.* Khusrau] is prisoner, he stayed the coach and called for him. He came and made reverence, with a

vented it, and that immediately after he was setled in that great service.'

From a letter of Kerridge's, in the British Museum, it appears that the cost of the coach in England was 151*l.* 11*s*. The coachman's name was William Hemsell, and he had been previously in the service of 'Dr. Farran and my Lord Bishopp of Coventrye and Lychfeild' [*i.e.* Dr. John Overall] (*Court Minutes*, 3 January, 1615). The 'very great pension' allowed by the Mogul was a rupee and a half per diem (*Letters Received*, vol. iv. p. 289) ! Hemsell died early in 1618.

[1] Umbrellas or sunshades (Port. *quita-sol*).

swoord and buckler in his hand; his beard grown to his
middle, a signe of disfavour. The King commanded him to
ascend one of the spare eliphants and so rode next to him, to
the extreame applause and joy of all men, who now are filld
with new hopes. The King gave him a thousand *rupias* to
cast to the people. His jaylor, Asaph Chan, and all the
monsters yet a foote. I tooke horse to avoyd presse and other
inconvenience, and crossed out of the *leskar* [*i.e. lashkar*, or
camp] before him, and attended untill hee came near his tents.
Hee passed all the way betweene a guard of eliphants, having
every one a turred on his back; on the fower corners fower
banners of yellow taffety; right before, a sling mounted, that
carried a bullett as bigg as a great tennis ball; the gunner
behind yt; in number about 300. Other eliphants of honor
that went before and after, about 600; all which were covered
with velvett or cloth of gould, and had two or three guilded
banners carried. In the way rann divers footemen with sckinns
of water that made a continuall shower before him; no horse
nor man suffered to approach the coach by two furlongs, except
those that walked a foote by; soe that I hasted to his tents
to attend his alighting.[1] They were walled in, about halfe
an English mile in compasse, in forme of a fort with divers
coynes and bulwarks, with high *cannatts* of a course stuff made
like arras, red on the outsyde, within which figures in panes,
with a handsome gate house; every post that beare up these
was hedded with a topp of brasse. The throng was great. I
desired to goe in, but no man was suffered; the greatest in the
land satt at the doore; but I made an offer, and they admitted

[1] The first halting-place was Dorāi, about four miles south of
Ajmer—the scene in 1659 of Aurangzeb's decisive victory over
Dāra. 'The tents pitch'd in that *leskar*, or camp royal, are for the
most part white, like the cloathing of those which own them. But
the Mogols tents are red, reared up upon poles, higher by much than
the other. They are placed in the middest of the camp, where they
take up a very large compasse of ground, and may be seen every
way; and they must needs be very great, to afford room in them
for himself, his wives, children, women, eunuchs, &c. In the
forefront, or outward part, or court within his tent, there is a very
large room for access to him, 'twixt seven and nine of the clock at
night, which . . . is called his *goozulcan*. His tents are encompassed
round with *canats* [Hind. *kanāt*], which are like our screenes, to

mee, but refused the Persian embassador and all the noble men. Here first the Persian embassador saluted me, with a silent complement only. In the middst of this court was a throwne of mother of pearle borne on two pillars raysd on earth, covered over with an high tent, the pole headed with a knob of gould; under it canopyes of cloth of gould; under foote carpetts. When the King came neare the doore, some noble men came in and the Persian ambassador. Wee stood one of the one syde, the other of the other, making a little lane. The King entering cast his eye on mee, and I made a reverence; hee layd his hand on his brest and bowed, and turning to the other syde nodded to the Persian. I followed at his heeles till hee ascended, and every man cryed ' Good joy and fortune,' and so tooke our places. Hee called for water, washed his hands, and departed. His weomen entered some other port [*i.e.* gate or entrance] to their quarter, and his sonne I saw not. Within this whole rayle was about 30 divisions with tents. All the noble men retired to theirs, which were in excellent formes, some all white, some greene, some mingled; all encompassd as orderly as any house; one of the greatest raretyes and magnificencyes I ever saw. The vale showed like a bewtifull citty, for that the raggs nor baggage were not mingled. I was unfitted with carriadge, and ashamed of my provision; but five years allowance would not have furnished mee with one indifferent sute sortable to others. And, which adds to the greatnes, every man hath a double, for that one goes before to the next remoove and is sett a day before the King riseth from these. So I returned to my poore house.

fold up together; those *canats* are about ten foot high, made of narrow strong callico, and lined with the same, stiffened at every breadth with a cane; but they are strongest lined on their outside by a very great company of arm'd souldiers, that keep close about them night and day. The tents of his great men are likewise large, placed round about his. All of them, throughout the whole *leskar*, reared up in such a due and constant order, that when we remove from place to place, we can go as directly to those moveable dwellings, as if we continued still in fixed and standing habitations; taking our direction from several streets and *bazars*, or market-places, every one pitched upon every remove alike, upon such or such a side of the Kings tents, as if they had not been at all removed.'—Terry, p. 421.

I demanded of Asaph Chan what remedy I should fynd against Zulphe[carcon], and showed his bill, desiring him to send to him or make complaynt to the King. He putt mee off to moove the Prince : that the King would not meddle with his servants. I yet, to my extreme trouble and woonder, heard noe newes from Suratt nor Agra ; resolved to follow the Prince on the morrow, and to complayne of our debts.

November 4.—I sent Mr. Bidolph and Jaddow to the Princes camp, to proove whither by fayre meanes Zulphe[carcon] would pay the debt ; for I knew how distastfull a complaynt against him would bee, and what I had suffered for this contention. They first went to Afzuld Chan [see p. 123 *n*], the secretary, and acquaynted him with my resolution to deliver his bill to the Prince. He answered hee doubted not but hee would give satisfaction without that course, and wishd them to goe speake with him ; which they did, and hee resolutly answered he would pay no more. When they urged his bill, hee slighted it, and bad demand it of the Prince, for whatsoever hee tooke from us was for him ; and that hee should pay it if he would, for that himselfe would not. Now the Prince was loose from the King, yow may judge that which I foresaw, that the delayes and pretences for want of certificatt from Suratt, which I had sent for six months, served only a turne to gett at liberty and to cosen us. I resolved in my tyme for no respect of danger or displeasure to leave such an example, but to hazard all to recover so little mony. If it had beene myne owne, I would have given it rather then undergone a new conflict ; but I purposed a fayre way without just exception, and that if I so suffered, it was a kind of martirdome : first to show his hand and seale to the Prince, and, if I found no justice, to deliver it to the King, with the full passage of all proceeding in yt.

November 5.—I rode to the Princes tents, about five mile, when he sate out. I usd some prefaces of respect, and desiered to take my leave of His Highnes, to whom I wished a prosperous journy, victorye over his enemyes, a glorious tryumph woorthy his greatnes, and a safe returne. I entreated him to beleeve I was his humble servant in all respects, reserving my duty to my soverayne ; and that hee would bee pleased to retayne our nation in his favour and protection. Then I presented to him Zulpheckarcons bills for 17,000 *m[amoodies]*, of which hee had payd 9,000 and the remayner hee refused after many delayes : that I had had long pacience for respect of His Highnes, but now the necessitye of his departure and my attendance on the King enforced mee to appeale to his justice, wherin I doubted not to fynd releefe. Hee read it over, and seemed to beleeve it had beene payd, demanding if Afsul Chan knew the account. I answered : yes : that hee was an instrument of the conclusion, and it was wittnessed by Mochreb-chan, Hoja Nassan, and divers, that knew wee lost for this end above 2,000 *m.*, and that his owne hand and seale and his *scrivanoes* bills would testefye against him. He desiered me stay till the secretary came and I should receive order. He rose before Afzul-Chan appeared, and retyred ; but sent Biram Chan [*i.e.* Bairām Khān], the commander of all his horse, to stay me a little. Within halfe an hower came answere that I should returne to my house, and two dayes after repayre to him : hee would examine the busines and pay mee himselfe : that then I should take my leave of him. He sate in the same magnificence, order, and greatnes that I mentioned of the King ; his throwne beeing plated over with silver, inlayd with flowers of gould, and the canopy over it square, borne on fower pillars covered with silver ; his armes, swoord, buckler, bowes, arrowes, and lance, on a table before him. The watch was sett, for it was evening. When hee came abroade, I observed him now [how ?] hee was absolute, and curiously his fashion and actions. Hee received two lettres, read them standing, before hee ascended his throne. I never saw so settled a countenance, nor any man keepe so constant a gravety, never smiling, nor in face showeing any respect or difference of men ; but mingled with extreame pride and contempt of all. Yet I found some inward trouble now and then assayle him, and a kind of brokennes and distraction in his thoughts, unprovidedly and amasedly answering sutors, or not hearing. If I can judg any thing, hee hath left his hart among his fathers women, with whom he hath liberty of conversation. Normahall in the English coach the day before visited him and tooke leave. She gave him a cloake all embrodered with pearle, diamonds, and rubyes; and carried away, if I err not, his attention to all other busines.[1]

November 6.—I received lettres from Mr. Browne at Amadavaz, advising mee of having gotten the Governor of Cambayas bill for the restitution of 1,100 ma[*moodies*] extorted last yeare, by virtue of a *firmaen* by me procured. So that I have recovered all bribes and extortions taken before my tyme with little losse. I suppose it wilbe a good example. He certefyed mee of a fray begun by the Portugalls, five of them setting on an English boy in Cambaya and disarming him; upon rumor wherof, John Browne and James Bickford [2] went to his rescue, and were assayled by seaven of them. One shooting a pistoll hurt John Browne in the hand, but his hart lay not thear. They defended them selves honestly, bravely, like English men, kylld one, hurt some others, and chased them up and downe the towne like beasts, to the great shame of such villaynes and reputation of our nation. To revenge this, the Portugalls beeing arrived in their frigotts, divers came ashore; no more English in towne but the three mentioned. The Governor understood the occasion, and sent the *Cuttwall* with a guard to our house and shutt the water ports, expelling the Portugall and commanding, upon payne of chasticement, not to meddle with the English; and so delivered them safe out of towne, who are returned to Amadavaz. By these I received newes from Suratt of a resolution to send to Jasques [3] without my

[1] There seems to have been no ground for the suspicion hinted here.

[2] Elected a factor in November, 1614. He was employed principally at Surat and Ahmadābād until his return to England in 1623.

[3] This decision was taken at a consultation held on board the *Charles* on 2 October, 1616 (see *Letters Received*, vol. iv. p. 189). Pepwell, who was himself unfavourable to the project, produced a letter from Roe (see *Add. MS.* 6115, f. 118), declaring that it would be useless to send to Persia until the issue of Sherley's mission to Spain were known; and that the *farmān* obtained by Steel and Crowder (see p. 110) was of little value, as it contained no undertaking on the part of the Shāh to send down silk to Jask, and no merchandise was obtainable at that port in the ordinary way. Against this Kerridge urged that the present opportunity was a good one, seeing that Sherley (who would be either a troublesome enemy or an expensive friend) was out of the way: that the Company had approved their previous measures and had encouraged them

knowledge, here beeing an ambassador of the Shawbas that offered mee all curtesy and whose advise would have given us great light to the busines; but in six weekes I never heard woord from them, neyther doe they thinck any body woorth the consulting but them selves. I sent downe the Kings *firmaen* procured by Crowther; but my advise that it was not woorth entertayning on so feeble conditions, with many reasons reserved to my selfe, not presupposing any man would have presumed a conclusion without mee; for that when I

to persevere: that, the war with the Turks having blocked commercial intercourse with Europe, there must be in Persia at once a dearth of cloth and a plethora of silk: that it was absolutely necessary to find some vent for the large stock of English goods in their warehouse for which no immediate sale could be hoped in India: and that one of the ships might just as well be employed in an experimental voyage as lie at anchor at Swally till the others were ready. Roe's opinion was set aside with the remark that 'in regard His Lordship in other particulers of his said letter is farr transported in errour of opynnyon concerning merchandizeing and merchants affaires in these parts makes us asured that hee is noe lesse transported from and concerning this Persian imployment'; and the expedition was decided upon. Edward Connock, the cape merchant of Pepwell's fleet, was chosen chief factor; Thomas Barker (then second at Surat) was made his principal assistant; and George Pley, Edward Pettus, William Tracy and Robert Gipps completed the party. The *James*, under the charge of Alexander Child, was told off to convey them to Jask, and she accordingly sailed on 8 November. The port was reached in safety a month later, the factors were landed with their goods, and the ship anchored again at Swally early in February, 1617 (Child's journal in *Purchas*, vol. i. p. 606; see also an account [by Pley] in *Egerton MS.* 2121). A Portuguese squadron had been despatched to intercept her, but had failed to do so (Bocarro's *Decada XIII*, c. 165).

How much Roe was angered at finding his opinion thus overruled may be gathered from his diary and letters; but neither he nor Pepwell could do anything in the matter. Keeling was still, by virtue of his commission, the chief director of the Company's affairs in the East, and in consequence the usual authority in matters relating to merchandise had been withheld from the general of the 1616 fleet. Pepwell, therefore, could not reverse the decision arrived at by the assembled factors, nor could he refuse to assist in carrying it out. Roe was equally powerless, and had to content himself with watching, in a decidedly critical mood, the outcome of the measures taken, while he awaited the result of his letters home of the previous year, complaining of his own want of authority.

motioned to send Shalbanke for 100 *rupias* overland to discover both Syndu and Jasques, to bee an eye wittnesse of the fittnes of the port and possibilitye of trade, and to have returned before the arrivall of our fleete with full intelligence, they rejected it, and braggd they had crossd all my advices ; and now have resolved to doe yt by a ship, at extreame perill and chardge, and without any ground, yea, against all reason ; without vouchsafing to acquaynt mee, but that I received the newes by collaterall enformation. Judge what respect your factors give mee : what the fruicts of division are, and seperating them from any relation to mee, though your last lettre signifyd yow required them to consult with mee before resolution of any matter of such importance. I must confesse it greatly discourageth mee, and my sincere payne, care, and toyle was not to serve to amend their follyes only at court, but hoped to have beene respected in my advice only for your profitt. For your cheefe factor [*i.e.* Kerridge] hath too much suddeyne fire and to great an opinion of his abilityes to give a temperate advise, as I can show abondantly and wee have had full experience, not once asking any mans advise from hence, but peremptorily commanding and ordering monyes to no purpose, too late and to extreame losse. Notwithstanding, this day I dispeeded a lettre from the Princes secretary, written in his owne name to Abram Chan, Salath Beage, and Isack Beage,[1] to oversee the Customer that hee wronged not the English nor suffered any other : that the busines might bee so ordered as should prevent all future complaynts : that the presents should be dispatchd to court without custome : that what soever was bought should not be taken by force, but the owner payd ready mony to content. The copy is registred.[2]

This day I wrote to the Governor of Cambaya to acknowledge his favour and my thanckfullnes : that I would acquaynt the King with his honorable respect of our protection.[3]

November 9.—The Prince, beeing to remoove, sent one of

[1] Ibrāhīm Khān, as already mentioned, was Governor of Surat. Of the other two, Sālik Beg was the *Dīwān* and Ishāk Beg the *Shāhbandar* (see *Letters Received*, vol. iv. p. 347).

[2] This does not appear to be extant. [3] See f. 134 of the MS.

his guard in hast for mee. I was unfitted to goe, but hee prest mee so farr that his master did stay out to speake with mee: that hee had commanded him not to returne without mee: that all the court did talk of the Princes favour to mee: that it was reported hee had desired the King to lett mee accompany him into the warrs, and that he had promised to use me so well as I should confesse his favour to our nation. This newes made mee take horse after dinner; but I found him newly risen and marching. I mett the Dutchman his jeweller [see p. 168 n]. Hee welcommed mee with good newes of some extraordinary favour from his master, who had sate almost an hower longer then his purpose to stay my comming, and such great promises that made mee beleeve none. Hee also confirmed the souldiers report of my attending the Prince. When I came up to the trayne I sent woord I was arrived, and had answer that I should passe before to the tents, and sitt untill the Prince came, and that hee would speake with mee. It was night before his approach. He made only a countenance to mee, sate a little, and went in among his woemen. As hee passd, he turned about, and sent a servant to desire mee to stay a while: that hee would com into the *guzelchan* and take his leave of mee. Within halfe an hower he sate out; but I could not gett any man to putt him in mynd of mee, and hee was falln to play, and eyther forgott it or put a tricke of state upon mee, that I stayd an hower. Beeing extreamly troubled, I went to the doore and tould the wayters the Prince had sent for mee: I came only to receive his commands: that I had attended long and must returne to my house, it beeing late: and if His Highnes had any busines, I desiered him to send it after mee, for I scorned such usage; and so departed to horse. Before I was up, ther came running messingers calling for mee, and I was sent for. I first complaynd of my stay: that I was come only to receive his command; that I had neyther bedd nor tent and six *course* home: that I could not procure entrance. I found him earnest at cards,[1] but hee

---

[1] A favourite pastime at the Mogul court. Akbar himself did not disdain to spend time in making fresh designs for them. There was at all events plenty of scope for variety, for the pack contained twelve suits of twelve cards each (Blochmann's *Aïn-i-Akbari*, vol. i. p. 306).

excused him selfe of forgetfullnes, and blamed the officers formally; but in show usd mee with more curtesy then ordinary, calling mee to see his cards and asking many questions. I expected hee would speake of my goeing with him, but, fynding noe such discourse, I tould him I was come only to obey him, and to take my leave: that I desired his pardon that I hasted away, for that I was to returne to Adsmere, beeing unprovided to stay all night. Hee answered hee sent for me to see me before his goeing: that I should presently bee dispatched. Then hee sent in an eunuch, and divers of his captaynes came smiling: the Prince would give me a great present, and if I feared to ryde late, I should have ten horse to guard mee, and made such a busines as if I should have received his best chayne of pearle. By and by came out a cloth of gould cloake of his owne, once or twice worne, which hee caused to bee putt on my back, and I made reverence, very unwillingly. When his ancester Tamerlane was represented at the theatre the garment would well have become the actor;[1] but it is here reputed the highest of favour to give a garment woorne by the Prince, or, beeing new, once layd on his shoulder. Then hee bowed him selfe and I had my dischardg; but I desiered to speake somwhat more. Using a preface of complements, I acquaynted him with the lettres I newly received from Suratt, wherin our factors acknowledge their good usadge and the receipt of the mony according to order: that as I had complaynd against the bad, I could not but acknowledge the justice and goodnes of Abram Chan, who in all poynts studyed to honour his master with noble actions and to protect us from injury. He replyed it was his command so to doe, and that hee was very glad that his servants and my countrimen agreed so well and were frends, which hee would continew by his expresse order: that in what I found my selfe agreeved hee would bee my judge him selfe and right mee. I desiered him to beginn his favour by commanding Zulphe-[carcon] to pay the merchants the 8,000 m[amodies] resting

[1] Doubtless Roe had often seen, in Marlowe's play,
   The Scythian Tamburlaine
 Threatening the world with high astounding terms,
 And scourging kingdoms with his conquering sword.

of his debt. He answered that he had undertaken to bee our
paymaster, and gave present order to give a bill to receive it
at Suratt; which I leave Mr. Bidolph to follow. So I tooke
my leave, and comming out was followed by all his wayters
and porters soe shamfully that I halfe paid for my cloake
before I gate out. By morning I gott home. In the way
thither I received an answer [1] of my lettres sent long since to
Suratt, which I supposed miscarried, but found that they
had kept my *pattamar* one month and fower dayes, only to
dispose their busines without my knowledge. They advise
mee of their sending the *James* to discover Jasques, with the
greatest quantity of cloth, lead, quicksilver, and teeth [*i.e.*
elephants' tusks], and divers factors, beeing forced to yt as a
comodity that would not vent in India (yet not many monthes
since they disputed with mee that these species would drive
the whole trade); notwithstanding that I had enformed them
that in Persia in the hart these kynd were lesse saleable, in the
sckirts (wher was no trade) not vendible at all. Next, that
they have made mony up to Agra, which cannot be returned
by the end of January. Thus, without once consulting any
man, they doe most absurdly all of their owne heads; which
I reprehended with some roundnes, and neede not repeat the
reasons I gave agaynst their courses nor my opinion, beeing
sent to the consultation and entered in its order among my
lettres [see p. 296 *n*]. They sent mee a copy of some clauses
of the Companyes commission which they pretend concerned
mee; but in the first, about the Persian employment, they
have proceeded as if it concernd mee not. The rest are
frivolous and, by misenformation into England, to no purpose;
and this is all it hath pleasd them to acquaynt mee with. They
confesse the receipt of the mony recovered by mee, of their
better usage at Suratt; but after I had procured order to
restore bribes, and brought the envy upon mee, they release
it in curtesy to procure favour for them selves. Concerning
Zulpheckarcons remayner they write mee they have not
leysure, and are loath to offend them that owe part, and so give
mee no account. Yet I have procured order for yt. But if

---

[1] See *Factory Records, Surat*, vol. 84, pt. i. f. 96.

I had received from them in six months a partition,[1] I had gotten ready mony; if now it be lost, I can doe no more; their negligence must answere it.

November 10.—All the towne beeing almost remooved, I was left behynd and could procure no camells nor carts, notwithstanding my warrant. The Persian embassador in the same case complaynd and had speedy redresse; upon notice wherof I sent to the court, and expect answere.

November 11.—I received two warrants for carts and camells at the Kings price; which I sent the officer.

November 13.—After two dayes search and layeing the townes ends, I could not bee fitted; so many wanted that usd force, the great men having souldiers every wayes out to catch all up; and it is a woonderfull matter to remoove the two *leskars* and all the citty at once. I despeeded my advise to the consultation at Suratt,[2] and to urdge them to such demands as were needfull.

November 14.—I received from Agra that, in barter of ould indico (a meane sort that lay on the owners hands) with halfe mony, they had putt off 20 clothes that were as heavy to us and as unsaleable; but I am of opinion if the indico will make any mony, it is no ill bargayne. Cloth is drye merchandice at best.[3]

---

[1] A statement showing the different persons from whom the money was due.

[2] See f. 135 of the MS. In this letter Roe says: 'the King is remooved seven *course,* and wantes for himselfe and the Prince 4,000 camells.' He blames the factors severely for sending a ship to Jask, which, he declares, 'is noe place of resort nor trafique. Noe silke growes within 1000 mile, nor none is like to bee brought downe for our sakes. The course of an ancient trade is not diverted by one offer. The port is not accessable by a leauge, if Newport bee a true man. Our goods are lesse vendible there then in India. This yeare came by Hispan to Adsmeere neare 100 broad cloths from Aleppo, that could not be putt off in Persia, and were sould here under the rate of ours two *rup*[*ees*] a *cobdy,* better cloth.' Further subjects of censure are the omission to consult him about the Persian project, the neglect to provide lading for the ships ere their arrival, the needless engagement of additional merchants, and the maintenance of unnecessary factories.

[3] In October, 1615, Kerridge wrote to Keeling that English cloth was much desired at Agra, but too expensive to find many pur-

November 16.—The King gave order to fire all the *leskar* at Adsmere to compell the people to follow, which was dayly executed.[1] I was left almost desolate ; and the Persian embassador, who had fought, chydd, brauld, complaynd, but could not gett remedy, in the same estate. Wee sent to bemone on a nother, and by his example I began to resolve to buy ; for many would sell, that at the Kings price would not hire ; and I cast it at the best hand I could, almost to save the hire, though the carts were deare ; for in three monthes the price was eaten. Necessitye enforced mee, for the towne was burnd and desolate. I was in danger of theeves that from the army came and robbd in the night, and I could not find bread to eate ; yet I sent a new to court, and resolved to abyde all the inconveniences of a hard seige.

November 17.—Notwithstanding the default of account from Suratt of the remayner of Zulph[ecarcon], yet I sent to the Prince for his promised bill, who undertooke the payment ; and so I received his lettre commanding to certefye what was unpayd of the 8,000 *m*[*amoodies*] demanded (for that some of it was chardged to Abram Chan), and the remayner to bee payd to the factor at Brampoor ; which lettre I sent the factors as a full conclusion. But withall I was certefyed that now the Prince was gone and I had tooke my leave (as hee thought) content with his promises, hee had given order to entercept all the presents and to force them to his *leskar*. I returned that first they should kyll the English that conducted them ; and purposed, so soone as I could gett carriadge to remoove, to complayne to the King. Judge now the fayth of this

chasers ; 'neither is it used at all in garments, but in coverings for ellophants, coaches, pallambkynes, saddles, &c. The country above aboundeth with course cloth made ther, better coullers and cheaper by far then in England ; so that ours is used more for novilty then for want' (*Add. MS.* 9366).

[1] In 1633 Peter Mundy saw at Ajmer 'many ruinated buildings formerly belonginge to the *Amrawes* in Jehanguerrs tyme, whoe resided heere about three yeres ; by whose *moholl* or pallace wee rested, which now lyes to ruyne. Shaw Jehan hath also his, hard by a faire tanck named Anasawgur' (*Travels*, vol. ii. p. 242). See *supra*, p. 217, for a reference to the Prince's house being near the Āna Sāgar.

Prince and my vexation. I received from Goa for truth that Don Emanuell de Meneses, with about 300 of those saved a shoare from out the Admirall, were arrived, poore, robbd, and rifled by the inhabitants of Angazesia, who had slayne many and forced some to circumsicion ; on the 24 of October not one of the fleete sett out from Lishbow arrived,[1] to their great woonder: the gallion of Mozambique was fought with by the Hollander that lately departed from Suratt, who lay off and on before Goa as shee came in to meete the ships expected ; she was rich in gould and other comodityes, but shee escaped, by nearnes of the port. Observe the bouldnes of the Hollander to attempt with one shipp and to brave the head of the Indiaes. I received a promise for camells to remoove.

November 18.—I could not procure carriadge, but was so dayly delayed that [I] feard to stay. Two carts I was enforced to buy, and camells I was constantly promised. Mr. Bidolph remayned in the Princes *leskar* to gett in mony. The King was yet but 12 *course* from Adsmere.[2] The Jesuite tooke his leave of mee, beeing forced to buy carriadg, notwithstanding his order for yt out of the Kings store ; but scarcetye punnished all men. This empty tyme offering no discourse of myne owne affayres, I shall digresse conveniently to mention the estate of Sultan Cursoronne, of whose new delivery into the hands of his enemyes every mans hart and mouth was full. The King, notwithstanding hee had so farr agreed to satisfye his proud sonne at his departure, yet it seemes ment not to wincke at any injury offered to the elder ; and partly to secure him in the hands of Asaph-Chan, partly to satisfy the people that murmered and feared the practice of some treachery against him, he tooke occasion to declare him selfe publiquely. Asaph-Chan had visited his new prisoner and in his fashion did not

---

[1] According to Faria y Sousa, three vessels started ; one sprang a leak and had to return ; a second lost company on the coast of Guinea, owing to a storm, but ultimately reached Goa in safety ; the third (the Admiral) was destroyed by the English fleet, as already narrated.

[2] At Rāmsar, about 20 miles south-east of Ajmer (*Memoirs*, vol. i. p. 342).

acknowledg him as his Prince, but rudely prest upon him against his will and with no reverence. Som are of opinion he pickt a quarrell and, knoweing the brave nature of the Prince, that hee would not beare indignitye, tempted him to drawe his swoord or to use some violence, which [the] guard should suddenly revenge, or ells it should be declared to the King as an attempt to kill his keeper and to escape. But the Prince was patienter; only he gott a frend to acquaynt the King with the manners of his jaylor. The King called Asaph-Chan at the *durbar* and asked when hee sawe his chardge. He answered: two dayes past. His Majestie replyed: what did you with him? He sayes: only visitt him. But the King pressd him to know what reverence and fashion hee carried toward him. Asaph-Chan found His Majestie knew what had passd, and confessed hee went to see him in affection and to offer his service, but that the Prince refused him admittance into his chamber; which, because hee had chardge of his safetie, hee thought it both necessary for him to doe and discurtesye in the other to deny; therfore he prest in. The King returns quick: when yow were in, what sayd yow, and what did yow? What duty showed yow toward my sonne? He stands blanck, and confesseth hee did not any reverence; wherat the King tould him hee would make his proud hart know him to bee his eldest and beloved heyre, his prince and lord: and if hee once heard of any the least want of reverence or duty toward him, hee would command his sonne to sett his feete on his neck and trample on him: that he loved Sultan Coronne well, but hee would make the world know he did not entrust his sonne among them for his ruine.

November 19.—I received from Agra that they received new bills from Suratt, when thyre car[a]van was out of towne; yet that they would execute their commission, though ther can bee no hope to arrive sooner at Suratt then the end of Januarye.

[*Thus farr went the journall for England. The next beginns the* 20 *of November this present month.*]

November 20.—I received from the court a new warrant for my carriadge, which procured mee eight camells from the officer, but misserable ones, such as would not suffice mee;

so that I was compelld to dispatch my selfe away, now left all alone to buy for my supplement.

November 22.—I remooved into my tents.

November 23 & 24.—I stayd for the merchannts; and received in answere from Spahan that my lettres were dispeeded for Aleppo: that our comming into Persia was expected, but on conditions to fitt the Shabas, so that it might advance his dessigne of diverting his silkes from the way of Turkye: that the generall of the Grand Signior lay with a mighty army at Argerome [Erzeroum], six dayes march short of Tavris [Tabrīz], uncertayne whether to assayle the citty or to enter Gorgeston [Georgia] and Gilan [Ghilān], the countryes of silkes, to wynn that by conquest which hee was prohibited by commerce: to meete both attempts the Shabas was encamped at Salmas,[1] a village indifferently seated in the way: but if in two monthes the armyes encounter not, winter approaching and the wants that will attend such multitudes will dissolve them both without any honorable action; or if they meete, the Persian, though by report 180 thousand, will not adventure battayle, but beeing light and able to march easely, without cannon and baggage, will fall on and off on every syde so on the Turks army as hee will breake and waste him without hazard.[2] With these I received a packett of lettres directed to on Jeronimo [3] Galecia, resident in Lahor, wherin I found divers commissions and lettres of deputation directed to him in the name of Bartholomew Hagatt,[4] consull in Aleppo, and others, constituting him as their procurator for the recovering of divers monyes and goods in the hands of Signor Bonelli,

---

[1] A village near the N.W. corner of Lake Urumiah, about 85 miles west of Tabrīz.

[2] The war is related at length in Von Hammer's *History of the Ottoman Empire* (vol. viii. of the French version).

[3] This should be 'Giovanni': see under 7 December. He was evidently the 'Joann. Galiseus, Venetus at whose house in Lahore Benedict Goës stayed at the close of 1602, when about to start on his fatal journey to China (see Du Jarric's *Thesaurus*, vol. iii. pt. i. p. 204).

[4] Appointed English Consul at Aleppo about 1611. He was a freeman of the East India Company, and sent them intelligence from time to time (*Letters Received*, vol. i. p. 273).

their factor resident in Lahor, who about ten months past was slayne and robbd; with divers notes of severall cargazons [*i.e.* inventories], bills of exchange and ready mony, verifyed by the seale and subscription of Jeronimo Foscarini, consull in Soria [*i.e.* Syria], and Stepheno Sala his chanceller, taken out of the registers of his office; all which amounted to a great summe, and were traded in Indya by the sayd Bonelli as agent for a partnership of the principalls of divers nations residing in Aleppo, to Padre Jeronimo Xavier. Which lettres and severall packets comming by error into my hands, I reserved with purpose to acquaynt the Jesuitte living at court, and so to proceed as befitted.

To the East India Company.[1]
(*Add. MS.* 6115, f. 140.)

Adsmeir, 24 November, 1616.

I received your lettre on the 12 of October, 1616, from the *Charles*, safely arrived with four ships at the barr of Suratt the 26 of the former month. Of what pasd at sea I doubt not yow will receive ample relation; only a little difference in the report of our fleete and the Portugalls I will mention: that wee began the fight, and that no viceroy beeing sent this yeare, an ancient souldier, Don Emanuell de Meneses, that had twice beene Generall of their forces, was in the Admirall, who, beeing beaten, ran her selfe ashore on Angazatia, the greatest of the islands of Comora, wher hee gott aland with the survivars of his force and caused the ship to bee fiered, which but for respect of him had yeilded; that the ilanders robbd them and sett them ashoare at Mosambique, and are nowe arrived at Goa. This tale hangs ill together; for that I know they first made five shot, and that it is impossible they could passe from Anguzesia to Mosambique in a canoe, or that the inhabitants, having robbd them, durst carry them into their strength; or that all this could bee effected and newes of their arrivall come from Goa in so little tyme.[2] So that my judgment is, they make their relation as neare ours as they can, with creditt, and are loth to confesse truth, that eyther all perished,

---

[1] A part of this letter was printed by Purchas (vol. i. p. 589), but with an incorrect date and many errors in the text.

[2] The story was, however, substantially correct. The survivors, after being plundered and ill-treated by the natives, were taken off by a Muhammadan trader, who carried them to Mombasa. There they embarked for Goa on 10 September.

or the Viceroy, which were the greatest losse and dishoner ever happened to them in India.

I shall not neede write yow any long discourse of your affaires, nor my opinion, for that in a continued journall I have sett downe all passages, and send yow the copyes of my lettres to your factoryes, wherin many poynts are disputed and opened; from both which yow may make best your owne collection and judgment; for in them casually all your businesse is handeled and discussed at full, and it may bee collected into such a method as yow may sitt at home and see it at once. But because some poyntes in my last lettres I swalowed at my first comming at others reports, which since I fynd vayne and frivolous, and others perhaps are yet unresolved in my generall discourse, I will runn over the materiall poynts with brevitye; for I extreamly desier that yow once understood the constitution of this trade, how to governe and settle it; that by varietye of fond opinions yow bee not councelled to unnecessary chardge, nor fall into grosse errors and damage.

But first I desire yow to receive in particular answer of your lettre that the unkindnes conceived betweene mee and Captain Keeling was not so far rooted that it was woorth your trouble or excuse. It is true I wrote to my honorable frend [Sir Thomas Smythe] somwhat that passd betweene us. I did only dischardge my hart, without purpose to have it spread as a complaynt; his favour to mee extended it beyond my meaning. Men cannot live without some distast, especially wher fawners and flatterers seeke to endeare them selves by others disquiett. Wee parted frends. It is lesse troublesome and easier to forgett discurtesyes then to lay them up or dispute them. I was not borne to a life smooth and easy; all my actions have beene mingled with crosses and rubbs, that I might rather say I wrestled then walked toward my grave. But God provides every man a portion fitt for his condition, and I am content. I never doubted your performance with mee in mony nor any other contract; I did averr soe much in that lettre and my answere to Captain Keeling. Nor will I complayne of any narrownes in my allowance. I made a covenant; I must abyde by it, and will endeavour to effect yt. I will acquaynt yow in tyme with all particulars of expence and referr my selfe to yow. I know yow ment not but that my labor should bee recompensd. My sincerity toward yow in all my actions is without spott; my neglect of privat gayne is without example, and my frugalitye beyond your expectation. I was never an ill husband of my creditt nor any trust committed to mee. My patrimoniall unthriftines only I feele and repent. I pray God I may so affect your desires as it may meritt what yow give. I will bragg of no industrie nor successe. Judge mee by my actions, not by the favour of an infidell King, with whom yet I stand on such outward showes of creditt as never any stranger did ; but want of language and an enterpreter that will deliver mee truly is an extreame prejudice.

Concerning the ayding the Mogoll or waffing [convoying] his subjects into the Redd Sea, it is now uselesse, yet I made offer of your affections ; but when they need not a curteyse, they reguard it as a dogg [doth] dry bread when his belly is full. The King hath peace with the Portugalls, and will never make a constant warr, except first wee displant them. Then his greatnes will step in for a share of the benifitt, that dares not partake the perill. When they have peace, they scorne our assistance, and speaks as lowed as our canon ; if warr oppresse them, they dare not putt out under any protection, nor will pay for yt. Yow must remoove from yow all thought of any other then a trade at their port ; wherin if yow can defend your selves, leave them to their fortune. Yow can never oblige them by any benifitt, and they will feare yow sooner then love yow. Your residence yow neede not doubt so long as yow tame the Portugall. Therfore, avoyd all other chardge as unnessesary, that resists not him ; hee only can prejudice yow. For a forte, at my first arrivall I received it as very necessarie ; but experience teaches mee we are refusd it to our advantage. If hee would offer mee ten, I would not accept one. First, wher the river is comodious, the cuntry is barren and untraded ; the passadges to parts better planted so full of theeves that the Kings authoritye avayles not, and the strength of the hills secures them in that life. If it had been fitt for trade, the naturalls would have chosen it, for they feele the incomoditye of a barrd haven ; and it is argument enough of some secrett inconvenience, that they make not use of it. But if it were safe without the walls, yet is it not an easy woorke to divert trades and to drawe the resort of merchants from their accustomed marts, especially for our comoditye, which is bought by parcells [*i.e.* in small quantities], and cannot be called staple. Secondly, the chardge is greater then the trade can heare ; for to mayntayne a garison will eate the profitt. It is not 100 men can keepe it ; for the Portugall, if hee once see yow undertake that course, will sett his rest [*i.e.* stake everything] upon it to supplant yow. A warr and trafique are incompatible. By my consent, yow shall no way engage your selves but at sea, wher yow are like to gayne as often as to loose. It is the beggering of the Portugall, notwithstanding his many rich residences and territoryes, that hee keepes souldiers that spends it ; yet his garrisons are meane. He never profited by the Indyes, since hee defended them. Observe this well. It hath beene also the error of the Dutch, who seeke plantation heere by the swoord. They turne a woonderfull stocke, they proule in all places, they posses some of the best ; yet ther dead payes consume all the gayne. Lett this bee received as a rule that, if yow will profitt, seeke it at sea, and in quiett trade ; for without controversy it is an error to affect garrisons and land warrs in India. If yow made it only against the naturalls, I would agree ; to make it for them, they are not woorth it, and yow should be veary warie how yow engage your reputation in yt. Yow cannot so easely make a faier retraict as an onsett ; one disaster would eyther discreditt yow, or interest yow in a warr of extreame chardge and doubtful event. Besides, an action so subject to chance as a warr is most unfittly undertaken, and with most hazard, when the remoetnes of place for supply, succors and councell subjects to unrecoverable losse : for that wher is most uncertaynty, remidies should bee soe much the nearer to occur to all occasions. At sea yow may take and leave ; your designes are not published.

The roade of Swally and the port of Suratt are fittest for yow in all the Mogolls territory. I have weyed it well, and deliver yow that shall never bee disprooved. Yow neede no more ; it is not number of ports, factoryes, and residences that will profitt yow ; they will encrease chardge, but not recompence it. The conveniency of one respectively to your sales, and to the comoditye of investments, and the well employing of your servants is all needfull. A port to secure your ships, and a fitt place to unlade, will not be found togither. The roade at Swally, during the season, is as safe as a pond ; Suratt, Cambaya, Barooch, and Amadavaz are better traded then all Indya, and seated comodiously. The inconveniencyes are—the Portugall at sea, and the landing of goods. To meete with which, first, yow must bring to passe that your ladings bee ready by the end of September at your port—which may bee effected by a stock before hand, or by taking up mony for three monthes—and so yow may dischardge and lade in one, and depart in excellent season for England ; and the enemy shall not have tyme with force to offend yow, who wilbe newly arrived ; and if the preparation be ancienter, wee can know yt. For the second, to land goods without danger of frigatts, and to save the carriadge over land, yow must send a pinnace of 60 tunne with ten pieces [*i.e.* guns], that drawes but seven or eight foote water, to passe up the river betwene Swally and Suratt ; and so your goods wilbe safe, and in your owne command to the custume house key ; and it will a little awe the towne. Shee may proceed after according to your appoyntment.

The comodityes yow sell passe best in that quarter. The goods yow seeke beeing principally indico and cloth, no one place is so fitt for both ; and the lesse inconveniences are to bee chosen. Of this yow shall gather more at lardge my opinion and reasons in my journall and discourses to your factors. Perhaps some of them will contradict it. But I am not deceived, nor have private ends, to keepe factories to employ and advance frends. The places and number of servants I have delivered my judgment in, and could manifest the past errors, but not mend them. Syndu is possesd by the Portugall; or, if it were free, were no fitter then Suratt, nor safer; as it is, it wilbe more subject to perill. Your factors sent me four or five clauses out of your commission, that concernd Persia, a fort, a plantation in Bengala, all which they knew were not of use; with no other purpose, proposition, or resolution they will acquaynt me. They cannot abyde I should understand or direct them. If they resolve of any thing in their opinion for your profitt, and send to mee, I will effect the court part; but yow will fynd in my lettres and journall how they use mee, which doubtlesse at first was sowed by some jealousy of yours, which will cost yow dearly.

For the settling your trafique here, I doubt not to effect any reasonable desier. My creditt is sufficient with the King, and your force will alway bynd him to constancy. It will not neede so much help at court as yow suppose; a little countenance, and the discretion of your factors, will with easy chardge returne yow most profitt. But yow must alter your stock. Lett not your servants deceive yow; cloth, lead, teath, quicksilver are dead comodytyes, and will never drive this trade. Yow must succor yt by change,[1] and yow will find my opinion discussed in lettres. I have this yeare passd many difficultyes by the perversenes of Sultan Coronne, Lord of Suratt; but by Gods direction I have overcome them. Articles of treaty on equall tearmes I cannot effect; want of presents disgraced mee; but yet by peices I have gotten as much as I desird at once. I have recovered all bribes, extortions, debts made and taken before my tyme till this day; or at least an honorable composition. But when I deliver the next guifts to the Mogoll, in the Princes absence, I will sett on a new for a formall contract. The presents sent are to few to follow examples; they will scarce serve the first day. The rule is at every arrivall of a fleete the Mogol, [and] the Prince during his signory in our port, will expect a formall present (and lettres from the King our sollicitor) from yow, which neede not bee deare if well chosen. Your agent must be furnished with a China shop [see p. 116] to serve little turnes, for often giving of trifles is the way of preferment. It cannot bee avoyded,

---

[1] 'The surest way to rayse a stock without losse to our country were from the sowth [Bantam, etc.], all China comodityes beeing as deare here as in England, and spices at good proffitt' (Roe to Capt. Pepwell, 10 September, 1616).

and I have beene scorned for my poverty in that kind. Particulars I have sent of such as I suppose will please. At my deliverie of the first sent by mee contentment outwardly appeared, but I will acquaynt yow with the cabinetts opinion, by which yow may judg. Three exceptions were taken and disputed by the King and his *privadoes*.[1] First, it was censured to name presents in a Kings lettre to bee sent by a principall man his ambassador and such poore ones delivered, meaner and fewer then when they came with lesse ostentation; that if they had not beene named as from a monarch, it had beene lesse despiceable; for such is the pride that, although the coach for the forme and for a modell gave much content, yet the matter was scornd, and it was never usd untill two other of rich stuff were made by it and that covered with cloth of gould, harnes and furniture, and all the tynn nayles headed with silver or hatched,[2] so that it was nine months a repayring; when I sawe it, I knew it not [cf. p. 284]. Secondly, it was excepted against that His Majestie did write his name before the Mogoll; but it matters not for that dull pride. Thirdly, that His Majestie in his lettre intimated that honor and profitt should arise to this Prince by the English or their trade, which hee so much despiseth to heare of that hee will willingly bee ridd of it and us if he durst. The forgetting to send mee lettres diminisheth my creditt, which is to bee mayntenyed by all ceremonyes; and Sultan Coronne expected one as an honor to him.

The suffering voluntaryes to passe in your fleetes is an extreame incomodity.... They are eyther some unruly youths that want ground to sowe their humors and are exposed to be tamed, and may doe mee and yow much prejudice in reputation ... or else they are sent at your chardge to learne to discover the streights and fittest places of interception of Indian goods for a future voyadge, and to enable them by experience to doe yow a mischeefe who bredd them to yt. I know many envy yow this trade, and would bee extreame glad to rove. Yow cannot doe better then, like the preists of Roome, to keepe all men in ignorance but your selves; at least as many as your owne necessitye useth not....

First, concerning Persia.... What my judgment is yow will find by my relations and lettres; how your factors have proceeded I hope they will advise. I sent a *patmar*, whom they kept a month without answer now in the heate of busines, because they would resolve the settling a factory at Jasques without my knowledge. I know they understand not the place, nor have any ground for what they did; and, besides

---

[1] An intimate friend, or in the case of a king (as here), a favourite. This was one of the Spanish terms current in England at the time.

[2] Ornamented with engraved lines.

the neglect of mee, I feare have sent a dead unvendible stock. I shalbe most glad if I bee in an errour ; but I know, if I err, it is upon better foundation then they can prosper in. If it had beene fitt to settle in that place, if once they had acquaynted mee with the purpose, I could have geven them lardge advise and much assistance from the Persian Ambassador resident at court, who offered mee his councell ; but now, as they beginn against my consent, they may proceede without my assistance. ... Sir Robert Shirly by contrary wynds lost his passadge for Lisbon last yeare and remaynes at Goa for the present returne of the fleete. His negotiation continewes full of hope to bring the Spaniard in to joyne with the Portugall. I have sent transcrips of my opinion which I first apprehended, and am constant to yt ; and God hath prevented him one yeare and given yow leasure for the future.[1] Next, I hould it woorthy your consideration to resolve somwhat for your safety and quiett in the road with the Portugall. Ther are but two wayes, a peace or a compulsion. The first I have a new undertaken by the mediation of a Jesuite, who foresees their ruine ; but I despayre of any successe, both that the Viceroy wants authoritie or is to proud to use yt. The next is force, which is allway to disadvantage when yow only defend. My opinion is that yow give order to all your fleetes to make price [*i.e.* prize] of them, and that, as yow nowe ride at Swally roade to protect one ship, that yow would send that guard next yeare to ride before Goa, to brave them or burne them, at least to stop them that they durst not putt to sea in December. So yow shall enforce them to loose their seasons ; one or two returnes hindered would undoe them. On my woord they are weake in India and able to doe your fleete no harme but by supplyes from Lisbon, which advertisement you must harken after and accordingly accommodate your strength.[2] Yow will add much reputation to your case, and force them to that which their pride will never suffer them to see they want more then yow, which is, a quiett trade.

My third proposition is for your trafique into the Redd Sea.[3]

[1] Roe had some hopes that Sherley 'might fall into the hands of our shipping.' 'That fleete,' he wrote to Pepwell (f. 120),' is easilye beaten ; one assault would more disharten them and give us more reputation then many prosperouse defences.'

[2] 'Some of their best frends here have advertised that, although they have not given over the quarrell but will attempt our subversion in this place, yet they confesse that their power here wilbe able to doe no good, having made experience of their greatest force ; but that they expect it from Lisbone, and to that end have advised and petitioned the King of Spayne' (Roe to Pepwell, 10 September, 1616).

[3] Roe had already urged this in his letter to Pepwell of 11 Nov.

It is more important then all other projects. My councell is that one of your smallest ships, with the fittest English goods and such other as this country yeilds, yearly goe in company of the Guzeratts and trade for them selves for mony, which is taken in abundance, and returne in September with them, to supply this place. The profit exceeds all the trades of Indya and will drive this alone. The danger is rather a jealousy [*i.e.* doubt or suspicion] then substantiall. When the Turcks betrayed Sir Henry Middleton,[1] our factoryes and courses in these parts were unknowne to them, and doubtlesse wee, beeing strangers in that sea, were mistrusted for piratts. Experience of us hath made them know better, and in company of the Guzeratts, for their sake (whom they cannot spare) wee should bee admitted. The King would write to the Admirall to entertayne our consortship, and they would be glad of it, and it were one of the best securityes of our frendship. The Dutch have practised it this yeare to great advantage and wer well received. Our owne warines might secure us. They must ride six months for wynds, tyme enough to send all the goods ashore by parcells, and never to trust above one or two factors and little comoditye at once. They will not declare their treachery for trifles ; and I doubt not yow might procure the Grand Signiors command to meete them. If I have any judgement, ther is not any matter for your profitt of such importance. Port Pequnua [see p. 194 *n*] in Bengala yow are misinformed in. Ther is no mart nor resort of merchaunts. It is traded by the Portugalls from Pegu with rubyes, topasses and saphiers ; and returnes cloth, which is fyne, but yow may bee furnished nearer hand. But if your factors require it I will send a *firmaen*. I would long since have done yt, but was discouraged by the consultation at Suratt.[2]

[1] See *Lancaster's Voyages*, p. 174.

[2] The following further entries relating to this subject seem to be worth recording :

' Concerning their [the Company's] advise for Port Pequina, in which the Portugals are seated, if yow write I will send downe a *firmaen*. But I lett yow first know that they are ill and falsly enformed, for it will vent no comoditye, neyther is ther any mart from Cathaya or Tartary, but a few peddling fellowes that carie packs ; and their advise may be censured by this only, that joyne Indolstan as a cuntry trading thither, which is a generall name of all the land betweene Indus and Ganges of such a language. It is true Bengala makes fine cloth, but the Company need not send a factory to buy that comoditye ; they may many wayes be supplyed at easier rates then to send a ship to yt, or passe it soe farr by land, at their owne ports of Mesolapatan and Guzeratt. For sugar, it is base, not woorth frait, and the wax in no plenty. The best comoditye

Yow have been wrongd in here maynteyning needlesse factoryes, by making new wages and entertayning servants unfitt and superfluous.... Yow were much wrongd in the *Hopes* returne. If I bee not misinformd, privat mens goods were shippd, and your owne sent about by Bantam for want of stowage. For indico I have scarrd all men, professing yow is a raw silke and pretty stuffs made therof, which are sould to Agra, but in small numbers' (Roe to the Surat factors, 12 Nov. 1616; *Add. MS.* 6115, f. 135).

'Heer is not nowe fitt shipping for the discovery of Port Pequino, which, according to Your Lordships informacion, we understand to be no fitting port for us. The Porting[alls] hath a citty one that part of Ganges, and with their boates comaund the river. Wee heare of another port, called Peepell [*i.e.* Pippli], about a dayes jornaye to the northwardes [*sic*] of the former, upon the coast of Orishaw [*i.e.* Orissa], belonginge to this Kinge; which reporte affirmes les daungerous and more usefull for sale of our como[dities]; wherof it maye please you particulerly to informe yourself, and, approving therof, procure the Kinges firmaen for that or any other of these parts against the next yeare; which this, for want of fitting shippinge etc. is unlikely to be attempted' (The Surat factors to Roe, 12 Dec. 1616; *Factory Records, Surat*, vol. 84, part i. f. 130).

'The port yow named at Bengala, this *Norose* I spake with the *Shabander* and with an ould man that had beene Governor. They protest it to bee an ill harbor, subject to the Portugall, for that Satagam [Sātgāon], where they are planted 1500, is but a nother outlett of the same river. Yt is in the protection of a *Raja* scarcely in good obedience. Finally, they wilbe glad of our comming soe wee can beate the Portugall quite out; otherwise, they say, wheras now they have quiett, theyr seas and trafique wilbe interrupted. They give noe hope of sale, except of spices; nor can warrant the transport up of them by river to Agra. Yet upon your next, if yow resolve I shall sett it afoote, I will; though I am resolved of a repulse before hand; all the great men are against us' (Roe to the Surat factors, 7 April, 1617; *Add. MS.* 6115, f. 180).

'Concerning Bengala, I mooved the fittnes of a residence to Lucas And[rinus] [Antheunis, see pp. 159, 193] at Mesolapatan, who yet gives noe encouragment upon any certainty of the place, but only wishes that, if such a *firmaen* be procured, it may bee sent over land to him, from whence best use may be made of yt, if any bee required. So that my purpose is to adventure for a generall grant of trad upon all the coast of Bengala, which, though I know it wilbe denyed for the trouble like to ensue by our dissention with the Portugall in those seaes, yet it will occasion mee to fall lower to some fitt port which the King may assigne, if hee will grant any; but I am dayly answered, for the comoditye wee bring wee hav too many already' (Same to same, 6 June, 1617; *Ibid.* f. 197).

have made a Persian law ir evocable, that whatsoever is sent is forfeyted.... I can find many faults, but yow give mee power to mend non; so that I might live at rest. The *dusturia* [1] in all bought goods (besides the brokars fee), which is due to the buyer, is a great matter. The first is in indico, two *ceare* to a *mand*; the second is so many *pice* upon a *rupy* when the account is cast up; [2] a third in some places at payment is one upon a hundred. Which of these or what yow receive, I know not; it is woorth your enquirye. It will make in a few years two rich men....

Now I may a little speeke concerning my selfe. First, for expence I send yow a yeares account, wherin I have traveld, kept yow two howses (sometyme seven and eight of your servants, their horses and *peons*, ever four of them), built and repayrd; so reasonable that, if yow compare it with others, I shall not neede to bragg of yt.[3] Two things I am sure of: the example did displease some; and that the stewardship is honestly carried, weekly examined by mee, and every parcell by my order, and that yow are not deceived of one *pice*. Next that, paying my mens wages all here (else they could not live) out of my allowance, and the desier to appeare handsome and honorable abroad, with liberalityes not brought to your account, make mee soe bare that yow neede not feare my trading nor growing rich. The Kings bountyes are rather markes of honor then of profitt. I have supplyed a yeare in presents of myne owne stock and aske not to deminish yours a penny in Indya. All your other servants part not with a knife but at four for one ready mony.... I shall not returne richer by 500*l.* for my stay, but in my honest deseart to yow; which I will bring under good certificatt and trust to yow for recompence. I will settle your trade here secure with the King, and reduce it to order, if I may be heard. When I have soe done, I must plead against my selfe that an ambassador lives not in fitt honor. I could sooner dye then be subject to the slaverye the Persian is content with. A meaner agent would among these proud Moores better effect your busines. My qualety often for ceremonyes eyther begetts yow enemyes or suffers unwoorthely. The King hath often demanded an ambassador from Spayne, but could never obteyne it, for too reasons: first, because they would not give presents un-

---

[1] Hind. *dasturi*, 'that which is customary,' *i.e.* a commission, fee, or allowance.

[2] Forty seers went to the maund, and from eighty to a hundred pice to the rupee.

[3] Biddulph wrote to the Company at the end of the year that Roe's household charges, with his servants' wages, amounted to 500*l.* or 600*l.* per annum (*Letters Received*, vol. iv. p. 286).

woorthy their kings greatnes ; next, they knew his reception should not answere his qualety. I have moderated it according to my discretion, but with a swolne hart. Halfe my chardg shall corrupt all this court to bee your slaves ; and I assure yow I can doe yow better service at home ; and so desire yow to bid mee wellcome whensoever I come. I will not leave your busines unsettled ; nor willingly loose tyme to no purpose. I desier yow will examine my actions and accept my endeavours, and beleeve my hart is sincere to doe yow service.

PS.—The best way to doe your busines in this court is to find some Mogol that yow may enterteyne for 1000 *rup*[*ees*] by the yeare as your solicitor at court. Hee must bee authorised by the King, and then hee will better serve yow then ten ambassadors. Under him yow must allowe 500 *rup*[*ees*] for a nother at your port, to follow the Governor and Customers and to advertise his cheefe at court. These two will effect all. . . . Concerning privat trade, my opinion is yow absolutly prohibit yt and execute forfeyture, for your busines wilbe the better done. All your loss is not in the goods brought home. I see here the inconveniences yow thinck not off. I know this is harsh to all men, and seemes hard ; men professe they come not out for bare wages. Yow shall take away the plea if yow resolve to give very good, to mens content ; then yow know what yow part from. But yow must make good choyce of your servants and use fewer. . . . My minister is dead. . . . My cooke, most of my necessary servants are dead, and I am very much unfurnished. . . . My surgion is a bedrid man with long sicknes, whom I leave at Adsmere. . . . I have lived in a continuall hospitall, but am now remoeving into the ayer. . . . I have drancke water this 11 months, and nothing els. Rack [*i.e.* arrack] I cannot endure, and your strong waters I would not meddle with. I hoped yow would have sent mee a peice [*i.e.* cask] of wyne ; but now it is to late to wish. Trye a cup or two of my liquor in a morning next your harts and then yow will remember mee.[1] But I hope yow will send for me home by the next expected fleete, the chardge being more then my employment can merritt, and therfore I begg none now ; though I could have beene pleasd that your servants aboord, that make very merrie, had afforded mee some. When I was aboord the *Lyon*, it was an errand from Suratt to come to drinck ; but I am farr from the well. . . .[2]

[1] Another comfort Roe had missed was tobacco. He had expected to receive some from his friends by the fleet ; but, this failing, he wrote to Pepwell to buy him a supply, ' sweet, but not very strong, some four or five pounds, not exceeding 12*s.* the pound ' (f. 126).

[2] Enclosed in the letter is the note already mentioned of goods fit for presents or for sale at the court. These include table-knives,

November 25.—Six *course*. Hither came Mr. Crowther from the caravan despeeded from Agra; of whom I received that the plauge was violent, and that the last bills were made up to be payd at 45 days sight, so that they were enforced for dispatch to give so many *jangiers* [1] for their owne mony : that by the last of November the goods was like to passe by Adsmere. Which made me resolve to stay to speake with some of them, and to send my lettres and papers for England with more safetye.

TO SIR THOMAS SMYTHE.
(I.O. Records : *O.C.*, No. 410.[2])

From the way, midnight,
27 November, 1616.

Sir,
An hower after I had sealed my lettr to yow [3] in the way, the long expected messinger returnd from Spahan, whom

swords, gilt armour, precious stones, cloth of gold, looking-glasses, arras, pictures, wine ('strong waters are unrequested now '), dogs, ostrich plumes, silk stuffs (' but no blew : it is the coulor of mourners ' —cf. Terry), and ' generally, any rare knack to please the eye. These people are very curious and can judge of woorkemanship well ; but yow must fitt them with variety, for they are soone cloyd with one thing.'

An undated copy of this list in the I.O. Records (*O.C.* 636) has been wrongly assigned to March, 1618, in the *Calendar of State Papers* (*E. Indies*), 1617-21 (p. 145).

[1] Jahāngīr rupees, *i.e.* those coined since the accession of Jahāngīr, and consequently bearing his name. The rupees of the reigning monarch were reckoned worth a little more than those of his predecessors (Ovington's *Voyage to Surat*, p. 220). In Biddulph's accounts (*Factory Records, Miscellaneous*, vol. 25) the Jahāngīr rupee is calculated at 2*s.* 7*d.*

[2] This is the original, in Roe's own hand. It has been printed in full at p. 245 of vol. iv. of *Letters Received*. There is a copy in *Add. MS.* 6115, f. 149.

[3] Of the same date (not printed). It is entered at f. 147 of the MS. In it Roe gives his opinion of the abilities of the various factors, urges the punishment of the fugitive Jones, and touches on other topics. He adds : ' I am subject by long drincking water to a stomack collick, which mightely afflicts mee.'

Although dated 27 November, it is clear from the companion letter given above that this one was completed before the packet from Ispahān arrived on 23 or 24 November (see p. 300). Evidently Roe

I dispatchd with my lettres over land, and with one to the Shabas; in answere of which William Robbins returnd mee a lettre, the materiall poynts wherof I send yow. He promiseth hope of trade to profitt, but withall sayth Sir Robert Shirly hath confirmd at Goa a peace with the Viceroy. But, Sir, the summe is this: except the Sha-bas bee assurd that wee will fetch all his comodyte by sea, he will not loose his other wayes; and this shipp now sent in the heate of his expectation, with such goods as are not pleasing to him, will disgrace our great promises and hopes. If he take any dislike and thincks this is our uttmost, or at least a sample of our best comodityes, he will reject us quite, and cast off all thought of us, and eyther the more constantly resolve to goe thorough with the Spaniard or to make peace with the Turke. One of them he must doe. If I had beene made privy to the purpose of your servants at Suratt in sending a ship to Jasques, I could have prevented the hasard they runne; but yow may now see their hast, and lack of respect to mee. If I left them as they are, it were just; but I am to account to yow, and therfore by the assistance of this embassador, I will speedely write to the Kyng, and certefye him the reason of this ships arrivall, that was not fitted for Persia, but only putt in to see the port, and to show our forwardnes. I will entreat a contract for trade, that silke may bee sent downe for tryall, and that these goods may bee vented, and that he wilbe pleasd to give mee directions for such lading as will fitt him. Two things I warne yow of in this trade; that to bring up your goods, and fetch downe theirs at your own chardge 1000 mile, I fynd by experience heare will eate up your profitt; and, though the hart of Persia bee quieter and better governed, yet the way to Jasques is thorough Lar, that is scarce in good obedience, and subject to the robberyes of the Balooches. Therfore all caravans must have great guarde of horse, and this marrs the trafique of merchants and leaves it only fitt for the Kyngs power to effect. The second thing is that yow bee not engaged at Jasques in the same trouble and chardges you are at in Suratt. For I am enformed the roade is woorse, open to Ormus (not above five leaugs distant); soe that yow must be enforced to maynteyne a fleete for defence of the trader, or hazard her yearly. These two considerations made mee doubtfull of sending yet wher was so small ground of profitt, or, if any, it is not woorth chardge; and whensoever the Turke and Persian make peace (for their warrs are too monstruous to continew), this trade wilbe agayne diverted, for the Turke will not make any

at times finished and signed a letter, but did not date it until an opportunity occurred of sending it off, perhaps with a hasty postscript.

conclusion but with the libe ty of the free and ancient entercourse of trade. And observe one thing well : the parts of Persia that vent cloth (which in Steeles judgement will not exceed 500 a yeare—a small matter—and the rest wilbe expected to be supplyed in mony) are the same that produce the silke, and are nearest Turky, as Gordgestan and Gilan ; and to those parts cloth can be brought cheaper by Aleppo then by Jasques, the voyadge at sea and land both shorter ; and consequently silke will returne cheaper the same way and that in tyme will turne back the passadge. But I would not discourage yow in that I so extreamely desire, but only lett yow know that wee seeke yt not right from England nor with English comodytyes ; for it will never bee a trade exept yow can undertake for a great quantetye, wherof the numbers of cloth speecifyed will not bee an eighth part. And I cannot learne that any thing in England will succour yt, but that it must rise from the southward, by callicoes, *baftoes*,[1] shashes, spices, rubies of Pegu, and such like, with some mony. The use [which] can be made with yow of this ship is that, seeing Sir Robert Shirly hath beene stayd at Goa by Gods providence this yeare, that His Majestie wilbe pleasd to command his embassador resident in Spayne to be attentive upon the arrivall of Shirly, that when he hath delivered his message (which I assure yow he had instructions for before his comming out of Europe),[2] he may require an audience, and take notice of the Perssian overture, and require the Kyng of Spayne in the name of His Majestie not to prejudice the subjects of England by this new contract, for that the Persian hath already, by his command sealed, given them free trade, and upon assurance therof yow have sent a ship : that it is a free kyngdome, and if the peace or leauge bee made to the expulsion of our nation, it is a just occasion of breach, at least a great discurtesye ; and withall to declare that, if they proceede to exclude us, they must resolve of a warr in that quarter, for if they[3] cannot trade like merchants, they[3] will like men of warr, and then perhaps our share may bee as good as theirs. Thus will I tamper with the Sha-bas, to keepe him from a resolution ; for, whatsoever your factors thincks, I am peremptory in opinion all is lost and in vayne untill the issue of Shirleys imployment bee broken, and a contract made for

[1] Pers. *bāfta* (' woven '), a term used for several kinds of calico, especially those made in Gujarāt.

[2] Compare a passage in a letter from Roe to King James, 28 Nov. 1616 (f. 152): ' I judge that the suddeyne entertaynment of the overture, soe contrary to the resolution in beeing, arose out of some assurance and instructions brought by Shirly out of Spayne.'

[3] " Yow ' in the copy. This seems to be what is meant.

an ample trade to come downe to the port at the Persians chardge; for all the silke is his, and whensoever he can be sure to pass yt any way but by Turky, he will readely embrace yt. This is my opinion, which I submitt to yow; and, however your factors love to runne without mee, I will looke out to mend their faults and, like patient Job, pray and sacrifice for them, as he did for his sonnes whiles they banquetted. I pray, Sir, remember my love to Sir Jheames Lancaster, and doe me the favour to communicat to him this and my former opinions and discourses concerning Persia, both in my journalls and lettrs. I promisd them to him; but I can write no more then I have, nor in one lettre so amply.

This ledger [1] in Spahan was Arnold Lulls servant, and I beleeve is out with his master. He hath no matter in him, but language; in that I thincke no English man equalls him —French, Spanish, Italian, Turkish, Persian, and some others. I trust him not much, for that he is Shirlyes procurator; but yet I fynd he would fayne interest himselfe into your service, hoping so to compound and to returne to his countrye by your creditt, and to that end I thincke he would deliver up all Shirlyes busines into my bosome and betray him. But he is not woorth yt; only I show yow what use yow may make of him, if yow please. Thus, Sir, I beseech yow, deliver mee to the Comittees; for I am weary on the way, and write on my knees. . . .

November 28.—Mr. Young arrived, with whom I had much conference about the inconveniences of passing downe our goods so late, so incommodiously on camells, at so terrible chardg; wherin I found that only this parcell of goods, by the residence of factors unnessesarily, by wages of *peons*, by hyre of camells, and other duties, besides customes on the way and the damage in condition by falls and other inconveniences, with new horse and expence on the way, would cost 500 [*li.*] starling; but it was to late to remedye it, and wherin he, that desiered reformation, was condemned of ignorance and crossd in his particular affayres.

November 30.—The carravan arrived at Adsmere. The

[1] William Robbins, of whom see p. 109. ' Leiger ' (one who ' lies ' abroad) was often applied to a resident ambassador, as opposed to one sent on a temporary mission. Cf. *Measure for Measure*, IV. i. :

' Lord Angelo, having affairs to heaven,
Intends you for his swift ambassador,
Where you shall be an everlasting leiger.'

factors and a Polack,[1] who with divers fardles of indico with two Italians kept company to sell it at Suratt, came to my tents, wher I dispatchd my lettres and sett forward.

To Mr. Secretary Wynwoode.[2]
(*Add. MS.* 6115, f. 150.)
From the Camp of the Great Mogol, Emp[eror] of India.
30 November, 1616.

If my last,[3] sent Your Honour by the way of Aleppo, bee miscarried, this present discourse wilbe undependent and obscure; which causeth mee to send a transcript that yow may command from Sir Thomas Smyth. How farre that dessigne of bringing in the Spaniard by Sheirly had proceeded, and my poore opinion, that will enforme; with the present estate of the warrs ther in preparation. What hath succeeded, Your Honour shall receive: that Sheirley was stayed at Goa, by falling short eight dayes of his passadge this past yeare, wher hee was entertayned with honor and mayntenance;[4] which makes mee judge his offers and negotiation is gratious. The Shabas yet so depends on that hope that hee continewes the prohibition of exportation of silkes by Turky. Some few dayes since, I received advise from Spahan that Sheirley hath written to the King, that with much joy and ready embracement hee hath soe farre proceeded with the Viceroy of Goa in a conclusion of this league as his [*i.e.* the Viceroy's] commission hath power, and that hee is ready to embarque for Spayne to accomplish yt fully. If it proceed and take effect, I can make it evident that it will revive and strengthen all the ruines and decayes of the Portugall in the Indies, and make all other

[1] This seems to have been a certain Johannes Baptista Steucksy, a Pole by birth, who had for twelve years been engaged in the indigo trade at Agra (Terpstra, p. 75; *English Factories*, 1618-21, pp. 291, 314).

[2] Printed by Purchas (vol. i. p. 588), but without the name of the person addressed, and, as usual, with many errors and omissions. It need scarcely be mentioned that Sir Ralph Winwood was Secretary of State from 1614 to 1617.

[3] Not extant, but no doubt sent in the packet despatched overland in the previous February.

[4] In the letter to King James already mentioned (p. 314 *n*), Roe says that the Viceroy is stated to have given Sherley ten thousand crowns, with a further allowance of one thousand per month. This report Roe believes 'not to bee punctually true, because it is Shirlyes owne glorious realation.'

wavering Princes accept them only. I will not presse the consequence, wher it wilbe soe fully understood. The Shabas is in the feild at Salmas,[1] a villadge indifferent to the ways of Tavris or Gordgestan, attending the Turkes generall, who, with a monstruous army (if it be not increased by fame) is encamped at Argerome, irresolute which of those two attempts hee shall beginn with, beeing not above five dayes from the one, and ten from the other. But these great armies will dissolve of them selves, and I am of opinion ther wilbe noe great effect of them, the wynter approaching; and that they will treate a peace, which the Turke will never embrace but with the opening of the trade and liberty of ancient commerce; which, though the Persian yeild unto, yet, if the Spaniard accept his offers, the liberty given the Turke wilbe uselesse, for that the silkes shall come downe to Ormus. But I hope Your Honors will prevent yt. God hath provided yow leysure. The King of Persia lately enquired anew after the English, for hee is indifferent what Christian hath the trade, so that the Grand Signior loose yt. But his first offer to the Spaniard will take his turne, and after wee may have the leavings. Wee have sent to Jasques a ship from our port of Suratt with cloth and English goods, to make the first offer of a residence, and to gett a kind of a possession. For wher it was free to refuse or accept us, it wilbe nowe an injurie to turne us out, beeing come upon assurance of his lettre received by mee. But though I did not consent to the goeing of this ship, because I knew both the port unfitt, the goods unvendible and prejudiciall to the great expectation and promises—which makes mee feare the Sha-bas will despise us, and judge us by this beginning, and so with the more roundnes eyther conclude with the Spaniard or make peace with the Turke (for his dessigne is eyther wholy to divert the trade or nothing)—yet I will mend yt as well as I can, by the helpe of an ambassador lately arrived at this court; who, I suppose by his humilitye, is come to gett ayd of mony, in which kynd hee often fyndes liberall releefes, and this King of India may better spare then any monarch of the East. The advantage to bee made of yt in England is (if I may give my opinion) that when Sir Robert Sheirley shall arrive in Spayne and negotiat his employment, the ambassador of His Majestie resident may crave audience, and produce the lettres of the Persian granted to us [2] and urdge our possesion of the port; and therfore requier, in the name of His Majesty, that in this new contract either the English may bee comprehended, or at least that nothing passe on the part

---

[1] See p. 300. 'The Persians armie is 180,000 strong; the Turks double' (*note in margin*).

[2] 'I have sent the copyes' (*marginal note*).

of the King of Spayne prejudiciall to the subjects of His
Majestie, nor contrary to the ametye of the two nations.
Which if the Spaniard shall enterprise, to the expulsion of us,
it is in my opinion (the trade beeing in a free kingdome granted
us) a just cause of such a breach as may produce lettres of
mart and reprisall in all the eastern parts to right our selves.
I will in the meane tyme amuse the Persian with as many
doubts as I can infuse into him of the Spaniard, and hopes of us.

In this court, which is now in the feild towards the conquest
of Decan (with an effeminat army, fitter to bee a spoyle then a
terror to enemyes), I shall so far effect my imployment as to
confirme our trade and people on equall conditions to the
inhabitants and borne subjects, who suffer them selves abuses
of governors which can never be remedyed but by a whole
change of the regiment and forme of dominion. For the
constancy I will no farther give my woord then our owne
prosperitye, and the others feare, and the Portugalls feeblenes
shall confirme to us.

The trade is profitable and fitt for England, but no way
understood by the Company how to effect it at best advantage;
and [as ?] yett wee have done little but discover errors. I have
no power to meddle in that; but if I were at home tenn dayes,
I could doe them better service then here now in ten years.
To prove and demonstrate every particular and circumstance
were rather the subject of a booke then of a lettre. But I
will doe my part every way, according to my abilitye and
judgment, faythfully and honestly. Besides (though they may
thinck I speake for myne own ends), I assure Your Honor it
is not fitt to keepe an ambassador in this court. I have
shuffled better out and escaped and avoyded affronts and
slavish customes clearer then ever any did. I am allowed
rancke above the Persian, but hee outstripps mee in rewards;
his master lyes neere us. But His Majestie commanded mee
to doe nothing unwoorthy the honor of a Christian king, and
noe reward can humble mee to any basenes. I see what the
Persian does and suffers. I know one that might creepe and
sue would effect more busines then I; for every little matter
cannot trouble the King, and his great men are more proud,
and expect that from mee I cannot give them. The King of
Spayne could never bee drawne to send any, and their experience hath taught them that, besides hee should not bee
received in honor correspondent to his qualetye, they know
an easyer way to effect their ends. I shall not returne a rich
man, and then many will condemne mee for want of providence
or witt to gett yt; but they know not the Indies, nor mee; it
growes heere in as rough wayes as in Europe. I will trust to
the Company, and to my meritt.

I could write Your Honor many remarckable accidents in

this goverment and kingdome. All the policye and wicked craft of the Divill is not practised alone in Europe; here is enough to bee learned, or to be despisd. But yow have not leysure to entertayne so forreyne discourses. That part which may bee woorth knowing—as the proceedings of the Jesuitts, the growth of their church, the commixture of this kingdome with Europe by trades, and the allyes it embraces—if I fynd not leysure to putt them into methode, I will weary Your Honor with them by a firesyde, in broken peices.

The Portugall pursues us here with violent hatred; but God doth chastise him, and his pride sees it not.[1] ... All these considered, mee thincks the heavenes conspire the fall of the Portugall in this quarter, if His Majestie would be pleased to bend only his royall countenance. But I shall (I hope) returne and not expect to see it effected in my tyme.

I will intreat Your Honor to preserve my name in the Kings memorie, not for any woorthynes, but an humble desire to serve him; and that yow wilbe pleased to accept of my endeavours, and esteeme mee such as I am, one that loves and honors yow, and that will pray to God, as the best expression of my affection, to encrease yow in all woorthy honor, and to blesse yow with His Holy Spiritt.

[PS.]—I humbly desire Your Honor to doe me the favour to thanck Sir Thomas Smyth in my behalfe, that he may fynde my gratitude in my frends.

To the East India Company.[2]
(I.O. Records; *O.C.* No. 411.)

December 1, 1616.

I have deferrd to write yow my full judgement of some particular to this day, that I might enforme my selfe fully of yt; which I could not doe untill your caravan despeeded from Agra with goodes this yeare were come neare mee, that I might speake with Robert Young.... Your goods are this day short of Adsmere 15 *courses*, and cannot arrive in Suratt before the end of January. The chardge is so unreasonable that I doubt not it will make evident the truth of my opinion for the disposition of factoryes. I have looked into the account, and the expence only of your factors (besides their wages), with the hire of camells, guards, and other chardge on the way before they arrive at Suratt, will cost yow 500 *li.* starling; and untill the investment, ther was not taken by

[1] An account of the destruction of the carrack is here given.

[2] Printed in *Letters Received*, vol. iv. p. 249. There is a copy in Add. MS. 6115 (f. 153).

residence there one *rupy*. I assure yow it is the like at Amadavaz in proportion, for every factory keepes servants, horses, and severall howses ; which beeing once yearly supplyed from Suratt, might in three monthes effect all the busines. If the court remoove to Agra, in respect of sales it wilbe necessary to keepe servants, and at Brampore during the warr ; but otherwise it will never pay horsemeate, and yow had neede save all unnessessary disbursments to advance your stock for tyme of imployment.

Wheras yow write for new factoryes, except the silkes of Bengala require yt (which yet in my opinion is had cheeper at Agra then yow will fynd it there, to maynteyne a factory for yt, beeing this people travell and live hardlyer then yours can), I am of opinion your residences are sufficient, and best chosen as they are ; and the disposure of them I have mentioned in my last to the consultation at Suratt, but what creditt it will carry I know not ; but I will lay this as a rule ; yow will sooner want stock to employ in these places then new residences to buy in. Agra alone sends 20 or 30 thowsand *chourlles* [see p. 237*n*] yearly to Persia and Turky ; many have three or foure years indico on their hands ; the *semianoes* are in abundance and cheape ; the silke of Bengala plenty at reasonable rates ; muscke, civitt, and many sorts of pretty stuffs which yow never saw, made in Bengala and other parts, which in my opinion would make good profitt. Amadavaz alone is able to lade yow two great shipps, and makes many stuffs. Cambaya nere yt, with fine grograms or chamletts. And Baroch is the best cloth in India ; for though Bengala and Syndu have as fine, yet it is farr fetchd, and here yow may bespeake what sorts yow will, what length, breadth, and finenes, and buy it from the loome at the best hand. So that in conclusion yow may employ a treeble stock to that yow send, in these places only, to the best advantage every way. And for sales of such grosse goods as teeth, lead, and cloth, the court only will vent the one and Suratt the other, in quantetyes. Tynn, if it bee fyne, is better sould then lead. I know not if yow send any, for I could never yet see any of your invoyces or commissions. Another rule is that yow dispose your factors in your commissions so to sort the buyinge of goods as they consider the places to fitt. Comodityes of greatest bulk, that eates much in carriadge, nearest your port ; finer goods will better beare the chardge. And this they ought to observe in disposition of places for sales ; for your transport up and downe is a terrible chardge, when yow cast it up. Make your observation only of these goods bought now at Agra and on the way.

I will venture one conceipt of myne more : that if silke at Agra bee fitt for your profitt, and *semianoes* and other small goods, that all your court stock bee imployed in them, and no indico ; for although the finest bee ther to bee had, yet the chardge is untollerable to bring it two monthes journy ; and the people of this country can transport it much cheaper then yow, and would, if that course were once begunn, to buy it off their hands at Suratt. Yow had better give four *rupias* in a *maune* more for it there then at Agra : the carriadge only of a fardell is five or six *rupies* downe, besides peons and expence on the way and many petty dutyes. To effect this, I could wish yow gave order to trye one yeare, and to forbeare buying at Agra, and to fitt your selves in Suratt ; though yow payd deare, it will quitt the cost. Ther is to bee had a shipps lading of the best sorts of ould indico, that lyes in the hands of chapmen to sell for the Redd Sea ; which if the English tooke off, and they once saw yow beginn that course and the other forborne, yow should bee fitted at better rates (your travell and expence considered) then yow can bee at Agra ; for yow beare much losse in passadge downe, and your goods often take damage. I assure yow this is a better course then yow yet thinck off ; and though perhaps some may be agaynst it, yet consider that men love to live at liberty and to travell ; the place unseene is ever best ; and that desier prevayles upon many mens judgements. But if ther be no remedy but to continew this course, then lett me perswade yow to command your servants to send downe your goods by cart, and not by cammell. One will carry three of the others loade, and will travell farther in a day ; for the cammell, lading and unlading with so little helpe, hath but five howers to goe ; the cart, which is never unladen, will march all day. Besides it is a third cheaper in the hier, they require not soe many attendants, and your goods take noe harme ; wheras from cammells they often fall, and every night at unlading catches bruses to great losse. Your goods, I know, wilbe in condition 100 *li.* better ; and lastly, lesse subject to theeves, who can slipp a cammell behynd a bush, in soe great numbers not easely missd, and one man cannot looke to five or six alwayes. Lastly, command to bring yow of all sorts of stuffs two or three peices. As farr as I am able, I will buy of everything somwhat ; and if I loose by them, yow (I hope) will ease mee. Here are many sorts and many kinds of callicoes which yow never saw ; and one like diaper of great breadth, fitt for tables, and narrow, for towells suteable. It is in vayne for mee to talke to your factors of these matters. They eyther love not that I should understand yt, or els crosse yt because I doe. But I could save yow so much yearly, by disposition only of your busines (if yow durst creditt mee), as would buy yow 500 *chuorls* of indico. When I come home, I will discourse it lardgely ; in the meane tyme I pray only compare the chardge of way of

S.T.R.   X

this caravan of 170 camells with others farr lesse, and yow shall fynd it is in the husbandry of your servants to ease many expences. My freedome in your busines I desier yow to take in good part. And for your priviledges, I will so watch, yow shall susteyne no wrong in silence, nor (I hope) without redresse. The past yeare is a good example. And what I write, when yow have considered it, make it not publique. Soe, in hast on the way, I committ yow to God.

December 1.—I remooved 4 *course* to Ramsor [see p. 298 n], wher the King had left the bodyes of 100 naked men slayne in the feilds for robbery ; and the caravan at midnight departed Adsmere.

December 2.—7 *course*.

December 3.—I rested, by reason of rayne.

December 4.—5 *course*. I overtooke in the way a cammell laden with 300 mens heads, sent from Candahar by the Governor in present to the King, that were out in rebellion.

December 5.—5 *course*.

December 6.—4 *course*. Wher I overtooke the King at a walled towne called Todah,[1] in the best country I saw since my landing, beeing a faire champion [*i.e.* level, open country]; at everie *course* a village, the soyle fruictfull in corne, cotten, and cattle.

December 7.—The King remooving, I sent for the Jesuite and communicated with him the lettrs received [see p. 300], who undertooke the conveyance and brake open that directed to Xavier,[2] as his sublegatt ; which concerned only the recovery of goods, prosecution of justice, and constitution of the factory under the sayd Jhoanni Galicio, and mentioned that the consull of the English had undertaken to procure my assistance, and to that end had sent lettres, which I never saw, and thought that, notwithstanding such promise made to his

[1] In Jaipur state, 63 miles S.W. of Jaipur and 65 E.S.E. from Ajmer.

[2] Xavier had recently proceeded to Goa (see *Letters Received*, vol. iv. p. 248). Roe's letter to Corsi (in Latin) on this occasion, dated 4 Dec., is given on f. 210 of the MS. It informs him of the receipt of the letters and invites his help in securing their delivery. Roe says that his tents will be found near the Ajmer road (*prope viam Adesmerinam*) and are distinguishable by the English flag, bearing a red cross.

partners, hee would neyther discover himselfe to mee nor that hee durst not to them. But finding my countriman interessed in yt, I resolved that Galicio should repayre to court, and furnish himselfe with what testemony he could concerning Bonellis estate; and in requiring justice of the King, I would testefye with him his authoritye to prosecute the cause, and give him all fitt assistance. To this end I caused the Jesuite to dispatch a currier with the particular lettres to the said Galicio and other instructions fitt, leaving the principall to bee copied and translated by the padre against his arrivall.

The King passd only from on syde of the towne to the other; which was one of the best built I ever saw in Indya, for that ther were some howses two storyes high, and most such as a pedler might not scorne to keepe shop in, all covered with tile. It had beene the seate of a *Raza Rasboote* before the conquest of Ecbarsha; and stood at the foote of a great rock, very strong, had many excellent woorkes of hewed stone about yt exellently cutt, many tancks, arched, vawted, and discents made, lardge and of great depth. By it stood a delicat grove of two mile long, a quarter broad, planted by industry with mangoes, tamerins, and other fruicts, devided with walkes, and full of little temples and alters of pagods and gentiliticall idolatrye, many fountaynes, wells, tancks, and summer howses of carved stone, curiously arched; so that I must confesse a banished Englishman might have beene content to dwell there. But this observation is generall, that ruine and distruction eates up all; for since the proprietye of all is come to the King no man takes care for particulars, so that in every place appeares the vastations and spoyles of warr without reparation.

December 8.—I received lettres from Adsmere that the *Cutwall* offered to turne the factors and our goods out of the house given us, which they resisted. I had not visited the King; but dispatchd a lettre to Asaph Chan for his prohibition, who was gone three *course* to hunt, and a note from him would suffice. My messenger mett him on the way, riding in hast to the King, but [he] desiered mee at night to come to the *gushelĭchan*. Which I did, and was well used and entertayned; but first demanded what present I had at my new comming, and answeering none, hee proceeded to ordinary questions of hunting. I found His Majestie so neere druncke (which hee finished within halfe an hower), that I had not oportunitye to move busines to him. He sate by a fier in furres by a tancke syde. Here I mett the Persian embassador, who telling mee a long tale in his language, I answered in English, much to our mutuall edification ; but I putt into his hand a copy of his masters command for the commerce of our nations, and at parting made him understand I desird a conference.

December 9.—In the morning I sent to him, that I would visitt him according to my offer and confer upon some busines which concernd his master, but that hee had neglected that civilitye which I expected ; or, if he durst not speake with mee, I would advise the Shabas of his fashion towards mee. He returned answer hee had beene in noe faulte, but the incomoditye of the journy and the forme of this kingdome had hindered him to performe that was fitt ; but entreated mee to come to his tents on the morow, which curtesye he would repay whensoever I called him, and hee would effect any desier of myne toward his master, and in all things further the ametye hoped for betweene our soveraynges.

I went to Asaph-Chan, and after mutuall complements and offering me a roome in his quarter (which I accepted off without purpose to use yt, for that it is impossible to observe limitts soe strictly as to avoyde quarrells, which dayly happen about them), I desiered his warrant for the continewance of our house in Adsmere ; which hee instantly wrote and signed, and I dispeeded. I acquaynted him with the faire and noble usadge of his brother in law, the Governor of Cambaya [see pp. 128 *n*, 290], which hee tooke gratefully, assuring mee that all the ports and officers in His Majestis dominions had order to entreat us frendly, and to protect us from injury, if wee drewe not occasion upon ourselves by misdemeanor. Returning I veiwed the *leskar*, which is one of the woonders of my little experience, that I had seene yt finished and sett up in four howers (except some of great men that have double provision), the circuitt beeing little lesse then 20 English mile, the length some wayes three *course*, comprehending the skirts ; and [in ?] the middle, wherin the streets are orderly, and tents joynd, are all sorts of shops and distinguished so by rule that every man knowes readely were to seeke his wants, every man of qualetye and every trade beeing limited how farr from the Kings tents he shall pitch, what ground hee shall use, and on what syde, without alteration;[1] which as it lyes togither may equall almost any towne in Europe for greatnes. Only a muskett shoott every way no man approcheth the *atasckanha* [see p. 262] royall, which is now kept so strict that none are admitted but by name; and the tyme of the *durbar* in the eveninge is omitted and spent in hunting or hawking on tanckes by boate; in which the King takes woonderfull delight, and his barges are remooved on carts with him, and hee sitts not but one the syde of one, which are many tymes a mile or two over. At the *jarruco* in the morning, hee is seene, but busines or speech prohibited. All is concluded at night at the *guzelchan*, when often the tyme is prevented by a drowzines which poss[es]eth His Majestie from the fumes of Backus.

Ther is now a great whisper in court about a new affinitye of Sultan Corsoronne and Asaph-Chan, and great hope of his liberty. I will fynd occasion to discourse it, for that the passages are very woorthy, and the wisdome and goodnes of the King appeares above the malice of others, and Normahall fullfill[s] the observation that in all actions of consequence in a court, especially in faction, a woman is not only alwayes an ingredient, but commonly a principall drugg and of most vertue; and shee showes that they are not incapable of conducting busines, nor herselfe voyd of witt and subtiltye. It will discover a noble prince, an excellent wife, a faythfull counceller, a crafty stepmother, an ambitious sonne, a cunning favorite: all reconciled by a patient king, whose hart was not understood by any of all these.[2] But this will requier

---

[1] In a letter of 24 Dec. 1616 (f. 157 of the MS.) Roe tells the Ahmadābād factors that ' your lettres will fynd mee in the *leskar* on the west syde from the Kings tents, but by my selfe, out of the throng; wherby I may be better found. I have two neighbours hould the same course. The one is Raja Bieman [Rāja Bhimma ?], by whose quarter I may bee alway discovered.'

[2] On the 30th of the preceding month Roe had written to Lord Pembroke (f. 152) that he hoped to reduce his observations ' into a

a place alone, and not to bee mingled amonge busines, which this day I received from Suratt, of extreame injuryes offered our nation and new broyles begunn to the hazard of our peace ; but as they only send mee complaynts, and deteyne the presents which should enable mee to effect their redresse, so they mingle their owne grevances with confession of misurable misdeameanors committed by the disorder of them selves, which noe warning of myne I see can prevent, when such liberty is given to all saylors and base rascalls to dishonor and disquiett us. Besides, I find not the principall free from all blame and occasion, for by want of judgment and an opinion of liberty neyther granted nor fitt for them to use, they incurr just displeasur, and yt breakes out into fury on both sydes ; for the officers as fast complayne of us as wee of them, and desier mee to send a sober discreet man to governe our nation, which I have noe power in ; so that I cannot tell at what end to beginn. The Prince is abscent ; our enterpreter cast off ; myselfe without presents or toong.[1] Yet I doubt not once more to reconcile this brawle to content of all sydes, if they please not to it on every occasion. This rule I ever lay : wee can never live without quarrell (which ingendreth often greater strifes, and the innocent suffer indifferently with the guilty) untill our commanders take order that noe man come to Suratt but on just occasion and of civill carriage, and the cape merchant so moderate such as come that, for the glory of open house, they give not liberty

meethood, and though this kingdome almost concerne not Europe, yet the historye may, as well as some of those that are farthar remooved by tymes past, and for subject perhaps as woorthy.' It is to be regretted that he never found the time to carry out his intention.

[1] ' Jaddow hath refused the wages assigned by yow and in our greatest neede forsaken us, and I am soe without any linguist that I cannot answere the King what it were a clock. . . . The plauge is at Agra in extreame violence, and this journy a worse plauge to mee, who, weakened by many crosses, decay in my strength and am by fluxes unfitt for travell or the feilds ; and. which is yet more troublesome, am sicker in mynd.'—Roe to Surat, 12 Dec. 1616 (*Add. MS.* 6115, f. 155).

The difference with the broker seems to have been smoothed over, for Roe on the 14th sent an urgent message to him, and he rejoined him on the 24th.

of excesse and drincking. For what civill town will endure a stranger by force to open in the streetes the close chayres [*i.e.* doolies] wherin their weomen are carried (which they take for a dishonor equall to a ravishment) ?[1]

December 12.—I dispatched the *patamar* back for Suratt, with order to direct the expected *caffela* [see p. 141] to court the shorter way. Concerning their complaynt, I wrote to the Governor and Admirall to give speedye redresse, or to expect such issue as the Kings justice would affoord mee. Meanes to enforme the King I had none, for want of our solicitor and linguist. With him I sent a lettre from the Prince, commanding his officers to certefye by the customers booke the debt of Zulphe[carcon], which I could not procure from our owne factors.

December 14.—I sent a *patamar* to Adsmere to hasten the comming of Jadow.

December 15.—Mr. Fettiplace arrived at the *leskar* from Agra, beeing out of busines and leaving Mr. Shallbanck with the goods, who determined to lock up the howse and to remoove to Fettipoore [Fatehpur Sīkri] for the vehement rage of the plauge, now their next neighbowre.

[1] The letters from Surat referred to will be found in *Factory Records, Surat,* vol. 84, part i., under date 18 and 20 Nov. 1616, and the principal one is printed in *Letters Received,* vol. iv. (p. 343). They record several quarrels between the English and the natives. One of these was caused by a sailor ' who (out of ignorance, not knowinge the costom) stopped and opened a *dowled* in the street to see whatt it contayned, but, seing therin a woman, desisted from further wronge and lett it passe.' Another, which led to a riot, personal violence to Kerridge, and a strict boycott of the factory, was due to a bell-turret which had been erected on the English house ; the matter was settled by its dismantlement. Yet a third was brought about by the action of the English admiral. Some Portuguese frigates hovering at the mouth of the river seized a native vessel laden with water-casks belonging to the English, whereupon Pepwell seized a vessel leaving Surat, which he believed to be Portuguese property. This was much resented by the natives, and the English factory was again boycotted until the prize was surrendered.

Roe's reply to the Surat factors (a quotation from which is given above) will be found at f. 155 of the MS. He mentions a rumour that Jahāngīr intended to make a stay at Ranthambhor for several months.

December 17.—Mr. Fettiplace departed to Adsmere to remayne with the goods.

December 18.—I visited the King, who having beene at his sports, and his quarry of foule and fish lyeing before him, hee desired mee to take my choyse ; and so distributed the remayner to his nobilitye. I found him sitting on his throwne, and a begger at his feet, a poore silly ould man, all ashd, ragged, and patched, with a young roage attending him. With these kinde of professed poore holy men the country abounds, and are held in great reverance ; but for woorks of chastisment of their bodyes and voluntary sufferings they exceed the braggs of all heritiques or idolatres. This miserable wretch, clothd in raggs, crownd with feathers, covered with ashes, His Majestie talked with about an hower, with such familiarity and show of kindnes that it must needs argue an humilitye not found easely among kings. The begger sate, which his [*i.e.* the King's] sonne dares not doe. Hee gave the King a present, a cake, ashed, burnt on the coales, made by him selfe of course grayne ; which the King accepted most willingly, and brake one bitt and eate yt, which a daynty mouth could scarce have done. After hee tooke the cloute and wrapt it up and putt in the poore mans bosome and sent for 100 *rup*[*ias*], and with his owne hands powered them into the poore mans lap, and what fell besides gathered up for him. When his collation of banqueting and drinck came, what soever hee tooke to eate, hee brake and gave the begger halfe ; and after many strange humiliations and charetyes rising, the ould wretch not beeing nimble, hee tooke him up in his armes, which noe cleanly bodye durst have touchd, embracing him ; and three tymes laying his hand on his hart, calling him father, hee left him, and all us, and me in admiration of such a virtue in a heathen prince. Which I mention with envye and sorrow, that wee, having the true vyne, should bring forth crabbs, and a bastard stock grapes : that either our Christian princes had this devotion or that this zeale were guided by a true light of the gospell.

December 21.—I received from Amadavaz of their dispatches for the fleete, as full of complaynts that they are kept in ignorance as I, and that they conveyed a command sent by mee for their redresse to Suratt; which I doubt not will appease all troubles.

December 23.—Being short about three *courses* of a citty called Rantepoore,[1] wher it was supposed the King would rest, and consult what way to take, hee suddenly turned toward Mandoa [Māndu], but without declaration of any resolution; in my judgment rather sent that way by the feare of the plauge in Agra, then any desire of approaching the warr; for wee marched every other day only about four *courses*, with a baggage almost impossible to bee ordered.

December 24.—I received from Adsmere that the factors continewed in their house and that our brookar Jaddow was in the way; for whose arrivall I deferred my intention of mooving the King to heare the busines of the severall complaynts from Suratt; for a redresse by *firmaens* from the Prince is but momentary and scarce effectuall. Jaddow my enterpreter arrived, and wee made new contract.

December 25.—I rested.

December 26.—Wee passed thorowgh woods and over mountayns, torne with bushes, tyred with the incomodityes of an impassible way, wher many camells perished. Many departed for Agra, and all complayned. I lost my tents and carts, but by midnight wee mett. The King rested two dayes, for that the *leskar* could not in lesse tyme recover their order; many of the Kings woemen, and thowsands of coaches, carts, and camells lyeing in the woody mountaynes without meate and water. Him selfe gott bye on a small eliphant, which beast will clime up rocks and passe such streights as noe horse nor beast that I know can follow him.

I received answere from Suratt full of dispute, but no certeyntye, neither of the expected presents nor conclusion

---

[1] Ranthambhor, a fort in Jaipur state, on an isolated rock. Jahāngīr's encampment appears to have been near the village of Kasthāla (called Khūsh Tāl in the *Memoirs*), about ten miles S.W. of Ranthambhor.

The Emperor's route, though given in some detail in his *Memoirs*, is by no means easy to follow on modern maps. For a list of the stages, see Beni Prasad's *History of Jahangir*, p. 287.

of Zulph[ecarcons] debt, nor busines of moment.[1] With it a lettre from Captain Pepwell, much complayning of disrespects towards him, of the cape merchannts obstinacye, and of opening and deteyning his lettres of advise sent to mee, his opinions of his future voyadge by want of stock, and requiring my opinions what course to runne if enforced as a man of warr. I dispatched a packett to Amadavaz.[2]

December 29.—Wee sate by the river of Chambett [*i.e.* the Chambal].

To Captain Pepwell.[3]
(*Add. MS.* 6115, f. 171.)

The *Leskar*, December 30, 1616.

.... Concerning the presents : though few in number and in kind ordinary, yet if they had beene dispeeded in tyme, [they] might have som way supplyed other defects ; but their deteyning hath not only disarmed mee of all meanes to sollicite the King, but so shamed mee that I forbeare to visitt him, beeing empty handed now six monthes, and yet dayly advised to give, and provokd to yt by his owne demands. Asaph Chan, that absolutly governs all, will not open his mouth untill his hands be filled. . . . If the strong waters only advised for had come heither by the middle of November, they had sould in the *leskar*, wher no wine can be brewed, at any rate such as will not bee seene in any suddeyne oportunitye. . . . These men [*i.e.* the Surat factors] doe and will make a great mistery of their sckill (like others in other kynds), but I pray lett them know I know, except in an account (wherin none of these can bragg), an easy man can doe all their busines, and that here is none such that can chalenge to him selfe any great profoundnes in the secretts of a true and good merchant. . . . It is happy that the gentellmen take no liking to stay here, for repentance to them, inconvenience to the Company, would ensue. . . . The minister and servants commended by yow I will willingly and thanckfully receive, and will use as befitts

[1] The letter referred to seems to be one of 29 Nov., for which see *Factory Records, Surat*, vol. 84, part i. f. 120.

[2] Containing two letters, dated 24 and 26 Dec. (see ff. 157, 158 of the MS.).

[3] A very long letter, answering Pepwell's complaints against Kerridge, and discussing the Persian venture, the proper relations between 'generals' of fleets and the chief merchants on shore, the disorders of the sailors, and so on.

mee and they deserve. I feare only they wilbe too fine and high to doe offices of servants, which I cheefly want, especially a cooke ; and in the Kings and Companyes service one might have beene commanded to attend mee, for I cannot want my meate with safety nor honor ; but if it cannot bee but by strong hand, I care not for such servants, and I will shift out. . . .

January 1, 1616-17.—I sent to Asaph-Chan to acquaynt him with the injuries of Suratt.

January 2.—Hee promised to write to the Prince, but desiered conference with me.

January 3.—I visited Asaph-Chan and propounded to him the substance of the complaynts : the taking a Portugall frigott, the reason, and the pressure of Sultan Caronns officers to deliver back. Hee went [1] from his woord to entermeddle in the Princes goverment, but if I would presse him, hee would make petition to the King ; but advised mee to waigh it well : the necessitie of the Princes favour (which hee would undertake was not acquaynted with this new brawle) : that if I complayned I might perhaps procure some checke to the Prince, but withall the busines would come to examination, and our owne faults would bee reckoned and objected, the issue of judgment doubtfull, and the Prince would remayne an unreconciled enemy. I answered I had forethought all this, and was as unwilling to complaynts as hee could bee, but that the desease was such as required a desperat remedy : but if in his wisdom hee would direct mee in a better course, I was ready to follow yt. This I did because, the injuryes beeing personall, they were recanted and reconciled, and my advertisements were soe in and out that I knew not whether they wished accusation or no, and we[r]e mingled not only with confusions [confessions ?] of our owne misdeameanors, but with intimations of greater layed to their chardge, which, though denyed, yet they feared would bee justifyed by perjurye, a small faulte among Moores. Asaph Chan replyed hee was very glad to see mee inclinable to a quiett way ; and though hee would not write, yet hee thus advised : that for the boate and goods taken wee should keepe her, for the Port[ugals] having begunn the injury, it was reason wee should requite it, and no exception

---

[1] Probably we should read : ' He said that he went.'

should bee taken at it ; the covetousnes of the Princes officers for some bribe was the reason of the remanding it, not any favour to them [*i.e.* the Portuguese] ; for the complaynts, hee wished mee to stay untill the presents arrived, and at their deliverie to the King to aske leave to goe to Brampoore to visitt the Prinnce, and, without mentioning particular offences, crave his lettre in generall tearmes to command his sonne to receive mee, to heare mee in what soever I desired, and to doe justice to our nation, suffering none to doe them force, and to grant what farther priviledges I should fittly propound ; which lettre hee would procure, and such a course would signifie my respect to the Prince, to whom I should, with some fitt present, deliver a breefe of all complaynts ; and having procured such justice as I desired and settled my busines with him, I might returne to court in double grace, and hee would write with mee to procure me content. This councell was such as I had taken before in myne owne purpose with little difference, and such as necessitye showed mee to bee the right way ; for I had experience by a Portugall what issue of complaynts against the Prince would follow, formall remedy but full revenge ; and seeing it was necessarie that I must visitt him, I was loath to exasperat him against my wellcome, and I found that, if my occasions would have permitted mee to give all my attendance and respect to him, *delinire ambitiosum*,[1] I should easiely compasse him ; so that I resolved to spare him as much as I could, and by myne owne travell overcum that I could not doe by opposition, and thus sett forward my purpose ; that the King was declared for Mandoa and the nobilitye sent all in hast to build, which beeing but eight dayes from Brampoore, it was as good as to sitt in the feilds ; and in that tyme I might provide a house by the Kings favour or buyld it if constrayned. At noone I visited the Persian ambassador, beeing the first tyme eyther of our leysurs would permitt yt. Hee receeved mee with great respect and curtesy. After complements, I generally propounded the settling of a trade, the conditions wee required, the comoditye to his master, and our forwardnes in sending a ship this yeare to Jasques upon his masters *firmaen*. Hee answered mee that his king greatly

[1] *I.e.* to flatter the Prince's pride.

affected the comming of the Christians, especially the English, but that Shirly was now sent to make offer of the ports to Spayne. But understanding from mee some inconveniences, wee resolved to dispeed a post to the Shabas ; and hee required mee to propound my desiers in writing, and hee would send them his master, as well to procure the salles of the cloth now landed as to provide in future for a fitt cargazon and residence on both parts. Hee made me a banquett of ill fruicts, but beeing a good fellow it appeared well. In his curtesyes hee exceeded all my entertaynment in India, rayled at the court, at the Kings officers and councell, and usd a strange libertye. I answered that I meddled [not ?] in cencure of other mens busines : I desired to effect myne owne. Hee offered to bee my linguist, desiered mee to pitch my tents by him, and whatever I would propound to the King hee would deliver ; assuring mee the King had divers tymes made honorable mention of mee, and expressed a desire to give mee all content. I seemed to accept of these favours, but suddenly knew not howe to trust them ; but determined to consider it, for it appeard a faire way and a harty motion. From hence hee proceeded to some vanetyes of his masters purpose to take Aleppo, that hee had conquered Babilon, and as his advises came hee would send them mee ; and desired mee to mention him to my soveraigne in my next lettres and in these to his master. The conclusion of busines betweene us is included in my advise to Kerridge in prosecution of his designe and in the demands to the Shabas, which was the substance agreed on in this conference. At my departur hee offered mee with much earnestnes a faire horse well furnished, which was brought to the doore, but I was as bountifull in refusing. Hee pressd mee the earnester, but not prevayling sent for nine peices of Persian stuffs, silke, and nine bottles of wyne, that I might not depart without some testemony of his love. I answered to effect my desiers with his master should bee the only pledges I would accept, wherin hee should do mee most frendship and him most service and honor : that I acknowledged his magnificence by his offers, but hee should not beginn a frendship at such cost : I could exchange a good hart, but had nothing, beeing a stranger, to requite curtesye of that nature. Hee looking earnestly upon my swoord, I offered it, but hee by example refused it. At night I visited the King, who spent his tyme sadly with an ould man after reading long lettres, and few spake to him. At his rising, he gave this gentellman that sate by him, a criple for age, 5,000 *rup*[*ias*], and with many embracements tooke his leave. Passing by, hee bowed to mee. The Persian ambassador mett here, where renewing complements, and repenting that hee refused my swoord, which hee fancied, hee fayerly beggd it, professing that liberty among frends was good manners in his countrye.

January 4.—I sent my swoord.[1]

January 5.—I dispeeded answere to Suratt with my advise and conference with the Persian ambassador, and his opinion; and to Adsmere what I conceived fitt for the disposure of that factory.[2]

January 6.—I translated the articles to send the Shabas, according to conclusion. Coppyes of all are regestred.[3]

January 7.—These dayes were consumed on the way, every other remooving about four or five *courses*. Wee sate on the goodly river of Shynd.[4]

January 8.—I dispeeded the articles to the King of Persia, with lettres to Robbyns, by a currier of the embassador, and sent coppyes.

[1] Value five pounds (Roe's Accounts).

[2] The letter to Fetiplace at Ajmer is given at f. 159 of the MS. In it Roe advises the factors to proceed to Fatehpur Sīkri, since the plague is raging at Agra, and Ajmer is both unsuitable and unsafe. He also asks that his surgeon, Christopher Green, may be sent on to him, if well enough, with some money for his expenses on the way.

For the letter to Surat see *Letters Received*, vol. v. p. 325. One to Capt. Pepwell, dated 4 Jan., will be found at p. 317 of the same volume.

[3] See *Add. MS.* 6115, f. 211. The articles have not been reproduced, as they are sufficiently summarised in the letter to Robbins. As will be seen later, they never reached the Shāh.

[4] The Kālī Sind, a branch of the Chambal.

To William Robbins at Ispahan.
(*Add. MS.* 6115, f. 166.)[1]

17 January 1616[-17].

... Breefly our desier is, first, that a port bee secured by the King, free for us alone or for all indifferently, wher wee may land our goods, and such priveledges granted to us as in such cases are requisite ; and next, that some agrement bee made and sett of prices indifferently on both sides, according to the condition of the comodityes ; lastly, that His Majestie command his silks to bee brought downe yearly, at the seazon, to the port (which is easier then the way of Aleppo), or to some indifferent citty, not far up, wher our factors may constantly and securely reside for a staple mart, as at Stoade or Middleborough,[2] that wee bee not enforced to seeke and travell to unprofitable marketts. A trad thus settled wilbe dureable, and by continuance increase, wheras shuffling and unstable courses one syde will relinquish by incomoditye. To this purpose, and to showe our forwardnes, wee have now sent a ship to Jasques, to unlade cloth and other goods, with our factors to attend the pleasure of His Majestie ; and though the comoditye bee not in quantety nor qualety such as may give the King any great encouragement, yet hee shall see our desiers and will not judge us by this beginning, for that wee came not purposely for the place, but to trye and settle our enterteynment. To this end I have sent His Majestie articles firmed by mee and commended by his embassador, which if yow will sollicite that the cloth may bee taken off, and, for the future, a certeyne course and residence dessigned, and a *firmaen* both what sorts and quantetyes of goods, eyther of Europe, India, Chyna, or the Sowth Islands, His Majestie will require, wee will then roundly and duly fullfill his desire, that hee shall find the profitt in his owne coffers and in the weakening his greatest enemy. If this cannot bee effected, it is not woorth labor ; wee shall both deceive and bee deceived. For wee ayme not at gnatts and small flyes, but at a commerce honorable and equall to two so mighty nations. Yow shall

---

[1] There is another copy in the I.O. Records (*O.C.*, No. 434), endorsed as received 5 March (at Ispahān ?) and in London, by way of Aleppo and Marseilles, 26 November, 1617. This has been printed in full in *Letters Received*, vol. v. (p. 50). The date of the letter is clearly wrong, though it appears in both copies. Probably the 7th is intended (see p. 371, where Roe says that the letter was actually despatched on the 10th).

[2] Stade, on the western bank of the Elbe ; Middelburg, in the island of Walcheren.

doe your countrie good service to acquaynt His Majestie freely with this motion ; open his eies, that hee bee not blynded with the smoky ayer of Spanish greatnes, who will never bee able alone to graspe all the world, and, if hee engage himselfe to them, they will tye him like a ward to their pleasurs. Yow are an Englishman : showe it rightly. This busines, discretly and sincerly handled, may bee a fortune to yow. . . . Deale in this clearly and substancially, and beleeve not that a trade will ever proceede that is not at first settled upon understanding grounds ; and if yow in your judgment and experience fynd that these conditions will not bee agreed too, the next best service yow can doe is to assure the King wee will not come like peddlears, and to advice us, that wee spend no more tyme and travell in vayne. . . . I shall not abyde in these parts (I hope) to see any great issue ; for in December 1617 I expect to turne my face homeward ; unlesse I be commanded by His Majestie my lord and soveragne to visitt the Shabas, which if it so happen, I will acquaynt him not only with the affection and power of my master to bee his frend, but with many things that are woorthy to bee knowne to so brave a Prince, wherin hee is yet unexcersiced, and expresse more fully my particular desire to doe him service. . . .

January 9.—Jaddow, finding by the invoyce small hope of sales, picked a quarrell that hee wanted water at midnight, and without taking leave forsooke mee. Soe that I resolved to bee no longer tyed to the servitude of such a villayne, who had so often notoriously abusd us ; but dispeeded a *pattamar* to Adsmere to procure the comming of a Greeke [see p. 341] that spake excellent language, to supply my use on the way, and to sollicite my determinations at the comming of the presents, and to assist Mr. Bidolph in the Companyes busines, hee propounding him as the fittest man in India ; but I purposed only to serve my use on him. and to prove him or to dismisse him so soone as I was settled. But for feare of his refusall or to bee destitute, I wrote to Mr. Shalbanck to practice with Jaffer [Jāfar], the brokar in Agra, to come downe and supply the place ; resolving soe to gett him into my power to answere the accusations laid by Jaddow that hee should deceive the factors of Agra in investments betweene 2 and 3000 *rup*[*ias*], which hee yet offered to justefy to Mr. Bidolph.

January 14.—I received from Agra that the plauge was fallen to 100 a day, and great hope of the clearing of the towne : that indico was like to bee at indifferent rates, and if mony could bee fitted in tyme, that all the cloth in barter might bee putt off; which lettres I answered, perswading to putt it in practice by the debts made and billes sent up to the creditors residing there.

January 16.—I sent a *patamar* expresse to Suratt, hearing nothing of the presents nor *cafala*, to require a resolution and to convey the packetts of Adsmere, which found now no passadge thence.[1]

To Sir Thomas Smythe.[2]
(*Add. MS.* 6115, f. 164.)

16 January, 1616[-17].

.... I am yet followeing this wandering King over mountaynes and thorough woods, so strange and unused wayes that his owne people, who almost know no other god, blaspheame his name and hers that (it is said) conducts all his actions. Ther is noe hope wee can settle any where this ten weekes; but at last our residence wilbe Mandoa, about 80 mile English from Brampoore, and nearer Suratt by 10 dayes travell. So that, although wee shalbe farr from Agra, it wilbe som way recompensed in other chardges. But I feare hee will not long stay any wher, whose course is directed by a woeman, and is now, as it were, shutt up by her soe, that all justice or care of any thing or publique affayrs either sleepes or depends on her, who is more unaccesable then any goddesse or mistery of heathen impietye. So that your servants had neede bee very circumspect how they engage them selves in any journy or residence. The chardge is such that is not supportable, if eyther I should follow the profusenes of examples, or your servants carry their heavy goods up and downe after him; wher nothing is vendible that I know, except it bee new and unseene, that may rather flatter curiositye then suffice uses or necessitie.[3] ... The trade [*i.e.* with Persia] (if it succeed at all) may be marrd at first settling by forwardnes, as was this of India; for I am perswaded wee might have brought it to passe that wee might have bought all our indico at the port, for that the Suratters would as well bring it theither (if

---

[1] The letter to Surat is given at f. 166 of the MS., where will also be found one to Capt. Pepwell of the same date. In this Roe says: ' The Kyng will tyre us all and teare us to peeces in the woodes.'

[2] Printed in full at p. 328 of vol. v. of *Letters Received.*

[3] Roe goes on to relate his controversy with Kerridge over the venture to Persia.

S.T.R.   Y

they were sure of vent) as to ship it ; and ther is ever enough
to lade a ship upon their hands, which wee seeke not. And if
it be sayd wee could not sell there, I answere : if the King had
beene at first held hard up, when the Portugalls had warr
with him, hee might have beene enforced to that hee will now
never bee perswaded too ; for hee cares not for busines, and
despiseth the consideration of his poore people. . . . Yow
might loade hence, if yow had stock, 10,000 *churles* yearly of
indico, and of cloth what quantety yow desire, and of what
sorts. So that, if yow could find means to accomplish this
trade, it were sufficient for this quarter ; and I cannot propound any way so probable as the Redd Sea, wher the Dutch
this yeare made a voyadge under English mens names and
had excellent usadg and great profitt . . . and secondly, by
spices and China ware from the south. . . . Thus much in
generall : yow shalbe sure of a trade on as good tearmes as
the subjects ; for such is the confused goverment that they
suffer under officers tyrranny such as they dare not offer us ;
and better I cannot hope for, unles the port were reduced into
the hands of a subject ; for Sultan Carroone is as absolute
by Normahalls power as shee, who is all ; for, if the King
did governe, his nature is just, easy, and good, and his opinicn
and favour to mee extraordinary, considering my barren hands
(which hath taught his the same toward mee) ; but hee, good
man, doates, and heares only by one eare. . . . Poore I am as
ever was any ambassador ; yet I will not hazard to runn in
debt. I spend my quarters allowance in a month, and take
patience two. Every thing that I can weare is dearer then at
the *Beare* in Cheapeside. And to acquaynt yow with our
necessities, while wee teare our selves in the woods, the King
suffers the mony changers to lett fall his coyne one fourth,
and others rayse their goods up to yt ; soe that four crownes
goe not so far as two and a half did. . . . Empart what yow
please of that I send yow, but conceale our wrangles.[1] . . .

January 18.—The King passed beetweene two mountaynes,
having cutt the way thorough the woods, but with soe much
trouble and inconvenience to the baggage that it was left
behind.[2] Without any refreshing, I found my tents by mid-

[1] In another letter to Smythe of 28 January, 1617, the ambassador
wrote that Kerridge had made apologies which he had accepted.
The letter has been printed at p. 333 of *Letters Received*, vol. v.

[2] The gorge here mentioned was the pass of Mukandwāra, memor-
able in later years in connection with Colonel Monson's retreat.
A description of the pass and its beautiful scenery will be found in
Tod's *Rajasthan*, vol. ii. pp. 702, 738.

night, having taken up my lodging first under a tree. T
countrie is full of theeves, and not in perfect obedience bu
they are kept by force. It belongs to a *Raja* that desiers
to see the King. *Haud facile libertus*[1] *et domini miscer*
The exactor complayned, and some few of the people that
beeing taken and chayned by the necks, were presented
King; the strongest keept the mountaynes. At night,
King fired the towne by which hee sate, and appoynted a
governor to the quarter, to reedefye and repeople it and re
it to civilitye. Hee left him some horse to effect it;
*neque quies gentium sine armis, neque arma sine stipei
neque stipendia sine tributis, haberi queant.*[2]

January 20.—The *Banditi* fled into the woods, in re
of their towne, sett upon a company of stragglers behind
divers, and robbd them.

January 22.—I received from Brampoore by Mr. Ban
advise of the safe passadge of the Agra *cafala* and their
but noe newes from Suratt; hee professing to have ser
expresse *patamars*, who were deteyned, and in two m
hee hard not any advise; having mony in cash unbes
to the Companyes losse and his greife. This made me de
of the presents expected, and resolved at night to vis
King to observe what countenance he would show mee
give occasion to aske after them. When I came, I fou
sate in a new order; so that I was to seeke what place to ch
loth to mingle with his great ones (which was offered), a
doubted to goe into the roome where hee sate, beeing cut
downe the banck of a river, and none neare him but Etimo
Dowlett (his father in law), Asaph-Chan and three or fou
others. Soe I went to the brimme and stood alone. Hee
observed mee and lett mee stay a while, and so smiling called
mee in and with his hand directed mee to stand by him;
favour so unusuall that it both gave mee some content anc
much grace, which I instantly found in others usadge. He

---

[1] *Libertas* is the reading of the original (Tacitus, *Hist.*, iv. (
'Liberty and lords go not well together.'

[2] 'For neither can the tranquillity of nations be obtained wit u
armies, nor armies without pay, nor pay without taxes.'—*Ibid.* i\ 4
The last word of the quotation should be 'queunt.'

provoked mee too talke, and I calling for an interpreter, hee refused it and pressed mee to use such woords as in Persian I had. Our discourse had not much sence nor dependance, but hee tooke it well, and with much curtesy demonstrated a good opinion.

January 23.—I returned answere to Brampoore.[1]

January 24.—Newes arriving at court that the *Decans* would not bee frighted out of their dominion (which Asaph Chan and Normahall had pretended, to procure this voyadge), but that they had sent their impediments into the hart, and attended in the borders with 50,000 horse resolved to fight, and that Sultan Coronne was yet advanced no farther then Mandoa, afraid both of the enemie and *Chan Channa*, these councellors changed their advise, and, declaring to the King that they conceived the *Decan* before his passadge over the last hills would have yeilded by the terror of his approach, but finding the contrary, perswaded him to convert it to a hunting journy, and to turne his face toward Agra, for that the other was not an enemie woorthy his person. Hee replyed this consideration came too late : his honor was ingaged : seeing hee had so farr passd, hee would prosecute their first councells and his purpose, and adventure the hazards of both. But hee dayly dispeeded fresh troupes toward his sonne, partly from his owne, the rest commanded from goverments, according to report 30,000 horse, but not by muster.

January 28.—I received from Suratt that the presents and goods for court were dispeeded the second of this month, and that if the Prince (which I feared) intercepted them not, I

---

[1] See f. 168 of the MS. In it Roe says that Kerridge's behaviour to Bangham is of a piece with his treatment of everybody else, 'my selfe having beene soe used that I am resolved to returne for England next yeare ; and I protest, if I thought it possible to come in tyme to the shipps, I would not rest a day.' He understands that Kerridge is manœuvring to go home next year with a great investment ; but he 'will returne in his company and prepare his reception, if hee mend not his courses.' The ambassador adds that, as soon as he has received the presents and given them to the King, he will proceed to Burhānpur for a stay of about ten days, in accordance with his promise to Prince Khurram.

might expect them by the 10th of Feabruary.[1] This late newes yet refreshed mee, who was soe weary of an idle journy that I had some hope to gett liberty to goe before and to dispatch at Brampoore with the Prince, according to a promise and a resolution taken, and the necessitye of our busines exacting that respeect too him ; so I attended in patience and expectation.

January 29.—The *patamar* I returned with a packett to Suratt.[2] At night arrived Diego Lopo, the Greeke, from Adsmere, with Mr. Fettiplace[s] lettres of his endeavoring carridg to remoove the goods for Agra ; of whom I purposed to make use during my necessitie, if I found him fitt for employment ;[3] for Jaddow in all this tyme never offered so much as to visitt mee, and I resolved never to use him. Water is become very scarce ; and though our *leskar* be halfe lessened, yet passing many dayes thorough a country wher the people were guilty of some disobedience, and for feare forsaking the villadges with their provisions, grayne and all other necessaries became soe deare, and the mony so abased by want of *pice*, that I was at double chardge of expence. The King, who feeles it not, takes no order. His *Channs* are followed with their owne provision and so enforme not. The strangers, the souldier, and the poore only, as woorst able, endure the burthen. Every other day the King remooved three, four, or five *course*. Short yet of Mandoa, 60.

January 30-*February* 2.—Every other day four *course*.

[1] The presents were in the charge of the Reverend Edward Terry, who, as already related (p. 216), had been chosen to fill Hall's place as chaplain to the ambassador. He was instructed by Kerridge to give Roe timely notice of his approach, and, if the Prince interfered, he was to invoke the assistance of Afzal Khān (*Factory Records, Surat*, vol. 84, part i. f. 142).

[2] With a letter recorded at f. 169 of the MS. Roe had now been mollified by the explanations tendered by Kerridge, and replied : ' I am veary glad to receive from you good woords ; so inclinable I am to peace.' He acquainted him with his intention of going to Burhānpur, and intimated that, if Kerridge could meet him there, he would welcome his assistance.

[3] He did not remain long. Writing to Burhānpur on 10 April, 1617, Roe said : ' Diego is gone from mee. He was to proud to serve a king.'

February 3.—Departing out of the rode of the *leskar* for ease and shade, and resting under a tree for the same comodityes, came upon mee Sultan Corsoronne, the Kings eldest restrayned sonne, riding upon an eliphant, with no great guard nor attendance. His people desired mee to give him roome ; which I did, but attended to see him, who called for mee, and with some gentle and familiar questions, full of curtesye and affability, hee departed. His person is good and countenance cherfull ; his beard growne to his girdle. This only I noted, that his questions showed ignorance of all passadges in court, in so much he never heard of any ambassador nor English.[1]

February 4 *and* 5.—Wee rested not.

February 6.—At night wee came to a little tower newly repayred, wher the King pitched in a plesant place upon the river of Sepra, short of Ugen [Ujjain], the cheefe citty of Malwa, one *course*. The place, called Calleada,[2] was anciently

---

[1] Terry (p. 431) gives the following account of an interview between Roe and the Prince. Although Terry speaks as if he had been present, and Roe is represented as having been at the court for two years, it seems to refer to the present occasion. ' Once he called my Lord Ambassadour to him as we passed by him, asking him many questions, as how far distant our country was from them, and what we brought thither, and what we carried thence, and how the King his father had used him since his arrive there ; whither or no he had not bestowed upon him some great gifts ? The Ambassadour told him that his business there was to obtain a free trade for his nation the English ; and that being granted him, he had reward enough. The Prince replyed that this could not be denyed us, we coming so far to trade there with him ; and the Prince further asked him how long he had been there ; the Ambassadour told him about two years ; the Prince replyed again, that it was a very great shame for the successor of Tamberlane, who had such infinite rules [riches ?], to suffer a man of his quality to come so far unto him, and to live so long about him, and not to give him some royall gift ; and he further added, that for himself he was a prisoner, and therefore could do him no good, but he would pray for him ; and so he departed.'

[2] Kāliyāda, about four miles north of the present city of Ujjain. It is described as an ancient palace, built on an island in the Sipra, and consisting of two square buildings, each covered by a cupola ; a bridge connects the island with the mainland, and below the bridge are several apartments on a level with the water ; the rocky bed of the river is cut into channels of various regular forms, such as

a seat of the Gentile kings of Mandoa, one wherof was there drowned in his drinck, having once before fallen into the river, and taken up by the hayre of the head by a slave that dived; and beeing come to him selfe, it was related to him to procure a reward. Hee called for the instrument of his safety, and demanding how he durst putt his hands on his soveraygnes head, caused them to bee stricken off. Not long after, sitting alone with his wife in drunkennes, hee had the same chance to slipp into the water, but so that shee might easely have saved him, which shee did not; and beeing demanded why, shee replyed shee knew not whither he also would cutt of her hands for her recompence.

February 8.—Wee rested.

February 10.—Wee remooved to a *course* beyond Ugen.

February 11.—The King rode to Ugen to speake with a *dervis* or saynt living on a hill, who is reported to bee 300 yeares ould.[1] I thought this miracle not woorth my examination. At noone by a foote post I received that the Prince,

spirals, squares, circles, etc., and the whole place formed a very cool and attractive retreat for the hot weather (Hunter's *Narrative of a Journey from Agra to Ujjain*, in *Asiatic Researches*, vol. vi.; see also *The Oriental Repertory*, vol. vi. p. 266, and Forbes's *Oriental Memoirs*, vol. iv. p. 6).

The building was erected by one of the Ghori kings of Mālwa, named Nāsir-ud-dīn (1500-12), the story of whose death is here related. The same tale, but with a few variations, is given in Jahāngīr's *Memoirs* (vol. i. p. 367). As Ferishta tells the story (*History of the Deccan*, Briggs's translation, vol. iv. p. 242), the king, while intoxicated, slipped into a tank, and was rescued by four of his women, who changed his wet clothes without his perceiving it. On awakening from his stupor, he complained of headache, and was thereupon told that he had been so drunk that he had fallen into the water. Enraged at what he thought (from the state of his clothing) to be a lie, and supposing them to be reproaching him for his inebriety, he put them all to death, in spite of their protests. But he did not die himself till many years after, and then of a fever.

[1] In his *Memoirs* (vol. i. p. 355) the Emperor relates this visit at great length. It was paid to a *sanyāsi* (ascetic) of the name of Jadrūp. A second visit was paid on the following day (*ibid.* p. 359); and several other interviews followed at later dates (vol. ii. pp. 49, etc.). A portrait of the saint, painted at this time, was reproduced by Mr. A. K. Coomaraswamy in the *Journal of the Royal Asiatic Society* for July, 1919. See also Beni Prasad's *Jahangir*, p. 276.

notwithstanding all *firmaens* and commands of his father, had entercepted the presents and goods sent up, to fullfill his base and greedy desier ; and that, notwithstanding any guift nor entreaty or perswasions of Mr. Terry, to whose chardge they were committed, would not part with them, but by force compelld them to returne with him toward Brampoore ; yet hee forbeare to breake any thing open, but pressed the English to consent ; which they refusing by my order, hee thought to wynn them by vexation. Such is the custome to see all merchannts goods, eaven before the King, that hee may first choose ; but I resolved to breake yt in our behalfe. The Prince, to satisfie his desire, before I could have knowledg, he sent a post to the King to certifye him that such goods hee had stayed, without mention of presents, and prayed leave to open them and to buy what hee fancyed. So soone as I heard of this faithlesse unjust usadge, I resolved I was justifiable before all the world, if I used the extreamety of complaynts ; that I had practised all meanes to wynne and purchase favour, and had suffered beyond the patience of a free man, my former courses will wittnes, and leave mee without blame in ill successes, though I found it in a rougher way, seeing I could fynd no better in the smoothest. Breefly, I resolved to appeale to justice by complaynt, but as calmely and warely as I could, to expresse my wholle greiffe, extreame injuryes, and long patience. To goe to Asaph-Chan, though to neglect him would displease him, yet to trye him I feared would prevent my purpose. To send to him that I desiered to visitt the King at the *guselchan*, I doubted what I entended might bee suspected, if hee had heard of the injurye ; so I practised first to avoyd prevention. The prophett whom the King visited offered mee occasion, and my new linguist was ready. I rode and mett His Majestie on his eliphant and allighted, making signe to speake. Hee turned his monster to mee, and prevented [*i.e.* anticipated] mee : My sonne hath taken your goods and my presents : bee not sadd ; hee shall not touch nor open a seale nor lock : at night I will send him a command to free them ; with other very gratious speeches, that hee knew I came full of complaynt, to ease mee hee begann first. Upon the way I could doe noe more ; but at night, without farther seeking to Asaph Chan, I went to the *guzelchan*, resolved to prosecute the complaynt of forcing back our goods in respect of the chardg and trouble, of the abuses of Suratt, and all our other greevances. Soe soone as I came in, the King calld my interpreter and delivered by his [means ?] that hee had written and sent his command very effectually that not a hayre should be deminished. I replyed the injury was such, and the chardge and abuses of our liberty by the Princes officers, that I desired redresse, for that wee could not longer suffer. It was answered what was past I must remitt to his sonne; but by Asaph Chans mediation I could procure nothing but very good woords, for hee smoothd on both sides. Soe that I was forced to seeme content, and to seeke an oportunitye in the absence of that my falce frend and procurator. The good King fell to dispute of the lawes of Moses, Jesus and Mahomett; and in drinck was soe kinde that hee turnd to mee, and said: Am I a king? Yow shalbe wellcome: Christians, Moores, Jewes, hee meddled not with their faith: they came all in love, and hee would protect them from wrong: they lived under his safety and none should oppresse them; and this often repeated; but in extreame drunkennes hee fell to weeping and to divers passions, and soe kept us till midnight.

Judg all men what travell I endured by reason the factors kept my presents four monthes and sent them eaven in the mouth of the Prince, arrived within two dayes of Brampoore; and hereby every way our chardg doubled. Yet I rested not satisfied, but seeing I had begunn and that the Prince was, as I feared, enough exasperated with a little, I thought as good loose him to some purpose as to none; at least to trie the King what hee would doe. Soe I wayted advantage; but sent back the messenger to Mr. Terry to stand out and attend the Kings answere, which I would speedely send him.

This journall from this 11*th February,* 1616[-17] *is posted into a nother booke* [1] *for want of roome.*

[1] Which unfortunately can nowhere be found; and henceforward we are dependent on Purchas's meagre extracts, together with such letters as have escaped destruction.

THE JOURNAL CONTINUED FROM 'PURCHAS HIS
PILGRIMES' (vol. i. p. 564).

And so resolved to dissemble that I hope to repay.[1] When
I came, with base flattery worse then the theft, or at least to
give me some satisfaction, because trouble was in my face
(for otherwise it is no injury heere to bee so used) he beganne
to tell me he had taken divers things that please[d] him
extreamely well, naming two cushions embroydered, a folding
glasse, and the dogges, and desired mee not to bee discontent,
for whatsoever I would not give him, I should receive backe.
I answered : there were few things that I entended not to
present him, but that I tooke it a great discourtesie to my
soveraigne, which I could not answere, to have that was freely
given seazed, and not delivered by my hands, to whom they
were directed : and that some of them were entended for the
Prince and Normahall, some to lye by me, on occasions to
prepare His Majesties favour to protect us from injuries that

[1] As Purchas commences this entry in the middle of a sentence and
gives no date, it may be surmised that some leaves were missing from
the MS. he used. The date it is impossible to supply, though it must
have been in the latter half of February. Terry says their journey
from Surat to Roe's camp lasted until the end of March, but he was
evidently mistaken in the month.

Some particulars of the seizure of the presents and their subsequent release are given in the following extracts :

'We were violently deteined in our journey by Sultan Caroon,
the Prince, whom we met in his march towards Brampore, and a
very marvelous great retinue with him. The reason why he interrupted us in our course was that he might see the presents we had
for his father the King ; but, we having command from the ambassador to tell him that we durst not open them till we came to the
King, we most humbly craved his pardon to spare us in that. So,
presenting him with a pair of rich gloves (though they be things they
wear not in those hot countryes) and a rich embrodered bag for
perfume (which amongst many other things of the like kinde were
brought from England to be given away for presents), after that he
had carried us back three dayes journey, he let us go, taking further
order for our safe convoy ' (Terry's *Voyage*, p. 194).

'The Prince seazed all the presents and goods and tooke them
into his tents, forcing back their attendants, but opened nothing ;
which newes arriving, I would not consoent hee should search myne
for the example ; and though it were reasonable to give leave to buy,
yet, noe merchant beeing present, and the goods sent up under the

strangers were daily offered, and some for my friends or private use, and some that were the merchants, which I had not to doe withall. He answered that I should not be sad nor grieved that hee had his choyce, for that hee had not patience to forbeare seeing them : hee did mee no wrong in it, for hee thought I wished him first served : and to my Lord the King of England hee would make satisfaction, and my excuse : the Prince, Normahall and he were all one : and for any to bring with me to procure his favour, it was a ceremony and unnecessary, for he would at all times heare me : that I should be welcome emptie handed, for that was not my fault, and I should receive right from him : and to go to his sonne, he would returne me somewhat for him, and for the merchants goods pay to their content ; concluding I should not be angry for this freedome : he entended well. I made no reply. Then hee pressed me whether I was pleased or no. I answered : His Majesties content pleased me. So seeing Mr. Terry, whom

name of supply to the court factory so base, so unwoorthy of the honor of the Company that I thought it would redound to much scorne to divulge their qualety. I desired the Kings lettre, which with many gratious additions hee gave, and all was dispeeded after long stay and much expence. When they came neare, the King beeing gone privatly ahunting, and my selfe in the *leskar*, the Princes *haddy* [*ahadi*, a gentleman-trooper], whom he sent with command to carry all to the King, betrayed mee ; and though I gott the merchants goods delivered to Mr. Biddolph, yet in the night hee stole away myne and carried them to the King as presents, who opened and tooke all that liked him. Next day I came, and hee made many excuses, offering mee restitution, but yet I cannot gett yt : and for some amends hee promiseth his lettres for redresse of abuses. But I never sawe what came up, nor have any thing for the Prince, except it bee returned ; so that this yeare I am barer handed then the last. All that I can urdge is answered with such promises, and, if they succeed, I am happely robbd ' (Roe to Surat, 10 March, 1617 ; *Add. MS.* 6115, f. 175 : printed in part at p. 355 of *Letters Received*, vol. v.).

From other letters of Roe's it appears that when the goods and presents reached the camp, the King was four *kos* away, hunting. The officer in charge at once rode to report to him, ' whose haste called for them and mee ; but the messengers at midnight carried all away, and His Majestie opened them and tooke everything before my arrivall ' (f. 177). Next day Roe reached the King's headquarters, and the interview here described took place.

I brought in with me, he called to him : Padre, you are very welcome, and this house is yours, esteeme it so : whensoever you desire to come to me, it shall bee free for you, and whatsoever you will require of mee, I will grant you.[1] Then he converted [*i.e.* turned] himselfe with this cunning unto me, naming all particulars in order : the dogges,[2] cushions, barbers case, you will not desire to have backe, for that I am delighted

[1] Terry's account of the incident (p. 440) is as follows : ' When I was first there brought into the presence of the Mogol, immediatly after my arrive at his court, I standing near the Ambassadour (for no man there of the greatest quality whatsoever is at any time suffered to sit in his presence) and but a little distance from that King in his *gozulcan*, he sent one of his grandees to me, to let me know that the King bad me welcome thither : that I should have a free access to him whenever I pleased : and if I would ask him any thing he would give it me (though I never did ask, nor he give). And very many times afterward when, waiting on my Lord Ambassadour, I appeared before him, he would still shew tokens of civility and respect unto me.'

[2] ' That year I went for East-India, the merchants here (as from the King of England, in whose name they sent all their presents) amongst many other things, then sent the Mogol some great English mastives, and some large Irish grey-hounds, in all to the number of eight, dispersed in our severall ships. . . . Only two of the mastives came alive to East-India, and they were carried up, each of them drawn in a little coach, when I went up to the embassador, that he might present them to the Mogol. The fiercest of these two, in our way thither, upon a time breaking loose, fell upon a very large elephant that was hard by us, fastning his teeth in the elephants trunk, and kept his hold there a good while, which made that huge beast extremely to roare ; and though the elephant did swing the mastive up and down above ground many times (as not feeling his weight) that he might throw him off, yet he could not suddenly do it ; but at last freeing himself from the dog, by throwing him a good space from him, there came a mungrill curr of that countrey towards our mastive, who then lost [left ?] this his most unequal match, fell upon that dog and kild him, by which means we recovered our mastive again into our custody, he not having received any apparent hurts. . . . This storie pleased the Mogol very much when the dogs were presented to him, and he allowed each of them four attendants of those natives to wait upon them, who by turnes two and two together carried them up and down with him in *palankees* . . . . to which they were tyed, and the other two went by them, fanning the flyes from off them ; and the King caused a pair of silver tongs to be made, on purpose that with them, when he pleased, he might feed those dogs with his own hand ' (Terry, p. 149).

in them ? I answered : No. Then, said he, there were two glasse chestes :[1] for they were very meane and ordinary, for whom came they? I replyed: I entended one for His Majestie, the other to Normahall. Why then, said hee, you will not aske that I have, being contented with one ? I was forced to yeeld. Next he demanded whose the hats were, for that his women liked them. I answered : Three were sent to His Majestie : the fourth was mine to weare. Then, said he, you will not take them from me, for I like them, and yours I will returne if you need it, and will not bestow that on me ; which I could not refuse. Then next he demanded whose the pictures were. I answered : Sent to me to use on occasions, and dispose as my businesse required. So hee called for them, and caused them to be opened, examined me of the women,[2] and other little questions, requiring many judgements of them. Of the third picture, of Venus and a satyre, he commanded my interpreter not to tell me what he said, but asked his lords what they conceived should be the interpretation or morall of that. He shewed the satyres hornes, his skinne, which was swart [*i.e.* dark-hued], and pointed to many particulars. Every man replyed according to his fancie ; but in the end hee concluded they were all deceived : and seeing they could judge no better, hee would keepe his conceit to himselfe, iterating his command to conceale this passage from me ; but bade him aske me what it meant. I answered : An invention of the painter to shew his arte, which was poeticall, but the interpretation was new to mee that had not seene it. Then he called Mr. Terry to give his judgement ; who replying hee knew not, the King demanded why hee brought up to him an invention wherein hee was ignorant ; at which I enterposed that he was a preacher, and medled not with such matters, nor had charge of them ; onely, comming

[1] These were two glass cabinets, which had arrived in a deplorable condition—' broken, meane glew woorke all to peices.' They had cost 70*l.* the two.

[2] The Lady Montague [wife of Sir Henry Montague, afterwards Earl of Manchester], and the Lady Molyneux [probably Frances, daughter of Sir Gilbert Gerard, and wife of Sir Richard Molyneux] (Kerridge to Roe, 12 December, 1616 ; *Factory Records, Surat*, vol. 84, part i. f. 128).

in their company, hee was more noted, and so named as their
conductor. This I repeate for instruction, to warne the
Company, and him that shall succeed me, to be very wary
what they send may be subject to ill interpretation; for in
that point this King and people are very pregnant and scrupulous, full of jealousie and trickes. For that, notwithstanding
the King conceited himselfe, yet by the passages I will deliver
my opinion of this conceit, which (knowing I had never seene
the picture, and by ignorance was guiltlesse) hee would not
presse hard upon me; but I suppose he understood the morall
to be a scorne of Asiatiques, whom the naked satyre represented, and was of the same complexion, and not unlike; who,
being held by Venus, a white woman, by the nose, it seemed
that shee led him captive. Yet he revealed no discontent,
but rould them up, and told me he would accept him also as a
present: for the saddle and some other small toyes, he would
fit me with a gift to his sonne, to whom he would write according
to promise, so effectually that I should need no sollicitor in
many [my?] businesses; with as many complements, excuses,
professions and protestations as could come from any very
noble or very base minde in either extreame. Yet he left not,
but enquired what meant the figures of the beasts,[1] and
whether they were sent me to give to him. I had understood
they were very ridiculous and ill shaped ordinary creatures,
the varnish off, and no beauty other then a lumpe of wood.
I was really ashamed, and answered: It was not my fault:
those that seized them must beare the affront: but that they
were not entended to him, but sent to shew the formes of
certaine beasts with us. He replyed quickly: Did you thinke
in England that a horse and a bull was strange to mee? I
replyed: I thought not of so meane a matter: the sender was

[1] These were six carved figures of a lion, buck, horse, greyhound,
bull and talbot (a species of dog noted for quickness of scent), and
had cost 57s. each (*Factory Records, Surat*, vol. 84, part i. f. 138).
Mukarrab Khān's list of goods suitable for presentation to the
King (sent home by Downton in 1614) included 'any figures of
beasts, birds, or other similes made of glass, of hard plaster, of silver,
brasse, wood, iron, stone or ivorye' (*O.C.* No. 183); and probably
the models referred to had been sent out in consequence of this
suggestion.

an ordinary man in good will to mee for toyes, and what he thought, I knew not. Well, said the King, I will keepe them, and onely desire you to helpe me to a horse of the greatest si:e : it is all I will expect, and a male and female of mastiffes, and the tall Irish grey-hounds, and such other dogges as hunt in your lands ; and if you will promise me this, I will give you the word of a King, I will fully recompence you, and grant you all your desires. I answered : I would promise to provide them, but could not warrant their lives, and if they dyed by the way, onely for my discharge, their skinnes and bones should bee preserved. Hee gave extraordinary bowes, layd his hand on his heart, and such kind of gestures as all men will witnesse he never used to any man, nor such familiarity, nor freedome, nor profession of love. This was all my recompence, that he often desired my content to be merry : that the wrong he had done me he would royally requite, and send me home to my countrey with grace and reward like a gentleman. But seeing nothing returned of what was seized, but words, I desired His Majestie to deliver backe the velvets and silkes, being merchants goods : that they were sent up among mine by His Majesties command, for that by that pretence they escaped the ravine of the Princes officers. So hee gave order to call Mr. Biddolph to agree with him, and to pay for them to content. Then I delivered a letter I had ready written, contayning my desire for priviledges and justice ; otherwise, I should returne as a fayzneane [a do-nothing (Fr. *fainéant*)] and disgraced to my soveraigne ; and desired some justice for Sulpheckarkons debt, lately dead. He replyed he would take such order with his sonne for Surat as I should have no cause to complaine, and that he should cleere it ; for which he gave instant order. For other places, he would give me his commands, and every way shew how much he loved me : and, to the end I might returne to my master with honour, hee would send by me a rich and worthy present, with his letter of my behaviour filled with many prayses ; and commanded me to name what I thought would be most acceptable. I answered : I durst not crave : it was not our custome, nor stood with my masters honour : but whatsoever he sent, I doubted not would be acceptable from so potent a king and so much loved of my lord. He replyed that I thought he asked in jest, to please mee, and that he saw I was yet discontent, but he conjured me to beleeve he was my friend, and would at conclusion prove so; and vowed by his head hee spake heartily concerning presents, but I must not refuse for his instruction to name somewhat. This earnestnesse enforced mee to say : If His Majesty pleased, I thought large Persian carpets [1] would be fittest : for gifts of cost and value my master expected not. He answered he would provide of all sorts and sizes, and added [add ?] to them what hee thought was fit, that your King may know I respect him. Next, having venison of divers sorts before him, he gave me halfe a stagge, with these words : Hee killed it himselfe, and the other halfe I should see bestowed on his wives ; which was presently cut out, in small pieces of foure pound, and sent in by his third [2] sonne and two women that were called out, to divers such mammockes [*i.e.* morsels] as if it had been a dole to the poore, and carryed by the prince bare in his hands. Now I had as much satisfaction and so abundant grace as might have flattered me into content; but the injury was above words, though I were glad of these, and of colour to dissemble, for hee sent as a conclusion to know if I were pleased, and did not depart discontent. I answered : His Majesties favour was sufficient to make mee any amends. Then, said he, I have onely one question to aske you, which is : I wonder much, now I have seene your presents two yeares, what was the reason why your King sent a merchant, a meane man [*i.e.* Edwards], before you with five times as many, and more curious toyes that contented all, and after to send you his ambassadour with a commission and his letter mentioning presents, and yet what you brought was little, meane, and inferiour to the other : I acknowledge you an ambassador : I have found you a gentleman in your usage : and I am amazed why you were so slightly set out. I would have replyed, but he cut me off : I know it is not the Kings

[1] Roe himself took home a 'great carpet with my [his] arms thereon,' which he afterwards bequeathed to his cousin, Sir Henry Roe (Roe's will, in Somerset House).

[2] A slip for fourth (Jahāndār) or fifth (Shahryār).

fault, nor yours, but I will let you see I esteeme you better
then they [who] employed you : at your returne I will send
you home with honour, with reward, and according to your
qualitie : and, not respecting what you brought me, will
like a king present your lord and master : onely this I will
require from you, and not expect it from the merchants, to
take with you a patterne of a quiver and case for my bow, a
coat to weare, a cushion to sleepe on of my fashion (which was
at his head), and a paire of boots, which you shall cause to be
embroydered in England of the richest manner, and I will
expect and receive them from you, for I know in your countrey
they can worke better then any I have seene : and if you
send them mee, I am a king, you shall not lose by it ; which
I most thankfully undertooke, and he commanded Asaph
Chan to send me the patternes. Then he demanded if I had
any grape wine. I could not denie it. He desired a taste
next night, and if hee liked it he would be bold ; if not, he
desired me to make merrie with it. So, spending this night
onely on me, he rose.

March 3.—Wee came to Mandoa,[1] into which the King
entred in state. But no man was suffered to goe in before
hee was set, by the advice of his astrologers ; so that wee
all sate without, attending a good houre.

[*March*] 6.—I came into Mandoa, having sent before and
found a faire court well walled, and in that a good church,
one great tombe. It was taken up by one of the Kings
servants, but I got possession and kept it, being the best

[1] Māndu, once the capital of Mālwa, now a deserted city in Dhār
State, 65 miles S.S.W. of Ujjain, 34 miles S.W. of the cantonment
of Mhow, and 15 miles N. of the right bank of the Narbada. Burhānpur lies about 90 miles to the S.E.
The city stands on the crest of the Vindhyas, nearly 2000 ft. above
sea level, overlooking the Narbada valley, while behind an abrupt
gorge cuts it off from the tableland of Mālwa. This strong position
led to its being chosen as the capital of the Muhammadan kings of
Mālwa, who adorned it with many splendid buildings, some of
which are still standing ; but after its capture in 1531 by Bahādur
Shāh, and its consequent incorporation with the dominions of
Gujarāt, it gradually declined in importance till at last it was
abandoned to the jungle. Of late years considerable attention has
been paid to its ruins by the Archaeological Survey of India.

within all the wall, but two miles from the Kings house, yet so sufficient that a little charge would make it defensible against raines, and save one thousand *rupias*; and for aire very pleasant upon the edge of the hill.[1]

[*March*] 11.—At night I went toward the court, but the King, upon newes of a lion that had killed some horses, was gone to hunt; so that I had leisure to seeke some water. For we were brought to a hill with a multitude of people (so great is the foresight, and so good the policie) where was no water, that men and cattle were like to perish. That little that was in pooles some great men possessed, and kept by force. I could get none. The poore forsooke the citie, and by proclamation many were commanded away, all horses

[1] Roe wrote to Surat that he had 'gotten a faire court with a church and other building in good place, which with some reparations may serve my turne; but farre from the Kings house and in such scarcety of water that the *leskar* is forced to goe out a *course* or two. Soe that wee suffer many incomodityes, but lesse then others' (f. 175 of the MS.). Another letter (see p. 359) he dates from 'Mando, on the sowth side, neare the edge of the hill, a *course* from the towne.' Terry (p. 196) adds that the ambassador's residence was 'one of those deserted *mosquites*, with some large tomb neer it, both vaulted overhead.' Following up these indications, in Jan. 1910 Mr. Henry Cousens and Col. Baker, R.E., found to the north-west of the Tārāpur Gate a mosque which seemed to them to answer to the description given. In Mr. Cousens' account of the search (*Annual Report of the Archaeological Survey*, 1912-13, p. 148), it is stated that the mosque is situated on the west side of a large tank and has in front of it the remains of a great tomb. Around the mosque are the ruined walls of smaller buildings and outhouses, and the remnants of an enclosing wall are still to be seen. The pillars of the mosque have been grooved to take trellis screens or something of the kind, showing that the building had at one time been used as a dwelling; and it is the only mosque in the neighbourhood which has been so treated. It must, however, be pointed out that the existence of a tank on the spot is hardly consistent with Roe's complaints of lack of water.

A writer in the *Calcutta Review* for 1857 (vol. xxviii. p. 254) mentions that some years previous Roe's name was to be seen on the walls of an old tomb among the ruins of Māndu, but he adds that it was generally supposed to have been scratched there at a comparatively recent date. It would indeed be hard to imagine the ambassador scribbling his name on the walls of his dwelling.

ROE'S SUPPOSED DWELLING AT MANDU

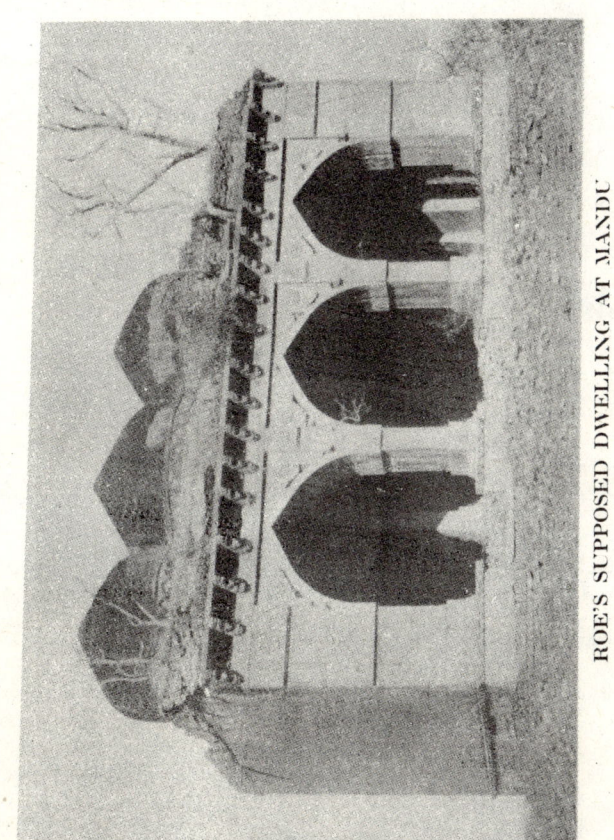

and cattel forbid ; and so those who were now in hope to rest were forced to seeke new dwellings ; who departed some two, three and foure *course* off, to the extreame trouble of all men, and the terrible rising of provisions. I knew not what to doe ; my roome and house was good, and though I were farre from markets, yet it was a lesse inconvenience then to sit in the fields without house or shelter; onely I wanted water. So I rode my selfe to seeke some, and found a great poole possessed by Chan, which was given by the King. I sent to desire him leave to draw,[1] who granted me foure load a day ; which satisfied me in such sort that, with selling away some of those jades [2] that were put upon me from Surat and putting off my cattell, I had hope to live ; to which purpose I sent two with them to lye out of towne. There was not a misery nor punishment which either the want of government or the naturall disposition of the clime gave us not.[3]

[1] ' The custome being such that whatsoever fountaine or tanke is found by any great men in time of drought, hee shall keepe it proper and peculiar to himselfe ' (Coryat's notes in *Purchas*, vol. i. p. 600, and *Early Travels*, p. 277). The name of the Khān seems to have been omitted.

[2] By an amusing press blunder, in the 1873 reprint of the Journal Roe is made to contemplate ' selling away some of those *ladies* that were put upon ' him from Surat.

[3] On 6 June the ambassador wrote to Surat : ' God hath directed me in the *leskar* to take my residence wher I have found a spring (and I know no more on the hill), which I keepe with some wrangle. The miserye of others is pitifull ; water sould in the streete at an incredible rate ; many perishing for want ; all begging that only as almes ' (f. 197). The discovery of the spring was due to Thomas Herbert, the youngest brother of Lord Herbert of Cherbury. This youth had arrived in Pepwell's fleet, and had joined Roe at the latter's invitation. He had been shipped to India as a ne'er-do-well by his despairing friends ; on the voyage out he behaved so badly that he was turned before the mast ; at Surat he was a plague to the factors ; and on the way to the court he endangered the safety of the party by first beating and then firing at a native, to the alarm of mild Mr. Terry, who characterized him as ' the most hasty and cholerick young man that ever I knew.' He behaved very civilly, however, during his stay with Roe ; and when, tiring of the hardships of camp life, he in Nov. 1617 returned to Surat, the ambassador made a special request that he should be well treated and accommodated with a passage (see *Letters Received*, vol. vi. p. 143). His

[*March*] 12.—I went to the King, and carried a new-yeares gift,[1] a paire of very faire knives of my owne, and six glasses of yours [*i.e.* the Company's]. The excuse I made was well received, and the King used mee with all grace; this onely was my comfort. He said whatsoever came from my hands was present sufficient: he accepted my love; and it was his part now to give me. I found a gainer[2] by him, who had so farre performed his promise that I perceived the King instructed in my desire, and gave present order to an officer to send for Mr. Bidolph to pay him to his content for such things as he claymed, and all the others were acknowledged to be received by name; and that when I went to the Prince, the King would write; but was loth to part with any thing, of which the best sweetbagge lay before him. I replyed: I was as loth to goe emptie-handed; so it rested. The King commanded I should come up and stand within, on the degrees [*i.e.* steps] of his throne by him, where I found on one side the Persian ambassadour, on the other the old King [of] Candahar [see p. 226], with whom I ranked; and he presently fell to begge a knife, which next day I sent. The King called for the Persian to come downe, to whom he gave a jewell and a young elephant, for which he kneeled and saluted the ground

subsequent career will be found in the *Dictionary of National Biography*. He is to be distinguished from the Sir Thomas Herbert who travelled in the East some ten years later.

Coryat, who records Herbert's discovery of the spring, mentions also that 'the day after, one of the Kings *haddys* finding the same and striving for it was taken by my Lords people and bound all, &c.; a great controversie being about it.' He also praises 'the charitie of two great men, that in the time of this great drought were at the charge of sending ten camels with twentie persons every day to the said river [Narbada] for water and did distribute the water to the poore, which was so deare that they sold a little skinne for eight *pise*.'

[1] The *Nauroz* festivities of this year are described at p. 370 of the *Memoirs* (vol. i.).

[2] This is evidently a copyist's or printer's error for 'Aganor' (Āgha Nūr), of whom see p. 143. He was master of the ceremonies at the *Nauroz* festivities, and 'new undertooke my court busines' (Roe's Accounts). The ambassador speaks of him later as having 'the oversight of strangers affaires.'

with his head. The throne was the same used the last yeare, and all the other furniture. At the upper end was set the King my soveraignes picture, the Queenes, my Lady Elizabeths, Sir Thomas Smiths and some others; two pieces of good and fine tapistrie below them, that came from Persia; a throne of gold set all over with rubies, emeralds and turqueis; and the old musicke of singing whores.

This day I dispatched to Surat my advice [1] of the Persian businesse and the new ambassadour, and some remembrance to Abram Chan the Governour; from whom I received a letter that in his absence our nation had beene wronged, against his knowledge, but that, his power being augmented by the Prince, he desired me to be confident in him: that while he lived in authoritie we should never suffer any such abuses, but we should live in all freedome.

[*March*] 13.—I sent a complement to Asaph Chan, a faire wrought night-cap of mine owne, and a rich paire of gloves, which he returned as uselesse in this countrey; the cap he received, and desired some Alegant wine, which I sent the next day at night. Aganor (whose diligence now gave me great hope and ease) sent a *Bannian* his secretary to tell mee hee had order for the dispatch of the merchants goods, and that his man should attend Mr. Biddolph to finish it: that the patternes should be sent me home: and that the King would give me a coat, and money to beare my charges to the Prince. I returned answere that I had no use of a Babylonish garment, nor needed money: if His Majestie were pleased to consider the injuries offered, of which the paper testified remayned in his hands, and to give me his letter to the Prince with some presents, or else to write in my excuse, it was all I would desire: but for his gifts I expected none but justice.

[*March*] 21.—I [2] yet could not at instant presse it further; only I discovered the Kings doubts, for he suspected my stealing out of his countrey, and breach with our nation: for

---

[1] See *Add. MS.* 6115, f. 175. The letter has been partly printed in *Letters Received*, vol. v. (p. 335). The 'new ambassador' is Connock, who was reported by Barker to have assumed that title; Connock himself vehemently denied it (*ibid.* pp. 196, 201).

[2] Here again Purchas's extract commences in the middle of a story.

the Prince, either out of guiltinesse or feare, or perhaps cunning, to make us the pretence of his owne dessignes, had newly enformed the King that next yeare the English purposed the taking of Surat and keeping it; of which our owne folly gave some colour, for lately upon one of their ordinary brabbles they caused two hundred musketers to land and march toward Surat, and being met by divers the joyfull mariners gave out they went to take it. This absurde bravado (for a handfull of men to passe twelve mile to a walled towne, able to put out a thousand horse armed and as many shot, a river to passe which a few men would defend against a good armie) gave just occasion of scorne and offence; and which the Prince apprehended for some other his owne ends, to refortifie the castle and towne, and to send downe ordnance for the defence: a good provision to keepe a doore open to flie out, if his brother live to correct his ambition. But this information occurring with my discontents heere, and some free language, my pressure to goe to Brampore, and flying newes that we had taken Goa and were preparing a great fleet in England, did cause some suspition in the King, which, though he concealed it, yet hee thought to discover by the former discourse,[1] with which hee rested fully satisfied, but

[1] This Purchas has evidently omitted; but some account of it is given in a letter of Roe's to Surat of 7 April (f. 180 of the MS.): 'The King, as soone as the rayns are finished, will make all hast to Lahor. Hee hath sent thowsands before, and it is doubted the water here will not last a month, but that wee must all remoove to the river or Brampoore way; and then, besides new chardge, I shall endure much miserye to sitt out with my meane provision in tents. The Kings departure thither is dayly expected; halfe the *leskar* is already gone. His goeing to Lahor hee tould mee him selfe, and therfore would not suffer me to goe to Brampoore; but first hee used policy with mee, thincking I had desiered to goe to slipp away (for such jealousyes hee conceives of us, enfused by the Prince); but when I mett him right, hee was well satisfyed, and assured mee it was better for mee to stay by him untill I were recalld home, for that hee was my best frend; urdging a promise to goe to Lahor with him, which condicionally I gave.' The Mogul thereupon wrote two letters to the Prince, one to excuse Roe's non-attendance, and the other to order redress of the abuses of which the ambassador had complained.

The greater part of this letter of Roe's has been printed in *Letters Received*, vol. v. p. 338.

I did not. I had beene long fed with words, and knew, as well as the heart that trembled, that feare of us only preserved our residence.

March 29.—This complaining of officers is a tune so new, so odious in court that it troubleth all great men; it beeing their owne case, who, living upon farming governments, in which they use all tyrannie to the naturals, are loth to suffer a way open to the Kings understanding of their practice; who ordinarily hang men by the heeles, to confesse money or to ransome themselves from no fault. This made all men envie my imployment, and avoid me as an informer.

To Nicholas Bangham at Burhānpur.[1]
(*Add. MS.* 6115, f. 177.)
April 1, 1617.

... My entent to come visitt yow is stayed by the King.... I desier yow to goe to the Prince and to desire him not to take in ill part my not coming, which I had a great affection too.... If His Highnes had beene pleased to lett myne owne goods come to my hands, I had long since visited him with a good present; but nowe empty handed I was ashamed to come.... If the Prince desier to knowe what was entended for him, yow may lett him know a rich saddle and furniture for a horse, a cushion to leane on of needle worke in gould, and a faire picture. Use your best diligence to keepe fayre quarter with that proud and unjust man; yow will fynd all wilbe to little. Now I proceed to engage yow in the prosecution of an ould debt of Zulpheckcarcons.... Among these [papers] yow shall fynd by a copy of Shawhussen, late Governor of the Custome House at Suratt, that hee is yet debtor to the English 500 *ma.* on the last years reckonings, besides 700 *m.* taken in bribes.... Now yow must also help to call him to account. .... The three palang posts [*palangposh*, a bed-cover] I have received from Mr. Terry: so good, soe fine as they give mee much content. I have not had my mony in some other places so well bestowed. I shall returne with nothing, but some toyes for my frends. I have made use of all my poore stock and creditt only in the Companyes service.... Now I wilbe bould to trouble yow; that if yow will lett mee eyther bee your halfe in the muske yow have bought, or provide for mee about 30 ounces, I will speedely make yow over mony. For bezars ... some I desier to have for my frends, though I pay

[1] From 'Mando, on the sowth side, neare the edge of the hill, a *course* from the towne.'

deare ; and what yow doe I will not mislike.... Next, I desire yow to provide for mee three or four carpetts of a kynd of cloth staynd, and wrought of severall sizes and fresh coulors and the best yow can gett at any price. Mr. Terry hath made me in love with them. Lastly, if yow light of any fine carpett or stuff or other toy which yow thinck is rare, of silke, gould, or other, that yow will buy it for mee ; and some six peices of fine cheates [*i.e.* chintz], spotted with fresh coulors in flowers or woorkes, not lawnes but close cloth ; the best are cheapest, in my estimation. And if a fine quilt, stitchd with silke, come in your way, remember your frend.... I heare yow have fine and curious China ware. If yow will spare me some dozen fine cupps and dishes (such as yow will choose), I will give as much as any man. All these I desier yow will keepe for mee till wee meete ; for I hope to pass downe by Brampoor toward England in October, and I would not trouble yow soe much but that I am resolved homward, and would willingly carry somewhat. My stock will not reach to things of profitt and trade ; therfore, seeing I shall not gett riches, I would yet pleasure my frends.... I am glad to heare the Prince useth yow well and that any hope of goodnes appeares in him. It makes mee beeleeve his father did not dissemble with mee in his late promises.... Wee [are] all, except Mr. Terry, in health, and H. Garrard. I have by Gods mercy recovered a good constitution of body. Wee live on a rock, allmost starved for water ; the *leskar* turned out and in miserable case. The King lately tould mee hee would depart to Lahor, and every day it is expected when hee will goe to the river, and returne at the raynes. This necessitye makes mee send away two horses ... which I desier yow either to putt off or send downe to Suratt.... Here they will not yeild a *pice*, for noe great man is suffered to keepe any, or not above two. The poore dye for thirst.... Such a cargazon as wee received, a pedler would have scorned in England to travell with ; wherby wee are become not only despised but they are weary of our company. I am ashamd when any man asketh what the merchants have to sell ; but it is my portion...

April 25.—I received from Dabull road from Captain Pepwell that according to advise he had stayed the juncke bound for Mocha,[1] but, weighing the caution given by mee

---

[1] In a letter to Pepwell of 4 Jan. 1617 (*Letters Received*, vol. v. p. 317), Roe had suggested, as a prize particularly worth taking, the vessel which yearly traded between Dābhol and the Red Sea. Dābhol, a town on the Malabar Coast, 85 miles S.E. from Bombay, was the principal port of the Bījāpur kingdom ; and in view of the war then being waged between the Mogul and the allied Deccan

to consider well what correspondence were betweene that Prince and Mozolapatan (in whose territorie the *Solomon* was and could not get to sea), finding both alliance and friendship, he freed her without spoile (alleaging the refusall of trade to Middleton) ; which courtesie procured him so good entertainment as the Indies affoords seldome : free trade, and promise to take three hundred clothes yearely, a good quantitie of lead sold for money, and some ordnance (which I like not : to arme the Indians, and the Portugals friends, enemies to the Mogoll) and all other courtesies, which (if this kindnesse proceeded not for that the juncke was yet under command) gives me good hope of some trade in sale yearely at the port. However, the freeing of the juncke assures me the commander will doe nothing by catching [*i.e.* prize-taking] prejudiciall to the Company, and deliver himselfe honestly from the jealousies cast upon him from Dabul.[1] Hee signifies his intent to proceed to Callicute ;[2] and if that factorie be not worth supplyes, to transmit it to Dabul.

[*April*] 27.—By the foot-post I received from Mesolapatan that the *Salomon* was got to sea, and the *Hosiander* from Bantam arrived, who brought the ill newes of the losse of the *Hector* and *Concord*, careening in the roade of Jacatra, on Java :[3]

princes, Roe thought that such a capture would be favourably received at court. Nor was a pretext wanting. At the time of Sir Henry Middleton's visit in February, 1612, the governor, while promising all friendly usage, had secretly prevented the merchants from trafficking with the English (*Lancaster's Voyages*, p. 197) ; and this action Roe chose to interpret as a mark of sympathy with the Portuguese and a sufficient reason for retaliation. He warned Pepwell, however, first to make sure that the capture of the junk would not embroil the English at Masulipatam with the King of Golconda, owing to the close relations between the latter court and Bījāpur.

[1] Probably this is an error for ' Surat ' (see Roe's letter in *Letters Received*, vol. v. p. 204).

[2] A factory had been settled at Cranganor (Kodungalur), near Cochin, by Captain Keeling on his way to Bantam in 1616, but after a few weeks the merchants moved to Calicut. However, the experiment was not a success, and Pepwell took the factors away.

[3] This report was afterwards corrected. ' The *Hector* was not cast away, but broke up by Captain Keeling, who the 10th of October,

in recompence, that the *Dragon*, *Clove*, and *Defence* were homeward laden from Bantam. I tooke this occasion to convey a letter to the Governour of Dabul over-land, to apprehend the overture newly made by him of the trade. Though I had little opinion of the place, yet I would not neglect that, nor encourage the next fleete to proceed but upon better assurance then a forced friendship and offers made while their juncke was in our power. The effect was to signifie the causes of our staying their goods for refusing trade to Sir Henry Middleton : but now finding in him a better inclination, and a desire to receive us and to establish a friendship and league, a promise to take cloth in good quantitie, I required, if these motions were hearty and such as befitted a man of honour, that he would write to the King his master to procure his *firman* with such priviledges as were fit for merchants, and his promise to buy our goods and to fulfill all the friendly offers made by him his officer, under his seale, and with expedition to send it mee to the court of the Great Mogoll, whereby I might receive assurance and encouragement that they entended faith ; and on such reception I did undertake on the behalfe of the King of England a good and firme peace toward his master, his subjects free passage in the seas from any oppression by our fleets, and that yearely I would either send a ship to his port for trade or (if it so required) leave and establish a residence in his government. I doubt not but yearely, for feare or love, some good trade by sales may bee made ; but for envestments it will not be worth it ; only I proceeded as I would have wished all men, not with too seeming eager a desire, nor to swallow any offers and conditions hungerly ; for strict care in the first setling is the best ad-

1616, sett sayle for England ' (Roe's letter to Burhānpur, 17 May, 1617 : *Add. MS.* 6115, f. 192). Keeling had received permission to return, ' such order comming from England by the *Swanne* that if hee would he might ' (*ibid.* f. 191).

Jacatra was the native town which was afterwards converted by the Dutch into their settlement of Batavia (Nova).

One of the letters received by Roe from Masulipatam was evidently that from Lucas Antheunis printed at p. 173 of *Letters Received*, vol. v.

vantage, and for misery [1] of ensuing times, it being a generall rule never to mend your first estate, often to empaire it. Every mans best houre is when he is new, a stranger, and at first seene ; after, the natural lenitie [levitie ?] of these barbarians finds all that brings not change fastidious. This dispatch I committed to Mr. Bangham,[2] and desired him to make diligent enquiry of the commodities, advantages, inconveniences, humours and affections of these Decannies towards us.[3]

[*April*] 30.—The time [4] that he brought me the excuses of the Persian ambassadour for failing in taking his leave of me, which he would not send by a servant, but uttered the truth that the ambassadour was not sicke, as he pretended, but receiving no content from the King in his businesse, he suddenly tooke leave ; and having given thirty faire horses at his departure, the King gave in recompence three thousand *rupias*,[5]

[1] The text is evidently corrupt. Possibly we should read : ' for preventing misery.'

[2] The chief factor at Burhānpur. Thevenot renders this sentence : ' Je mis cette depesche entre les mains de nostre Bangan ' ; adding, as a marginal note : ' Bangam signifie interprete.' This amusing confusion appears to have resulted from the Company's broker (who generally acted as linguist) being mentioned as a *Banyan*.

[3] Roe's letter will be found in *Add. MS.* 6115 (f. 190). The Governor's reply was received in June. In this he reiterated the promises made to Pepwell, but would not commit himself to buy any specified quantity of goods yearly ; as for the desired *farmān*, he had sent Roe's letter to the King, and would communicate to the ambassador his reply (Roe to Bangham, 21 June, 1617). This answer seemed to Roe sufficiently encouraging to follow up the matter ; and he accordingly arranged in the following February that the *Anne* should call at Dābhol on her way to the Red Sea ; this, however, was found to be impracticable, and nothing more was done till the sailing of the fleet in 1619, when Captain Bonner, doubtless at Roe's suggestion, put into Dābhol road on his way down the coast. No sales were effected, but the authorities were so lavish in promises that the English forbore to enforce a trade and sent word to Surat advising a further attempt in the following year.

[4] Something has been omitted here. Āgha Nūr seems to have been the person referred to.

[5] Jahāngīr says that he gave the ambassador a sum equal to 30,000 rupees, and that the presents sent to the Shāh were of the value of 100,000 rupees (*Memoirs*, vol. i. p. 374). The ambassador died at Agra a few months later (*ibid*. p. 398).

which he tooke in great scorne; whereupon the King prized all that the ambassadour had given him at meane rates, and likewise all that the King had returned since his arrivall, even to slaves, drinke, mellons, pines, plantanes, hawkes, plumes, the eliphant and whatsoever at extreme high rates, and sending both bils made it up in money. This base usage and scorne caused him to excuse his not seeing Asaph Chan and Etimon Dowlet on a fever; which having done, hee could not come through the towne to mee without discoverie, but desired him to acquaint me with the truth, and to make all excuse and profession that hee would recompence this discourtesie by double friendship to my countrimen in Persia; with some bitternesse against the King, which Aganor as freely delivered, and I seemed as unwilling to heare. I presented them with some Aligant and knives, and we parted.

May 12.—I received newes of a great blow given the Persian by the Turkes army, so that Tavris [*i.e.* Tabrīz] was rased, and the Shabas not able to keepe the field.[1]

To the Factors at Surat.
(*Add. MS*. 6115, f. 194.)

May 22, 1617.

... Upon your last complaynt, sent up in Persian, and my delivery to the King, His Majestie wrote a lettre to the Prince not many dayes past (for I procured Aganor to moove it anew) as full of favour as I could desire, commanding us to bee used in all sorts as respectively as his owne subjects: that wee came only to see him and his cuntrie, and therfore hee would not endure any wrong to bee offered to us. Hee tooke particular notice of your restraynt in victualls, and customes for victualls, and the detention of the presents and the sealing them to bee directed to the Prince, and many other circumstances. Besides, hee gave order to Asaph-Chan to write four lettres to fower of the Princes officers by name, to take knowledg of the complaynt made against them and to signifie at lardg His Majesties pleasure and what himself had written the Prince. These lettres Aganor voweth hee saw written and read them, and sayth they are sent away; but I feare Asaph-Chan did only blind us both (though the other vowe fayre play, and that the

---

[1] An account of the campaign, written by the Turkish Grand Wazīr, will be found in *Purchas*, vol. ii. p. 1612. See also Knolles's *History of the Turks* (1687 edn., vol. ii. p. 950).

King would bee extreame angery at any fraud after his order), because they came not to my hands. I desier yow to make all enquiery what lettres or *firmaens* came lately to any in Suratt concerning us; for if our great solicitor have fayled, I will not faile to make the King understand yt. I am confident his desire is now to satisfye us, and I would not lett it coole. The last newes that came to this court from Persia is not good for us. The Shabas, sending part of his armie to entercept a convoy of the Turkes, was betrayd by one of his owne captains and cutt to peices 12,000 of his choyce guards, wherby the Turks armie advanced into the feild toward Tawris, and the Shabas, not able to abyde him, razed it and desmantled it wholy, and, wasting the cuntrie about, keepes the strengths of the hills. The truth of newes that comes soe far is doubtfull; but the King received it from the governors of his borders. . . . I have buried a servant, and my surgeon lyes at Gods mercy. . . .

[*May*] 25.—A lion and a woolfe used my house and nightly put us in alarume, fetching away sheepe and goats out of my court, and leaping a high wall with them. I sent to aske leave to kill it, for that no man may meddle with lions but the King, and it was granted. I ranne out into the court upon the noyse, and the beast, missing his prey, seized on a little Island dogge before me,[1] that I had long kept. But the woolfe one of my servants killed, and I sent it the King.

June 14.—Certaine goods of the Jesuites were sent from Cambaya in a cabinet, phisicke and necessaries and a letter, which were betrayed by the bringer, and delivered the King; which he opened and sent for the Padre to reade the letter, and to see all in the boxes, of which nothing liking him, he returned all; which I observe as a warning to all that deale in this kingdome, to bee wary of what they write or send; for such is the custome and humour of the King, that he will seize and see all, lest any toy should escape his appetite.

[*June*] 18.—I received letters from Amadavar of the hope of the fall of indico, by the failing of the Goa *caffila*,[2] and that

[1] 'A little white neat shock, that ran out barking at him' (Terry, p. 197). An Iceland dog was 'a shaggy, sharp-eared white dog, formerly in favour as a lap-dog in England' (*Oxford Eng. Dict.*). While at Māndu the English found it necessary to keep a fire burning at night outside their dwelling to scare away wild beasts.

[2] The non-arrival of the usual fleet of Portuguese frigates to buy supplies for Europe.

there was plentie to be bought, but deare : that the unicornes horne was returned as without vertue, concerning which I gave him new advice [see p. 254 n] : many complaints against Surat and others, which I meddle not with. I received from Brampoore two letters, how doubtfull the debt of Ralph [1] stood, and newes of the returne of Spragge from the *leskar* of Decan.[2] The Generall Melickamber,[3] with much shew of honour, gave instant order for privie search in all his campe for the Persian fled, and by me remanded [*i.e.* demanded back] ; but finding him departed to Vizeapoore [Bījāpur] by testimony, that businesse was pursued no further, but by a letter to a Dutch there resident. The Generall desired Spragge to be a meanes to bring him English cloth and swords to his campe for the supply of his souldiers, which lye within sixe dayes of Brampoore. In my opinion, that had beene a good employment of some idle men and a way to vent our dead commodities.

To Nicholas Bangham at Burhānpur.
(*Add. MS.* 6115, f. 201.)

Mandoa, June 21, 1617.

.... I desier yow to write me ... what way your factions lye among the great men. Wee heare divers rumors, but cannot beleeve none. Yow may easely sound Mahobett-Chan, and yow shall doe me a great pleasure to visitt him in my name and to tell him that I alway wish his presence heare ; and (as if it came of your selfe) lett him know that I many tymes complayne of discurtesyes showed mee by Asaph-Chan, and that hee is soe great noe man dares informe the King ; my selfe, wanting language, suffer many tymes that which the King in his goodnes would redresse ; and that I have long hoped for his comming. By this discourse yow may gather some what of his affection ; and perhaps hee may offer to

---

[1] A printer's error for Zulph, *i.e.* Zūlfakār Khān.

[2] He had been sent in pursuit of a Persian named Mīrzā Abbās, whom Fetiplace had trusted at Agra to the amount of 1700 rupees. The debtor had promised to make repayment at Māndu, but fled thence in the night, intending, it was supposed, to take refuge in the enemy's camp.

[3] Malik Ambar, the well-known generalissimo of the Ahmadnagar kingdom.

write to the King in my behalfe and to lett him know that which all wee cannot, for want of a bould toong; if not for love to us (which I never expect harty from a Moore), yet for spight to the other, against whom (it is sayd here) he letts slipp no occasion to utter all hee knowes. I may perhaps this way startle our hollow frend, or how ever it is but one labor lost. I am with the King in the same termes that ever; but Asaph Chan and I had lately some little wrangle. Hee, suspecting I came to complayne against Groo [see p. 381 n], whom hee protects, hindered mee from comming up to the King so neare as to deliver or make signes to speake. I had noe entention then to say any thing, but excepted at the trick. Wee parted faire; but I should bee extreame glad so farr to awaken him as to lett him see I would seeke other meanes when hee playd falce, and that I neither feared him nor would be bound to observe his rules nor to endure his affronts. . . .

To the Same.
(*Add. MS*. 6115, f. 202.)

Mandoa, July first, 1617.

. . . Mahobett-Chan, I understand, expects I should doe as Edwards did; but hee is deceived, and, if his memory fayle not, hee tooke knowledge of mee on the way, for I mett him, but would not visitt him whom I knew not; and his lettre to mee is of a nother stile. Besides, Edwards went by Bramport to take his leave of him and reape the last cropp of the liberality hoped for. But if hee bee so proud, I can as soone forgett him. . . . I thancke yow for the two China cupps, and doe extreamely like them for the curiositye. Their price I must bee content with, because the buyer cannot make yt; but they are dearer here at that rate by much then in England. I doe not desiere any more of that sort so small; but if yow can fitt mee out of the rest with a parcell of fine dishes or cupps for use, or any peece, as a bottle or eywer, and of the best sorts . . . to make up this summe 100 or 80 *rup*., I desier yow to make your choyce for mee. . . .

To the Factors at Surat.
(*Add. MS*. 6115, f. 203.)

Mandoa, July first, 1617.

. . . I would wish yow not to take so suddeyne alarums at any rumor. See first order and proclamation made to expell yow. Yet to advise what yow heare is not amisse, to make mee looke about. But assure yourselfe the Prince dares not doe such an affront to his father without his privetye, and the King would not consent without sheweing some effect of his reasons to mee ; and I live not heare so idle as to bee ignorant of that concerns us. I know well our enemyes have tryed the Kings affection ; but Asaph-Chan hath opposed it, if not for frendship, yet for reason of state. Neyther are the Portugalls in so good creditt here as to bee able to hurt us ; it is enough they can procure them selves liberty, the King noe way gracing them, the Prince lately affronting and using them uncivilly, seeasing their goods and persons. All these are conjectures. If wee have any deadly enemy, it is our owne disorder, that giveth such as wish our absence advantage against us. ...

To FRANCIS FETIPLACE AT AGRA.
(*Add. MS.* 6115, f. 205.)

20th July, 1617.

. . . I desier much newes from Mr. Shalbanck, and with yt knowledge whether my lettres dated in January, with one to Thom. Coriat, by his owne expresse, came to hand ; and that I might by it know his purpose for England, or stay, or, if I take any new course, whither hee will goe with mee.[1] I hope hee is now long since returnd. ... At court I have not beene this month for extreamety of weather. ...

July 30.—I received from Surat of the casting away of two Dutch ships on the coast of Damon, that, having come from the southward with spices and China silkes, were bound for the Red Sea, but, losing their season with much extremitie of weather, beating many weekes about the entrance for harbour, attempted the like at Socatra and upon the coast of Arabia, but being not able to get in any way, they resolved for Surat, hoping by the last yeares good successe to be able to ride safely ; but the yeares differ, and beeing forced to

[1] Roe was of course expecting either to be sent to Persia or to be allowed to return to England. It was doubtless in consequence of this invitation that Coryat rejoined him at Māndu, though in so weak a state of health that one day he fainted in the ambassador's presence and was with difficulty brought to his senses. He left Māndu with Roe ; but, when it became evident that Jahāngīr's destination was Ahmadābād, Coryat set out for Surat, hoping probably either to get a passage to Persia by sea or to go home by the next ship. However, the hospitality of the Surat factors, who plied him with sack, proved too much for his enfeebled constitution, and (says Terry) ' he overtook death in the month of December, 1617, and was buried under a little monument like one of those are usually made in our churchyards.'

anchor in extremitie their greater ship cut her masts by boord, and after, her cables breaking, shee went ashore upon the coast, ozie ground within musket shot. The ship kept upright, but having lost their long boat, and their skiffe not able to live, by rafters foure men got ashoare, and the tydes heaving her in upon the spring, they saved much goods and all their people. Her pinnasse of sixtie tunne was beaten to pieces.[1]

August 21.—The King of Candahòr came to visit me and brought wine and fruit, sate halfe an houre, and for one jest of his begged a bottle of wine.

The Prince Sultan Corseroone had his first day of hoped libertie, and came to take ayre and pleasure at the banquetting house by me. The Prince at Brampoore had made a marriage [2] without the Kings consent, and gotten displeasure; besides, some practice of his was discovered against his brothers life, but this as a secret. He was called for to court. Normahall and Asaph Chan, by their fathers advice, came about to make a peace with Corsoroone and alliance, and with infinite joy his libertie is expected.[3]

---

[1] These ships were the *Middelburg* and the *Duif*, under the command of Pieter van den Broecke, the captain of the ship which had visited Surat in the previous year. With him came Pieter Gillis van Ravesteyn and Adriaan Willemsz. Goeree. They left Bantam on 8 March, 1617 (N.S.), and after calling at Mauritius, stretched across to the coast of Melinde and into the mouth of the Red Sea. Then, as the *Middelburg* had sprung a leak, Van den Broecke made for Sokotra; but, missing it, was obliged to run before the wind in the hope of getting into Surat. The storm increased in violence, and the ship struck on the coast near Damān. As narrated by Roe, the crew reached the shore in safety, where they constructed a barricade to defend their goods. Shortly after, they were joined by the company of the *Duif*, which had stranded a mile off. Van den Broecke burnt the wreck of his vessel, and the whole party marched to Gandevi, near Surat, where they took up their quarters (Van den Broecke, *Op sijne Reysen*, p. 73; Terpstra, *Opkomst*, p. 63). There is an interesting account of the shipwreck in a letter from the Surat factors to the Company (*Letters Received*, vol. vi. p. 162).

[2] With the daughter of Shāhnawāz Khān, son of the Khān-khānān.

[3] On 12 Dec. 1616, in writing to Surat, Roe had mentioned a rumour that 'Sultan Curserone shall marrie Normahalls daughter, and have liberty, and that all the faction will adhere to him' (cf. p. 325). The lady in question was the daughter of Nūr Mahal by

[*August*] 22.—The King feasted at Asaph Chans. I received from Aleppo and Persia passages of the warre, the Turkes retrait, but no word of our English, only that the Captaine of Grinins [1] had written to practise their disgrace.

To Libby Chapman, Consul at Aleppo.
(*Add. MS.* 6115, f. 206.)

August 21, 1617.

... Your newes is very acceptable as newes, for my life is more solitary and retired from any then any hermitt. ... Our trade here is a fickle thing, depending on the unconstant will of a prince that hath noe laws, nor understands no bonds and obligations of honor nor amitye but such as brings him some pleasure or content to his appetite. Our English goods are in could request, and it is impossible for any rethorique to alter nature. Toyes to please phancy, or were [ware] fitt for women and children, are the soder and life of this trade. In hope of them the other is permitted us; and some good success by Gods blessing over our enemyes hath given a kind of creditt, of awe rather then love. The Portugalls decay in India, and by their fall wee may rise. One prosperous day with them against us will turne the face of these princes into frownes. ... I may allmost safely say that the Mogol is the greatest prince of Asia, if China contradict it not (of which wee knowe little). ... His greatnes substantially is not in yt selfe, but in the weaknes of his neighbors, whom like an overgrowne pike hee feedes on as frye. Pride, pleasure, and riches are their best discription. Honesty and truth, discipline, civilitye, they have none, or very little. ..

her former husband, Shīr Afgan, and there seems little doubt that, had Khusrau accepted the proffered alliance, he would have regained his liberty, and perhaps his rightful place at court. But he was devotedly attached to his existing wife, and refused to listen to any proposal of the kind. His intended bride was therefore transferred to his youngest brother, Prince Shahryār, whom the empress endeavoured (though unsuccessfully) to set up as a rival to Prince Khurram (cf. *Della Valle*, Hakluyt Soc. edn., vol. i. p. 56, and *The English Factories*, 1624-29, pp. xvii, xxiv).

[1] 'Geroon,' the old name for 'Ormus,' is probably meant. There is some confusion as to the date on which these letters were received. As will be seen from Roe's reply, they arrived on the 20th, not the 22nd.

To WILLIAM ROBBINS AT ISPAHAN.[1]
(*Add. MS.* 6115, f. 207.)

Mandoe, August 21, 1617.

Both your mentioned lettrs I have received by long passadges; this last arrived the 20 present, by which I understand your honest and effectuall care of the trust committ[ed] yow.... I doubt not yow have long since received my lettrs by the post of Mahomet Raza Baege, the Shaw-bas his ambassador, dispeeded from court the 10th of January, 1616, and since yow are fully possessed of our intents to prosecute the negotiation of Persia by the arrivall of our factors. I can yet proceed to no farther engagement then by way of advise to wish yow as a faythfull Englishman to deale clearly with the Prince what wee seeke and what wee will performe. I feare, as this beginning was rash, it may receive some disgrace, especially if any of our servants either overlash in their woords and promises or in their titles. Therfore, that yow may truly know what yow may safely deliver: Edward Connock was sent from Suratt as a factor to beginn and make offer of the amety, unprovided either of instructions, goods, or meanes fitt for such an enterprise. Therfore the Prince wilbe pleasd not to judg us by this attempt, which was rather to showe our affection then any proofe of our abilitye. Neyther will it bee ever embrased by the English, unlesse a port bee seecured or mart established, prises agreed on for such quantetyes of both sides as that neither be deceived, wee in fitting and putting off of our comoditye, nor the Prince of vent for his. Upon these tearmes yow may bee bould to say whatsoever hee desiers may bee accomplished; but a straggling, peddling, uncertayne trade will neyther profitt nor become so great nations. My last is more lardge in this particular. Only I find in all your lettres yow have a beleefe that Sir Robert Sherley is a well wisher to his countrie and an enemie to the Portugall. I would perswade yow out of this error. His actions showe little reason; he hath not only procured for them a peace, but is engaged to procure for them the whole trafique, and to that end is he imployed. I doubt not the Sha-bas may have a good affection to us; but yet hee will deale like a king and come fayre off from his first offer. It is not good to bee blind, nor by blinding others to hope to atteyne our ends; therfore I would not wish any Englishman to undertake that the English will deale for all the Kings goods, except hee will exchang it for cloth and our English comodityes; then bee bould; the rest I knowe what wee are

---

[1] A copy sent overland by Robbins to the Company is in the I.O. Records (*O.C.*, No. 530). It has been printed in *Letters Received*, vol. vi. (p. 75).

able to performe. Nor that wee will take Ormus and beate the Portugall out of those seas : these are vanityes.[1] The Company entend a trade, not a warr, but in their owne defence, and that bravely and honestly. It were better for the Prince to ayme only at that free commerce ; so he should understand the sweetnes of a trade and the difference of nations. But I professe I know not upon what tearmes any way to bee engaged, the Company not yet knowinge of the enterprise ; therfore I will farthar spare my opinion untill I can doe yt upon good grownd, and only advise yow to assist this beginning with all force and yet with all moderation ; to cast off all hopes of Sir Robert Sherley advancing us, and trust to our selves and our owne honest wayes. Thus yow shalbe sure to fynd a just recompence to your desarts.

I feare it wilbe my hard fortune this yeare to visitt yow by order from His Majestie, and to help to build upon this foundation ; for by this fleete I expect a resolution from England, and suppose I shall receive full commission to treat effectually. If it fall out so, yow shall fynd a frend that will deserve well your paynes. In the meane tyme, let no newe inventions putt yow out of the way to show the King my lettrs and the last articles sent His Majestie, wherof yow have a copy in English, and they were agreed unto here by his ambassador. I neede not send a transcript, for, if they miscarried, now they will arrive too late, for I shall almost bee in Persia as soone as this.[2] If I come not, I returne for England, and these affayres will no more concerne mee. So, in expectation of farther newes from the true founteyne, I commit yow to God.

[*August*] 25.—I advised to Agra my proceeding in the Armenians businesse ;[3] backe to Surat and Brampore of all occurrents.

[1] Yet in less than five years the English did both.

[2] As will be seen, the letters from England contained no definite instructions to Roe to proceed to Persia, and he contented himself therefore with authorising the factors already on the spot to act on his behalf. It was, however, believed in London at the beginning of 1619 that Roe had either gone (*Cal. State Papers : E. Indies*, 1617-21, No. 532) or was going (*ibid.* No. 536) to Ispahān, and this has been accepted as a fact by the editor of the *Calendar* (preface, pp. xxx and lxix), and others.

[3] An Armenian had bought cloth at Ajmer from the English factors to the value of 7,500 rupees, but had failed to pay the last instalment of his debt (see *Letters Received*, vol. vi. p. 244). The letter to Agra is given at f. 209 of the MS. ; those to Burhānpur and Surat, at ff. 209, 261. In the one to Burhānpur Roe says : ' At this present the Prince is called for up in displeasure. . . . The newes here is that the King will for Guzuratt ; but I thinck necessitye and scarcety will send him for Agra.'

This day Asaph Chan feasted Normahall [and ?] the Prince Sultan Corsoroone ; as is reported, to make a firme alliance, and that he will bring away a wife, by his fathers importunitie. This will beget his full libertie, and our proud masters ruine.

To the expected Generall which shall arrive this yeare.[1]
(*Add. MS.* 6115, f. 258.)

August 30, 1617.

... The generall estate of our establishment here is safe enough as long as wee keepe our reputation up against the Portugalls ; for though the King in his owne disposition bee willing to enterteyne us, his subjects importunitye and wearines would soone eject us, if feare restrained not their complaynts. Besides, if wee should be putt to a defence, I have nothing to flye unto, wherby I might maynteyne to the King that our comming into these parts is any way comodious to him or his subjects, but the contrarie manifould and manifest ; for our cloth, nor any other comodityes of England are not requested. It is often cast unto mee : what breing yow but trash that wee esteeme not ? Another strength alsoe wee fayle in, which were to fly to the nobilitye to assist mee. But for what reason ? Upon what ground ? They answere : wee expected from yow fine, rare, and rich stuffs and toyes to buy from yow, to serve the King with at the *Norose* and other feasts, wherby wee might be furnished at hand, and eased of the labor and chardge to seeke and send abroad ; but yow fitt us with nothing but knives and ill looking glasses. What advantage have wee by yow ? The fault of this hath beene ill enformation, ignorance of their factors, or willfullnes in the owners. At once if this place were but fitted with goods as it ought to bee, wee should not only rayse a great stock tymely to provide our ladings, but bee acceptable to the King and his nobilitye, desiered and sought after ; wheras now wee are wearisome to them and dispised. ... The last fleete brought with them a dreame of building forts and maynteyning garrisons ; which if yours doe, it must bee awakened. The King will not give away his land, nor become subject to them whom hee may now command. If wee were all aboord and their shipps on returne, they would talke with us of such a matter, but never performe it. Now they laugh at the motion, as they have good cause. Or if the King would grant one, I would not accept yt. I know what kind of chardg the profitt of the trade can bare and our stocke compasse. Neyther would the port aymed at ever be

---

[1] The 'expected General' proved to be Martin Pring, of whom see later.

haunted with merchannts. . . . The next thing that occures to my mind is the abuses of the last fleete, the ill goverment, both in Christianitye and moorall civilitye. . . . I could never open my mouth for wrongs offered us but I was stopped with lettres of woorse complaynt agaynst our barbarous disorders, in so much that it hath occasioned the Prince to send downe a *firmaen* to order us by force this yeare (for which hee tooke my woord in writing last, and fynds it of no force). This hee doth, not only for order sake, but to pick a just occasion to turne us out with shame ; therfore your wisdome and goverment must soundly prevent. . . . The presents sent this yeare . . . I desier yow to keepe them all aboord untill I can send some expresse order and resolution. . . . I knowe not mine owne purpose for returne or stay, untill I see my lettres and instructions. . . . I doe for some reasons expect order from His Majestie to goe for Persia ; which, if it come, I must obey, very unwillingly, to follow such a beginning and such a person [*i.e.* Connock], who hath made ambassador already ridiculous there, and, I feare, the Companeys stock very thinne. . . . The Dutch at Suratt will plant in spite of us ; but I know no reason why wee should not beate them off at sea. Their insolencyes would be requited, especially of this man, who hath robbd with English coulors. If his ship bee yet alive and by search such could bee found, shee would [should ?] bee fired, her goods seased, and as many as yow could take carried home to England to answer it. However charitye now pittyes their estate of nawfrage [*i.e.* shipwreck], enquire of Mr. Kerridge their courses to the sowthward and yow will find they merritt noe curtesye. Therfore my advice is to woorke upon their necessitye ; no way to releeve them, but to buy their comoditie fitt for the Redd Sea, to fitt our selves if that attempt be thought on, or for Persia ; if that last yeare they sould spices at such rate in Suratt as wee might well make profitt on . . . it is wisdome to use the present to best advantage.[1]

[1] Roe's advice was acted upon. As soon as the English fleet arrived Van den Broecke went on board and begged that Pring would either give his men passage to Bantam or sell a Portuguese prize for this purpose. Both requests were refused, and the Dutchmen thereupon started to march overland to Masulipatam. They reached their destination in safety on Christmas eve, after a journey of a month and twenty-five days (Van den Broecke, pp. 73, 80 ; Terpstra, p. 67). Van Ravesteyn and Goeree had been left in charge of the factory at Surat.

Roe seems to have changed his mind later, for on 8 Nov. 1617, he wrote expressing regret that Pring had not sold to the Dutch one of the prizes (*Letters Received*, vol. vi. p. 152).

In 1620 Van den Broecke returned to Surat as Director for Arabia,

Now I shall come to a more generall consideration of the whole estate of the Companies affaires, which wilbe very requisite well to ponder.... First, at the place wher yow are, I confesse it is now the fountayne and life of all the East India trade, and therfore principally to bee respected; but not soe as to robb all others, except it could suffice to loade all your shipps; which, seeing it will, with the stock it hath, but compasse one (and that not the greatest), the other emptie bellies must bee cared for; els it will proove a deare bargaine. It is true the feare of the Portugalls will compell us to arrest all for defence of this; but that may bee better borne if yow after know how to dispose the rest. The factors at Suratt, as men respecting in the principall place their owne estates, will drawe from yow all they can, for that they shall have the creditt of this, and the misery of the residue they shall not feele, or not so soone; but wee reguard not creditt singly, but profitt and creditt universally, in the consideration of the whole voyadge. Therfore, as yow must bee liberall in sparing whatsoever may bee spared for this, soe yow must bee veary circumspect to save what yow can for the sowthward; I meane mony, for your comodity (if as other years) is only fitt for this and is lost forward, so that yow may dischardge of that as much as they will take, and keepe that redy comodity, coyne, for Bantam, wherin the Dutch are soe furnished that they will overlay yow or make yow buy at unreasonable price. Persia, I feare, will demand some, for the King will never tast us without yt, for that is his end, to vent his silkes to rayse a revenew, for the silke is all his and the best part of his income. His ambassador tould mee hee might buy some cloth to pay his souldiers with, but no quantety, neyther would hee truck, nor wee effect any great woorke unlesse wee resolved to bring two thirds mony, the rest in spices and fine ware. Our cloth is sould cheaper in Spahan then heare; to my knowledg the Persians bring quantetyes, which lye now at their *seray*, of the same sorts and best coulors, bought at Aleppo and not vendible at home, and here affoorded at a *rupie* and two in a *cobdee* under ours. This will make yow see what hope ther is of raysing that way a stock by cloth. But, with the best husbandry yow can use, fitting this factorie as it wilbe requisite, yow wilbe so fleeced as yow cannot have hope by all the remayner and the proceed of the others to take in to lade one of your greatest ships, or but one at most; and yow shall

Persia, and India, a post which he held till April, 1629. Della Valle, who met him there in 1623, speaks of him as 'a gentleman of good breeding and very courteous' (vol. i. p. 25). An engraving of Franz Hals's portrait of him is given in Valentyn's *Oud en Nieuw Oost-Indien*, vol. iv. part II. p. 224.

fynd divers before yow attending to bee served, like men at a founteyne in scarcety of water. What then is to bee done with your fleete ? First, I will propose to yow the Red Sea. Though your stock bee not great, the returne may, beeing reimployed here, and so one ship may bee occupied and fitted ; and yow shall have in your way these chances : the Dabull shipps, or of the Samorin [of Calicut], or any other where wee trade not. Beleeve me, Sir, to chasten any of these people makes not only them but any their neighbors the better. If it bee doubted how the Mochars will take it or how admitt yow trade, I answere to the last : very willingly, in company of the Guzeratts. Necessitie will enforce them to give yow content, least yow molest others by whom they profitt ; and ther is noe great doubt, for the Dutch had trade last yeare and good usage in our names,[1] and upon that made this second attempt which is miscarried this yeare, as if oportunitye envited us to that in our owne persons which others did in our shadowes. Besides, the treachery used to Sir Henry Middleton was the first apperance and notice of any of our forces in that seas ; they tooke us for piratts, which now they better understand, and dare not offend us, because they know wee can bee revenged, if but by keeping others from trading with them. For the former, to deale with any others that may bee safe prise, it may bee done after trade at the [Red] Seas mouth. It wilbe long before it bee knowne, and, when it is, it matters not ; the suffering the Guzuratts to come peaceably is favour enough, because they are the mayne traders on that coast. Concerning the rest of your fleete, yow may keepe company on this coast and take your hazard about Zeilan [Ceylon]. If the King of Achin bee fickle and our factorie not flowrishing, hee must bee chastised too, and this one way, by threatening him not to suffer the Guzeratts to supply him, whom yet yow may not meddle with. From thence yow may attend the passadg of the Chineses and other traders in the sowtheren streights and chandg with them at the best hand. If yow stand soe low as China or toward Mocaa [Macao] it selfe, suerly all is prise ; and this may either gett yow a trade or at least serve the present, and cannot leave the whole in woorse estate then it is, for as good wee doe it as beare the envy for no profitt, for the Dutch practise it under our English crosse. Japan I doubt yow will not see ; or, if yow doe, I feare yow shall fynd cause enough to bidd yow thinck nothing frye that

---

[1] This is doubtful. The Surat factors told Roe that the Dutch had been taken at first for Englishmen, but they did not assert that they had pretended to be so ; while Van den Broecke distinctly avers that he hoisted the Stadtholder's flag over the Dutch factory at Mokha.

abides in the nett. The Portugalls I neede not any way mention; their injuries and your owne commission will guide yow. Some will say this course will in tyme overthrow all trade. I am of another opinion, considering the nature of this people, that have no sence of honor, but only profitt. Wee shall in tyme teach them to know their superiors; and if they will not give us trade, wee can yet choose whither they shall enjoy it or no. Necessitye and feare will enforce them with whom no curtesy nor reason can prevayle. Necessitye alsoe pleades now for us; for, were wee admitted trade, wee want meanes for soe great fleetes to use it and the losse at hand wilbe heavie. The gaine by good bootye once pursed will bare out the couldnes of trafique a yeare or two; and some kind of springs [*i.e.* young growth] are the fresher for cropping. Thus yow have my opinion, which use according to your discretion; for I doe not decree but only propose.[1] ...

To the Surat Factors.
(*Add. MS.* 6115, f. 261.)

30 August, 1617.

... [Your letter] of the 13th [July] advised of the Dutch misfortune, which when I signifyed at court I found little care or respect of such busines; only in complement it was answered: if they were not English, it mattered not. ... The debts at court are yet all unrecovered. ... The cloth taken by the King is well neare spent. ... I suppose the King may take 100 more at his arrivall at Agra; not before, for never was soe great a company soe poorly provided of carriadges. ... What yow remention concerning Zulph[eckcarcon] I am satisfied in ... but must forbear by necessity all farther pursute untill the Princes arivall, when I may dispute it face to face, which for noe respect I will forbeare. Bengala depends on the same thred. Everie tyme I mention it, Asaph-Chan

---

[1] The rest of the letter is occupied by a criticism of the policy pursued by Downton, when attacked by the Portuguese, of keeping on the defensive, in 'the hole at Swally.' Roe maintains that it would be far safer, instead of allowing themselves to be 'beseeged in a fish pond,' to 'putt out ... and attend them in sea roome.' 'Captain Best with lesse force mett them and beate them like a man, not by hazard; and if he had had that force which Downton had, I beleeve had brought away a better trophee.' Pring agreed with Roe, and in a letter to the Company of 12 Nov. 1617 (*Letters Received*, vol. vi. p. 175) he stated that if the rumour proved true that seven Portuguese ships had arrived, it was his intention to go to meet them, 'where I may be in a more spatious place then the poole of Swally.'

perswades mee to goe to the Prince and deale with him first, for that nothing wilbe granted without him to the prejudice of his port ; soe that I should bee tossd in and out to noe end. When hee comes, I will demand a *firmaen* before him, that soe I may answere to any objection. . . .

September 1.—Was the Kings birth-day, and the solemnitie of his weighing,[1] to which I went, and was carryed into a very large and beautifull garden ; the square within all water ; on the sides flowres and trees ; in the midst a pinacle, where was prepared the scales, being hung in large tressels, and a crosse beame plated on with gold thinne, the scales of massie gold, the borders set with small stones, rubies and turkey [*i.e.* turquoises], the chaines of gold large and massie, but strengthened with silke cords. Here attended the nobilitie, all sitting about it on carpets, untill the King came ; who at last appeared clothed, or rather loden, with diamonds, rubies, pearles, and other precious vanities, so great, so glorious ! his

[1] Roe had missed this ceremony the previous year, owing to the mistake of a messenger (see p. 221). It was an old Hindu custom, adopted by Akbar, and is still in use in Travancore and elsewhere.

Terry, who was present on this occasion, thus describes the scene (p. 395) : ' The first of September, which was the late Mogols birthday, he, retaining an ancient yearly custom, was in the presence of his chief grandies weighed in a balance ; the ceremony performed within his house or tent, in a fair spacious room, whereinto none were admitted but by special leave. The scales in which he was thus weighed were plated with gold, and so the beam on which they hung by great chains made likewise of that most precious metal. The King sitting in one of them was weighed first against silver coin, which immediately after was distributed among the poor : then was he weighed against gold : after that against jewels, as they say ; but I observed (being present there with my Lord Ambassadour) that he was weighed against three several things laid in silken bags on the contrary scale. When I saw him in the balance, I thought on Belshazzar, who was found to light, *Dan.* 5, 27. By his weight, of which his physicians yearly keep an exact account, they presume to guess of the present estate of his body ; of which they speak flatteringly, however they think it to be. When the Mogol is thus weighed, he casts about among the standers-by thin pieces of silver and some of gold, made like flowers of that countrey, and some of them are made like cloves and some like nutmegs, but very thin and hollow. Then he drinks to his nobles in his royal wine (as that of Ahasuerus is called, *Esth.* 1, 7) who pledge his health. . . .'

sword, target, throne to rest on correspondent ; his head, necke, breast, armes, above the elbowes, at the wrists, his fingers every one with at least two or three rings, fettered with chaines, or dyalled dyamonds, rubies as great as wal-nuts (some greater), and pearles such as mine eyes were amazed at. Suddenly hee entered into the scales, sate like a woman on his legges, and there was put in against him many bagges to fit his weight, which were changed sixe times, and they say was silver, and that I understood his weight to be nine thousand *rupias*, which are almost one thousand pound sterling. After with gold and jewels, and precious stones, but I saw none ; it beeing in bagges might bee pibles. Then against cloth of gold, silke, stuffes, linnen, spices, and all sorts of goods, but I must beleeve, for they were in fardles [*i.e.* bags or bundles]. Lastly, against meale, butter, corne, which is said to be given to the *baniani*, and all the rest of the stuffe ; but I saw it carefully carryed in, and none distributed. Onely the silver is reserved for the poore, and serves the ensuing yeare, the King using in the night to call for some before him, and with his owne hands in great familiaritie and humilitie to distribute that money. The scale he sate in by one side. He gazed on me, and turned me his stones and wealth, and smiled, but spake nothing, for my enterpreter could not be admitted in. After he was weighed, he ascended his throne, and had basons of nuts, almonds, fruits, spices of all sort, made in thinne silver, which he cast about, and his great men scrambled prostrate upon their bellies ; which seeing I did not, hee reached one bason almost full, and powred into my cloke. His noblemen were so bold as to put in their hands, so thicke that they had left me none if I had not put a remayner up. I heard he threw gold till I came in, but found it silver so thinne, that all I had at first, being thousands of severall pieces, had not weighed sixtie *rupias*. I saved about twentie *rupias* weight, yet a good dishfull, which I keepe to shew the ostentation ; for by my proportion he could not that day cast away above one hundred pound sterling. At night he drinketh with all his nobilitie in rich plate. I was invited to that, but told I must not refuse to drinke, and their waters are fire. I was sicke and in a little fluxe of bloud, and durst not stay to venture my health.

September 9.—The King rode to the river of Darbadath [Narbadā], five *course*, on pleasure; and comming by my house, I rode out to meete him. The custome is, that all men by whom hee passeth neere their gate make him some present; which is taken as a good signe, and is called *mombareck*,[1] good newes or good successe. I had nothing to give, nor might fitly goe with nothing, nor stay at home without discourtesie; which made mee venture upon a faire booke well bound, filleted and gilt, Mercators last edition of the maps of the world;[2] which I presented with an excuse that I had nothing worthy, but to a great king I offered the world, in which he had so great and rich a part. The King tooke it in great courtesie, often laying his hand on his breast, and answering: Every thing that came from mee was welcome. Hee asked after the ships arrivall, which I told him I daily expected. Hee told me hee had some fat wild hogges sent him from Goa, and, if I would eate any, at his returne he would send me some. I made him due reverence, and answered: any thing from His Majestie was a feast to me. He rode on his eliphant, and the way was stonie; and I offering to bring him toward the gate [*i.e.* of the city], hee bade God keepe mee, and returne to my house, demanding which it was, and praysing it (indeed, it was one of the best in the *leskar*, yet but an old church and large tombe inclosed). Iterating his farewell, he said the way was ill, and desired me to goe home; and with much shew of courtesie tooke leave.

[*September*] 16.—I rode to repay the visit of Marre Rustam [see p. 369], the Prince of Candahor; who at my arrivall sent word he durst not see mee, except hee asked leave of the King or acquainted Etimon Dowlet or Asaph Chan, which at the *durbar* he would. I answered: he should not need, for I never meant to trouble my selfe with a man so uncivill, nor to come a second time: I knew well it was a shift out of ill manners: that the King would bee no more angry for his bidding mee welcome to his house then for his comming to mine: but that

---

[1] *Mubārak*. Bernier speaks of the Dutch embassy sent to congratulate Aurangzeb on his accession as going to present him 'with the *Mohbarec*' (p. 127).

[2] 'Cost in England 7*l.*' (Roe's Accounts).

I cared not to see him, but came in civilitie to requite that I took so in him. His man desired me to stay untill he told his master my answere; but I would not, and returned. At night, I rode to court to visit the King, who questioned about the booke of maps; but I did forbeare any speech of my debts.

[*September*] 25.[1]—I rode to the court, very weake, to make triall of the King about our debts;[2] for that Muckshud had also newly answered he had mist his *prigany*,[3] and knew not how to pay, but by his house. I delivered the King the merchants petition, which hee caused to bee read aloud, and the names of the debtors and sureties and summes distinctly, by Asaph Chan; which done, he called Araddat Chan,[4] the chiefe of his officers of houshold, and the *Cutwall*, and gave them order; but what I understood not. Reading the names, hee questioned their abilities and qualities, and what goods they received, finding some dead, some strangers: concerning Rulph [Zūlfakār Khān] Asaph Chan offered to speake to the Prince at his arrivall to finish it. My interpreter was now called in, and the King converted [*i.e.* turned] to mee, giving this answere: that the merchants had made debts at their owne wills, and not brought a note of their goods to him: therefore, if the men were insufficient, it was at their perill, for that it was no reason to expect the money from him (which,

[1] The 23rd, according to Roe's letter to the Surat factors of the 29th idem. See *Letters Received*, vol. vi. p. 304.

[2] Two of these—14,000 rupees due from Mukshud Dās, and 30,000 owed by 'Groo' [Guru]—were for cloth sold in Ajmer in October, 1616. There was also a sum of 2,000 rupees due from 'Hergoven' [Har-Gobin], who had made over some elephants to satisfy the claim; but, he dying at this time, all his goods were seized for the King's use. Roe's correspondence at this time is full of references to the recovery of these debts.

[3] His *pargana*, *i.e.* the tract of country assigned by the King for his maintenance. Purchas, in a marginal note on p. 455 of his first volume, explains that '*prigonies* are lordships.'

[4] Irādat Khān, the title of a Persian named Mīrzā Muhammad Bākir (the 'Mirza' of p. 143). He was introduced at court by Āsaf Khān, and later on assisted him materially in securing the accession of Shāh Jahān. The latter gave him the title of Āzam Khān, and bestowed upon him in turn the governments of Bengal, Allahābād, Gujarāt, and Jaunpur. He died in 1649.

I suppose, he spake of his servant Hergonen, who being dead, his goods were seazed for the Kings use) : but seeing it was the first time, he would now assist me, and cause our money to be payed : but if hereafter the English would deliver their goods to his servants without money or acquainting him, they should stand to the hazard : but if, when their commodities came to the court, they would bring a bill to him of all, he would first serve himselfe, and after distribute the rest to such as should buy that and [1] if any of them failed, he would pay the money himselfe. This is indeed the custome of Persia merchants, to bring all to the King (which I have often seene), who takes his choice and delivers the rest to his nobilitie, his *scrivanoes* writing to whom, and his officer cutting price ; a copy of which is given the merchant, and hee goes to their houses for money ; if they pay not, there is an expresse officer that hath order by currant course to force them. Then was it told my interpreter what command the King had given : that Arad [Araddat ?] Chan should call the debtors before him, and cause them to pay ; but this pleased not our merchants. I thought it both a just and gratious answere ; better then in such cases private men can get of great princes.

The King, hearing I had been sicke and wished for wine, gave me five bottles, and commanded, when I had ended those, to send for five more, and so as I wanted : and a fat hogge, the fattest I ever saw, sent up by Mochreb Chan, that came from Goa, which at midnight was brought home by a *haddy* with this message : since it came to the King it had eaten nothing but sugar and butter. I tooke this as a signe of favour, and I am sure in that court it is a great one. Then he sent for the map-booke, and told me he had shewed it his *mulaies*, and no man could reade nor understand it ; therefore, if I would, I should have it againe. I answered : at his pleasure ; and so it was returned.[2]

[1] Probably we should transpose this and the preceding word.

[2] ' The Mogol feeds and feasts himself with this conceit, that he is Conqueror of the World ; and therefore I conceive that he was troubled upon a time, when my Lord Ambassador, haveing businesse with him (and upon those terms there is no coming unto that King empty handed, without some present or other) . . . and having

[*September*] 26.—There being a *raja* in rebellion in the hills, not past twentie *course* from the *laskar*, the King lately sent out two *umbras* [1] with horse to fetch him in ; but he defended his quarter, slew one of them and twelve *maancipdares*, and in all of both sides about five hundred ; returning scornefull messages to the King to send his sonne, for he was no prey for ordinary forces.

To the Commander of the Fleet.
(*Add. MS.* 6115, f. 263.)

Mandoa, September 29, 1617.

... Some alteration is hapned in the project of Dabull, for that I understand Fearne [2] hath robbd their great shipp. It at that time nothing left which he thought fit to give him, presented him with Mercators great book of Cosmography (which the Ambassador had brought thither for his own use), telling the Mogol that that book described the four parts of the world, and all several countreys in them contained. The Mogol at the first seem'd to be much taken with it, desiring presently to see his own territories, which were immediately shewen unto him ; he asked where were those countreys about them ; he was told Tartaria and Persia, as the names of the rest which confine with him ; and then causing the book to be turn'd all over, and finding no more to fall to his share but what he first saw, and he calling himself the Conqueror of the World and having no greater share in it, seemed to be a little troubled, yet civily told the Ambassadour, that neither himself nor any of his people did understand the language in which that book was written, and because so, he further told him that he would not rob him of such a jewel, and therefore returned it unto him again. And the truth is that the Great Mogol might very well bring his action against Mercator and others who describe the world, but streighten him very much in their maps, not allowing him to be lord and commander of those provinces which properly belong unto him.'—Terry, p. 367.

[1] Properly a plural word (Arabic *Umara*, pl. of *Amīr*), but often used, as here, to signify a grandee or military commander of rank. Fryer styles the *Mansabdārs* 'petty *Omrahs*.' The expedition referred to may be that described at pp. 390-2 of the *Memoirs* (vol. i.).

[2] In the spring of 1615 the Company had been alarmed by a report that Sir John Fern and others (of whom Pepwell was one) were meditating a voyage to the Red Sea under a commission from the French King. The aid of the Privy Council was invoked, and royal

will stirr up the consideration of this people, but crosse our designe, for I feere they will not venture out, nor beeleeve us free. If yow purpose not to trie the port, wee shall have leysure to consulte of that in tyme of a nother course at your departure. That which I would most impresse into you is the consideration of the Redd Sea, the rather for that it is reported the King sends his sister to Mecha, which, if true, wilbe the fittest oportunitye to treat of those conditions which pride now will not admitt off. I assure yow shee is the best price that ever was taken in India. The King is fully resolved to visitt Guzeratt, Cambaya, and Amadavaz, and there will spend this yeare. The nearenes will some way advance our expedition. I receive good woords and good usage, but without presents shall fynd drye effects. Now is the last triall; for our comoditye is badd, our conditions unstable; and if it mend not, wee must showe them a nother countenance. . . . A few dayes since dyned with mee an Italian that long hath used Persia. I enquired the estate of trade. His answere was it was not *tierra de negocio*: [1] all the trafique lay betweene Aleppo and Casbin [Kazvin], for silke and mony: that only wilbe accepted: that our cloth will never vent, for in experience it hath beene often tryed from Turkye and sould at extreame losse. The disposition of the King is to bee very familiar with strangers if they bee in cash, in hope to gett; no man can escape him; when hee hath suckd them, hee will not knowe them. . . .

letters were obtained commanding Fern to desist. He thereupon fled into France, and the scheme came to nothing. The Company, however, feared that he would renew his attempt, and in the royal commission to the leaders of the 1616 fleet (*First Letter Book*, p. 463), a clause was inserted authorising the capture of interlopers, Fern being particularly mentioned. Doubtless their letters to the East contained a warning to their servants to prepare for troubles from this source, for on 30 May, 1617, Roe wrote to Kerridge: 'I much feare some ill newes from the Redd Sea that will bringe us all in trouble by the fugitive Fearne. Possesse all men with an opinion of French piratts. God turne his wayes from offending us. If hee touch any of this country goods, the Prince will prosecute revenge and satisfaction with all malice' (MS. f. 195). Roe's fears were, however, groundless, for, at the date when he was writing thus, Fern was in command of a ship in Ralegh's ill-fated expedition to Guiana (see Hume's *Life of Ralegh*, p. 325; Gardiner's *History of England*, vol. iii. p. 128; etc.).

[1] No country for trade.

To the Surat Factors.[1]
(*Add. MS.* 6115, f. 264.)

Mandoa, September 29, 1617.

... Your lettres arrived in Mandoa the 28th at night, and this morning came to my hands, with very wellcome newes of the safe arrivall of our fleete. ... The answere of Asaph Chan [2] is an implicite denyall, and I expect no better when the Prince arrives. The reasons are : the people will petition against yt for troubling their seas ; and the Prince will keepe us to his port by necessitye. But I will putt it to triall. I am sorry to heare the newes from Mesolapatan. I know not what that factorye is good for ; and their project into Orixa or Bengala I cannot conceive. It were necessarye to know yt before they proceede. They are young men, and would bee doeing perhaps they know not what. Suer I am none of our comoditye will sell there ; not our cloth, for that bought in barter was dessigned for tryall [and] since upon better advice the owners have sent it to the *laskar*, and it is heare arrived. I will assist yow in all I can, with charitable and indifferent consideration of mens desarts and travells, to hynder such a course of privat trade as was practised last yeare. I hav[e] yet not meddled ; but have, under the Companyes seale, a warrant to seaze any such goods, and am bound in 4000 *li*. to execute yt. This I will publish, hoping mens discretions will not enforce mee to see too much. ... I should thincke yow did mee a great curtesye and the Company a great service, if yow could plott the landing of the presents so secrettly that they might come unknowne to my hands ; reserving halfe by yow till farther order ; which I suppose by boate secrettly might bee effected. ... I will not bee abused as last yeare, nor serve their turnes that will snatch all at once and expect new daylie. ...

October 2.—The Prince entered the towne, and all the great men, in wondrous triumph. The King received him as if he had no other, contrary to our expectation.[3] Brampore left

---

[1] Printed in full at p. 301 of *Letters Received*, vol. vi.

[2] About trade in Bengal.

[3] The campaign against the Deccan princes had now been brought to a close by the submission of the King of Bījāpur, which forced Malik Ambar also to make terms by the surrender of Ahmadnagar and other territory which he had reconquered from the Mughals. Roe's account, contained in a letter to the English ambassador at Constantinople, 21 Aug., 1617 (*Add. MS.* 6115, f. 207), is rather scornful : 'The King is at present in that they call an army ; but I see no souldiers, though multitudes entertaynd in the qualety.

almost emptie under *Chan Channa*. I had sent to Asaph Chan [1] to excuse my not meeting him, for I was not able to stirre, nor had no present. All the great men, and the Kings mother, received him foure *course* off. I sent also some of my servants with my just excuse, which his pride only nodded at.

To Nicholas Bangham at Burhanpur.
(*Add. MS.* 6115, f. 266.)

Mandoa, October 3, 1617.

... The Prince yesterday arrived in all glory, such as was never seene. I went not to meete him, partly for lack of a present, but principally for weakenes, having had a scouring twenty weekes, which hath brought mee soe low I can but walke up and downe my dining roome, nor forbeare above an hower, having the emralds [*i.e.* hemorrhoids, or piles] still bleeding. But I hope I am now by Gods mercy beginning to recover, and will pursue all busines with expedition. ... I could wish that yow sent the copy of this to the Generall with speede, that I desier if hee can stay the Princes ship at Suratt, or send over one to Goga and seaze that. It will bring our busines to some conclusion, provided they take nothing, but only keepe the shipp and goods, that by complaynt hither I may bee questioned for yt. I am content also that hee say hee doth it because I have written him that wee cannot procure payment of those goods taken from us by Zulph[eckcarcon] and Shaw Hussen two yeares past. ...

To Thomas Kerridge at Surat.
(*Add. MS.* 6115, f. 267.)

Mandoa, October 4, 1617.

... So soone as yours came, the King had newes of the arrivall of our fleete, and sent to call Jaddow, demanding if I had knowledge of yt and why I came not with the advise to

The purpose was the oppression of the united Decan kings, who are perswaded to part with some rotten castles that may pretend a shadowe of yeilding somwhat, for which they are pleasd here to thinck themselves woorthy of the glorious prayses due to an honorable conquest.' (The whole letter is printed at p. 298 of vol. vi. of *Letters Received*.)

It was on this occasion that the Prince received the title of Shāh Jahān, by which he was ever after known. His reception by his father is described at p. 393 of the *Memoirs* (vol. i.).

[1] This is probably an error for Afzal Khān, the Prince's secretary (see p. 123 *n*). The same mistake occurs on a later page.

him ; who answered truth : that I was unfitt to come abroad. Then hee asked if I know [sic] what goods or comodityes were brought ; to which he replyed that I had received no lettres, but only a generall report that the shipps were seene upon the coast. At this conference stept in the Princes procurador, sayeing the English brought nothing woorth His Majesties sight nor fitt for the countrye, but swoords and cloth, of which they had no neede. Asaph-Chan interrupted him, answering it would be seene this yeare, for that hee had spoken to mee for divers things to please the King, and that hee did beleeve that wee would come noe more unfurnished, for wee had better experience of the country ; at which the King sayd it was good, and commanded Jaddow to tell mee I should bring him a note of what soever wee had in our shipps so soone as I received yt, and that hee would choose and appoynt such as he liked ; the rest wee might dispose at our pleasure. Thus I abyde in expectation ; but cannot tell which way to turne mee among this people, for that this day I sent to feele Asaph-Chan how I should proceed, promising that I would reserve any thing for him that I knew he liked ; who answered that it could not bee, for the Prince would have all that was landed. I understand it not, but it is a good warning. Hee shall have nothing from mee, nor my consent on such conditions. Therfore I desier nothing may come ashore but your grosse goods or such as yow will sell or send up to him at adventure. . . . If yow can send mee some good toyes of small bulke, landed at Barooch, or by an Englishman sent thither along the water undiscovered . . . I will trye what I can doe with a little. The rest it is better to conceale then bee robbd off, and to give out ther are noe presents come. . . . I stayed your servant a day to heare an end of a rumor that a complaynt was come against us to the Prince, that the English had taken the Beagams shipp in the Redd Sea ; which I supposed was Fearne (if true), but that wee should not easely proove our innocency. Since I learne that it is come from Suratt that our fleete hath stayed that shipp at the barr, untill the Generall knowe our estate ; which, if true, I am very glad off. Any thing that would stirr these people to know us and feare us will woorke better effects then all the faire wayes of the world. I shall heare fynd the woorst of displeasure, but I care not. . . . I had rather bee before hand then a sutor. Yf they bee enforced to come to mee to gett loose their goods, though they lay mee in irons, they shall give good conditions before I yeild. . . . If I had only to deale with the King, I were happy ; but with these ravens it is a misserie unexpressable. . . .

[*October*] 5.—I received from Surat newes of our shippes arrivall, the Admirall missing, and her prize of Mosambique;[1] the rest well, who had taken two English rovers, set out by (   )[2] who were found in chase of the Queene Mothers ship returned from the Red-sea, which they fortun-

[1] Presumably Roe means that he received fuller details. He had heard nearly a week earlier of the arrival of the fleet (see p. 385). It consisted of five vessels, the *Royal James, Royal Anne, New Year's Gift, Bull* and *Bee*, commanded by Martin Pring, an old acquaintance of Roe. Pring, whose Virginian voyages are well known, had been master of the *New Year's Gift* in Downton's fleet of 1614, and the ambassador was not without hopes that he would find him in charge of one of the incoming ships; his pleasure when 'the expected general' turned out to be his desired friend is shown in the letter which follows.

Part of the fleet reached Swally on 20 September; but Pring himself, whose ship had a bad leak, did not arrive till five days later. Three prizes had been taken: one a Portuguese ship from Mozambique, laden with ivory and gold, and bound for Diu; the others, two English interlopers, who, when they were seized, were on the point of capturing the great junk which was yearly sent from Gogo (in Kāthiāwār) to the Red Sea, and was now on her return journey. These two ships were the *Francis*, of 150 tons, commanded by Samuel Newse, and the *Lion*, of 100 tons, under the charge of Thomas Jones, who had been formerly boatswain of the *Hector*; they were the joint property of Sir Robert Rich (who afterwards as Earl of Warwick was a prominent leader in the Civil War) and Philip Barnardi, an Italian merchant resident in London, and had been set out under the protection of a commission from the Duke of Savoy. Roe strongly advised resolute action, and Pring, acting on his advice, confiscated both ships and goods for the use of the Company. This course was entirely approved by the latter; but it involved them in a long dispute with the noble owner, who claimed damages amounting nearly to 20,000*l*. The King, who could not deny that the Earl had infringed their patent, yet pressed them to give compensation. In the controversy, Roe earned the gratitude of the Company by taking upon himself the responsibility of the seizure, and justifying it to the Privy Council. In the end, the matter was referred to arbitration (see *English Factories*, vol. vi. p. 174, etc.; *Cal. State Papers, East Indies*, 1617-21, preface, pp. lxxvi-lxxx; Gardiner's *History of England*, vol. iii. p. 216, etc.; *Historical MSS. Commission, Fourth Report*, Lords' Papers, p. 19; *Journal of John Jourdain*, p. 340; Court Minutes, *passim*).

Extracts from Pring's journals of his two voyages to the East will be found in Purchas's first volume, p. 629. For Pring himself see an article in the *Dict. of Nat. Biography*, and a pamphlet by Dr. James H. Pring, published at Plymouth in 1888.

[2] Thus in the original. Purchas was unwilling to mention in this connexion so exalted a person as the Earl of Warwick.

ately rescued and brought safe in (if shee had bin taken, we had all bin in trouble); with these the Companies letter, invoice, instructions for Persia, and divers other notes of advise, that by reason of the Admiralls absence they knew not what course to take with the men of warre. I dispeeded to Surat orders about all businesse, as appeares in my letters.

To Captain Martin Pring.
(*Add. MS.* 6115, f. 268.)

Honest Man, [5 October, 1617.][1]

God, that knowes my hart, wittnesse yow are the wellcomest man to this country that could here arrive to assist my many troubles. ... The Company have, it seemes, entrusted more to mee then I am willing to undertake; for receiving a commission about Persia,[2] it is soe limitted, and with soe good reasons, that I cannot proceed with such hast as a supply would requier; neither dare I thinck it requisite to seperate your fleete, nor convenient to venture more goods before advice, and advice from a soberer man then Connaught, who was sett out without my knowledg and, I am sure, upon such conditions as the Company have restrayned mee in. I am of a nature not to hurt; it was the rashnes of our merchants last yeare, whom I would now excuse and helpe out, if any thing committed that may prejudice them. I understand the Company to entend noe farther yet then a treaty of conditions, which they heare [*i.e.* the Surat factors] have begunne, but never sent

[1] No date is given in the original.

[2] From Carew's *Letters* (p. 77) we learn that Roe's despatch to the Company of 14 Feb. 1616 (see p. 110) had reached England in good time by an express messenger from the consul at Aleppo; those to the King and Council were entrusted by the same official to John Pory, and did not come to hand till later. On 16 Jan. 1617, Sir Thomas Smythe and other leading members of the Company presented Roe's letter at the Council-table. 'The Lords like so well of it,' wrote Carew, ' and the marchants so willinge to finde itt, as thatt it is concluded thatt a tryall thereof shall be made'; and the result is seen in the letters now received. Carew suggested three possible objections to the venture: that Jask was an unsuitable port: that the Grand Signor might be offended by a compact with his enemy, and retaliate on the Englishmen in his dominions: and that the need of ready money to drive the trade (600,000*l.* he thought would be necessary) would exhaust the treasure of the kingdom. The resulting instructions to Roe (here referred to) will be found in *The First Letter Book*, p. 455.

me a copy how they limited them. For feare of their forwardnes I sent to the Shabas by his embassador an overture of a treaty, strict enough and wary on our part, the answere wherof I expect, if Mr. Connocht, who is ambassador, have not taken upon him to enlardg yt and promise that wee cannot performe. Therfore, the busines thus perplexed, it can from mee receive noe farther authoritye then that I shall not crosse any supply, if the merchants hould it necessarie. But I see no fitt cargazon to send but will weaken this too much. . . . Steeles projects [1] are idle and vayne, smokey ayrye imaginations. His owne relations of Persia contradictorye and silly, magnifying his owne woorks. I never sawe him ; but I suppose I understand him, and woonder how the Company are so deceived if they putt much trust in him. . . . That which causeth my present writing is conserning two men of warr taken by yow, of which it seemes some make doubt to stay, by reason of their commissions and the greatnes of their owners. Yow know your strength, what yow may doe to men of their qualetye ; and I know the Companies lettres patents, prohibiting any of the subjects of England to trade this way, much more to rove [*i.e.* play the pirate]. And if it prohibit it, it consequently giveth power to execute such prohibition ; els

[1] Richard Steel's mission to Persia, and his journey overland to England, have already been mentioned. The loss of the Court Minutes for 1616-17 prevents us from following his subsequent negotiations with the Company, but their main purport may be gathered from a letter written by him to the court which is printed in *The First Letter Book* (p. 457). In this he refers to his advocacy of ' the trade of raw silkes from Persia,' and then unfolds four more schemes : first, the transportation of the goods of Asiatic merchants from Sind to Persia by sea, thus saving the long overland journey via Kandahār ; secondly, the carriage to India and Persia of spices and other products of the Far East ; thirdly, the convoying of the Gujarāt ships to the Red Sea ; fourthly, the erection of waterworks at Agra, to supply that city with water from the Jumna in the same way as part of London was supplied with Thames water by a pumping engine at Broken Wharf. For this he doubted not ' but either the King will give a good gratification, or the people of that cittye pay quarterly or yearly for yt.' He himself was willing to venture 300*l*. in the scheme, and he was also prepared to serve the Company for five years at a salary of 200*l*. If Roe should be sent to Persia to conclude a treaty, Steele would gladly ' keep him companye in so worthey buisines and be a help for obteyning many favours from the said Sophey.' Apparently the Committees were unwilling to take a part in his waterworks scheme ; but (in an unhappy hour for their long-suffering ambassador) they engaged his services in a general capacity, and allowed him to take out with him in Pring's

LETTER TO PRING

were it in vayne. Therfore I desier yow not only to stay them, but to take out their officers and some of their men and change them with yours for safetye, least they make escape. They will steed yow well with the Portugalls, whom yow may expect to bicker with. The reason of this strict dealing is, besides the right of the Company and the equitye of nations, the Kings honor is engaged that wee shall not molest free merchants, not our enemyes. I am here a pawne, and represent his person ; assure yow, what damage soever any of these subjects shall susteyne by us, our bodyes and goods shall answere. If for any occasion of our owne yow deteyne the said ship of Suratt, it is in our owne power to free her : that is another case. I heare one Captain Newse is in one. Hee, if I mistake not, is a follower of my lord Davers,[1] himselfe a souldier and a valiant man. Deale with him to bee content to referr himselfe to mee. I will use him well and like his qualetye, and, if wee might bee assured of his fayth, perhaps some way employ him. . . . Sir Robert Rich is my frend ; but I am now a publique minister, and cannot see any thing with those eyes ; yet hee shall fynd I will not use any extreamety in the end. Ther are many better courses then this, to wrong his soveraynge and his nation. . . . Assure them they shall be better used, and may

fleet a number of workmen, on the chance of his being able to interest the Mogul in his very visionary project.

With him came other troublesome adventurers, viz. Captain Towerson and his wife and Mrs. Hudson. Towerson (well known in after years as the chief of the English factors put to death at Amboyna) had been in the Company's First Voyage, and had been chief at Bantam, 1605-08 ; in 1611 he had commanded the *Hector* in the Eighth Voyage, and on his return had married the widow of William Hawkins. As will be remembered, she was an Armenian girl whom Hawkins had espoused at Agra at the instance of Jahāngīr ; and it was in the hope of pushing his fortunes in India with the help of his wife's relatives that Towerson had persuaded the Company to grant them passages. Mrs. Towerson brought with her her friend Mrs. Hudson, and a maid named Frances Webbe. The latter was secretly married to Steel during the voyage ; and their son, born at Surat soon after the fleet's arrival, may be safely set down as the second English child born in India (the first was the infant of Sir Thomas and Lady Powell, Sir Robert Sherley's companions). Mrs. Hudson was probably the widow of William Hudson, who was in India in 1610 and returned to Europe in the following year (*Journal of John Jourdain*, p. 137). From her association with Mrs. Towerson and this visit to India, it may be surmised that she was of Indian origin.

[1] Lord (Henry) Danvers (1573-1644), afterwards Earl of Danby. Roe seems to have been mistaken in this identification of Newse.

thanck God they fell into our hands ; for as men of warr they shall have honest shares, if wee purchase [*i.e.* make prize] upon our enemies ; if not, I can tell them where to make a voyadge they shall justefye. Deale effectually with them to make them frends and faythfull ; and write mee your opinion whither wee may trust or no. . . . There is one pearle [1] in a box directed to mee, and somwhat concerning it concealed from the merchants. That may bee sowed so in cloth that it may come safe and speedily by the first English ; but take heed yow bee cunning hiders, for here are cunning searchers. All the other pearle, or some of the best, may bee so convayd in quilted coates ; but lett the men bee trusty. . . . I pray love that little woorme John Hatch,[2] and commend mee to him. If no lettres from the King to the Mogol nor Prince, a great error. . . . [*PS.*] I know not Captain Andrew Shilling [3] but by fame to be a brave honest man, and therfore I am bound to love him and to wish him all good. If hee will trye mee, hee shall fynd I remember some of his actions. If Captain Adames bee our ould Virginia Adams,[4] hee is my good frend. Commend mee to him whosoever, and to all our countrimen.

[1] A valuable pearl weighing 29½ carats, ' shaped like a pare, very large, beautifull, and orient ' (Terry, p. 393). Four strings of small pearls were also sent (Biddulph's Accounts).

[2] Master's mate in the *Lion* when Roe came out in her. The latter wrote to the Governor of the Company in his favour, and Smythe, with a jest about turning plain John Hatch into Master Hatch, sent him out in the present fleet as master of the *Bee*. In her, a little later, he made a voyage to Jask. When the fleet was leaving Surat, the ambassador made it his special request to Pring, that he would either take Hatch home with him, or send him back to India that he might be with Roe. In April, 1618, however, Hatch was made commander of the *New Year's Gift*, and did not return to England till 1621, when he was censured by the Court for having ' carried himself very weakly in the fight with the Flemings.'

[3] Shilling, the commander of the *Anne* (in which Roe made his homeward voyage), has earned a place in the *Dictionary of National Biography* by his action with the Portuguese off Jask, in which he lost his life (Jan., 1621). An account of him will also be found in the preface to Sir Clements Markham's *Voyages of William Baffin*.

[4] Robert Adams, commander of the *Bull*. He was sent home with her from Surat in February, 1618, and went out again to Bantam the following season with the news of the agreement made with the Dutch. Frequent references to him will be found in *Cocks's Diary*.

A Captain Adams is mentioned by Purchas (vol. iv. pp. 1733, 1756) as going out with Gates's Virginia fleet of 1609, and doubtless it is to him that Roe refers ; but whether he was identical with the commander of the *Bull* does not appear.

To Thomas Kerridge at Surat.
(*Add. MS*. 6115, f. 269.)

Mando, 5 October, 1617.

I have received lardge instructions from the Company, and commission to deale farther in their affairs then I am now willing ; yet in my advise I will not bee niggardly. First for Persia. That sent mee is signed by some of the Lords of the Councell, to tye me, I suppose, to warines ; with yt divers reasons against the trade, but not to diswade yt, but by caution. . . . I referr yow to Martyn Prinns lettre sent herewith. . . . Only I will touch Mr. Steele. I know him not ; but I ever doubted by his lettres his judgement was vast and uncollected. His relations and projects are to mee wynd and smoke ; yet if hee can make them good in reason, I will assist him. His bringing a wife secrettly I mislike, and I know the Company will. Keepe no houses here. Shee is come ; use her with charety and curtesy, and house her with convenience, but not at our chardg (except ther come privat warrant) ; neyther consent to her comming up, if desired. . . . Captain Towerson is welcome, and his wife. I will doe them any curtesy. His hast to court wilbe convenient, for his wife may assist mee to Normahal better then all this court. . . . Abram, her father [*sic*], is here arrived. . . .

[*October*] 6.—I rode to visite the Prince, at his usuall houre, to give him welcome and to acquaint him with our businesse ; determining to make offer of all respect to him, and to that end not to come emptie handed, and bought a fine chaine of gold, China worke. I sent in word. He returned that I should come next morning at sunne rise, when he sate to be worshipped, or stay till his riding to court, which I must have done at his doore. This I tooke in extreame scorne, his father never denying me accesse ; and his pride is such as may teach Lucifer ; which made me answere roundly : I was not his slave, but a free ambassadour of a King, and that I would never more visite him, nor attend him ; hee had refused me justice : but at night I would see him with the King, to whom only I would addresse my selfe ; and so departed.

At night I went to the King, who received me graciously. I made a reverence to the Prince, but he would not once stirre his head. Then I acquainted the King that, according to his order, I had brought an abstract of our ladings, desiring his command. After his manner he asked what and what, and was so wonderfully satisfied, especially with arras, that he promised mee all favour, all priviledges, all that I would desire. He enquired for dogges, which I could not answere ; and for jewels, which I told him they were dearer in England then in India, at which hee rested satisfied. I durst not name the pearles for many reasons ; if I had, our people had beene waylaid for by the Prince, and such snatching as I could not avoyd infinite trouble ; I knew I could bring them ashoare and to court by stealth : that the lesser expected, the better welcome : but my maine reason was, I would make a friend by them. Therefore, when Asaph Chan pressed me to know, I desired him to make that answere of dearenesse, and that I would speake with him alone. He soone understood me, and made excuse.

The King being well pleased, I thought it good time to moove againe for the debts ; and, having my petition ready, opened it, and offered it up. The King not marking others discovered what it was, and knew the King would bee enraged that his order was neglected ; whereat one stept to me, and clapt downe my hand gently, desiring me not to doe so. I answered : Aradake Chan [Irādat Khān] had absolutely refused me justice ; at which he, being by, came in in much feare, calling Asaph Chan, desiring him to hinder me from complaint. I answered : our ships were arrived, and we could not forbeare nor endure such delayes. So they consulted together and called the *Cutwall*, giving order to execute the Kings command ; who that night at midnight beset their tents, and catched some of them. So that now we shall have reason.

I had great thanks of all the *Umreies* for protecting the Queenes ship, and our courtesie to their passengers, which they enformed the King, who tooke it kindly ; and they all promised that they were obliged to love our nation, and would doe them all service ; but they wondered we could not governe our people, but that theeves could come out without the Kings leave.

At the Kings rising, Asaph Chan carryed me with him to his retyring place, and there first we translated the abstract into Persian, to shew the King an houre after ; in which I inserted the money with some addition,[1] because the King might perceive was brought profit to his dominions ; next the cloath and sorts ; then the fine wares in generall : lastly the grosse commodities ; desiring His Majestie to order what he would buy, and to give us liberty for the rest. This finished, Asaph Chan renewed the reason why I would speake alone, bad me be free, vowed and protested such friendship as I never could expect. I replyed : the reason why I desired it, was to aske his counsell ; for it was true I had somewhat, but my usage last yeare was so bad, that I durst not trust any ; but, that he might see how I replyed [relied ?] on him, I was willing, on his oath, to reveale it ; which he presently gave. I told him I had a rich pearle, and some other ropes faire : I knew not whether it was fit to tell the King, lest the Prince were displeased ; I told him how in the morning I had been to visite him, and his discourtesie, and my resolution : but that I knew his favour was so necessary for us, that I hoped I might recover it by this one respect that I kept the pearle for him. This, I said, was my purpose and reason I concealed it : he was father-in-law to him, and favorite of the King : I was ready to please both, and desired his advice. He embraced me, and began : I had done discreetly, but I should acquaint neither : if I did, I should never want trouble : the King would use me well, but keepe such a stirre to see it and get it into his hand, according to custome, and then I must sue for mine owne : the Prince was ravenous and tyrannicall, and wearied all nations. He bade mee steale all ashoare, trust none, and shewed mee many conveyances [*i.e.* furtive contrivances] ; bade me observe the usage of the Portugalls, how they were ransacked ; and desired to buy it, which if I would grant it, I should have money in deposito, what I should aske ; and he would, for this trust of him, sollicite all my desires ; that without him I could doe nothing. Now was an oportunitie to make a friend. I answered : I was willing, but I feared hee would reveale it ; which having received his oath, and a ceremony of covenant by crossing thumbes, we embraced. I promised to be directed by him ; and he to doe all that I required for the comming up of the rest : he would take order to give me *firmans* : no man

[1] An astoundingly frank admission.

should touch any thing, but all come to me, to dispose of at
pleasure : the Prince he would reconcile to me, and the next
time he visited him, he would take me, and make him use me
with all grace ; and for other businesse it should not be in his
power to crosse me : but, if he did, he would assigne us a
syndic,[1] which was in his government, or procure any other
port at my desire : and whatsoever I demanded should be
performed faithfully. He also advised me to give his sister
Normahall some toy. He said he would make the King give
me money ; to which I answered : I desire you to convert it
into the well usage of my countrey-men : I asked no more.
Thus we rose, and he carryed me in to the King, with the note
translated, who gave mee all good usage ; asked if the arras
were a present. I answered yes (lest it should be seazed, for
the Prince was by). In conclusion, hee said hee would buy all
the parcell of cloath, and many other things, appointing me
to send for it speedily ; Asaph Chan to take order for a *firman*
from the Prince.

Thus I had a good night ; and I knew, though they are all
[*blank*], yet in this he [*i.e.* Āsaf Khān] would deale truely,
because it was to helpe himselfe, and durst not betray me till
he had the pearle, for feare to misse it ; nor after, for having
himselfe betrayed the Prince.

To the Factors at Surat.
(*Add. MS.* 6115, f. 270.)

Mandoa, 8 October, 1617.

I perceeave yow conceive that either the Company hath putt
a new authoritie into my hands or that I am very willing to
assume one. First, lett mee desier yow not to mistake mee nor
them ; they have given no more then I thought ever I had, nor
will never take more upon mee, which is, frendly to joyne with
all their good servants in advice, not to governe or overrule nor
to doe any thing of myne owne head, except in such case that
any by grose misdemeanor should abuse the Company. . . . I
doe first as my opinion deliver that, if Mr. Kerridge thinck his
authoritie is any way lessened, that he bee perswaded to the
contrarye, for that both his deservings and experience will

[1] Syndu (*i.e.* Lahrībandar) is meant.

protect him from any such matter....[1] If the ship of Goga bee free, I am pleased. If not, before shee passe, gett, I pray, a letter into your hands of acknowledgment, to bee sent mee to show the Prince, whose pride only will take no knowledge of any curtesye. The first thing to be considered is the supply of Persia, which I hould necessarie not to bee neglected, though wee shall runne blyndly on, having no reason from them last yeare imployed.... That yow may the better understand the Companyes purposes, I have sent yow two copies directed to mee, wherby yow may see both their desier to follow and procure that trade, the objections against it and the restrictions of their conditions ; out of which I gather that they suppose yet no undertaking,[2] but desier some established conditions and articles and some assurance of vent of theirs and easie rates of the comodityes of Persia before they would engage them selves, or at least not farr ; which limitations of theirs agreeing with the want of supply in cargazon.... I am of opinion that it is fitt to forbare any supply of goods this yeare ; yet if yow all thinck otherwise I yeild willingly. But that wee must not lett the project sleepe I am resolute in ; first, not to disgrace our nation ; next to releive our countriemen, who will expect us ; and to make a judicious experience of the profitts and possibilitye of that trade, for the encouragment or satisfaction of our imployers. But the question is how it may bee done.... Use your discretions ; I will agree, consent too, and confirme whatsoever Captain Prinne, Mr. Kerridge and those merchants joyned with them shall thinck in this case most requisite to bee donne ; and this is all in that poynt I can say.[3] I mention not Mr. Steele for this employment of Persia

[1] Roe's remarks on the suspicious attitude of the Company towards him, and on the evils consequent on his powerlessness to control their factors, had had their due effect; and by a letter dated 6 Feb., 1617 (no longer extant), the factors at Surat were notified that the ambassador was authorised ' to instructe, directe and order all the factors in the Mogulls country in all the affaires and buisines of the said Honourable Company ' (O.C., No. 538; *Letters Received*, vol. vi. p. 95). Apparently Kerridge, resenting this, had announced his intention of returning to England, waich he was at liberty to do, as his stipulated period of service was nearly at an end. Roe, who, in spite of their differences, fully recognised Kerridge's abilities and knew the difficulty of replacing him, did his best to dissuade him ; and, somewhat grudgingly, he consented to stop.

[2] The Company were, of course, ignorant of the despatch of Connock and his fellow-factors to Jask.

[3] The letters brought by Pring's fleet had amply vindicated Roe's authority in this matter. ' Persia,' he wrote to the factors at Agra, ' is also wholy referred to mee, the Company no way thinckhing any

suddenly, because I thinck his speedy repayre hither of more use. As I was writing came in your servants with other letters from England, wherin receiving from the Kings Majestie my gratious master his favorable lettres and instructions, I have order to prosecute the project of Persia, but still with restraynt only to conclude and contract, if I thinck it fitt, not to send any goods until the next joynt stock, according to the Companyes orders. . . . Disperse the pearle [*i.e.* pearls] so in stitched clothes, or the great one in the stock of a peice, bored and finely stopped and blacked that it cannot bee seene ; and if Mr. Steele will come speedely with them, lett him soe convey these pearles that hee may passe up with them (which matter is very easy to doe) and not to stay for the goods and presents ; for his projects requiers speedie conference. . . . If hee will not come so soone . . . convey this pearle up speedely by some honest Englishman, well sowed in his clothes soe as they may not bee found. . . . If one of the swoords sent mee by the Company may come up with Mr. Steele, or any other thing of the Companyes by stealth, I shalbe woonderous glad. I pray warne Mr. Steele that noe man speake a woord of pearle in any kind ; for I have denied any such, and will never revele it untill I see my tyme. . . .

To the Factors at Surat.[1]
(I.O. Records : *O.C.*, No. 548.)

Mandoa, October 11, 1617.

. . . It hath pleased God to rayse mee unexpected frends ; soe that I am almost confident to doe all yours and my busines to ease and contentment, and that noe reasonable thing wilbe denied mee of the King, who soe gratiously now useth mee. The Prince I have yet refused to visitt, but treated by a third person. I received from him a messuage of better tast then

man had meddled in yt without mee.' But, for the reasons stated in the text, and in the absence of any news from Connock, he judged it inexpedient to send any goods this season. In case, however, it should be decided at Surat to send a ship to Jask for intelligence, he drafted full instructions to Connock and his associates, as also a formal commission authorising Connock to negotiate a treaty with the Shāh. These two documents are printed in full at pp. 107-113 of *Letters Received*, vol. vi. With the signatures of Pring and Kerridge added, the originals were despatched to Jask in the *Bee*, which sailed on 14 Nov., under the charge of John Hatch, with Edward Monnox and Francis Tipton as factors.

[1] Printed in full at p. 116 of *Letters Received*, vol. vi.

former, but not such as I will relie upon. One of his desiers is a mastye [*i.e.* mastiff]; which, if any in the fleete, I desier yow to deliver to his Governor, to bee speedely sent him by them, desiering him to advise it was my order, for I will not bee at chardge to cart nor convey such cattell, as formerly. On Sunday next, the 12, I am with Asaph-Chan to visitt the Prince, to bee reconciled, to receive a *firmaen* and all other reasonable conditions, by the Kings desier and Asaph-Chans mediation. This I knowe : I shall never recover his hart ; but I dare allmost say I shall ease yow all, and from the King obteyne more then yow expect. . . . Your debts at court I have procured, and found so good and round execution of justice that I hope to recover most of the mony in ten dayes ; which wee will make for Agra. The two principall are prisoners, fetched by force, and have obteyned three dayes to make satisfaction, or they will ly very hard in could irons. These three are granted by the *Cuttwall* to trie their frends. . . . I should bee gladder then all yow to come amonge yow ; but till I can bring an olive leave to the arke (that is, peace and securitie to our nation), I dare not stirr. My soveraigne hath written gratiously to mee, for which I am indebted; for hee takes in good part that nothing I have done, which binds mee to give him a better account. . . . The presents may rest untill the *firmaen* come ; then yow shall have my resolution, and it shall all bee upon my head. I have the Kings honor engaged toward my assurance ; but still with the same resolution formerly mentioned. . . . The King persists to buy all the cloth ; his officers aske for it, for they want. This is true ; therfore with the presents dispeede all. Make but one busines and chardge. I suppose it must come to Amadavaz and no farther, for that the Kings tents are out, to remoove within 14 dayes thither. Wee beleeve it constant. Therfore Mr. Steele must knowe this, that he may accomodate his journy. Yf hee either hath or doe nominate the pearle by lettre or woord to any man, hee doth ill service and more then hee can answere. Lett him bee veary warye, for I feare hee hath mistaken himself already, and given out that which hee is not, nor must not expect ; for the Prince demanded if ther was not a new agent come for the English, and what hee was. Hee was fully answered ; but I feare hee received some vayne newes from below. I am loath to bee rough, but will have every man knowe himselfe. Concerning his wife, I knowe not his meanes ; but if the Company gave her not leave as his wife, I will not consent shee shalbe a chardge to them, nor travell this way. I pray advise him to take such a course as I bee not enforced to see his faulte. Captain Towerson and his wife wilbe wellcome hither ; but if the King continue his purpose, it will ease them much to meete us at Amadavaz. Commend me to them.

They shall fynd the Companyes respect in mee ; but for chardge I hope yow understand their conditions. . . .

[*October*] 12.—According to promise, Asaph Chan carryed mee to the Prince, into his private roome, where I presented him with a small China gold-chaine,[1] in a China cup. He used me indifferently.[2] Asaph Chan perswaded him to alter his course towards us, telling him hee gained yearely by us a *lecke* of *rupias* at his port : that it appeared we yearely encreased our trade, and it would in time bring profit : that if the hard measure were continued, we would quit both that and the countrey, of which inconvenience would ensue : that we were his subjects (such words he must use) : if, for desire of toyes, he gave us discontent, we would practise to conceale all from him : but if hee gave us that libertie which was fit, wee would strive to bring all before him, for that I only studyed his content and favour : for my particular, that he should receive mee, when I came to visite him, with honour and according to my qualitie : it would encourage mee to doe him service, and content my nation. Finally, hee moved him for a *firman* for our present ease, and obtained it, promising all manner of content, and at instant gave order to Asaph [3] Chan, his secretary, to draw it in every point according to my owne desires, and to write a letter to the Governour in recommendations of it : and that I should at all times have any other letter, when I called for it. It is easily seene with how base and unworthy men I traffique. Asaph Chan, for a sordid hope only of buying some toyes, was so reconciled as to betray his sonne [*i.e.* son-in-law], and to me obsequious, even to flattery ; for the ground of all this friendship was that he might buy the gold taken in the prize,[4] and some other knackes. To which end he desired to send downe a servant, which I could not deny without losing him I had so long laboured to get ; neither was it ill for us, for his payment is good, and it will save us much charge and

[1] For the chain see p. 393. The cup was one that Roe had procured from Bangham, and cost eight rupees (Roe's Accounts).

[2] *I.e.* neither well nor ill.   [3] ' Afzal ' is meant ; cf. p. 386 *n*.

[4] See p. 388 *n*. Its value was about 350*l*. (*Letters Received*, vol. vj p. 166).

trouble to sell aboord, especially wine and luggish [1] that spoiles in cariage ; and he obtained leave under false colours, and wrote to the Governour in our behalfes, with all manner of kindnesse. There is a necessitie of his friendship : his word is law ; and therefore I durst not see his unworthinesse ; and hope by this course to winne him, at least to make present good use of him. Upon this occasion I moved for a *firman* for Bengala, which he promised, and would never before hearken to. And this effect of his greatnesse [*i.e.* friendliness] I found : that hee prosecuted our debtors, as if his owne ; and, passing by the *Cutwalls* on his elephant, called to command dispatch, which was an unusuall favour ; upon which Groo was imprisoned, and Muckshu had two dayes libertie only to pay us ; and I doubt not but to end that in ten dayes, the summe being foure and forty thousand *rupias*, and the debtors most shifting false knaves in India.

[*October*] 21.—At this instant came in to me from Asaph Chan a servant, in the name of Normahal : that shee had moved the Prince for another *firman* that all our goods might bee in her protection, and that shee had obtained it, and was readie to send down her servant with that, to see and take order for our good establishment : that shee would see that wee should not bee wronged : that Asaph Chan had done this for feare of the Princes violence, and because of his delayes : that now, hee was sure, that his sister had desired to bee our protectresse, that the Prince would not meddle : that upon his honour I should receive all things consigned to mee : that shee had written such a command, and charged her servant to assist our factors, so that we should have never more cause to complaine of Surat : therefore hee desired of mee two or three words to the captaine and factors to use him kindly, and to let him buy for her some toyes, such as I would spare. This I durst not deny, though I saw the greedinesse ; and gave him a note,[2] on condition to see the copy of the *firman*, which was sealed and I could not without leave ; and so he was dispeeded. But you may by this judge this place, how easie it were to raise a stocke. Last yeare, wee were not looked after. Now,

[1] Luggage (heavy goods).
[2] Printed at p. 136 of *Letters Received*, vol. vi.

because I translated the cargazon [*i.e.* invoice] of fine wares (yet concealed the pearle) and gave it the King, every one is ready to runne downe to buy ; Normahall and Asaph Chan studying to doe me good offices ; many great men desiring a letter to send their servants downe ; so that, if you had treble this stocke, it would be bought up aboord, and save you custome and carriage and spoile. For which purpose out of this I have ordered your factory to sell to the servants of Normahall and her brother whatsoever may bee spared, so that I may bee fitted at court in any proportion. Thus I shall save trouble and you charge ; the Prince prevented, and our friends confirmed, and yet I hope sufficient for to please the King and his sonne ; at the delivery of which Asaph Chan hath undertaken the *firman* for Bengala, or any port, and a generall command and grant of free priviledges in all his dominions.

To THOMAS KERRIDGE AT SURAT.[1]
(I.O. Records : *O.C.*, No. 552.)

Mandoa, October 21, 1617.

... The King remooves on Thursday the 24th present ; it is yet said, to Amadavaz, but it is much labored to alter yt ; wherby wee stand in great uncerteynties. For your desier of my speedye repayre to Suratt, it is neither necessarie, so long as yow abide, nor possible for mee to effect ; for that, if the King should for Agra, I must of force returne, and spend the whole yeare in travaill ; and if for Amadavaz, I must there meete him, to finish my great expectations by Asaph-Chans freindshippe earnestly continued ; wheras, at the comming of the presents, I hope to make a finall conclusion at court to good content, and soe to take leave and visitt yow ; which if not done untill wee come to Amadavaz, yet I shall arrive before your fleetes departure ; I doubt not, to the satisfaction of the Companie and us all. The debt of Zulph[ecarcon] and Shaw Hussen I will one way or other finish before my departure. Yow doe very well to lett your Governor knowe that which his proude master will not heare. Now I stand upon new hopes ; but assure yow, if I bee abused, I will in effects revenge it. I am in a very great confidence of a change ; yet if the Princes shipp come in, I doe much desier that shee bee stayed, either untill yow can gett the Governors letter to the Prince to pay our debts, or untill the Prince himselfe demand her

[1] Printed in full at p. 127 of *Letters Received*, vol. vi.

freedome, for then I shalbe heard to speake. I knowe what tearmes theise people are best treated with ; and of this I will advise the Generall. Asaph Chans denialls are all turned into sollicitations in my behalfe ; soe that I hope to effect that of Bengala, as in my last advised. . . .

Your mony for Agra remitted is past by. I would yow continued the same course of exchange ; for if yow send by convoy, it wilbe as deare and more unsafe, and cost exchange after from Brampoore, as much as perhaps at first. Yet for ease of any trouble at Daitatt, in the countrie of Partappshawe, I have gotten his *firmaen* to lett passe our goods without any exaction but what shall be willingly bestowed on the watchmen, and that at pleasure alsoe ; which I will send downe to Brampoore, to lie for occasions. . . .

. . . Asaph-Chans man is alsoe, I hope, arrived with yow ; who comes with the like notes from mee, but principally for gould. The content yow give him is of more consequence then all others. I have acquaynted him with Mochreb-Chans offer of Goga ; but hee assures me today I shall not neede. Besides the *firmaen* sent heerewith, hee hath caused Normahall to speake to the Prince for a new, to such effect as gives mee great content, and it shall come in her name ; with which Asaph-Chan will write to his servant to see execution. Breefly, hee heapes upon mee all present curtesies ; and at this instant, doubting Choja-Jehan[1] at Agra would favour the Banian [*i.e.* Mukshud], writes another command to the *Cuttwall* to whippe his servants, if they avoyd not the house, or pay not in five dayes after sight. . . . I have hearewith sent yow the Princes *firmaen* ; as it is enterpreted to me, very ample for our generall good usadge ; and warranted by Afsul-Chan that, after receipt of this, wee shall neede noe more question. The three poynts principally are : to suffer and helpe our shipps to freesh victualls without custome, and to assiste us in yt : what marchandize soever shall be brought to the *alfandica*, without all delay to dispatch with yow, and to let yow take it to your house and dispose it : that whatsoever comes as presents unto mee shall not bee searched, nor opened, nor hindered, but dispeeded with the English to be brought directly to mee, that I my selfe may goe with yt to the King and Prince. Thus Jaddow justifieth it is written. Therfore now I desier yow to dispeed what yow may. . . . As I was writing this, came Asaph-Chans servant from him and Normahall ; but I understood him not clearly but that hee desiered a lettre to bee written that shee might buy somwhat in the shipps. I per-

[1] Khwāja Jahān, a title conferred by Jahāngīr on Dost Muhammad of Kābul, whose daughter he married. He was much employed by the Emperor in superintending the erection of buildings.

swaded her to stay; butt Jaddow comming tould mee that Asaph-Chan had done it to this end, that shee should undertake the protection of our goods, and that shee had procured a nother *firmaen*, sent by her owne servant, to command our faire usage, and had entreaded of the Prince that shee might pleasure the English in this, and that all might come in her name to be delivered to mee. Thus Asaph-Chan perswaded mee he hath done, knoweing the Princes humors and fearing hee would seize; which now hee undertakes hee will not, and that all shall come to mee that yow send, untouched and without custome. How to beleeve or not, I knowe not, but am resolved to venture; for I am sure I finde heere all frendship. . . . Many great persons have urdged mee to give leave to send downe. When the presents come, Asaph-Chan promiseth upon the deliverie hee will deliver my petition for priviledges, and procure the *firmaen* for Bengala or any other place. Hee assuers mee the King will not denye, and that the Prince hath referrd all concerning us to himselfe. . . . Thus, very wearie, never in more hope of good successe, I committ yow and all our endeavours to Gods blessing, desiering Him to direct us; for such ravenous people I never wish to see, if I escape these. . . .

[*October*] 24.—The King departed Mandoa foure *course* and, wandering in the hills, left us irresolute what way to take, no man knowing his purpose.[1]

[*October*] 26.—I got a warrant for ten camels at the Kings price.

[*October*] 29.—I removed after: forced away by the desolations of the place.

[*October*] 31.—I arrived at the Kings tents, but found him gone with few company for ten dayes a hunting,[2] no man to follow without leave; the *leskar* divided and scattered into many parts; ill water, deare provisions, sicknesse and all sorts of calamitie accompanying so infinite a multitude; yet nothing remooves him from following this monstrous appetite. Heere

[1] Jahāngīr's route appears from the *Memoirs* (vol. i. pp. 401-23) to have been by way of Dhār to near Rāmghar; thence to Dohad, and thence to the banks of the Mahi (see map). Here Roe left the camp and went direct to Ahmadābād, arriving 15 Dec., 1617. The Emperor proceeded by way of Nariād to Cambay, reaching that port on 19 Dec. He left again on the last day of the year, and entered Ahmadābād on 6 Jan., 1618.

[2] He had made an excursion to Hāsilpur (*Memoirs*, vol. i. p. 404).

I understood the Kings purpose was uncertaine, whether for Agra or Guzerat; the latter given out; the former more probable, because his councell desired to be at rest; but that, however, for the dispatch of my businesse, seeing hee would linger heere about a moneth, I was advised, and thought it as fit to send for the goods and presents as to deferre it upon uncertainties; being that dispatched, I had hope of some quiet in this course. I wore out my body, being very weake, and not like to recover upon daily travell in the fields, with cold raw muddie water.

November 2.—Arrived Richard Steele and Mr. Jackson,[1] with the pearle [*i.e.* pearls] and some other small matters stollen ashoare, according to my order, which I received and gave quittance for. With him I had conference about his projects, which because I would not rashly reject them, as he had set them afoot, after having made him see his fancies and understand the qualitie of these people, how for the water-worke, if to bee effected, it must bee begunne at our charge, and after triall, we shall not enjoy the profit, but the naturalls taught and our people rejected; neither our commoditie vented by it, for that the lead will treble his price by portage over-land, and cannot bee delivered at Agra so cheape as found there: yet I was content hee should make triall for satisfaction by carrying his work-men to Amadavas, to meete mee there, where by assistance of Mocrib Chan, who only is a friend to new inventions, I would make offer to the King of their industry and make proofe what conditions may be obtained; but in my judgement it is all money and labour cast away. The Company must shut their eares against these projectors, who have their

[1] A gentleman who had come out in Pring's fleet with letters of recommendation from Sir Thomas Smythe and 'many honourable lords of His Majestys Councell.' He seems to have decided very quickly not to remain in India, for on 3 Nov., 1617, the ambassador wrote (*O.C.*, No. 556) to the Surat factors to assist him ' to goe to the sowthward, if hee desier it, to seeke a better fortune, [and] to advise him which way he may reape some honest recompence of two years travell without injurie to the Company.' Probably he was the John Jackson who at the end of 1618 lost a leg by a shot from the Dutch castle at Jacatra and died three days later (*O.C.*, No. 784, and *Purchas*, vol. i. p. 656).

owne employments more in their ends then their masters profits. Many things hold well in discourse, and in the theorique satisfie curious imaginations, but in practise and execution are found difficult and ayrie; especially to alter the constant received customes of kingdomes, where some drinke only raine-water, some of a holy river, some none but what is fetched by their owne cost.[1] His second, of reducing the *caffilaes* and merchants of Lahor and Agra by the River Indus, that used to passe by Candahor into Persia, to transport by sea in our shipping for Jasques or the Gulph, is a meere dreame; some man in conference may wish it, but none ever practise it. The river is indifferently navigable downe; but the mouth is the residence of the Portugalls; returnes backe against the streame very difficult. Finally, wee must warrant their goods, which a fleet will not doe; neither did the Portugall ever lade or noise [*sic*] such goods, but only, for those of Sindie and Tatta, that traded by their owne junckes, they gave a *cartas* or passe to secure them from their frigats, and traded with them; for which they payed a small matter, and that onely which came to the purses of the Grand [2] of Diu, Damon and Ormus. Or if all other difficulties were taken away, yet will the Lahornes never bee drawne downe, being that *caffila* consists most of returning Persians and Armenians that knew the passage from Jasques almost as bad as from Candahor; and for that little on the confines of Sinde not worth mentioning. Notwithstanding, for his better satisfaction, I was content hee should by experience learne his owne errours, so it were not at the Companies charge; but I suppose hee will let it fall, not knowing at which end to beginne.

A third project, for to joyne the trade of the Red Sea with this, I recommended to him, for that it was alreadie in use, and the perill for the Guzurats very apparant;[3] therefore I doubted not some merchants might be drawne to lade in our ships at freight; whereby wee should make our selves necessary friends to these people, supply our owne defects, save export of monies, and finally, for this yeare employ one ship of the olde

[1] Should be ' caste.'   [2] Elsewhere called the Captain.
[3] As we have seen, Roe had proposed this to the Company quite independently of Steel.

account that should returne in September and receive the proceed of the remaynes of this joynt stocke,[1] which will be sufficient to re-lade a great ship ; otherwise to transport it over will be extreame losse. This I opened and urged the consequence, shewed which way to effect it, and commended by him to the commander, the cape merchant, and your factors with all earnestnesse, as by my letters appeares. The consequence I will make evident in your profit, if they follow it. For were the goods and estate all my owne, if I could not procure somewhat towards charge by freight from the Guzurats, yet having so many emptie vessels for so small a stocke, and two fallen into your hands of men of warre, I had rather goe emptie, and for company with them, then to omit that. There are many chances in that sea and in the way ; her returne onely of our owne remaynes shall requite all forbearance, and be readie in time ; for employed she must be if we intend to send the rest upon this account, for that here is no harbourage. At his arrivall, I found him high in his conceits, having somewhat forgotten me; Mr. Kerridge and him at warres, which I endeavoured to temper on all parts ; but for his wife I dealt with him cleerely : she could not stay with our safety, nor his masters content : that he had ruined his fortunes, if by amends hee repayred it not : that shee should not travell nor live on the Companies purse (I know the charge of women) : that if he were content to live himselfe like a merchant, as others did, frugally, and to be ordered for the Companies service, and to send home his wife, he was welcome : otherwise, I must take a course with both against my nature. Having to this perswaded him, I likewise practised the discouragement of Captaine Towerson about his wife (you know not the danger, the trouble, the inconvenience of granting these liberties). To effect this, I perswaded Abraham [see p. 168 n], his father in law here, to hold fast : I wrote to them the gripings of this court, the small hope or reliefe from his alliance, who expected great

[1] The first joint stock had been brought to an end, and a second started. The goods belonging to the former had either to be exchanged for native commodities and these sent home, or else they must be carried over (' transported ') to the new stock at a valuation. The former course was obviously the more profitable.

matters from him. Finally, I perswaded his returne quietly. To further this, I wrote to your chiefe factor that such things as hee had brought and were vendible should bee brought to your use by bill of exchange, to such profit for him as both might save ; and this inconvenience you bring on your selves by liberties unreasonable. But to take tye of his trash to lye upon your hands, upon any condition I did prohibit.

I find by your letter your strict command in private trade, as well for your owne servants as others ; whereby I collect you meane not that he shall have that libertie hee expects, for he is furnished for above one thousand pound sterling, first penny here, and Steele at least two hundred pound, which he presumes, sending home his wife, his credit and merit is so good towards you, that you will admit in this case to be rid of such cattell. I will not buy, but order that it be marked and consigned to you, that you may measure your owne hand. You discourage all your olde servants. Some may doe all things for faire words ; some nothing for good actions. I could instance some gone home two yeares since that onely employed their owne stocke, did no other businesse, and live now at home in pleasure ; others that raise their fortune upon your monies, from port to port, and returne rich and unquestioned. Last yeare a mariner had six and twentie churles of indico : others many fardles : a third seven thousand *mamudes*, first pennie, in Baroach bastaes [baftaes], chosen apart (for hee invested your monies, and it is probable hee chose not the worst for himselfe) : a fourth,[1] above one hundred and fiftie pound, first pennie. These I mention, not for spight, but to move you to equalitie ; neither by their example these may escape, for they swallow you up ; but that an indifferent restraint be executed upon all. For the effecting of all these purposes, the sending home the woman and the prosecution of the Red Sea, I send [*sic*] backe Richard Steele with orders to Surat, having altered my purpose of the goods and presents from the *leskar* ; it beeing declared that the King will for Guzurat, where I have appointed Richard Steele, after having dispatched other matters, to meete, with

---

[1] ' The names are omitted ' (*marginal note by Purchas*). They are, however, partly supplied in Roe's letter of 14 Feb., 1618 (*infra*).

them and his ingeniers. I also sent my advice and directions
to Captaine Pring, to take an inventorie of all the monies and
goods in the two men of warre : to make it over to your stocke
and land it : to sell or dispose of the ships, as his occasion shall
require (the monies, if sold, to be put to stocke) : to grant
passage to some of the chiefes, to entertaine the rest and to
referre it to you at heme, whom [how ?] you will deale with the
owners that set them out. My opinion is peremptory that their
surprize is just and justifiable, all their goods forfeited ; if you
will restore anything, at your courtesie ; but with the more
rigour you deale with these, the better example you will leave
for such barbarous piracies ; for, if this course be practised,
take your leave of all trade about Surat and the Red Sea, and
let the Company of Turkie stand cleere of the Grand Signors
revenge, and we heere must expect cold irons.

To Thomas Kerridge at Surat.[1]

(I.O. Records : *O.C.*, No. 556.)

Six *course* of Mandoa, 3 November, 1617.

The alterations of humors here change mee as the wynde
doth the best seaman. The King is declared for Amadavaz,
and doubt not but must winter it in Guzeratt. This causeth
mee to alter my last of the 1 of November [*not extant*], because
of avoydeing charge and that incomoditie wee may fall into
by followeing the *leskarr*. Therfore my desier is that all the
presents and other fine goods, with the cloth and all for the
court, may be stayed to be sent thither ; but seeing it wilbe
two months before the Kings arrivall there, yow neede not
hasten, but soe that they meete mee just, least others play
with us falsly ; of which I will give yow (as I see wee proceede)
just advise in sufficient tyme, and will meete them two dayes
journy, to prevent miseusage. Mr. Steele hath safely in eight
dayes delivered the pearle. I feare not soe fitt for this markett ;
the great fowle, of black water, well knowne in Indya : the
others small, and to my experience here (that have bought)
deare ; but I hope to passe them, beeing come soe privatly, and
soe returne the mony to Agra speedily. I have dealte with
Mr. Steele very faierly and clearly, and opened my mind. Hee
gives mee satisfaction in his promises, and I doubt not to
accomodate all soe well as wee may live like frendes. The
principall difference wilbe about his wife. . . .

[1] Printed in full at p. 140 of *Letters Received*, vol. vi.

[*November*] 6.—I went to Asaph Chans, having received his passe ; unto whom I shewed the pearle according to promise. Though the sorts fit not the countrey just (as I was informed hereafter), yet their performance with him gave him such content that I am confident I may use Pharaohs words : The land is before you, dwell where you will, you and your servants. For the price wee talked not, but he vowed such secrecie ; and for my sake, who have shewed this confidence in him, hee will give more then their worth, and not returne one, and pay readie mony, of which hee professeth not to want, and to lend mee what I want. His sister I have promised to visit, whom hee hath made our protectresse ; and briefly whatsoever contentment words can bring I receive, and some good effects. When the presents arrive, assure you I will not be liberall to your losse ; little shall serve. Asaph Chan admonisheth mee himselfe : so they came with somewhat to induce them, as well accepted, bought as given ; experience of others makes mee to approve of this doctrine. Finishing these complements with him in his bed-chamber, he rose to dinner, having invited me and my people; but he and [his] friends dined without, appointing mee a messe with him apart, for they eate not willingly with us ; where I had good cheere and well attended ; the reversion for my servants.[1] After dinner, I moved Groos debt, told him the delayes. Hee answered : I should not open my lips : he had undertaken it : that Groo by his meanes was finishing accounts with a jeweller : that hee had ordered, as money was paid,

[1] This appears to be the dinner spoken of by Terry (p. 207) :

' Once my Lord Ambassador had an entertainment there by Asaph Chan, who invited him to dinner (and this was the only respect in that kinde he ever had, while he was in East India). . . . This Asaph Chan entertained my Lord Ambassadour in a very spacious and a very beautifull tent, where none of his followers besides myself saw or tasted of that entertainment. That tent was kept full of a very pleasant perfume ; in which sents the King and grandees there take very much delight. The floor of the tent was first covered all over with very rich and large carpets, which were covered again, in the places where our dinner stood, with other good carpets made of stich't leather, to preserve them which were richer ; and these were covered again with pure white and fine callico clothes, and all these covered with very many dishes of silver ; but for the greater part of those silver dishes, they were not larger than our largest

it should rest in the *Cutwalls* hand for us ; which I found true, and the *Cutwall* promised to finish it in three dayes, desiring mee to send no more to Asaph Chan.

I cannot omit a basenesse or favour, according as you will interprete it. The King, when his prisons are full of condemned men, some he commands to be executed, some he sends to his *Umraes* to redeeme at a price. This he esteemes as a courtesie, to give meanes to exercise charitie, but he takes the money, and so sels the vertue. About a moneth before our remove, he sent to mee to buy three Abassines [*i.e.* Abyssinians] (for fortie *rupias* a man), whom they suppose all Christians. I answered : I could not buy men as slaves, as others did, and so had profit for their money ; but in charity I would give twenty *rupias* a piece to save their lives, and give them libertie. The King tooke my answere well, and bade them to be sent me. They expected money, and I was not hastie ; hearing no more of it, I hoped it had beene forgotten ; but his words are written decrees. This night the officers, seeing I sent not, delivered the prisoners into my procuradors power, and tooke his *screete* for sixtie *rupias*, which at my returne I payed, and freed the slaves.

To the Factors at Surat.[1]
(I.O. Records : *O.C.*, No. 558.)

Leskar, six *course* from Mandoa, 8 November, 1617.

. . . Mr. Kerridge his readines to stay and to here my poore advise, to joyne with mee to assist in the Companies affayres, trencher-plates, the brimms of all of them gilt. We sate in that large room as it were in a triangle ; the Ambassadour on Asaph Chans right hand, a good distance from him ; and myself below ; all of us on the ground, as they there all do when as they eat, with our faces looking each to the other, and every one of us had his several mess. The Ambassadour had more dishes by ten, and I less by ten, than our entertainer had ; yet for my part, I had fifty dishes. They were all set before us at once, and little paths left betwixt them, that our entertainers servants (for onely they waited) might come and reach them to us one after another. . . . At this entertainment we sat long, and much longer than we could with ease cross-leg'd, but, all considered, our feast in that place was better than Apicius, that famous epicure of Rome . . . could have made with all provisions had from the earth, and air, and sea.'

[1] Printed in full at p. 145 of *Letters Received*, vol. vi.

I take very gratfully. I professe it is his abilities and experiences that urdgeth it from mee to have pressd him; and I doe undertake not only the continuance of him in qualetie of cheefe factor, which hee was before, but suppose it to be the Companies intent, and that trust they have committed to mee is but a superintendance over all their servants, not to hinder and wrong them, but to farther and direct them in that which I shall see requisite, and to dispose their endeavors for the benifitt of their masters; which power yow shall see I will use with all modestie, or rather never lett yow see but in case of necessitie; hoping yow will suffer mee to advise, and either follow it or show mee a good reason wherin I err (which for me is very easie); and I shall endeavour to leave in the Company so good impression, both of his and all other mens good deservings, that may encourage such as shall follow to the like industrie and performance.... The cloth must accompany the other goods to Amadavaz (whither yet they say the King will goe), by the convoy of Mr. Steele, whom I wish yow to use faierly.... I knowe not what the *firmaen* will doe; for that I complayned since, especially about the cryeing downe the roy[all] of eight, and I was answered: stay untill yow heare the success of this: if it faile yow, yow shall have remedie. Beleeve mée, I want not the best frends in this court. I was within two dayes invited to dinner to Asaph-Chan, carried into his private roomes, and used honorabley. Our debts are a stalling [*i.e.* being collected in instalments], that is, the *Cuttwall* collects the mony from other debtors, and shall pay us.... For your house, the Governor will not putt yow out, and I cannot trouble the Prince for such matters. Keepe your possession. If they use force, then I will step in, upon good reason.... If yow cannot sell quantety of your wyne, I pray send mee a small vessell, two or three. I had rather have sack then red wyne, yet some of that.... All this is vanetye, to talke of authoritie. Lett us all despise all authoritie to controll us from any ill, and yow shall all fynde me a tame lyon.... You may try Goga, Sindu, Bengala: but noe port so fitt as Suratt, if yow practise to send our goods up by our owne pinnace.... I am most glad Captain Towerson affects not the court. Keepe and nourish that resolution. Hee wilbe deceived in expectation here, and others in him. And his wives helpe I neede not. Normahall is my sollicitor, and her brother my brokar.... Thus, extreame faint and weary, and no helpe, I committ yow all to Gods direction. ...

To Captain Pring.[1]

(I.O. Records : *O.C.*, No. 559.)

Leskar, six *course* from Mandoa, 8 November, 1617.

... I am agreed with yow in opinion that force from Goa will not molest you this yeare, and that yow may the boulder attempt the Red Sea with the lesse force ; for if noe gallions come, none can attend her that way employed ; others wee neede not feare. Therfore for the project a lesse ship may serve, and one wilbe sufficient. To moove the Prince is in vayne. Hee scornes to confesse wee can helpe him ; and will never command it to his servants, but leave it free. I have divers wayes tried him. What must bee done must proceede from our readines and their owne necessities. If yow [will] take my opinion, publish it yow will send a ship for trade to Mochae ; if any will freight or passe in her, they shall partake fortunes with us, such as wee doe ; if not, yow will not bee tyed any way to stay to keepe company or defend them, but shift for your selves. I doubt not yow will have many offers, or els Mr. Steele is wyde. If not, I should bee doeing for goodfellowship, because I would fynde a ship woorke to relade the next yeare.... It is impossible I should leave the court and returne ; my body will not endure hard travell, and ther is noe neede of mee in those where Martine Pring is.... I want (I thanck God) nothing but my health (which is all). Your wyne will refresh mee. But for that I hope to come to Suratt, I would send for it. In the meane tyme a little cheese, two bottles of the oyle, four or five bottles of sack and red wine, and a quart of synoman water will keepe mee alive. Lett the remayner of your favours be kept at Suratt ; where if I arrive short of seeing yow, yet I will remember yow often. But when the goods come up (of which I am yet uncerteyne), I pray cause two of the least runletts of wyne to bee sent ; for a frend one, the other for the way. If any of your surgions have a little sirrope of violetts or lemons, halfe a pint to bee left at Suratt. Mr. Kerridge and I shall well agree. Though last yeare I was sett behynde the door, nothing can make mee forsake justice. I know his abilitie, when it is tempered ; and the want of him, if hee depart, I shall repent.... Yow may perhaps use the *Bee* to send for Bengala (yf the King give mee his *firmaen*) that wee may satisfie the Company ; but in my judgment it is tyme cast away....

[1] Printed in full at p. 151 of *Letters Received*, vol. vi.

To Thomas Kerridge at Surat.[1]

(I.O. Records : *O.C.*, No. 573.)

Leskar in Rannas Wood,[2] December 2, 1617.

My last dated the 17th of November [*not extant*], I doubt not hath signified the Kings hast to Amadavaz, which hee continewes without rest, by soe miserable wayes as I beleeve never armie or multitude ever went. Hee purposeth to enter it about the 13th present. That brought yow my desiers of Mr. Steeles dispeede to meete mee there with the goods and presents. I hope yow finde noe difficultie in their passadge, for that Asaph-Chan stands obliged on both sides beteene the Prince and mee ; the King drincks and is indifferent. . . . The pearle I feare is over rated or over bought in England ; for the smaller sort, losse to a halfe, for the greater to a third, and for the greatest but 12,000 rup. I hope to gett more for that ; else I will not sell it, nor the rest, to any losse. I pray advise mee by the first what yow thinck fitt to doe, if they will not yeild their owne mony : to keepe or returne them. . . . Groo will yeild us yet noe money ; but today I had a nother order for him, for hee goes at liberty. Asaph-Chan commanded his detention close, if hee satisfie us not instantly (which by his unckle hee is about to doe) ; and frendly sent the *Cutwall* woord our debts were his and hee should noe other esteeme of them. Beleeve me, but for his frendship it might bee writ in lettres easye to wype out, or not recovered this twelve months, and that by sales at long day. Nowe ther is noe doubt in a month it wilbe mony, though wee are promised an end the next resting day. . . . Wee travell daylie. I have scarse leasure to eate, or noe meate, but ill water. A little glasse of yours would helpe a weake stomacke.

PS.—Abram-Chan is called up, upon the complaynts of Shaw-Hussen and Sale-Beage. The *firmaen* was sent before

[1] Printed in full at p. 208 of *Letters Received*, vol. vi.

[2] Apparently near Dohad. Terry (*Purchas*, vol. ii. p. 1481) says there were ' no lesse then 200,000 men, women and children in this *leskar* or campe (I am hereof confident), besides elephants, horses and other beasts that eate corne : all which notwithstanding, wee never felt want of any provision, no, not in our nineteene dayes travell from Mandoa to Amadavar, thorow a wildernesse, the road being cut for us in the mayne woods.' It will be seen that he differs from Roe as to the discomfort of the journey ; but his account (written after his return to England) is continually inaccurate in detail. Thus he speaks of the length of the present journey as nineteen days, which is obviously too short a period ; in his later narrative, on the other hand, he gives the date of departure from Māndu as 20 September, which is over a month too early.

I had knowledg. I went to Asaph-Chan about it, who knewe it and supposed I was glad, for that hee thought wee could not make soe many complaynts and the Governor honest. I made him understand the contrarie, and his goodnes and his justice, which hee protests hee will deliver in his defence; and if hee desier to returne wilbe his frend and helper. . . .

[*December*] 10.—I visited Asaph Chan,[1] having received advice from Surat of a new *firman* come downe to disarrive [disarrme] all the English, and some other restrictions of their libertie ; upon a complaint made to the Prince, that we intended to build a fort at Swally, and that our shippes were laden with bricke and lime for that end (which suspition arose only by bringing a few on shoare to found the ships bell [2]) ; yet the alarum came to court so hot, that I was called to answere ; which, when I made it appeare how absurd the feare was, how dishonorable for the King, how unfit the place for us, without water or harbourage, yet the jealousie [*i.e.* suspicion] was so strongly imprinted, because formerly I had demanded a river by Goya [Gogo] for that end, that I could hardly perswade the Prince we intended not some surprise. By this you may judge how easie it were to get a port for our selves, if you affected it, which I can [*sic*] neither so profitable for you, nor a place tenable. Notwithstanding all remonstrances, this furnace must be demolished, and a *haddey* of horse sent downe

[1] From Biddulph's accounts (*Factory Records, Miscellaneous*, vol. 25) we learn that on this occasion Roe gave Asaf Khān a 'riche standishe' [inkstand] which had cost 12*l*. 10*s*. ; while on the 30th of the same month he presented him with a large picture of the value of 6*l*. 13*s*. 4*d*.

[2] 'Moreover, our bell beinge broken, there was a few bricks landed at Suallie to new cast the bell, at which ther was great murmuringe amongest the countrie people, who said we went aboute to buyld a castell ; of which some did write to the Kinge, and the Kinge tould it the Prince, who presentlie sent downe a chiefe man from the courte to forbidd us buyldinge our castle and also to take order that not above 10 Englishe should be suffred to com into the towne together and those 10 to leave their armes at the customhouse ; and the Governour, Abram Chan (who to his power hathe bin ever a friend to our nation) was in danger to be displaced, yf not quite thruste oute, for that he had not written his master of our buyldinge a castle (in the ayre).'—Monnox and Tipton to the Company, 28 Dec., 1617 (*O.C.*, No. 586).

to see it effected. The disarming of our men, being all that our people stomacked (though it was only to leave their weapons in the custome-house, and that only of the ships company), though it were quieter for us, except they were often more civill: yet I told Asaph Chan wee would not endure the slavery, nor I stay in the countrey: that one day the Prince sent a *firman* for our good usage and grant of priviledges, the next day countermanded it; that there was no faith nor honour in such proceedings, neither could I answere my residence longer. He replyed: at night hee would moove the King, before the Prince, and give me answere.

To Thomas Kerridge and assistants at Surat.[1]
(I.O. Records: *O.C.*, No. 575.)
The woods, 30 *course* short of Amadavas, December 6, 1617.[2]

Yours nowe received of the 21th November mentioneth one of the 9th that never came to mee; with this the copy and note in English and Persian of what delivered to Asaph-Chans servant, the weight of gould, and prises as by invoyce.... His payment is better then any mans, though his prises hard made. By this I am sure I have saved custome, contented a frend, and not borne the hazard of portage.... Your bills for Agra are received and mony almost all invested; 200 camells on the way this 13 dayes; cloth bartered; creditt for about 25,000 *rupees*, three monnths; the proceede much enlardged, double to former years (as they write), in best commoditie, and all things ther performed much to my content, and (I hope) their creditt and the Companyes profitt; the number of semians enlardged (a new sort of cloth) [see p. 233 n], and carpetts not yet gotten but in hand. Their day I will not faile on, nor have they found difficultie, as wee supposed, in trust nor prises hoysed [*i.e.* raised] out of reason; and I make noe question, by this yeares and the next practise, to enter soe into good opinion as to buy on tyme for a *leecke* of goods; by which the ships shalbe supplied in tyme, and, if care taken to preserve the foundation, it shall proove an advantage of better use then to bee so good husbands as to venture nothing.... A *firmaen* from [for?] Bengala cannot be had while the Prince hath

---

[1] Printed in full at p. 213 of *Letters Received*, vol. vi.

[2] Though thus dated in the original, it is clear from the contents that it was written (or finished) on 13 December (cf. p. 419).

Suratt, unles wee will quitt it and rely on the other only. Hee pretends that all our fine goods shall come thither and his port beare the burthen of trash and hinder others. ... For privat trade yow know my orders, and I the Companyes pleasure. The prime comoditie [*i.e.* indigo] no man, I hope, will deale in upon any pretence ; cloth, if they doe and consent to acquaynt the factors with it and remitt it to their masters, it may passe, and by your and my advise may bee favored ; but for all such as are obstinate, I require execution of commission to the utmost, notice of their names, and I will use my creditt to bring them to repentance by losses.... Mr. Steele hath satisfied him easely that loves not contentions. But I can discerne woords and shawdowes from truth and substance. I hope well of all men, of him, and would not put my finger to the ruyne of any. I cannot so soone help a man as destroy him ; it is a tender thing in a mans conscience. Yet I am not soe easye as to bee abused much. You shall see I see both wayes and will choose the best. ... Your Governor is recalled (as by my last advised), perhaps for our sake. But I will proove a more active frend to him then hee was to us, when hee arrives. Abulhassan [1] pretends to bee sorrie for the Princes usage of us ; sayes hee dare not stur in his [*i.e.* the Prince's] owne *prigony* [see p. 381], but if hee weare remooved would make a new Suratt for us at Swally. To night I will question with him of that dissimulation ; but I knowe the complaynt came to the Prince, by him to the King, and disputed before my face not long since ; to which Abulhassan sayd nothing nor seemed to bee concerned in yt. The King was not pleased at the folly ; but, after his manner, gave us no satisfaction, but only bad his sonne use strangers better. I complayned of this new trouble before your lettres arrived ; am promised a lettre downe of new favour, but on the way unpossible to sollicite it. If that were the woorst, to take away their [2] weapons and restore them, except they were more governed, itt matters not ; or if yow would shew them in a glasse their folly, the Generall may disarme their boates and, beeing demanded reason, may say wee doubt they are bound for the conquest of England and the taking of London. ... Yf they dispatch your goods, that yow may proceede in your busines, lett them tyrannize over presents as much as they will. If sent up, I will trye for them and will not loose them ; or, if I doe, I will dye on the coast, if not repayred both in honor and mony. ... Mesolapatan is a new question. I thought them soe bare as they needed noe shippe to fetch any proceede. They speake of some on creditt ; I knowe not what it is, nor whether it be fitt goods [for one ship ?], much lesse two. In

---

[1] Āsaf Khān (see p. 93 *n*).   [2] The English sailors' (see p. 416).

this poynt I wish your due consider[a]tion ; for, if the factorie shalbe continued as profitable, and that bee the Companyes intent, some supply they must have, but whether from us or Bantam I knowe not custome [1] ... I thinck if the stocke were kept togither, and that disolved, it were better for the owners. But this must come from themselves ; I will goe noe further then Mogolls India. ... Yow mistake mee if yow thinck I would relye on the Suratters for a whole supply [of indigo]. But I would buy all they had, if at any reasonable rates. I doubt not, if it were practised, the quantetie would encrease ; and they will venture here wher they find gaine. But the venture is nothing from Agra to Suratt, and I suppose it bought up (for to that end I mooved it) ; and, if bought, what doe they adventure ? Privat merchants make their owne provision ; but wee are a company and may sweepe a towne. And if they could bee brought to it, then yow must pardon mee from thincking wee could buy or bee furnished at our owne travell soe cheape as they. What they gett on us, that live on rise and *chaule* and *donna*,[2] wilbe easelie saved in our expences of horse and guards and peons and exactions. To buy that which is, if at any rate, is no harme. To see what it will encrease too, and to encouradg them to bee furnished, if it faile, wee are wher wee were ; not relying upon it, but using it for our advantage. And yow see now, if 200 *churles* were there, whether not better take that deare then the worst sort of Barooch in all India cheape. ...

... Your despatch for Persia I understand ; but sawe noe cause to spare two factors to carry lettres, both, it seemes, soe sufficient as to doe all if the woorst happen. All I shall farther add in it is to putt yow in mynde it is to mee His Majestie hath referrd it, and the Company entrusted it. I cannot answere for England until the returne of this voyadge to any satisfaction. That therfore I expect the first sight and receipt of all that comes, except your privat lettres and accounts of sales for the bookes perfecting ; but relations, treaties, priviledges, projects and all of that qualetie, are noe mans to judg off but myne ; and I shall either receive them whole or not meddle in them. ...

Your *pattmars* will now finde mee in Amadavaz or Cambaya. If they find not my tents, if on the way on a remooving day in the Kings way, they cannot misse my English servants with the camells. ... The cheese and wyne, if not come with [the] presents, I hope to live to drinck and eate with yow. That sent

---

[1] Pring, on his way from Surat to Bantam (April, 1618), detached the *Bee* with a supply of money for Masulipatam (*O.C.*, No. 784).

[2] *Chāul* and *dhāna* likewise mean rice, the former term being mostly applied to husked rice and the latter to unhusked (paddy).

by *cahar* [1] is in great perrill, nine dayes in unhabited woods, and all that falls short robbd ; but I willingly beare the hazard. . . .

Thus I conclude answer to your lettre, wherin I fall into consideration of the paynes by myne owne wearines. Yow may suppose I write not at ease in a house ; remoove every other day ; forgett to answer none ; have much to prepare for England, and no helpe. Therfore what is written in hast must not bee severly censured. I am long in some instances ; it is to lett yow see my motions come not at adventure without consideration, though they bring not allway their reasons.

Nowe I come to our estate here. I have recomplayned ; to night visitt the King with his Majesties lettre translated ; deferred till nowe for extremetie of wayes, that made all in confusion ; at which tyme I hope to dispute our owne cause anewe. Asaph-Chan remaynes the same ; hath feasted mee, and wee meete often. The Prince against his will shalbe left at Amadavaz ; hath that goverment geven him and Cambaya. This is doubtles an ill signe that the King remooves him. It is out of doubt true. The good to us is : Asaph-Chan hath enformed hee [the Prince] quittes divers small *jaggers* [*jāgirs*] to the King, of which hee [Asaf Khān] will procure Suratt may bee one, which hee will take ; and then I doubt not to see all amended. This will suddenly bee tryed, and upon these changes the Prince will not have cause of oposition. Asaph-Chan then promiseth to procure the *firmaen* for Bengala (for hee suspects not us to seeke it to betraye Suratt, but to encrease our trade) and all other my just demands, and voweth hee will make Englishmen content and happy. Thus in new hopes I rest a tyme ; and so I must from writing, for I am not able scarce to write my name. I committ yow all to Gods mercy.

[*December*] 13.—I revisited Asaph Chan. He told me wondrous matters of the Kings affection to my sovereigne, to my nation, and to mee : that hee had ventured the Princes disfavour for our sakes, and had full promise for a new reformation : but because he feared the Princes dealing, he gave me this assurance, that he would take the *prigany* of Surat, which the Prince must leave, being made Governour of Amadavas, Cambaya, and that territorie ; and to give me satisfaction that he had not dissembled with me, he desired me to come at night to court, and bring the King my masters letter [*not extant*] and the translation : the oportunitie was faire to

---

[1] *Kahār*, a porter who carried goods for long distances balanced at each end of a long bamboo.

deliver it ; upon the occasion of which he bade me persist in my complaints, and offer to take leave : I should then see what he would say for us, and so I should beleeve my selfe. At evening I went to the King, it beeing a very full court, and presented my letter, which (the King sitting on the ground) was layd before him ; and he, busie, tooke no great notice. Asaph Chan whispered his father in the eare, desiring him to reade the letter, and to assist us, for that he might better begin that then himselfe. Etimon Dowlet tooke up both letters, gave the English to the King, and read the translated ; to which when the King had answered many words of complaint, to that point of procuring our quiet trade by his authoritie among the Portugals, he demanded if he [sic] would make peace. I answered : His Majestie knew long since I offered to be governed by him, and referred it to his wisdome, and had expected his pleasure. He replied : hee would undertake absolutely to accord us, and to make agreement in his seas, which he would by answere to my masters letters signifie, and therein give him content in all other his friendly desires. Notwithstanding, I demanded leave to goe before to Amadavas, to meet the Kings presents and to prepare for my returne. Upon which motion, the question grew betweene the King and the Prince, who complayned that he had no profit by us, and that he was content to be rid of us. Asaph Chan tooke the turne, and very roundly told the King that we brought both profit to the port, to the kingdome, and securitie : that we were used very rudely by the Princes servants, and that it was not possible for us to reside without amends : it were more honourable for his Majestie to license us [to depart ?] then to intreate us so discourteously, for it would be the end. The Prince replyed very cholerickly that he had never done us wrong, and had lately given mee a *firman* at his entreatie. He replyes : it is true, you gave a *firman* to his content, and in ten dayes sent another, in effect, to contradict it : that he stood surety betweene both : had undertaken from the Princes mouth our redresse, but now he had the shame and dishonor of it : that he ought me nothing, nor I him : he spake for no ends but for the Kings honor and justice ; in that which he [*i.e.* the Prince] said that he did us no wrong, he must appeale to me, who complayned that our goods were taken by force : that two yeeres past Rulph [Zulphecarcon] had begun it, would never pay us, and his officers continued every shipping : that if the Prince were weary of us, he might turne us out, but then he must expect we would doe our owne justice upon the seas. He demanded if the King or Prince gave mee meanes to eate, or who did ? That I was an ambassadour and a stranger, that lived and followed the King at great charge : that if our goods were forced, and after we could get neither goods nor money, how should I live and maintayne myselfe ?

This delivered with some heate, the King catched the word, force, force, redoubling it to his sonne, and gave him sharpe reprehension. The Prince promised to see me paid all : that he had taken nothing, but only caused the presents to be sealed, because his officers had no custome : and desired to have them opened before him. I absolutely refused it ; also I told the King I would only doe my dutie to my master, in delivering his presents free : after I would give the Prince all content. Etimon Dowlet, who is always indifferent, and now by his sonne made our friend, whispered with the King, and read a clause or two in my masters letter ; at which the King made his son rise and stand aside. Asaph Chan joyned in this private conference (which they told me was for my good) and in conclusion the Prince was called, commanded to suffer all the goods to come to my hands quietly, to give me such priviledges as were fit, which Asaph Chan should propound. The Prince would not yeeld the presents except Asaph Chan would stand surety that he should have a share, which he did ; and then we all agreed upon that point ; the King giving mee many good words, and two pieces of his *pawne* [1] out of his dish, to eate of the same he was eating. Then I tooke leave to goe to Amadavas to meet the presents ; and so we parted. At night, I set on my journey, leaving my tents, supposing the next day to reach the citie ; but I rode two nights, a day and

[1] Betel-leaf, chewed by the natives with the dried areca-nut. The Hindustāni term here used is in full *pān-supāri*, which is generally employed for ' the combination of betel, areca-nut, lime, etc., which is politely offered (along with otto of roses) to visitors, and which intimates the termination of the visit ' (*Hobson-Jobson*).

a halfe, with one baite upon straw, and the fifteenth at noone arrived at Amadavas.[1]

To Thomas Kerridge and Assistants at Surat.[2]
(I.O. Records: *O.C.*, No. 578.)

Amadavaz, 18 December, 1617.

Your lettres come soe quick upon mee in this huddle of trouble and journy that I know not which or what is answered; but rather double then omitt any thing necessarie. That of the 11th dicto by your expresse touchd in part; by which yow understand of my arrivall in Amadvaz. The complaynts therin I cannot speedelie redresse, the King beeing turned to Cambaya and not expected here this 13 dayes; at which tyme I will soe lardgly enforme in all kinds as, if ther bee any honor or sence or common understanding, I shall procure amends, or licence to depart. The motion to leave the bringing of corrall or any comoditie that will sell [3] is all one as to moove the expulsion of us; for if wee bee debarrd our trafique free, wee will not stay. My answere the last brought round: if they seeke our embarque [*i.e.* embargo] wee will trade into the Red Sea in spight of them and upon them. Unlesse wee professe this, they will bee still cavilling. I perceave, by some heare, a resolution in Captain Towerson to goe to the sowthward [*i.e.* to Bantam]; to which I never can nor will consent. . . . Hee is here arrived with many servants, a trumpett, and more show then I use. . . . With him is arrived Captain Newse, of whose comming the commander advised mee noething; thence I gather it was without his knowledge. Hee is very wellcome to mee, seeing hee is come; but I mannerly refused it to him, for reasons not expressed which were very materiall. I had professed to the King, to give him the more feeling of our service and affection, that wee had taken the ships and their company that offered to robb the *Beagams* [4] junck. Our enemies replied

---

[1] Ahmadābād, the principal city of Gujarāt, where Roe spent (with a short interval) the remaining period of his attendance on the Great Mogul. It is situated on the left bank of the Sābarmati river, about fifty miles from the sea; and was at this time a large and populous city, with flourishing manufactures and a considerable commerce. A good description of it is given by Della Valle (vol. i. p. 95), who was there in February, 1623.

[2] Printed in full at p. 227 of *Letters Received*, vol. vi.

[3] Apparently the Surat merchants had objected to the threatened competition of the English in the Red Sea traffic, and had endeavoured to secure its limitation.

[4] The Begum's, *i.e.* the Queen Mother's.

to my face it was a trick : that wee weie all theeves : now wee could not doe it faierly, and therefore sett a counterfeyt show upon it. The King questioned how any English durst offer such an injurie and come soe bouldly, if not by consent of His Majestie; which when I had answered, I delivered on my creditt that what wee had done was bona fide and sincerly : that the captains were made prisoners in our ships, kept in irons : and that I would soe send them home to His Majestie, who would make them an example of such bouldnes to dare to disturbe the allies of his crowne. Hee is knowne here by merchants come upon the same junck and in companie with him, who I doubt not will betray him, and in him mee. With what face can I answere this, if I bee questioned ? To send him back is discurtesie, beeing admitted as Captain Towersons companion; nor what to doe in it doe I well knowe. I should bee much eased if yow were more reserved in this kind belowe. Hee is very conformable to all reason ; offers to returne ; but it is knowne already, and I may have the shame, yow the losse, of that curtesie which before was thought wee had done them. Since, on the 16, arrived with mee safely your goods and presents and all the company (more then I wished) ; and for Mr. Steeles reasons for them, they are veary carefull ones, wher there is noe neede. I am sorry for all such chardges, that wee can doe nothing without the utmost of expence. They [*i.e.* the presents, etc.] remayne with mee yet unopened, by reason of the Kings absence ; and I doubt not but to have peace with them and by them. With these are arrived Mr. Steeles artificers, with whom I have spoken and tould them my judgment. Hee is confident to doe somwhat woorthy his labor and answerable to his hopes ; if I barely sayd noe, hee might lay his owne errors upon mee. Therefore I have consented hee shall have a little roome apart, keepe house with them, oversee them, and sett them to woorke in triall two months. If he can doe it, hee shall have all the honor and due prayse ; if not, they shall returne and hee will undergoe the shame. This will cost the Company some mony, against my will ; but they that adventure must sometymes pay for their crudulitie, and his owne reckonings shalbe apart. Secondly, hee tells mee hee hath brought up some merchaunts that sue for passadge into the Red Sea and promise to drawe in many more ; to which I harken most willingly, for ther shall never bee any good trade in Guzeratt for us, nor any thing tye them by the noses, but our mingling with them in the Red Sea, or eating them out of that trade and serving them by necessitie of what they want. I knowe that their trade in the Red Sea without us is more profitable for them, and in hope of that wee live as wee doe. But it is all naught ; wee must teach them by constraynt and necessitie, and talke with them of leaving that trade when wee

have possessed it to our gaine and their want ; then will they
begg the conditions which they now will not harken after. In
this employment I have both interested Mr. Steele and designed
him the cheefe merchant ; for lesse then some cheefe will not
content him, and it cannot bee in this countrie to the injurie of
any. I hope the commander, yow, and hee will finde some
employment of a shipp that way. If it were myne owne
busines, I would goe spend tyme only for hopes, though I had
noe helpe of the Guzeratts ; and this I have often declared. . . .
The supplyes for Agra wilbe lardger then your monies, Mr.
Fettiplace having assured me of 25,000 *rup.* creditt, and if
tymely will goe farther. Hee urdgeth keeping creditt soe
pressively, and it is of such consequence to us, that I have
sould the great pearle for 12,000 *rup.*,[1] without abatement to
bee payd 10,000 *jangeries* in Agra ; which mony I have made
up. I knowe the pearle somwhat better woorth, not much,
neither could I ever procure it esteemed at that rate ; but for
our present use, and for some other very good reasons, I have
yeilded to please in it Asaph-Chan. Considering the royall
of eight at Suratt and in England, the price equals almost
1,400*li.* in that mony at 4*s.* 6*d.*, and is paid clear in Agra without
abatement of exchange with *shraff*, which is profitt allsoe. It
paid noe custome, and cost in England, as Mr. Steele avowes,
but 1,000*li*. This made mee yeild ; els I would have ventured
to have taken it back. . . . The other pearle I cannot make
away to save ; but [hop]e to rayse them at the Kings comming,
to fullfill my creditt in Agra.

Mr. Browne shall and will doe all in his power. The Governor
hath much hindered, not for our cause nor for more toyes, but
to gripe a *leecke* [*i.e. lakh*] or two from the inhabitants.[2] Hee
is departed to the King, wher[by] I cannot gett a liberty for
our selves. This wicked travell hinders all busines. But our
people are at Serquese [Sarkhej], and I have sent messages and
am in promise that the restraynt shall not hinder us, who will
deale upon all ready made. I will please the ould foole upon
any conditions when hee comes ; but my store is little, those

[1] Apparently these were *khazāna* (' treasury ') rupees (the usual
currency at Ahmadābād), six of which were equal to five *Jahāngīris*
(see p. 312). Roe appears to have reckoned the 12,000 rupees as
equal (roughly) to 6,000 rials, which at 4*s.* 6*d.* apiece would be
equivalent to 1,350*l.* ; and in this he was following the factors' own
practice. Steel was wrong as to its cost, which was 2,000*l.* (see
Factory Records, Miscellaneous, vol. 25) ; there was thus a considerable loss on the sale. Āsaf Khān paid on 11 December (*ibid.*).

[2] Mukarrab Khān had forbidden all dealings in indigo, intending
to engross it and make his profit from the sale (see *The English
Factories*, 1618-21, p. 28).

beeing behynd ; therfore I pray consider the supply with what hast you may. Yf Mochreb-Chan doth not fitt mee with a parcell when wee meete, or give full libertie, I will petition in the name of all the owners against him. The next Governor wilbe the Prince, or rather is. Wee shall trade quietly enough under him in that kinde. It is these presents that make all the stirr. . . .

January 8, 1617-18.—There was some question about presents. The Prince asking for them, I answered : they were readie, if hee pleased to receive his. Then hee demanded : why I brake his seales ?[1] I told him : it was dishonorable for me to bring a Kings gifts in bonds, and great discourtesie to set seales upon them : I expected and attended his licence twentie daies, but seeing no hope, I was enforced to doe it. Some heate began ; at which appeared a gentleman of the Kings, who was sent to observe the passage, and to stickle,[2] and told us both the King commanded wee should come before him at a garden, where he sate, a *course* out of towne, upon the river.[3] So the Prince tooke his *palankee*, and I a coach, well attended by servants both of father and son. When I came to the gates the women were entring, and then no man can but the Prince ; who made within a bitter complaint against mee, that I had dared to cut his seales, and to take out what I list. Asaph Chan was called for, who was my suretie, and the Prince laid it on him ; he, as the custome is, denyed it, excused himselfe ; yet I had not accused him, but tooke it upon me, as knowing my selfe better able to beare it, and that he would denie it. Then I was sent for to the water-side, where the King sate privately, where I entered, with mee the presents ;

[1] It would seem that the presents had been sent up from Surat sealed with the Prince's seal (see p. 421) ; and Roe, after applying in vain for permission to open them, had cut the bonds and taken possession.

[2] To accommodate matters. The old meaning of ' stickler ' was one who attended on combatants, to see fair play and part them when they had fought enough.

[3] Apparently the *Shāhi Bagh*, about a mile and a quarter to the north of the city. Jahāngīr, on his arrival at Ahmadābād, had taken up his residence in the *Bhadar* or citadel, situated on the river bank. The buildings on the spot had been furbished up, and others added, for his use. We have no information where Roe stayed.

but the King was within amongst his women. Asaph Chan chafed at mee for breaking his word; told mee the Prince had shamed him. I replyed by Jaddow: you know I had your consent; this man is witnesse. He denyed it to us both. I replyed: though I would not cast it upon him, it was true, for I had witnesse. Jaddow would not returne the answere, but told me he might not tell him he lyed to his face. And this is usuall; if any command come from the King that he forgets, he that brought the message will disavow it. I bore up as high as I could. The great men told me it was a great affront; no man durst doe such a thing. Others smiled. I answered: not so great as the Prince had done me often. Thus we spent the day, and the King appeared not, but privately stole away, leaving us all sitting in expectance. At night word came the King was gone, and I offered to goe home; but was so well attended, I could not but by force. In the way new messengers came to seeke mee, and I arrived backe at the Kings court, not having eaten or drunke; but the King was not come in, nor could I get loose of my attendants, but they used me very respectfully. We sate an houre. Suddenly newes came to put out all lights, the King was come; who entred on an open waggon, with his Normahall, drawne by bullocks, himselfe carter, and no man neare. When hee and his women were housed, the Prince came in a horse-backe; and entring in, called for me. I found them alone with two or three capons [*i.e.* eunuchs]; and about mid-night the King set on it an angrie countenance: told mee I had broken my word: that he would trust me no more (the Prince had desired him to doe so). I answered as roundly: I held it fit to give freely: I had done nothing of offence in my owne judgement: if their customes were other, it was ignorance, and I must bee pardoned. Wee had many disputes. At last the Prince interposed, offered his friendship, and wee were all reconciled fully, and promises too large. Then I opened the chests, gave the King his presents, the Prince his, and sent in that for Normahall. We were above two houres in viewing them. The arras he tooke well, but said it was course, desired to have a sute of such as the sweet bagge; and wee concluded that in the morning I should come to the Prince, that he should be my protector and procurator. The goods (except three things) more then [*i.e.* other than] presents were there returned mee ; for those three the Prince told me he would pay, seeing his father tooke them.

January 10.—I went to the Prince, was received with all favour, had order for a *firman* for the man murthered,[1] a declaration of his reconcilement in publike, command to all his officers to take knowledge, and to his chiefe *raja* to be my procurator, and to draw what *firmans* so ever I desired. I presented Captaine Towerson and some English, whom hee used with grace ; and for a signe of this peace, gave me a cloth of silver cloak, and promised to be the protector of our nation in all things. I told him of Mr. Steele and his work-men. Hee desired me to bring a small present to his father at night : hee would present them ; which I did. Hee kept his word, and spake for us to him, who was willing enough. I presented Captaine Towerson to the King, who called for him up ; and after a few questions rose. At the *gushel choes*, I presented Mr. Steele and his work-men. The King sate in a hat I gave him all night, called for Mr. Paynter,[2] and after much discourse, gave him ten pounds, and promised to entertayne the rest.

January 13.—The Dutch came to court with a great present of China ware, sanders [*i.e.* sandalwood], parrots and cloaves ; but were not suffered to come neere the third degree. At last the Prince asked me who they were. I replyed : the Hollanders resident in Surat. Hee demanded if they were our friends. I replyed : they were a nation depending on the King of England, but not welcome in all places : their businesse I knew not. He said : for being our friends, I should call them up ; and so I was enforced to send for them to deliver their present. They were placed by our merchants, without any speech or further conference.[3] Finally I had all granted I

---

[1] Presumably in some brawl at Surat.

[2] The painter brought by Steel. His name was Hatfield. Roe would have sent him home, but feared that Steel would complain to the Emperor that ' I cross his pleasure in paynting ' (*O.C.*, No. 611).

[3] The Dutch embassy was headed by Pieter Gillis van Ravesteyn (see p. 369 *n*), whose report to the Directors at Amsterdam will be found in *Hague Transcripts*, 1st Series, vol. iii. No. 96. He says they

desired.[1] I attend the perform ince and money. And thus I conclude that without this contestation I had never gotten anything; for I told the Princes messenger, in the presence of all the English, that if he used force to me or my goods, he might doe his pleasure, but it should cost bloud : that I would set my *chop* upon his masters ship, and send her for England.

January 18.—I received from Surat of the imprisonment of Spragge and Howard at Brampoore, their house and goods seized, their lives in question, for drinking with the *Cutwall* in their house : that one of the *Cutwalls* men dyed that night, upon which they stand accused of poyson : and the *Cutwall*, to free himselfe of comming into the house, pretended that he came to fetch a mans wife away from Thomas Spragge. What the truth is I know not. Information is come to the King against them ; and I went to the Prince (who undertooke all my causes), but could not speake with him. With the same came complaint of a force used to the *caffila* upon the way, notwithstanding the *firman* sent, by the *raja* of the countrey.[2] In both which to night I will make petition to the King. My toyle with barbarous unjust people is beyond patience. At the Princes I found the *firman* promised, drawne, but halfe the conditions agreed on left out ; upon which I refused it, and desired nothing but leave to depart to treat with these in the sea.

[*January*] 21.[3]—A command to free the English and their goods, and that if the Moore came into their house to drinke, if they killed him with a dagger, hee had his just reward. The

were well treated, and obtained a *farmān* from the Prince granting them a number of privileges, though not all for which they had asked. He records a conversation he had with Roe, who complained of the hostility of the Dutch towards the English in the Moluccas, and said that King James was very angry about it, and would take steps to avenge his subjects' wrongs ; ' but,' adds the Dutchman, ' I am not at all afraid of that.'

[1] Evidently Purchas has omitted something here.

[2] Partāb Shāh (see p. 66 *n*). As the Surat-Burhānpur road ran partly through his territory, he claimed the right of levying a toll at Dhāita. Roe, however, had procured a *farmān* freeing the English from this imposition (see p. 403).

[3] This is evidently part of the record of a further interview between the Prince and the ambassador. Purchas has omitted the first portion of the account.

second to *Raja* Partapshaw, to repay us all exactions whatsoever : not to take hereafter any dutie upon the way towards his [*i.e.* the Prince's] port : and in case of failing, that he would deliver his sonne into my hands.[1] He further ordered the delivery of the *firman* for Surat, the articles by mee demanded, and to pay us all our debts of Surat, and to cut it off upon his *mancipdaries*, that had taken that, without delay. He called to account his old Customers, charged the new to use us as his friends, shewed as much favour publikely as I could require. I mooved expedition. He replyed : to morrow by nine in the morning all should be delivered into my hands.

[*January*] 22.—I went my selfe to receive them ; and carryed the merchants with some pearle that the Prince had bin instant to see, pretended to be Master Towersons. But he had received some uncertaine information of pearles to the value of twentie or thirtie thousand pound, which he hoped to draw from us. When his secretarie saw the small sorts, hee replyed : the Prince had *mands* of these : if we brought no better commoditie, wee might be gone, he cared not for our custome. How basely false and covetous are those of jewels, you may judge. I undertooke reply : that I had procured those from a gentlewoman to satisfie them : if they liked them not, they could not be made better : it was incivility to be angry with merchants for their goodwill ; but told him I came for my *firmans*, and expected them. I was answered : wee had deceived their hopes, and the Prince would deceive ours : *firman* I should have none : I had asked leave to depart : I might come and take leave when I pleased. I answered : nothing contented mee more, but that I would visit their unjustice in an indifferent place : that I would speake with the King, and depend no more on them, for I saw all was covetousnesse and unworthinesse. So I rose and parted. But he recalled me to come to the King and Prince together the next day : I should have content.[2]

---

[1] Partāb Shāh had visited Jahāngīr at Māndu, and on leaving had been ordered to send his eldest son to court (*Memoirs*, vol. i. pp. 396, 411).

[2] Here Purchas's extracts come to an abrupt end. 'For the whole,' he says, ' my selfe could have wished it, but neither with the

To THOMAS KERRIDGE AT SURAT.[1]
(I.O. Records : *O.C.*, No. 612.)

Yours received the 21 January.... All delivered [to] Asap-Chans servant is acknowledged, and an end therof. For the Red Sea, I understand your conclusions ; and it seemes yow thinck Dabull will vent all your dead comodities for feare... but I am perswaded, if wee fynd not a juncke at port, they will not bee drawen to take off such comodities as I ayme at to vent.... I declare my opinion that, in case I traded not at Dabul for goods fitt for Mocha, I would more then trade wherever I mett them.... All which take *cartasses* of our enemies and pay them duties for licence as lords of the sea, which wee will not acknowledge, and as their allies, I would make them prize. If we doe it not, the Dutch will. I had rather wee begunn to compell them to take us for their protectors then another ; and by this course wee shall hinder and bridle the Portugall of his profitts, and force him to some composition with us, when hee sees wee beginn soe round a course. Now he letts us rust and decay in reputation ; while hee getts creditt and hart. The companie of our shipps will awe the Guzeratts (as I have often urdged) and make them see our frendship necessarie to them. For my opinion is wee cannot hould long in peace with them. For any juncke or ship of Dieu whatsoever, I would take her. They live under our enemies, as subjects to them ; and the woorst is, if the Mogol quarrell it, to compound as did the Portugalls [2]... Mr. Steele [is] entreauged into a woorke without end.... His ayd to the Red Sea is quite given over. Hee never did nor could doe any thing in it. What hapned yow shall know. Here hath beene some question about the voyadge among them selves, and all merchants loath to adventure. Asaph-Chan hath encouraged some soe farr as to fraight from Goga the *Gehangier*. Shee hath her *cartasse*, without stopping at Suratt ; and upon conclusion sent to mee for my passe, els the merchants

Honourable Company nor else-where could learne of it ; the worthy Knight himselfe being now employed in like honourable embassage from His Majestie to the Great Turke.'

[1] An incomplete copy, without date. From internal evidence the beginning of February may be assigned. An abstract is given at p. 2 of *English Factories*, 1618-21.

[2] Roe goes on to intimate that he will not actually order the voyage to the Red Sea to be undertaken. If Kerridge disagrees, the project had better be dropped, each side recording the reasons, for the satisfaction of the Company. He then refers to the choice of merchants for the venture.

would not stirr; that only stuck. At which I went to court, and found them with Etiman Dowlett and Asaph-Chan sitting in the *amkass*,[1] making of *screetes*, the captain, *malum*,[2] and principall adventurers. Presently they tooke occasion to renew their feares of us; and Asaph-Chan, without any promise of mee, undertooke for us. At which I replyed: they had experience of us, that wee defended them: that the subjects of the King durst not wrong them while our masters were in peace: but that was not all the danger: the Dutch, French, or piratts might, and the jealouzie after wrong us: therfore I desiered a declaration in the poynt, whither they nor the King would not expect and require at our hands the faults of other men, those trading under His Majestie[s] authoritie beeing newtralls. The father, sonne, and merchants replyed: it was all reason: the King expected not any thing from us but for our selves. Then I showed him the danger of others, and made publique our offer, two years made to the King in the name of His Majestie, to safe conduct their goods and shipps to our powers: that wee had now a fleete: wee were ready with one or two to serve His Majestie or the Prince, to goe with them, or to take in their goods: and this I thought a full proofe of my masters affection and our intents to them. To this Etimon Dowlett replyed: hee never hard so noble an offer: no brother could say more: and that he would enforme the King of it. The merchants first tould him: for freighting in our ships, they never would: wee would bee masters of our shipps, and they could not have that libertie nor content they desired: and besides the ships of the countrie would by that meanes decay, and wee enter into their trade: soe that utterly they refused to freight in us. To goe with them, they thancked mee and accepted of it; but desiered Etimon Dowlett to know if I expected noe pay. I replyed: reason would enforme them that, if wee spent our tyme, paid our men, consumed our provisions and victualls, it was fitt we should have recompence: it was enough wee fought for them: but that, if they would propound any thing, they should see how ready I would bee to show this offer was for love, not for profitt. The merchants as roundly answered: they would rather sitt at home then give us any thing: they knew our chardge, and they would not venture their goods to give us the profitt. At this all were blanck. I asked if they would move the King. Etimon Dowlett replyed: not: hee thought wee had gone for love only: and the merchants would give us nothing. Then they proceeded upon the first poynt: if I would give a passe; which I could not deny, beeing yet in peace. I promised I

---

[1] The Emperor's reception hall (*ām-o-khās*); see *Bernier*, p. 261.
[2] Arabic *mu'allim*, a pilot or sailing master (see p. 13 *n*).

would, upon these conditions : that, if wee came into the Red Sea, they should be contented with our company and trade, helpe us and assist us as frends, as wee would doe them ; and so it ended. Since which tyme, for the sayd ship, captain, and merchants I have geven my lettre to all English, specifieing the conditions;[1] which, if wee break with them, is voyd, for it depends on the peace here. This I am fallen upon to lett yow see how little hope from them ; yet that they feare us and, when they see wee will joyne with them, will fynd they must seeke us on better tearmes. I see noe reason but why wee should take *cartasse* mony as well as any ; for wee are lords of the ports : the Portug[alls] dare not appeare in them.[2] . . .

To the East India Company.

(I.O. Records : *O.C.*, No. 610.)

My Honourable Frends, Amadavaz, 14 February, 1617[-18].

Your lettres mentioned upon the *Charles* safely arrived at Swally Roade in Sept. 1616, and came to hand October following ; were answered by the *Globe*, dispeeded from the Coast the 7th of March after,[3] to which I referr yow ; coppies whereof I cannot now send (and by Gods mercy there is no cause), for I, beeing fully determined to returne, was unprovided of them, or of any but my booke, and beeing in continuall travell have beene much streightened to send you these of newer dates and soe more necessarie, having but one hand to assist mee, and that oftener weake then able.

For the passadges of your business in court or factories (as much as I was made acquaynted with), the one yow shall receive by a journall, and the other yow may collect out of transcripts of lettres directed to your severall factories by mee ; all which are punctually sent yow ; wherin yow may see what wayes I held, and what my opinions were. In reading these, yf yow compare the dates with those of your servants corresponding, yow shall have more light, and judge of all as if yow were present. I make no question others send their owne, for

[1] A copy of this document, dated 20 Jan., 1618, forms *O.C.*, No. 597. It provides for the junks being detained, on their return to Surat, until the escorting vessel has learnt from shore ' how our trade continewes ' (see *English Factories*, 1618-21, p. 2).

[2] Roe then discusses the choice of merchants for the Red Sea voyage, and the ' course of trade ' to be adopted there ; gives his opinions about the organization of the factories in India ; and concludes by expressing his satisfaction at Kerridge's decision to remain, assuring him of his support.

[3] Roe's letter referred to is no longer extant.

soe I advised tymely ; and I could perswade yow to appoynt one to view them togither, to collect the reasons and conclusions for your full enformation. Yow may in some clauses fynd mee sharp and censuring your advises from home ; but yow will find my reasons justifiable and my ends honest and upright. To the particular of your last received by the *James Royall* by my frend Captain Pring, and to all instructions sent therby, yow shall receive answere either in this or in some single papers to that purpose ; and in all yow shall see my judgment of all your trades, for I have dealt openly and freely, as well before yow committed to mee any thing as since. As this bringeth a coppy of yours [of] the former yeare, so I will runne along with yt in the poynts mooved. The little doubts that rose betweene mee and Captain Keeling soone vanished. I found him in all things a reasonable and discreet man ; nor want of any performance on your parts of any thing promised mee. Wee have this yeare, for suffering the insolencies of the Prince, made triall of Goga and searched all the Bay,[1] but can fynd noe place fitt for your head residence but Suratt ; soe that question is at an end, and wee must study to make the best of that place. To waft the Mogolls subjects into the Red Sea will never give your men bread and water. They neither desier it nor will admitt it, except wee doe it of curtesie ; for they pay their *cartasse* notwithstanding, beeing compounded with the Portug[alls], and they feare none but piratts, which is a new trade of a yeares standing ; yet that feare will sooner make them not trade (for in all they are but slaves to the lords of the ports, who cutt upon them) then give us the remayner of their profitt for their safe conduct, as in Mr. Steeles projects yow will perceive my triall (for hee had other ends). The motions of building a fort have begott such jealousies in these Moores that, upon bringing brick ashore to found a shipps bell, it rang to court, our people disarmed in Suratt, and I am not yet cleare of liberties lost upon yt, though I have made the Prince ashamed at the weakenes of the suspition, to confesse a handfull of men could take a part of their countrie by force. But it is true wee would bee lords there, and have committed soe many insolencies that I have woondred at their patience ; yet wee complayne. The last yeare for another folly our people were restrayned in the towne, and they sent from [the] ships 200 naked [*i.e.* unarmed] men ashore to take Suratt, who as brutishly bruted it in their march ; yet ten men would have kept them from passing the great river. This yeare wee have offered upon *puntoes*[2] to force the custome house, and twenty drawn their

[1] See Pring's account of this (*English Factories*, 1618-21, p. 29).

[2] Ital. *punto*, a point, a small matter : hence, minute observances, or, as we now say, punctilios.

swoords in yt. If these bee not just causes of jealousy, I am silent; yet I patch it up. The Commander [*i.e.* Pring] now by his great modesty and discretion hath both reformed many abuses, gayned yow much good will, himselfe all mens love and his owne creditt. An honester man I suppose yow cannot send, and that his actions will approove : one that studies your ends, is ready to joyne with any, without insisting upon disputes and tearmes.

To returne to a fort. There is noe place to bee obteyned. They are weary of us as it is ; and indeed wee see wee have empoverished the ports, and wounded all their trades, soe that by much perswasion of the Governors the merchant goes to sea. Or, if there were licence granted, ther is none fitt for your shipping except one that lies out of all commerce and hath more inconveniences in yt then this, which, when your goods are ready by September, wilbe easie enough. And if yow began to build and plant here, quarrell would arise, the enemie [*i.e.* the Portuguese] exasperated, who may now bee drawn to composition, and all your proffittes eaten in garrizons and dead payes. It is noe way to drive your trades by plantation. The Dutch have spoyled the Moluccoes which they fought for, and spent more then they will yeild them, if quiett, in seaven yeares. Syndu [*i.e.* Lahrībandar] yow may freely goe too, lade and relade ; but it is inhabited by the Portugall ; lies noe way well for your stock (except yow scatter it) ; it ventes only your teeth [*i.e.* ivory] and affoordes good cloth and many toyes. But if the sorts yow have seene serve your marketts, yow are nearer seated and may have what quanteties you please ; and for your teeth the marchant will fetch them at Suratt. Bengala hath noe ports but such as the Portugalls possesse, for smalle shipping. It will vent nothing of yours. The people are unwilling, in respect of the warr (as they suppose) like to ensue in their seas ; and the Prince hath crossed it, thincking wee desired to remoove thither wholy, and that, if wee stay in India, hee takes to bee an affront. But now I may obteyne one ship to come and goe, upon hope of rubies from Aracan and Pegu ; but I knowe not what profitt yow can make by any residence there ; and I speak upon searching the bottome of all the secretts of India. If yow will have patience to try one yeare, yow shall see one thing effectually done is woorth twenty by fragments. Yow will find it is not many factories here that getts yow a penny. I will forecast your ease, and by Gods grace, settle not only your priviledges but your profitts. This two yeare the Prince hath beene my enemie ; and if I had yeilded, I must have been his slave. This last I have stood out to the last and adventured the feircnes of his wrath. It hath succeeded better then I expected. Wee are soe reconciled that hee is now my effectuall mediator and will procure mee content.

Indeed, hee only can give it. His father growes dull and suffers him to write all commands and to governe all his kingdomes. [*Marginal note by Roe.*—When I wrote this, I had woords enough ; but such delayes in effects that I am weary of flatteries as of ill usadge.] Yow can never expect to trade here upon capitulations that shalbe permanent. Wee must serve the tyme. Some now I have gotten, but by way of *firmaens* and promise from the Kynge. All the goverment depends upon the present will, where appetite only governs the lords of the kingdome. But their justice is generallie good to strangers ; they are not rigorous, except in scearching for things to please, and what trouble wee have is for hope of them, and by our owne disorders. In both I have propounded to yow a new course, and will here practise it.

The presents last yeare were all seazed by the Prince in the way. I gott them realeased, but to spight mee hee sent them to the King. What I chalenged of yours was returned ; a good part went for Persia. The remayner the King had in a base fashion, as my journall will relate.

The Fleminge is planted at Suratt, [and] hath obteyned a *firmaen* upon as good tearmes almost as wee. I did my endeavour to crosse him ; but they come in upon the same ground that wee began, and by which wee subsist, feare. And if I fynd not all performed with mee now promised, I shalbe as bould as to chasten them once agayne ; els the Duch wilbe before hand and doe it first, and then hee wilbe the brave man. Assure yow I will not leave this coast but upon good tearmes.

I perceive my lettres overland came to your hands, but they gott a flaw in the way. My Lord Ambassadors [*i.e.* Connock] care was very great ; which in the future I shall prevent, not by charactar [*i.e.* secret cipher] (for yours is ould and knowne) but by such conveyance as busie men shall not intercept. Ther wilbe smalle occasion from hence ; and yours seated in Persia will give account of their proceedings. I will not omitt any matter of new consequence. The coppy of my lettre to the Sha of Persia by negligence was left out of the packett ; which, finding, I sent by the *Globe*. The substance was only to amase [*i.e.* frighten] him from any sudeyne conclusion with the Portugalls, [and] to offer in generall tearmes our shipping upon his coast ; for without instructions I durst not enter into particulars, neyther was my experience in these parts sufficient for yt. [*Marginal note by Roe.*—This letter, the Sha beeing in the feild, Mr. Connok gott after, and usd it as his owne.]

What I have done in reformation of particular wrongs and recovering of debts my journall will enforme ; how my lardge demands were rejected and my selfe tyed to observe the custome to make sute upon new occasion. I have done my endeavor, and though yow will find many yet unpayed, many yet unreformed, notwithstanding it will appeare not my fault, for I neither spared labor nor meanes ; and in many things the error hath beene our owne, by negligence or disorder. The substance is : I have gotten many bribes restored, many debts, many extortions, and commands to take noe more ; that by little and little I shall ease all : now I am upon best tearmes, and, if the court were settled, would soone finish these my teadious labors. Yow shalbe sure of as much priviledge as any stranger, and right when the subject dares not plead his. The troubles at Suratt depending upon covetousnes of curiosities to satisfie the Prince (for your grosse goods passe with ease) I will reforme by yeilding him content ; but it is privat men that make the broyle and then exclaime most.

The advise I gave to procure a place of securitie at the first face seemed good to mee, and I gave it as I received it ; but yow must excuse mee of recanting twenty things which I could not knowe but from others. There is none fit, nor to bee had. The *Bee*, sent to transport your goods up the river of Suratt, hath fullie tried it and cannot performe it, for the many shifts of sands, without grounding, and then subject to bee fiered.[1] Wee must sticke to Swally Roade, and, if I can effect my purpose to provide your ladings ready, yow shall not feele the other inconveniences. The renting your customes I have endeavoured ; but as your servants in former yeares would never answere niee in the poynt, soe these demand twise more then ever yow payed ; supposing then wee would double our trades.

Your land men will most returne, except such as your shipps will neede by great mortalitie this yeare ; and, which I feare more in tyme to come, the trade for refreshing at the Cape [*i.e.* of Good Hope] beeing utterly spoyled, either by ours left or by some violence of others, your fleetes must seeke short, or about. It cannot bee but ther are many better places ; for these base people are but the brokars or sellars of the cattell at second hand. I hope my last lettres will ease yow of the chardge of land men.

A peace with the Portugall here were the best service I could doe yow. I made, as by enformation yow know, an overture to the Viceroy, which his pride never answered. Since wee have given them a knock or two ; and at this instant I am upon hopes of treatye. But, that yow may understand the true estate of this busines, yow shall know the passages. First, the attempts made upon your fleets were not, as I collect, by expresse order from Spayne. The ould Viceroy who came in

[1] By the Portuguese frigates. Pring wrote to the Company to the same effect (*Letters Received*, vol. vi. p. 178). Presumably the pinnace had been sent in consequence of Roe's suggestion on p. 73.

person, 1614, against Captain Dowton discontented the wisest of his councell and all the inhabitants of Goa in yt; his insprosperitie made his action the more hatefull, and hee is now prisoner in the castle, to bee returned to answere, I know not whither that hee did no more, or for doeing so much; but for that busines only.[1] The new Viceroy declares not himselfe, but prepares a fleete to supplant, as hee pretends, the Dutch in Cormandeil. The Jesuite here, who much affects an agreement,[2] wisely foreseeing they maynteyne it more by stubbernes then reason, hath often mooved lately to mee a peace, and to that end hath written to his superiors in Goa, but received no direct answere. I have demanded to show mee a power that the Viceroy hath authoritie to conclude it, but in the poynt could not bee satisfied; but that the merchant, the coaster, the inhabitant, and the discreeter sort, all desired it, only the glorious souldier withstood it. Since, the arrivall of his Majestie[s] lettre, which in one clause mooved the Mogoll by his authoritie to enforce the Portugalls, or to secure his owne coast that wee might have safe and quiett recourse unto yt, hath ministred occasion. It seemes the Portugall stood upon a *punto* that he would not offer us that which hee once would not answere; but by that motion (which I signified to the Jesuite to show our desiers were sincere to accord with Christians) I drew from him that hee supposed theirs were the like, but that a third person wanted [*i.e.* was needed] to moove it; but that was happelie by this lettre offered, that the Mogol would bee meadiator betweene both; to which end, after the lettrs deliverie, the Padree followed it to Asaph Chan, as a man

[1] Upon the arrival of the news of Azevedo's unsuccessful attack upon Downton, the King appointed D. João Coutinho, Conde de Redondo, to succeed him as Viceroy. The latter arrived at Goa towards the end of 1617, and, acting upon orders from home, arrested Azevedo and sent him to Lisbon, where he died in prison (Bocarro's *Decada XIII*, c. 186; Faria y Sousa's *Asia Portuguesa*, Stevens' translation, vol. iii. p. 274). Faria y Sousa says that the chief charge against him was his failure to fight the Dutch.

[2] Cf. p. 248. In a letter to Agra, dated 8 Oct., 1616, Roe says that 'the Padre hath entreated and promised that if any injury bee offered, on the least woord of complaynt to them wee shall receive full satisfaction.' Not long before the date of the present letter, Corsi had taken the opportunity to render Roe a service, for the following entry appears in Roe's accounts under the date of 18 Nov., 1617: 'Geven to the Padre, in recompence of a smalle present geven mee and of a great curtesie done mee in court, one foulding case with combes richly embrodered, cost 5*li*., and the embrodred girdle and hangers with pearle sent me by the Company.' What the 'great curtesie' was, does not appear.

of peace, for the quiett of the seas and to avoyd effusion of blood. On our parts it was declared by His Majestie, on theirs no way but by the Jesuite; and therefore, before the King would moove it to bee refused, it was demanded if the Jesuite would undertake the Kings desiers should upon reasonable tearmes take effect; which hee could not promise but by advise from Goa. Soe it rested; only betweene us some speech upon what tearmes and how farr wee intended this treaty; generall in the Indyes was improbable to effect; for a couple of shipps upon all this coast, it might bee granted. At first I stood upon no restraynt, to come as wee listed; but after promised that when I saw power to treat I would agree unto conditions reasonable and honorable. Returne of these are not come, in the direct poynt; but, the King beeing neare the sea, the Viceroy (which never before was done) sent an ambassador toward the court to congratulate in the name of the King of Spayne. He yet stayes at Baltasare,[1] the confines of this territorie below Suratt. The Jesuitt mooved his admittance, and the King replied: if hee come with presents fitt for his master to send and mee to receive, he is wellcome: if not, I shall not acknowledge him for the person hee pretends nor give him honor. This answere was strange; but, getting noe better, it was returned, and as yet wee know not whither hee will proceed or not. By him, as the Jesuite subtilly tells mee (for hee sayes hee cannot averr it for truth, having not received it authentically), is come some authoritie to enter into communication of peace, if the King motion it, and that it is one of his ends. I have answered: I can acknowledge no ambassador from a Viceroy to treat on equall tearmes, and that I must see power from Spayne. Att last, this is the truth: the Viceroy is woone by the inhabitants to consent to a treaty, but hath noe power to conclude it; but, as his masters deputie generally, he hath authoritie to doe much at his discretion; and if wee can agree upon fitt tearmes, to make a conditionall truce for three years, with reference to the confirmation of our masters in Europe; and this is all wee can hope for. If hee come, wee may proceed; if not, they shall not coosen mee; I am wher I was. I have to Mr. Secretarie and some of the lordes againe mooved this poynt; but the effecting and full aggreation must come from Spayne. The Viceroyes will for their glorie hardly enforme their true estate; but make the King beeleve they can woork woonders, untill they have lost India. If it were fully questioned at home whither they make this warr by expresse command or by a generall pretence of I know not what

[1] Bulsār, a town 40 miles south of Surat, on the river Auranga. De Laet speaks of it as 'ad limitem Daman.' This embassy does not appear to be mentioned by the Portuguese historians.

title to all the world, I thinck it would soone bring it to issue, at least to a declaration ; for I am perswaded the King of Spayne hath not given expresse commission for yt and will disavow yt. I am sure, were I in Spayne, I could make it evident to any cast Viceroy that perswades the warr, that hee abuseth his master and that pride only and folly began and continues it. In conclusion of this : I know how fitt a peace or truce were for yow. If I can, upon safe and honorable tearmes, effect it, I shall thinck it of good meritt toward yow. If it bee still war, the force of India will not wrong us (except from the Manillas), but putt yow to many inconveniences ; if greater strength prepared in Lisboa, yow must discover and provide accordingly. To enforce the Portugall to consent I have tried many wayes, and find the best by chastising their neighbowrs for their sakes ; but the roundest is, if the King wilbe insencible of his honor, to suffer his subjects to pay for leave to trade in his owne seaes (which he seemes not to care for),[1] then must wee in the Red Sea force them alsoe to give us as much ; for the Portugall hath noe other right but as lords of the sea, which it is evident now he is not, and therfore the tribute due to us. Then eyther wee shall have all the trade and the Portugall loose his contract (for the merchant will give over), or the Mogol wilbe enforced to see it is necessarie for him to bring us to accord, that both may give over that quarrell and leave the seas free for all. This I have often urdged, but they have pawnes and presume wee will not beginn. For my part, it should bee my first woorke, if I durst hazard your trade, which I suppose I could restore to perfection in six months. But, to minister occasion, I have pressed to your factors the employment of a ship to Mocha in company, though at first wee have no ease by the Guzeratts ; my reasons are at lardge in lettres. But their resolution I cannot gett, and will doe nothing alone. The feare of us already makes them requier my passe ; which though I have given to one ship (to satisfie her owner, whom I could not refuse, beeing in tearmes of peace), yet the demand shall give us title to more, if wee bee tyed to former incon-

[1] The English had several times endeavoured to rouse the pride of the Mogul by pointing to the indignity put upon him by the claim of the Portuguese to control the navigation of his seas, ' as yf both yourselfe and your countreys were assubjected to the crowne of Spaygne ' (Letter from James I, in *First Letter Book*, p. 349) ; but their efforts were in vain. ' He is not sencible of the dishonor, giving reason : he conquered Guzuratt and keepes it in the same condition he found yt, and upon the same articles and contracts made by Bahud [Bahādur Shāh], kyng of Guzuratt, who made them with the Portugalls before this monarchy was united ' (Notes by Roe in *O.C.*, No. 611).

venience. The second way is by riding with our fleete at Goa the tyme wee spend at Suratt; which Captain Pring was willing to doe, but by the disaster of the *James* [1] and absence of the *Bee* hee was both weakened and tyme lost.

I well know what losse, hazard, and inconvenience yow runn by the stay of your fleetes. My last lettres to yow and many to your servants to prevent it will fully declare my prevision in yt; but, as yow will fynd, I had no power; what I propounded was countermanded; I might not meddle. But since yow have entrusted somwhat to mee, I dare promise yow to provide your ladings ready by October; and soe yow shall prevent the Portugall, who cannot bee fitt for an attempt two months after. It was never beleeved I could effect that done. Wittnes the returne from Agra, treble almost to former yeares, provided in a month, part by creditt (which I have kept, and therby entered yow into more), part by barter of 100 clothes that lay by the wall two years, as the motion did. The same course I will take in tyme to come, not to defer investments till our shipps arrivall and the indicoes swept away. Yow will fynd your returnes short of expectation, by reason that wee stayed for comoditie yet unmade; but much shorter if Mr. Fettiplace had not ventured on my wayes. Aprill and March are the seasons to buy; and the most of our provisions shalbe fitted in their due seasons. Your servants cannot deny this error. Want of stock is some excuse; but it had beene as good to have dealt in creditt, to pay at the fleetes arrivall, as to send up that mony to invest after. Your remaynes of the ould stock are very great; enough to relade the *An*. To transport it were great losse. I have urdged the use of her to Mocha for many ends, but principally to fetch off upon her owne account our proceed of yt. If the factors crosse mee not, I will fitt her loading by the arrivall of the next fleete; and then, if yow wilbe before hand, goods only must bee landed and returnes forborne one yeare; so, by the courses I will sett, yow shall for ever bee before, and if yow encrease by jewells your stocke to make mony, may easely relade for 3 or 4000 fardles of indico, and cloth [*i.e.* calico] to any fitt proportion. Amadavaz will fynd yow lesse, by reason of the Dutch and the trade open to the Red Sea; but, creditt mee, at Agra yow may every yeare have your whole *partido*.[2] There is of ould store sufficient yet, and ther is made betweene that and Lahor at least 30000 fardles yearly, most wherof is carried away by land. All these my intents, my reasons and orders yow will find in severall lettres opened and discussed with your servants; to which I refer yow.

[1] The leak already mentioned.

[2] *Partito* (Ital.), 'bargain,' investment.

The discontents, if I tooke any, were soone disgested. This place provides mee dayly new to put out the ould. If I may in conclusion doe your busines, I doubt not yow will esteeme mee rightly. I never desiered to know any of your secretts in trade, but for your good. I am satisfied in your opinion of mee, and shall, I doubt not, fullfill part of yours of mee. A little experience will confirme both. Mr. Bangham hath done yow better service then hee could with mee. Everie man seekes his owne preferment. I cannot blame him, if hee desired to bee in a course more to his creditt then my bookes or accounts, seeing hee saw I had so little creditt to prefer him. He hath done better, and I not amisse. I hope my reckonings will content yow. The consultation upon good reasons have dissolved his factorie, as of no profitt now the army is dissolved; upon which hee tooke occasion to bee earnest for his returne: soe earnest that I thought not fitt to denye him, though he was a very good servant and an honest man, and for such yow will receive him. I had some ground to suspect that yow doubted my providence and thrift; but I found noe restraint in your servants toward mee, for I gave noe occasion. Now that yow have enlardged to mee in creditt, I shall not abuse it. As I begann, I will proceede; and neither aske nor take more. My servants allowance hath pinched mee; but seeing I have borne the burthen, I will not for one yeare shrinke. I must trust to yow at my returne; therfore I will not wast your favours in petty matters. Only I am bould to take 24 yards red cloth for liveries; which I will allow for price cost.

Privat trade hath gotten such head last yeare that I shall hardly suppresse it. Every man pleads it lawfull, and I gett ill will which in tymes past was a stranger to mee. What I have ordered, and how strictly, yow will find by coppyes sent; but if yow beginn not at home, all men will presume. It is not the gaine of their trade hurtes you, but the inconveniences [that] follow. I have more distastes for them then all yours. They follow their owne busines, with neglect of yours and at your chardge. Under coulor of guarding your goods, every fleete sends his factors up to Amadavaz. This I must prevent for the future. A good example I will leave next yeare; but if yow doe not second it at home, yow make mee beare the envy to noe purpose. The truth is yow should bee indifferent [*i.e.* impartial] to all. Last yeare the master of the *Globe* [*i.e.* Nathaniel Martin] can ryott. Hee laded 26 *churles* indico, a great quantetie of cloth, and other goods. Your fleete brought lead, teeth [*i.e.* ivory], quicksilver, and sould freely. Mittford by information invested for 8000 ma[hmūdis] and passed it at your chardge, returning in your debt; used your purse at his owne pleasure. Waldoe was not behynd for his portion. These stick in all mens stomacks: that I should bee now so strict to them, and such libertye to others. Yow write yow have mett with some goods; they jest at yt. I offer some liberty, upon condition to marke it, with advise, and referr it to yow; but all men avoyd the motion. Att my returne I shall see it done; few will assist mee now, or obey it as an order.

What power yow gave to Captain Keeling was upon good knowledge of his abilitie and experience; in which yow had no proofe of mee. I was desierous to know the proceedes of your busines for good affection toward it, not for ambition of authoritie or trouble, but to keepe my selfe in creditt to doe yow better service. Now that yow have entrusted the care to mee, yow will find I use it with modestye, and take not more upon mee then is fitt; nothing but with advise of your factors, which I instantly [*i.e.* pressingly] in all occasion require, and am as ready to yeild to reason as to propound it. This wilbe evident to yow by my course held with your factors, declared by my lettres, that I runn not single, nor diminish their creditt or power, and shall not use any of myne but when I see they neglect their dutie. Generally your servantes are in good order. Mr. Kerridge I have stayed; but could not doe it but by continuance of his contract with Captain Keeling; which I consented too by necessitie. Hee is quick, and will doe yow great service, and could not now bee spared.... Mr. Browne is well content with his first agreement; and for payment of your royalls,[1] though all murmur att yt, I have ordered it according to your desier.[2] ... Some other your servants have beene out of order. I am loath to undoe any. Some I have cleared yow off, whose disorder brought themselves in trouble and your goods in hazard; and in generall I will have an eie to all. They shall not wrong yow; if they will wrong themselves, I shall dismisse them and ease yow. If I any way transgresse, it wilbe in preferring one of myne, bred a merchant with Alderman Gore, that hath taken much paynes in writing, as by his hand will appeare.[3] He is sufficient; beene practised in Barberie; and desiers your service

[1] Rialls of eight. The Company had recently ordered that, in paying the factors the third of their wages which by agreement they were to receive in the East, the rial was to be reckoned at 5s. instead of at 4s. 6d.

[2] Roe goes on to discuss the expenses of the Ahmadābād factory, and an increase of wages granted to Fetiplace at Agra.

[3] The reference is to Edward Heynes, Roe's secretary, whose neat and legible hand is to be seen in most of these letters and in *Add. MS.* 6115. As intimated later, Roe sent him to Mokha in the *Anne*. Heynes afterwards served in several of the factories in India, and died as agent in Persia (August, 1632).

as a reward. I will not exceed to him the lowest rate yow give —30*li*. (a third for mayntenance) ; but hope yow will give him encrease according to his meritt.

Persia hath now taken many of your supplies last yeare and this. Most of your ould servants are ready to returne. Every man claymeth your promise to stay here. Some wee must plant ; but such as may serve yow and not disfurnish other places.

Biddolph followes the court by reason of many debts ; which though I neither counselled nor consented to the making, yet I must approove the course, if the men had beene good. The abuse was in the brokars. But such a course I have taken that I hope to recover all or most. The most desperat I have secured ; some payd ; and shall cleare all the extortions of Suratt. Part of the mony is collected, and I have a *firmaen* for all. The course in this yow will fynd in my lettres and journall. If the cloth had beene kept, it had perished, and in these remooves cost yow much chardge. It was sould soe deare that it payes the forbearance. The King promised mee to buy all this parcell ; but his officers protract, by reason of the trouble and toyle in carriadge (the King ever remooving), and would defer us for their case untill a settling. A present must helpe it off. [*Marginal note by Roe.*—I gave the Master of the Wardrop a good present and he sent for cloth, but prised it so basely that I was forced to demand my guift agayne (it is the custome here) ; wherupon he anew offers to take our cloth. If it bee followed, it may bee done before remoove.[1]] That comodite wee cannot bring into request. The price exceeds ordinarie purses ; and your quanteties of stamells [2] will hardly passe, for they will give but one price. My hope is by bartar with mony to putt yow off a hundred yearly at Agra, besides the King, who with great men may take a hundred more of a better sort. But those for Agra must bee cloth of 10 and 12*li*.,[3] because they will not sell above six *rupias* the *cobd*. And soe yow may a little encrease your principall there, though to noe great profitt. The coullors must bee of all, reed, greene, yellow, or popingey [*i.e.* parrot-green].

[1] It was not until 22 July, 1618, that the broadcloth was bought for the Emperor (see Biddulph's accounts in *Factory Records, Miscellaneous*, vol. 25).

[2] A woollen cloth (usually red), coarser and cheaper than the ordinary broadcloth. 'Stamet' is another form of the same word. Both terms were also used to denote the particular shade of red used ; hence there were 'stamet' broadcloths of rather a high price.

[3] Broadcloth was made up in lengths of about thirty yards, and the piece cost anything from 10*l.* to 20*l.* or more.

It is not in your sales that yow must stand upon price, soe yow may vent to rayse a stock. It is the great and quick returnes that must advance your gaynes; part of which must arise by providence here in expence, in fitting the seasons both to buy and send downe.

What hath beene done in Persia yow will fynd. The capitulations and Kings lettre sent. How I proceeded, and upon what reason, my lettres to your factors, instructions, and commission will give accompt; my opinion to the objections and answere to the instructions.[1] All I can say is it is not now to bee given over, though begunn unperfectly. The King[s] honour, in whose name it was sett afoote; yow have goods and your people engaged; to the mayntenance of which I have thought fitt to lett the ship dessigned for the Red Sea touch there to bring off your silkes and mayntenye your creditt, to supplie them and keepe life in the busines untill by your better meanes and full tryall wee may proceed more roundly. What is past I will not aggravate, nor tread on the dead [*i.e.* Connock], whose vanetye and follies, wast, and irreligion I did too justly suspect. To the busines, your freedome and admittance is very faier; the next consideration is how yow may securely use this trade by want of a port and compasse it without export of great quanteties of monies; for doubtles, if to bee done, it is the best trade of all India and will yeild yow most certeyne profitt. For the safetye of your fleetes, I doubt the Sha will not fortefie for yow, except yow can satisfie his ends, to pass all his comoditie and to furnish him with silver. Ormus lies upon advantage. Yow must woorke your peace at home with them [*i.e.* the Portuguese], and then yow cannot trade in these parts upon ill conditions. Toward this I will exasperatt the Sha to my uttmost against them that would hinder free trade. To surprise or take their seate by force is not easely

---

[1] The *Bee* had returned from Jask in the middle of January, bringing news of concessions obtained from the Shāh by Connock and of the death of the latter. The concessions, however, did not cover all the points stipulated for in the Company's recent orders; and therefore Roe drafted a fresh set of instructions to Barker (Connock's successor) and Monnox to negotiate further with the Shāh. This document (*O.C.*, No. 608) was printed in the first edition of the present work (p. 462). Roe had intended that the *Anne* should leave the instructions at Jask on her way to Mokha, but this was found to be impracticable; and so they were sent to Kerridge for transmission overland 'by way of Sind.' Later in the year, on the arrival of Bonner's fleet at Surat, the *Expedition* was sent to Jask, where she arrived on Nov. 22. She returned to Surat in January, 1619, with about seventy bales of silk, in time for Roe to take them home in the *Anne* as the first-fruits of the Persian trade.

done. I confesse that were an end of the question ; but it will cost a great chardge, and such enterprises are uncerteyne ; and after it would engage yow into a warr. Therfore I can see no way sure but a composition in Spayne, which to my poore understanding His Majesties authoritie might effect. I knowe not by what pretence the King of Spayne can prohibitt yow trade in a free princes countrie to which he hath no pretence. If this were effected, yow need not insist upon a contract with the Sha, but, having lycence, trade for as much as yow could and by what meanes yow could. But the meanes to furnish this trade will not arise from England, neyther by our cloth nor any other comoditie. It is folly to deceive yow with hopes that will fayle. Of these some may yearly be vented by contract with the Shaw, and some tynne will sell well, quicksilver, and vermilion ; but not to compasse a tenth part of that by yow aymed at. By spices yow may well assist your selves ; they give as good profitt as in England within 30 per cent, as I am enformed. China ware is in good request, and from India great profitt to bee made by sugars, cloth, steele and other comodities, by all which yow may rayse a good part of whatsoever yow contract for, or, if yow trade at libertie, toward your provisions ; the rest must bee supplied in monie, to the furnishing wherof I must referr yow to your owne meanes. One considerable thing is the distast of the Grand Signior, who doubtlesse will seeke to hynder the passadge of the Persian commerce by sea, hee reaping as much by custome as the Sha by the prime comoditie. Mr. Steele is settled upon water woorkes, rather for his owne ends then any profitt to yow. I have proposed to him his helpe in Persia ; but hee hopes hee is settled, and letts all other projects fall. Assure yow I will doe my endeavor to settle yow in this trade, if I may doe it upon such grounds as I may have creditt by, and yow profitt. If your factors agree to the little supplie I now moove, with it I will send provision for omissions ; and, if your fleete come next yeare provided, will proceed roundly and effectually according to our advise. If wee see the danger and chardge unavoydeable and no meanes to enter into yt but by mony, and that we cannot vent ours and sowther ae goods to profitt and returne yow a fitt *partido* of silkes to beare your expence and hazard, then wee will tymely recall your servants and advise yow by land with expedition. If yow proceede in these two trades fully, yow must furnish both with spices, for all we can forecast will not rayse your stocke excepte only jewells, if yow can fitt them to profitt. In these poynts of the peace and other that may help yow, I have beene lardge alsoe to Mr. Secreatarie Wynwood [*not extant*], and playne according to my understanding.

Of Mr. Steeles other projects yow will find the generall opinion in your servants lettres and other discourses ; for that of lead, which hee only followes, the King hath taken the woorkmen at dayes wages, but I see no hope (nor end of his) to vent your lead. Yow must beare the hazard for giving soe easy creditt. I must bee playne. He came hither expecting to command us all, ever mentioning his desarts and creditt with yow ; but I have a little humbled him. The great wages yow gave him made all your factors eager to return ; who say they travell heare, and a light-braynd man that goes home and fills your ears with fables shall returne in better estate then they for paynfull service. Yow must pardon mee for my directnes. He neither can nor intended to performe any of his great braggs. I can gett noe reason of him for any one [and ?] was enforced to lett him trie which hee would. For that of freight into the Red Sea, wee have all experience nothing wilbe given, nor shipt in ours if wee would aske nothing ; [1] if we once compell them, they will know us. To that end I desire one of your shipps employed in companie ; they shall make better conditions with them when they are abroad with them and in perill then wee can heare ashore wher they are safe ; and this way I advise to proceede. To bring goods by the river of Indus to Lahor is an ould project but very hard to bee effected when we must wring it from the Portugal, who makes some profitt, but not the tenth mentioned by Steele. If wee trade into Persia wee may effect yt, and it may ease chardge ; but to hope of profitt by the conduct [*i.e.* convoying] alone is absurd. The trade is not soe great as to find your men rise [rice] ; and yet if it must bee done by strength, they will feare to adventure with yow. Ther is nothing but a peace can settle all these. Ther is noe settled trade betweene Lahor and Syndu woorth the mentioning ; only a few *Banians* that shipp in frigots for Ormus ; whom it is hard to perswade to change their customes, the woorst wherof they know. It is true ther passe yearly 20000 camells by Lahor from Agra and other parts with spices, indicoes, sugars and goods for Persia ; but the most of these bring goods on camells and sell and invest for returne, and will not bee drawen to the sea, except it were open and secure. I am perswaded, if yow had the trade of Persia free and the Portugall frends, many would take that way ; [2] but this is a woorke of tyme ; what may bee done in yt shall not bee omitted.

[1] ' For the waftinge of the Guzeratt shipps to Moha or other places,' wrote Fetiplace and Hughes sarcastically to the Company (*O.C.*, No. 581), ' we thinke they put soe much confidence in our nation as that they had rather goe alone.'

[2] This expectation was realised. When the English were settled at Gombroon, their vessels were freely used by native traders between that port and Surat.

Mr. Steele will, I hope, fall into consideration. I daylie presse him; but he would bee delivered of mee. I urdgd him to agree for a woorke by great, that yow might have some returne of your chardge; but he is yet only in woords. Hee will not once name the renting of his woorke, it beeing soe absurd. Noe cast here will drinck of the water, but fetchd by his owne cast; or, if they would, the profitt should not bee allowed you.[1] The King is desierous of all new arts, will entertayne the artificers, and soone learne their sckill and cast them off. However, I will provide hee shall not spend yow more then hee shall earne. His wife I have bound to Mrs. Towerson at her sute. [*Marginal note by Roe.*—But he hath fetchd her away and keepes house perforce. I have mad a protest agaynst him; but I feare he cares not.] I was resolved to send her home; but shee hath one child sucking and (as they say) forward of a nother; it were unfitt to send her home alone among men. If her husband had returned, it had beene more convenient; yet hee would have tould yow hee would have performed all. Now hee is kept to triall; and I beleeve by the next yow may expect him, rich in children and not unprovided of other meanes, for hee brought in goods and jewells above 400*li.*, and tooke of Mochreb-Chan 5000 *rup*[*ias*] impresse upon them, in hope of more, without my knowledge. Thus hee presumes he may trade freely: that his creditt is greater with yow then such trifles. Or, if hee had not stock, hee layed his owne plott well; for hee brought a paynter, stole him aboord at the Downes, [who] is bound to him for seven years (a very good woorkeman both in lymming and oyle) to devide profitts; him hee preferred to the King in his owne trade, pretended to mee for an engineer in water woorkes. His smith makes clocks; of all hee shares the moyetie. I required to bynd them to yow by covenant, which hee could not refuse;

[1] Steel's projects are further criticised in a separate paper of about this date in the I.O. Records (*O.C.*, No. 611; see *English Factories*, 1618-21, p. 12). Roe, in explaining to the court after his return the absurdity of the waterworks scheme, pointed out that 'first, the River Gemini [Jumna] was unfit to set a myll uppon, raging with vyolence of waters three months together, overflowing his bounds a myle from his banks, so that it appered unpossible to settle such a worke either at the highest or lowest tyme therof, when he falls within his banks againe. Secondly, the *Banians* in Agra (who are the greatest part of the inhabitants) will not touch nor meddle with any water that is brought or handled by any other then themselves. Thirdly, the King and nobilitie have as excellent and artificiall waterworks of their owne as can be desired. And, lastlye, lead may be had at Agra better cheape then can be brought uppon camells from Surat' (*Court Minutes*, 10 November, 1619).

but his paynter would not, and when I offer to send him home, I dare not for the Kings displeasure, to whom Steele by his toong to my face may wrong mee, and hath already practised it.[1] But I shall defend myselfe and yow, if God blesse mee.

Captain Towerson and his wife find could reception here. Her frends are poore and mean and weary of them. Hee came with hopes of great diamonds, and they looke for guifts of him. I am sorie for him and his little vanetie. I have used my best advice to perswade his returne. He sees his owne abuse, and yet hath not power to recall yt. Hee thought to bee esteemed here a great man; God send him to returne as hee came; which, if I would consent, hee might in estate better, for his purpose was, it seemes, to invest here in indicoes for about 1000li.; pretends your licence, and his meritt to bee such as yow will deny him nothing. I shall gett an ill name by refusing such easye requests. I woonder why yow should grant him this favour and bynd all our hands: and yow could not but foresee his ends was trade, or, if he say true, yow allow yt. Yow may assure yourselves it makes all your servants grudge; and till I see under writing it was your pleasure I will not bee overcome with pretended desarts that I know not. Mrs. Hudson claymes the like for her proportion, about 120li. I am the same to man and woeman. Lastly, when they sawe my resolution, they intended to the sowthward and soe make five returnes for one. But I understood your prohibition to be generall; I knowe what injurie that course would doe yow, and have alsoe denyed yt. Now hee is resolved to stay, perhaps till I am gone, to find an easier man. Hee may be deceived. I offered him to returne this yeare and, to ease us of his weomen, liberty to invest his stock in cloth and other goods, indico excepted, provided to bee consigned to yow; but hee hath better hopes, and I assure yow I feare hee will spend most of his stock and ease mee of refusing him unreasonable demands. By suffering such adventurers yow putt mee to much inconvenience, discontent your servants, and hazard more then yow consider; everie man is for himselfe, and I the common enemie. He hath many ends never to yow propounded; but bee assured I will looke to him. Yow neede not doubt any displeasure hee can rayse yow by her kindred, nor hope of any assistance. They fence one upon a nother and are both weary. The mony mentioned of Captain Hawkings is fallen by misenformation from 2000 *rup[ias]* to 200; not woorth recalling, ells I had beene dooing before your dischardge came.

What I have employed for yow of myne, I will account when

---

[1] Steel was able to speak Persian, and had been used by Roe as an interpreter, an opportunity of which he did not fail to take advantage (see p. 455).

I come home, and not aske mony out of your stock. I desier every way to lett yow know I ayme at creditt, not at mony. The presents yow sent are in their kynds some good, others ordinarie. Noe man can tell what to advise for ; they change every yeare their fancy. It is all come to hand with some trouble, as my journall will enforme ; part given, part putt to good profitt, sould and to sell ; part to putt off your heavy goods. But if yow expect that I make good my woord upon these, that they shall give five, ten, etc. for one profitt, yow will find I was deceived in part, and yow in understanding mee soe. It is not to bee expected upon woorke or things they can judge off ; but a new raretie or curiositie never seene here and of smalle price in Europe, such as I have seene sould soe, as a glasse to showe many coulors, and Venetian toyes. But now your shipps have made all things common ; knives bought at 10 *rup[ias]* offered for 6 *mamoodies* ; and yearly ther comes as many toyes of all kyndes as yours, which sould in hast by marriners or others bound to the sowthward hath made all cheape and common. They imitate every thing wee bring, and embroder now as well as wee. What my opinion changeth too for goods and presents is in a paper severall ; but noe man can advise certeynly except upon jewells. These people will covett any thing ; when they see it, disgrace it, and not come to halfe the price. Yet yow shall finde sould of these many at two for one, some at 50 per cent, some at three and four, and halfe shalbe putt to profitt. Many things alsoe, as gloves, will give nothing nor bee accepted as guift, but as patterns to picke out woorke.

The tokens yow sent mee I receive most gratfully ; but all beeing not for my use, I take only two feathers and one hatt and band, a sworod and hangers, and lace for bands. The rest yet lye by mee, that may serve your turne ; if not, I will weare them for your sake, or sell them and put to your account. Your love to mee is sufficient present. I dare not perswade yow to send any quantetie of such ware as these ; the kinds in its owne place I have mentioned. Ammell [*i.e.* enamel] is fallen in price, yet it will give good profitt ; but it must bee good. Ther is noe salle till the court bee settled. About this quantetie yearly will passe at most, for the Portugall now overlayes it.

I was fully resolved to returne by this fleete, as yow may perceive by many passadges ; but your earnest desier prevayles above myne owne occasions. Sir Thomas Smyth had power to send mee out, and hath lost noe part of his interest in mee. I doubt not His Majesties lettre too mee was procured by yow, wherin I find his gratious acceptation above my meritt, which bindeth mee to endeavour above my abilitie. I must acknowledge the favour yow did mee in relations to His Majestie.

That is the reward I labor for and expect ; and yow shall finde I will not fayle yow in my uttmost endeavours. When my experience was raw I wrote yow many things by report, and I am not ashamed to recant ; but the end shall judge of mee and of my endes. The next yeare I shall take your offer to returne in one of your shipps and to command her. If wee agree not here, I shalbe busie with her ; but will not doe it but for that end which no fayre way can procure. Ther was never fayerer woordes and lesse fayth among the Cretans then in these people.

What the valew of pearle and other *pedreria* [*i.e.* jewels (Sp.)] is I have specified in a tariff here inclosed. Those yow sent, except the great, of which I have given reason, are yet unsould and will never give the mony yow rate them att ; [1] yow must either buy cheaper or invoyce your goods right, that your servants may know what to doe. I know these are over valewed. But to the poynt. At the rates by mee given, if they hould weight and bewtie, I give yow assurance yow may sell for 50000*li.* yearly ready mony, and for as much more in any sort of stones by mee specifyed ; [2] and this way only rayse a stock, and your free recourse bee desiered by the King and Prince and great men ; and if they are pleased, the crie off a million of subjects would not bee heard.

The rates and prises of your pearles could not bee kept secrett by mee. Before I heard of them, the newes was in Brampoore and Amadavaz ; and Mr. Steele published an invoyce, the great pearle at 1000*li*.

My opinion of cloth yow find in many places. Kersies are

[1] These pearls, after their first rejection by Āsaf Khān, were offered to Mukarrab Khān, but were ' disgraced in the Kings presence by Assuff Can, as being his refuzalls ' (*The English Factories*, 1618-21, p. 9) ; whereupon, it would seem, they were returned. Most of them were finally sold in June, 1618, to Āsaf Khān for Rs. 8,092, ' haveinge beene offered to many and none wold give soe muche for them togeather.' As they had cost 1521*l.* 17*s*., there was a considerable loss on the transaction (Biddulph's accounts in *Factory Records, Miscellaneous*, vol. 25).

[2] The Portuguese relied largely on jewels for their trade with Hindustān : ' We never heard of any other commodity the Portingalls doe bringe to Goa then jewells, ready mony and some few other provisions of wine and the lyke, except the marfeel [ivory], gold and amber which they bringe from Mozambique. Those factors which come from Goa to the court, Agra, and Brampore bringe nothinge but jewells, which they retorne imployed in indico, both of Biana and Cirkeis [Sarkhej], semanaes, carpetts and the lyke ' (The Agra factors to the Company, 20 Dec., 1617 ; *O.C.*, No. 581, printed in *Letters Received*, vol. vi. p. 241).

more uncerteyne sale. Some are of opinion white Devonshires would sell, as beeing a light and fine cloth. I dare not advise in any thing upon hopes of these people, except such as I see ordinarie vent or use. Lead you have furnished for five years. Tynn is good ware in Persia, and fynds but easy marketts here. Teeth will yearly sell to a small quantetie ; by reprisall and specie from England I suppose here is enough for three years. Corall will give yow reasonable profitt, and not lie upon your hands, except the merchant of Suratt prohibitt your sale ; which hee endeavoreth, but I have answered : if wee cannot sell, hee shall not bring in. This is your surest comoditie. Spices sell to good profitt. I have advised to Suratt for the marchants price, as the Dutch hath sould. I knowe in the shopp it is almost as deare as in London. I wish wee had yearly 100 tunns pepper, 40 of cloves, 20 of mace, and 20 of nutmegs. Cinamon is cheape, and makes noe profitt. In these particulars I am not well read. I have this yeare beene in the woods. By my returne I will bring yow an exact survey of all the trafiques of India, and bee by yow to answare any misinformation. Ther is no complaynt by the Mogolls subjects that wee buy not their comoditie, but contrarie, that wee buy so much that their owne merchants want for the Red Sea. I knowe it true. Wee have raysd the price of all wee deale in, and now wee feare the Dutch will make it woorse.

I have runn over your lettre, and to my understanding answered all the parts of yt. Wher I err, yow must consider I cannot see all ; wher I am playne, that I wish all well, and yow will excuse mee. My conclusion is : I will have reguard to your mayne busines, both in Persia and in India. I will give yow a good account of your trust, and by altering the courses lett yow see a change that shall ease and profitt yow.

I have only two poynts to touch. That these seas beginn to bee full of rovers, for whose faults wee may bee engaged. Sir Robert Rich and one Phillope Barnardoe sett out two shipps to take piratts, which is growne a common pretence of beeing piratts. They missed their entrance into the Red Sea (which was their dessigne), and came for India, gave chase to the Queene Mothers juncke, and, but that God sent in our fleete, had taken and rifled her. If they had prospered in their ends, either at Mocha or here, your goods and our persons had answered it. I ordered the seisure of the shipps, prises, and goods, and converted them to your use ; and must now tell yow, if yow bee not round in some course with these men, yow will have the seas full and your trade in India is utterly lost and our lives exposed to pledge in the hands of Moores. I am loath to lie in irons for any mans faults but myne owne. I love Sir

Robert Rich well,[1] and yow may bee pleased to doe him any curtesie in restitution, because hee was abused ; but I must say, if yow give way, yow give encouradgement. I had rather make him any present in love then restore any thing in right. For Barnardo, I doubt not yow wilbe sencible of his plott, and call him into question. Hee getts the Duke of Savoyes commission, but the faces are all English. Jhons, the captain of the *Lyon*, was a projector. The Mootams[2] enveigled Sir Robert Rich and after mutined, tore his commission, disarmed his captain, and are breefly villaynes woorthey to feede in the Marshalsy one yeare. Such an example would deter others ; els yow give them both title and hart. The captaine of the *Francis*, Mr. Newse, sett out by Sir Robert Rich, I will commend to your favour as an honest discreet gentleman, who neaver consented to your injurie, but was forced by his disordered gyng [*i.e.* crew] ; the rest I leave yow to deale with as in your judgement yow shall find requisite. But if yow suffer rovers in these seas, ther must bee noe traders. It is hard to proove to these people the difference of merchants and piratts, if all of a nation ; or, if yow could proove it, I am unwilling to lye for a pawne untill certificatt came out of Europe.

The second is the Dutch. They wrong yow in all parts and grow to insufferable insolencies. If wee fall foule here, the common enemie will laugh and reape the fruict of our contention. There must a course bee taken at home, which, by His Majesties displeasure signified, were not difficult, if he knew how they traduce his name and royall authoritie, robb in English coulors to scandall his subjects,[3] and use us woorse then any brave enemie would, or any other but unthanckfull drunckards that wee have releeved from cheese and cabbage, or rather from a chayne with bread and water. Yow must speedelye looke to this maggat ; els wee talke of the Portugall, but these will eate a woorme in your sides. I neede not counsell

[1] Rich afterwards married Roe's cousin, Susanna, widow of Alderman William Halliday.

[2] James Mootham was master of the *Francis* ; John, possibly a master's mate. The latter was taken by Pring into his fleet in that capacity, and died some thirteen months later ; James, probably as the more guilty of the two, was sent home a prisoner in the *Bull*, together with Newse and Jones. Bangham recommended him to the Company for employment, but apparently without success, and the last heard of him is that in 1620 the Company procured a warrant against both him and Jones for hiring away divers men from the *London* to serve the King of Denmark in the East Indies.

[3] Cf. p. 376. This was generally believed by the English factors in the East ; cf. *Cocks's Diary*, vol. i. p. 260, vol. ii. p. 41, and *Letters Received*, vol. ii. p. 199.

yow which way; only advise yow never to joyne stock to profitt and losse, for their garrisons, chardges, losses by negligence will engage yow to beare part of their follyes for no profitt. But your accord must bee by a stint at those parts common to yow both, and agreement to what ports yow may resort without offence one to the other. If they keepe yow out of the Moluccoes by force, I would beat them from Suratt to requite it. In both these I have beene lardge to Mr. Secretary and some of the lords, that they may have feeling of the injuries and bee assistant to yow.

This second February arrived with mee the footmen sent from Spahan by Edward Connaught with lettres of eight months date, directed to Mr. Kerridge and to noe other.[1] I opened them. In generall I fynd no more then the coppies that came by the *Bee*; some particulars [*i.e.* private letters] by which I discover more of their triumvirat faction[2] and privatt plotts then matter of busines. In one I find a new charactor [*i.e.* cipher], which giveth mee some suspition; but I will understand it before I accuse. In others I and yow will find that there was a resolution taken to conceale all the proceedures in Persia from mee; and the better to enter creditt with yow, the lettres I sent the King of Persia in February 1615 and January 1616 [see pp. 109 and 334], with divers advises to yow, both reasons and objections, the full declaration of our entents in pursuing this trade, all directed for deliverie or conveyance to William Robbynns, Connaught gott into his power, opened, and suppressed them; and, not supposing I sent coppies other wayes, out of myne makes his use and writes yow these lettres of his propositions to the King. Yow may compare them poynt to poynt, the phrase not altered. Reading them I knew myne owne, and, though not woorth the challendging, yet yow may see how these new ambassadors and agents packd [*i.e.* conspired] against mee. All coppies fitt for yow, which I doubted others would conceale, I send yow; all which might informe, or did concerne, the factoreis I dispeeded the same night, that no pretence of delay might hynder my present desiers for a little supply thither; wher if a trade may bee settled with securitie and compassed with your fitt meanes, I shalbe gladder then all they who would have kept mee in ignorance. I can spare them the creditt of yt that want yt; and my manner of prosecution shall give both account of my affection to yt and your good, and of my judgement in the possibilitie and profitt.

Since the finishing of the former intent of supply for Persia,

[1] Probably the letters of 15 and 16 May, 1617, which form *O.C.*, Nos. 480-481.

[2] Barker reviling Connock, and Pley blaming Barker.

I received full answere from the shipps that it was impossible to bee performed untill the next change of monzone, and hereby wee are enforced to leave it in imperfection. By your next fleete I doubt not wee shall understand the resolution of our hopes and bee furnished to releeve the wants, and either to settle it or recall it. In the interim I will send to your factors such direction as is requisite, and to the Sha excuse of our fayling: that yet wee know not nor were agreed upon the quanteties of goods nor prises on both parts. I received to day newes from Ormus of a revolt of all the Mahometans subject to the Portugalls for the stealing an *Alcaron* [i.e. a Koran] out of their *moschee*; which the Sha takes alsoe for a breach of peace, it beeing one of the articles that the Moores should not bee offended nor injured in poynt of their religion. Yf it bee not suddenly appeased, it may occasion the Sha to take the fort into his hands; which by a little help might bee effected, and for him easy by our assistance; without joyning, very difficult for either of us.

The new pretended Spanish ambassador is refused audience, beeing come as far as Cambaya, within two dayes of court; principally because his presents were not of great valew. But the King, shaming to insist upon soe base a reason, used for a full deniall a later pretence, that hee was no right embassador; having of mee demanded by Asaph-Chan if I would avow him for one, to which I replyed if I saw his masters lettres I was bound; if not, I should not acknowledge him but as a messinger. The King demanded of the Jesuite if he had lettres, who replying truth: none from Spayne, and, to avoyd the affront, professed alsoe that hee came but from Damon, a citty of the Portugalls, but soe suddenly as the new Vizeroy could neither prepare a fitt present nor lettres: that his comming was to congratulate in the Vizeroy and cytties name his approach into these parts; at which hee had his full dismission, but with good tearmes: that if hee came to see him, hee should bee wellcome; but if the Vizeroy would send him or any other with presents and authoritie in the name of the King of Portugall, hee would receive him with honor. The Jesuite is somwhat troubled; and the embassador, who came on in great braverie, takes himselfe scorned. They pretend to mee that a nother shall returne with ampler lettres and full power to treat with mee; which Asaph-Chan from the King gave in chardge. For my part, I am not sorry for any distast begunn, and thinck not that the Portugall will stoope so farr as to send a nother nor presents upon such a demand and affront; neyther that if any come that hee shall bring authoritie to make yow a secure peace. The issue I attend.

Mr. Steele hath now fully delivered himselfe and his woorke-men into the Kings power, and them into his pay; hath had speech of the like for himselfe; and it is all our opinion hee will upon that sett up his rest. In woords he protesteth not; but hee hath gotten his wife up with Mrs. Towerson, as her servant, and vowed to mee shee should live in her house, to which end I tooke a covenant from them. But the first day hee brake it, carried her to a house of his owne, where hee lives with coach, *palinke*, seven horses, and ten servants; and, beeing stayed in my house as prisoner, to search into his entents, he confessed hee said any thing formerly and consented to the covenants to deceive mee and to gett his wife into his owne power. The excuse of all is affection. [*Marginal note by Roe.*—Now he followes the court with as great expence as I and as many servants.] Send them home by force I cannot, or is now too late, untill the King bee satisfied in his expectation of great promises from Richard Steele. Neyther will hee proceed upon the woorke of Agra (which was my condition), but follow the *leskar* to make picturs, clocks, coaches and such devices, by which hee hopes to creepe into great preferments. I assure yow I write of his courses very modestly. Wee are not yet wise enough to see any hopes nor any-entents of his to effect a woork out of which yow may make any advantage. He hath professed the woorkemen are his servants: that he spent 500*li*. to bring them for the King. They have not language to denye it, nor will to follow him; but now they are engaged, having received horses and mony; and when I moove their true employment, it is replyed they are in the Kings pay, and must obey his pleasures, they and their guide. [*Marginal note by Roe.*—When he was my toong to the Kyng he would deliver his owne tales and not a woord what I commanded.] The next difference is that hee will alsoe carry up his woman; which I refuse, requiring her stay with her mistris, according to yours and my intent. If hee consent, I shall give him some employment and allowance from yow; if not, that hee will runne in all contrarie, then hee gives mee such assurance of that all men suspect, that I shall neither trust him with your goods nor pay him any wages untill I have meanes to send him home; which will soone bee, if hee continew his expence and attend the bounties of this King. You see I desier noe weomens company, but labour to leave such incumberances behynd. Beleeve mee the scandall already is not easely wyped off. Your securitie shalbe, at the woorst yow shall loose no more by him; I will looke to your estate.

William Hempsale, the Kings coachman, is dead. I send yow the coppy [of] his will. A hundred *Jangier rupias* hee disposed to his mother or brothers, to be delivered to mee. I have given it to cash,[1] received bills of exchange, and desier

[1] On 13 Jan., 1618 (see Biddulph's accounts, f. 11).

yow to enquire of his frends, that they may receive what is their due, and I discharged. It is mony for mony 12*li*. 18*s*. 4*d*. If yow among them ad any liberalitie, in reguard it was not converted to profitt, they will pray for yow. Hee served the Bishop of Chichester [*sic*], Doctor Overall. Except in his house, I know not where to enquire after him.

If Mr. Young returne, I wilbe a mediator for him, and will deliver truth. No man hath taken more paynes, lived more frugally and fayerly; and I am confident hath passed his service honestly. Yf hee errd in Mr. Edwardes yeare, consider that a superior may easely prevayle, that promiseth protection. Least by mistakings of my entents any error should bee committed in my project of the Red Sea, I have sent my servant Edward Haynes as one of the merchantes, because he hath transcribed all my discourses in that busines and should bee perfect in yt. This I hope yow will allow, and shalbe his probation. I have taken bond of him to your use of faythfull service. Mr. Wallys I am forced to send home (his body is unperfect); and some others for disorders. I am in this very sparing to undoe any; but if all bee suffered, most wilbe undone by example.

The King is anew gone into the woods, toward Mando as reported, but wee are not certeyne. I am entering into the miserie and chardge of following. What conclusion I shall have I cannot presage. Hee is good to mee; his sonne latly better, who is absolute King. Hee hath granted mee a few priviledges, and reconfirmed our trade and liberties at Suratt, but will heare of noe more ports; his *firmaen* also for recoverie of customes taken on the way and for your goods and servants at Brampoore that were seized by the justice. He hath ordered all your debts in *cerkar*,[1] and promised execution of the Kings sentence against other our debtors; which if wee could settle, in a month I should doubtlesse finish. I was not consenting to the making, yet will not leave them alone that did mee. I am soe weary of the wayes of this court, which are governed by no rule, that I must open to yow my full resolution. If this *Norose* I can finish my desiers of universall priviledges that shalbe of power in all parts of his dominion, and recover our debts, I shall desier to retyre and rest mee untill the arrivall of your fleete; for the next raynes, if I lye in the feilds or in an open house, will finish my travells. If not, I will take my leave, and bee ready at Suratt to meete with the ship I expect from the Red Sea, who shall both pay mee all that is due and

[1] *Sarkār*, a word used in several diverse senses, but having here, as in many other cases, the meaning almost of our 'privy purse.' What is implied is that the Prince had ordered the immediate payment of all sums due for goods taken for his or the King's use.

make those conditions bee offered which now I seeke with despayre. Assure yow, I knowe these people are best treated with the sword in one hand and caducean [1] in the other.

If I have erred in my judgment yow will easely fynd one man cannot see all. My affection to doe yow right and honest service shall excuse many escapes. But in generall I desier yow to preserve in your opinion this thought of mee: that whatsoever I conceive good for yow I will practice: neither feare nor paynes shall divert mee: and that when I shall be present to give yow reason of any thing I have written, noe man shalbe soe impudent as to contradict it: and for my life, it will not bee ashamed of any search and enquirie. The issue of all yours and our endeavors I committ to Gods blessing, who is able to make rich and poore, and to convert the successes of all to His glorie.

Your honest frend to doe yow service, THO. ROE.

ADVISE FOR GOODES FOR SURRATT.[2]
(I.O. Records : *O.C.*, No. 637.)

Broade cloathes : everie two yeres 200, or every yere 100 ; red, greene, yallowe, poppingey ; no stammetts, or not above ten. Corrall : as much as yow cann provide ; the rates and sortes Surratt must informe. Lead : none theis two yeres. Quicksilver : for 1000*li*. yerely. Vermillion : a small quantitie. Wine, hott waters, swordes, knives (except great and rich), glasses (looking nor glasing) : none, nor anie such like trash. Pearles : anni great well bought ; chaines of pearles, between three carr[ats] and ten, the greatest the best. Rubies give the best proflitt, from three carr[ats] upwardes of all sizes, so high in coullour and faire. Ballasses : faire and greate, of 60 carr[ats] upwardes. Cattes eyes : if yow knewe the right stone. Emrauldes : of the old and new rocke,[3] the greatest.

---

[1] The wand or rod carried by Hermes as the messenger of the gods.

[2] A copy, endorsed : 'Advise from Sir Thomas Roe of Goodes and Presents for Surratt, 1617.' In the *Cal. of State Papers* (*E. Indies*), this is assigned (with a query) to March, 1618 ; but there seems to be sufficient ground for assuming that it is the enclosure referred to in the preceding letter (p. 449).

[3] These terms were probably used first of diamonds (cf. Garcia da Orta's *Coloquios*, ch. 43), those from 'the old rock' (or mine) being considered superior to the other variety ; but the same distinction was made in the case of emeralds (as here) and turquoises (see Constable's *Bernier*, p. 148).

Aggats : some fewe well cutt, the faces white. Armletts : anie made to lock onn with one joint, sett with stones, diamondes and rubies, good worke, will give yow proffit.

Of this kinde of goodes, if yow would finde anie rich stone to the value of 20,000*li.* to equall the Portugall, would give yow great proffit and credit. It is howrely objected and required. By this meanes only yow can compas a stocke and make your trade desired ; upon such a rare peece yow maie get anie condicions, for their coveteousnes of them is unsatiable. If yow can send yerely in great stones of theis kindes or pearles 100,000*li.*, I dare be bownde it would vent to proffitt and make yow highly requested. Without this the Kinge wilbe wearie ; and it will save yow presents. All other things will faile yow, and with theis yow may putt of anie thing. The Towre, I ame perswaded, could furnish yow with manie great olde stones that are useles.

Arras : fresh and good coullours, for one or two yeres yow maie vent to some proffitt for 10,000*li.* Cloath of gould and silver branched, grograines or sattins, that make a fine shewe, mingled with fresh coullours, will raise monie, but to no great proffit. Gould lace is much inquired after by the King. I thinck it will yeld 30 per cento proffitt. Chamblets [1] of Turkey, red, greene, yallowe, purple : they come in quantityes from the Red Sea. Shirtes of male : a hundred, so they be lyght, arrowe proofe, and neately made. Imbrodered coates of the Indian fashion, for our wastcoates they canot use here. I have patterns of the King of divers sortes sent yow. Cases for round bucklers. Quivers for bowes and arrowes, Indian fashion. And generally I give yow this rule : whatsoever yow send in this kinde must be made by Indian patternes, for then they are of use and every bodies monie. Gloves, hangers, scarfes : by theis only they picke out the workes. In steade of sweete baggs, rownde cushions gathered like cloke bags, to leane on. Any of theis in needleworke or imbroiderie will sell cent. per cent. or not much les ; all imbroderie being fallen in value, for they have learned by ours to do as well. Boxes imbrodered will sell to proffitt ; and great glasses. Some light coullored Norwich stuffes wrought in flowers for triall, the lighter the better. I ame perswaded manie would vent, if chosen fitlie.

Concerning Presentes.

Not to followe the course of presenting yerely in the Kings name. Once in three yere a letter and a good present. If yow bring stones yow shalbe welcome to all.

[1] Camlets, a light stuff said (though this is disputed) to have been originally woven from silk and camel's hair.

Furnishing yerelie 2 or 3,000*li*. in other fine ware or cloath of gould, silver, etc., yow must yelde to have it seene at customehowse, and sent all to the King or Prince, with whome must go a merchant, and when opened before the King (which is the slaverie here) he maie give one or two toyes (such as he seeth pleaseth) and, after, all the rest to sell. I assure yow they wilbe all bought and good paiment, and the King better content then in this course ; for our trouble is all aboute the presents, which, if all came to sell, were finished at once. I am inforced by experience to change the course. I have tried all waies and hazarded this yere a quarrell to avoyd an affront. I will sett downe a course to prevent their greedines and to tourne it all to proffitt, seeing they have no honour. This counsell Asaph Chan first gave, telling me we were fooles and had brought up a custome to our owne hurt : the King expected nothing of merchantes but to buy, and at entrance (as fashion) a toy, and when anie peticion, the like : that when we gave in the name of the King it should be seldomer, and then befitting his honour. He demanded who practized this course but yourselves, neither Duitch, Persians, nor Armenian merchantes ; neither did the King expect it. I knowe this both wise and thriftie counsell, but your agent resident wilbe against it. For ther is no man but will ayme at his owne proffit, my self excepted, as by my retourne it will appeare ; I never gave a knife for myne owne endes, nor used the least basenes of begging ; my riches are accordingly.

Fitt presentes from the King.[1]

once in three yere, four or five of theis, with one of good value.

Some good stone for once, or some rich peece of arras, silke and gould, but one or two at most. A rich peece of tissue or clothe of gould. A fine crowne, sett with small stones. A faire bed feild, with lace or some worke. A rich feild caparason and sadle ; the patterne from hence. An imbrodered bowe, quiver, and arrowes : patternes from hence. A coate of sattin imbrodered ; the paterne from hence.

With theis : Some cushions, cabbennetts, glasses, standishes and toyes of use for others. Pictuers of all sortes, if good, in constant request; some large storie ; Diana this yere gave great content.

Goodes from the southwardes.

Spices of all kindes give great p[r]offit. China dishes and all sortes of fine ware, as chestes, cabbennetts, bedsteades etc. to as

[1] i.e., to be presented in the name of the King of England.

good proffit as in England. Taffaties imbrodered with gould silke in flowers, vearie well requested and rated. From theis partes for presentes in toyes yow maie be better furnished then from Europe.

Cochenel will never sell a certenty. Few knowe it. For a pownd or two some may give a good price ; but it is no comoditie of use. Those of Sinda only buy it. The Persians bring a little and retaile it at 35 *ruppies* the great *seere*. Ammell hath sould : the red, if verie fine, ordinarily for twice the waight in gould. The Portugales have theis two yeres from Goa brought some, of which Francisco Swart[1] 18*li.*; the red sould at 45*s.* the ounce, blewe, white and greene att 18*s.* The King being in the feild, all the workmen, both of the court and the great men, are retourned to Agra, where I must sende it. It may yeld yow, the red (against the *Norouse*) nere the waight of gould, the rest ¼ the waight in gould.

To Captain Martin Pring.
(I.O. Records : *O.C.*, No. 613).

February 14 [1617-18].

... By way of provision I have sent instructions [2] for the voyadge into the Red Sea, to which Mr. Kerridge must add his for marchandizing affayres and deliver yow goods to beginn our trade. The mayne objection is that there is noe great foundation to beare chardge ; to which I answere wee have many dead comodities wee must seeke to put off, and may either sell them by frendship or teach a trade by force. With whomsoever the ship meetes of the allies of the Portugalls, which are the Decannines or Samoring [see p. 376], they are to us as enemies. If shee should meete with no booty, yet I suppose they shall not bee denyed traficque at Mocha, wher certeynly will bee juncks, both of Diue and Dabull and of other southern ports, with which (if the Mochers will not accept of our goods) they should [trade ?] for indicoes and other comodities fitting England or Suratt. The returne of a smalle stock

---

[1] Francisco Soares, a Portuguese merchant who was apparently engaged in bringing jewels to the court from Goa and other places. In a letter to Surat (*O.C.*, No. 556) Roe calls him ' the prodigall Portugall,' and says that he is about to marry an aunt of Mrs. Towerson.

[2] These form *O.C.*, No. 598. They were printed in the first edition (p. 492), but are now omitted to make room for more important matter. They are summarized in *English Factories*, 1618-21 (p. 19).

from thence will pay the expence of the ship, toward which Mr. Kerridge sayth hee can procure freight for 15 or 16,000 *mamoodies*, which I would accept off as a beginning. Hee doubts it will hynder, the stay at Dabull, but I see noe reason, if wee sett so much the sooner out then usually the juncks doe for the same voyadge off this coast. Goeing into the Bay of Jasques is more doubtfull ; of that I cannot judge, but referr it to your consideration if one ship may doe all, or any two, of which I thinck Jasques and the Red Sea of most consequence. . . . A second objection is that the Grand Signior will embargue our English in his dominions for our molesting his trades ; to which I say wee goe to offer peace, to secure his seaes, and not to disturbe any but our enemies that deny us trade, and by our usadge many may bee encouraged to augment that way who are now afrayd of rovers and overlayd with tribute or the exactions of the Portugalls. In the Red Sea itselfe shall wee best make the Guzeratts understand their danger and the benefitt of our offer ; ther they will bee spoken with at leysure, where now wee seeke to them at their houses. Nature is easier to deale with when it is a little afrayde.[1] Or, if wee are soe jealous of our frends at Constantinople, how can wee proceede in Persia, the stealing away of which trade will more sharpen the Turk then the rifle of a junck or two of rascalls that hee takes noe notice off ? . . . I once mooved yow to keepe close the sowth shoare [2] for the chances of the Malaccoas ships and others that in March come in to Goa. Now I advise yow to bee warie, for the Vizeroy (as wee heare) prepares a fleete to goe about the Cape for the Coast of Cormandell and wilbe ready this month.[3] If yow bee alone it is not good to tempt them. Concerning the juncks of Diu, I understand that Mochreb-Chan and some Mogolls freight from thence. Wee cannot take notice of on mans from anothers that mingle with our enemies. I would not spare any of that port upon the best pretence. Our warienes wilbe to keepe the junck it selfe ; to putt a merchant and purser upon it untill returne to Suratt. If it bee prooved Mogolls goods and that the King stirr in yt, I know this people ; restitution alway makes peace, and wee shall have the advantage of some good condition for restitution, and make them feare to freight in the Portugalls and rather offer them

---

[1] The Bantam factors wrote to the same effect (19 Jan. 1618 : *O.C.*, No. 595) :—' For the troubles and abuses of our people by the Governor and great men, remedy may be sooner found in the Redd Sea amongst their neighbour junkes then at the Mogulls court, and better cheape. Nothing but feare keepes a Moore in awe ; use him kindly and he will abuse you, but deale with him in smooth words and nipping deeds and he will respect and reverence you.'

[2] In proceeding to Bantam.   [3] Cp. p. 437.

selves to us. Until wee show our selves a little rough and busye, they will not bee sencible.

The woemen [1] are almost arrived at court, but I hope I shall depart this towne before, the King goeing out suddenly, which makes mee now take my leave. I am in your debt for your love above all your other kindnesses, which now yow close up with new. ... I assure yow honestly I have loved yow seven yeares for the good disposition and woorth I found in yow. If it were any way in my power I would make it manifest. My woord or report in England yow neede not; yet perhaps not soe well knowne to all as to the Companie. Whatsoever I can add to give yow right, either to them or any higher, assure yow I will not fayle; or, if I did, it is your fault not too lett mee know which way. But I am gladd both of your assurance and modesty. Wee live in a barberous unfaythfull place; yow in the sea with more securitie and constancye. Pray for us, that God wilbe pleased to keepe us, that among heathens wee may bee as light in darknes; at least that wee shame not the light. I will hope to live to see yow safe returned, and for your happy voyadge, health (above all temperall comforts), wealth and good successe according to your owne desiers, and a joyfull arrivall into your countrie. All the blessings that attended Jacob, when hee went out with a staff and returned with troopes of servants and heards of cattell, accompanie yow, that in the seas yow may find *Machinyma* [2] and at your returne *Bethel*.

... Since the finishing this former came your lettre of the 4th January, by which I perceave that which I doubted, that it was impossible to supply Jasques; and soe that unfortunate busines must lye in its wounds until better occasion. I have sent a declaration and instructions of my intents into the Red Sea, which is as much commission as I can give; if Mr. Kerridge can add to yt any enformation, wee are all for one end. For the ship or ships I referr it to yow, and am very well assured of Captain Shillings sufficiency. For merchants I know not how

---

[1] Mrs. Steel, Mrs. Towerson, and Mrs. Hudson. They were accompanied by the Rev. Mr. Golding, the chaplain of the *Anne*, who had at the Cape solemnised the marriage of Steel. The reverend gentleman's devotion to the ladies while at Surat had caused some scandal, and he had been ordered to return to his ship; but, instead of obeying, he slipped out of the city disguised as a native, and went 'after the women' to Ahmadābād. Roe sent him back in company with Heynes and the rest, but he escaped from them on the way. Subsequently, he returned to Surat and obtained pardon (*English Factories*, 1618-21, pp. 19, etc.).

[2] Mahanaim (*Gen.* 32, 2).

Mr. Rastall[1] can bee spared nor with what qualeties the fleete is provided. I have sent my servant Haynes for one, because by offten discourse hee knowes my entents. I hope hee will proove diligent and honest. . . .[2]

. . . In assurance of right I rest quiett, as farr as Mr. Steele, the woemen and the indiscretion of Mr. Goulding will suffer mee. I woonder to see him here and shall as soone resend him. I must labor to mend all. I gave consent for the best to Mrs. Steele, but never for the minister. Now her husband discovers himselfe ; but one of us must breake in this busines. I expect noe more to heare from yow, for the King is entering into the woods. The God of heaven blesse yow and all your company, and send mee once more to live among men of honesty.

To King James.

(Public Record Office : *C.O.* 77, vol. i, No. 58.)
The Camp of Ghehangeer Sha, Greate Mogoll,

May it please Your Majestie,   15 February, 1617[-18].

The most gratious reception of my travells and the commands which Your Majestie hath vouchsafed to mee, your unable and unworthy vassall, have given new life and quickened mee almost in the grave. There is no bond more stronge

---

[1] Thomas Rastell had come out in the 1616 fleet, and was now second at Surat. On Kerridge's departure for England in 1622, Rastell became chief, a post which he held at the time of the visit of Della Valle, who warmly praises him (vol. i. p. 19). He returned to England in 1625, and went out again in 1630, dying at Surat a year later. His wife's mother (widow of Alderman Gore) became the second wife of Sir John Coke, who was for some time Secretary of State.

[2] Roe goes on to complain of two of his servants who had left him and gone down to Surat. One of these was 'an idle boy,' named Hill, who had been dismissed for lying. 'I desier that he may have at the mayne mast three barricoes of water powered in his neck.' The other, his surgeon [Green], whom he describes as 'a drunken, perjured, malitious knave, no surgeon but a mountebanck imposture,' had been spreading slanderous reports concerning him. Roe begs Pring to arrest him and force him to make public recantation, after which he should be 'duckd for example,' or at least prevented from taking a passage to England. Green made some amends, and was allowed to go home in the *Bull*. On his arrival he was soon involved in a dispute with the Company over the goods he had brought home. A settlement was steadily refused until Roe's return ; when the ambassador, with his usual generosity, used his influence in Green's favour.

then that by which I am tied to Your Majestie as your subject; but that it hath pleased you out of your royall grace to give occasion to my weakenes, that also addeth strength and couradge to a minde already wholy devoted and offered up to Your Majesties service.

The negotiation of Persia, by Your Majestie to mee committed, was begunn a yeare past by the factors of India and overture made in the name of Your Majestie, of which proceedinge I was utterly ignorant; but had written some letters and sent divers propositions in myne owne name, as Your Majesties minister, unto the Sha-bas, to give him understandinge of your desires in generall and to discover to him somwhat of the Portugalls dealings with those who too easily granted them admittance or retraicts of strength. The succeds of both is: the Sha hath sent Your Majestie a very noble lettre, procured by Edward Connock, with divers lardge and ample priviledges granted unto Your Majesties subjects for there acceptance and quiett commerce, directed for deliverie unto Sir Thomas Smyth. There yet are many difficulties, unconsidered in the beginning, which forbidd mee to give judgment, eyther of the conveniency or possibilitie of this trade, untill upon knowledge of the merchants meanes to compass it without prejudice to Your Majesties kingdomes and to their owne profitt and securitie, their farther resolution bee declared. The particulars are both too many and of too low an elevation to troble Your Majestie, your generall commande beeinge obeyed. I have opened my poore understanding in the rest unto Your Majesties principal secretarie, from whom you wilbe pleased to receive lardger enformation. If I finde by one yeares experience more that this trade may bee made, by vent of the comodities of Your Majesties kingdom or by the industrye of your subjects from divers ports, without greater exports of mony or bullion then Europe is able to beare, considering how many wayes it bleedeth to enrich Asia, I wilbee bould to confirme in Your Majesties name the treaty already begunn, and to add to yt some other conditions which shall as well make it profitable for Your Majesties estates as easy for your subjects; to which end I have sent under the limitations received from Mr. Secretarie Wynwood, and instructions from the East Indya Companie, a commission to proceede in and perfect this affayre, or tymely to foresee the hazards and inconveniences, that wee may retyre without dishonor.

To the monarch with whom I reside Your Majesties minister I delivered your royall letters and presents, which were received with as much honor as their barbarous pride and custtoomes affoord to any the like from any absolute prince, though far inferior to that respect due unto them. I have stroven, somtimes to displeasure, with their tricks of unmeasured greatenes rather then to endure any scorne. I dare not dissemble with Your Majestie their pride and dull ignorance takes all things done of duty, and this yeare I was enforced to stande out for the honor of your free guifts, which were sceazed uncivilly. I have sought to meyntayne upright Your Majesties greatenes and dignitie, and withall to effect the ends of the merchant ; but these two sometyme[s] cross one another, seeing ther is no way to treate with so monstrous overweening that acknowledgeth no equall. He hath written Your Majestie a lettre [*see Appendix B*], full of good woords, but barren of all true effect. His generall [authorities ?] are yet to publish ; what hee will doe I know not. To article on evven tearmes he avoyds, and houlds mee to his owne customes of government by new *firmans* upon new occasions, in which hee is just and gracious. It may please Your Majestie to accept the translation, being faythfull. The original in Persian, as yet of use to us to urge him to performe it, I am bould to keepe untill I shalbee made happy by falling at your feete.

Greater matters then truth I dare not boast of, neyther will steale vayne prayses by false reports. What my endeavor is and how faythfull, what my travell in the camp of confusion, I hope Your Majestie will graciously conceive. This I will presume to avow that I will not live and suffer Your Majesties royall name to bee diminished for any consideration ; and, for the success of my employment, that I will establish Your Majesties subjects in as good tearmes for theire trafique and residences as any strangers or the naturalls themselves enjoy, or at last by our force teach them to know Your Majestie is lord of all the seeaes and can compell that by your power, which you have sought with curtesie ; which this King cannot yett see for swelling.

The Portugall is not yet wise enough to know his owne weakenes, who rather enviously hinder us then like noble enemies hurte us. Lett Your Majestie bee pleased to give mee leave to enforme want of a peace with them (which by your royall authoritie were easyly commanded) makes all these trades of Indya and hopes of Persia heavy and dangerous to the undertakers.

I dare not troble Your Majestie with more unnecessarie discourse, but humbly crave pardon for so much intrusion ; and that you wilbee pleased not to bee offended, after five yeares pilgrimage, that I take leave to enjoy the happines of those which attend your presence, desiring the Almightie God to make your reigne so long, so blessed, and so glorious, that your name may bee the object of all envy and the example of all prosperitie.

Your Majesties most humble vassall and devooted servant,
THO. ROE.

To Sir Thomas Smythe.
(Public Record Office : *C.O.* 77, vol. i, No. 59.)
Amadavaz, 16 February, 1617[-18].

Your acceptation of my endeavours is a confirmation of the same affection which you began towards mee when I had merited nothing. I now feare I shall fall into another evill and bee prejudiced by too much expectation. These Princes and customes are so contrarie to ours that I shall travell much in myne owne eies and performe little in yours. Ther is noe treaty wher ther is soe much prid, nor no assurance wher is no fayth. All I can doe is to serve present turnes. The people are weary of us. The King hath no content, who expects great presents and jewells, and reguards no trade but what feedes his unsatiable appetite after stones, rich and rare peices of any kind of arte. The breefe is I have sent you a lettre which will show his promises, but they hould not one minute. Feare only keepes us in, and untill they feele us once more and that his owne subjects petition for us, wee shall never obteyne more then to rubb out in a chardgable trade, with much servitude. My employment is nothing but vexation and trouble ; little honor, lesse profitt. Whatsoever I have done and my opinion in all your affayres, you will fynd in generall lettrs, [di]scourses, and other papers directed to you. Only, I protest, to give you testemony of your power in mee, I changed resolution to stay this yeare, which will fullfill my banishment of five years. In this tyme what I can add to you I will, for my owne creditt is deeply engaged, and yet is ther noe way to release me, but by a little force.

The presents sent this yeare were too good ; but (to deale playnly with my frends) soe farr short of their greedy expectation that they rather disgrace then helpe mee. Yet I cannot bee without untill the whole course bee changed. I will use none but for your busines, and (if I may advise) I wish you send noe more in the Kings name, but only proceed as other merchants doe, which is to fitt goods that they desier, and the merchant that goes to court at the showing to give one toy for his entrance. This way hath less trouble and chardge. Wee only have begott our selves a custome of slaverie now duly expected.

I was not soe desierous of command over your servants as to procure my self trouble and envy. Mr. Kerridge was sufficient. Now they joyntly cast all upon mee, hoping to over lay mee, under couler of humilytie. I will dischardg my selfe honestly of all I can doe, and may show you an example, if they which should assist crosse me not. I have stayed Mr. Kerridge in the countrie and am therby obliged to promoove the Companies recompence which he pretends. I must say truth his paynes is very great and his parts not ordinarie; only hee loves dominion, and you shall perceave by my courses with him and all others I will not robb him of yt. In the mayne poynts I wilbe assistant to provide your lading in season, and to direct the courses of your trades. The mechannicque part I must refer to others as burthensome.

I have received from yow and the Company some tokens. Such as I shall use I will make bould with, the rest convert to their use, with as many thancks as if I had in them received a pledge and assurance of your affections. The pearle lies upon our hands, as beeing either over rated, or dearer in England then here. The sizes are too small. With great pearle and stones according to the tariff sent you, you may compasse this trade to content, and by no other way.

I have recovered, by the kindnes of your captains, a better constitution of health then formerly; but I feare this new remoove will make mee relapps. Gods wilbe done.

I thank you for Jhon Hatch, your bible, peice, and oyle—all your particular love and kindnes. Beleeve me, Sir, I have noe barren and unthanckfull hart. Yet I send you nothing but the common phrases of such as are indebted. If I live, you shall find what impression your love hath made in mee; and if I dye, you shall loose more then yet you know of, because you cannot know my hart.

The ship by mee sent out wherein you were an adventurer is returned rich, but I cannot here who hath shared her. I left all her writings with Sir Jhon Brookes. I am not yet soe rich as to send home any mony. If Mr. Christopher Brookes neede any for my use, you wilbe pleased to pay him the 100li.[1] due for my servants wages, which I have supplyed here. If not, I hope you will enter it as an encrease into the Joynt Stock, and at the devision of the last soe order mee and my part of adventure as it may become profitable to mee. These courses I understand not; but as by you I came to have interest, soe unto you I referr mee.

What was done in the busines of Persia the last yeare and since by Edward Connaughts, many relations will signifie; wher I should beginn I know not. The priviledges are very good, but the port, and ground to proceede in the trade, are yet

---

[1] There seems to be no information extant as to this ship or its destination. On 20 Feb. 1618, Mr. Christopher Brookes applied to the Company for 1000l. to meet a debt for which he and Roe were pledged, he having a general power of attorney from the latter. The court granted the request, on the condition that Brookes gave a bond for repayment should Roe disapprove of the transaction.

uncerteyne. If you send next yeare meanes to supply it, wee shall proceed, I hope to generall content. The neglect of mee last yeare makes me unwilling to bee too f[orw]ard and hath stirrd up Mr. Kerridge, who takes himselfe wronged that any thing is committed to me, to many perverse disputes. I know not how I stand in his favour. Having opened Connaughts lettres to him for my information, which I could not send and bee tymely enformed, he takes it hotly; but I have done nothing but what is just. I looke into no more then your busines, and in that I will not bee kept in ignorance. This is the benefitt, that if wee cannot agree (which I by all meanes endeavor) yet wee shall both bee wary of doeing ill; and when ever I shalbe accused, it wilbe my honor. I write this because Mr. Kerridge doth magnifie his owne successe in Connock, and I proceede as if it concerned not mee; but upon the grounds of reason whatsoever in that busines can bee effected shall have both our helps : he for love to his owne project, I for your generall good.

I have signified in my generall lettres that I have sent home Anthony Wallys and some others.... The rest of your servants are for the most very civill. If any overspend, I cannot abbridge that which they pretend necessarie. What I can doe, not to drawe all mens ill will upon mee, I shall by counsayle ; if I find dangerous or grosse faults, I will stop them.

The first is Mr. Steele, who brought to sea a mayd, Captain Towerson[s] servant, but great with child, and married her at the Cape under a bush. I could not perswade Captaine Towersons returne nor his wives, though I offered conditions of your losse, nor send her home alone and anew with child among men. He pretended great matters. All your servants were willing to disgrace him. I was both unwilling and afrayd to doe yt, but consented to bring up his artificers, who proove his servants for his owne ends. I presented them to the King; but Steele getting accesse as linguist to his paynter in privat [1] (who was

[1] Of this incident Purchas (who heard it from Steel himself) gives, in his *Pilgrimage* (p. 534) the following account : ' Master Steele, having a project of water-works, to bring the water of Ganges [*sic*] by pipes &c., carried five men with him to the Mogol, who gave them entertainment with large wages by the day and gave to each an Arabian horse. One of these was a painter, whom the Mogol would have to take his picture; and because hee could not speake the language, Master Steele (who could speake the language of the court, which is Persian) was admitted (a thing not permitted to men) into the Mogols lodgings, where he did sit for the said limner. At his entrance, the chiefe eunuch put a cloth over his head that he should not see the women (which hee might heare as hee passed, and once

pretended to mee to bee your servant, sent by you as cheefe in the water woorke) entreaged them and himselfe so into the Kings service that I cannot without hazarding much displeasure enforce them eyther to retyre or to follow that they promised you. He surely either hopes to supplant mee, and to succeed (for so some tyme his vanetie pretends), or els he hath quitted his countrie. I dare not trust him with goods, seeing hee will follow the court with his wife, notwithstanding all oathes and covenants, and at as great chardge as I almost. How he pretends to maynteyne it, I cannot foresee. This only I will trye him with patience; keepe your purse from him; if he runn right, I will assist him; if not, I will doe my utmost next yeare to force him home, when the King is as weary of him as all wee. I assure you hee is now our affliction, and may bee my shame, for ever yeilding to suffer him to land.

Captain Towerson pleads leave to trade. Hee wilbe deceived in expectation of his frends and I know not what in these cases [to] doe. All the ill offices are cast upon mee. You, Sir, must bee pleasd to beare part of the burthen. I will consent noe farther then I may defend my selfe, and yet would not bee ill spoken off of all men. . . .

To conclude, Sir, I am infinitely weary of this unprofitable imployment, the successe wherof is not that I aymed at for you, and that which I hate in others, to gett an ill name. But hee that will please all men can never please the honestest. My comfort is you professe you wilbe as carefull of mee as of your owne sonn; and at that I take you as a father. Examine all my courses; if I shame you in any, renounce mee and this name of
<blockquote>Your truly unfeyned frend and adopted sonne,
THO. ROE.</blockquote>

Remember my service to your ladie, and I beseech Almighty God to blesse you and all your famelie. Mr. Jhack[s]on will I hope give testemonie of my desieres to doe him any pleasure.

<blockquote>To CAPTAIN MARTIN PRING.
(I. O. Records : O.C., No. 628.)
Baroch, March 10, 1617[-18].</blockquote>

Yt is now a month and more since I heard from yow or Surratt; soe that I was confident the ships were dispeeded.

also saw them, the eunuch purposely putting on a thinner cloth over his head), there being of them some hundreds.'

Purchas also relates the friendship which sprang up between Mrs. Steel and the daughter of the Khān-khānān. The interest this lady took in Steel's wife no doubt strengthened his position at court.

The misery of these wrongs are insufferable, yf yt be the true cause that your goods could nott be dispatched, which I by a former heard was donne upon the arivall of Shaher-mull [Shāhār Mall]. I hope to finde a way out for my self and others. Steele will soon vanish and come to nothing ; affliction must humble him.

I am sorry to heere the *Ann* hath no other cargason then the refuse of India. I meddled nott in the subservient parts of trade to apoint what other goods, butt expected the wisedom of the factors would have sent a tryall of other sorts. I can make no other collection but that they desire nott any great prosperity to yt. God will mend us all and turne honest wayes to the best. I am confident on the grounds that Surratt will never be a trade unles the Red Sea both supply yt and awe the Guzeratts. This yeare I only sought the way and occasion ; but I know well by private provizions they are nott ignorant what had been fitt, and yf yt fayle I shall well acquite my self. Those of Messolapatan I feare write at randon, or els there is great change since their last. . . . Greenes recantation is a poore on. Yow know him nott. He us a most mallitious knave and will say any thing for feare. I as much scorne revendge of him as to feare his tongue ; butt yf yow can see him, I desire yow to give him warning how he useth me, for I have provided for his wellcome into England. Your later desires my resolucion for the *Annes* keeping company to Dabull. Yf by advice or other former experiences the juncks of that porte be departed or that yt be dangerous to loose tyme for getting in, then yow may direct hir right for hir course ; butt yf nott, the surprize of any goods there fitt for the Red Sea would much advantage hir and be fittlier donn then att the roade at Mocha for interuption of quiett trade, which I ayme att. Butt yf yt soe fall out, yet I wish yow to doe somewhat yf yow may, and to send the Persians lettres as parte of payment. The noise of yt will doe good heare. I know in former yeares the ships of this coast have sett out later ; butt in that point I cannott resolve, but must leave yt to them who know the voiadges. I am well pleased that Joseph Saltbanck undertakes the voyadge. Heynes stands nott upon place, and the ould man loves me.

Yow are nott soe desirous to see me as I to confer with yow. Beleeve me, I am reddy to breake for want of an honnest free conference and advice in the Companies buissines. But I am weary ; yt is impossible, and I will not stay yow an hower. God in heaven blesse yow, and send me once among men ; for these are monsters. The trouble and falce hartednes of our owne I will trample on in tyme. Yow know nott these men nor, I hope, never shall. The God of heaven again and againe blesse yow and all your fleet.

[PS.] I wish nott that the *Ann* wayt upon the Princes ship outward, though she goe nott to Dabull, butt loose her and leave hir to her fortune, and that they know that their detention of our goods was the cause, and that we will nott doe them courtesye for such usadge. Yf we doe, they will yearely practice ytt.

To the Agent and Factors at Surat.[1]
(I.O. Records : *O.C.*, No. 645.)

Crowda, April 26 [1618],
Sunday night, if the raynes have not washt away a day.
Your coppie and letter I received tonight att Crowda. By myne yesterday yow will know I mett your two servants and missed myne, but now have all I expected. Your offer to meet mee shortens all answers. I shalbe att Baroch, God willing, on Tewsday night, not resting att Uncleseare,[2] because my tents must attende passage. Yow shalbe welcome to the

---

[1] Jahāngīr, accompanied by his son Khurram, left Ahmadābād on 10 Feb. 1618 for Agra, intending to take Māndu on his way ; but at the beginning of April, when he had got a little beyond Dohad, he abandoned the journey, on account of the heat, and returned to Ahmadābād, which was reached on the 17th of the month. Roe's movements are more difficult to follow. On 16 Feb. he was at Ahmadābād, preparing to follow the Emperor ; and four days later he was still there, for at that date Jahāngīr's letter to King James was delivered to him (see Appendix B). On 10 March he was at Broach ; and now on 26 April we find him (on his way back from Burhānpur to Broach) at ' Crowda,' which was probably Kathodara, a little village 15 miles N.N.E. of Surat, on the road from Burhānpur to Broach *via* Māndvi. Some light is thrown on the matter by an entry in Biddulph's accounts (f. 15), from which we learn that a quantity of broadcloth, hides, etc., was carried at this time from Ahmadābād to Burhānpur and back, but that, ' before wee came neere the Kinge, he was retorned, and His Lordshipp retorned from whence hee came.' From this it may be surmised that, since Jahāngīr was proceeding (as before) by a devious route through rough country over which laden carts could not easily travel, the ambassador judged it best to take the goods by the ordinary roads through Broach to Burhānpur and thence to Māndu to meet the court there. At Burhānpur he would learn of Jahāngīr's change of plan, which necessitated his own return to Ahmadābād. It has been thought best not to overcrowd the map of Roe's journeyings by including this excursion ; but no difficulty will be experienced in following it.

[2] Ankleswar, on the south bank of the Narbadā, opposite Broach.

remaynes of my wine. I forgott not to trie the pearles, but finde the price as farr below the courte as the proffitt of laying out mony two months will aske. I will not consente that yow pay Isack Beage a *pice* of any new dewty nor ould, if unjuste. Bid him, if hee dare, tell the Prince I will have right for all injuries, and that uppon his shipp.

Mr. Steele doubtlesse hath had a fall. His owne wayes were enemye enough. He followed mee to Brampoore,[1] and receaved once more good councell. I pittie him, whether he take it or no.

I perceave your latter servant carried a good supplie number one, and that yow have passed a better by Amadavaz. Though uppon creditt, yow have taken a course that will in your comodetie only helpe, pay your intreste, besides the imployment now in best season. I have not heard from Agra since the second bills I sent for their debts acknowledged receaved. Yours firste by Amadavaz were new written, returned by their owne two expressers that brought their accounts downe. I doubt not come safe, and suppose that in my packetts yours are miscaried. I dessigned him to direct to Amadavaz, because that factorie would beste know my wayes, and I heard of one uppon the way, that is gone to Mandoe. Muddo [Madho] will returne within tenn dayes to Amadavaz, I truste with good newes of Gods mercy to them.

I sent Sprage to Gulchanda uppon good reasons.[2] Itt had bene fitter hee had gone sooner, and in my opynnyon Mr. Saltbanke should have procecuted my order, which was indeede more needefull then the Red Sea without my knowledge. I could not conceave that there was any neede of more helpe att Agra, when yow lessened one of the number I appoynted and yow consented to sende thether. Whensoever hee goes, I am sure hee can serve no other turne then come downe with a *caffila*. His merchandiz I have tryed, and yow have seene his writeing. Hee will returne tyme enough for that hee is fitt. Captain Shilling hath neyther bill nor coppie of the debts,[3] butt a letter written to mee to forbeare two months (now four

[1] Steel had set out from Ahmadābād after the Emperor, but on the way quarrelled with the official who had been told off to look after him and his workmen, with the result that his camels were taken away and he was left to shift for himself (*English Factories*, 1618-21, p. 60).

[2] The object of Sprage's mission was the same as in the previous year, viz., the recovery of the debt due from the fugitive Persian (p. 366). His subsequent adventures may be followed in *The English Factories*, 1618-21.

[3] The Persian's debt, which was to be recovered from any Dābhol vessel met with.

expired). If wee bee paid, itt is worth labour ; if nott, itt will justefie any reprisall, because wee have demaunded justice. If both, wee are once aforehand, which wee were never with a Moore. Mr. Fettiplace is of opynnyon it had bene recovered if prossecuted laste yeare ; and soe am I.

I hope soe soone to meete as that I neede say nothing of the teeth ; but I wish yow remember no price will recompence the stay of our fleete for three fourths ladeing. Six months day is not for us ; but if yow were sure of mony att three, I am sure of creditt, if Fetteplace live.

When your advices come from the south [*i.e.* from Bantam] I pray send me full coppies, and soe I shalbe att large informed.

That I had a full parte of the raynes my laste will signifie ; but the domage of the cloth yow neede nott feare, though the merchants were in a house. I saw itt thatched. If that gone for Agra [1] had such another as I attendeing, it might bee drie in a ryver.

I hope to meete yow within two dayes, to laugh away my journy ; till when God keepe yow.

I pray you bring the coppie of this with yow, for I am weary.[2]

[1] In view of the Emperor's departure for Agra, a large consignment of broadcloth and hides was dispatched thither from Ahmadābād on 23 Feb. 1618, under the charge of John Young and John Bangham (Biddulph's accounts, ff. 13, 14).

[2] From this date we hear nothing more of Roe until August. One incident of the time, has, however, been preserved for us by Terry (p. 242), viz., an outbreak of disease, from which the English suffered considerably. Jahāngīr, who, as well as Shāh Jahăn, was laid up with it, says (in his *Memoirs*, vol. ii. p. 10) that although widespread it was not generally fatal. ' The city Amadavar,' says Terry, ' (at our being there with the King) was visited with this pestilence in the month of May, and our family was not exempted from that most incomfortable visitation ; for within the space of nine dayes seven persons that were English of our family were taken away by it ; and none of those which dyed lay sick above twenty houres, and the major part well and sick and dead in twelve houres, as our surgeon (who was there all the physician we had), and he led the way, falling sick at mid-day and the following mid-night dead. And there were three more that followed him, one immediately after the other, who made as much hast to the grave as he had done. . . . All those that died in our family of this pestilence had their bodyes set all on fire by it, so soon as they were first visited, and when they were dying, and dead, broad spots of a black and blew colour appeared on their breasts ; and their flesh was made so extreme hot by their most high distemper that we who survived could scarce endure to keep our hands upon it. It was a most sad time, a fiery

TRANSLATE OF THE FIRMAN FOR COJA ARABS HOUSE IN
SURATT, SENT DOWNE 3D AUGUST, 1618.[1]

(I.O. Records : *O.C.*, No. 675.)

There hath come to us a petition from the English resident in Suratt : that there was a house belonging to Coja-Arab Turbethee,[2] lying in Suratt, for the which the sayd English have, as they affirme, given mony for the tyme of three yeares to the people of Coja Arab, and accordingly have taken a writing in testemony of the same of the sayd Coja Arab or his assignes. [Whereof ?] take knowledge ; and if it bee so, and that the owner of the sayd house bee content that the English shall

trial indeed. . . . All our family (my Lord Ambassadour only excepted) were visited with this sickness ; and we all, who through Gods help and goodnes outlived it, had many great blisters, fild with a thick yellow watry substance, that arose upon many parts of our bodyes, which, when they brake, did even burn and corrode our skins, as it ran down upon them.'

What the particular form of disease was cannot be determined. Col. D. G. Crawford, in his *History of the Indian Medical Service* (vol. i. p. 44), notes that it was evidently not cholera and that the symptoms described do not correspond with those of the plague in its modern form.

Speaking generally of such experiences, Terry says (p. 244) : ' Death made many breaches into my Lord Ambassadors family ; for of four and twenty wayters [*i.e.* attendants], besides his secretary and my self, there was not above the fourth man returned home. And he himself by violent fluxes was twice brought even to the very brink of the grave.'

Terry also mentions (p. 380) that while at Ahmadābād he witnessed the spectacle of a malefactor being stung to death by snakes. On this see the *Memoirs*, vol. i. p. 453.

[1] This transcript is in Roe's own hand. In *Home Miscellaneous* 628 (No. ix.) will be found a copy (made in 1789) of an earlier order from Afzal Khān, dated 13 July, 1618, in these words : ' Whereas I wrote you to take Coja Arab's house for the Prince, being anciently his mint house, and to give the English another, I will you to give them as good a house as that, such as may content them, and to use them like friends ; and in no case to let them be unprovided of a house to remove unto.'

The dwelling here referred to had been hired for three years from Khwāja Arab in the middle of 1616 (*Letters Received*, vol. v. p. 74). Apparently he had now died, and the house had escheated to the Prince, who had decided to turn out the English factors.

[2] Probably Tūrbati, *i.e.* of Tūrbat (perhaps Tūrbat-i-Haidarī, in N.E. Persia).

remayne and abide in the sayd house, then is it our pleasure that they abide in the sayd house ; but if the sayd English have not payd or given the sayd rent aforehand for the tyme of three yeares, but that they remayne therin by force, contrarie to his likinge, upon receipt hereof yow shall putt the sayd English foorth therof and deli[ver   ] therof into the hands of the sonne of the sayd [   ] therof according to his will ; and in lieu therof shall [give the ?] sayd English another fitt house, such as shalbe to their content ; and hereof signifie unto mee the answere of the premises.

ARTICLES PROPOSED TO THE PRINCE SULTAN CORONNE, LORD OF AMADAVAZ AND SURATT, BY THE AMBASSADOR, UPON THE BREACH WITH THE PORTUGALLS, AUGUST 15, 1618.[1]

(I.O. Records : *O.C.*, No. 678.)

1. That the Prince had received the English nation into his protection and favour, and had concluded peace and ametie with them, according to the command of the Great Kyng, and hereby doth give notice to all his Governor, Leiutenant and other officers of Suratt and all his other signories, to pu[b]lish the same and to obey it.

2. In consideration of this treaty, and that the Portugalls are common enemies to their peace and traficque, it shalbe lawfull for the English to land with their armes and to pass with them for defence of their persons and goods ; and if the sayd Portugalls should attempt any thing by sea agaynst the sayd English or the ships of the Kyng and Prince, that then the Governors of Suratt should deliver to the English as many frigatts as they should need for their mutuall succor, and in all poynts of releeve and succour should assist them as frends and as the naturalls of these kyngdomes.

3. That it should bee lawfull for the English to buy or hyre any house in his ports, where they might quiettly dwell and no man to disturbe or displace them ; and therin house their goods sufficiently and safely ; and that neyther Governor nor other officer should entermeddle neyther with them nor their goods, but, in case they were not or could not of them selves provide sufficient housing, that then the Governor should assist them and procure for them a safe and quiett habitation.

[1] In Roe's own hand. Endorsed : ' Articles and treaty with the Prince, Amad., August, 1618.' The occasion of the ' breach with the Portugalls ' is not clear, but possibly it arose from the dispute described in the Surat letter quoted later (p. 485). From this it would appear that the Indians for a time resisted the payment claimed for the *cartaz* of the Gogo junk, and ' made greate shew off warrs.'

4. That the Governor of Suratt and other officers should receive and dispeed the English ambassador with honor and curtesie, and see him well housed during his stay in Suratt, and that he [be ?] offered no force nor affront to him nor to any of his servants, but they might live, goe, and pass at their pleasure.

5. And if it should fall out that they could not agree with the owner for the house they now resided in, having paid mony before hand, the Governor should cause the remayner to bee repayd to the sayd English.

6. That it should bee lawfull for the sayd English to land any sort of goods and to relade, at their pleasure ; and upon the land in any part to trade, traficque, buy and sell according to their owne will ; and that the judges and officers of the *alfandicaes* should not deteyne their goods longer then to take account and to agree for customes as by former treaty, and therin should give them dispatch, and in no sort nor upon any pretence should stay or take by force or deteyne any of their goods contrarie to the owners will, nor should doe them any injurie or violence whatsoever ; and that for jewells, pearles and all sorts of that nature they should demand no custome nor duty ; and that upon the wayes to and from their ports no exaction or duty should be taken nor demanded, but only at their port, according to custome.

7. That the sayd English might live in their owne houses and among them selves according to their owne religion and lawes, and for that respect no Governor, *Kazy*, nor other should doe them any affront nor in any sort trouble or molest them.

8. That if any quarrell or other controversie whatsoever did arise among the English, that the Governors nor any other officers should not intermeddle, but leave it wholy to the president of their owne nation ; and if any English did escape or flye away from their obedience and service, the Governors should assist to take and deliver him into the hands and power of the English to doe in all thing[s] among themselves justice according to their owne lawes ; but that in case any difference of what kynd soever happened betweene the English and any Moore or *Banyan*, the Governors and other officers in their place should take notice and doe justice according to the offence or complaynt of eyther syde.

9. That the linguist and brokars serving the English should have free libertye to speake and deliver any thing in the behalfe of their masters, and should have licence to bargayne, traficque, sell, or buy for them, and to doe them any other service ; and for such occasion should not bee subject to any question or account, nor any way prohibited nor molested.

10. That all presents beeing showed at the custome house, that the officers might avoyd deceipt, beeing *chopped* by both

parts, should bee delivered to the hands of the English to send to the court at their pleasure.

11. That in all causes of complaynt or controversie the Governors and *Kazies* of the place should doe them speedy justice and protect them from all injuries or oppressions whatsoever, and should ayd and entreat them as frends with curtesie and honor; for that so it is the command of the Great Kyng, who hath given them his securitie, and that therfore it pleaseth the Prince to make declaration and confirmation of the sayd treaty by this writing, agaynst which no man shall presume to doe contrarie.

written under-neath :

That which I demand is bare justice and which no man can deny that hath a hart cleare and enclined to right, and no more then the lawes of nations doth freely give to all strangers that arrive, without any contract; and in no case so much as the Great Kyng doth promise and command. If it please the Prince to confirme these articles freely and without ill meaning or collusion and to command that they bee obeyed precisely, I shall rest content and shall give satisfaction to my master and to my nation; but if not, and that any part bee refused or written fraudulently, according to former experiences, then I desire the Prince to take knowledge that I wilbe free of my woord given the Great Kyng in his presence and of all blame or inconvenience that may happen after it, having given promese upon these conditions or els to bee at liberty.

After almost three yeares experience of the pride and falshood of these people, that attended only advantage and were governed by privat interest and appetite, I was forced to relinquish many poynts often insisted upon, when I could gett nothing, and to make offer of these few as the most necessarie to settle a trade and which might give the least offence and might pass with ease, leaving the rest to the generall order of the Kyng to receive justice from our procurador generall; and therfore seemed content and delivered it up to the Princes *Divon* for consideration and answere; who excepted almost agaynst all, or agaynst all that might serve to give us ease. But after many disputes I went to the Prince and had there read and discussed the articles as followeth :

To the first, it was wholy agreed unto.

To the second, to lend us frigatts was agreed unto, but more for the defence and bringing in of their owne ship then for good will to us; yet it passed sufficient for both. But in no case would the Prince consent that wee might land or weare armes in Suratt. First, they offered mee and my servants liberty; after, for ten merchants, and to more would not yeild, but that they should leave their armes in the custome house to bee delivered at returne. They instanced the disorder and quarreling of our people, the offering to take Suratt, anno 1616, the erecting a bell, and many woords given out that the English would fortefie their house or surprise the castle, with many more foolish jealousies arising from our owne faults. So that I consented, to cleare all, to the grant of ten at a tyme and the merchants residing, on condition that other articles were granted sufficient for our securitie, and that our people going in defence of their goods to any other inland cytty might pass with their armes for their guard agaynst theeves and exactions upon the way.

To the third, it was absolutly refused upon no conditions that wee should buy or build a house, nor hyre none neare the castle or upon the water ; but that wee should have given us in the cytty, in convenient place, a good, strong and sufficient house, one or more as wee needed, wher wee should live for our rent, as wee could agree, and no man should putt us out ; and that the Governor should see us furnished and provided of such habitation to our owne liking.

To the fourth, it was fully agreed unto.

To the fifth, it was agreed unto ; but withall they declared that that house of Coja Arab wee should not have upon any conditions ; first, because our earnest sute gave them suspition; next, because it was the ancient mynt ; thirdly, because it stood agaynst their great *mesquite*, and offended the Moores, especially our people pissing rudely and doing other filthines against the walls, to the dislike of the Mahometans, who with reverence reguard their holy places ; lastly, because there was a rumor that wee ment to surprise the said *mesquite* and being of stone and flatt at the topp it was supposed that wee intended to make [it ?] our fort and to annoy the castle therefrom ; which though it was a most frivoulous, idle, impossible suspition, yet they averring it arose from som rash speeches of some of our owne, they would not yeild ; and that, seeing they offered us the choyce of all the towne, wee could show no materiall reason why only that house would serve us.

To the sixt, it was fully agreed unto.

To the sevventh, it was [a]greed unto.

To the eight, it was agreed unto that in causes of difference among ourselves it should wholy bee referred to the English ; but in case the controversie were with More or Gentile, it should bee referred to the Governor or officers proper to doe justice. But to deliver up any English that fled, it was refused, upon pretence if they turned Moore they could not refuse them protection ; to which I replyed that wee would never consent that any should leave his fayth, for under that coulor they might robb us of all our goods. After much contention it was yeilded unto, because I utterly refused all if that libertye were left to any ill-mynded person.

To the ninth, it was fully agreed unto.

To the 10, it was agreed unto, the presents beeing opened and seene (that under coulor of them the Prince should not bee deceived of his rights) and sealed, should bee delivered to the English. But they added that if the sayd pretended presents were not given, that then in future tymes they should eyther pay custome or not bee delivered to the English; which, though most base, and in our power to give any or none, I consented too; but especially because ells I could have nothing, for these presents trouble all our busines.

To the 11, it was agreed unto.

Having thus gotten what I could, a draught was made to this effect and given to the secretarie writer of *firmans* to bee digested into forme, and was sealed and sent unto mee. But comming to reade yt, I found prohibition to land with any sort of armes, nor no English in Suratt to weare swoord, dagger, or other weapon but a knife, my selfe only excepted and nine that I would nominate as my servants, and in all other poynts with the like falshood and show of wicked cunning malice, not once mentioning free trade nor libertye upon the way to pass without exactions, nor any other poynt faythfully sett downe according to meaning and good intention, but mixed with exceptions and cavills to bring us into more danger and trouble. I had taken leave of Kyng and Prince [1] and could not come to complayne without leave, and they would also know or feare my intention that should aske yt, and so hynder mee. Wherupon I sent backe the *firmaen*, utterly refusing it, and withall these reasons ensuing:

First, that for this unwoorthy suspition of our ill intents to disarme us utterly, it was a signe of no frendship, good meaning, nor favour toward us, and for no respect I would take any so disho[no]rable conditions, but keepe our armes and use them agaynst our enemies or any that should wrong us. Neyther could I see the face of my soveraygne lord the Kyng of England and report to him I had made peace with the Ghehangier, who had given us full libertye of trade, and to that effect had written his lettres, and at the same instance bee contradicted by an under treaty with the Prince, for that one of these must needes seeme false and counterfayt; and the later most unjust and such as our enemies could show no more malice; that eyther wee would be frends as wee ought to bee, or enemies declared. How could I command my countrimen to draw their swoords in defence of the Kyngs and Princes

[1] This seems to show that the negotiations were prolonged well into September.

ships at sea, which I had promised, when the Prince will not suffer them to weare their armes for their owne defence ? That my nation were men and reguardfull of their honor, and would never obey mee that had so neglected them, nor doe any service for them that so mistrusted and disgraced them. That in the tymes of peace with the Portugalls they never demanded nor offered any such condition ; nor yet did command the like unto the Hollanders,[1] who were crept in and offered no service nor assistance to the Kyng, and who in all parts sought to gett footing and to build forts, as was experienced in Mesolapatan, Belligate,[2] the Moluccaes and other places, but that the English never desired nor needed any such retraicts, but came in peace to traficque in all these parts as merchants under the protection of the kyngs or lords of the same. That hereby wee were exposed unto the power of all theeves and robbers on the wayes ; wee passing yearly to Amadavaz and other parts with great summes of mony and goods, could not keepe them, in a countrie so ill governed, with knives ; and that it was an infinite shame and scorne to the Prince to feare that a few men could surprise or take so populous a cytty as Suratt, and build forts in an hower, especially wee having many pledges of our fayth and good meaning in so many parts of Indya by the residence of our people and goods, one of whose lives wee would not loose for 1000 Mores. Lastly, that all other poynts agreed unto were left out or falsifyed utterly, which demonstrated ill meaning toward us ; and that it was more honorable to deale clearly and to prohibitt us all trade, giving us license to depart ; which now I only desired, and I would soone contract our people, or settle them in Goga and Cambaya, under the protection of the Kyng, whose gratious grants were to us sufficient securitie and under whom wee were assured to live in safety ; for upon no tearmes I would eyther accept this *firman* or stay in the port of Suratt, nor goe downe to yt, but seeke another way to ship my selfe, and after to doe that which was reason ; recalling the promise and woord I had given before the Kyng, and did make protestation that I was guiltless of all the evill that might succeed by this unfaythfull dealing.

To this I added a commission sent to the next fleete to disarme all the shipps and frigatts of the Princes ports (as appears by the coppy), which I translated into Persian and sent with these former reasons and protestations to the Princes officers and the originall to Suratt to bee published there ; and left *firmaen* and all these in the hands of Afzull Chan.

[1] ' Upon this was sent a *firmaen* to disarme the Hollanders, and that none of them in Suratt might wear armes, nor other Christian.'— *Marginal note by Roe.*

[2] Pulicat, on the Coromandel coast, seems to be intended.

AGREEMENT WITH KHURRAM

A day after, new consultation was called ; and in the night I was sent for and had lardge dispute upon all particulars, pronoun[cing] that, if any woord were written of disarming us, I would refuse [it ?] and if all the mentioned conditions were not clearly granted I would proceed according to the declaration made. At last Afzull Chan freely confessed the truth, that the *firmaen* was written with no good meaning, showing their feares more at lardge ; and wee came to agreement that the clause of disarming should bee left out on their parts, but that I should covenant that our people should not land in hostile manner to annoy the peace, and many other articles which appears by my contract given [1] ; which was urdged in respect of the *Ann* in the Red Sea, who had well followed directions, and was the only cause which drew these to agreement, showing them the way to seeke justice. Upon my agreement and covenant to which articles demanded on their part, and after many intricate and perplexed disputes, a new draught was made of all my demands, and anew agreed unto, with promise that, now they had received satisfaction by my reasons and opening the course of our trade and intents, they would satisfy the Prince and procure

[1] No contemporary copy of this contract has been preserved. There is, however, at the India Office (*Home Miscellaneous*, vol. 628, No. xii.), what appears (though this is not certain) to be a transcript of it, made in 1789, which runs as follows :

'The cause of this writing is that Sir Thomas Roe, ambassador of the King of England, hath given his word and faith for the business underwritten in certain articles that it shall be accordingly performed.

'First, that the English shall not build any house in or about Suratt without leave obtained of the King ; but only hire a convenient house for their merchants and merchandise, in which they shall abide till their ships arrive. Moreover, that no goods that come in the ships, that may serve for the King's use, be hid or concealed from the officers of the haven of Suratt. And for such things as the Governor will buy for the King's pleasure, if they cannot agree upon the price, they [shall ?] be sealed up with the officers' seal and sent to the court to the English there residing, who shall shew them to the King, and if he shall like them they shall agree of price. Further, that no man shall touch or open any of those things that shall be brought for presents to the King or Prince ; but that they shall be brought untouched to the English ambassador at the court to deliver to the King. Lastly, that during the abode of the English at Suratt they shall do no wrong or hurt to any, but shall pay the dues and customs agreed on heretofore ; and on these conditions it shall be lawful for them to come and go freely, in the same manner as the King's subjects or other Christians that abide there.' *Endorsed* : ' Articles required by Sultan Coronne, and signed by me.'

confirmation with loyall and true meaning, and that, all jealousies layd aside and forgotton on both parts, wee should live in full quiett and peace and bee received as frends, and justice done in all our occasions; with many protestations of fayth and complements, not to bee hoped after in performance.

The next day, Afzull Chan sent to mee that he had acquaynted the Prince at lardge with this conference and the contract on my part, which had given him satisfaction, and that he had commanded to give me a *firmaen* according to my desire, and professed fayth and good observance in all poynts; desired that I would make ready that on my part under my seale; and to show his true dealing had therwith sent me a draught of the new *firmaen*, which the Prince had yeilded too, with a warrant sealed to the secretarie to pass it accordingly: and that now I might bee assured of good meaning. And it was the first tyme that ever I could gett sight of any *firmaen* before it was passd, they alwayes giving what they please.

I caused this draft to bee translated, and found it according to promise, effectuall in most poynts according to their formes and stile, and no materiall thing left out, and written clearly and rightly, only some clause inserted, not much to purpose, for which I was not willing to have a new brawle, and the Prince gone. I tooke one coppy and sent the other to the secretarie with warrant to pass yt.[1]

[1] Jahāngīr left Ahmadābād for Agra early in September, 1618, and in the same month Roe took his departure for Surat—probably about the 26th, on which date a payment to him is entered in Biddulph's books. One incident of the journey down is mentioned by Terry (p. 182). Near Baroda the party was assailed about midnight by a band of robbers, who were, however, met with so sturdy a resistance that they quickly disappeared. At Surat the ambassador seems to have been treated with respect, and a suitable dwelling assigned to him, in accordance with the 'articles' given above; for Terry, after describing (p. 201) the pleasant abodes of the native functionaries, with their gardens, tanks, and bathing-places, adds: 'in such a garden-house, with all those accommodations about it, my Lord Ambassadour lay with his company at Surat the last three moneths before he left East India.'

Egerton MS. 2086 (Brit. Mus.) contains at ff. 47, 49 and 50, three letters of Roe's which belong to this period. The first and longest, dated 14 Dec. 1618, is apparently addressed to Brown at Ahmadābād. The second is written to Capt. Bonner (the commander of the 1618 fleet, which had arrived on 20 Sept.), and bears date the 16th of the same month. The third is to Heynes, reproving him for being 'so busy a factor for all men,' and not attending more to the Company's business; this is dated 17 December. Apparently all three were signed by Roe, but only in the case of the first has the signature

To the Governor of Mokha.
(I.O. Records : *O. C.*, No. 755.)

Honorable and Great Governor of the Port of Mocha, Raja Baga [Rajab Āghā], health and greeting.

I received your honourable lettres [1] with much joy by the hands of Joseph Salbanck and Edward Heynes, who doe give great testemonie of your noble disposition and good affection to our nation, wherin yow showe your selfe to bee a woorthy and discreet man. Ther hath alway beene good respondence and ametye betweene His Majestie of England and the Grand Sinior, and it is reason all their good subjects should by all meanes maynteyne it ; and wheras entercourse and trafique is the principall bond of ametye, wee doe desier on our parts to resort yearly to your port, ther to trade in love and frendship as honest merchants, not doubting but yow will confirme the priviledges by yow last yeare granted [2] and procure the like and more ample from the Grand Sinior and his Viceroy the honourable Pashaw of Synan [Sana], wherby wee may bee encouraged to bring yow all sorts of comodities, as well from Europe as spices from the sowthard and cloth from India, by which meanes your port wilbe more famous and become the mart of all Asia ; and this I promise yow in the honor of His Majestie of England that wee meane faythfully to performe and to keepe your seaes and ports from all troubles to our uttmost, and not to molest nor doe injurie to any people or merchants your allies trading to your port (the Portugalls, our utter enemies, only excepted), but to maynteyne with yow a firme and true leauge. According to your desier, I have sent unto yow the same men that last yeare were with yow, desieringe yow to receive them as frends and to suffer them quiettly upon the conditions agreed on to land their goods and to sell them and reship themselves at their pleasure. Herein yow shall doe according to your honourable

escaped destruction. Their mutilated state makes them difficult to decipher, but they seem to contain nothing of importance.

One or two minor incidents of Roe's stay at Surat are referred to on p. 485, and in the extracts from the Court Minutes given in the previous edition.

[1] Brought back by the *Anne* in her voyage the previous year. The letter, for which see *The English Factories*, 1618-21, p. 44, assures Roe of the Governor's wish to be friends with the English nation and to afford them every advantage for trade. It was accordingly arranged that the *Lion* should be despatched to Mokha, and she sailed (carrying the above letter) in company with the *Anne* and the rest of Bonner's fleet on February 17.

[2] See *op. cit.*, p. 33.

name and procure great proffitt and quiett to your port. The great God of Heaven and Earth make your honor to encrease.

From Suratt, February 16, in the yeare of Jesus the Sonne of God 1618[-19].

THE FACTORS AT SURAT TO THE COMPANY.[1]
(I.O. Records : *O. C.*, No. 777.)

Surat, the 12th March, 1618[-19].

... Per the *Bull* wee certefie[d] you directlie and truly the tearmes itt [our residence] then stood on ; which since as per coppies of our registers per the *Ann* (wherto for more ample relacion of sundrie affairs wee referred you) you will perceave the poore remedie wee have receaved, not only of our former injuries butt many others since ; and therby alsoe bee ascertained of the meane grace His Lordship stood in with this King and Prince, that, after three yeares attendance, att his departure by earnest intercession could not procure the guifte of a house nor ground nor lycence to build us a habitation nor soe much as continue us in this, from whence (our tyme neerely expired) wee shortly expect to bee remooved. Wee have already sought oute and obteyned from the owner another ; but these cheefes will not consente wee shall have any nere the waterside ; and elcewhere, in the inner parte of the towne, there is not any strong nor for us conveniente, excepte such as belonge to *bannyanes*, who will nott lett them. Soe where to be accomodated, as yett wee know nott.

The depts remayning at courte and manner of His Lordships lycence you have no doubt receaved relation from then [*sic*] presente. What hee heather brought for the establishing of your trade (his capitulations refused, as per our laste advised [2]) was only a *firmaen* from the King [3] and another from the Prince; the first gennerall, for our reception and continuation in his domynnyons, as many others (more ample) heeretofore receaved ; the latter particuler for this porte of Suratt. The

---

[1] Roe left Surat in Captain Shilling's vessel, the *Anne*, on 17 Feb. 1619 (*O.C.*, No. 817).

This parting shot from Kerridge and his associates (Biddulph, Rastell, and Giles James) is given partly because it shows their continued hostility to Roe, in spite of his endeavours to smooth over previous differences, and partly because it mentions one or two additional particulars of the events of his stay at Surat.

[2] See *The English Factories*, 1618-21, p. 59. The passage contains no additional information.

[3] Cf. p. 506. This *farmān* is not extant.

fruicts which both have produced you may please to perceave by your goods detention these six months in customehouse and yett unreleaced, and our dwelling uppon every triviall humor subject to change; wherof, att his coming to Suratt, discerning the discomodoties, hee endeavored by letters and presents to the King, Prince and nobillity to releeve us, and receaved another *firmaen* from the Prince to as little purpose as the former, wherby itt is evident they have commaunds of sundrie kindes and know which to obay; otherwise the Princes se[c]uritye could not be jested with by his servants. The consideration and laste tryall wherof caused a cleerer sight of the omission paste, and himselfe to propose the juncks detention next yeare, wherin by reason of the many difficulties beeing opposed, hee lefte itt to the discretion off councell (if not releeved in the premises), whoe will not easilie bee induced to attempt itt without expresse order from Your Worships to warrant itt, aswell for the affiance you had in His Lordships wisedome, who, though hee had authoritie, could not bee induced therto himselfe, as the Kings present remote residence,[1] which perhapps through the stoping of your buisnesse err the questions decyded might cause many inconveniences and expose the actors to more then is convenient for them to hasard. Itt may please you therfore well to consider this pointe. The debts are unlikely to be soone recovered, and these are a people that curbd wilbe brought to any reason and if suffered in their owne wayys grow insolente and insupportable, which they excersise not on the Portingalls, that incroacheth asmuch on them, permitt none of their shipps to saele without lesence, and even now since the *Anns* departure have forced the Goga junck, appertaineing to the beloved Queene, to pay them 65000 *mamoodes* for custome to the porte of Dieu (an antient dutie), which, striveing to infringe, loste her voyage the laste yeare, and made greate shew off warrs, yett after much contention have submitted againe to the yoake....

In this shipp [the *Anne*] is returned Sir Thomas Roe, to whom wee have delivered a box sealed, maled and covered, containing the accoumpts, letters and registers and invoeces and sundrie other writeings, both from this and the Agra factory, directed unto Your Worships, which wee hope hee will safely deliver in the same condition; others of your servants, distrusting that convayance,[2] have delivered theirs to Captain Shilling, master of the shipp.

[1] Jahāngīr, on leaving Ahmadābād, proceeded to Fatehpur Sīkri, near Agra, and thence, in October, 1619, started for Kashmīr.

[2] The innuendo shows the malignant feelings with which Roe was regarded by the factors.

In His Lordships company is alsoe gone home Gabriell Towreson and Richard Steele, his wife, and Mrs. Huddson [1]. . . .

ROE TO THE PRESIDENT AT BANTAM.[2]

(Public Record Office : *State Papers, Holland*, vol. 95, 29 May, 1620.)

Coppy of the writing I gave to Fredericque Hoftman to bee delivered to the President of the English in East Indya.

Sir,
Meeting here with Fredericque Hoftman, admirall of a fleete of eleven ships of Holland bound for Bantam, but now two only in company, of good force and well manned, the rest disperced on the coast of England, wee have had some con-

---

[1] Mrs. Towerson had elected to remain behind with her relatives, and she afterwards gave some trouble to the Agra factors by her applications for the loan of money until her husband's return. He, however, had evidently no intention of rejoining her, for in January, 1620, he sought for and obtained employment as a principal factor for the Moluccas. As already mentioned, while holding this post he was executed by the Dutch at Amboyna, in February, 1623.

Steel, his projects having completely failed, had judged it best to return. His reception by the Company was a cold one, for ' he was much condemned for his unworthie carriage abroad, having perfourmed nothing that was intended and resolvd of at his departure, but hath brought home a great private trade, put the Company to an extraordinarye charge by a wife and children, and wrongd my Lord Embassador by a false and surmised contestation and arrogating a higher title and place to himself then ever was intended ' (*Court Minutes*, 17 Sept. 1619). His offers of service in October, 1623, were declined ; but later on he was more successful, and in January, 1626, was once again in the employment of the Company. He desired to return to the scene of his former employment, but was sent instead to Bantam. The last fact recorded concerning him is a resolution of the court, in 1627, to recall him for private trading.

Mrs. Hudson also came in for censure, as she, after going out at the Company's expense and living in India in their house for five months, had brought home a considerable amount of private trade. However, after some delay, she was allowed, by the intercession of her friends, to have her goods on payment of thirty pounds for freight.

[2] Printed in the *Calendar of State Papers (East Indies)*, 1617-21, Preface, p. xxxi. This letter, written from the Cape, explains itself. Roe's action in thus advising the factors at Bantam of the negotiations proceeding in London between the Dutch and English was

ference about the bad humors begunn betwixt us in Indya. Hee professeth affections of peace and that he hath no instructions to the contrarie and avoweth the arrivall and reception of the States commissionars in England to treat an accord. Wee have agreed mutually to send our advices, I to you by him, he to his Generall by the *Beare*, of what wee heare and that it is probable an union wilbe made ; hereby on both sides to prevent, if possible, any farther occasions which will not bee so easely quenched. If you fynd in effect as much as he professeth, a man of his place and authoritye may much advance our desires, so it may bee done with due respects of honor and the Companies service. So I committ yow to God.

THO. ROE.

Master Barwicke,[1] Admirall of two good ships, the *Beare* and *Starr*, ready to depart, the 11 May, 1619.

commended by the Company ' for a very wise and worthy course ' (*Court Minutes*, 17 Sept. 1619). His earnest wish for the settlement of the differences between the two nations is reflected in a letter from Van Ravesteyn (the Dutch chief at Surat) to his employers, under date of 4/14 Feb. 1619 (I.O. Records : *Hague Transcripts*, series 1, vol. iii. No. cxv.). After mentioning Roe's courtesy to him, both at Ahmadābād and at Surat, he says : ' I found him a very peace-loving man, who is very sorry for the differences between us and the English, and would gladly see an agreement arrived at ' ; Roe has asked him to write to recommend the settlement of these troubles, and has undertaken, for his own part, to do his utmost to bring this about. Another letter to the same effect from Van Ravesteyn to Batavia, dated 12/22 Feb. 1619, has been printed by Dr. Terpstra (p. 221). In this he speaks of Roe as being well known in Holland and well inclined towards the Dutch.

A letter from Tiku, dated 10 Nov. 1619 (*O.C.*, No. 822), states that ' my Lord Row would have taken two Flemishe shipps, had not Master Barwicke informed My Lord that some of the Committees told him at Gravesend that he mighte boldly reporte that Your Worships and the Flemings were agreed ' ; and another letter from the same place and of the same date (*O.C.*, No. 821) says that ' had nott those in the *Beare* perswaded Sir Thomas Roe that peace was concluded with the Hollanders, hee had resolved to have taken four [*sic*] Holland shipps att the Cape, which hee might easily have done, they comming in butt one and one, wee having three good shipps well manned in the roade.' It is, however, highly improbable that any such action was contemplated by the ambassador ; nor does his letter bear out the statement that Barwick had made him believe that peace was actually concluded.

[1] The commander of the *Bear*, to whom a copy of this letter was entrusted for delivery. The original, as above stated, was given to

[1619]

Roe to the East India Company.[1]

(I.O. Records: *Factory Records, Miscellaneous*, vol. i, p. 12.)

Arivall of the *Ann* into Plymouth from Surratt. She was 17 daies beating up in the Sowndings with contrarie windes. Their biskett badd, dirt, and rotten.[2] She was 12 weekes comyng from St. Hellena. He settled the priviledges, and left all things in good order at Surrat at his comyng away. He bringeth a letter and a present to our Kings Majestie from the Great Magull. He resetled trade in Persia. He hath setled a more proffitable trade in Mocha then anie you have, and sent the *Lyon* thither. The benefit of Mocha trade related, to vend there 100,000*li.* a yere at 100 per cent. proffitt. The *Expedition* sent to lade 300 tonn of pepper contracted for. He procured the Magoll to banish all the Portugales from all his portes, but contynued not. They met the *Beare* and *Starr* at the Cape, who for Bantam, and the *Ann* for London, sett saile from the Cape the 15 of May. The *Anns* navigation from the Cape. Arived at St. Hellena 1 June; sett saile from thence the 6 June, and arrived at Plymouth 29 August. A report at St. Helena of the fight between the Inglish and Holland fleetes at Bantam.[3] The bringing home of Steele and his wife, of Mrs. Hudson, with the reasons of the same.

the Dutch admiral, who handed to Roe in return a similar notification to be transmitted to the Dutch chief (see *Holl. Corresp.*, as above, and *Dom. Corresp., Jac. I,* vol. cxvi. Nos. 19, 191). Barwick had come out to India in the same fleet as Roe (see p. 2 *n*).

[1] 'From aboard the *Ann* at Plimouth, 29 August, 1619.' This is an abstract only, the original letter being missing.

[2] From an entry in the Court Minutes of 1 Oct. 1619, there seems to have been something like a mutiny on board.

[3] In December, 1618 (see Jourdain's *Journal*, p. lxx.).

APPENDIX A.

ROE'S GEOGRAPHICAL ACCOUNT OF THE MOGUL'S TERRITORIES.[1]

The severall kingdomes and provinces subject to the great Mogoll Sha-Selim Gehangier, with the principall cittyes and rivers, the scituation and borders, and extent in length and breadth, as neere as by description I could geather them. The names I tooke out of the Kings register. I begin at the north west.

[1] From *Add. MS.* 6115, f. 256. This interesting document was printed by Purchas in his first volume (p. 578). Terry has a similar list, but arranges the provinces in a different order, and substitutes 'Jeselmeere' for 'Roch.' From this and from the differences in spelling, it is evident that, while he had Roe's list before him (having probably obtained a copy from the ambassador), he relied chiefly upon Baffin's map. His version may be consulted in Purchas's second volume, p. 1467 (reproduced in *Early Travels in India*, p. 288), and in his own volume of 1655 (p. 78). He mentions in the latter that the provinces 'antiently were particular kingdomes, whose true names . . . we there had out of the Mogol's own records.'

This description of the Mogul's territories is evidently quite different from the systematic survey, based on fiscal divisions, which we get in the *Aīn-i-Akbari*. Though always taken as topographical (and apparently he himself so understood it) the list copied by Roe seems rather to have been (as hinted by Terry) of an historical nature, enumerating roughly the states which had fallen under the sway of the Mogul emperors. Hence, we find several petty Himālayan states, such as Sība, Jaswān, Chamba, and Nagarkot, figuring on the same plane as Bengal and Gujarāt; hence, too, Ajmer and Oudh—though the latter is included under the general term of 'Purp'—are not specifically mentioned; while Gaur is differentiated from Bengal, Narwar from Agra, and Bukkur from Multān. The names Roe says he 'tooke out of the Kings register,' and he seems to have re-arranged them in what he understood to be their geographical order, commencing from the north-west, and to have added

APPENDIX A

1. CANDAHAR. The cheefe citty soe called. Lyes from the hart of all his territory north-west ; confines with [*i.e.* borders upon] the Shā-bas [dominions of Shāh Abbās, *i.e.*, Persia] and was a province of Persia.

2. TATA [Tatta, or Sind]. The cheefe citty soe called. Is divided by the river Indus, which falls into the sea at Syndu [Lahrībandar] ; and lyes from Chandahar sowth ; from the middle of which I suppose Agra west, somewhat sowtherly.[1]

3. BUCKAR. The cheefe citty called Buckar Suckar [Bukkur-Sukkur]. Lyes upon the river of Syndu or Indus, to the northward somwhat easterly of Tata, and west confines upon the Baloaches [Baluchis], a kind of rude warlike people.

4. MULTAN. The cheefe citty soe called. Lying alsoe upon Indus, sowth east from Candahar, northly from Backar.

5. HAAGICKAN.[2] The kingdome of the Baloaches, to the

such further particulars as he was able to obtain. As will be seen from the notes, these were frequently erroneous, and the list in general contains a number of discrepancies which it is impossible to reconcile. However, with all its imperfections, it was the earliest published attempt to supply European readers with an account of the political divisions of the Mogul empire ; and subsequent writers were content to adopt it almost in its entirety. In 1824 Robert Kerr (*Voyages and Travels*, vol. ix. p. 378) endeavoured to explain Roe's erminology, but without much success.

In the present reproduction, the modern names of the various provinces, cities, etc., have been mostly added within brackets without further annotation. In identifying the names given by Roe, considerable help has been derived from a series of articles by Professor Blochmann, on the geography and history of Bengal during the Muhammadan period (*Journal of the Bengal Asiatic Society*, vol. xlii. pt. 1, p. 209 ; vol. xliii. pt. 1, p. 280 ; vol. xliv. pt. 1, p. 275), in the course of which he deals briefly with Roe's list as given by Terry and De Laet. Sir Roper Lethbridge also discussed the list in his interesting articles on De Laet in the *Calcutta Review* (vol. li. p. 336 ; vol. lii. p. 67). It would seem, however, that neither had Roe's version at hand, or was aware of the extent to which Terry's (and consequently De Laet's) list had been influenced by the locations adopted in Baffin's map.

[1] Here, as elsewhere, the cardinal points are confused.

[2] Baluchistān, or more specifically the lower Derājāt, ruled by the descendants of Hāji Khān, whose overlordship was recognized by all the Baloch tribes.

TERRITORIES OF THE GREAT MOGUL

west of Tata and Backar, and confines west upon the kingdome of Lar [Lāristān], subject to the Sha-bas. Indus wyndeth it selfe into the Easter syde of yt. It hath no renowned citty.

6. CABULL. The citty soe called. A great kingdome, the northermost of this Emperors dominion ; and confineth with Tartaria.

7. KYSHMIER [Kashmīr]. The cheefe citty is called Sirinakar [Srīnagar]. The river of Bhat [Bihat or Jhelum] passeth thorowgh it and findeth the sea by Ganges [1] or, some say, of it selfe in the north part of the Bay of Bengala. It bordereth Cabul to the east sowtherly. It is all mountaynes.

8. BANKISH.[2] The cheefe city is called Beishur.

9. ATACK [Attock]. The cheefe citty so called. It lyeth on one syde the river Nilab,[3] which runneth [from ?] the northwest into the river of Indus.

10. The kingdom of the KAKARES [4] lyes at the foote of the mountaynes. It hath principall cittyes Dankely [Dangāli] and Purhola [Pharwāla]. It bordereth north-east on Kishmier.

11. PEN-JAB [Punjab], which signifieth five waters, for that it is seated within five rivers. The cheefe cytty is called Lahor. It is a great kingdome and most fruictfull. The citty is the mart of India for trafique. It borders north-east on Multan.[5]

12. JENBA.[6] The cheefe citty soe called. It lyes east of Pen-Jab. It is very mountanous.

13. PEITAN.[7] The cheefe citty so called. It lyeth east of

[1] This is, of course, an error. The Jhelum flows into the Indus, and is so shown in Baffin's map.

[2] Professor Blochmann identifies Bankish with Bangash, in N.W. Kohāt, on the Punjab border, and Beishar with Bajaur, a district still farther north. Possibly, however, Peshāwar is intended.

[3] The term is generally applied to the upper Indus. In the map, as here, it seems to be identified with the Kābul river.

[4] The country of the Ghakkars, in the north of the Punjab, subdued early in Akbar's reign.

[5] 'Upon the north-east of Multan ' is intended.

[6] Chamba, one of the Punjab hill states, lying between Kashmīr and the British districts of Kāngra and Gūrdaspur.

[7] Professor Blochmann says : ' This is Paithān, the form used by Abulfazl for Pathān or Pathānkot. Terry evidently means the whole

Jenba, and from the north-west of Bengala it is full of mountaynes.

14. NAKARKUTT.[1] The cheefe citty so called. The north eastermost confine of Mogor. It lyes to the north-east of the head of the Bay of Bengala. It is very mountaynous.

15. SYBA.[2] The cheefe citty soe called. It borders with Nakarkutt sowtherly. It is all mountaynes.

16. JESUAL.[3] The cheefe citty is called Ragepur. It bordereth with Bengala sowth-east; north with Syba and Nacurkutt. It is full of mountayns.

17. DELLY [Delhi]. The cheefe citty so called. It lyeth on the north-west syde of the river Jemny [Jumna], which falleth into Ganges and runneth thorough Agra. It is an ancient cytty and the seat of the Mogolls ancestors. It is ruined. Some affirme it to have beene the seat of Porus, conquered by Alexander, and that ther stands a pillar with a Grieke inscription.

18. MEVAT.[4] The cheefe citty called Narnol. It lyeth on the east of Ganges.

hill-tract of the Sirmūr range, as far as the Alaknandā. It is, however, possible that he meant the Markandā; but this river does not flow into the Ganges.' The identification is probably right; but it is not necessary to stretch the boundaries of the district in order to account for Terry's statement that 'the river Kanda waters it, and falls into Ganges in the confines thereof'; for here, as elsewhere, Terry is merely inserting what he has found in Baffin's map.

[1] The Kāngra district in the N.E. of the Punjab. Its historic capital, which now bears the same name as the district, was formerly known as Nagarkot.

[2] Sība, now part of the Kāngra district, but formerly an independent principality. The town of that name is about 17 miles S.W. of Kāngra.

[3] The ancient Rājput principality of Jaswān, which centred in the valley of that name in Hoshiārpur district (Punjab). 'Ragepur' is Rājpura, not far from Amb.

[4] Mewāt lay to the south of Delhi, and included parts of the present Muttra and Gurgāon districts and portions of Alwar, Bhartpūr, and Patiāla. It was subdued by Akbar, and was included in the *sūbah* of Agra. Its geographical position is very incorrectly given, for it was considerably to the west of the Ganges. In the map it is still further displaced.

Nārnaul, its chief town, which was for a time one of the strongholds

TERRITORIES OF THE GREAT MOGUL

19. SANBALL. The cheefe citty soe called.[1] It lyeth betweene Ganges and Jemna to the north-west of their meeting.

20. BAKAR [Bikaner]. The cheefe citty is called Bikanir. It bordereth north-west one Ganges.

21. AGRA, a principall and great kingdome. The citty soe called, the hart of the Mogolls territorye, in north latitude about 28d½. It lieth most on the sowth-west syde of Jemna, the citty upon the river, wher one of the Emperors treasuries are kept; from Agra to Lahor beeing 320 *course*, which is not lesse then seven hundred mile. It is all a playne and the highway planted on both sides with trees like a delicate walke; it is one of the great woorks and woonders of the world.[2]

22. JENUPAR.[3] The citty soe called, upon the river of Kaul, which I suppose to bee one of the five rivers enclosing Lahor; and the country lyeth betweene it and Agra, north-west from one, sowth-east from the other.

23. BANDO.[4] The cheefe citty so called. Yt confineth Agra to the west.

24. PATNA. The cheefe citty so called. It is inclosed by fower great rivers: Ganges, Jemna, Serseli[5] and Kanda [Gandak]; so that it lyeth from Agra sowth-east toward the Bay of Bengala, where all these pay tribute.

of the famous George Thomas, now forms part of Patiāla, having been bestowed upon the Mahārāja in recognition of his services during the Mutiny.

[1] Sambhal, in Moradābād district, United Provinces. Under Akbar it was the capital of a considerable *sarkār*. Roe is mistaken in placing it between the Ganges and the Jumna.

[2] No doubt Coryat, who had travelled along this road, had described it to Roe. It will be seen that this ' Longe Walke ' is a prominent feature of the map. Its length is much overrated in the text.

[3] Jaunpur, formerly a considerable Muhammadan kingdom, extending from Budāun and Etāwah to the frontier of Bihār. By Kaul (Kāli) may be meant the Gogra; but the city of Jaunpur is on the Gūmti, and both streams are tributaries of the Ganges.

[4] Bāndhu (Bāndā), now a district of the Allahābād division of the United Provinces.

[5] Professor Blochmann identifies this with the Sarsuti (Saraswati). ' According to the legend,' he says, ' the Saraswati, which is lost in the sand east of Bhatinda district, joins the Ganges below the ground at Allahābād.'

25. GOR [Gaur]. The cheefe citty soe called.[1] It lyeth toward the head of Ganges.

26. BENGALA. A mightie kingdome enclosing the western syd of the Bay on the north and wyndeth sowtherly. It bordereth on Cormandell. The cheife cittyes are Ragmehhal [Rājmahāl] and Dekaka [Dacca]. Ther are many havens, as Port Grande [Chittagong], Port Pequina [see p. 194 n], traded by the Portugalls, Piliptan [Piplīpatam], Satigam [Sātgāon]. It conteyneth divers provinces, as that of Purp and Patan.[2]

27. ROCH.[3] It hath noe citty of note, and bordereth the sowth-east of Bengala, and the Bay.

28. VDEZA.[4] The cheefe citty called Jekanat. It is the utmost east of the Mogulls territories beyond the Bay, and confines with the kingdome of Maug,[5] a savuage people lyeing betweene Udeza and Pegu.

29. KANDUANA.[6] The cheefe citty is called Kerhakatenkah. It lieth sowth-west of the sowth of Bengala.

[1] The ruins of this, the ancient capital of the Muhammadan kings of Bengal, are still to be seen in Mālda district, 25 miles S.E. of Rājmahāl.

[2] ' Purp ' (Hind. *pŭrb*, from Sanskrit *pūrba*, ' the east ') was used loosely to signify Oudh, Benares, and Bihār. Finch applies the term to parts of Oudh (*Purchas*, vol. i. pp. 436, 438); Jourdain (1611) says, ' Pierb is 400 *cose* longe and hath beene the seate of four kinges '; Van Twist (1648) calls it Purbet, ' a province on the borders of Tartary '; Manrique (1649) carries it as far west as Agra (' llamose esta provincia antiguamente Purrop '). Patan may be a duplication of Patna, or a confused notion of Bhotān.

[3] Sir Roper Lethbridge (*loc. cit.*) suggests that this is meant for Koch, *i.e.* Kuch Bihār. Professor Blochmann, however, holds that it is Arakan, which is often called Rukh by Muhammadan historians. I incline to the former opinion, because Arakan could not have been considered at this time part of the Mogul empire, whereas part of the Koch kingdom had been conquered as recently as 1612. Probably Roe had merely the name (miswritten), and on making inquiries about ' Roch ' was given a rough outline of the situation of Arakan.

[4] Were it not for the mention of Jagannāth, this would scarcely be recognised as Orissa, especially as the latter duly appears on the map (as ' Orixa ') in something like its proper position.

[5] The Maghs are a tribe inhabiting the northern part of Arakan.

[6] Gondwānā, nearly all of which is now comprised in the Central Provinces. Kerhakatenkah is Garhakatanka, near Jabalpur, but the name was often applied to the whole district.

30. KUALIAR [Gwalior]. The cheefe citty soe called. It lyeth to the sowth-east [1] of Kanduana, and bordereth on Burhampur.

31. CKANDES [Khāndesh]. The cheefe cittye called Burhanpur. A great kingdom; one of the ancient seates of Decan, and conquered from them. It lyeth east of Guzaratt, sowth of Chytor, west of Decan. It is watered with the river Tabeti [Tāpti], which falleth west into the Bay of Cambaya. It is now the seat of the Decan.

32. MALVA [Mālwa]. The cheefe cyttyes called Ugen [Ujjain], Narr [Dhār?], and Seringe [Sironj]. It lyeth west of Chandes, betweene that and the countrie of Ranna; on the west of the river of Sepra,[2] which falls into the Bay of Cambaya, not farr from Suratt.

33. BERAR. The cheefe cytty is called Shahpur.[3] It bordereth on Guzeratt and the hills of Ranna.

34. GUZRATT. A goodly kingdom enclosing the bay of Cambaya. The cheefe city is Amadavaz [Ahmadābād]. It conteynes the city and goverment of Cambaya, the bewty of India, the territorye and city of Suratt, and Barooch [Broach]. It is watered with many goodly rivers, as that of Cambaya [the Māhi], falsely supposed to bee Indus, the river of Narbadah, falling into the sea at Barooch, that of Suratt, and divers others. It trades to the Red Sea, to Achyn, and many places.

35. SORETT [Sorath, in Kāthiāwār]. The cheefe citty called Gunagur [Junāgarh]. Lyeth to the north-west of Guzeratt.

36. NARVAR.[4] The cheefe citty called Ghehud. Lyeth sowth-west from Chitor.

[1] North-west.

[2] The Sipra. It falls, not into the Gulf of Cambay, but into the Chambal, a tributary of the Ganges.

[3] Shāhpur, six *kos* south of Bālāpur, in Akolā district. It was for a time a place of importance as the head-quarters of Sultān Murād (son of Akbar), but is now a heap of ruins.

[4] Narwar, now part of Gwalior state. It is classed in the *Aīn* as a *sarkār* of Agra. Ghehud might be taken to be Gohad, but that town is both at a considerable distance from Narwar and (according to the *Imperial Gazetteer*) of a date much later than Roe's time.

37. CHYTOR [Chitor]. An ancient great kingdom. The citty soe called on a mightie hill, walled about ten English mile. Ther stands yet above 100 churches, the pallace of the Kings, many brave pillars of carved stone. Ther is but one assent, cut out of the rock, passing fower magnificent gates. Ther remayne the ruines of 100,000 howses of stone. It is uninhabited. It was doubtlesse one of the seats of Porus and was woonne from Ranna, his issue, by Eckbarshaw, the last Mogoll. Ranna, flyeing into the strength of his kingdome among the mountayns, seated him selfe at Odepoore [Udaipur]; who was brought to acknowledg the Mogol for his superior lord by Sultan Coroonne [Khurram], third sonne of the present Emperor, in the yeare 1614. This kingdome lyeth north-west from Chandes, and north-east from the north-west of Guzaratt, in the way betweene Agra and Suratt. Ranna him selfe keepes the hills to the west, nearer Amadavaz.

The length is north-west to sowth-east: from Chandahar to Lahor 350 *courses*, about 800 miles; from Lahor to Agra, 320 *courses*, about 752 miles; from Agra to Hhagipurpatna [1] 300 *courses*, about 680 miles: from Hhagipurpatna to Kirasunder,[2] 300 *courses*, about 670 miles. In all, *courses* 1270, miles about 2872.

The breadth in all is north-east to sowth-west, from Hardvar to Duarsa,[3] 630 [4] *courses*, about 1500 miles.[5]

[1] Hājīpur-Patna, *i.e.* Patna. Hājīpur was the original city, on the northern bank of the Ganges.

[2] This seems to be Kiyāra Sundar, which is mentioned in the *Aīn* (vol. ii. p. 124) as a township in the *sarkār* of Sonārgāon in S.E. Bengal.

[3] Dwārka, on the N.W. point of the Kāthiāwār peninsula.

[4] Purchas's 'sixe hundred and fiftie' is the more probable reading.

[5] As Purchas noticed, the figures given are irreconcilable, both as regards the total mileage and the ratio of the *kos* to the mile; and he endeavours to explain the discrepancies by the fact that 'as for *courses*, they are diversly taken (as southerne and northerne miles with us), in some places longer, in others shorter, which causeth scruple in the computation.'

NOTE ON THE MAP.

WITHIN a few months of Roe's return to England, and while his embassy was still a subject of general curiosity, appeared the *Indolstani . . . Descriptio*, a reduced facsimile of which, from a copy (probably unique) in the British Museum, is herewith placed before the reader. Quite apart from the fact that it is the earliest English attempt to delineate the territories of the Mogul emperors, the map is of great interest, alike from the circumstances of its production, the information it embodies, and the extent to which it has guided (and misguided) the work of later geographers. We will briefly consider it under these three heads.

First, however, a few facts concerning the map itself may be mentioned. The original, which is known at the British Museum as K 115 (22), measures (exclusive of margin) about nineteen and a quarter inches by fifteen. The full title (in the bottom left-hand corner) is INDOLSTANI *Imperii Totius Asiæ ditissimi descriptio : ex indagatione Ilust : Dom : Tho : Roe Equitis Aurati in Regia Mogollanica Legatum agentis Illustrata : Anno Sal :* 1619. *Vera, quæ visa : quae non ? veriora.* At the top of the map is a short title, *A Description of East India conteyninge th' Empire of the Great Mogoll* ; and in the upper right-hand corner appear the Mogul's standard and his seal, with the Persian names given in English characters. Along the lower margin we find the names of the engraver (*Renold Elstrack sculp :*) and of the vendor (*Are to be sold in Pauls Church yarde by Thomas Sterne, Globemaker*), and, in a small label between them, the significant inscription : *William Baffin deliniavit et excudebat.*

Although generally known, in after years, as Sir Thomas Roe's map, it bears, as we have seen, the honoured name of William Baffin as its draughtsman. This fact at once affords a clue to its history. For Baffin, who was an indefatigable surveyor and map-maker, was a master's mate on board the *Anne*, the ship in which Roe returned to England [1] ; and we may surmise that the acquaintance which would naturally spring up during the voyage between the ambassador and a navigator of Baffin's experience had led to a project for the publication of an accurate map of India, and that for this purpose Roe had placed at Baffin's disposal all the information in his possession. It may be that the map was actually drawn during the voyage, and that the ambassador assisted Baffin in locating the interior cities and provinces ; but the character of

[1] This interesting conjunction, and also the fact of his connection with the first English map of Hindustān, appear to have escaped the notice of Baffin's biographers.

APPENDIX A

some of its inaccuracies, and the fact that it is not mentioned among the maps submitted to the East India Company by Baffin shortly after his return (for which they voted him a gratuity),[1] militate against this view ; and it seems more probable that it was compiled during the few months that elapsed between the arrival of the *Anne* in September, 1619, and Baffin's departure as master of the *London* at the beginning of February, 1620.[2]

It is important to note in this connexion that Roe had himself intended at one time to prepare a map of the country to which he had been accredited. There is no reference to the subject in his extant letters or journal, but the fact is placed beyond doubt by a passage in one of Lord Carew's letters to him (Maclean's edition, p. 123). ' Lett me entreat you,' wrote the latter, ' to be carefull to make the mappe of the Mogolls territorie, as you have intended ; itt will be a worke worthye of your sellfe and adorne your travell and judgement, and leave to the world a lasting memorie when you are dust.' Doubtless it was with this purpose in view that Roe had compiled (some time before October, 1617) the geographical compendium which has been printed in the foregoing pages. Probably he intended to supplement this by the collection of fresh information as opportunity offered, but was prevented by ill-health and the many other troubles of his mission from following up the matter ; and the slenderness of the material he had obtained may have made him all the more willing to commit the task to other hands.

The extent of the assistance afforded to Baffin by Roe must remain largely a matter of conjecture. On the one hand, the manner in which the map differs from the list, often without apparent reason, seems to negative the idea that he had any voice in the matter. On the other, it is almost incredible that

[1] As the Company had specially desired the preparation of a map of India, Baffin had every reason to exhibit his if he had it ready. The instructions given to Downton in the 1614 voyage had contained a clause directing him to send some fit person to discover ' the river of Sinda ' and the surrounding country with a view to the preparation of a ' trew mapp for our better understanding of the same ' ; ' and the like mapp ' (they continued) ' wee would have hime drawe exactly of *all the whole contrey of the Great Magoll*, for the setuation of Agra, Lahor, Byana, etc., and all the rivers whereuppon ther cittyes stand and which come downe to Cambaya and other places, *which to this daye we cold never have* ' (*Marine Records, Miscellaneous*, vol. 4). Downton, however, had found no opportunity of carrying out this project.

[2] Of course either January or February, 1620, would be included in 1619 in the old style of reckoning.

NOTE ON THE MAP

Baffin should not have shown at least a draught of the map to the person at whose suggestion (probably) it was undertaken, and who would certainly feel the liveliest interest in such a matter. The fact, too, that Narwar, which is stated in the list to be S.W. of Chitor, should have been changed to the N.E. instead, suggests the influence of Roe, or of someone who, like him, knew enough of western India to make the correction; and the introduction of the ' Longe Walke ' between Agra and Lahore, of the Cow's-head gorge at Hardwār, and of ' Jallamakee, the pilgrimage of the Banians '—all obviously derived from the narratives of Tom Coryat—may also have been due to the ambassador. Terry's statement that the map was ' first made by the especial observation and direction ' of Roe would of course settle the question, if it could be relied on; but it was made many years after the date of publication, and (as we have seen) the reverend gentleman's memory was not to be trusted implicitly. The general attribution of the map to Roe is sufficiently explained by the use made of his name in the title, and the fact that what fresh matter it contained was undoubtedly derived from information supplied by him.

That that information, though often inaccurate, constituted on the whole an important advance, may be seen on comparing Baffin's map with the one given in the standard atlas of the period, viz., the *Gerardi Mercatoris Atlas denuo auctus*, of which a fourth edition was published by Hondius at Amsterdam about 1612.[1] A glance at the latter will shew how little was previously known as regards the interior of the Indian peninsula. The coast line and the chief ports had been given with fair accuracy in Linschoten's map (see the English edition of 1598), from information drawn from Portuguese charts; and in the atlas this is copied fully, though somewhat carelessly. But the interior is still a region to be filled in almost at random. The Indus falls into the Gulf of Cambay (an error which Roe specially emphasizes), while its proper place is occupied by a river called the R. de Diul Sinde. Even the best known of the up-country cities—Lahore, Delhi, Agra, Patna, etc.—are located by guesswork; and the whole country is portrayed in a most rudimentary fashion.

In these respects the map drawn by Baffin was a great advance upon its predecessor. The Indus for the first time assumes somewhat of its proper shape, and it is duly identified with the river entering the ocean near Diulsind (Lahrībandar). In fact, the whole of western and the greater part of central India may be said to be portrayed with fair, though far from complete, accuracy. Where the difficulty came in was to locate

[1] This was the atlas presented by Roe to Jahāngīr and returned by him, as related on pp. 380, 382.

the provinces—such as Jenupar, Bankish, Syba, etc.—which were known only from Roe's list. In that document the indications given were often either too vague to be of use, or else irreconcilable with other statements. The map-maker seems therefore in desperation to have filled them in almost at random, and, as we have seen, most of his guesses were very far from being successful. Vdeza, again, was not recognized as the Orixa of the Portuguese charts; and its erroneous location in Roe's list (' the utmost east of the Mogulls territories beyond the Bay ') led to its insertion between Bengal and Burma, while ' Orixa ' occupies its proper position.

There was at least one re-issue of the map in its separate form. Mr. C. G. Cash possesses a map of India similar to the one under discussion, except that its date is 1632, and that the copies are stated to have been *Printed for Henery Tombes and Benjamin Fisher and are to be soulde at the Talbut without Aldersgate*. This issue was reproduced and described by Mr. Cash in *The Scottish Geographical Magazine* for February, 1902. The two maps are identical in all but the date (which bears traces of alteration in the later edition) and the publisher's imprint; and it is clear, therefore, that the plate had been passed on from the first proprietor to Messrs. Tombs and Fisher, who had then issued a fresh impression, after altering the date and inserting their own names.

Some six years after its publication, Baffin's map was re-engraved on a reduced scale for *Purchas His Pilgrimes*, and as the form in which it there appeared is the only one which has hitherto been generally accessible, it may be useful to make a brief comparison. The same engraver, Renold Elstrack, was employed, but his work had nothing like the accuracy of the first edition. In the one case he was working (we may assume) under the superintendence of Baffin; in the other he was left to his own devices. Hence we find that in the later map signs of haste and negligence abound. Elstrack has, in the first instance, marked the Ganges delta as Sinde, for in spite of attempts to erase the name from the plate it may still be read; the frontier of Bengal has had to be corrected, and the alteration has left part of the name outside the boundary of the province; while Hajacan has been turned into Halacan, Brodera into Brodem, Jallamakee into Illamakee, and so on in at least half a dozen instances. In other respects, the copy follows the original with fair accuracy; but it must always remain a careless and untrustworthy version of Baffin's handiwork.

The next appearance of the map (on a still smaller scale) was in Terry's work in 1655. In this, many of the names of provinces and towns have been omitted; and amongst other mistakes ' Ugen ' has become ' Upen,' ' Cambay ' ' Campay,'

NOTE ON THE MAP

'Buckor' 'Bucko,' and 'Jeselmeere' has been shortened to 'Jesel.' But the (unknown) engraver avoids some of the errors of Purchas's version, and it is evident that he worked not from the latter but from the 1619 map. Ten years later (1665) the same plate was made use of in the version of Terry which was published as a supplement to Havers's translation of Della Valle's letters. The copy, by the way, given in the 1777 reprint of Terry's book is still more inaccurate than its predecessor.

To follow in detail the influence of Baffin's map on the work of succeeding geographers would carry us beyond our limits. It may suffice to say that it is writ large upon every map of India, English or foreign, which was produced for quite a century. Roe's name lent the map an authority which probably he would have been the first to deprecate; and though later geographers might doubt the accuracy of some of its details, it was only after great hesitation that they ventured to amend them. Consequently, Siba, Nakakutt, Jenupar, Peitan, Kanduana, Jesuall, Mevat and the two Orissas—mostly in the positions assigned by Baffin—appear in turn in the maps of Blaeu, Van den Broecke (Valentyn's *Oud en Nieuw Oost Indien*, vol. v), Sanson, Ogilby, Bernier and even Catrou (1715); and it was not until the advent of scientific map-making with Rennell (who went back for his political divisions to the *Aīn* itself) that Indian geography shook off at last the incubus of these and similar errors.

APPENDIX B.

I. LETTER FROM KING JAMES TO THE GREAT MOGUL.

(Purchas's *Pilgrimes*, vol. i, p. 580.[1])

The Kings Letters sent to Selim Shagh,[2] the Great Mogor, in the yeare 1614[-15] *by Sir Thomas Roe.*

James, by the Grace of Almightie God, the Creator of Heaven and Earth, King of Great Britaine, France and Ireland, Defendor of the Christian Faith, etc.

To the high and mightie Monarch the Great Mogor, King of the Orientall Indies, of Chandahar, of Chismer and Corazon, etc. Greeting.

We having notice of your great favour toward us and our subjects, by your great *firma* to all your captaines of rivers and officers of your customes, for the entertaynment of our loving subjects the English nation with all kind respect, at what time soever they shall arrive at any of the ports within your dominions, and that they may have quiet trade and commerce without any kind of hinderance or molestation, etc., as by the articles concluded by Suc Suff,[3] Governour of the Guzerats, in your name, with our loving subject Captaine Thomas Best appeareth: have thought it meete to send unto you our ambassadour, which may more fully and at large handle and treate of such matters as are fit to be considered of, concerning that good and friendly correspondence which is so lately begunne betweene us, and which will without doubt redound to the honour and utilitie of both nations. In which consideration, and for the furthering of such laudable commerce, wee have made choice of Sir Thomas Roe, Knight, one of the

---

[1] From a copy found by Purchas among Hakluyt's papers.

[2] Salīm Shāh, the Emperor's proper name. He is, however, always known by the title of Jahāngīr, which he assumed upon his accession to the throne. [3] Shaikh Yusuf.

principall gentlemen of our court, to whom wee have given commission under our great seale of England, together with directions and instructions further to treate of such matters as may be for the continuance and increase of the utilitie and profit of each others subjects : to whom we pray you to give favour and credit in whatsoever hee shall moove or propound toward the establishing and enlarging of the same. And for confirmation of our good inclination and wel-wishing toward you, we pray you to accept in good part the present, which our said ambassadour will deliver unto you. And so doe commit you to the mercifull protection of Almightie God.

II. LETTER FROM KING JAMES TO ROE.
(Public Record Office : *C.O.*, 77, vol. i, No. 57.[1])

To our right trustie and well beloved servant Sir Thomas Roe, Knight, our ambassadour resident with the Grand Mogull. JAMES R.

Right trustie and welbeloved, wee greete you well. Wee have seen your letters written unto us in February last [2] and we have bene also more particularly informed by our principall secretary of the adverticements which came from you at that tyme in your other private letters ; which have given us very good contentment, being resolved to retaine in a gratious memory the dilligences and dexterity which you have used in your negociations there. In particular we do approve of the entrance of a treaty which you have begon to make with the Sophy of Persia for the opening of his Gulfe and inlarging the trade of our subjects into his dominions, especially for the traffique and commerce of silke ; beinge resolved to prosecute the same to effect, according as we shall judge it requisite upon the further advertisements that we shall heerafter receave from you. In the meanetyme we do authorize you to proceed in your good beginnings and to dispatch into Persia some fit persons with such instructions as you shall receave from the Governour and Committies of the East Indie Company, to ripen and prepare that busines. And moreover, if you shall find all

[1] Printed in the *Calendar of State Papers, E. Indies*, 1617-21, Preface, p. xxvi.

[2] See p. 113. The present letter was written at the instance of the East India Company, as Roe guessed (p. 449). A note from Smythe to Winwood, asking his assistance in procuring it, is among the MSS. of the Duke of Buccleuch (*Reports of Hist. MSS. Commn.*, 1899, vol. i., p. 180). Its receipt by Roe is noted on p. 398 ; and his reply will be found on p. 463.

things there so well prepared that you may come to the conclusion of a treaty to the purpose above-named, without further circumstance we do in such case heerby give you power to perfect and conclude, or cause to be perfected and concluded, a treaty of comerce betwixt the said great Sophy and us, for the mutuall good of the subjects and dominions of us both, without attending from hence any other directions then a confirmation only of that treaty, which shalbe by us foorthwith ratified, according as you shall in our name undertake the same.

Given under our signet at our Pallace of Westminstre, the 4th of February 1616[-17].

III. LETTER FROM THE GREAT MOGUL TO KING JAMES.[1]

(British Museum : *Add. MS.* 4155, f. 100.)

When Your Majestie shall open this lettre, lett your royall hart bee as fresh as a sweete garden. Lett all people make reverence at your gate ; lett your throne bee advanced higher ; amongst the greatnes of the kyngs of the prophett Jesus lett Your Majestie bee the greatest, and all monarchques derive their councell and wisedome from your brest as from a founteyne, that the law of the majestic of Jhesus may revive and flourish under your protection.

These salutations are much amplified in phrases in the originall.[2]

---

[1] This is the document mentioned in the ambassador's letter to King James of 15 Feb. 1618 (see p. 465). The text here given is from a copy in Roe's handwriting, and may therefore be accepted as authoritative. Mr. Sainsbury has printed a slightly different version in the preface to his *Calendar of State Papers, E. Indies*, 1617-21, taken from an undated copy in the Public Record Office (*C.O.* 77, vol. i., No. 68) ; a third copy, also presenting some unimportant variations, is in *Add. MS.* 29975 (f. 37) ; and a fourth (as also a French version) will be found among the *State Papers, Foreign* (vol. 40), at the Public Record Office. There is further, among the Marquis of Salisbury's MSS. at Hatfield, a document containing (as Mr. R. T. Gunton was kind enough to ascertain for me) copies of both this and the following letter on a single sheet endorsed, ' Two letters from the Great Mogol to his Majesty, 1619 ' ; and yet another copy of the two is among the Carte MSS. in the Bodleian Library (No. 103, f. 280). Terry quotes the opening lines of both, and says (not quite correctly) that one was written a year before the other.

[2] These are, of course, marginal comments by the ambassador.

LETTER FROM THE GREAT MOGUL

The lettre of love and frendship which yow sent and the presents, tokens of your good affection toward mee, I have received by the hands of your ambassador, Sir Thomas Roe (who well desserveth to bee your trusted servant) delivered to mee in an acceptable and happy houre; upon which myne eyes were so fixed that I could not easelye remoove them to any other object, and have accepted them with great joy and delight.

In the originall are many titles of honor and prayses cast away upon mee.

Upon which assurance of your royall love, I have given my generall command to all the kyngdomes and ports of my dominions to receive all the merchants of the English nation as the subjects of my frend; that in what place soever they choose to live they may have reception and residence to their owne content and safety, and what goods soever they desire to sell or buy, they may have free libertie without any restraynt; and at what port soever they shall arrive that neyther Portugall nor any other shall dare to molest their quiett; and in what cytty soever they shall have residence, I have commanded all my governors and capteynes to give them freedome answerable to their owne desires: to sell, buy, and to transport into their countrie at theire pleasure.

For confirmation of our love and frendship, I desire Your Majestie to command your merchants to bring in their shipps of all sorts of rareties and rich goods fitt for my pallace; and that yow bee pleased to send mee your royall lettrs by everye oportunitie, that I may rejoyce in your health and prosperous affayres; that our frendship nay bee enterchanged and eternall. Your Majestie is learned and quicksighted as a prophett and can conceive much by few woords, that I neede write no more. The God of Heaven give yow and us increase of honor.

Written in Amadavaz, the cheefe cytty of Guzuratt, sealed in a case of gould satten, sent to the ambassador the 20 day Feb. 1617[-18] (the coppy firmed by the secretarie), in answere of a lettre by His Majestie of Great Brittayne dated 1616[-17]; which should have beene sent for England by the fleete returned in March 1617[-18], but deteyned because ther was nothing performed according to the contents therof, that therby the ambassador might urdge the Kyng of Indya to performance, or refuse the lettre.

IV. LETTER FROM THE GREAT MOGUL TO KING JAMES.

(Public Record Office : *C.O.* 77, vol. i, No. 67.[1])

Many of these phrases beeing in the Arabicque (sic) cannot bee expressed litterally in English woords : but they import the height of honor and are in their owne dialect very elegant. The translation beares the full sence, many flourishes beeing omitted for the difficultie.

How gratious is Your Majestie, whose greatnes God preserve. As upon a rose in a garden, so are myne eyes fixed upon yow. God maynteyne your estate that your monarchy may prosper and bee augmented and that yow may obteyne all your desires woorthy the greatnes of your renowne ; and as your hart is noble and upright so lett God give yow a glorious reigne ; because yow strongly defend the law of the Majestie of Jhesus, which God make yett more flourishing, for that it was confirmed by miracles. And the same honor which God hath given unto Moses and to Jesus, the same God give unto yow.

This clause in the originall is adorned with many curious prayses.

The lettre of frendship which yow wrote unto mee I have received and have understood all that was conteyned therin ; and all the presents and rareties which yow sent mee are delivered unto mee, which I have accepted with much delight, love and great content, and have received them as if the Kyngs my ancestors had sent them to mee. And in whatsoever I may give yow the like content I have given my command to all my kyngdomes, subjects and vassalls, as well to the greatest as to the least, and to all my sea ports, that it is my pleasure and I doe command that to all the English marchants in all my dominions there bee given freedome and residence ; and I have confirmed by my woord that no subject of my kyngdomes shall bee so bould to doe

---

[1] In Roe's hand, and endorsed by him : 'Coppy of the lettre of Ghehangier-sha, Great Mogol ; and of his agreement and contract for reception of the English, made with Sir Thomas Roe, His Majesties Ambassador, and sent by him to His Majestie, Anno 1618, 8° die August.'

A second copy, containing a few unimportant variations and without the marginal notes, forms part of No. 68 in the same volume. A third copy, as also a French version, will be found in *State Papers, Foreign*, vol. 40.

This is the letter delivered to Roe before his departure from Ahmadābād (p. 479) as the Mogul's reply to King James's further letter (of which no copy is extant) presented in December, 1617 (pp. 419, 420).

any injurie or molestation to the sayd English, and that their goods and merchandise they may sell or traficque with according to their owne will and to their owne content, and that of all things which they desire in my kyngdomes whersoever they may buy, carry foorth and trade freely, for that it is my good will and pleasure that they may soe doe ; and that all their ships may come and goe to my ports whersoever they choose at their owne will. And I have commanded the great lord Asaph-Chan that he take this contract and busines into his care ; that he may farthar give or enlardge in all mattres belonging to the land or seas, according as I have given my securitie and made agreement ; and whatsoever the sayd great lord Asaph-Chan shall doe shall stand in force as well in any articles of contract as in all other their desires or occasions ; and that whatsoever goods shall come from your kyngdome hither unto mee of any kynd or shall goe to yow from my kyngdome shall receive no hinderance nor impediment, but shall pass with honor and frendship.

[margin: This is expressd in the originall by a woord that signifies they shalbe so free as that no man shall meddle att all, but lett them pass without casting an eye upon them.]

[margin: To whom is added many high titles.]

[margin: The woords carry a sence that Asaph Chan shall grant to the English all their desires, and in those tearmes he received his commission.]

So God give Your Majestic health.

    Written in Amadavaz, the cheefe cytty of Guzeratt, Anno Domini 1618, Mense August, die 8vo.

Sowed in a purse of gould and sealed up by the *Divon* at both ends ; sent to the ambassador and the coppy off the records testefied by the secretarie.[1]

---

[1] From a note by Purchas (vol. i., p. 591), it appears that the seal was not impressed in the usual fashion on the letters sent to James I, but was sent separately, engraved on a silver plate. The note is as follows :

'I have heard that Sir Thomas Roe at his returne, desiring the Great Mogor or Mogoll his letters of commendation to His Majestie, easily obtayned that request, but found him very scrupulous where to set his seale ; lest, if under, hee should disparage himself, if over, it might cause distast to the King. His resolution and prevention therefore was this : to send the letter unsealed, and the great seale it selfe, that so His Majestie might according to his owne pleasure affixe it. The scale is silver.'

A somewhat similar plan had been adopted with the royal letter delivered to the English factors in March, 1615. Kerridge writes (*O.C.*, No. 270) that the seal was ' putt loose therein, which is the

APPENDIX B

costome, for if itt were on the top itt sheweth superyoryte; if underneathe, inferyoryte; butt beinge loose, equallytye. The seale is sett in inke, having therein eight severall names in signetts and himselfe the ninth placed in the middest, deryvinge himselfe from Tamberlayne, the firste of the nine.'

Purchas (*loc. cit.*) adds the following illustration of the seal. This may be elucidated by the aid of the English version given on Baffin's map.

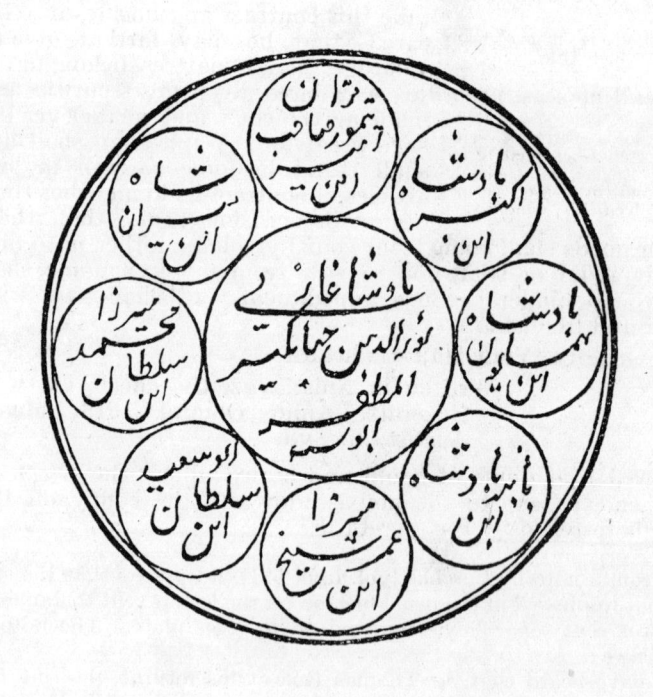

INDEX

Abbās, Mīrza, 366 n, 470, 472 n.
Abbās, Shāh, 130 n, 247, 445, 503, 504; character of, 384; his wars with the Turks, 92, 103, 110, 111, 115, 259, 273, 291 n, 300, 313, 316, 317, 333, 364, 365, 370; conquers Georgia, 92, 103; campaign against the Uzbegs, 92; subdues the Kurds, 273; relations with the Portuguese, 454; blockades Ormus, 56, 79, 92, 103, 110; his negotiations with Spain, see Sherley; kills his son, 92, 103; protects the Deccan kings, 259; Jahāngīr's interest in, 111; his letter to Jahāngīr, 258-60; his envoy to, see Muhammad Riza Beg; inquires for the English, 317; Roe's letters to, 109, 112-4, 313, 334, 390, 435, 453, 454, 464; negotiations with, 76, 79, 110, 111; his *farmān* for trade, 110, 112, 290 n, 291; letter from King James to, 444; his letter to King James, 464. *See also* Connock *and* Persia.
Abbot, George, Archbishop of Canterbury, Roe's letters to, 104, 114 n, 176 n, 271.
Abbot, Sir Maurice, 104 n.
Abd-el-Kuri, 17-19, 24.
Abdullah Khān, Governor of Gujarāt, 150-3; Roe writes to, 153; recalled, 242; pardoned, 242; to go to the Deccan war, 243; visits Khurram, 255, 261.

Abdurrahīm, Mirza, 69, 70 (2), 70 n, 171, 206 (2), 386; notice of, 69 n; Roe and, 68, 72; objects to Khurram's appointment to the Deccan, 238, 243, 340; recalled, 243, 256; accusations against, 242; Jahāngīr tries to poison him, 243; his son, 369 n; his daughter, 469 n; his kinswoman, 243.
Abraham the Dutchman, 168, 293, 393, 407.
Abūl, 153.
Abūl Hasan, Khwāja, 164, 190, 236; Roe visits, 182.
Abyssinia, 14.
Abyssinians, 23, 411.
Achin, 254 n, 376; Indian trade with, 376, 495.
Acosta, Joseph, 5.
Adams, Robert, 392.
Admiral (ship), 3, 19 (3), 248, 298, 298 n, 301.
Adriaensen, Hendrik, xxix.
'Affront,' 170.
Afzal Khān. *See* Shukrullah.
Agates, 458.
Āgha Nūr, 143, 356 n, 357, 363 n, 364 (3); his brother, 143 n.
Agra, *passim*; position of, 91, 493; well built, 105; Roman Catholic church at, 275, 277; plague at, 268, 312, 326 n, 327, 328, 334 n, 336; Governor of, 108, 157, 184, 201; his brother, 157 n, 158, 184, 201; *Kotwāl* of, *see* Āgha

Nūr; Jahāngīr expected to go to, 239, 320, 340, 372 n, 377, 402, 405; proceeds thither, 482 n; Portuguese trade at. 161, 162 n, 450 n; English factory at (*see also* Fetiplace), 82 n, 108, 143 n, 152, 188 n, 399, 416, 440, 472 (2), 485; letters from, 152, 184, 201, 220, 238, 247, 265, 299, 366; factors and goods sent to, 141, 232, 240, 266, 472, 473; money sent to, 403, 409, 416, 424; caravan from, 312, 315, 319, 320 trade at, 201, 220, 237, 238, 295, 296 296 n, 309 n (2), 320 (2), 341, 406, 424, 443; English broker at, 241, 336. *See also* Waterworks.

Agulhas, Cape, 7.

Ahadi, 347 n, 356 n, 382, 415.

Ahmadābād, 135, 304, 441, 450, 495, 505, 507; note on, 422 n; directly under Jahāngīr, 94 n; plague at, 473 n; Governor of, 50, 94 (2), 95 n, 172; *Kotwāl* of, 150; Dutch at, 427, 440, 487 n; Jahāngīr goes to, 372 n, 384, 399, 402, 405, 408, 409, 412, 414; arrives, 404 n, 425 n; leaves and returns, 471 n; departs for Agra, 482 n, 485 n; Roe makes for, 399 (2), 402, 405, 414, 418, 420, 421; arrives, 404 n, 422 (2); leaves, 482 n; factory at, 44, 50, 60, 108, 150, 153, 202, 236, 290, 320, 328, 365, 442 n, 472; Roe writes to, 45, 153 n, 172, 214 n, 330; trade at, 233, 237, 320, 440; abuses at, 94, 95 n, 106-8, 150, 152, 153, 172.

Ahmadnagar, 366 n, 385 n.

Ajmer, 29, 83, 296 n, 311; described, 91; fort at, 85 n, 91, 282; tank at, 217, 297 n; fires at, 154, 155, 235; floods at, 217; Khurram's house at, 217, 297 n; Roe's house at, 91, 98, 116, 125 n, 154, 191 n,

201, 217, 218, 287, 310; *Kotwāl* of, 323; factors at, 241, 268, 323, 324, 327, 328, 334, 341, 372 n, 381 n; Roe reaches, 84; leaves, 300; Jahāngīr's departure, 282-7, 296 n, 297.

Akbar, xv, 84 n, 125 n, 166 n, 209 n, 226 n, 245, 262 n, 293 n, 378 n, 491 n, 492 n, 493 n; captures Chitor, 82, 496; character of, 275; his religion, 275.

Akbarpur, 81.

Alabana, Cape, 17.

Aldworth, Thomas, xvii; death of, 50, 53, 95 n; notice of, 50 n; his servant, 51.

Aleppo, 83 n, 92, 296 n, 300, 301, 314, 333, 335, 370, 375, 384; letters sent via, 316, 335 n; English consuls at, *see* Chapman *and* Haggat.

Alexander the Great, 82 (2), 90, 270, 492.

Alfandica, 49, *and passim*.

Ali, the Prophet, 274, 280.

Alicante wine, 141 (2), 185 (2), 190, 357, 364.

Almonds, 212, 225, 379.

Aloes, 22-5.

Amānat Khān. *See* Cambay, Governor of.

Amar Singh, 270; reduced to submission, 42 n, 82, 84 n, 90; sends Karan to court, 127.

Amara, 83 n.

Ambassador (an) unnecessary, 310, 311, 318.

Amber, 14, 116, 143 n, 193 n, 450 n.

Ambergris, 13.

Ām-o-khās, 431.

Amr-bin-Said. *See* Sokotra, Sultān of.

Āna Sāgar, the, 217, 297 n.

Angaziya, 9 (3), 15, 16, 248, 298, 301 (2).

Animals, figures of, 350.

Anīrāi Singh-dalan, 246, 256.

Ankleswar, 471.

Anne, Queen, portrait of, 125, 357.

INDEX

Anne, the, 363 *n,* 388 *n,* 392 *n,* 462 *n,* 497; sent to the Red Sea, 363 *n,* 440, 442 *n,* 444 *n,* 456, 460-3, 470 (2), 471, 481, 483 *n,* 488; sails for England, 483 *n,* 484, 485; Roe goes home in, 444 *n,* 484 *n,* 485; her voyage and arrival, 488, 498.
Antelopes, 4.
Antheunis, Lucas, 159, 160 *n,* 309 *n,* 362 *n.*
Antwerp, 84 *n,* 168 *n.*
Anūp Rāy. *See* Anīrāi.
Ape, story of an, 280.
Aquaviva, Rudolph, 275 *n,* 279 *n.*
Arab, Khwāja, 474; his house hired for an English factory, 474, 474 *n,* 478, 484.
Arabia, 20, 368; horses from, 259.
Arabic language, the, 13, 275, 506.
Arabs, 9, 20, 22.
Arakan, 434, 494 *n* (2).
Aravād, 68.
Areca, 11, 421 *n.*
Aristotle, 275.
Armada, 102, 105.
Armenians, 36 *n,* 100, 168 *n,* 391 *n;* merchants, 51, 74, 372, 406, 459.
Armlets, 283, 458.
Armour, 312 *n,* 458.
Armstrong, Thomas, 98 *n,* 99.
Arrack, 311.
Arras, 286; trade in, 181, 312 *n,* 458; price of, 181; as presents, 151, 160, 259, 263, 394, 426, 459.
Arrows, 262, 283, 289, 458, 459.
Āsaf Khān, *passim;* notice of, 93 *n;* his rise, 236 *n;* his character, 138, 180, 330, 400; related to Khurram, 97, 236 *n;* slights Khusrau, 298; rumoured reconciliation with, 325; his son-in-law, 128; his house, 137, 161, 175 (2), 188 (2); his servants, 152, 188, 191, 400, 401, 403, 411 *n,* 416, 430; solicitor for the English, 160, 229 *n;* friendly to the Portuguese, 162, 229, 236; Roe's letters to, 138, 139, 163, 185; pearls sold to, 395, 410, 424, 450.
Ascension, the, 81 *n.*
Astrologers, 171 *n,* 275, 353.
Attock, 491.
Aurangzeb, 380 *n.*
Averrhoës, 275.
Āzam Khān, 381 *n.*
Azevedo, Jeronimo. *See* Goa, Viceroy of.
Azud-uddaula. *See* Jamāl-uddīn.

Baboons, 4.
Babylon. *See* Bagdad.
Baffin, William, 489 *n,* 490 *n,* 491 *n,* 497-501.
Bāfta, 314, 408.
Bagdad, 103, 273, 333.
Bāglān, 66 *n.*
Bahādurpur, 68.
Bahādur Shāh, 353 *n,* 439 *n.*
Bailie, ——, xx.
Bairām Khān, 289.
Bajaur, 491 *n.*
Bakhshi, 71, 72, 142, 143, 153 (2), 265.
Balass rubies, 89, 149, 161 (2), 162, 162 *n,* 259, 457.
Balochis, 313, 490 (2).
Baluchistān, 490.
Bandell, 110, 111.
Bāndhu, 493.
Bangash, 491 *n.*
Bangham, John, 473 *n.*
Bangham, Nicholas, 62, 178, 339, 400 *n,* 441, 452 *n;* notice of, 62 *n;* Roe writes to, 157 *n,* 340, 359, 363, 363 *n,* 366, 367, 372, 386.
Banians, *passim.*
Bankish, 491, 500.
Bantam, 254 *n,* 305 *n,* 309, 375, 391 *n,* 392 *n,* 418, 422, 473, 486; ships go to, 247, 252, 361 *n,* 487, 488; ships from, 361, 362; Dutch at, 202, 219 *n,* 369 *n,* 374 *n,* 486, 488 *n;* fight at, 488.

INDEX

'Barb,' to, 180.
Barbary, 1, 6, 442.
Barber's case, a, 348.
'Barde,' 244.
Barker, Thomas, 291 n, 444 n, 453 n.
Barnardi, Philip, 388 n, 451, 452.
Baroda, 482 n, 500.
Barrica, 463 n.
Barwick, Thomas, 2 n, 24, 487, 487 n (2), 488 n.
Basins, 63, 64, 151.
Batavia. See Jacatra.
Bāyasanghar, Prince, 176 n.
Bāzār, 287 n.
Bear, the (sign), 338.
Bear, the (ship), 487 (2), 487 n (2) 488.
Bedawīn, 22.
Bed-field, 459.
Bedsteads, 99, 459.
Bee, the, 388 n, 392 n, 413; sent to Persia, 392 n, 398 n, 440; returns, 444 n, 453; useless at Surat, 436; sent to Masulipatam, 418 n.
Beer, Roe asks for, 96; Jahāngīr inquires about, 199.
Beishur, 491.
Bengal, 90, 280, 494; Parwīz sent to, 219, 235; products of, 193 n, 308, 308 n, 309 n, 320; proposed trade in, 79, 134, 148, 193, 193 n, 305, 308, 309 n, 320, 377, 385, 401-4, 412, 413, 419, 434; leave refused, 228, 385, 416, 434, 456; Dutch and Portuguese in, 193 n, 252, 308, 308 n, 309 n, 434, 494.
Bengal, Bay of, 270, 491-4.
Berar, 495.
Berkeley, George, 33, 38, 53.
Best, Captain, xvi, xvii, 73, 94 n, 377 n; his agreement, xvi, 28 n, 31, 45 n, 47, 502.
Betel, 11, 421 n.
Bezoar stones, 157 n, 254 n, 359.
Bhadwār, 67 n.
Bhagwān Dās, 262 n.
Bhimma, Rāja, 325 n.

Bhotān, 494 n.
Biāna, 450 n, 498 n.
Bickford, James, 244 n, 290.
Biddulph, William, 27, 28 (2), 298, 310 n, 484 n; notice of, 27 n; at Ajmer, 125 n, 140, 141, 152, 156, 159, 167 (2), 198, 209, 255, 288, 295; follows the court, 268 n, 336 (2), 347 n, 351, 356, 357, 443; his accounts, 415 n, 443 n, 450 n, 455 n, 471 n, 482 n.
Bihār, 209 n, 494 n.
Bihārī Mal, Rāja, 262 n.
Bihat (river), 491.
Bījāpur, city of, 366.
Bījāpur, King of (Ibrāhīm Ādil Shāh II), 360 n, 362, 363 n; submits, 385 n; embassies from, 89, 99, 212, 244, 256; and to, 209 n. See also Deccan.
Bikaner, 493.
Bikangāon, 81.
Birds of Paradise, 264.
Blochmann, Professor, 293 n, 490 n, 491 n (2), 493 n, 494 n.
Blue the mourning colour, 312 n.
Boars, wild, 84, 88, 98, 116, 117, 138, 155 n, 220, 225, 247, 380, 382.
Bojador, Cape, 1.
Bone lace, 99.
Boncili, Signor, 300, 301, 323.
Bonner, Robert, 59 n, 363 n; his fleet reaches Swally, 444 n, 482 n; departs, 483 n.
Bonner, Thomas, 58.
Boots, 284, 353.
Borgāon, 80.
Boughton, Humphrey, 21, 22 (2), 33, 35; notice of, 21 n; at Burhānpur, 69 n, 72; his death, 80.
Bows, 21, 183, 258, 262, 283, 289, 353, 458, 459.
Boxes for presents, 458, 459.
Brahmans, 92, 171, 221.
Brass goods, 151, 160.
Bread, 67.
Broach, 60, 61, 73, 74, 387, 408, 418, 495; its importance,

INDEX 513

178, 233, 304, 320 ; English house at, 177, 178, 192 ; proposed removal of English headquarters to, 177, 178, 192, 217 ; exactions at, 172, 177, 290 ; Roe at, 469, 471, 471 n.

Broadcloth, trade in, *passim* ; as presents, 77, 99 n ; length and price of, 443 n.

Brokers' allowances, 310.

Brookes, Christopher, 467.

Brookes, Sir John, xx, 467.

Brothers, the, 18.

Brown, John, 50, 51, 184, 202, 254 n, 290, 424, 442, 482 n ; notice of, 50 n ; wounded, 290.

Bucklers, 283, 286, 289, 458.

Bukkur, 489 n, 490.

Bull, the, 63 n, 388 n, 392 n, 452 n, 463 n, 484.

Bulsār, 438.

Burhānpur, 62 n, 68, 88, 91, 177, 192, 207, 215 n, 385, 403 (2), 450, 450 n, 495 ; *sarāi* at, 68-70 ; castle at, 68 n, 70 n, 80 ; Khurram at, 359, 360, 369 ; Roe at, 68-80, 456, 471 n, 472 ; his proposed visit to Khurram, 332, 340 n, 341, 341 n, 357-60, 369 ; factory at (*see also* Bangham, Nicholas), 70-2, 80, 81, 178 n, 233, 240, 253, 297, 320, 339, 340, 366 ; dissolved, 441 ; affray at, 428, 456 ; *Kotwāl* of, 68-72, 80 (2), 428.

Burning glasses, 77.

Cabinets, 99, 259, 349, 365, 459 (2).

Caducean, 457.

Calico, trade in, *passim* ; private trade in, 417.

Calicut, English at, 361 ; Zamorin of, 376, 460.

Cambalu, 76, 118.

Cambay, 73, 74 n, 91, 172, 304, 365, 454, 495, 498 n ; vessels of, 27 ; trade of, 320 ; Governor of, 29, 128 n, 172, 290 (2), 292, 324 ; makes overtures for trade, 29, 30, 40, 41 (2), 43, 44, 480 ; fight with Portuguese at, 290 ; Jahāngīr visits, 384, 404 n, 422 ; Roe may go to, 418.

Cambay, Gulf of, 270, 433, 495 (3), 499.

Camels, *passim* ; disadvantages of transport by, 315 (2), 319, 321.

Camlets, 147, 320, 458.

Canary Islands, 1, 2.

Canning, Paul, xvii, 94 n.

Cannon, sale of, 361.

Canoes, 9, 301.

Canterbury, Archbishop of. *See* Abbot, George.

Caparison, a field, 151, 459.

Cape, the. *See* Good Hope.

Cape merchant, 407 ; position of, 96.

' Capon,' 190, 426.

Carckga, 66 n.

Card-playing, 293, 294.

Careless, R., 27.

Carew, Lord, Roe's letters to, 88, 88 n ; his letters to Roe, lxxi, 92 n, 159 n, 210 n, 223 n, 389 n, 498.

' Cargazon,' 301, 333, 390, 397, 402, 470.

Carmelite friar, 112 n.

Carpets, 416, 450 n ; as presents, 96, 116, 259, 352 ; Persian, 96, 126, 352 ; Roe buys, 352 n, 360.

Carrack, a Portuguese, destroyed, 247 n, 248, 250, 251, 274 n, 298, 301, 319 n.

Cartas, 406, 430 (2), 432, 433, 475 n.

Cash, Mr. C. G., 500.

Caste, 406 n, 447.

' Catching,' 361.

Cathay, 92, 308 n.

Cats' eyes, 457.

Cattle, *passim* ; draught, 67, 74.

Cavalleiro, 199.

Ceylon, 376.

Chamba, 489 n, 491.

Chambal (river), 330, 334 n, 495 n.

S.T.R. 2 K

'Champion,' 322.
Chapes, 262.
Chapman, Libby, 370.
'Character' (cipher), 115, 280, 435, 453.
Charles, Prince, lxxix, 269.
Charles, the, 290 n, 301, 432.
Chaul, 14 n, 15, 56, 204.
Chāul, 418.
Cheese, 413, 418.
Chess, 212.
Chhāp, 65, 136 (2), 137, 151, 175, 177, 179 (2), 181, 184, 428, 476.
'Chicken,' 202.
Child, Alexander, 291 n (2).
China, 203, 335, 370, 376; trade with, 21 n, 76, 181, 305 n; goods from, 49, 99, 284 n, 368, 393, 400; no intercourse between India and, 92; Emperor of, 21 n, 76.
'China shop,' 116, 305.
China ware, 99, 116 n, 148 n, 181, 338, 360, 367, 400, 427, 445, 459.
Chintzes, 100, 360.
Chitor, 82, 90, 496.
Chittagong, 194 n, 494.
Chopra, 67.
Choultry, 80 n.
Christians, royal princes made, 176.
Churls, 237, 320, 321, 338, 408, 418, 441.
Cinnamon, 451.
Cinnamon water, 413.
Circumcision, 270, 274, 276, 298.
Civet, 23, 116, 193 n, 320.
Civet cats, 23.
Cloak bags, 458.
Clocks, 447, 455; as presents, 94, 259.
Clove, the, 362.
Cloves. *See* Spices.
Coach, 297 n; sent as a present, 48, 49, 76, 78; presented, 90, 98; altered, 284, 306; imitated, 282, 284, 306; cost of, 285 n; given to Nūr Mahal, 285, 289.
Coachman. *See* Hemsell.

Cochin, 252.
Cochineal, 460.
Cocks, Richard, 58 n.
Coco de mer, 13.
Coco-nuts, 9, 11, 13; milk of, 12; the tree, 11, 13.
Coffee, 22.
Coke, Sir John, 463 n.
Comorin, Cape, 461.
Comoro Islands, 7-15, 248. *See also* Angaziya, Johanna, *and* Mohilla.
Concord, the, 361.
Connock, Edward, sent to Persia, 291 n; his proceedings there, 357, 371, 374, 389, 390, 398 n, 435 (2), 444, 444 n, 453 (2), 464, 467, 468; Roe sends him a commission, 398 n; death of, 444.
Constantinople, 461; ambassador at, 109; Roe writes to, xliii, 385 n.
Cook, Roe's, 36, 311, 331.
Coral, 422, 451, 457.
Corn, 67, 270, 379.
Coromandel Coast, 432, 494; Dutch on, 437, 461. *See also* Masulipatam.
Corsi, Francesco, 105, 121, 124, 131, 162, 260, 301; account of, 276 n; Jahāngīr and, 99, 276-9, 365, 438; Roe and, 248, 277 n, 278, 280, 322, 322 n, 323, 437 n; leaves Ajmer, 298; mediates with Goa, 249, 307, 437, 438, 454.
Coryat, Thomas, 274 n, 276 n, 355 n, 356 n, 368, 493 n, 499; at Ajmer, 83, 89 n, 115; Jahāngīr and, 83 n; goes to Agra, 232; reaches Māndu, 368 n; his death, 368 n.
Cotton yarn, 178.
Coutinho, João, 437. *See also* Goa, Viceroy of.
Covado, 100, 181 (2), 184, 296 n, 375, 443.
Covert, Robert, 81 n.
Cows venerated, 275.
'Crake,' 199.
Cranganor, 361 n.

INDEX

Crawford, Col. D. G., 474 n.
Criali, 66 n.
Cross, —, 6 n.
'Crotch,' 20.
Crowder, John, lxi, 108, 201, 290 n, 291, 312.
Crown as present, 459.
Crystal, 99, 127 n.
Curtis, John, 2 n.
Cuscus, 12.
Cushions, 346, 348, 353, 359, 458, 459.
Cutwork, 99.

Dābhol, 15, 360, 361; trade at, 361, 363 n, 430, 461, 470, 471; ships of, 376, 383, 430, 460, 470, 472 n; Governor of, 361 n, 362, 363 n.
Dacca, 494.
Da Costa, Father, 279 n.
Da Fonseca, Gonçalo Pinto, 74 n.
Daggers, 259, 282.
Damān, xxv, 14, 15, 26 (4), 56, 204, 368, 369 n, 406, 454.
Damask, 126.
Dangāli, 491.
Daniell, John, 1 n.
Dāniyāl, Prince, sons of, 176 n, 277, 278.
Danvers, Lord, 391.
Darbār, 84, and passim.
Darsani ceremony, 270, 276.
Dastūri, 310.
Dates, 23.
Dayānat Khān, 242 n.
Deccan, the, 90; Abdullah Khān's campaign in, 150; Khurram sent to, 164, 171, 172, 177, 183, 220, 237, 238, 242-4, 256, 274, 318; course of the war, 340; its close, 385. See also Bījāpur.
Deer, 108, 155 n.
Defence, the, 362.
'Degrees,' 356, 427.
Delhi, 239, 492; pillar at, 82, 492.
Delishi, 20 (3).
Della Valle, Pietro, 91 n, 375 n, 422 n, 463 n, 501.

S.T.R.

De Meneses, Emanuel, 298, 301.
Denmark, King of, 452 n.
Dervish, a, 343.
De Silva e Figueroa, Garcia, 111 n.
Devonshire kerseys, 451.
De Wolff, Jan (or Hans), xxix.
Dhāita, 67, 403, 428 n.
Dhāna, 418.
Dhār, 404 n, 495.
Diamonds, passim; 'dyalled,' 379; 'drild,' 283.
Diana, picture of, 459.
Dioscorides, 20.
Dipsall, 3, 16.
Discalsato friar, 112.
Diu, 25 (2), 406, 485; ships of, 388 n, 430, 460, 461.
Diul-Sind, 75 n, 91, 104 (2), 499. See also Lahrībandar.
Diul-Sind (river), 75, 490, 498 n, 499.
Diwān, 292 n, 477, 507.
Dodsworth, Edward, 6 n, 7 n, 32 n.
Dogs, Jahāngīr asks for, 160, 251, 351, 394; Khurram desires one, 399; as presents, 312 n; some presented, 346, 348; one attacks an elephant, 348 n; used in punishment, 201; Roe's dog, 365.
Dohad, 404 n, 414 n, 471 n.
Doolies, 327, 327 n.
Dorāi, 286 n.
Dos Baixos, Cape, 16.
Downton, Nicholas, xvii, xxv, 350 n, 498 n; defeats the Portuguese, xxvi, 7 n, 14, 40, 102, 105, 377 n.
Dragon, the, xviii, 18 (2), 19, 59 n, 362.
Drums, 21, 285.
Ducks, 4.
Duffield, —, 6 n.
Duif, the, 368, 369.
Dulce (river), 4.
Dutch, the, 366, 430, 431, 459; at the Cape, 5; at the Comoros, 9; in Bengal, 193 n; at Surat, see Surat; embassy, 427; hostilities with

2 K 2

INDEX

the Portuguese, 79, 102, 106, 298, 437, 461; to be excluded from India, 74 n, 203 n, 214, 453; their policy criticised, 303, 428 n, 434, 453; Roe and, see Roe. See also Ahmadābād, Bantam, Coromandel, and Mokha.
Dwārka, 496.

East India Company, passim; Roe's letters to, 72, 98, 101, 106 n, 110, 301, 319, 432, 488.
Ebony, 143 n.
Edwards, William, xvii, xxvi, 32 n; notice of, 27 n; at court, xxvii, 27, 63, 64, 75 n, 78, 94 n, 117, 126 n, 154, 229 n, 234, 352; Roe writes to, 29, 46, 60, 61; he writes to Roe, 77; meets him, 83, 98; leaves Ajmer, 84, 367; Roe's opinion of, 96 (2).
Elephant, the (storm), 217.
Elephants, passim; as presents, 89, 99, 128 n, 187, 282, 356, 364; reviews of, 222, 270, 281; carry guns, 286; fights between, 85, 91, 270; used for executions, 87, 104, 153 n, 191; wooden, 91.
Elephants' teeth. See Ivory.
Elizabeth, Princess, xxi, xxii, 157 n; portrait of, 125, 357.
Elks, 120.
Elstrack, Renold, 497, 500.
Embroidery, 99, 129, 284, 346, 348 n, 353, 449, 458.
Emeralds, 127 n, 162, 222, 225, 283, 285 (2), 357, 457.
Enamel, 285, 449, 460.
Erzeroum, 300, 317.
Euclid, 275.
Eunuchs, 85, 190, 191, 270, 282, 285, 286 n, 294, 426, 468 n, 469 n.
Expedition, the, xviii, 10 n, 82 n; her voyage out, 1 n, 18, 19, 26, 28, 58; sent to Persia, 444 n; and to Sumatra, 488.

Fainéant, 351.
Fardles, 379, 408.
Faria y Sousa, Manoel, 298 n, 437 n.
Farīd Bukhāri, Shaikh, 211.
Farmān, 31, and passim.
Farran, Dr., 285 n.
Fartāk, 20.
Fatehpur Sikri, 327, 334 n, 485 n.
Feathers, 260, 282 (2), 283, 449; as presents, 143, 261, 264, 312 n, 364.
Fern, Sir John, 383, 387.
Fernoso, Cape, 7.
Fetiplace, Francis, 152, 191, 196, 473 (2); at Agra, 232, 366 n, 424, 440, 442 n, 446 n; at Ajmer, 268 n, 328, 341; visits Roe, 327; Roe writes to, 239 n, 334 n, 368.
Fiador, 242 n.
Fish ceremony, 283.
Fisher, Benjamin, 500.
Flamingoes, 4.
'Flory,' 16.
Flux, 141, 326 n, 379, 474 n.
Fortaventura, 1, 2.
Fortified base, English desire a, 73, 250, 305, 433; objected to, 252, 434; Roe advises against, 303, 373, 415, 434, 436.
Foscarini, Jeronimo, 301.
Fowls, 12, 13, 22, 24, 66.
Francis, the, 388 n, 389-91, 407, 409, 451, 452.
Frankfurt, 99.
French, the, 115, 211, 383 n, 384 n, 431.
Frigates, 73, and passim.
Fruit, artificial, 126, 262, 378 n, 379.
Fumbuni, 12.
Furs, 324.

Gabell, 57.
Gago, 6.
Gala, 14.
Galaxia, the, 2.
Galecia, Giovanni, 300, 322, 323 (2).
Gallinhas, Cape, 2.

INDEX

Gandak (river), 492 n, 493.
Gandevi, 154, 369 n.
Gangamora, 13 n.
Ganges (river), 270, 308 n, 491-4; revered, 271, 274.
Garhakatanka, 494.
Garrard, Henry, 360.
Gates, Sir Thomas, 392 n.
Gaur, 489 n, 494.
Geese, wild, 4.
'General,' 3 n; post of, 95.
Gentiles, 105, 270, 274-6, 478.
Georgia, 314; subdued by Persians, 92, 103; the Turks and, 300, 317.
Germans, lii, 51, 141.
Geroon, 370.
Ghakkars, the, 491 n.
Ghi, 91, 379, 382.
Ghilān, 300, 314.
Ghiyās Beg, 150, 166, 237, 245, 339, 364, 369, 380, 420, 421, 431 (5).
Ghusl-khāna, 85, *and passim*.
Gimbals, 282.
'Ging,' 452.
Ginseng, 5 n.
Gipps, Robert, 291 n.
Glass, a folding, 346.
Glasses, trade in, 13, 373, 457, 458; as presents, 122, 356, 459.
Globe, the, 61 n, 248, 432, 435, 441.
Gloves, 283, 458; as presents, 211 n, 346 n, 357, 449.
Goa, 15, 44, 56, 79, 204, 358, 365, 380, 382, 413, 450 n, 460, 461; news from, 298, 301; Roe proposes a blockade of, 307, 440; Sherley at, 252, 274, 307, 313, 314, 316.
Goa, Viceroys of, 74 n, 102, 302, 313, 316, 436-9, 454; new, expected, 27, 56, 248; none sent, 301; Roe's overtures to, lii, 56, 57, 97, 101, 124, 137, 248, 249, 307, 420, 434, 436-9; present to Jahāngīr from, 161.
Goats, 9, 12, 13, 23, 24 (2), 117, 365.
Goeree, Adriaan W., 369 n, 374 n.

Goës, Benedict, 300 n.
Gogo, 74 n, 415, 433; offered to English, 403, 412, 480; junks from, 386, 388 n, 397, 430, 475 n, 485.
Gogra (river), 493 n.
Gohad, 495.
Golconda, 361 n, 472.
Gold, *passim*; trade in, 6, 14, 388 n, 400, 403, 416, 450 n.
Gold, cloth of, *passim*; price of, 100, 181; trade in, 151, 181, 312 n, 458, 459.
Gold lace, 458.
Goldie, Father, 276 n.
Golding, Rev. —, 462 n, 463.
Gollonsir, 18.
Gombroon, 111, 446 n; captured, 110.
Gondwānā, 494, 501.
Good Hope, Cape of, 4, 8 (2), 436, 468, 486 n, 487 n, 488. *See also* Table Bay.
Gopi-talāo, the, 58, 90.
Gore, Alderman John, 442, 463 n.
Greek, a. *See* Lopo.
Greek inscription, a, 82, 492.
Green, Christopher, 311, 334 n, 365, 463 n, 470.
Grograms, 147, 320, 458.
Guardafui, Cape, 16, 17 (2), 24 (3).
Guiana, xxii, 384 n.
Gujarāt, 308 n, 495; conquest of, 439 n; Governors of, *see* Abdullāh Khān, Khurram, Farīd, *and* Mukarrab Khān.
Gujarātis, 21, 23, 25, 202 n, 308, 376.
Gunners wanted, 255.
Guns as presents, 195, 467.
Guru, debt of, 367, 381 n, 394, 399, 401, 410, 412, 414.
Gwalior, 495.

Hāfah, 20 n.
Hāfiz Jamāl, 121, 141, 143, 166, 175, 176, 182, 215, 219, 264; Roe at, 211.
Haggat, Bartholomew, 109, 300, 322, 389 n.

518   INDEX

Hāji Khān, 490 n, 500.
Hājīpur-Patna, 496.
Hakewill, William, 92.
Hall, Rev. John, 12, 35, 213; death of, 216, 311.
Halliday, William, 452 n.
Hangers, 437 n, 449, 458.
Har Bilas Sardar, 217 n.
Hardwār, 496, 499.
Har-Gobin, 381 n, 382.
Harris, Capt. Christopher, xviii, 31, 55 (3), 56, 59.
Hāsilpur, 404 n.
Hatch, John, 3, 392, 398 n, 467.
'Hatched,' 306.
Hatfield, —, 427, 447, 448, 468, 468 n.
Hats, 117, 349, 427, 449.
Hawkins, William, xv, xvi, 69 n, 78, 391 n, 448; his widow, *see* Towerson, Mrs.
Hawks, 325, 364.
Hector, the, 10 n, 62 n, 361, 361 n, 388 n, 391 n.
Hemsell, William, 99, 282 (2), 284, 284 n, 285 n; death of, 455.
Henry, Prince of Wales, xxi, xxii.
Herbert, Thomas, 355 n.
Herbert of Cherbury, Lord, 355 n.
Hertford, Lady, 83 n.
Heuten, Wouter, 219 n.
Heynes, Edward, lxxii, 258, 267, 442, 474 n; sent to the Red Sea, 442 n, 456, 462 n, 463, 470, 483; Roe writes to, 482 n.
Hides, trade in, 184, 200, 471 n, 473 n.
Hill, —, 463.
Hindustān, meaning of, 308 n.
Hingona, 68 n.
Hoftman, Frederick, 486, 487 n.
Holland cloth, 13.
Honey, 12.
Hope, the, xxvi, 14, 309; at the Cape, xxv, 5 n, 6 n, 7.
Horses, *passim*; Jahāngīr desires an English, 129, 151, 251, 351; care of, 91; trained for the coach, 284, 284 n.
Hosiander, the, 361.

Hosten, Father, 124 n.
Howard, Nicholas, 428.
Howdahs, 283, 286.
Hudson, Mrs., 391 n, 448, 462, 463; goes home, 486, 486 n, 488.
Hudson, William, 391 n.
Hughes, Robert, 187-9, 268 n, 446 n.
Hūgli, 194 n.

Ibrāhīm, 8, 13, 17.
Ibrāhīm Khān, 62-4, 66 (2), 196, 209; Governor of Surat, 62, 107 n, 145, 170, 178 n, 218, 228, 231, 232, 252, 253, 260, 292, 297, 400-2, 412; summoned to court, 414, 415 n, 417; the Dutch and, 202 n, 219; Roe writes to, 146 n, 327, 357; he writes to Roe, 219; character of, 253, 294, 415.
Iceland dog, 365.
Idu'l Fatr festival, 239.
Indigo, trade in, *passim*; private trade in, 408, 417; from Lahore, 23; from Agra, 201, 321.
Indus (river), 75, 148, 270, 308, 406, 446, 490 (3), 491 (2), 491 n (2), 499; wrongly mapped, 76, 91, 104, 495, 499.
Interlopers. See *Francis*, the, *and Lion*, the.
Interpreters, Roe's difficulties with, 100, 124, 160, 211, 266, 303, 326, 327, 366, 367, 448 n, 455.
Irādat Khān, 143, 381, 382, 394.
Ishāk Beg, 241, 292, 327, 472.
Ispahān, 76, 83 n, 274, 296 n, 315, 372 n, 375, 453; letters to, 109, 335, 371; letters from, 300, 312, 316, 370.
Italians, 316, 384, 388 n. *See also* Corsi, Venetians, *and* Veronese.
Itimād-uddaula. *See* Ghiyās Beg.
Ivory, 143 n; trade in, 14, 63, 147, 228, 295, 305, 320, 388 n, 434, 441, 450 n, 451, 473.

INDEX 519

Jacatra, 361, 362 n, 405 n.
Jackson, John, 405, 469.
Jacob, 51, 141.
Jacobite Christians, 22.
Jadrūp, 343 n.
Jādu, broker at Ajmer, 124, 128, 196, 197, 218, 220, 268, 288, 336; his negligence, 191; proposed transfer to Surat, 241; acts as Roe's interpreter, 100, 109, 119, 198; leaves him, 326 n, 336, 341; again employed, 326 n, 327, 329 (2), 386, 387, 403, 404, 426.
Jāfar, broker at Agra, 241, 336.
Jāfarābād, 73.
Jagannāth, 494.
Jāgīr, 419.
Jahān, Khwāja, 403.
Jahāndār, Prince, 243, 285, 352.
Jahāngīr, the Emperor, *passim*; his character, xxxi, 105, 226 n, 257, 259 n, 273, 325, 328, 338, 447; his delight in animals, 30, 129, 151, 160, 251, 351, 394; his interest in painting, 187-90, 199; his religion, 105, 270, 276, 278, 279, 345; his cruelty, 87, 104, 265, 322; his parsimony, 116, 225, 342 n, 364; his love of sport, 325, 404; his addiction to liquor, 86, 86 n, 99, 190, 222, 226, 240, 245, 265, 324, 325, 345, 353, 414; dislikes Wednesdays, 166 n; never circumcised, 276; his mode of government, 86, 89, 102, 104, 105, 201; extent of his empire and resources, 90, 102, 105, 270; his stock of jewels, 116, 222, 270, 378, 379; his respect for Shāh Abbās, 111; portraits of, lxxviii, 200, 201, 212, 214; his standard, 497; his seal, 497, 507 n, 508; his wives (*see also* Nūr Mahal), 270, 282, 283, 285, 286 n, 287, 329, 349, 352, 425; his mother, *see* Maryam-zamāni; his sister, 384; to go to the Deccan, 125 n, 235, 238-40,
274; leaves Ajmer, 282-7, 296 n, 297; interviews with ascetics, 328, 343; at Māndu, 353-404; birthday festivities, 221, 378; leaves Māndu, 402, 404; goes to Ahmadābād, 372 n, 384, 399, 402, 405, 408, 409, 412, 414; arrives, 404 n, 425 n; his illness there, 473 n; leaves and returns, 456, 460, 462, 463, 471 n; departs for Agra, 482 n, 485 n; his correspondence with King James, *see* James.
Jahāngīr, the (ship), 430.
Jahāngīrī rupees. *See* Rupees.
Jaisalmer, 501.
Jaitāpur, 66 n.
Jamāl-uddīn Husain, entertains Roe, 209-12; visits him, 215; made Governor of Sironj, 215.
James, King, 281, 319, 388 n, 428 n; portrait of, 125, 357; letters to Eastern princes, 24, 232 n; letters to Jahāngīr, xv, xvii, xxiii, xxvi, lviii, 87, 98, 100, 305, 306, 392, 419 (2), 420, 437, 439 n, 464, 502, 504-6, 506 n; letters from Jahāngīr to, 166, 189, 465, 466, 488, 504, 506; presents from Jahāngīr to, 201, 503; letter to Khurram wanted, 305, 306, 392; letter to Shāh Abbās, 444; the reply, 464; letters to Roe, 398, 399, 449, 503; Roe writes to, 102, 113, 314 n, 316 n, 463, 503.
James, Giles, 484 n.
James, the, 291 n, 295. *See also Royal James*, the.
Japan, 76, 376; goods from, 99, 181.
Jask, 76, 110, 114, 118, 148, 193 n, 217, 292, 313, 389 n, 392 n, 406 (2), 467; ships sent to, 290, 295, 296 n, 306, 313, 314, 317, 332, 335, 392 n, 398 n, 440, 444 n, 461, 462.
Jask, Cape, 76 (2).
Jaswān, 489 n, 492, 501.
Jaunpur, 493, 500, 501.
Jawāla Mūkhi, 499, 500.

INDEX

Jesuits, the, xv, 77, 236 n; at court, 75 n, 124; intrigue against the English, xviii, xix, 78, 102, 275 n; their work in India, 272, 275-9, 319. *See also* Aquaviva, Corsi, and Xavier.
Jet, 143 n.
Jewels, 191; as presents, 89, 99, 129, 138 n, 312 n, 356, 394, 459; trade in, 149, 161, 162, 263, 440, 445, 449, 450 n, 457, 467; desired at court, 99, 450, 458, 466; Jahāngīr's stock of, 116, 222, 270, 378, 379. *See also* Diamonds, *etc*.
Jews, 345.
Jharokha, 85, 87, 242, 282, 325.
Jhelum (river), 491, 491 n.
Johanna, 8, 9 (3), 15.
Joint Stocks, First and Second, 407, 467.
Jones, Robert, 124 n, 158, 159, 164, 312 n.
Jones, Thomas, 388 n, 391, 392, 423, 452, 452 n.
Joseph, Benjamin, 248, 253.
Judia, Bassas da, 8 (3).
Jugglery, 271, 280.
Jumna (river), 390 n, 447 n, 492, 493 (3).
Junāgarh, 495.

Kābul, 491.
Kābul (river), 491 n.
Kāfila, 141, *and passim*.
Kafir, 14.
Kahār, 419.
Kakares, the, 491.
Kāli (river), 493.
Kāli Sind (river), 334.
Kāliyāda, 342.
Kanāt, 286, 286 n, 287 n.
Kandahār, 90, 226 n, 390 n, 406 (2), 490, 496, 502; district of, 490; Governor of, 322. *See also* Rustam, Mīrza.
Kāngra, 212 n, 492 n.
Karan, Prince, 127, 132, 133.
Karod, 66 n.
Kashmīr, 485 n, 491, 502.
Kathodora, 471.

Kāzi, 476, 477.
Kazvin, 384.
Keeling, William, xviii, xix, 193 n, 233, 291 n, 361 n, 442; notice of, 9 n; on the voyage out, 6 n, 9, 11, 21, 24; Roe's relations with, xxv, 10 n, 77, 95, 302 (2), 433, 442; at Swally, 27-31, 33 (2), 39, 41, 42, 44, 45, 51, 52, 56, 59-62, 78, 93 n; captures a Portuguese vessel, 252; at Bantam, 361 n; returns to England, 362 n.
Kerridge, Thomas, *passim*; notice of, 94 n; his character, 292, 326, 330, 467; at Ahmadābād, 94, 108; agent at Surat, 94 n, 178 n; ill-used there, 327 n; his letterbook, 94 n; goes home, 463 n.
Kerseys, 450.
Khāndesh, 495.
Khān Jahān Lodi, 171.
Khānkhānān, the. *See* Abdurrahīm.
Kharrāb Khān, 52, 59.
Khazāna rupees. *See* Rupees.
Khilats, 226 n, 242, 243, 256, 259, 284 n, 357, 427.
Khumbāriā, 65.
Khurassan, 502.
Khurram, Prince, *passim*; his character, 93, 247, 273; fond of drink, 99; an enemy to Christians, 88, 146, 176, 247, 279; favours Portuguese, 146, 161; yet ill-treats them, 368; his wives, 97, 369; death of his daughter, 166; a son born, 179; subdues Udaipur, 82 n, 123 n, 496; made Viceroy of Gujarat, xxvii, 28, 40, 73, 88, 93, 419 (2), 425; orders English to leave Surat, 55, 60, 93 n, 174; denies it, 93; his relations with Parwīz, 235; and with Nūr Mahal, 289, 338; aims at the throne, 244; attempts to secure custody of Khusrau, 245, 246; succeeds, 256; tries to murder

him, 262, 369; suspected of complicity in his death, 247 n; his house at Ajmer, 217, 297 n; to go to the Deccan, 164, 171, 172, 177, 179, 183, 220, 237, 238, 242-4, 256, 274; leaves Ajmer, 281; gives Roe a cloak, 294; desires English gunners, 255; dispute with Corsi, 279; given title of Shāh. 282 n; his campaign in the Deccan, 340, 385; at Burhānpur, and Roe's proposed visit, see Burhānpur; in disfavour, 369, 372 n; summoned to Māndu, 369, 377; arrives, 385, 386; receives title of Shāh Jahān, 386; his increased influence, 435; at Ahmadābād, 425-9; his illness, 473 n; leaves Ahmadābād, 471 n; Roe's agreement with, 475; Roe takes leave of, 479; letter wanted from King James to, 305, 306, 392; his ships, 202, 204, 206, 207, 213, 241, 386, 402, 428, 471, 472; portrait of, lxxviii.

Khusrau, Prince, 171; his character, 247, 299; his rebellion, 211 n; popularity of, 244, 256, 286; Jahāngīr intends him to succeed, 244 n; makes him ride with him, 285; Khurram tries to secure custody of, 245, 246; succeeds, 256; attempts to murder him, 262, 369; Āsaf Khan slights, 298; their rumoured reconciliation, 325, 369, 373; he is released, 369; and offered Nūr Mahal's daughter, 369, 373; Roe's interview with, 342; his sister, 256; his wife, 325, 370 n; his death, 247 n.

Kishin, 20 n.
Kiyāra Sundar, 496.
Knives, trade in, 13, 146, 149, 373, 449, 457; given as presents, 41, 46, 76, 98, 124 n, 143 n, 311 n, 356, 364, 459.
Koran, the, 454.

Kos, passim; explained, 65 n, 84, 496 n.
Kotwāl, 68, and *passim*.
Krieger, George, lii.
Kuch Bihār, 494 n.
Kurds, the, 273.

Lace, 99, 449, 458, 459.
Lafer, —, xxix.
Lahore, *passim*; proposed factory at, 148, 193 n; Venetians at, 300, 301; Governor of, 211; Jahāngīr thinks of visiting, 358 n, 360. *See also* Indigo.
Lahrībandar, 10 n, 75 n, 208, 406, 490; proposed factory at, 193 n, 292, 396, 412; disadvantages of, 305, 434; Portuguese at, 76, 193 n, 305, 406, 446. *See also* Diul-Sind.
Lakh of rupees, *passim*; value of, 89.
Lancaster, Sir James, 9, 315.
Lane-Poole, S., 223 n.
Lar, 313.
Lāristān, 491.
Larks, 4.
Lashkar, 286, and *passim*; the royal, described, 324.
Lawn, 283, 360.
Lead, trade in, *passim*.
Leather goods, 262. *See also* Hides.
'Leiger,' 315.
Lemons, 9, 13, 225.
Lemons, syrup of, 413.
Leske, Rev. William, 216 n.
Lethbridge, Sir Roper, 490 n, 494 n.
Levant Company, the. *See* Turkey Company.
Liège, 195.
Limes, 13.
Linschoten's map, 499.
Lion, the, xviii, xxiv, 2 n, 3 n, 10 n, 141, 148 n, 247, 311, 392 n; sent to the Red Sea, 483 n, 488.
Lion, the (interloper), 388 n, 389-91, 407, 409, 451, 452.

INDEX

Lions, 354; only the king may kill, 365; a tame, 176; Roe troubled by a, 365.
Lisbon, 274, 298, 307 (2), 307 *n*, 439.
Loadstones, 91.
'Longe Walke,' the, 493 *n*, 499.
Looking-glasses, 50, 76, 77, 457; as presents, 108, 259, 262, 312 *n*.
Lopo, Diego, 336, 341, 341 *n*, 344, 345, 349.
Lulls, Arnold, 109, 315.

Macao, 376.
Mace. *See* Spices.
Madagascar, 7, 13, 15.
Madho, 472.
Madrid, 57, 113.
Magadoxo, 14 (4), 15; people of, 8, 11, 15, 17.
Magellan clouds, 2.
Maghs, the, 494.
Magini, Giovanni Antonio, 22.
Mahābāt Khān, 82 *n*, 162 *n*, 171, 178 *n*, 280 *n*, 366, 367; notice of, 171 *n*; his character, 178, 192; dislikes Khurram, 192 *n*; Roe writes to, 177, 193; his reply, 192.
Mahal, 297 *n*.
Maheza, 14.
Mahi (river), 404, 495.
Mahmūdis, passim; value of, 145 *n*.
Mail, shirts of, 458.
Malacca, 461.
Malik Ambar, 366 (2), 385 *n*.
Malim, 13.
Mālwa, 342, 495; kings of, 343, 353 *n*.
Mammocks, 352.
Māndu, 343, 429 *n*; described, 81, 220, 353 *n*; Jahāngīr goes to, 219, 238-40, 328, 332, 337; arrives, 353; his residence, 354; Roe's quarters at, 332, 353-5, 359 *n*, 360, 365, 380; Coryat at, 368 *n*; Khurram at, 340, 385, 386; banqueting house at, 369; scarcity of water at, 354, 355, 356 *n*, 358, 360; Jahāngīr leaves, 402, 404; Roe leaves, 404.
Mango trees, 323.
Manilla, 439.
Manohar Dās, lxxviii.
Mansabdār, 383, 383 *n*, 429; system, 89, 105.
Maps, presented, 45, 46, 84 *n*; Roe's map, 497. *See also* Linschoten *and* Mercator.
Marcasite, 5.
Marfil, 14, 228, 450 *n*.
Marshalsea prison, 452.
Martin, Nathaniel, 441.
Maryam-zamāni, the Queen-mother, 262, 386; her ship, 74 *n*, 387, 388, 388 *n*, 394, 422, 451.
Masulipatam, 157 *n*, 308 *n*, 361; English factory at, 159 *n*, 160 *n*, 417, 418 *n*; letters to and from, 158 *n*, 159, 193, 252, 309 *n*, 385, 470; Dutch at, 203, 206, 207, 374 *n*, 480.
Maund, 310, 321, 429.
Mauritius, 369 *n*.
Mayotta, 9 (3).
Mecca, 74, 384.
Melinde, 369 *n*.
Melons, 150, 152, 364.
Mercator's maps, 1, 3, 7, 15, 91, 104, 499; incorrect, 383 *n*; presented to Jahāngīr, 380, 381, 383 *n*, 499 *n*; returned, 382, 383 *n*.
Merchant's Hope, the. *See Hope, the.*
Methwold, William, 224 *n*.
Mewār. *See* Udaipur.
Mewāt, 492, 501.
Middelburg, 335.
Middelburg, the, 368, 369, 374.
Middleton, Sir Henry, xvi, 24, 361, 361 *n*, 362; his voyage to the Red Sea, 81 *n*, 308, 376.
Mildenhall, John, xv.
'Minion,' 172, 178, 197.
Mīr Mīrān, 130.
Mīrza Beg, 128.
Mitford, Thomas, 61, 441.
'Mogoll,' origin of, 274.

INDEX

Mohilla, 7, 16, 24, 25 ; the fleet at, 8-15 ; Sultān of, 9, 12.
Mohurs, 128 n.
Mokha, 376, 413, 430, 460 ; Dutch at, 202, 308, 338, 368, 374, 376, 376 n ; Roe's correspondence with the Governor, 483. See also Red Sea.
Moles, 4.
Moluccas, the, 428 n, 434, 453, 480, 486 n.
Molyneux, Lady, 349 n.
Mombasa, 301 n.
Monkeys, 121, 280.
Monnox, Edward, 398 n, 415 n, 444 n.
Montague, Lady, 349 n.
Mootham, James, 452.
Mootham, John, 452.
Moses, 280, 345, 506.
Mosques, 13, 90, 274, 353, 354 n, 454, 478 ; spelling of, 13 n.
Mota, 66 n.
Mother of pearl, 126, 287.
Mozambique, 13, 14, 298, 301 (2), 387, 388 n, 450 n.
Mu'allim, 13 n, 431 n.
Mubārak, 380.
' Muff,' 117, 151, 251.
Mughals effeminate, 92, 318.
Muhammad, the Prophet, 12, 270, 276 (3), 280, 345.
Muhammad Bākir, Mīrza. See Irādat Khān.
Muhammad Husain, 157 n, 158, 184, 201, 233.
Muhammad Riza Beg, Persian ambassador, 247 ; received, 258-60, 274, 285 ; delivers his presents, 262, 283 ; at court, 264, 287, 296, 297, 310, 318, 356 ; presents to, 264, 266 356, 364 ; Roe and, 267, 287, 291, 307, 317, 324 (2), 332-5, 363, 371, 372, 375, 390 ; leaves the court, 363 ; death of, 363 n.
Mukaddum, 30.
Mukandwāra, pass of, 338 n.
Mukarrab Khān, xxv, xxvi, xxvii, 27, 188 n, 350 n, 461 ; notice of, 27 n ; his character,

180 ; concludes peace with Portuguese, xxvii, 74 n ; his relations with Roe, 122, 130, 138, 166-9, 175 (2), 176, 230, 234-6, 289 ; Roe visits, 180, 234, 236 ; made Viceroy of Gujarāt, 230, 242 n ; with superintendence of Surat, 236 n ; at Ahmadābād, 382, 405; 424, 425, 447, 450 n ; his offer of Gogo, 403 ; refuses to buy the unicorn's horn, 254 n.
Mukshud Dās, 381, 394, 399, 401, 403, 412.
Mules, 259, 263.
Mulher, 66.
Mulla, 274, 275, 382.
Multān, 490.
Mundy, Peter, 66 n, 85 n, 297 n.
Murtaza Khān, 212 n.
Musician. See Armstrong.
Musk, 116, 182, 193 n, 213, 320, 359.
Muskets, 21, 183, 259.
Muslin, 116.
Muzafarābād, 73.

Nagarkot, 489 n, 492, 492 n, 501.
Nails, 284 n, 306.
Nandurbār, 67.
Nārāyanpur, 67.
Narbadā (river), 81, 353 n, 356 n, 358 n, 360, 380, 495.
Nariād, 50 n, 404 n.
Nārnaul, 492.
Narwar, 489 n, 495, 499.
Nasabar, 67 n.
Nāsir-uddīn, 343 n.
Nassau, the, 202, 206, 219 n, 298.
Nauroz, the, 121, 124, 309 n, 373, 456, 460 ; ceremonies of, 125, 131, 132, 356 ; meaning, 125.
Nautch-girls, 128, 132, 357.
' Nawfrage,' 374.
Needlework, 262, 359, 458.
Newport, Christopher, xviii, 10, 11, 110, 117, 296 n.
Newse, Samuel, 388 n, 391, 391 n, 392, 452, 452 n ; at Ahmadābād, 422, 423.

INDEX

New Year's Gift, the, 6 n, 388 n (2), 392 n.
Night-cap, a, 357.
Nilab (river), 491.
Nimgul, 67.
Ningin roots, 5.
Nizām, Khwāja, Roe and, 101, 106, 118, 122, 150, 152, 153, 155, 175, 177, 179, 289; nominated as Governor of Surat, 106.
Norwich stuffs, 458.
Nūr Mahal (Nūr Jahān), xxxii, 88, 97, 137, 154, 155, 190, 218, 236 n, 256, 340, 347, 373, 393, 396, 426; her influence, 88 n, 89, 235, 252 n, 256, 270, 337, 338; her character, 325; visits Khurram, 289, 338; joins in plot against Khusrau, 245; makes overtures to him, 369, 373; shows favour to Roe, 401-4, 410, 412; sends him a present, 150; presents for, 99, 108 n, 252 n, 346, 349, 426; English coach given to, 285, 289; her ship, 485; her daughter, 369 n, 370 n, 373.
Nutmegs. See Spices.
Nuts, 379.

Odola, 14.
Oliver, Isaac, 190 n.
Oranges, 9, 13, 23.
Orchilla, 14.
Orissa, 309 n, 385, 494, 500, 501.
Ormus, 44, 77, 313, 317, 444, 446; blockaded by Persians, 56, 79, 92, 103; revolt at, 454; possible cession to English, 103; attack on, deprecated, 372, 444; Captain of, 370, 406.
Orris root, 5.
Ortelius, 104.
Ostrich plumes, 312 n.
Oudh, 489 n.
Overall, Dr. John, 285 n, 456.

Pagod, 158, 323.
Painter, an English, see Hatfield;

Jahāngīr's chief, 189, 190, 199, 200.
Paithān, 491, 501.
Palangposh, 359.
Palki, 80 (3), 116, 242, 284 n, 285, 297 n, 348 n, 425, 455.
Palmetto trees, 28; wine, 12.
Pān, 421.
'Pane,' 211, 263, 286.
Paradise, birds of, 264.
Parakeets, 285.
Pargana, 381, 417, 419.
Parliament, 148 n.
Parrots, 427.
Partāb Shāh, 66, 67, 67 n, 403, 428, 429; his son, 429.
Partito, 440, 445.
Partridge, William, 141.
Partridges, 4.
Parwīz, Prince, at Burhānpur, 69, 70, 72, 88; Roe visits, 70, 79; farmān from, 81; recalled, 171, 177, 179, 242; sent to Bengal, 219, 235; character of, 70 n, 72 n.
Pathānkot, 491 n.
Patna, 188 n, 209, 210, 493, 494 n, 496.
Pattamar, 240, and passim.
Peacocks, 121.
Pearls, passim; trade in, 116, 149, 161, 263, 450, 457, 458; as presents, 89; sent by the Company to Roe, 392, 394, 395, 402, 414, 424, 429, 450, 467, 472; brought up by Steel, 398, 399, 405; sold to Āsaf Khān, 395, 410, 424, 450.
Pedreria, 450.
Pegu, 193 n, 308, 314, 434, 494.
Peking. See Cambalu.
Pembroke, Earl of (William Herbert), Roe writes to, 83 n, 114 n, 325 n.
Penguin Island, 2-5, 6 n.
Penguins, 4.
Peons, 65, and passim.
Pepper, 451, 488; for Persia, 111, 113.
Peppercorn, the, xviii, 2 n, 18, 19, 21, 26 (2).

INDEX 525

Pepwell, Henry, 216 n, 383 n; events of the voyage, 247 (see also Carrack); he is wounded, 248 n, 253; arrival of his fleet, 240, 241, 247; his powers, 291 n; opposes the Persia project, 290 n; seizes a boat, 327 n, 331; at Dābhol, 360, 361; at Calicut, 361 n, 363 n; Roe writes to, 10 n, 197 n, 232, 234, 252, 253, 305 n, 307 n (3), 311 n, 330, 334 n, 337 n, 360 n; his letterbook, 134 n, 227 n, 229 n, 232 n.

Persia, 383 n, 384, 451, 490, 491; King of, see Abbās; benefits of English trade with, 76, 113, 445; Turkey's trade with, 445; trade between India and, 92, 320, 382, 390 n, 406, 446, 459, 460; horses from, 29, 263; silk from, 76, 112-4, 290 n, 296 n, 300, 314-7, 335, 375, 384, 390 n, 444, 444 n, 445; envoys from (see also Muhammad Riza Beg), 87, 90, 92 n, 180, 214, 259 n; attempts to open up relations with (see also Jask), 108-12, 295, 300, 305, 306, 313-5, 330 n, 334-7, 357, 371, 374, 375, 390, 435, 443, 444, 503; Roe's possible visit to, 336, 368 n, 372, 374; his commission regarding, 389 (2), 393, 398, 418, 464; his consequent action, 397, 418, 444, 445, 453, 454, 461, 462, 464, 467, 488; Portuguese and, 372, 435, 444-6, 465; friars in, 111, 112. See also Ispahān, Jask, Ormus, Sherley, Spices, etc.

Persian the court language, 100, and passim.
Peshāwar, 491 n.
Pettus, Edward, 291 n.
Peyton, Walter, xviii, 58, 59; his journal quoted, passim.
Pharwāla, 491.
Pheasants, 4.

Philippines, the, 439.
Pice, passim; scarcity of, 341.
Pictures, 211, 455; as presents, 77, 99, 123, 129, 132, 143, 167 n, 200, 215 n, 227, 263, 312 n, 359, 415 n, 459; displayed at court, 125, 357; Jahāngīr and, 189, 199, 222-4, 349.
Pierce, Samuel, 108.
Pineapples, 48, 364.
Pinnace wanted, 73, 304, 412. See also Bee, the.
Pintadoes, 100, 193 n, 240.
Pippli, 309 n, 494.
Pistachio nuts, 212.
Pistols, 21, 200, 290.
Plague at Agra, 268, 312, 326 n, 327, 328, 334 n, 336; at Ahmadābād, 473 n.
Plantains, 11 (2), 34, 364.
Pley, George, 291 n (2), 453 n.
Plush, French, 117, 151.
Plymouth, 488.
Pole, a, 316.
Polo, 59.
Popinjay green, 443, 457.
Porcelain. See China ware.
Porto Grand, 194 n, 494.
Porto Pequeno, 194 n, 308, 308 n, 309 n, 494.
Portrait-coins, 215.
Portuguese, the, 332; position in India, 15, 74, 79, 101, 102, 105, 146, 185, 186, 269, 272, 303, 319, 368, 370, 373, 395, 430, 432, 439, 465, 466; war with the Indians, xxv, 40, 43; peace concluded, xxvii, 44, 49, 74, 430; grant passes to Indian vessels, 430, 432, 433, 439, 475 n, 485; send an envoy, 438, 454; fresh disputes, 475 n, 485, 488; trade in India, 149, 151, 161, 162, 449, 450 n, 458, 460; in Bengal, 193 n, 252, 308, 308 n, 309 n; at Ajmer, 161, 162, 235; in Africa, 13; at Sokotra, 23; in Persia, see Persia; intrigue against English, 27, 73, 102,

103, 106; Roe urges action against, 79, 103, 106, 269, 303, 304, 307, 377; defeated by Downton, xxvi, 7 n, 14, 40, 102, 105, 377 n, 437; other hostilities between English and (see also Carrack), xvi, 252, 291 n, 327 n, 331, 388 n, 375, 391, 392 n, 413, 440, 460, 483, 505; English not to molest, 97, 101, 107, 109, 123, 130; Dutch and, see Dutch. See also Cambay, Goa, Lāhribandar, Lisbon, Ormus, etc.
Porus, King, 82, 90, 270, 492, 496.
Pory, John, 389 n.
Powell, Sir Thomas and Lady, 391 n.
Prester John, 14 (3), 23, 83 n, 116.
Pring, Martin, 377 n; arrival of his fleet, 385-9; his proceedings at Swally, 386, 388 n, 397, 398 n, 407, 422, 433 n, 436 n, 440, 452 n; and afterwards, 418 n; Roe's letters to, 373, 374 n, 383, 389, 392 n, 393, 403, 409, 413, 460, 469; Roe's friendship for, 388 n, 389, 433, 434, 462; his journal, 6 n.
Privado, 306.
Procurador, 300, 387, 411, 427 (2), 477.
Pulicat, 480.
Punjab, the, 491.
Punto, 433, 437.
Purchas, Rev. Samuel, lxxii, 22, 388 n; errors in his version, lxxiv, 5 n, 9 n, 104 n, 199 n, 257 n, 301 n, 316 n, 386 n, 400 n, 414 n, 428 n (2); his map, 500.
'Purp,' 489 n, 494.
Purses, 262.
Pushkar, 158 (2), 166.

Queen-Mother, the. See Maryamzamāni.

Quicksilver, 5; trade in, 12, 228, 295, 305, 441, 445, 457.
Quilts, 360.
Quitasols, 285.
Quivers, 258, 262, 283, 353, 458, 459.

Raīpur, 80.
Raisins, 212, 225.
Rajab Āghā, 483.
Rājmahāl, 494.
Rājpura, 492.
Rājputs, 245, 246, 274, 323.
Ralegh, Sir Walter, xxi, 384 n.
Ramazān, 12, 41, 53, 239.
Rāmghar, 404 n.
Rāmsar, 298 n, 322.
Ranthambhor, 327 n, 329.
Rastell, Thomas, 463, 484 n.
Rāver, 68 n.
Recife, Cape, 8.
Red Sea, Indian trade to, passim; Roe advocates trade in, 307, 338, 376, 384, 406, 409, 413, 423, 424, 430-2, 439, 440, 444, 446, 461, 470; voyages to, see Anne, the, and Lion, the; interloping voyages to, 383 n, 451. See also Mokha.
Redondo, Conde de. See Goa, Viceroys of.
Rehamy, 14.
Religions, Indian, 102, 105, 270-2, 274-6.
Reynolds, Mr. L. W., 217 n.
Rhubarb, 118.
Rials of eight, passim; value of, 134 n, 424, 442; quantity sent in Keeling's fleet, 103.
Rice, 11, 22, 23, 193 n, 213, 418.
Rich, Sir Robert, 388 n, 391, 451, 452 (3).
Rings, 280, 283.
Robben Island. See Penguin Island.
Robbins, William, 112; notices of, 109 n, 315; Roe writes to, 109, 114 n, 334, 335, 371, 453; his replies, 313, 371.
'Rock,' old and new, 457.

INDEX

Roe, Sir Thomas, *passim*; his antecedents, xxi; his appointment, xviii-xxiii; his commission, xxiii, xxiv *n*, 43, 87, 88, 98; his salary and allowances, xxiii, 302, 310, 338, 467; his outfit, xxiv; wears English dress, 84 *n*; his household arrangements, 122 *n*, 216, 331; his suite, xxiii, 310, 311, 441, 474 *n*; his secretary, *see* Heynes; his chaplains, *see* Hall *and* Terry; his expenses, 310, 441; his age, 118; his religious sentiments, 216, 281 *n*; his ill-health, xxxi, 72, 80, 84, 96, 98, 115, 312 *n*, 326 *n*, 360, 382, 386, 405, 413, 467, 474 *n*; portraits of, lxxvii, 84 *n*, 85 *n*; Jahāngīr's presents to, 201, 212, 214, 225; his little knowledge of Persian, 340; predicts civil war, 246; wishes for wine, 311, 382, 412, 413; anxious to return, 96, 281, 311, 336, 340 *n*, 360, 372, 402, 449, 450, 456; desires to command the ship in that event, 96, 450; his views on the silver question, 146-8; his dealings with Persia, *see* Persia; and the Red Sea, *see* Red Sea; increased powers from the Company, 386, 387 *n*; his dealings with the Dutch, 202-9, 217, 218, 427, 486, 487; his voyage home, liv, 444 *n*, 484 *n*, 485-8; his reception, liv; gratuity to, lvi; his subsequent career, lvi, lxvii; his connexion with Baffin's map, 497, 498.
Roe, Lady, xxii, 223 *n*; supposed portrait of, 222-4.
Rose, the, 247.
Rosewater, 259.
Royal Anne, the. *See* Anne, the.
Royal James, the, 388 *n*, 433, 440.
Rubies, *passim*; trade in, 162, 308, 314, 434, 457. *See also* Balass.

Rupees, *passim*; value of, 74 *n*, 89, 210, 379; *Jahāngīri*, 225 *n*, 312, 424, 455; *khazāna*, 424 *n*.
Rustam, Mīrza, 226, 356, 369, 380.

Sack, 96, 368 *n*, 412, 413.
Sackbuts, 36.
Saddles, 151, 262, 264, 297 *n*; as presents, 350, 359, 459.
Sadler, Richard, 172, 173.
Safi, Mīrza, 92, 103, 130 *n*.
Saīd-bin-Saīd, 20.
St. Augustine, Cape, 7-9, 15.
St. Helena, 488 (3).
St. Lawrence. *See* Madagascar.
Sala, Stephano, 301.
Salām, 86 *n*, 92.
Salbank, Joseph, 99 *n*, 274 *n*, 276 *n*; notice of, 81 *n*; in attendance on Roe, 68, 81; to go to Sind, 118, 148, 292; at Agra, 184, 327, 336, 368; sent to the Red Sea, 470, 472, 483.
Sālik Beg, 292, 414.
Salīm Shāh. *See* Jahāngīr.
Salisbury, Lady, portrait of, 126.
Salmas, 300, 317.
Samāna muslins, 233, 283, 320(2), 416, 450 *n*.
Samarkand, 83 *n*, 92, 116.
Sambhal, 493.
Sana, 483.
Sanders (Sandalwood), 427.
Sanguis draconis, 23.
Sanyāsi, 343 *n*.
Sapphires, 308.
Sarāi, 68-70, 375.
Saraswati (river), 493.
Sardār Khān, 153 *n*.
Saris, John, 12, 16 *n*.
Sarkār, 456.
Sarkar, Professor Jadunnath, 85 *n*.
Sarkhej, 108 *n*, 424, 450 *n*.
Sātgāon, 194 *n*, 309 *n*, 494.
Sati, 105, 271.
Satin, 285, 458, 459, 505.
Savoy, Duke of, 388 *n*, 452.
Scarves, 458.

INDEX

Scrito, 51, 151, 196, 197, 411, 431.
Scrivano, 152, 153, 177, 179, 289, 382.
Seal, the Mogul's, 507, 508.
Seals, 5.
Seer, 254 n, 310, 460.
Semiano. See Samāna and Shāmiyāna.
Sempervive, 23.
'Sentences,' 194.
Sequins, 202.
Serraglio, 51, 236 n, 243, 256.
Shāhār Māll, 470.
Shāhbandar, 309 n. See also Surat, etc.
Shāh Husain, customer at Surat, 414; relations with Roe, 39, 46, 53; accusations against, 142 (2), 172, 173, 218, 228, 231; removed, 153 n, 156, 209; his debt, 359, 386, 402, 429.
Shāh Jahān. See Khurram.
Shāhnawāz Khān, daughter of, 369 n.
Shāhpur, 495.
Shahryār, Prince, 176, 243, 285, 352; marriage of, 370 n.
Shaikh, 21, 22 (2).
Shāmiyāna, 125.
Sharīf, 12 (2), 13, 21, 274.
Shash, 198, 226, 283, 314.
Sheep, 13, 23, 24, 117, 131, 365; price of, 100.
Sherley, Sir Robert, 10 n, 268, 391 n; a Roman Catholic, 111; assists Steel, 112; at Ajmer, 133; his mission to Spain, lxi, 76, 111-4, 290 n, 307, 313-7, 333, 371, 372; his previous mission, lx, 314; at Goa, 252, 274, 307, 313, 314, 316.
Shīa sect, 105.
Shilling, Andrew, 392, 462, 472, 484 n, 485.
Shīr Afgan, 370 n.
Shock (dog), 365 n.
Shoes as presents, 262.
Shot (of cable), 19 (2).
Shroffs, 233, 338, 424.
Shuja, Prince, born, 179.

Shukrullah, Mīrza (Afzal Khān), passim; notice of, 123 n; his character, 123, 143, 232.
Sība, 489 n, 492, 500, 501.
Sīdī Hāshim, 23.
Sijdah, 214, 258, 259, 264, 267.
Silk, raw, trade in, see Persia; from Bengal, 309 n, 320 (2); from China, 368.
Silk goods, 100, 147, 148 n, 181, 309 n, 312 n, 333, 351.
Silver, 126, 127, 289; exportation to India, 147, 186.
Silver, cloth of, 129, 282, 283, 284 n, 285, 427; trade in, 151, 181, 458, 459.
Sind, 90, 118, 406, 444 n, 460, 490; trade in, desired, 134, 148, 193 n; refused, 228. See also Lahrībandar and Tatta.
Sindkhera, 67.
Sipra (river), 342, 495.
Sironj, 215 n, 495; calicoes from, 215 n.
Slaves at Sokotra, 22, 23; in India, 132, 154, 266, 267, 364, 411; from Madagascar, 13.
Smythe, Sir Thomas, 112, 157 n, 316, 389 n, 392 n, 405 n, 464, 503 n; portrait of, 126, 357; Roe writes to, 6 n, 95, 116, 223 n, 302, 312, 337, 338 n, 466; his friendship for Roe, xx, 319, 449, 467, 469; his wife, 469.
Snakes, execution by, 474 n.
Soares, Francisco, 460.
Sokotra, 14, 24, 218, 368, 369 n; Keeling's fleet at, 18-25; the Portuguese and, 23; Sultan of, 20-5.
Soldado, 261.
Soldania. See Table Bay.
Solomon, the, 361 (2).
Somerset, Lady, portrait of, 125.
Somerset, Earl of, 114 n, 125 n.
Sophy, the, see Abbās, Shāh; term explained, 109 n.
Sorath, 495.
Sorcery, 271.
Southampton, Earl of, xxi; Roe's letter to, 115; his family, 116.

INDEX

Spain, 307, 452 ; King of, 307 *n*, 314, 436, 437 *n*, 439, 445 ; never sends an ambassador to the Mogul, 273, 310, 318 ; Sherley's mission to, *see* Sherley.
Spaniards in Africa, 6.
Spencer, Lady, 116 *n*.
Spices, 148 *n*, 202, 368, 379, 427, 483 ; for India, 305 *n*, 309 *n*, 338, 374, 390 *n*, 445, 451, 459 ; for Persia, 111, 314, 375, 390 *n*, 445 (2), 446.
Spirits, 50, 311, 312 *n*, 330, 379, 457 ; as presents, 45, 71, 124 *n*, 259.
Sprage, Thomas, 366 (2), 428 (2), 472.
Spurs, 143.
Srīnagar, 491.
Stade, 335.
Stamells, 443, 457.
'Standish,' 415 *n*, 459.
Star, the, 487, 488.
Steel, Indian, 445.
Steel, Mrs., 393, 399, 407-9, 447, 455, 462, 463, 469, 469 *n* ; her marriage, 391 *n*, 468 ; goes home, 486, 488.
Steel, Richard, 166 *n* ; his mission to Persia, lxi, 108, 110, 112-4, 290 *n*, 314, 390, 462 *n*, 468, 470, 472 ; offers to go again, 390 *n*, 397 ; his projects, 390, 393, 405, 413, 423, 433, 445-7, 454, 455, 468, 469 ; arrives in India, 390 ; differences with Kerridge, 407 ; joins Roe, 398 (4), 399, 405, 409 ; is sent back, 408 ; at Ahmadābād, 408, 412, 414, 423, 424, 427 (2), 430, 455 ; his relations with Roe, 417, 423, 424, 427 *n*, 445-8, 450, 455, 463, 468, 469 ; his private trade, 408, 447, 486 *n* ; his knowledge of Persian, 448 *n*, 455, 468 *n* ; goes home, 486, 488 ; his subsequent history, 486 *n*.
Sterne, Thomas, 497.
Steucksy, J. B., 316 *n*.

'Stickle,' 425.
'Stone' priest, 13.
Suffolk, Earl of, 114 *n*.
Sugar, 91, 213, 382, 445, 446 ; Bengal, 193 *n*, 308 *n*.
Sugar candy, 213.
Surat, *passim* ; importance of, 375 ; well built, 90, 105 ; castle at, 35, 208, 368, 478 ; tank at, 58, 90 ; minthouse at, 474, 478 ; the Kāji Masjid at, 478 (2) ; best port for English, 304, 412, 433 ; factory at, 412, 474-8, 481 *n*, 484, 485 ; Roe's house at, 28, 29, 35, 36, 39, 48, 476, 482 *n* ; English not to build at, 101, 144 *n*, 481 *n*, 484 ; English disorderly at, 36 *n*, 119, 145, 252, 253, 326, 327 *n*, 368, 374, 433, 478 ; rumour of their taking, 358, 433, 478, 480 ; dispute over their wearing arms, 415-7, 433, 475, 477-81 ; duties payable at, 137 ; English imports, 186, 400 ; Roe offers to compound for customs at, 185-7, 191, 194, 195, 197, 436 ; English broker at, 241 ; Dutch at, xxix, 202-9, 214, 217-9, 368, 374, 377, 435, 451-3, 487 *n* ; disarmed, 480 *n* ; *Bakhshi* of, 142, 153 ; Chief of Customs at (*see also* Shāh Husain), 144 *n*, 252-4, 260, 292, 429 ; *Dīwān* of, *see* Sālik Beg ; Governors of, *see* Ibrāhīm Khān, Nizām (Khwāja), and Zūlfakār Khān ; *Shāhbandar* of, *see* Ishāk Beg.
Surgeons, 413, 473 *n*. *See also* Green.
Susan, the, 10 *n*, 81 *n*.
Swally, passim ; advantages of, 304 (2), 436 ; rumoured intention of building a fort at, 415 ; *Mukaddum* of, 30.
Swan, the, 6 *n*, 247, 362 *n*.
Sweetbags, 356, 426, 458.
Swine, English, 29, 30.
Swordblades, trade in, 13, 25, 50, 64, 70.

Swords, 21, 117 ; trade in, 147, 149, 181, 184, 312, 366, 387, 457 ; as presents, 98, 99, 151, 200, 259, 262, 282, 334 ; the Company send one to Roe, 398, 449.
Syria, 301.

Table Bay, 25, 247 ; the fleet at, 2-7 ; Roe sets up a pillar at, 4 n ; felons left at, 6 ; natives at, 4. See also Good Hope, Cape of.
Table book, 200.
Table Mountain, 4, 5.
Tābrīz, 300, 317, 364, 365.
Taffeta, 85 n, 100, 126, 285, 286, 460.
Talbot, a, 350 n ; sign of, 500.
Tamarīda, 20-23, 25.
Tamarind trees, 323.
Tamberlane. See Timūr.
Tanks, 58, 90, 121, 211, 217, 323-5, 354 n, 355 n, 482 n.
Tapestry, Persian, 357. See also Arras.
Tāptī (river), 495 (2).
Targeteers, 255.
Targets (shields), 258, 262, 379.
'Tariff,' 467.
Tartary, 83 n, 116, 118, 308 n, 383 n, 491.
Taslīm, 118, 119, 258, 259, 262, 264, 265.
Tatta, 406, 490.
Taurus Mountains, 90, 270.
Telescopes, 77.
Tents, Jahāngīr's, 286, 287, 324 ; double shifts of, 240, 324.
Terpstra, Dr. H., xxix.
Terry, Edward, lxxiv, 342 n, 359, 360 (2) ; notice of, 216 n ; appointed chaplain, 216 n, 330 ; goes up with the presents, 341 n, 344, 345, 349, 355 n ; arrives, 346 n, 347 n ; Jahāngīr and, 347, 348 n, 349 ; his dress, 85 n ; his map of India, 500 ; his narrative, 500 ; quotations from, passim.

Thālner, 67.
Thevenot, Jean de, 363 n.
Thieves, punishment of, 201.
Thumbs, ceremony of crossing, 395.
Timūr, 82, 83 n, 270 (2), 274, 294, 342 n, 508.
Tin, 147 n, 252, 320, 445, 451.
Tinta roxa, 14.
Tipton, Francis, 398 n, 415 n.
Tissue, 181 (2), 459.
Tobacco, 11, 311 n.
Toda, 322, 323.
Tolā, 162.
Tombs, Henry, 500.
Tombstones, 50 n.
Topaz, 308.
Tornado, 2.
Tower of London, 458.
Towerson, Gabriel, arrives, 391 n ; Roe and, 393, 399, 407, 412, 422 ; at Ahmadābād, 422, 427 (2), 429, 448, 468, 469 ; goes home, 486 ; his subsequent history, 486 n.
Towerson, Mrs., 168 n, 391 n, 393, 399, 407, 412, 447, 448, 455, 460 n, 462, 463, 468 ; remains in India, 486 n.
'Toyes,' 221, and passim.
Tracy, William, 291 n.
Trade, private, Roe on, 77, 309, 311, 385, 408, 417, 441, 448.
Travancore, 378 n.
Tricanados, 263.
Trumpets, 21, 285.
Trunks, 99.
Turbans, 21, 259, 260, 282, 283.
Tūrbat, 474 n.
Turkey, 147 n, 300, 320, 384, 458 ; Sultān of, 140, 308, 317, 389 n, 409, 445, 461, 483 ; sends envoy to India, 87, 92.
Turkey Company, the, 148, 409, 461.
Turks, the, 118, 129 ; masters of Arabia, 20 ; wars with Persians, see Abbās, Shāh.
Turquoises, 225, 260, 357, 378, 457 n.
Turtle doves, 121.

INDEX

Udaipur, 495 (2) ; city of, 82 n, 496 ; Rānā of, see Amar Singh.
Udeza, 494, 500, 501.
Udi Singh, 82 n, 496.
Ujjain, 342, 343, 495.
Umara, 259 n, 297 n, 394, 411 ; term explained, 383 n.
Umar-bin-Ādil, 12.
Unicorn's horn, a, 254, 366.
Uzbeg Tartars, 92.

Van den Broecke, Pieter, 202 n, 203 n, 369 n, 374, 374 n (2), 376 n, 501.
Van Deynsen, David, xxix, xxx.
Van Ravesteyn, Pieter Gillis, xxix, xxx, 369 n, 374 n ; at Ahmadābād, 427 ; on Roe, 487 n ; his journal quoted, 52 n, 55 n, 66 n, 67 n, 68 n, 80 n.
Vārāha, image of, 275.
Velvet, passim ; trade in, 25, 49, 147, 351 ; Chinese, 49, 284 n ; Persian, 285.
Venetians, 115, 300, 301.
Venice, goods from, 259, 449 ; 'King and Queen of,' 263.
Venus and a Satyr, picture of, 349, 350.
Vermilion, 5, 445, 457.
Veroneo, Jeronimo, 124 n.
Veronese, John, 124, 128-31, 158.
Viāra, 66.
Violets, syrup of, 413.
Virginals sent as a present, 48, 49, 76, 98.
Virginia, 388 n, 392, 392 n.
Voider, 127.

'Waft,' 250, 303.
Waldo, Lawrence, 441.
Wallis, Anthony, 34, 456, 468.
Watches, 22, 25, 227.
Watchet blue, 117.
Waterworks, 447 n ; Steel's project for, 390 n, 393, 405, 445, 447, 455, 468 n, 469.
Wax, trade in, 308 n.

Webb, Frances. See Steel, Mrs.
West Indies, 127 n.
Whales, 5.
Wheat, 193 n.
White water, 16.
Whipping, 265, 266.
Wine, passim ; as presents, 99, 141, 142, 150, 184 (2), 191, 259, 312 n, 333 ; Armenian, 36 n. See also Alicante and Sack.
Winwood, Sir Ralph, 503 n ; letters to, 114 n, 316, 438, 445, 453, 464.
Witchcraft, 271, 275.
Withington, Nicholas, 275 n.
Wolves, 365.
Women as guards, 85.

Xavier, Jerome, 74 n, 275, 301, 322.
Xerafins, 74 n.

Yādgār, Khwāja, 153.
Yātīsh-khāna, 262, 325.
Yāval, 68 n.
Young, John, 51, 473 n.
Young, Robert, 157 n, 184, 201, 232, 315, 319, 456.
Yusuf, Shaikh, 502.

Zamāna Beg. See Mahābat Khān.
Zamorin of Calicut, 376, 460.
Zūlfakār Khān, 93 n ; notice of, 42 n ; character of, 30, 44, 196 ; Governor of Surat, xxvii, 27 ; Roe's relations with, 28, 29, 35-42, 45, 46, 49-57, 62-5 ; visits Roe, 42, 48 ; Roe visits, 46, 59 ; letter to, 54 ; his misgovernment, xxx, 58, 119, 154 ; superseded, 106 n, 153 n ; arrives at court, 139 ; Roe's proceedings against, 93, 97, 122, 138-145, 149, 150, 152-160, 163-9, 172-7, 179, 182-5, 191, 194-8, 209, 215, 217, 232, 238, 241, 255, 282, 288 (2),

289, 294, 295, 297, 327, 330, 351; Roe's interviews with, 195, 197; accompanies Khurram to the Deccan war, 164, 172; dies, 351; further attempts to recover his debt, 359, 366, 377, 381, 386, 402, 421; his brother, 35, 36 n, 39, 40; his servants, 143, 144, 152, 153, 177, 179.